Strangers in the Land

Strangers in the Land

*Exclusion, Belonging, and the
Epic Story of the Chinese in America*

Michael Luo

Doubleday  New York

Published by Doubleday, a division of Penguin Random House LLC,
1745 Broadway, New York, NY 10019.

DOUBLEDAY and the portrayal of an anchor with a dolphin are
registered trademarks of Penguin Random House LLC.

Library of Congress Cataloging-in-Publication Data
Names: Luo, Michael, author.
Title: Strangers in the land : exclusion, belonging, and the epic story of the
Chinese in America / Michael Luo.
Description: First edition. | New York : Doubleday, [2025] |
Includes bibliographical references and index.
Identifiers: LCCN 2024026731 | ISBN 9780385548571 (hardcover) |
ISBN 9780385548588 (ebook)
Subjects: LCSH: Chinese Americans—History | Chinese—United
States—History. | United States. Chinese Exclusion Act. | United States—
Emigration and immigration—History. | United States—Ethnic relations.
Classification: LCC E184.C5 L84 2025 |
DDC 305.8951073—dc23/eng/20250106
LC record available at https://lccn.loc.gov/2024026731

penguinrandomhouse.com | doubleday.com

PRINTED IN THE UNITED STATES OF AMERICA
1 3 5 7 9 10 8 6 4 2

The authorized representative in the EU for product safety and compliance
is Penguin Random House Ireland, Morrison Chambers, 32 Nassau Street,
Dublin D02 YH68, Ireland, https://eu-contact.penguin.ie.

For

Madeleine and Vivienne

The question is: Who gets to be an American?
What does an American look like?

—Charles Yu, *Interior Chinatown*

Contents

A Note on Usage

For the most part, the romanization of Chinese names and organizations in this book is consistent with the way they are rendered in the historical archives. Exceptions are made for prominent place names and the names of Chinese officials, which are spelled out using the modern Pinyin romanization system. In such instances, where helpful, I also include the historical usage—typically in the Wade-Giles system, or a Cantonese transliteration—either in the text or in a note. Names are also, generally, rendered, according to the Chinese custom, with the surname first.

Strangers in the Land

Introduction

In the beginning, the door was open. The Founding Fathers celebrated the multiplicity of difference in their young republic and recognized that filling the country's vast, open spaces with newcomers was necessary for securing its future. As Thomas Jefferson put it: "The present desire of America is to produce rapid population by as great importations of foreigners as possible." In the 1840s, some states on the Atlantic seaboard took steps to exclude poor Irish Catholic immigrants, who were arriving by the thousands, but there were no federal laws restricting immigration. The story of how that changed begins on the Pacific coast. At the time, the verdant land that Spanish conquistadors called Alta California was still a Mexican province. Only a few hundred Americans had made their way to the region. They found a land of almost unfathomable natural resources, blessed with temperate climes and abundant bays.

In 1844, James K. Polk won the presidency as a proponent of American expansion, a vision informed by practical necessity—the country's population had boomed—as well as a religion-infused conviction about the superiority of white Americans. Polk embraced the belief that it was America's "manifest destiny" to extend from the Atlantic Ocean to the Pacific. In May 1846, a skirmish between American and Mexican troops in a disputed area on the border between Texas and Mexico became Polk's pretext for war. Less than two years later, under the Treaty of Guadalupe-Hidalgo, Mexico ceded California to the United States, along with the broad sweep of land that today comprises Nevada, parts of Arizona, and New Mexico. The fledgling town of San Francisco then consisted only of a collection of wood-frame and adobe buildings. Fewer than a thousand hardy inhabitants, many of them Mormons fleeing religious persecution, occupied the sandy, windswept settlement. That changed with remarkable suddenness.

On the morning of January 24, 1848, a carpenter named James Marshall was inspecting progress on the construction of a sawmill on the banks of the American River, in a forested river valley about 130 miles east of San Francisco. He spotted some glints in the water and picked up several metallic fragments. He studied them closely and realized that they might be gold. Several days later, Marshall returned to New Helvetia, a remote outpost in the Sacramento Valley, where he asked his business partner, John Sutter, to meet with him alone. The two men conducted some tests and satisfied themselves that Marshall's find was genuine. Sutter implored those working the mill to keep the discovery quiet, but one day in May 1848, a Mormon leader named Samuel Brannan, the owner of a general store at the settlement, traveled to San Francisco, heralding stunning news. "Gold! Gold! Gold from the American River!" Brannan shouted as he strode the streets, holding aloft a jar full of gold dust and waving his hat. Within a few weeks, three-quarters of San Francisco's male population had decamped for the mines. The cove that carved in from the sandy shoreline soon filled with abandoned ships whose crews had rushed off in search of wealth. A local newspaper, *The Californian*, reported: "The whole country from San Francisco to Los Angeles, and from the seashore to the base of the Sierra Nevada, resounds to the sordid cry of gold! GOLD!! GOLD!!" The next day, the newspaper shut down, as its entire staff departed for the diggings.

It is uncertain how exactly word of the gold rush reached China. According to Chinese lore, a merchant named Chum Ming, a recent arrival in America, was among the legions who ventured into the foothills of the Sierra Nevada mountains. He wrote an excited letter to a friend back home, Cheong Yum, a fellow villager from the Sanyi district of Guangdong province, about the wealth to be had in the mines. Cheong Yum told others about Chum Ming's good fortune and set off across the Pacific himself.

A more verifiable fact is that a ship carrying California gold—

specifically, a packet containing two and a half cups of gold dust—arrived in Hong Kong on Christmas Day 1848. (A San Francisco agent of the Hudson's Bay Company, the fur-trading concern, had requested that British experts in China evaluate it.) On board the ship as well were copies of the *Polynesian,* a Honolulu newspaper, with news of the gold rush. Soon, word had spread throughout the Pearl River Delta, a populous enclave in southeastern China. Men began scraping together funds, often using their family's land as collateral for loans, and crowding aboard ships bound for *Gum Shan*—Gold Mountain.

Gold Mountain riches set in motion a cycle of migration across the Pacific. Fathers sent word for sons to join them; brothers wrote to brothers and cousins; returning villagers inspired others to venture to the distant land on the other side of the ocean. Advertisements from American shipping companies that circulated in China declared that "Americans are the richest in the world and welcome Chinese." They promised "big houses to live in" and assured people considering the trip that "everyone is equal" in America. By 1860, Chinese immigrants made up just under 10 percent of California's population. The state teemed with white Americans, Californios—the state's Spanish-speaking settlers who were granted citizenship after annexation—Indigenous peoples, Black Americans, Hawaiians, English, Scottish, Irish, German, French, and Chinese migrants, and others, brought together by an unprecedented mass movement of people from around the world to the United States. They became the substrate for a nettlesome experiment in multiracial democracy that had little precedent in the country's history.

This book tells the story of how the United States responded to the influx of tens of thousands of people from a distant land, who spoke a different language, had different beliefs and customs, and did not fit into the country's existing racial stratification. Americans initially welcomed the Chinese arrivals, but as their numbers grew, the sentiment turned ugly. While the debate over slavery roiled the eastern half of the country, a different kind of racial conflagration broke out on the West Coast. Horrific episodes of racial violence erupted in the minefields; lawmakers passed laws targeting Chinese immigrants; California's highest court ruled that Chinese testimony was inadmissible in court against a white person. Politicians recognized an opportunity in the rising anti-Chinese sentiment and began calling for their removal. They cast Chinese immigrants as a threat to Anglo-Saxon civilization. They twisted the principle of "free labor," an ideology that took shape in response to slavery, into a weapon of racial oppression, condemning all Chinese as "coolie" laborers. Crucially, lawmakers decided to bar Chinese immigrants from naturalized citizenship, even as they extended the privilege to "persons of African descent." A prolonged economic downturn that idled legions of white workingmen helped create the conditions for what came next. Congress enacted a series of exclusionary laws to prevent Chinese laborers from entering the country. Each one was more onerous than the last. As shiploads of Chinese people continued to cross the Pacific, their opponents turned to violence, resulting in some of the ugliest episodes of racial terror in our nation's history. Later, in the twentieth century, after Chinese exclusion became permanent, a sprawling federal bureaucracy took shape to keep Chinese immigrants out. Lawmakers also took steps to ban other Asian immigration, establishing, in 1917, a "barred zone" that stretched from the Middle East to the Pacific islands; only Japan, which had already negotiated an agreement with the United States limiting immigration, and the Philippines, which was an American territory, were excepted. In 1924, as arguments based on eugenics declared the inferiority of Jews, Italians, and other immigrants from southern and eastern Europe, new legislation imposed strict quotas on immigration from those regions. It also excluded "aliens ineligible to citizenship," closing America's gates to all Asian immigrants based on their race.

Yet the Chinese in America persisted. They spread out across the American West and made their way eastward as well. A population of Chinese Americans even took root in the Mississippi Delta, operating grocery stores that catered to Black customers in the Jim Crow South. Chinese immigrants continued to journey across the ocean and evade the racist laws designed to keep them out. A native-born generation emerged, whose members found themselves caught in the familiar wrenching contest between their parents' culture and the forces of assimilation and acculturation. Unlike the descendants of Irish, German, and other European immigrants, Chinese Americans carried the additional burden of race.

This book is, principally, their story. It is the biography of a people, the participants in the first large-scale Asian immigration to the United States, who then withstood the crucible of racism and exclusion in this country. Call them the first Asian Americans, even though that term did not yet exist. The voices of individual Chinese who arrived in America in the second half of the nineteenth century can be difficult to find in the historical archives, but this absence should not be mistaken for their silence. The Chinese in America were not simply the victims of barbarous violence and repression; they were protagonists in the story of America. They pressed their adopted homeland to live up to its stated ideals. Their experiences serve as a reminder that a democracy's promises should always be measured against how it treats its most marginalized members. Chinese immigration in the late nineteenth century took place during a crucial period of formation for the country after the Civil War, a time when noble visions of liberty and equality in America foundered. The Chinese Question followed the Negro Question and coincided with the vanquishing of Reconstruction, the spread of Jim Crow, and the subjugation of Native peoples on the western frontier. These histories, whose legacies continue to refract in American life, should be considered alongside each other. That belief wraps under and around this book.

In the end, it was not an overdue reckoning with the country's egalitarian values that led to the repeal of Chinese exclusion but a shift in the geopolitical order. China became an ally of the United States in its war against Japan. Lawmakers allocated a largely symbolic number of slots for Chinese immigration. It was not until 1965, when a sweeping new immigration law set aside the national-origins quota system, that America's gates finally swung open to Chinese immigration. The legislation prioritized relatives of U.S. citizens and permanent residents, as well as immigrants with skills and "exceptional ability" in various fields. It set in motion the ethnic transformation of the country that is still unfolding today. Nevertheless, even that legislation was made possible only because of proponents' mistaken impression that it would do little to alter the nation's demographics. Absorbing this historical reality is necessary for understanding the cleavages over immigration that continue to rend this country.

When I first started thinking about the need for a book like this, it was the fall of 2016. I was standing in the rain with my family and some friends, in front of a restaurant on Manhattan's Upper East Side, when a woman brushed past us, evidently aggravated we were in her way. Partway down the block, she yelled, "Go back to China!" For a moment, I was stunned. *Did she really say that?* I abandoned my younger daughter in her stroller and rushed after the woman. We exchanged words, and when I walked away, she screamed, "Go back to your fucking country." Because I could think of nothing else, I said, "I was born in this country!" There was something about the woman's words that caused a tremor inside me. The election of Donald Trump was just a few weeks away. A curtain of nativism seemed to be descending across America. Growing up in mostly white suburbs, I was accustomed to the feeling of disconnection that often comes with being Asian American, but I began to wonder whether my children, two generations removed from the immigrant experience of my parents, would ever feel like they truly belonged in this country.

In 1889, when the Supreme Court upheld a measure excluding Chinese laborers from this country, Justice Stephen Field characterized the Chinese as "impossible to assimilate with our people." They were, Field concluded, "strangers in the land." More than a century later, the "stranger" label remains imprinted on Asian Americans. Today, there are more than twenty-four million people of Asian descent in the country; people of Chinese descent make up the largest contingent. By the middle of the century, Asians are projected to be the largest ethnic group in the United States. Much of this recent immigration has been linked to skills-based allocations, contributing to the stereotype of Asian Americans as the model minority, yet no other ethnic or racial group experiences greater income inequality—or perhaps feels more invisible. Then came the Trump presidency, with his racist sneers about "kung flu" and the "China virus," and the wave of anti-Asian violence that swept the country during the COVID-19 pandemic. As I write this, politicians from both parties seem to be engaged in a contest of bellicosity over the threat posed by China. Every shrill denunciation adds to the tinder of racial suspicion.

The anti-Asian attacks generated a remarkable outpouring of energy and emotion from the Asian American community and beyond, but the sense of emergency soon dissipated. It's unclear whether anything lasting will come of the moment. The reality is, Asian Americans do not fit easily into the narrative of race in America. Evaluating gradations of victimhood, and where feelings of estrangement end and structural barriers begin, is complicated. In examining the history of the Chinese in America, I've come to realize the precarity of the Asian American experience has never fully subsided. Throughout American history, we have been told to go back to where we came from. The surge in violence towards Asian Americans was only the latest reminder that America's present reality reflects its exclusionary past. That transforms the work of making legible the long, ugly history of anti-Asian racism—and the related experiences of Black Americans, Native peoples, and other marginalized groups—into a search for a more inclusive future.

My aim in writing this book was to furnish an accounting of this traumatic period in American history and render it in narrative form, with all its pathos and humanity, for modern readers. Yet it's worth noting that the events of this book are more immediate than one might initially suppose. The grandchildren of Chinese immigrants who survived the bigotry and violence of the late nineteenth century in America are the grandparents of fifth-generation Chinese Americans today. Until I embarked on this project, I knew very little of this history. Both of my parents emigrated from Taiwan—my father came in the late 1960s and my mother in the early 1970s—for graduate school. My father began working as an electrical engineer in Pittsburgh, where my twin brother and I were born. We both graduated from Harvard. I went on to a career in journalism, mostly at *The New York Times* and then at *The New Yorker*. The turbulent decades of violence and exclusion seemed distant to me, even foreign. Yet, when I began immersing myself in the archives, I found myself engrossed, in part, because of how relevant the history felt to our present moment. This is not just the story of the Chinese in America; it's the story of any number of immigrant groups who have been treated as strangers. It's the story of our diverse democracy. It's the story of us.

Part I

Arrivals

CHAPTER 1

Gold Mountain

Huie Kin grew up in Wing Ning, a tiny village of about seventy people, all from the same clan, tucked away in the hills of Taishan, an impoverished, mountainous county in the Pearl River Delta. At one end of the village was a bamboo grove; on the other was a fishpond; housewives gossiped at the communal well, near the entrance to the village. Huie's house was made of sun-dried bricks and had a thatched roof. He lived in one room with his father and the family cow. His mother slept in the other room. They shared a compound with another family, separated by a courtyard. Because the space was so cramped, Huie's two brothers stayed in the village shrine at night; his two sisters spent their nights at a home for unmarried girls. Rice fields surrounded the village. During harvest season, the men worked in the fields, while the women tended to the home. At the age of eleven, Huie started attending the village school but dropped out after a few years.

One day, a member of Huie's clan returned from America with stories of gold found in riverbeds. Huie grew obsessed with traveling to Gold Mountain, as the faraway land was called. He and three cousins vowed to go to America together. To Huie's surprise, his father readily agreed to their plan—he had also heard the tales of people who had returned from abroad with gold in their pockets. Huie's father borrowed the money for his son's passage from a wealthy neighbor, using their family farm as security on the loan. On a spring day in 1868, the cousins left their village before daybreak, each with just a bedroll and a bamboo basket carrying their belongings. Huie was in his early teens. His mother packed them biscuits for their journey. They caught a small boat to Hong Kong. While waiting for their ship to America to depart, Huie idled in Hong Kong, spending his days on the waterfront, where he saw his first Europeans, "strange people, with fiery hair and blue-grey eyes." Finally, they set sail for America on a large ship with three heavy masts and billowing sails.

A vast majority of Chinese immigration to America in the nineteenth century would originate from just four counties, the Siyi, in the western part of the Pearl River Delta: Taishan, where a quarter of the population would ultimately leave for overseas; Kaiping; Enping; and Xinhui. The inhabitants of the Four Counties were mostly farmers, though the land was hilly and rocky. The climate was temperate all year round. The mountains that surrounded the Siyi on three sides meant its people were isolated from the rest of the country. Why this parcel of China, no bigger than the state of Connecticut, drove so much emigration to America remains the subject of some debate. When the people of Siyi began making their way to America, it was a time of upheaval in their homeland. The population of Guangdong had surged in the first half of the nineteenth century, making land increasingly scarce. Political tumult was also roiling China. The worst unrest came from the Taiping Rebellion, which killed at least ten million people between 1851 and 1864. In Guangdong province, an insurgency by a secret society, who became known as the "red turbans," and a savage conflict between the native Punti population and the Hakka, a minority group, contributed to the turmoil. Yet these explanations alone seem inadequate. Other regions of China experienced greater economic privations that did not lead to widespread migration. The timing and geography of the political disturbances do not correspond neatly with the exodus overseas. A decisive factor seems to have been that the inhabitants of the Pearl River Delta were unusually familiar with the West. Some of the earliest Chinese writings about the United States, dating back to the early nineteenth century, came from the region. Guangzhou, the provincial capital (known then as Canton), had a long history as an important trading port and was a frequent destination for American merchants and missionaries. Hong Kong, a hub of trade and commerce, was just a few days' journey away by boat.

Most of the vessels crisscrossing the Pacific early in the gold rush were cargo ships that lacked passenger quarters. Shipmasters stuffed the Chinese sojourners into overcrowded holds that lacked sanitation; food and water were usually meager. In 1854, a ship arrived in San Francisco harbor with a hundred dead Chinese passengers, a fifth of those on board. One captain contracted to carry Chinese to America aboard his ship, the *Santa Teresa,* encountered an epic storm. He rushed to lower the sails and seal all the openings to the hold where the Chinese were confined, so that the ship would not sink if it capsized. The ship lay helpless to the waves and the wind. After several days of this, the storm began to subside. A terrible odor, screaming, and wailing came from belowdecks. "The Chinese were scared, thirsty and hungry from the ordeal of several days of living in an inferno of darkness and agony, not knowing where they were and what would happen to them," an account later said. Several people had died. The crew commenced feeding rice to the Chinese, a process that took several hours. The dead below the hatches were brought up by the Chinese themselves, and after a prayer was read, they were slid into the sea. "There can be no excuse before God or man for the terrible mortality which has occurred on some of the vessels containing Chinese passengers," William Speer, a Presbyterian missionary who cared for many Chinese after they disembarked in San Francisco, later wrote. During Huie Kin's trip, his eldest cousin, Huie Ngou, the leader of their band of travelers, suddenly became feverish and struggled to breathe. He passed out and later died; his body was wrapped in a sheet and lowered into the ocean. Huie and his other cousins stood for hours staring out into the inky blackness of the sea, overwhelmed by grief. When the fog lifted, on a cool September morning, and they finally sighted land, Huie later wrote that the feeling was indescribable: "To be actually at the 'Golden Gate' of the land of our dreams!"

The individual stories of the earliest Chinese arrivals in America have mostly slipped through historians' grasps. In 1878, a reporter for the *San Francisco Chronicle* set out to investigate how the "Mongolian octopus developed and fastened its tentacles upon the city." The reporter's first stop was the offices of the Sam Yup Company, one of the mutual aid associations that looked after the interests of Chinese immigrants, on Dupont Street, in the city's Chinese quarter. (Sam Yup is the Cantonese romanization for Sanyi, the three counties that surround Guangzhou.) Interviews with an official there who spoke good English, as well as other "leading Chinamen," yielded the account of the merchant Chum Ming, who they said had come to America in 1847.

On February 2, 1848, a pioneering merchant named Charles V. Gillespie arrived in San Francisco aboard the American brigantine *Eagle*. Several years earlier, in 1841, Gillespie had become the first American resident in Hong Kong. He traveled frequently between Guangzhou, Hong Kong, and Macau, and had made a trip to California the year before to sell Chinese goods. On this trip, he brought with him a cargo of silk handkerchiefs, velvet slippers, rhubarb, and tea. Two Chinese men and one woman accompanied Gillespie. He later described them as "the first Chinese who came here." After the discovery of gold, the two men went off to the mines; Gillespie himself became a gold dealer, choosing to remain in America. The Chinese woman, who went by the name Maria Seise, stayed on as a servant with his family for more than thirty years, joining the Trinity Episcopal Church and becoming a close companion of Gillespie's wife. Seise's story was unusual. She had run away from her home in Guangzhou and made her way to Macau, where she worked for a Portuguese family. She later married a Portuguese sailor, who never returned from a sea voyage. Seise traveled to the Sandwich Islands as a servant with another American family, before returning to China and eventually finding employment with the Gillespies.

In July 1849, the manifest of a British sailing vessel, the *Swallow*, recorded that an elderly Chinese merchant named Yuan Sheng arrived in San Francisco, along with two other Chinese passengers. Notably, this was not Yuan's first trip across the Pacific. He had previously spent time in New York and then gone on to Charleston, South Carolina, before returning to China. In America, he went by the name Norman Assing—also spelled, variously, Ah-Sing and Asing. He spoke fluent English and wore a stovepipe hat atop his queue. In San Francisco, he opened a restaurant and trading company.

By the beginning of 1850, there were about eight hundred Chinese in San Francisco. In the fall, three hundred of them had gathered at the Canton restaurant on Jackson Street and appointed Selim E. Woodworth, a former naval commander and businessman, as their adviser. They adopted a resolution acknowledging their vulnerable position: "strangers as we are, in a strange land, unacquainted with the language and customs of this, our adopted country," the Chinese needed a counselor "in the event of any unforeseen difficulties arising." For the new arrivals from China, America was a foreboding place. In 1850, a Chinese merchant named Luchong sailed through the Golden Gate, the narrow strait that marks the entrance of San Francisco Bay. Luchong reflected later in a letter to a cousin about his soaring optimism after glimpsing land. Soon after dropping anchor, however, a fleet of pirates on boats scrambled aboard, intent on robbing the passengers. They hurled Luchong into a dinghy, where an oarsman tried to rob him. After a struggle, his attacker tied him to a post on the wharf by his long braid. Luchong managed to cut himself loose with a small blade from his pouch. He wandered along the streets of San Francisco, marveling at the entertaining costumes of the people. Luchong later, however, found himself being summoned by a distinguished-looking man, whom he followed, only to find himself under arrest, suspected of being an accomplice in a robbery. "I was seized by the nape of the neck and hurried down a dark staircase and thrown like a sack into a dirty, dingy cell." He ended his first day's adventures in California on the floor of a jail cell.

Notwithstanding Luchong's experience, at least initially, the reception for the Chinese was generally positive. In the summer of 1850, city leaders in San Francisco held a public ceremony to welcome them. On August 28, the Chinese assembled in Portsmouth Square, in front of other residents, and were presented with Chinese books, Bibles, and religious tracts that had been printed in Guangzhou. Frederick Woodworth, the vice consul of the San Francisco port, Mayor John Geary, and two pastors, the Rev. Albert Williams, of the First Presbyterian Church, and the Rev. Timothy Dwight Hunt, the moderator of the Presbytery of San Francisco, delivered remarks. Norman Assing, the merchant who had arrived on the *Swallow,* translated the speeches into Cantonese. Williams later wrote that the speakers were united in conveying "the pleasure shared in common by the citizens of San Francisco, at their presence" and the hope that more of their brethren would cross the ocean to join them in America, where they would enjoy "welcome and protection." Geary, the city's mayor, invited them to join a funeral procession the next day honoring President Zachary Taylor, who had died seven weeks earlier. The news had only just arrived in California.

At eleven in the morning the following day, a procession of city personages escorted a funeral hearse pulled by four white horses. A band played a solemn dirge as the procession wound its way through streets crowded with mourners. Bringing up the rear of the procession were the Chinese, dressed in their native finery. The next day, Assing delivered a formal message to Geary, thanking him for his invitation to take part in the ceremony: "The China Boys feel proud of the distinction you have shown them, and will always endeavor to merit your good opinion and the good opinion of the citizens of their adopted country."

In January 1852, during his state of the state address, Governor John McDougal called for more Chinese to come to California. McDougal, a Democrat, had advocated at the state's constitutional convention for excluding from California certain classes of Black people. He also supported a fugitive slave law, which the legislature later enacted, ensuring that formerly enslaved Africans who escaped to California could be reclaimed by their masters. But he believed the Chinese could be a source of cheap labor for white Americans. He urged the legislature to focus on the issue of land reclamation and the drainage of swampland, suggesting the Chinese, "one of the most worthy classes of our new adopted citizens," could help with this work.

Many California businessmen envisioned a golden age of trade between China and the United States and embraced Chinese immigration as part of that interchange. A few months after McDougal's address, the *Alta California*, the first daily newspaper in California, took note of the growing number of "Celestials," as the Chinese were often called, arriving in the city. "Scarcely a ship arrives here that does not bring an increase to this worthy integer of our population," the article said. "They are among the most industrious, quiet, patient people among us." The article predicted that one day the halls of Congress would be "graced by the presence of a long-queued Mandarin sitting, voting, and speaking," and that "China Boys will yet vote at the same polls, study at the same schools and bow at the same Altar as our own countrymen."

In the early days of the Chinese migration, San Francisco, or *Dai Fow,* "Big City," as they called it, was mostly just a stopover, a place to stock up on provisions before heading to the mines. New arrivals encountered a city under construction. There were canvas tents and makeshift houses made of corrugated iron, alongside more permanent brick buildings. Soon, a Chinese quarter, dubbed "Little China," sprang up, with stores stocked with tea, dried foods, and other goods. Signs with Chinese characters and festooned with red ribbons hung over doorways. Performances went on in a Chinese theater. Throughout the town, there were Chinese hand laundries, or wash houses, in which men ironed with copper pots made hot by burning charcoal. Processions of Chinese heading for the mines passed through town, their carts laden with equipment. The men were often carrying boots, the one concession to Western fashion that Chinese miners made.

In the mining districts, the Chinese tended to congregate together. Many of the white prospectors who encountered the Chinese early on viewed them as curiosities. Timothy Coffin Osborn had sailed around Cape Horn to San Francisco from New York with two cousins. They made their way to the Southern Mines on the Merced River. In a journal entry from December 26, 1850, Osborn wrote about a group of Chinese building a log cabin nearby. He described them as "apparently of good 'blood' and very polite." One man in the group spoke English, and Osborn peppered him with questions. In his diary, Osborn included a sample of the man's writing: a scrap of paper with fifty Chinese characters and their English translations. Ezra Gregg wrote to his brothers and sisters back home in Vermont that the Chinese he spent so much time with in the California wilderness, outside of Downieville, sounded like a "flock of black birds" when they talked amongst themselves but that "they are very good neighbors."

Even so, the racial hierarchy in the mines was always clear. Chinese miners typically only worked claims abandoned by white miners, patiently scratching out earnings of two or three dollars a day. One of the few surviving accounts from the early days of the gold rush that contained extended observations of the Chinese came from John D. Borthwick, a Scotsman who arrived in San Francisco in 1851 and later boarded a steamer for Sacramento. He made his way by stagecoach to the town of Placerville—a single street of clapboard houses and log cabins, built into a hollow at the side of a creek. Miners in Placerville were mostly working on surface diggings, in which they'd sift through layers of dirt—a practice known as placer mining—often using a long wooden trough known as a long tom, or a cradle that they'd rock back and forth. A group of Chinese had recently arrived at the creek, setting up camp near a cabin where Borthwick was staying, about two miles outside of Placerville. "They did not venture to assert equal rights so far as to take up any claim which other miners would think it worth while to work; but in such places as yielded them a dollar or two a day they were allowed to scratch away unmolested," Borthwick wrote. "Had they happened to strike a rich lead, they would have been driven off their claim immediately." Nevertheless, some Chinese stumbled upon unimaginable fortunes. At Moore's Flat on the Yuba River, a company of Chinese miners found a 240-pound nugget valued at $50,000. In another abandoned claim on the Feather River, Chinese miners found a 40-pound nugget. To avoid garnering unwanted attention from white miners, they sanded it down into smaller pieces and sold it with the rest of their gold dust.

The first mass expulsion of Chinese from the mines took place in the fall of 1849, in a hilly encampment that became known as Chinese Camp, above Woods Creek, in Tuolumne County, near what is today Yosemite National Park. A ship's captain had persuaded the Chinese crew members of a stranded ship to come help him sift for gold. The encampment began to attract other Chinese. Several dozen were working there for an English company, when a group of white miners, whom the California historian Theodore Hittell later characterized as "lazy and shiftless," forced them out. Hittell wrote that a few other, isolated expulsions occurred but no larger movement because "the Chinamen had not as yet come in such numbers as to cause apprehensions in the mind of any except a comparatively very few."

.   .   .

In 1852, the number of Chinese passing through San Francisco's Custom House jumped to more than twenty thousand from less than three thousand in the previous year. One miner commented in his diary: "Chinamen are getting to be altogether too plentiful in the country. Six months ago it was seldom one was seen, but lately gangs of them have been coming in." Goodwill towards them dissipated rapidly. In April, the State Assembly's Committee on Mines and Mining Interests issued a report that warned about the "vast numbers of the Asiatic races, and of the inhabitants of the Pacific Islands, and of many others dissimilar from ourselves in customs, language and education." In what would become a recurring theme against the Chinese, the committee described them as unassimilable, with no interest in becoming citizens, nor "would it be wise to promote such a wish, should any exist." Governor John Bigler, a Democrat facing a difficult re-election the following year, recognized a political opportunity in the growing anti-Chinese sentiment. On April 23, 1852, just before the close of the legislative session, he called on the legislature to halt Chinese immigration. His message was filled with racial overtones, alluding to a coming inundation from China and misleadingly depicting Chinese immigrants as coolie laborers, bound by oppressive contracts. Bigler's opprobrium of the Chinese as a "coolie race" would prove to be a resilient epithet, becoming a convenient political instrument whenever white Americans needed a racial scapegoat. The label likened them to enslaved Africans; their low wages and condition of servitude made them a threat to free white labor. This turned opposition to Chinese immigration into a matter of principle, even though it was rooted in racial difference. Bigler explicitly differentiated the Chinese from white European immigrants, arguing that the Chinese had not come to America seeking the "blessings of freedom" but only to "acquire a certain amount of the precious metals" and then return home. He also doubted that the "yellow or tawny races of the Asiatics" could become citizens under the country's naturalization laws that restricted the privilege to "free white persons." Anti-coolieism became a kind of shape-shifting, racist cause.

Bigler's call to halt Chinese immigration prompted a remarkable pair of rebuttals from the community. Shortly afterward, two Chinese merchants, Hab Wa and Tong Achick, issued a response that was republished in newspapers across the country. Growing up, Tong had been one of a handful of the original students at the Morrison Education Society school, founded by Protestant missionaries, in Macau. Tong was eleven at the time, the oldest of three brothers, from a nearby village. The school, along with its students, later moved to Hong Kong, occupying a hillside overlooking the harbor. Tong became fluent in English and, after graduation, worked as an interpreter for the chief magistrate's office in Hong Kong. He also converted to Christianity. In 1852, he traveled to the United States with an uncle, bringing with him letters of introduction from Western clergymen in Hong Kong. Protestant leaders in San Francisco were captivated by Tong's English fluency and refined manner. Even though Tong was only in his early twenties, he quickly became an influential figure in the Chinese community, particularly in its dealings with Americans.

Tong Achick and Hab Wa went to great lengths in their letter to dismantle Bigler's allegations about Chinese coolies, emphasizing that the aspirations of their countrymen were like those of other immigrants to the country. "The poor Chinaman does not come as a slave," they wrote. "He comes because of his desire for independence, and he is assisted by the charity of his countrymen, which they bestow on him safely, because he is industrious and honestly repays them. When he gets to the mines, he sets to work with patience, industry, temperance, and economy." They insisted, too, that Bigler was wrong that the Chinese were not interested in citizenship. "If the privileges of your laws are open to us, some of us will doubtless acquire your habits, your language, your ideas, your feelings, your morals, your forms, and become citizens of your country," they wrote.

The citizenship issue underscored the ways in which the Chinese complicated America's racial stratification. The Nationality Act of 1790 restricted naturalization to "free white persons of good moral character," but there was some ambiguity in the way judges interpreted the law. Norman Assing, the merchant who served as a translator when city officials welcomed the Chinese, was apparently able to take advantage and become a citizen, as were some other Chinese arrivals. Assing's response to Bigler was published, in early May, by the *Alta California*. Assing, who described himself as "a Chinaman, a republican, and a lover of free institutions," assailed Bigler for a message that threatened to "prejudice the public mind against my people, to enable those who wait the opportunity to hunt them down, and rob them of the rewards of their toil." The framers of the Constitution, he maintained, would never have countenanced "an aristocracy of *skin*."

In early May, Tong Achick went to Sacramento to meet with Bigler, bearing gifts of silk, handkerchiefs, and shawls. Bigler introduced the Chinese emissary to other senior officials. Tong later reported to his fellow Chinese that he had been "very honorably entertained." Bigler, however, suddenly broke off his engagement with Chinese leaders. A follow-up letter to the governor from Tong Achick and Hab Wa is filled with alarm about the change in tenor in the mines. They reported a violent incident at Weaver's Creek, a settlement of a dozen log cabins in gold country, in which white miners had held long ropes between them and dragged them across a Chinese encampment, sweeping it away. "At many places they have been driven away from their work and deprived of their claim," they wrote. "Many hundreds of Chinamen have thus been reduced to misery and are now wandering about the mountains, looking for new places, where they may be allowed to dig, and fearful that they will be driven away again."

In the town of Columbia, in Tuolumne County, miners held a mass meeting and enacted a series of resolutions decrying those flooding the state with "degraded Asiatics." The miners voted to bar Chinese from mining in the district and convened a "vigilance committee" of twenty local officials to enforce the rule. A similar meeting was held at a hotel at Foster's Bar, on the Yuba River, in which the miners decreed that "large numbers of foreigners, and Chinese especially, are overrunning and now occupying a large portion of the mining lands in this vicinity, to the injury and disadvantage of American citizens." The Chinese would be required to "*vamose the ranche*," the miners resolved. In El Dorado County, white residents turned away stagecoaches carrying Chinese miners and passed resolutions barring them from working in the mines; at Weber Creek, tents and mining equipment belonging to Chinese were burned. Along the banks of the north fork of the American River, several dozen white miners, accompanied by a band playing music, drove off two hundred Chinese miners, and then headed down to a different encampment to do the same to four hundred other Chinese.

By this point, Chinese leaders in San Francisco had become convinced they needed to send an urgent message to their countrymen. A clipper ship, *Invincible,* left San Francisco for Hong Kong, carrying circulars with a warning about what was happening in America: Chinese were no longer welcome.

CHAPTER 2

Indian, Negro, or Chinaman

In early 1853, the members of the California State Assembly's Committee on Mines and Mining Interests traveled to San Francisco for an unusual meeting. The mining committee was an eclectic group, a product of the diverse assemblage of people who had thronged to the state during the gold rush. The committee was led by a Democrat, James Gardner, a native of South Carolina who had arrived in California in 1849 by way of the Isthmus of Panama and made his way to the gold-fields along the Yuba River. Others on the committee included Benjamin B. Redding, a twenty-nine-year-old who had organized a company of fortune-seekers who sailed around the tip of South America to reach the Pacific coast from Yarmouth, Nova Scotia, and Thomas Thompson Cabaniss, a twenty-seven-year-old doctor who would later be appointed the physician of Siskyou County and then its coroner. They had traveled from Benecia, where the legislature was in session, at the request of the heads of the four houses, or *huiguan,* that represented the interests of Chinese immigrants. The *huiguan,* essentially mutual aid associations, were the anchors of the expanding Chinese community. Each of the *huiguan,* also known as companies, served members from a different region or dialect group in Guangdong province. They met new arrivals when they disembarked, offering them room and board and advancing money to buy tools and other supplies. If a member died in America, the *huiguan* made sure their bones were shipped back to China for burial. Merchants from Sanyi, the three counties surrounding Guangzhou, and others from Siyi, the four counties in the western part of the Pearl River Delta, had established the first two *huiguan*. Norman Assing later helped to found the Yeong Wo Association, which included members from the Zhongshan region, east of the mouth of the Pearl River on the South China Sea, near Macau, Guangzhou, and Hong Kong. A fourth *huiguan* represented emigrants from Guangdong who overwhelmingly spoke the Hakka dialect, instead of Cantonese and its variants. The Yeong Wo Association soon became the largest and most influential of the associations, occupying a striking, light-blue-painted building on Telegraph Hill in San Francisco, whose wide entrance and portico were guarded by a pair of wood-carved lions. Assing served as its first president, but health issues forced the elderly Chinese leader to resign after only a brief tenure. He was replaced by his young protégé, Tong Achick.

In the meeting with the lawmakers, Tong served as the *huiguan* leaders' translator. Through him, they conveyed their upset to Gardner and the other committee members about the mistreatment of Chinese in the mines. They complained that they had been paying large sums in taxes to the state—foreign miners were required to pay a license fee to the state of $3 a month—but failed to receive the protections that should come with their payments. The houses had been keeping a record of the abuses endured by Chinese miners. A partial accounting provided later by one merchant: "Yu Lin-shing, a Chinese, was shot and killed by an American. The murderer was apprehended and brought to the place of justice. He was released without condemnation." Another one: "Liu Kiu was put to death by an American; the murderer was captured and put in prison; but, as usual, was released without trial." In his subsequent report about the meeting, Gardner wrote that the merchants were focused, in particular, on the fact "that in disputes which have arisen between our citizens and Chinese," often their testimony was not allowed in court because of "the color of their skin."

At issue was a statute, enacted in 1850, that stated no "black or mulatto person, or Indian, shall be permitted to give evidence in favor of, or against, a white person." The law was part of a host of measures passed by the legislature that were aimed at ensuring that white Californians remained atop the state's racial hierarchy. During the state's constitutional convention, in 1849, delegates had voted to ban slavery from the state, but a vigorous debate had ensued over whether to exclude free Black people. A faction of Democratic delegates argued that the white and Black races could not co-exist together. The measure was defeated, in part because delegates feared it would jeopardize California's chances at statehood. Instead, the first legislature set about restricting the rights of Black people in the state. Foreigners were targeted as well, through the enactment of the tax on foreign miners. That law, too, became overtly racial in its orientation when Mexican and other miners from Latin America became the ones overwhelmingly targeted. (Mexican American residents, who accounted for about a tenth of the state's population in 1850, occupied an ambiguous status in California, defined as white under the state's constitution but often enduring bigotry and discrimination as well.) Many California judges had been excluding Chinese testimony in their courtrooms, but others had been giving them greater latitude under the law. The members of the mining committee believed the language of the statute meant Chinese testimony was inadmissible and tried to explain this to the *huiguan* leaders, Gardner later wrote, but "without the desired effect."

Despite Bigler's denunciations of the Chinese the year before, the members of the committee were skeptical that America was in any danger of being overrun by Chinese. The committee pressed the merchants, however, about Bigler's allegations about coolie labor. The heads of the houses explained that a vast majority of Chinese in the country had come voluntarily. The *huiguan* leaders had a variety of their own suggestions for ameliorating the tensions in the mines—notably including bolstering the effort to collect the taxes required of Chinese miners. Rather than seeing the license fees as a discriminatory burden, the merchants saw them as a way of purchasing peace. They even offered to furnish interpreters to assist the tax collectors and promised to do what they could to persuade their members to pay the fees. They also vowed to do their utmost to discourage more of their countrymen from coming. "We have no authority there, but very confidently believe we could exert much influence," Tong Achick said, suggesting that emigration would soon taper off.

.   .   .

It is unclear whether the *huiguan* leaders had any real ability to stand in the way of the boatloads coming from China. The discovery of gold in Australia in 1851 temporarily diverted tens of thousands of Chinese to the goldfields there. In 1853, the number of arrivals in San Francisco fell, only to rebound the following year. A kind of truce developed in the mining districts. The legislature made a variety of amendments to the foreign miners tax, including raising the fee by a dollar to $4 a month per person. The resulting infusion of cash helped to deliver a begrudging tolerance for the Chinese presence. In many of the locations where they were driven out—Columbia, Foster's Bar, Woods Creek, and elsewhere—the Chinese eventually returned. In a letter to his parents, from Jones Bar on the north fork of the American River, one miner described two hundred Chinese miners being driven out two weeks earlier, only to return "as thick as ever." Individual prospecting in creeks and streams had begun to give way to larger companies of miners working in concert. Chinese miners built elaborate "wing dams" that partially redirected rivers and streams onto diggings below. Miners learned to use nozzles and hoses to direct pressurized water at hillsides and riverbanks to dislodge gravel and sediment and send slurry through sluice boxes.

It fell to local sheriff's departments to collect the $4 per month license fee that filled the coffers of mining districts. Many tax collectors were brutal in their tactics. One sheriff's deputy kept a diary of the mundane violence he inflicted: "Went down to the little Yuba thence up shot a Chinaman had a hell of a time returned home by way of Fosters." Another entry: "hunted Chinamen in the night, done very well, collected about 80 licenses." A few months later: "Loafing around doing nothing but picking up a few Chinamen whom their bad luck and my good threw in my way."

In San Francisco, where the Chinese quarter was growing rapidly, random violence meted out by white Americans on Chinese residents became routine. In one brutal assault on Dupont Street, described in a newspaper account, a white American held a Chinese man by his braid and "kicked and beat him until he was tired," while a large crowd watched. The victim managed to straggle away, only to be picked up by a policeman who saw his bloody face and put him in jail for the night; his assailant was not arrested. Another article decried the "valiant rowdies" who were frequently practicing their "pugilistic skill" on the "helpless Chinaman." *Huiguan* leaders like Norman Assing sometimes served as court interpreters and advocates for the Chinese, but cases were often dismissed because no translators were available. Chinese merchants, the most affluent members of the community, began offering rewards for information about the death of their countrymen. In one case, Tong Achick and another merchant, Chun Aching, posted a thousand-dollar reward, on behalf of the "storekeepers of Sacramento Street," for any information leading to the "arrest and identification of the man who shot and killed the Chinaman, Yu Awa, on the corner of Jackson and Davis Streets."

In the face of near-constant strife, the Chinese concluded they needed an American champion. In March 1853, they approached the Rev. William Speer, a Presbyterian missionary who had arrived in San Francisco several months earlier. The Chinese asked Speer to become their "chief in this country," he later wrote. According to Speer, the Chinese needed a "general superintendent," someone who could shield them from the "acts of injury and plunder, to which they are now daily liable." Speer had previously spent almost four years in Guangzhou as the first Presbyterian missionary to the region. His first wife, Cornelia, had died while giving birth to their first child, Mary Cornelia, soon after the couple's arrival; six months later, the infant died as well. But Speer had stayed in the field for several more years, until health issues forced him to sail back to the United States. As the numbers of Chinese arriving in San Francisco steadily grew, the Rev. Albert Williams, pastor of the First Presbyterian Church, wrote to his denomination's Board of Foreign Missions, imploring them to dispatch someone with language skills to minister to the Chinese. The board decided to send Speer and his new wife, Elizabeth. After a difficult voyage from New York, by way of Panama, the Speers arrived in San Francisco in November 1852. Soon after their arrival, the pastor met with both Norman Assing and Tong Achick. Speer seemed to view Assing with suspicion, writing his "character was not good." Hints of Assing's darker side can be found in reports from Recorder's Court, where he appeared regularly after various violent encounters. Speer was relieved that Tong succeeded Assing in his leadership position. In his letter to the board, explaining the request from Chinese leaders, Speer expressed surprise at their willingness to trust him, even though he was an outsider.

In early 1853, at churches and for civic groups, Speer began a series of lectures for white Americans about the Chinese. He extolled their history and civilization and encouraged trade between the two countries. But he also saw the Chinese as a solution to the labor shortage in the South that had resulted from the end of African slavery, replacing the "sons of Ham" with the "diligent descendants of the old and world-renowned dynasty of the 'Han.'" Speer believed God had conferred upon America the privilege of being "agents of the regeneration of two dark continents of heathenism." Africa had sent millions of "ignorant sable sons and daughters" to be schooled in America, and as the education of one race was nearing an end, a new door had opened. "Another, but ancient, wealthy, and intelligent, in comparison, is brought to seek us of the same boon," he said. He urged the citizens of California to take their awesome responsibility seriously. They may have come in search of gold, but there was a far greater purpose in store for them.

In the fall of 1853, Speer's ministry to the Chinese brought him to a spare courtroom in Nevada City, a bustling gold-mining town in the foothills of the Sierra Nevada. Miners heading down to Sacramento had first discovered gold in the area four years earlier. The town was situated in a grassy valley fed by Wolf Creek, a tributary of the Bear River. Within a year, the settlement consisted of some 250 buildings. Stagecoaches frequently ran through town, carrying supplies to the mining camps in the neighboring hills. By 1852, about four thousand Chinese had settled in Nevada County.

On the night of August 9, 1853, on Greenhorn Creek, near the Bear River, two brothers, George and John Hall, and a third man, Samuel Wiseman, fell upon a Chinese miner and tried to rob him. The man managed to flee and cry out for help, as the Americans trailed behind. A cousin, Ling Sing, emerged from his tent, and rushed to his aid, but George Hall, a married midwestern native who was about thirty years old, with a dark complexion and blue eyes, shot Ling Sing in the back with a shotgun. The Chinese man was left with several deep wounds near his spine and fifteen other smaller cuts in his back from the buckshot. He later died. The only witnesses were several Chinese miners. The prosecutor on the case, William Stewart, was a twenty-seven-year-old district attorney who had never practiced law before he was appointed to his post several months earlier. Stewart, a native of New York, had arrived in Nevada City in 1850. After ranging across the region, working the diggings as a miner and later running a sawmill, he decided to study law in Nevada City under the tutelage of J. R. McConnell, the district attorney. When McConnell resigned his post several months later, Stewart was admitted to the bar and appointed to fill the job on the same day. Stewart interviewed the Chinese miners and found they all told the same story. The prosecutor obtained an allowance of $5,000 for use in the trial and made sure the witnesses were held in separate rooms, so they couldn't communicate with each other before trial. Finally, he recognized that he urgently needed to find a Chinese translator. He traveled to San Francisco and, at considerable length, persuaded Speer to attend the trial. William T. Barbour, the district court judge presiding over the case, later issued a subpoena for Speer to appear. According to a letter Speer wrote recounting the trial, Barbour wanted to ensure the evidence in the case was properly interpreted and was also worried about the "prejudices of the mining community," since "the Chinese are so often suspected of scheming and falsehood." Barbour, a native of Danville, Kentucky, was a colorful presence in the community, known to frequent a saloon on Main Street with other lawyers. He once got into an argument with a gambler, who drew a pistol and was about to kill him before another lawyer rushed into the saloon with a pine root and struck the man over the head. Nevertheless, Speer described Barbour as an "upright and intelligent gentleman."

Before departing San Francisco, Stewart asked Speer for his suggestions about what form of oath would be binding upon the Chinese. The prosecutor had heard that cutting off a chicken's head or burning paper would serve the purpose. Speer told him that would work as well as any other method, Stewart later recalled. On October 4, ten white men were seated as part of the trial's jury, but the candidate pool was exhausted, prompting Barbour to order the sheriff to bring in a new group of potential jurors the next day. Two more men were selected, and the trial began. Stewart called at least three Chinese witnesses, who were all sworn in with a pledge, written on yellow paper, to tell the truth; the paper was then burned. Speer later described the Chinese testimony as "direct, clear and, after severe cross-examination, to every mind unbiased, convincing." The defendants marshaled more than twenty white witnesses. After four days of trial testimony, the jury began their deliberations on Saturday evening. Finally, at two o'clock in the morning, the jury returned to the courtroom and pronounced George Hall guilty. (His brother was acquitted.) The sentencing was set for late November, when court was back in session in Nevada County.

In late October, the mutilated body of another Chinese miner was found near Goodyear's Bar, along the North Yuba River. No arrest was made. When the day of Hall's sentencing arrived, the courtroom was crowded. He insisted upon his innocence. "It seems hard that because I was so unlucky as to be there when that Chinaman was killed, I should be put down as his murderer," he said. "Those Chinamen, because I had a difficulty with one of them, swore my life away. I must now leave my wife and friends and all I hold dear because I was so unlucky as to have trouble with them." Barbour, however, said that he had little doubt that justice had been properly rendered. He spoke stirringly about the colorblind nature of the law. "Many persons here, have supposed that it is less heinous to kill a Negro, an Indian or a Chinaman, than a white person," he said. "This is a gross error. The law of our country throws the aegis of its protection upon all within its jurisdiction, it knows no race, color or distinction." Barbour sentenced Hall to death by hanging.

Hall appealed his case to the California Supreme Court, a three-member panel that met in San Jose. A petition began to circulate in the community for the governor of the state to commute Hall's sentence to life in prison. During the hearing before the Supreme Court, McConnell, Hall's lawyer, introduced a new argument: that the testimony of Chinese witnesses should not have been considered by the jury, under the law that barred testimony of an Indian against a white man. Stewart argued no objection had been raised in the trial, which meant it could not be considered on appeal; moreover, he argued that the witnesses were not Indians but of the Chinese race. But Chief Justice Hugh Campbell Murray, a twenty-eight-year-old former trial judge in San Francisco who had a reputation as a drinker and gambler, and Associate Justice Solomon Heydenfeldt, voted to reverse the guilty verdict. Murray wrote the majority opinion, delivering a lengthy disquisition about his belief that the term "Indian" in the 1850 statute should be understood broadly as encompassing "the whole of the Mongolian race." He argued that the legislature's intention was to cover "every known class or shade of color" in the law, in order to "protect the white person" from testimony "other than that of persons of the same caste." Even if Indians did not include the Chinese, Murray wrote that the words "black person" should be understood to be "contradistinguished from white," which meant that it excluded "all other races other than Caucasian." Murray's focus was not just on the statute but on the dangers that would arise if the rights of a "race of people whom nature has marked as inferior" were not properly circumscribed. He feared the establishment of a precedent that would lead to the awarding of other privileges to the Chinese. "The same rule which would admit them to testify, would admit them to all the equal rights of citizenship, and we might soon see them at the polls, in the jury box, upon the bench, and in our legislative halls," he wrote. Murray remanded the case back to the trial court. One of the principal white witnesses in the case had died, and another could not be found. Without the Chinese testimony, Stewart, the prosecutor, decided not to retry the case. After more than a year in jail since his trial, Hall was freed.

Speer later wrote an impassioned appeal to the legislature to remedy the Supreme Court's decision, pointing out that a large percentage of the state's population was now open to being attacked, robbed, and otherwise abused with impunity. He also asserted that, with the way people of "Mongolian stock" made "countless Westward migrations since the earliest ages," Asian immigrants were as close to "the people of Europe" as they were to Native Americans and Black Americans. "If the Chinese are Indians, then *we* are Indians; if the Chinese are negroes, then *we* are negroes," Speer wrote. In fact, over the next few years, the question of Chinese testimony was often debated alongside that of Black Californians. The Chinese were considered by many to be lower on the racial hierarchy because of their status as "heathens." Black Californians themselves often emphasized this point. In 1863, as the Civil War raged and California sided with the Union, the state legislature finally ended its ban on testimony of Black Americans, but it amended its statutes to explicitly disqualify Chinese and "Mongolian" witnesses.

After the Hall trial concluded, Speer returned to San Francisco. Several months later, he opened a chapel for the Chinese, built in part with contributions from Chinese merchants. On Sundays, he held a morning Bible class and services in the afternoon and evening. Speer also established an evening school for the Chinese and a medical dispensary. Perhaps his most enterprising initiative involved the establishment of a Chinese and English newspaper, *The Oriental*. While his superiors at the Presbyterian Board of Foreign Missions were skeptical of the newspaper's value, Speer insisted it represented an "incalculable advantage to the Chinese." A Chinese immigrant, Lee Kan, who had been educated at an American missionary school in Hong Kong, produced the issues in Chinese, while Speer took care of the English. Chinese merchant leaders agreed to be responsible for acquiring subscribers for the newspaper. Speer explained to the board that it was intended as a vehicle for conveying "our customs, religion, laws, and general news" to the Chinese population. He viewed the English-language section as equally vital: "No people are so little known and comprehended, even in our own midst."

In the first issue, Speer wrote about the court's ruling on Chinese testimony, responding to a writer who had blamed the "mendacity of the Chinese" for the way they were persecuted. "If the 'mendacity' of the Chinese be the cause of the flagrant wrong inflicted upon them by excluding them from the privilege of protection of our laws, when abused, plundered, cheated, murdered, by native Californians, Mexicans, Chilenos, Irish, Dutch, American, or by any other individuals of European Extraction, then why does not the notorious mendacity of the three first mentioned classes exclude them also?" he wrote. "All testimony should be received in judicial trials, and allowed to go for just what it is worth. Even the wickedest have social rights, to violate which is to endanger the community, and every man in it."

Speer's most tangible accomplishment on behalf of the Chinese came in 1855, when he lobbied against a proposal to raise the foreign miners tax to $6 a month and, every year thereafter, an additional $2 a month. Speer produced another lengthy monograph, "An Humble Plea Addressed to the Legislature of California in Behalf of the Immigrants from the Empire of China to the United States." He sent copies to legislators, newspaper editors, and other Christian believers throughout the state. "Scarce any persons here care [to] speak out in their behalf, and it seemed important as a missionary, and one who has lived among them and whom they besought, so to lift up a word for them," he later wrote. The tract was full of details about the Chinese, countering the "coolie" label and outlining the benefits they brought to the state. He described the violence inflicted upon the Chinese by sheriff's deputies enforcing the license fees and strenuously argued that the safety of the Chinese was beneficial to all citizens. Speer appealed to the legislators' concern for the spiritual welfare of the Chinese. "I can scarce hope for success as a minister of the gospel in leading them to adore *our* God, or love *our* Savior, so long as the present state of things continues," he wrote. The legislature voted overwhelmingly against the measure.

For all of Speer's energetic ministration, he struggled to accomplish his chief aim: the conversion of souls. His letters record only one baptism of a Chinese convert, a young man named Yeung Fo, who wrote in his statement of faith that he had in the past believed in the "doctrines of Buddha" and had been "licentious, disobedient, covetous, malicious, spoken falsehoods, and broken the Sabbath, times without number" but had been awakened by the "preaching of the truth." Speer's ministry was ultimately short-lived, ended prematurely by health issues, including exhaustion and pulmonary disease that led to a chronic cough and chest pains. In the spring of 1856, he decided to pause his mission work in San Francisco and embark on a trip to the Sandwich Islands, known today as Hawaii, in hopes that the change in climate would be beneficial, but the five-month stay yielded little improvement. He complained in his letters about the caustic effect on his lungs of the raw, cold winds of San Francisco. In early 1857, the Presbytery in California ordered Speer to close the mission and directed him to recuperate in the South. When the Chinese learned that Speer was to depart, a stream of them came to the mission to bid him farewell. Speer delivered a final address that was printed and distributed throughout the city and even to the goldfields. In a concluding letter to the Board of Foreign Missions, Speer once again mentioned the issue of Chinese court testimony but expressed optimism that their station was improving. "At no period have the Chinese stood fairer in California than at present, since they began to come in large numbers," he wrote. "Their rights, their customs, and their importance are better understood."

Here, Speer seemed to be naive, or was perhaps being sanguine about an otherwise disappointing end to his ministry. There were certainly some hopeful signs. The California Supreme Court struck down an onerous tax imposed on shipmasters for the landing of every passenger who was not eligible for citizenship. The depletion of placer mines also relieved tensions somewhat in the state's mining districts, causing many white miners to drift elsewhere in search of better opportunities. Even so, the troubles of the Chinese were only beginning.

On February 5, 1859, miners gathered at Excelsior Hall in the town of Shasta, the "Queen City of the Northern Mines," to deliberate on what to do about the "vast hordes" of Chinese miners who were "depriving the American Miner of what his own country's blood, and toil, and treasure have bequeathed to him." They agreed to set a deadline of March 1 for the expulsion of the Chinese. A few days before the deadline, however, an armed mob of two hundred white miners charged through an encampment of Chinese at the mouth of Rock Creek. They captured about seventy-five Chinese miners and marched them through town, down Main Street, and into the Chinese quarter. The mob clubbed and beat several Chinese miners; one was killed. The county's young sheriff, Clay Stockton, arrested a handful of men and issued warrants for twenty-five others. In the following days, roving bands of men throughout the region rounded up Chinese miners. "There is at present, in this County, some three hundred armed men, whose object is to expel the Chinese," Stockton wrote in a telegram to the state's governor, John B. Weller. He explained that arrests were ineffectual because the accused were invariably acquitted. Stockton asked the governor to arm the 150-man posse he had assembled. Weller sent a shipment of 113 rifles and 2,500 ball cartridges by steamer. "This spirit of mobocracy must be crushed out, no matter what it may cost," Weller wrote. The sheriff and his men were eventually able to restore order. The skirmishes came to be called the Shasta Wars. The rioters were put on trial but quickly acquitted. "Quiet once more reigns in the Republic of Shasta," a local newspaper reported.

The peace was deceiving. The white men of Shasta remained unbowed, intent on barring Chinese miners from the county. Elsewhere, organized opposition to the Chinese was spreading. Miners in Colville, near the border with Nevada Territory, passed a resolution banning the Chinese. In San Francisco, agitators established an "Anti-Coolie Association." "John Chinaman must leave," one witness to the Shasta troubles wrote in a newspaper account, "and the sooner he emigrates the better."

CHAPTER 3

The Great Army and the Iron Road

The moment deserved pomp and circumstance. Shortly after noon on January 8, 1863, Leland Stanford, the governor of California and president of the Central Pacific Railroad company, appeared on a small platform that had been erected at the corner of K and Front Streets in Sacramento. On Stanford's right and left were American flags; a ten-piece brass band on a hotel balcony across the street played patriotic tunes. Two years earlier, Stanford and other local businessmen had agreed to back the building of a railroad that would start in Sacramento, ascend the mountains of the Sierra Nevada, and make its way eastward to the Nevada Territory. The line was to be the western link to a railroad spanning the two halves of the country. The officers of the Central Pacific had resolved that a proper ceremony be held to mark the beginning of construction. Rain, however, had turned the streets into sodden corridors; several carriages carrying dignitaries and other invited guests to the event had become stranded in mud. Organizers had scattered straw around the speakers' stand in hopes of giving the assembled a dry place to stand. Some listeners balanced on a plank bridging the watery street. Stanford, who had a fleshy face, bushy eyebrows, and an imposing frame, was a plodding speaker. On this day, he kept his remarks mercifully brief. "Fellow citizens: I congratulate you upon the commencement of the great work which, in its results to the State of California and the Pacific coast, and to the nation itself, is to be what the Erie Canal was to New York and the Western States," Stanford said. "The work will go on from this side, to completion, as rapidly as possible. There will be no delay, no halting, no uncertainty in its continued progress. We may now look forward with confidence to the day, not far distant, when the Pacific will be bound to the Atlantic by iron bonds, that shall consolidate and strengthen the ties of nationality, and advance with giant strides the prosperity of our state and our country." Two horse-drawn wagons, draped with bunting and laden with earth, trundled forward. Stanford deposited a shovelful on the muddy embankment, a ceremonial first act of exertion on a project that would demand prodigious feats of physical labor over the next six years.

Many in the country believed the railroad to the Pacific was a hopeless fantasy. There were the physical obstacles: multiple mountain ranges, vast stretches of desert, and innumerable river valleys and gorges. The cost of building the railroad was also exorbitant. Complicating matters further, the Civil War was nearing the end of its second year. Nevertheless, the project had long been a priority of California's leaders. The journey of nearly every adult resident to the West Coast had been lengthy and hazardous. Sailing from New York, around Cape Horn, could take four or five months; the trek overland by wagon across plains and mountain ranges was even more arduous; a third option involved a transit across Central America, in which death from disease was common. When Stanford himself first traveled to California from New York, in 1852, he left his wife of two years, Jane, behind with her parents in Albany and embarked on a more-than-month-long odyssey that included a nearly two-week expedition across Nicaragua. Stanford's brothers were grocers in Sacramento and furnished him with the goods to open a branch in Cold Springs, a mining camp in El Dorado County, where white miners' resentment of the Chinese was growing. Nevertheless, Stanford made a point of marketing his wares to the latter. Above the store's doorway was a large sign that read in their native language: "This store always has Chinese goods." Mining claims in the area had been largely exhausted, so the following spring Stanford tried again, this time in Michigan Bluff, in Placer County, where miners were still arriving in droves. In May 1855, Stanford learned his father-in-law had passed away in Albany. He hurried back across the country to be by his wife's side, only to make a transcontinental journey once again, after the couple decided to start their lives anew in the West. This time, the trip took more than three weeks. Stanford took over his brothers' wholesale grocery business in Sacramento. Through the store, as well as some fortuitous mining investments, Stanford accumulated a small fortune. He also began getting involved in the state's fledgling Republican Party, falling in with a circle of local shopkeepers, many of them transplants from New England and New York. They included Collis Huntington and Mark Hopkins, partners in a prosperous hardware business, and Charles Crocker, a successful dry goods merchant.

In 1860, Theodore Judah, a young railroad engineer, came to Sacramento looking for backers of a Pacific railroad. Judah was convinced that he and Doc Strong, a druggist and mountaineer from the mining village of Dutch Flat, in the Sierra Nevada foothills, had found a viable route across the mountain range through the Donner Pass. In 1845, the pass was the site of a tragedy, when a group of settlers from Illinois trying to reach California became trapped by snowfall; several dozen of them had died. Judah believed the deep snow could be overcome. He convened a meeting with merchants at the St. Charles Hotel on J Street and another one above the Huntington & Hopkins hardware store nearby. Many were eager to contribute but the commitments were relatively modest. Huntington was among those who held back, but he told Judah that he was open to hearing more. "If you want to come to my office some evening, I will talk to you about this railroad," he said. The next day, Judah and Huntington met in a room above his store. Huntington pressed him about the feasibility of the project. Finally, Huntington said he would organize a group to pay for a proper instrumental survey of a route from Sacramento to the Nevada border. "I don't promise to do anything now but make a survey," Huntington said. Huntington approached his partner, Hopkins, and then his friend, Stanford, about joining him. Stanford was cautious but, after two nights of discussions, agreed to take part. Several other merchants filled out the small syndicate.

Several days later, Judah got to work mapping the route, starting on Front Street, near the hotel where he and his wife were staying. His proposed path followed an unbroken ridge line to the summit of the Sierras at a maximum grade of just over a hundred feet per mile; the descent from the summit to the valley floor continued along mountains on the south side of Donner Lake to the Truckee River. He estimated that about eighteen tunnels would need to be dug, many of them through solid granite. Judah's painstaking work lasted into the spring. Finally, on June 28, 1861, the merchants, along with Judah, formally incorporated the Central Pacific Railroad and chose Stanford to be the president.

At the time, Stanford was preoccupied with his political aspirations. In 1859, he had campaigned unsuccessfully as the gubernatorial candidate for the nascent Republican Party in the state, finishing last in a field of three. As the country tipped towards civil war, however, the Democratic Party's grip on power in the state began to weaken. Stanford called the union's preservation a "holy cause," as he traveled across the state in 1861, during his second gubernatorial campaign. This time, he prevailed.

Stanford had become close with President Lincoln and believed slavery to be an evil that needed to be eradicated, but there were limits to his racial tolerance. "I prefer the white man to the negro as an inhabitant of our country," he said. "I believe the greatest good has been derived by having all the country settled by free white men." During his inauguration, in January 1862, Stanford urged the legislature to take steps to discourage Chinese immigration. He warned of the need to protect the "character of those who shall become settlers" in California and decried the Chinese as "a degraded and distinct people." Several months later, Stanford signed a measure that imposed a tax of $2.50 a month on every person "of the Mongolian race." (There were certain limited exceptions for Chinese who worked in industries that were undesirable to white laborers.) An appellate court later invalidated the bill.

Yet, even as Stanford publicly railed against the Chinese, in private Stanford and his wife, Jane Lathrop Stanford, had a very different relationship with them. In 1861, the couple moved into a rambling mansion in Sacramento. Soon after, they hired a Chinese cook, Moy Jin Kee. He had come to America several years earlier, at the age of twelve, making the journey with an uncle who was a tea merchant in San Francisco. With placer mining mostly exhausted, it had become increasingly commonplace for Chinese to work as household help. A year into his employment by the Stanfords, Jin Kee sent for his younger brother, Jin Mun, who had recently arrived in America and had just turned fifteen. The Stanfords took in Jin Mun as a gardener. Jane Stanford grew attached to the teenager and eventually offered to adopt him. His older brother, however, forbade it. After all, their parents were still very much alive in China. When Jin Mun left the family's employ three years later, Jane gave him a gold ring with his name engraved on the inside as a memento of their relationship.

In 1862, Jane Stanford became seriously ill with a lung infection. As her husband grew desperate, Jin Kee suggested consulting Yee Fung Cheung, a Chinese herbalist who worked in Sacramento's Chinese quarter. Stanford agreed, and Jin Kee rushed there in a carriage and found Yee playing mah-jongg behind a grocery store. The pair returned to the mansion, and Yee treated Jane with an herb that eased her labored breathing. She eventually recovered.

That same year, in July, President Lincoln signed the Pacific Railway Act, designating the Central Pacific Railroad, along with another company, which would later be organized as the Union Pacific Railroad, as the recipients of government funds for the construction of a railroad across the continent. The Union Pacific would work its way westward from Omaha, Nebraska, while the Central Pacific proceeded eastward. The legislation effectively pitted the two companies against each other. The more miles of track each laid down, the greater share of government money it garnered. That would, in turn, mean wresting more profits from the operation of the railroad itself. The race was on to build the railroad. Stanford did not know it at the time, but the people who had saved his wife's life and whom he had called "degraded" would be the ones he would come to depend upon.

The construction on the Central Pacific portion of the railroad demanded an army of workers. The dirt to level the terrain would need to be delivered one handcart at a time; every boulder dislodged by a man swinging a hammer, or carefully placing a charge of gunpowder; every piece of iron track dragged into place by teams of horses driven by men; each tunnel cleared by pick and shovel. Charles Crocker, the dry goods merchant, quit his position on the Central Pacific's board and became the principal contractor for the railroad. It would be his task to marshal the labor force needed. Crocker, an intimidating, temperamental figure, weighing more than 250 pounds, knew nothing of railroad construction, but he brought a relentlessness to the task. He later talked about the insomnia he suffered nightly while building the railroad, his mind constantly "pushing and crowding ahead." He believed a ruthlessness was necessary with the workers. "I used to go up and down the road in my car like a mad bull, stopping along wherever there was anything amiss and raising old nick with the boys that were not up to time," he later said.

Initially, Crocker put some two hundred men to work on grading the route, across five different locations, between the American River and the Sierra Nevada foothills. Huntington traveled to New York to buy the materials they needed for construction. The most serious obstacle in the early going was funding. By law, the two railroad companies needed to finish forty miles of track in two years, before any federal funding would become available to them. The directors of the railroad had to rely upon their own funds—and personal credit—to finance the initial construction. The other major impediment was workers. The 1858 discovery of silver in Nevada and gold strikes in places like the Fraser River and the Cariboo Mountains, in British Columbia, had led to an exodus of surplus labor from California. Many of the desultory workers who remained behind would agree to work for one payday and then walk off the line, on their way to the next boom town. One by one, other contractors abandoned their sections, but Crocker persisted. Largely due to his doggedness, by October 1863, the first tracks were finally ready to be laid. Some in the company suggested holding a ceremony to mark the occasion but Huntington demurred. "If you want to jubilate driving the first spike here, go ahead and do it," he said. "I don't. These mountains look too ugly, and I see too much work ahead."

It was around this time that an enterprising Chinese labor contractor named Hung Wah placed an advertisement in the *Placer Herald* offering his services. Hung Wah's life can only be sketched in outline, but he likely arrived in California as a teenager during the gold rush. He had initially worked as a miner and made his way to Auburn, about thirty-five miles northeast of Sacramento, but he eventually became a supplier of Chinese workers to American companies that needed legions of workers to sift through vast quantities of gravel and dirt in their hydraulic mining operations. Hung Wah's advertisement, which appeared in successive weeks, in late August and early September of 1863, read: "I will furnish any number of Chinese laborers to work on Rail Roads, Wagon Roads, or Mining Claims, at the lowest cash rates. Having experience in the business, I have facilities for obtaining any required number of men." He even offered a reference, listing William McDaniel, a local store owner and mining executive, as someone who would vouch for him. He signed the ad "Hung Wah, Auburn." In January 1864, Hung Wah began working for the Central Pacific. The payroll record for the month credits him and his crew with 587 days of work, which amounts to a crew of 23 men working 26 days; they were paid $1.19 per day. The ledger separately records payments to a Chinese foreman, Ah Toy, who had previously worked on the ranch of James Harvey Strobridge, a thirty-seven-year-old Irishman who had become Crocker's construction superintendent. The Central Pacific paid Ah Toy for 24 days of work in the month, at a daily rate of 96 cents. The two men appear to have been the first Chinese employees on the Central Pacific's payroll.

Construction progressed slowly until late February 1864, when the first eighteen miles of track were completed, between Sacramento and the town of Junction, and the first locomotives carrying passengers and freight began to run on the tracks. By June, an additional thirteen miles were finished. But even with the railroad finally beginning to bring in operating income, a shortage of cash to pay laborers often brought construction to a near standstill.

The company's financial outlook brightened in the new year. On January 2, 1865, the California Supreme Court affirmed the constitutionality of a measure authorizing the state to provide payment of interest on Central Pacific bonds. Later that month, the company advertised that it was looking for five thousand laborers, "for constant and permanent work," and distributed flyers at every post office in the state. Interested men were to apply to Strobridge, a terrifying taskmaster who considered his workers to be "as near as brutes as they can get." For all the company's strenuous recruitment, Strobridge found himself with only around eight hundred men. After the first payday, more than a hundred quit. Strobridge struggled to replenish his workforce, only to see the pattern repeat itself after the next payday.

It was reportedly Crocker who first encouraged Strobridge to try Chinese labor. Crocker had a talented manservant, Ah Ling, who was constantly by his side. Some reports suggest it was Ah Ling who nudged his boss. Strobridge initially refused to consider it. "I will not boss Chinese," he said, adding that he did not believe that they were fit to build a railroad. It was the threat of a strike by Irish workers that prompted Crocker to suggest to Strobridge again "You can get Chinamen." In Crocker's telling, it took several more months before Strobridge finally came around. He began by hiring fifty Chinese laborers just north of Auburn; before long, he hired fifty more; and then another fifty. (Central Pacific's payroll ledgers indicate the first large-scale hiring of Chinese workers began in March 1865.)

At first, Strobridge tried the new workers on simple tasks such as filling dump carts; then, he began letting them drive the carts. He didn't believe the Chinese, with their slender frames, had the strength to swing sledgehammers, but he soon found they were more than capable. At one point, when railroad officials were dealing with further labor trouble, this time among Irish masons, they began training the Chinese in that trade as well. When Strobridge expressed skepticism, Crocker told him, "Did they not build the Chinese wall, the biggest piece of masonry in the world?" Soon Chinese workers were doing all the tasks involved in laying down tracks. In his report on construction progress, dated October 8, 1864, Samuel Montague, then acting chief engineer, said that the Chinese had become experts in "drilling, blasting, and other departments of rock work." Crocker arranged with a San Francisco labor agent, Cornelius Koopmanschap, who had a business in Hong Kong, to hire as many men as he could in China. "I told him all he would bring, up to 2,000," Crocker later recalled. "He brought 500." Most of the Chinese workers for the railroad early on would be recruited in America, by men like Hung Wah. In March 1865, Hung Wah supplied the Central Pacific with about fifty Chinese laborers; the next month, his crew grew to more than 130, and then to nearly 250 the month after that. His responsibilities would only continue to enlarge. By July 1866, he would be entrusted with supplying more than nine hundred men to the railroad.

In April 1865, E. B. Crocker, the company's legal counsel and Charles's brother, wrote a letter to his friend Cornelius Cole, a member of Congress and another early investor in Judah's venture, and offered an indication of how reliant the Central Pacific had become on Chinese workers. "We have now about 2,000 men at work with about 300 wagons and carts and I can assure you they are moving the earth and rock rapidly," he wrote. "A large part of our force are Chinese and they prove nearly equal to white men in the amount of labor they perform, and are far more reliable." The following month, Mark Hopkins, one of the Central Pacific's "Big Four," told Huntington in a letter that the Chinese workforce had become essential. "Without them, it would be impossible to go on with the work," he said.

The Chinese were initially paid a dollar a day, or $26 a month, with the cost of their housing and provisions deducted from their pay. White workers received $35 and had their room and board covered. But they were lucrative wages for Chinese workers, more than they could earn in other trades in America and certainly more than they could make back home. Their wages edged upwards to $30 and then $35 a month. They worked from sunrise to sunset, six days a week. The Chinese were organized into groups of twelve to thirty, each with a "head man" who handled the wages for the group, paid out once a month by a white foreman. There was a practical reason for this arrangement. "We cannot keep the names of the Chinamen," Crocker said later. "It is impossible. We would not know Ah Sin, Ay You, Kong Won." The head man also bought all of the supplies used by the group each month. The workers ate a surprisingly varied Chinese diet of dried oysters, dried cuttlefish, dried bamboo, salted cabbage, vermicelli, dried seaweed, Chinese bacon, and pork. They drank vats of lukewarm tea that was kept in wooden barrels and placed alongside the railroad route.

In a report to stockholders in July 1865, Stanford reported that the Chinese were "found to be good laborers and, at the price at which they are to be had, full as cheap as any other." Stanford added that "regular and prompt pay, with kind usage" would help secure the confidence of the Chinese, and that should enable the Central Pacific to "obtain to the extent that white labor shall prove inadequate, the necessary force to prosecute the work vigorously." The Central Pacific's railhead was now progressing steadily eastward, first to Auburn, and then on to Colfax, fifty-four miles from Sacramento. The work getting steadily more difficult as it crept up the slopes of the Sierra Nevada. In the summer of 1865, Stanford led a contingent of guests on a sojourn to inspect the railroad's progress. They traveled to the terminus of the line in Colfax and then rode horses for a dozen miles towards the summit, watching the Central Pacific's four thousand laborers at work along the way. "They were a great army laying siege to Nature in her strongest citadel," wrote Albert D. Richardson, a journalist invited along on the trip. "The rugged mountains looked like stupendous ant-hills. They swarmed with Celestials shoveling, wheeling, carting, drilling and blasting rocks and earth, while their dull, moony eyes stared out from under immense basket-hats, like umbrellas." Carving narrow, snaking paths into bluffs that climbed, nearly perpendicular, above deep ravines, the work demanded feats of daring. One traveler through the region published an account of watching Chinese workers on the face of a more-than-two-thousand-foot precipice, lowering themselves over the edge in baskets and drilling holes in the mountainside to place black powder charges. "At one time there were 460 of these charges connected by a fuse, exploded at one time," he wrote. "Masses of rock weighing many tons, fell to the bottom with terrific fury. When the debris had ceased to fall, the echoes were still reporting among the distant hills. So stunning was the shock that I would never willingly witness the like again."

The leaders of the Central Pacific believed they had solved their labor problem. In October, Stanford issued a detailed report to President Andrew Johnson, who had assumed the presidency after Lincoln's assassination in April, about the state of the Pacific railroad. Stanford's public reversal on the Chinese was now complete. "Without them it would be impossible to complete the western portion of this great national enterprise, within the time required by the Acts of Congress," Stanford wrote. "As a class they are quiet, peaceable, patient, industrious and economic—ready and apt to learn all the different kinds of work required in railroad building, they soon became as efficient as white laborers." He concluded with assurances that the Central Pacific would be able to procure during the next year more than fifteen thousand laborers, enabling the company to be able to proceed swiftly with construction.

The granite spurs of the Sierra Nevada are composed of an interlocking lattice of mica, quartz, and feldspar crystals, formed after magma deep within the earth solidified and then rose to the surface. The result is a stone that is classified as a seven out of ten on the mineral hardness scale, the equivalent of hardened steel. Chinese workers would need to bore fifteen tunnels through it. Tunnel #6, the Summit Tunnel, represented the most formidable challenge, stretching 1,659 feet. The lengths of the other tunnels varied from just under a hundred feet to more than five hundred; the total length of tunneling would amount to more than six thousand feet.

The digging began in earnest in the fall of 1865. Strobridge sent gangs of workers ahead to begin work on the opposing ends of the summit tunnel. They worked in teams of three, in close quarters; one man held a drill and two others swung sledgehammers. After drilling several deep holes, the workers inserted black gunpowder, lit a fuse, and retreated back down the tunnel. Once the dust had cleared, the crews resumed their hammering. The work was dangerous. On April 17, 1866, a spectacular explosion killed "three whites and three Chinamen," a newspaper account reported the next day. The foreman, Phil Hagen, was "blown to pieces and part of him not found"; another victim's body was found a hundred feet from the blast. The Chinese workers who died went nameless.

In August 1866, the Chinese began work on a seventy-two-foot shaft in the center of Donner Summit, so teams could dig on four fronts simultaneously. A small, fifty-foot square house was built over the shaft, and an old locomotive was brought in to power the hoisting engine to remove debris. The shaft took eighty-five days to complete. At this point, Crocker recruited a group of experienced Cornish miners to work on the tunnel. They were pointed in one direction and the Chinese in the other. "We measured the work every Sunday morning;

and the Chinamen without fail always outmeasured the Cornish miners," Crocker later said. In the end, the Cornish miners quit, leaving the work entirely to the Chinese.

In November and early December, the snow arrived, blanketing the rocky slopes. Unlike the previous winter, which was relatively mild, it would turn into one of the harshest winters on record. Railroad engineers kept meticulous records, counting forty-four snowstorms in all; drifts measured as deep as fifteen feet. In late February, during a storm that lasted nearly two weeks, ten feet of snow fell. The snow made the wagon road impassable at times; men without snowshoes would sink up to their shoulders. Chinese laborers braved the elements in only their cotton jackets and blue jeans. They constructed elaborate snow tunnels, with chimneys, air shafts, windows, and stairs, so the work could continue. Avalanches were common. As the snow began to melt in the spring, the danger increased. "The snow slides carried away our camps and we lost a good many men in those slides; many of them we did not find until the next season when the snow melted," Strobridge later said. At night, the mountain would be illuminated only from the fires that lit the tunnels, casting shadows on the tall firs, drooping with snow. All was quiet, except for the tapping of hammers and the occasional blasts of powder.

In the summer of 1867, the Central Pacific's leaders confronted an unexpected problem. On Monday, June 24, three thousand Chinese, up and down the summit, refused to come out of their camps. Strobridge telegraphed company officials with the news that "the Chinamen have all struck for $40 & time to be reduced from 11 to 10 hours a day." It was a remarkable feat of collective action, unrivaled in scale at the time. The Central Pacific's leaders had been growing worried about their ability to retain their Chinese workforce. Many had been migrating to Idaho, Montana, and other territories, in search of more lucrative opportunities. Just a few weeks earlier, E. B. Crocker had written to Huntington, informing him they had decided to raise the wages of the Chinese to $35 a month from $31. "The question of whether we can get all the Chinamen we need is very important," he wrote. Charles Crocker, however, now moved swiftly to crush the strike, cutting off supplies to the Chinese camps. He gave them until the following Monday to return to the line, or they would be fined. On July 2, Hopkins reported that Crocker had relayed that the strike had been resolved. "All have gone to work again on terms in all respects same as before," he wrote. On Monday morning, at 6 a.m., the summit was once again abuzz with Chinese workers. A month later, the Summit Tunnel was finally pierced. The most difficult passage in the construction of the railroad, scaling the Sierra Nevada, was now behind the Central Pacific.

The labor unrest seemed to do little to diminish the Central Pacific leaders' admiration for the character of their labor force. Years later, Crocker would praise the orderliness of the work stoppage. "If there had been that number of white laborers on that work in a strike there would have been murder and drunkenness and disorder of all kinds," he said. "It would have been impossible to have controlled them; but this strike of the Chinese was just like Sunday all along the work. These men stayed in their camps; that is, they would come out and walk around, but not a word was said, nothing was done; no violence was perpetrated along the whole line." Over the next few years, the Central Pacific's leaders would continue to do their utmost to encourage Chinese immigration, even going so far as to send Chinese labor agents back to their homeland to encourage more to venture to Gold Mountain. "I like your idea of getting over more Chinamen," Huntington wrote to Charles Crocker on October 3, 1867. "It would be all the better for us and the State if there should be a half million come over."

On June 17, 1868, a train left Sacramento at 6:30 a.m., bound for Reno, Nevada, 154 miles and a mountain range away. Snow on the tracks forced passengers to disembark at the Summit Tunnel and wait as Chinese workers scrambled to clear the tracks. Several more snow slides caused further delays. Finally, the train descended from the mountains towards Donner Lake and eventually Truckee Station, before rushing onward, as night was falling, into Reno, a new town in the Nevada desert. A "long, shrill, joyous shriek of the locomotive" announced its arrival, a newspaper correspondent later wrote. "Thus ends the story of the trip of the first passenger train over the Sierra Nevada."

The Central Pacific was now surging through the Nevada desert, finishing four miles of track a day. The choreography unfolded at a gallop. A horse-drawn flatcar loaded with rails advanced to the end of the line; teams of Irish workers used rollers to drop the iron, weighing 560 pounds each, onto the ties; gangs of Chinese workers then wrestled them into place across the grade and hammered in the spikes; the empty car was then lifted off the track, making way for a fully loaded one to be dragged forward. One observer timed how long it took for a half mile of track to be laid and found that it was completed in less than twenty-eight minutes.

A pitched back-and-forth ensued between the Central Pacific and the Union Pacific. One day, the Central Pacific laid down six miles of track in a day, only to have their rivals counter with eight miles. "We must take off our coats," Crocker told Strobridge, vowing to lay down ten miles. Strobridge was skeptical that it could be done. Crocker outlined a plan of constant forward motion, with horses dragging forward materials in a continuous cycle. "Just as fast as one train drops its load, you will send it forward just as fast as your men can carry it; and take it off just as fast as you can; then run another train-load up and take that off just as fast as you can, and so on," he said. "Then you are going to have your men to spike: the first man drives one particular spike and does not stop for another; he walks right past that rail and drives the same spike in the next rail; here another man follows him and drives the next spike to that in the same rail; and another follows him, and so on." The spikers would be followed by the straighteners, then the levelers, the fillers, and the tampers. At dawn, on April 27, 1869, the Central Pacific's battalions leapt into action, laying down track as fast as a horse could walk. When the whistle blew at dusk, the mostly Chinese crew of workers had completed ten miles and fifty-six feet of track, an astonishing feat.

Two weeks later, about fifteen hundred people gathered at Promontory Summit, Utah, to mark the completion of the transcontinental railroad. The setting was a remote, mountainous location on the northern end of Great Salt Lake. A group of Irish tracklayers from the Union Pacific maneuvered one half of the final pair of rails into place; a crew of eight Chinese workers from the Central Pacific then did the same. The assembled doffed their hats for a prayer. Governor Stanford, who had arrived in Utah several days earlier on a train from Sacramento, and

Thomas C. Durant, vice president of the Union Pacific, tapped a golden spike into place. Stanford's blow closed an electric circuit that transmitted a telegraph message to the world: "Done." Afterward, in his private train car, Strobridge entertained members of the press and officers of the Twenty-First United States Infantry, who had attended the ceremony. He made a point of introducing his Chinese foreman—presumably, Hung Wah—and his team of laborers and invited them to join in the banquet. The assembled guests gave the Chinese three rousing cheers.

The individual stories of the Chinese who built the railroad are like silty river bottom passing through a sieve. Payroll records of the Central Pacific account for only a fraction of the company's Chinese workforce and offer only the barest of details. In June 1866, for example, when it's likely some fifteen thousand Chinese were employed by the railroad, informal names associated with only a few dozen Chinese were scattered throughout the company's ledgers, recorded in neat cursive. They were usually referred to by the diminutive "Ah." In Camp No. 15: "China Ben," a cook; "China Tim" and "China Thomas," dishwashers. In Camp No. 9, "Ah Tom" and "Jim Chinamen," stewards. In Camp No. 24, "Ah Show" and "Ah Sam," waiters. The names of Chinese laborers on construction crews, the bulk of the workforce, were mostly absent. Records associated with Sisson, Wallace, and Co., and Egbert Co., two companies that were major procurers of Chinese workers, furnished only the names of Chinese headmen and labor contractors. The fates of most of these workers are unknown. It's uncertain who lived or died, whether they stayed in America, whether they had children and grandchildren.

Yet some stories have emerged from the Central Pacific's records. One name appearing on the Sisson list from June 1866 is that of Ah Chuck in Camp No. 22, who is listed alongside Abe Callaway, his Irish foreman. Ah Chuck, whose real name was Mock Chuck, arrived in America in 1864 at the age of seventeen. He had been trained as an herbalist in China, which gave him a facility with numbers. His uncle was hired as a cook for the railroad; with his help, Mock Chuck became a headman. He appears repeatedly in payroll records, always next to Callaway, a testament to the closeness with which Chinese laborers worked alongside their white bosses. Mock Chuck persevered through the early work on the summit tunnel, before quitting just before the winter of 1866–1867. In June 1866, according to the company ledgers, his crew logged 786½ days of work. Mock Chuck later became a partner in a Chinese goods store in San Francisco and worked as a supplier to Chinese laborers working on railroads in Texas. When the Southern Pacific, which absorbed the Central Pacific Railroad, began work on a new line to connect San Francisco to Los Angeles, Mock Chuck became a major labor contractor.

Towards the bottom of payroll no. 214, from June 1866, is the listing "Jim King & Co." At first, the name might be mistaken for that of a white railroad worker, but it is actually a reference to a Chinese immigrant, Jow Kee, a twenty-seven-year-old native of the Pearl River Delta, who had come to America more than a decade earlier as a teenager. After his arrival, Jow Kee found work with an American mining company, where he learned to speak English and worked for eleven years. They called him "Jim King." When the Central Pacific needed workers, King became a valuable conduit. He was able to hire Chinese laborers and serve as a translator. The payroll record indicates the company paid Jim King & Co. for 631 man days in June, which suggests that he recruited a team of roughly two dozen men. King went on to build levees in the Sacramento River delta and eventually became a tenant farmer. One day, on a visit to Chinatown in San Francisco, he encountered a young girl, Hel Shee, weeping on the street. She had been enslaved as a child and brought to America as a prostitute; she was trying to escape her master. King bought out her contract and married her. They raised eight children together. Near the turn of the century, King went missing near Isleton, a town in the Sacramento River delta where the Chinese occupied the western district. His body was never found.

The vast majority of the Central Pacific's Chinese laborers drifted back to California after they were discharged, finding work in farming, or in cigar or woolen factories, or as laundrymen and domestic workers. The railroad retained a small group of Chinese workers to perform maintenance on the line and to construct new branches. Hundreds of others found work building railroads in places as far-flung as Louisiana, Virginia, and New Jersey. For a moment, amid the glow of their accomplishment, it seemed possible that Chinese immigrants might finally find acceptance in America. Yet there were signs that any goodwill towards the Chinese would be easily sluiced away. The Civil War had distracted from some of the resentment that simmered among the laboring classes in California. During the late 1860s, anti-coolie clubs had begun proliferating in San Francisco. On February 12, 1867, a large crowd gathered on a hillside opposite a construction site, where a contractor was employing more than two dozen Chinese laborers for some excavation work. The crowd began raining rocks down upon them. The hurled missiles bloodied several workers and forced the group to flee. The crowd of white men, which had grown to about four hundred, marched en masse towards a nearby woolen factory that employed dozens of Chinese workers. They all fled ahead of the mob's arrival. A few in the crowd surrounded a hapless Chinese man they happened upon and beat him. Others set fire to the factory. Eventually, a band of police officers restored order and arrested several in the mob.

In the years after their achievement at Promontory Summit, the memory of what the Chinese railroad builders had accomplished faded quickly. Hung Wah, the great Chinese foreman of the Central Pacific, is believed to have died in 1931, at the age of ninety-six, in a county hospital in Placerville. Obituaries described him as a "survivor of the horde of Chinese who came to California in the excitement following the discovery of gold at Coloma." Known by his nickname, "Rock County Charlie," Hung Wah had apparently become a ward of the hospital and a kind of town eccentric, who hobbled around the nearby streets, collecting tinfoil and other items and carrying them back to his room. There was no mention in any of the articles of his years of service on the Pacific Railroad.

CHAPTER 4

Colorblind

Perhaps the truest measure of a country's values can be found in whom it is willing to admit into its family of citizens. In the aftermath of the Civil War, as the newly reunited states struggled to establish an egalitarian society, the Chinese migration to the Pacific coast posed a conundrum that the country had not yet had to confront. For nearly a century after America's founding, the mores governing citizenship were surprisingly indistinct. The phrase "Citizen of the United States" appears three times in the original Constitution but is never fully explained. The founders recognized that immigration was essential for their young republic, so circumscribing who could become a citizen made little sense. Yet they also fretted about what an influx of outsiders, with different customs and culture, might do to "warp and bias," as Jefferson put it, the American experiment. Naturalization laws represented a way to establish a protective fence around America's body politic. The act to "establish a uniform rule of Naturalization," enacted in 1790, merely required people to have lived in the United States for two years and to be of "good character," but it also limited eligibility to "free white persons." In this way, the statute was, at once, remarkably expansive and shockingly narrow. European immigrants of all nationalities were welcomed, but free Black people, American Indians, and others who could not pass as white were left out. Congress later adjusted the residency requirement several times, before finally settling on five years. Notably, the racial boundaries around naturalization remained entirely uncontroversial.

When the Civil War ended in 1865, four million formerly enslaved Black people became free men and women. Suddenly, the need to clarify the contours of citizenship became urgent. The boatloads of Chinese disembarking in California and populating the American West presented a new complication. In 1866, Congress passed a law conferring citizenship on "all persons born in the United States," overcoming the veto of President Andrew Johnson, who had questioned the fitness of formerly enslaved people and other groups, like the "Chinese of the Pacific states." Senator Lyman Trumbull, the chairman of the Judiciary Committee and the bill's sponsor, had made clear during the debate over the measure that he believed it applied to the new arrivals from across the Pacific Ocean. "The child of an Asiatic is just as much a citizen as the child of a European," he said. The fears some in the Senate chamber harbored about the threat posed by the heathen Chinese were allayed by the fact that it seemed unlikely that the overwhelmingly male Chinese immigrant population would give rise to significant numbers of American-born progeny.

Two years later, the ratification of the Fourteenth Amendment enshrined in the Constitution the principle of birthright citizenship and barred states from enacting laws that infringed on the "privileges or immunities" of citizens, or deprived any person of "life, liberty, or property, without due process of law." The amendment left unresolved, however, the question of whether the most basic rite of American democracy, voting, was permitted for all citizens. The question consumed Congress during the winter of 1868 and into the early part of 1869, as the Pacific railroad was nearing its completion. The proposed language of the Fifteenth Amendment was brief and straightforward: "The right of the citizens of the United States to vote shall not be denied or abridged by the United States or by any State on account of race, color, or previous condition of servitude." The debate among lawmakers was ostensibly over the rights of Black Americans, but animus towards an entirely different race and people—the Chinese—nearly derailed the amendment's passage and led to some of the most vile denunciations ever uttered in the halls of Congress. George Williams, a Republican senator from Oregon who would in a few years become the attorney general of the United States under President Ulysses Grant, warned that the very character of the United States would be endangered if Chinese immigrants acquired the right to vote. "Every ship that comes across the Pacific brings its hundreds and lands them upon our shores," he said. "They are a people who do not or will not learn our language; they cannot or will not adopt our manners or customs and modes of life; they do not amalgamate with our people; they constitute a distinct and separate nationality, an *imperium in imperio*—China in the United States; and, sir, they are and continue to be the ignorant and besotted devotees of absolutism in politics and the blind disciples of paganism in religion." Congressional support for Black suffrage was overwhelming, but passage of the amendment was only made possible by repeated assurances that it would do nothing to alter the status of Chinese immigrants, because they were not eligible for naturalization. Even then, both the assembly and the senate in California overwhelmingly rejected the amendment; the legislature in Oregon did as well.

Were Chinese arrivals even interested in becoming Americans? Most of their detractors were skeptical, depicting them as sojourners, intent only on extracting as much of America's wealth as possible, before heading home. "I presume no application on the part of a single one of them has been made to become a citizen of the United States," Senator Cornelius Cole, a California Republican, said, during the debate on the Fifteenth Amendment. "So wedded are they to their native country, to the Celestial Empire, that even the dead are taken back there." But Cole was mistaken.

Some Chinese immigrants had indeed come to embrace life in the United States and planned to settle in the country permanently, despite the travails. In late 1854, a Chinese immigrant named Chan Yong applied for citizenship at the federal court in San Francisco. Newspaper accounts noted that he was lighter skinned than most Chinese, but his petition was rejected. There is evidence, however, that judges across the country were perplexed by how to handle Chinese petitioners. At least some managed to become naturalized. According to naturalization records in New York City, on January 11, 1860, a Chinese man, presumably a seaman, who listed his residence as the barque *Virginia,* at Pier 39, and called himself "John Charley," renounced his allegiance to the "Emperor of China" at the Court of Common Pleas. He applied his signature with an "X." Six years later, another Chinese seaman, who identified himself in court as "George Abut," did the same. It's unclear, however, if he was granted citizenship. A clerk scrawled on the document "Not admitted," followed by a notation, in parentheses: "Chinaman." In 1867, John A. Wing filed his declaration of intention to become a citizen, witnessed by his brother and roommate at 65 Cherry Street, James E. Wing, who was apparently already naturalized. In the census of 1870, the rolls for the seventh district of the city's sixth ward, in Lower Manhattan, identified at least two Chinese residents as citizens: Charles Ahchung, a twenty-three-year-old seaman who lived with his American wife, Ellen, and a one-year-old child, John; and John Ahtong, a forty-five-year-old cigar maker.

In the postwar era, a time of rapid industrialization and economic expansion for the United States, the Chinese were not the only immigrants arriving in waves. Migration across the Atlantic, mostly by German and Irish immigrants, had resumed in earnest after the war. The Germans mostly made their way to the Midwest, while the Irish poured into northeastern cities. For these white European immigrants, citizenship helped to secure their place in America. During the middle of the nineteenth century, nativism was a potent force that shadowed the lives of impoverished Irish Catholic immigrants, in particular, but vitriol towards them began to subside as they were able to assert themselves politically. Skin color proved to be an important legal buffer.

Frederick Douglass, the formerly enslaved man and famed orator, became an unexpected advocate for the Chinese in America. When the Chinese first began arriving to the Pacific coast, his newspaper, *Frederick Douglass' Paper*, based in New York City, had been critical of Governor Bigler's efforts to stop Chinese emigration and California lawmakers' discriminatory laws targeting the Chinese. In the late 1860s, as Congress was wrestling with the Chinese question, Douglass was barnstorming through northern cities on the lecture circuit. In 1867, he tested out a new speech in Boston on America's "composite nationality," and appears to have begun delivering it in earnest in late 1869. The address is a stirring celebration of the country's heterogeneity and a call for the United

States to fulfill what Douglass believed to be its peculiar mission in the world, serving as the "perfect national illustration of the unity and dignity of the human family." With the end of the Civil War, Douglass's optimism for the country was almost boundless. "The storm has been weathered, and portents are nearly all in our favor," he said. But he admitted the unique challenges facing the country, given its panoply of races, ranging "all the way from black to white, with intermediate shades which, as in the apocalyptic vision, no man can number." The relations between Black and white Americans had not yet been satisfactorily settled, Douglass said, and now a "new race is making its appearance within our borders, and claiming attention."

He urged the embrace of the "Chinaman," as a "new element in our national composition," and predicted, in the not too distant future, that the Chinese population would number in the millions. Douglass believed it to be inevitable that the Chinese would "cross the mountains, cross the plains, descend our rivers, penetrate to the heart of the country and fix their homes with us forever." He reminded his audience that it was natural to feel repugnance for the foreigner. The way to override this feeling was to "work for the elevation of those deemed worthless, and thus make them worthy of regard and they will become worthy and not worthless." Like a preacher imploring his flock, Douglass urged Americans to work to overcome their darker passions. "Do you ask, if I favor such immigration, I answer I would," he said. "Would you have them naturalized, and have them invested with all the rights of American citizenship? I would. Would you allow them to vote? I would. Would you allow them to hold office? I would." He rested his belief on basic human rights, "the right of locomotion; the right of migration; the right which belongs to no particular race, but belongs alike to all and to all alike." His hope was for the Chinese to "feel at home here," he said, "both for his sake and for ours."

On July 2, 1870, Congress finally confronted the question of Chinese naturalization directly. For two years, Charles Sumner, the crusading Republican senator, had been trying to attract support for his proposal to eliminate race as a criterion in the country's naturalization laws. Sumner, a former abolitionist who was perhaps most famous for the brutal beating he suffered at the hands of a pro-slavery colleague on the floor of the Senate, believed the requirement to be at odds with the country's founding ideals. During the previous Congress, while lawmakers were consumed by the debate over the right to vote for Black Americans, Sumner had introduced a bill excising the word "white" wherever it occurred in naturalization laws, but it failed to advance beyond the Judiciary Committee. He had tried again at the outset of the new congressional session, but the bill stalled again.

Lawmaking sometimes demands temerity, and Sumner, who stood six feet and four inches tall, possessed large reserves. It was approaching five o'clock, on a Saturday evening, and the senators in the chamber had been haggling over legislative business for six hours, when Sumner realized he had an opening. The senators had agreed to vote on a House measure that overhauled certain naturalization procedures. The bill was mostly technical, addressing the way fraudulent naturalization claims were handled. It was a relatively straightforward matter, and lawmakers were eager to dispense with it. The senators had a long list of bills to get through before Congress adjourned in the middle of July. As the deadline to vote drew near, however, Sumner had a surprise for his Senate colleagues. He proposed a new section that he read aloud: "And be it further enacted, that all acts of Congress relating to naturalization be, and the same are hereby, amended by striking out the word 'white' wherever it occurs, so that in naturalization there shall be no distinction of race or color."

Suddenly, the previously sedate chamber stirred. George Williams, the senator from Oregon, requested to "amend the amendment." Oregon's Chinese population was growing—the 1870 census tallied more than three thousand in the state—and anti-Chinese sentiment was mounting with it. A clerk read aloud Williams's proposal: "But this act shall not be construed to authorize the naturalization of persons born in the Chinese empire."

William Stewart, a second-term Republican senator from Nevada, demanded to be heard as well. Stewart was a vigorous former frontier lawyer and a gifted raconteur who possessed a long, untamed beard. During his political ascent, he had switched parties repeatedly and was even briefly a member of the nativist Know-Nothing Party in Nevada. His views on race embodied the contradictory impulses in the Senate chamber with regard to the Chinese. In 1853, Stewart had been the district attorney in Nevada City who successfully prosecuted a white man, George W. Hall, for killing a Chinese miner, only to have the verdict overturned by a ruling of the California Supreme Court that the testimony of Chinese eyewitnesses was inadmissible. Stewart had gone on to become the attorney general of California and later moved to Virginia City, in the Nevada Territory, where he became a wealthy man acting as the counsel for mining corporations. In 1864, when Nevada achieved statehood, Stewart was elected to the Senate. Stewart had played a leading role in the passage of the Fifteenth Amendment. The senator also, ostensibly, prided himself on his friendship to the Chinese, declaring that he had always "stood by" them. Earlier in the year, he had helped to ensure that the Civil Rights Act of 1870, legislation intended primarily to protect Black Americans in the South from the violence of the Ku Klux Klan and guarantee them certain rights, covered foreigners in the country as well. Stewart said at the time that his hope was to "extend the strong arm of the Government to the protection of the Chinese."

For Stewart, though, a path to citizenship for Chinese immigrants was beyond the pale. In March 1869, Nevada had been the first state to ratify the Fifteenth Amendment. Stewart had been at pains to make clear to legislators in Nevada that the measure granted no rights to the sizable Chinese population in their midst, because they were not citizens. He had insisted to his Senate colleagues during the suffrage debate that "the idea of naturalizing" the Chinese was "entirely out of the question." When he rose this evening to address Sumner's proposal, he made clear that he was willing to bring a halt to the proceedings with a filibuster, if the Sumner amendment was added. He issued a stern warning: "Do not put it on this bill."

Senator Oliver Morton, a Radical Republican from Indiana, chided Sumner. "This amendment involves the whole Chinese problem," he said. "Are you prepared to settle it tonight?" Sumner delivered a brief riposte. "The Senator says it opens the great Chinese question," he said. "It simply opens the question of the Declaration of Independence and whether we will be true to it. 'All men are created equal,' without distinction of color." Later, Sumner took the floor again to argue that he was simply seeking to eliminate from the naturalization process "a requirement disgraceful to this country and to this age." The Senate eventually voted to add Sumner's amendment to the bill under discussion.

Stewart was now adamant that the chamber take the time to debate the issue at length. He launched into a disquisition about the "condition of the Chinese," raising the familiar bugbear of Chinese laborers toiling under coolie contracts. He argued that Chinese residents should be liberated, before they were naturalized. He also tried to cast his argument against naturalization as one of concern for the safety of the Chinese in America, warning of widespread bloodshed if "pagans" were put on the path to citizenship. "Do you want to have the Chinese slaughtered on the Pacific coast?" he said. "Do you want their extermination? Do you want to make us utterly powerless for their good? Then pass this bill." Debate on Sumner's amendment went on for two hours, before the weary senators adjourned for the evening.

On Monday, July 4, the Senate resumed its deliberations. The crush of legislative business was so urgent that lawmakers elected to keep working through the holiday. Stewart continued his filibuster, even as his colleagues grew restless. Stewart warned his fellow Republicans of the political costs if they backtracked on the promises they had made during the suffrage debate about not conferring any new privileges on the Chinese. His tone was paternalistic, as he complimented the Chinese as an "honest people" and a "very industrious people," but he deemed them unfit to become Americans. "They are a pagan people; they are hostile to our institutions," he said.

Stewart's colleague from the Pacific coast, George Williams, scoffed at Sumner's invoking of the country's founding documents. "I ask the Senator, and I ask every candid man in this body, does the Declaration of Independence mean that Chinese coolies, that the Bushmen of south Africa, that the Hottentots, the Digger Indians, heathens, pagan, and cannibal, shall have equal political rights under this Government with citizens of the United States?" he said. He argued that the passage of time would change nothing about the Chinese in America: they were unassimilable. "Mongolians, no matter how long they may stay in the United States, will never lose their identity as a peculiar and separate people," he said. "They never will amalgamate with persons of European descent."

The Chinese did have their defenders. Trumbull, the Judiciary Committee chairman, pointed out the hypocrisy among anti-slavery Republicans in their opposition to the Chinese. Trumbull had started his political career as a Democrat. In 1855, the state legislature elected him to the Senate, and, soon after, Trumbull switched parties over his opposition to the expansion of slavery to U.S. territories. He later pressed Lincoln to more aggressively prosecute the Civil War. Trumbull co-authored the Thirteenth Amendment, which gave enslaved Black Americans their freedom, and took a leading role in shepherding legislation protecting the rights of Black Americans through Congress. He made the point that the country's standards for naturalization should be uniform. "When foreigners come here, whether from China or Japan, from England or Ireland, from Germany or Africa, no matter whence they come, if we allow them to settle among us and have a law under which they may naturalize according to the Constitution and the principles of our Government, all should be permitted to naturalize alike," Trumbull said. "If a person comes here from China, conforms to our laws, adapts himself to the condition of things in this country, he has the same right to become a naturalized citizen under any laws we may pass as if he came from Europe. Why not?"

In the end, as the debate stretched into the evening, the senators realized that without a compromise there was no way to bring an end to Stewart's filibuster. The supporters of Sumner's amendment eventually conceded, with several choosing to sit out a vote on its reconsideration and others switching sides. A separate vote on an amendment extending naturalization to "aliens of African nativity and to persons of African descent" narrowly passed. Trumbull made one last attempt on behalf of the Chinese, moving to amend the amendment that was just adopted to include "persons born in the Chinese empire," but the resolution was easily defeated. The naturalization bill was read a final time and approved. Just after eleven o'clock in the evening, the Senate was finally adjourned, and, with it, the chance for Chinese immigrants to become naturalized citizens was extinguished for more than two generations.

Stewart had warned of bloodshed in western states if citizenship was made available to the arrivals from Asia. "Every precinct officer, every officer from the highest to the lowest, on the Pacific coast, in every town, village and city will be a Chinese hater," he said. "What will be the fate of the Chinamen then?" Congress had deemed the Chinese to be unworthy of admittance to the American republic, but hate for them was still coming, a venomous, unstanchable tide.

CHAPTER 5

Rope! More Rope!

On January 15, 1851, John R. Evertsen, a government agent, set out across the dirt paths of the former Mexican pueblo of Los Angeles to record the name of every inhabitant. The seventeenth dwelling Evertsen visited that day belonged to a merchant, Robert Haley, and his wife, Mary. They listed four people in their household: themselves, and two male servants, "Alluce," likely Ah Luce, age eighteen, and "Ahfou," or Ah Fou, age twenty-eight. These were the first recorded Chinese in Los Angeles. Among the 8,329 total residents that Evertsen eventually counted in the town and its environs, 295 of them foreigners, Ah Luce and Ah Fou were alone.

A few years later, Joseph Newmark, a dry goods salesman who would become a leading figure in Los Angeles's nascent Jewish community, and his wife, Rosa, brought their own Chinese servant to the frontier town when they arrived from San Francisco. In the years that followed, as placer mining in gold country declined and the Pacific railroad was completed, other Chinese arrivals migrated southward.

By 1870, the Chinese population in Los Angeles County numbered more than two hundred. The town was isolated and had a reputation for lawlessness and disorder. Its streets, lined with yellow adobe buildings, were often choked with dust; after rainstorms, giant mud holes opened that trapped mule teams; stray dogs infested the town. The Chinese opened laundries, or worked as household cooks and servants; some leased small plots of land to farm vegetables that they peddled on one-horse wagons. Most settled on a squalid stub of a street, near the former city center, called Calle de Los Negros. The name apparently originated during the period when the city still belonged to Mexico, a reference to the dark-skinned mulattos who once populated the thoroughfare. The white settlers who came later referred to it as "Nigger Alley." It was a narrow dirt byway, about five hundred feet long, notorious for violence and vice, populated by saloons that sold beer for five cents, gambling halls, and brothels. One observer described it as "the chosen abode of the pariahs of society." Here, the Chinese arrivals in the city lived alongside a population of Californios—descendants of Alta California's Spanish and Mexican settlers—Native Americans, and poor white residents. (Despite the street's appellation, it does not appear that Black Americans inhabited the neighborhood.) To the north was the city's old plaza, built by Spanish settlers, that had become a weed-filled expanse. On the street's southern end was a crumbling, low-slung building that belonged to Antonio Francisco Coronel, an early settler in Los Angeles from Mexico City who in 1853 served as the city's first mayor. Coronel divided his building into separate storefronts, from which various Chinese merchants ran their businesses and where many also lived. Chee Long "Gene" Tong, a popular herbal medicine doctor, maintained a storefront facing south, with a signboard hanging outside. According to census records and contemporaneous accounts, Tong was in his twenties or thirties; he spoke fluent English and was an unusually enterprising businessman. He had previously operated a store on Main Street, catering to a white clientele, in a house belonging to William Abbott, a furniture dealer. Tong had advertised his services in the local newspaper as a "Chinese physician"—an herbalist—and as an employment agent, who could furnish "farmers, gardeners, cooks, etc." He lived in the Coronel building with his wife, Tong You, a roommate named Chang Wan, and a pet poodle. Two doors down from them was Wing Chung Co., a restaurant and store selling Chinese wares, owned by a Chinese *huiguan* leader, Sam Yuen.

Just like in San Francisco, the Los Angeles *huiguan* knit together an immigrant population made up almost entirely of single men. Yuen headed the Ning Yung Association, a company composed of emigrants from Taishan, the poor, hilly region in the western part of the Pearl River Delta that accounted for the largest number of Chinese in America. Fractiousness in the Chinese community had birthed Yuen's company. Natives of Taishan had previously belonged to the Sze Yup Company, one of the first two Chinese *huiguan* established in San Francisco. When the company was founded, in 1851, it represented all four counties from the Siyi region. (Sze Yup is the Cantonese romanization for Siyi.) In April of 1854, however, a dispute caused more than three thousand members from Taishan to withdraw and establish their own association. The rupture left the Sze Yup badly weakened, and at least two other groups, the Kong Chow and the Hop Wo, eventually emerged from the company. In Los Angeles, acrimony among the rival factions began to escalate during the summer of 1870. The longtime head of the Sze Yup Company in Los Angeles was a colorful merchant named Sing Lee, who had been in the city for a decade. He had once been the unchallenged leader of the Chinese community, described in the local press as the "boss Chinaman." As his company splintered, however, he found himself in a feud with one of his former lieutenants, a stocky, loquacious cigar factory owner named Yo Hing, who led the Kong Chow Company. Yo Hing was a former cook in the household of a local judge, A. J. King, who later became the editor of the *Los Angeles Daily News;* the Kong Chow leader had also once leased a vegetable farm from John G. Nichols, the city's former mayor, before finally turning to "manufacturing choice brands of cigars," as he put it in one of his newspaper ads, in a factory on Los Angeles Street. Yo Hing had long arms, an imposing frame, and a knack for cultivating white patrons, even as he became increasingly ruthless in his tactics to consolidate power in Chinatown.

In the fall of 1870, several Kong Chow henchmen brutally assaulted a Chinese prostitute in a wooded area, on the outskirts of San Bernardino, a town of three thousand people, about sixty miles east of Los Angeles. The woman had been purchased by the men from the Kong Chow Company in San Francisco. (Prostitution was part of the business portfolio of all the Chinese *huiguan* in Los Angeles.) She had refused to turn over some money to them, so they hauled her by the hair, through wet grass and swampy land, to a remote spot outside of town. They stripped her naked and tied her to a tree, binding her hands behind her, so her feet were barely touching the ground, and commenced whipping her. They lit some paper with a match and burned her bare breast with the makeshift torch. After a while, they took her down and abandoned her, but she staggered after them, apparently afraid of being left alone in the wilderness. They tied her back up again and began torturing her with burning sticks. The torment went on for two hours. Close to midnight, some people who happened to be passing through the area heard her cries and rescued her. The episode horrified residents of San Bernardino, who passed a resolution banning Chinese from the town. A jury convicted four of the men on assault charges, only to have the verdict overturned by a judge in Los Angeles on a technicality. Nevertheless, the events set in motion a campaign by Yo Hing to punish people he believed had informed the authorities about his men. He targeted Sze Yup members, shaking them down for money and harassing them with frivolous lawsuits and contrived criminal complaints. On March 7, 1871, a group of Kong Chow men entered the home of Hing Sing, a wealthy Sze Yup member, and carried off his wife, Yut Ho. One of the men, a cook named Lee Yong, obtained a marriage certificate and became legally betrothed to Yut Ho. A legal skirmish ensued over who should properly be considered her husband.

The press delighted in reporting on this marriage between "lovers" from "rival companies, which hated each other like Christians." The internecine dispute between the companies played out in dueling public statements. In a letter addressed "To the Public," published in a local newspaper on March 10, 1871, Sing Lee and others from the Sze Yup identified Yo Hing as the leader of a breakaway Chinese company and the "prime mover and originator of all of these disturbances." Yo Hing responded in his own defense, insisting that he had always been a "peaceable, quiet, and humble" resident of Los Angeles.

Over the next few months, tensions seemed to dissipate in the Chinese quarter. By the summer, Sing Lee had returned to China, turning over the proprietorship of the Wing Chung store to Sam Yuen. Meanwhile, Coronel announced plans to raze the dilapidated building in Chinatown where the store was located. Civic leaders cheered the plan, hoping that the alley would be restored to respectability and its Chinese quarter disbanded. But Yuen was plotting a decisive move against Yo Hing. In the fall, gun dealers in Los Angeles noticed that Chinese customers were steadily acquiring weapons. One day, in late October, several hired killers traveled to Los Angeles from San Francisco by steamship. They were so-called hatchet men, from one of the tongs, secret societies that controlled gambling, prostitution, and other Chinese underworld activities. At nine thirty in the morning on October 23, Yo Hing was standing outside the home of an acquaintance in Negro Alley, when two of the tong members confronted him. Yo Hing was unarmed and ran inside. The men chased after him and opened fire. One bullet passed through Yo Hing's coat and shirt; another slammed into a clock on the wall.

The authorities arrested the two men from San Francisco. Yuen offered to act as their bail bondsman. When an officer visited his store to confirm his ability to pay, Yuen opened a trunk under the counter filled with gold and silver coins worth two or three thousand dollars. Yo Hing was placed under arrest as well, after one of the gunmen, a man identified as Ah Choy, filed a complaint that identified him as a shooter in the melee. Two of Yo Hing's American patrons acted as guarantors for his bond. The following afternoon, the three men all appeared in court, pleaded not guilty, and were released. They returned to a tense Chinese quarter. According to Yuen's subsequent account, at around four thirty in the afternoon, Ah Choy was sitting down for dinner inside a house on the eastern side of Negro Alley when he heard a commotion outside. At the front door, he found Yo Hing and a group of Kong Chow men waiting for him. One of them shot him in the neck. He crumpled to the ground. A gunfight erupted on the street.

When the shooting began, a police officer named Jesus Bilderrain was at C.C. Higby, a saloon nearby. Bilderrain was one of a handful of men—all political appointees—attached to the city's police force. Bilderrain had previously served as the city assessor and had a reputation as an effective lawman. The officer was accustomed to breaking up violent disputes in Chinatown and had heard that there might be a confrontation that afternoon. He later said this was why he had been stationed at Higby's that afternoon, though it's possible he was simply having a drink on the job. He hurried over on horseback. He and two other arriving officers separated the combatants and captured one gunman. Bilderrain then chased another into Sam Yuen's store inside the Coronel building, only to find himself face-to-face with the shooter inside a dark hallway, a gun aimed at his chest. The officer grabbed the weapon just as it fired, and the hammer came down on Bilderrain's thumb, likely saving his life. He was about to strike the man with his own gun, when someone else shot Bilderrain in the right shoulder. As several others in the store opened fire on him, Bilderrain tumbled back onto the street. He called out to warn a bystander, Adolfo Celis, who had rushed to help him, to stay outside. Bilderrain grabbed hold of a wooden veranda post and blew his police whistle. Robert Thompson, a longtime resident, clattered onto the porch. Thompson, a native of Arkansas, was a well-liked former saloon proprietor turned cattle rancher. Most accounts describe him as merely a concerned citizen who arrived on the scene, but the county sheriff, James Franklin Burns, would later recall that Thompson was there in an official capacity as a deputy constable. (Another version of the events, reported by Major Horace Bell, a Los Angeles attorney, said that Bilderrain and Thompson were acting on a fictitious warrant and were in the process of trying to rob Yuen. But Bell's account is contradicted by sworn testimony and other firsthand accounts.) While an officer named Estaban Sanchez aimed his pistol at the doorway, Thompson leaned against the door, reached around with his arm, and fired. A gunman inside pulled his trigger nearly simultaneously. Thompson staggered, struck in the chest. "I'm killed," he said.

Gunfire erupted from inside the store and outside. A fifteen-year-old boy was shot in the leg; another man was struck in the hip. Onlookers dragged Thompson to a nearby drugstore, Wollweber's, on Main Street. A restive crowd began to gather in front of the Coronel building. Many hurried home to retrieve weapons. Word soon spread that Thompson had died. He had a pregnant wife at home, Rosario, who would give birth in November to twins, and the couple also had an eight-year-old daughter, Cecilia. Packs of men began streaming towards Chinatown. "The whole city seemed moved by one grim and tacit purpose," one account later said. A line of men encircled the Chinese quarter. Some began chanting "Hang them!" Frank Baker, the city marshal, hurried over from his soda factory nearby and ordered several men to stand guard in an alley behind the house and others to station themselves in front and on both ends of the street. They were to ensure that no one escaped. At the southern end of the block, where the alley met Los Angeles Street, one of Baker's men caught a fleeing Chinese man. He seemed to have come from the building on the east side of the block, where the initial shootout between Ah Choy and Yo Hing's men had occurred. Baker searched the man and confiscated a pistol but let him go. Burns, the county sheriff, had also made his way to the Chinese quarter. The sheriff took charge of the front of the Coronel building, along with two patrol officers, Emil Harris and George Gard. Their orders were to prevent anyone from leaving or entering the building.

Harris, a German Jewish immigrant who was also a member of the fire department, was stationed on Los Angeles Street when a Chinese man came running towards him. It was the man Baker had earlier searched and released; this time, he wielded a hatchet. (In subsequent accounts of the evening, the man was identified variously as Wong Chin, Ah Wing, and Wong Tuck. He was an employee at the Pico House, a hotel in the alley.) A member of the mob captured him; Harris, along with another constable, Richard Kerren, began escorting the man to the county jail. The group only made it a few blocks to the intersection of Main and Spring Street, when a horde of men descended. They pinned Harris's arms behind him and seized his prisoner. The mob dragged the man up the hill on Temple Street, where Harris eventually lost sight of him. Cries of "hang him" and "shoot him" became an overwhelming din. Another cry soon went up: "A rope!" A man ducked into a store and emerged with a coil. At Temple and New High Streets, across the street from an Episcopal church, the double doors to Tomlinson's, an old corral that had become a lumberyard, turned into an improvised gallows. On both sides were posts about twelve feet high; a thick crossbeam connected them. A. R. Johnston, a shoemaker who was known as "Crazy Johnston," shouted, "Hoist him up." The Chinese prisoner had remained silent throughout his ordeal but now began mewling plain-tively. The mob strung him up, only for the rope to snap. They dragged him up again. The rope held, but one of his captors commented that he didn't seem to "hang right" and proceeded to clamber up one side of the gate. He jumped forcefully on the man's shoulders. The crowd hooted. Johnston was later overheard delighting that "the cheap labor was done away with now, the sons of bitches were hanged."

When Harris returned to Negro Alley, he joined Gard, his fellow officer, in front of the Coronel building. A group of men propped lad-ders against the adobe walls and clambered onto the flat, tar-covered roof; they passed up axes and stalked back and forth, as the rioters below hooted their approval. The group on the roof included Californios like Refugio Botello, a butcher who had been nominated several months earlier for county assessor, and Jesus Martinez, the sexton at the city's Catholic cemetery; L. F. "Curly" Crenshaw, a stable boy, was another rioter who patrolled the top of the low-slung building, with a pistol in hand. Witnesses later heard Crenshaw bragging that he had killed three Chinamen. They used the axes to chop through the thin roof and began shooting at the Chinese huddled inside, as well as others who tried to flee into the yard in the back of the building. A member of the mob tossed a burning pile of material into the building through a doorway to a front room. After it burned for several minutes, someone dashed inside and tossed the flaming material back out onto the street. Gard and Harris begged the mob not to set fire to the block. At one point, likely with the help of George Fall, a city councilman and the head of the volunteer fire department, the rioters connected a fire hose and directed a stream of water onto the roof, during a brief attempt to flush people out that way. A Chinese man came running out of the building and was immediately shot down.

Harris watched as the mob proceeded apartment by apartment, breaking down doors and dragging Chinese occupants out. When they reached the doorway for apartment no. 6, they pulled out a husband and wife. This was Gene Tong, the herbalist, whose store was next door to Sam Yuen's. His spouse, Tong You, clung to him. The rioters also dragged from the apartment Chang Wan, a roommate. The mob later released Tong You but thrust the two men up New High Street to the old corral, this time to the western gate, where the town's vigilance committee had lynched a notorious murderer, Lachenais, less than a year earlier. Two other Chinese victims, Leong Quai, a laundryman, and Ah Long, a cigar maker, were already dangling, half-naked in the moonlight. Tong told the men he had nothing to do with the shooting of Bilderrain and Thompson and begged them to release him. He had money, several thousand dollars in gold, he said. But someone in the mob shot him in the face, and he was strung up, his pockets ransacked. The mob hauled him up and down, smacking his head repeatedly against the crossbeam. Joseph Mesmer, a teenage boy who witnessed the lynching, later said the sound reverberated "like the breaking of a watermelon." When the mob tried to hang Chang Wan, the rope snapped and he tumbled back to the ground. A stronger rope materialized. "All right, pull away," someone said. His captors jerked him violently upward several times, smashing his head into the beam.

Back at the Coronel building, the mob continued to drag cowering Chinese onto the street. At one point, two women came to the door of the Wing Chung store and the crowd opened fire on them. Michael Rice, an employee at the Pico House, was sitting in the lobby when a man ran inside and shouted, "Get your guns an' come quick. The Chinks are gonna slaughter us." The hotel's manager strapped a revolver around his waist and motioned for Rice to join him outside. They encountered a welter of men surging toward the alley. "I remember one fellow, big, hatless and coatless, with bulging, maniacal eyes as he ran past us, brandishing huge butcher's axes," Rice later recalled. A Californio on a horse, brandishing a carbine, urging the crowd on. Rice watched the crowd brush past several sheriff's deputies and barge into Chinese establishments in the alley. He watched as the rioters raised and lowered one victim six times. After the corpse was left dangling, a young boy—Rice guessed he was six or seven years old—threw his arms around the legs. "Come down papa, come down," he said. "I stood and stared stupidly, ashamed for the first time of my own race," Rice later said.

A group of men used a piece of timber as a battering ram against the adobe walls of the Coronel building, while others wielded axes and picks. Frenzied men plunged through a hole they'd opened, firing their pistols wildly. Rioters pulled a Chinese man out by his hair and placed a rope around his neck. The mob towed him through the streets. Fists, clubs, and the butts of guns battered him, until he died. The awning in front of John Goller's blacksmith and carriage shop, a few blocks away on the southside of Commercial Street, became another gallows site. "Rope! More rope!" became the urgent call. A woman who ran a boardinghouse across the street gave the mob her clothesline. They hung four men from the sides of a large prairie schooner wagon. Henry T. Hazard, an attorney, climbed atop an adjoining wagon as a group prepared to string up one man, demanding if they knew for certain the man was guilty. "He's a Chinaman," they replied. When the crowd began to turn on Hazard, firing shots in his direction, friends pulled him down. Rioters suspended other Chinese victims from an iron bar supporting the sidewalk roof in front of a boot and shoe store, on the corner of Commercial and Los Angeles Streets. The store's owner, William Slaney, locked his Chinese employees inside for their protection and stood guard.

There were other residents who tried to stop the frenzy. Robert Widney, an attorney, was returning home when a neighbor called out to him with the news: "They are killing all of the Chinese off." At first, Widney thought he was joking. Widney was the head of the Law and Order Party, a committee of concerned citizens that had recently been convened to fight rising crime. When Widney realized the loud sounds he was hearing were gunshots, he told his neighbor to gather others from the committee at a meeting spot on Arcadia Street. He then hurried to his law office in search of his revolver and a single-shot pistol. He returned empty-handed, but he joined about eight to ten others from the committee as they headed into the Chinese quarter. Just as they were starting to fan out around the Coronel building, people began breaking down the doors and yanking out Chinese. Widney tried unsuccessfully to intervene with a group of rioters who had captured several Chinese men and were heading to the old corral. He watched as they brought out ropes and hung their prisoners, including a boy who appeared to be about fourteen years old. The rioters then headed back down Temple Street in search of more victims. At the intersection of Temple and Spring Streets, Widney encountered another knot of people, heading north with more Chinese captives. He realized that a massacre was underway. As he continued to cast about for a weapon, his nineteen-year-old brother, William, found him in the crowd. It turned out that William had his brother's revolver and pistol. William gave over the revolver to Robert, who waded into a group of rioters who had captured a Chinese man. He grabbed hold of the coat lapel of one of the rioters and pointed his gun at his breast. The man slunk away. One by one, Widney subdued the Chinese man's captors and sent the freed man off with a clutch of other Law and Order men so they could deliver him to the county jail. Widney later diverted another group of twenty men heading up Temple Street. By the end of the night, according to Widney, he had rescued nearly two dozen Chinese. There were others who defied the mob: Frank Howard, a lawyer, dashed into a knot of men and pulled free a woman, frozen in fright; William H. Gray, a justice of the peace who was known to be fair-minded with the Chinese, hid several Chinese residents in the cellar of his home on the outskirts of town.

Around nine thirty in the evening, Sheriff Burns mounted an embankment and called upon those who wished to "preserve the peace" to follow him. About twenty-five volunteers positioned themselves around the Coronel building. By then, however, the killing was over. Rioters were picking through the detritus. The Wing Chung store had been pillaged: trunks were open and rifled; bags of rice were strewn everywhere; clothes, broken furniture, joss sticks, tossed. Blood smeared the walls. The dining table was set for a large meal; a bowl of rice sat in the center, alongside two bowls of chopped fish, a vegetable dish, and other Chinese delicacies. Officers Gard and Harris, who would later receive a gift of appreciation from the Chinese community, had managed to get inside the store and were guarding it overnight. Next door, at Gene Tong's store, "human gore could be traced in all directions," a later account said. Thieves had cut open all of his valises and sliced through the pockets on his clothes, looking for his gold. There were broken chairs and tables; Tong's supplies of herbal medicine were strewn all over the floor. The couple's poodle was found whimpering under a counter, with a broken leg. In the courtyard of the Coronel building sat the shell of a trunk, whose lock had proven too difficult to pick, so instead thieves had cut open its sides to make off with its contents.

Members of the mob crowded inside the city's drinking establishments, crowing about the evening's events. At J. H. Weldon's, a saloon on Commercial Street, a man with blood on his shirtsleeve bragged that he was "satisfied now," because he had killed three Chinamen. At Higby's, where Bilderrain had been getting his drink when he heard the gunshots in the Chinese quarter, the drunken shoemaker, Johnston, joked about how "some of the long-tails" had "gone up." At half past one in the morning, his neighbor heard Johnston and some other men fumbling to get inside his house. "I have killed some Chinamen," Johnston said.

The following morning, along a fence on the north side of the courtyard at the county jail, the victims of the massacre were laid out in two rows. The bodies were horribly mangled; those that had been lynched still had the cords around their necks; many were only partially clothed. There were seventeen corpses in all. (An eighteenth body had been deposited at the city cemetery early on in the massacre.) Wooden coffins were stacked nearby. About a dozen Chinese men and women huddled together inside a cell at the two-story jail. Some of them had been arrested the night before; others had come seeking protection. An injured Chinese man, identified as Gene Tong's brother, lay moaning on a dirty blanket in an adjoining cell; he had been shot in the neck. In the press, horror about the night's barbarism was on display but also animosity towards the Chinese. The headline "The Chinese Outrage" greeted readers of the *Los Angeles Star*. "The horrible assassinations which were perpetrated in our city last night by the brutal, uncivilized barbarians that infest the country, is an indication of what the consequence would be were their race transmigrated in larger numbers upon this coast," the unsigned article said. The newspaper referred to the city's Chinese residents as a "living curse." The *Daily News* condemned "mob rule" and the "horrible feast of indiscriminate death," but also hastened to make clear: "We are opposed to the Chinese."

At eight o'clock in the morning, the county coroner, Frank Kurtz, began his inquest into the death of the lone white man killed, Robert Thompson, before a jury of a half-dozen men. They heard from only one witness, Officer Bilderrain, who had recovered enough from his injuries to testify. The jury concluded that Thompson had been shot while assisting Bilderrain by an unknown Chinese man "from the house of Sing Lee," referring to the tong fighters recruited by Sam Yuen. The inquest into the deaths of the Chinese followed, before a new jury of eleven men. Throughout the morning, groups of distraught Chinese residents had been arriving at the jail in search of friends and loved ones. The coroner went through each body in the jail courtyard, recording a name and a manner of death. The first body belonged to Gene Tong, who had been shot in the head and hanged; the second was Wa Sin Quai, who had lived in Los Angeles for five years and was shot eight times; the third was Chang Wan, the housemate of the herbalist; the fourth was a man named Leong Quai, a laundryman who had died from hanging; the fifth was Joung Burrow, shot through the head and left wrist; the sixth was Ah Long, a cigar manufacturer, who had been hanged; the seventh was Wong Chim, who had also been hanged; the eighth was Tong Wan, who had arrived only recently from San Francisco and had been shot, stabbed, and hanged; the ninth was Ah Loo, a recent arrival from China who had been hanged; the tenth was Wan Foo, who had been hanged; the eleventh was Day Kee, hanged; the twelfth was Ho Hing, hanged; the thirteenth was Ah Wang, hanged; the fourteenth was Ah Cut, a liquor manufacturer, who had been shot in the abdomen; the fifteenth was Lo Hey, hanged; the sixteenth was Ah Wan, hanged; the seventeenth was Wing Chee, of the Sam Yup company, hanged; the eighteenth body, at the city cemetery, was the first person hanged in the massacre and was unidentified.

Afterwards, the bodies were released to mourners for funeral preparations. The names of the dead were written on wooden slats and nailed to the coffins. Gene Tong's was the first body taken by wagon to the cemetery. A small group of mourners accompanied the hearse; they burned sticks of incense and, from the wagon, tossed bits of paper, inscribed with Chinese characters. Other mourners gathered at the cemetery, where several coffins were placed inside a single grave. A pair of sandals and a shirt were placed inside one coffin. At the foot of one grave, a woman knelt and keened.

Over the next four days, the jury heard from seventy-nine witnesses, many of whom, it would become clear, had participated in the riot. Most insisted they were unable to identify specific culprits. Nevertheless, certain names came up repeatedly: Johnston, the drunken shoemaker; Refugio Botello, Curly Crenshaw, and Jesus Martinez, who had all been on the roof; Patrick McDonald, who had drawn his pistol on the sheriff; Andreas Soeur, a butcher, was seen with a cleaver in his hand and overheard boasting that he had helped to hang five Chinamen. When it was over, the dozen members of the jury issued a statement: "We find the mob consisted of all nationalities as they live in Los Angeles, and find that we have sufficient evidence to accuse the following persons as having taken part in the destruction of the lives and property of the Chinamen." The jury then appended a list of more than a hundred names, but the press elected not to publish them so, as one newspaper put it the next day, as "not to defeat the ends of justice."

On November 8, County Court Judge Ygnacio Sepulveda convened a special grand jury of a dozen men to weigh indictments on the massacre. He urged the group to "set a true example of courage in the performance of your duty." The grand jury deliberated for twenty-three days and returned forty-nine indictments, twenty-five of which were for murder, or accessory to it; the rest were for other felonies on the night of the massacre. The indictments named over 150 people, most of whom had not been arrested. The jurors also singled out the sheriff's office and the city police force for opprobrium, condemning them for failing to make any attempt "to arrest any of those, who in their presence were openly, and grossly, violating the law, even to the taking of human life."

The task of obtaining justice for the massacre's victims fell to Cameron E. Thom, the district attorney of Los Angeles. Thom, a forty-six-year-old native of Virginia, had arrived in the Sacramento valley by wagon train during the gold rush, but he headed back east to fight in the Confederate army during the Civil War. When he returned to Los Angeles after the war, he opened a successful law practice and then was elected a state senator. He became district attorney in 1870 and would later become the city's mayor. On the night of the massacre, he had hurried to the Chinese quarter with a neighbor, John G. Downey, a former governor of the state. Thom had climbed atop a box and urged the rioters to go home. Notably, the presiding judge on the riot cases would be Robert Widney, one of the heroes on the night of the massacre, who had personally confronted at least some of the indicted. The first case to go to trial, on January 5, 1872, accused a constable, Richard Kerren, of aggravated assault for allegedly shooting at two Chinese women, identified in the court records only as "Cha Cha" and "Fan Cho." During the coroner's inquest, a witness had said Kerren was among a group of rioters who fired fifteen to twenty shots at two Chinese women when they appeared in the doorway of the besieged Wing Chung store. Testimony lasted only a day, and Kerren was quickly acquitted. The prosecutor turned his attention to potential cases against the rioters alleged to have been responsible for the massacre itself. Thom decided the best strategy was to focus on the murder of Gene Tong, who had been so well known in the community, narrowing the prosecution to a small group of defendants. These included some of the most visible rioters on the night of the massacre, such as Johnston, the shoemaker, and L. F. Crenshaw, Refugio Botello, and Jesus Martinez, who were among the men spotted on the roof. Thom also elected to prosecute Adolfo Celis, who had rushed to help Bilderrain and witnessed the shooting of Thompson but was named by the grand jury as an accessory to murder. On February 16, Crenshaw's case was the first to go to trial. Newspaper accounts characterized Crenshaw as a troubled, shiftless young man. He was twenty-two years old but looked several years younger. He possessed a head of light-colored ringlets, which earned him his nickname, "Curly." Crenshaw had been born in Illinois, but his family had made their way to Nevada. He ran away from home and drifted south to Los Angeles. He had been working as a laborer and a stable boy but fell in with the wrong crowd in the city. "His favorite resort was the rendezvous of lewd women, pickpockets and cut-throats," one account said. Thom's case against Crenshaw, however, was problematic from the start. The witnesses he called to the stand included Henry M. Mitchell, a reporter for the *Los Angeles Star* who had reportedly joined in the calls on the night of the massacre to hang the Chinese, the attorney Henry

Hazard, and Officer Emil Harris, but none could connect Crenshaw directly to Tong's murder. One witness testified that he had overheard Crenshaw at a saloon afterwards boasting about killing three people and "shooting Chinamen," but Thom had no one who had witnessed Crenshaw carrying out violence. When Crenshaw testified in his own defense, he insisted that he'd only gone up on the roof of the Coronel building when he heard cries of "fire" and that he'd assisted an officer in escorting a Chinese woman to the jail, before retiring to the bar for some drinks. Nevertheless, the jury deliberated only twenty minutes before returning a guilty verdict of manslaughter. Eleven of the jurors had reportedly favored a murder conviction, while one voted for acquittal, before they compromised on manslaughter, a lesser charge that did not require premeditation.

Thom turned to the cases against nine other rioters, agreeing to a request from the defense to try them simultaneously. Selecting an impartial jury proved unusually difficult. In late February and into early March, the lawyers went through a pool of 255 people, before settling on a panel. The trial finally commenced on March 18. Over the course of seven days, Thom examined more than two dozen witnesses; the defense chose not to call anyone. On March 26, throngs of onlookers crowded the courtroom for closing arguments, which consumed nine hours and ended around ten o'clock in the evening. After deliberating into the early-morning hours, the jury returned to the courtroom to pronounce seven of the defendants—Louis Mendel, A. R. Johnston, Charles Austin, Patrick McDonald, Jesus Martinez, Refugio Botello, and Estaban Alvarado—guilty of manslaughter as well. Two of the defendants, Adolfo Celis and D. W. Moody, were acquitted. The verdict seemed to demonstrate that the city could overcome its worst impulses. "It has been the universal belief of the entire country that a conviction of the perpetrators of the outrage that cast such a blot upon the fair fame of our city, could never be obtained by any jury impanelled in the country," a newspaper editorial said afterward, adding that the verdict would do "much toward appeasing the indignation aroused by the commital of the outrage." During the sentencing of the defendants two weeks later, Crenshaw asked for clemency, given his age, but Widney ordered him to serve three years in state prison. Johnston, the shoemaker, delivered a rambling defense, highlighting his "life of industry" and blaming his indigence. He also described a dream in which he saw the jury as a rose with green leaves, attacked by a bee, which took the rose's honey and caused its decay. Widney sentenced him to six years. Johnston's attorneys filed a motion to have him examined for an insanity defense. He even went so far as to write a letter to the judge, claiming that he had not wanted to "make known of my accounts of being slightly deranged in public" but asked that the judge visit him to evaluate his mental status. "As I have been wounded twice in the head and at present there is still a piece of lead a laying on my brain which you can feel with your own hands and it is liable to hurt me at any time," Johnston wrote. Widney dismissed his motion. The other convicted men received sentences ranging from two years to six years. They all filed appeals.

Other legal proceedings related to the massacre foundered, including a complaint filed by Tong You, Gene Tong's widow, against Yo Hing for inciting the riot, as well as a case against Sam Yuen for manslaughter in the death of Robert Thompson.

In early August, the Chinese in Negro Alley observed *tachiu*, a festival that coincided with Daoist and Buddhist feasts for the dead, meant to restore peace to the spirits of victims who might be suffering in the afterlife. Members of the Chinese community contributed $1,000 for the commemoration, and several Daoist priests traveled from San Francisco to help with the ceremonies, which took place over four days. The adobe building on the east side of Negro Alley, opposite the Coronel, became a kind of improvised shrine. Drawings were hung on the walls, illustrating the manner in which victims of the massacre had died; the rioters were depicted as demons. The priests chanted and performed ritual acts for the spirits; mourners marched to the cemetery, playing gongs and drums; they placed dishes piled with meats, fruits, and tea in front of the graves. A group of men made a circuit around the cemetery, firing pistols into the air at the evil spirits. Several women—paid mourners—wailed lamentations. If the massacre marked any kind of chastening in the way the Chinese were treated by other residents of the city, the press accounts of the ceremonies offered little sign of it. "This morning winds up the affair, and the civilized portion of Los Angeles will certainly be glad of it, as the dim [*sic*] and confusion contributed by these barbarians have simply been abominable," one article said.

Nine months later, on May 19, 1873, the Supreme Court of California issued its decision on the convicted rioters' appeal. The court ruled the indictments against the men were "fatally defective," because they never specified that "a person was actually murdered." Based on this technicality, the defendants were ordered to be discharged from prison.

One survivor of the massacre, Chung Sun, wound up in Watsonville, in northern California, where he found work digging trenches. He asked a white man he had befriended to write a letter on his behalf to the editor of the *Pajaronian,* the region's newspaper. Chung Sun explained he had only recently come to the United States, in search of "freedom and security," and had made his way to Los Angeles in hopes of becoming a tea planter. Even before he journeyed across the Pacific, Chung Sun had been familiar with America's history. "We have heard of your great and good Washington—his justice, wisdom, and unselfish patriotism," Chung Sun said. "We are conversant with your literature, science, and philosophy. Your wonderful skill, enterprise, and material progress commands our respect." But he said he was disappointed by his experience in America. "Just as I had reached my destination, at a town where I knew no one, while peacefully walking the street, I was assaulted in the most brutal manner by a mob, severely beaten, and robbed of all my money, and for my knowledge of the language of your country would doubtless have been murdered, as no one came to my assistance, and more than twenty of my countrymen of the more humble class were that very night butchered in cold blood," he said. "I applied for but could get no redress." With no funds, he fled the city. A week after publication of the letter, Chung Sun's friend updated readers that a deputy constable had recovered $600 from the robbers and sent the Chinese man $100 and kept the rest for himself. Chung Sun was grateful but was planning to return to China on the next steamship. The newspaper published a second letter from him, this time written to a friend in China. Chung Sun described his confusion about Americans. "The more I see and learn of this strange country and people, the more puzzled I am now to understand their peculiarities and, to me, seeming contradictions," he wrote. Chung Sun characterized Americans as "half-civilized." In certain areas, they'd made notable advances, Chung Sun wrote, "but in civility, complaisance, and polite manners, they are wholly wanting and are very properly styled barbarians."

Part II

———

Passages

CHAPTER 6

The Cauldron

It was a Georgia planter and congressman, Thomas Butler King, who first proposed, in May 1848, that the federal government establish a steamship line to the Far East. King owned a sprawling plantation in coastal Georgia and imagined a future in which hundreds of millions of Chinese purchased American-grown cotton. As chairman of the House naval affairs committee, King published a report on "Steam Communication with China, and the Sandwich Islands," in which he laid out the vast commercial possibilities of the Celestial Empire. "Certainty and rapidity of intercourse only are wanted to bring these two great nations nearer together, to give them a more perfect knowledge of each other, develop their resources and build up a commerce more extensive than has probably ever heretofore existed between two nations," he wrote. The route failed to materialize then, but by the 1860s the value of goods exchanged between China and the United States was doubling by the year. In 1865, Senator Cornelius Cole, a California Republican, revived King's proposal. During a speech on the Senate floor, Cole told his Senate colleagues that trade with the Chinese empire was "the richest prize ever placed before a nation." The only question, he said, was "have we the wisdom to grasp it?"

Less than two years later, on a fall morning in 1866, about two thousand people gathered at a shipyard in Greenpoint, Brooklyn, to witness the launch of the *Great Republic,* the largest wooden steamship ever constructed in the United States. From stem to stern, the ship measured 380 feet. Its steerage compartment could hold fifteen hundred people. The ship, powered by two enormous paddle wheels, was the first of four vessels constructed for the Pacific Mail Steamship Company, subsidized by the federal government, enabling the establishment of a monthly route that ferried cargo and passengers across the Pacific, with stops in San Francisco, Hong Kong, Yokohama, Japan, and Honolulu in the Sandwich Islands. On September 3, 1867, a crowd of Chinese and Americans assembled along the shoreline in San Francisco to watch the ship churn out of the harbor, carrying about seven hundred Chinese passengers.

On the other side of the Pacific, America's top diplomat in China, Anson Burlingame, a charismatic former congressman from Massachusetts, had been working to establish a more cooperative relationship with China. Officials of the ruling Qing dynasty vacillated between contempt for "foreign devils" and the need to deal with them as equals on the world stage. The skirmishes that became known as the Second Opium War had ended in 1860, with the storming of Beijing by British and French forces. Even after enduring that humiliation, Chinese rulers continued to believe in the superiority of their civilization. A few influential reformers, however, realized that China would have to accommodate the West. In January 1861, an imperial edict ordered the creation of the Zongli Yamen, the foreign affairs office of the Qing government, under the supervision of Prince Gong, the half brother of the Xianfeng Emperor. Soon after, President Lincoln appointed Burlingame to his post. He arrived in China, at the age of forty-one, knowing little about the country. Burlingame had grown up poor, the son of a deeply religious schoolteacher, in Ohio. He attended Harvard Law School and became a lawyer in Massachusetts. A magnetic public speaker, who possessed muttonchop sideburns, a full beard, and a fleshy face, Burlingame quickly rose to prominence as a devoted member of the radical faction of the Republican Party and a zealous opponent of slavery's spread into western territories. Unlike some other Western emissaries, Burlingame refused to treat the Chinese as "conceited barbarians," as he put it in a letter to Secretary of State William Seward. Over time, Burlingame grew close with Prince Gong, who was seeking to overhaul China's relations with the West. In November of 1867, Burlingame resigned his diplomatic post, with the intention of returning to the United States. Prince Gong hosted a farewell dinner for him in Beijing. Wenxiang, a reform-minded official in the Zongli Yamen who favored Western engagement, approached Burlingame with an unusual proposition. Would he consider representing China, officially? Burlingame, who did not speak Chinese, initially thought the idea was a joke and laughed off the request, but Wenxiang persisted. "You must be our friend in foreign lands where we are so misunderstood," he said. Several days later, Prince Gong extended an official appointment by royal decree, a document on yellow paper, placed inside a yellow box. Burlingame formally resigned as the American minister to China and became "Envoy of His Imperial Majesty's Government" to the West. The Burlingame mission was born. The Chinese empire would venture forth into the Western world to establish closer ties.

On March 31, 1868, Burlingame, accompanied by a retinue of Chinese officials and servants, arrived in San Francisco aboard the Pacific Mail steamship *China*. Burlingame had been anxious about how his decision to lead the Chinese mission would be received by his fellow countrymen, but a porter who came down the gangplank reassured him. "The whole city is here to welcome the new Chinese minister," he said. The crowd's excitement came from the belief that China, which had been impenetrable for so long, was finally joining the family of civilized nations and opening itself to the advance of Christendom. Several weeks later, Governor Henry Haight, who had waged a vigorous campaign against the Fifteenth Amendment because he feared Chinese immigrants gaining the right to suffrage, hosted a sumptuous dinner for the Burlingame mission for more than two hundred guests. "For centuries this people has remained almost entirely excluded from intercourse with Europe and America," he said, during his toast. "A wall of separation has prevented them from contact with the civilization, arts, commerce, polity, and religion of the Western world." He hailed the opportunity for the "young, impulsive, progressive civilization of America" to interact with the "ancient, venerable and peculiar civilization of Asia." A few days later, Burlingame and his party departed for New York, by way of the Isthmus of Panama, arriving several weeks later.

On June 2, Burlingame arrived in Washington and promptly called upon his former boss, Seward. The sixty-seven-year-old Seward was recognizable by his unruly hair and pronounced nose and chin. He had come to national prominence in the U.S. Senate, where he represented the state of New York for a dozen years and became an intellectual leader of the anti-slavery movement. "From him we received the battle-cry in the turmoils of the contest; for he was one of those spirits who sometimes will go ahead of public opinion instead of tamely following its footprints," Carl Schurz, his Senate colleague, later said. Seward had been widely expected to win the Republican nomination for president in May 1860, but was supplanted by the less heralded former congress-man from Illinois, Abraham Lincoln. After winning the election in November, Lincoln appointed Seward to be secretary of state, the most prestigious position in his cabinet. A gregarious personality and gifted raconteur, Seward became a close confidant of Lincoln's during the Civil War. On the evening of April 14, 1865, when John Wilkes Booth shot and mortally wounded Lincoln at Ford's Theatre, a co-conspirator in the plot attacked Seward inside his home, stabbing him in the face and neck with a Bowie knife. Seward eventually recovered and stayed on as secretary of state under President Andrew Johnson.

Seward was a fervent champion of American commerce to the Far East. In 1867, he negotiated the purchase of Alaska and the Aleutian Islands from Russia, an important step in his Asia maritime strategy. With Burlingame's arrival in Washington, Seward arranged for a cer-emonial welcome at the White House. He took it upon himself to draft a new treaty that recognized China's territorial sovereignty and prom-ised its subjects in the United States the same "privileges, immunities and exemptions" as those bestowed upon citizens of the most favored nation. In the middle of July, Seward and Burlingame agreed upon the terms, and the Senate quickly ratified the treaty. Prince Gong and other Chinese officials were initially stunned by the speed with which an agreement had been reached but found it to be "thoroughly advanta-geous to China." They expressed hope that the Burlingame Treaty, as it came to be known, would finally mean that the "Chinese in California will cease to be subjected to the ill-treatment they have hitherto met."

The new treaty contained a clause that stated both countries "recog-nize the inherent and inalienable right of man to change his home and allegiance, and also the mutual advantage of free migration and emigration of their citizens and subjects respectively from one country to the other for the purpose of curiosity, of trade, or as permanent residents." It was a provision that Seward, an ardent proponent of the effort to build the Pacific railroad, reportedly crafted himself. He believed that Chinese emigration to the American continent would inevitably benefit the economies of all Western nations. He was also convinced that China's ability to shed some of its surplus population would help open the kingdom to Western influence, including evangelization.

During the mid-1860s, the Chinese population in the United States seemed to ebb. The San Francisco Custom House had begun recording more Chinese departures than arrivals on an annual basis. With the Burlingame Treaty, however, a new era of Chinese immigration commenced.

A pell-mell scene greeted Pacific Mail ships every month as they arrived in San Francisco harbor. One day in 1869, a writer for the *Atlantic Monthly* made his way down from Rincon Hill, a fashionable neighborhood situated on a steep incline overlooking the waterfront. He navigated his way through a knot of people waiting outside the steamship company's gate. On a long, covered wharf, representatives of the various mutual aid associations—known collectively as the Six Companies—waited to receive the passengers of the *Great Republic*. The deck of the ship was "packed with Chinamen—every foot of space occupied by them," the writer later wrote. Workers hoisted gangway planks onto the decks, and officers from San Francisco's Customs House climbed aboard. A small group of American naval officers, returning from the Pacific, came down a rear gangway. The forward planks were reserved for Chinese arrivals. A petite woman, dressed in a satin blouse and trousers and wearing a small wreath of artificial flowers atop her hair, descended, covering her face with a pair of fans. She was the new bride of a Chinese merchant, who escorted her into a waiting carriage. Soon after, a stream of men dressed in blue cotton blouses, baggy pants, and stockings, with their possessions dangling from bamboo poles across their shoulders, poured down the planks. "There is a babel of uncouth cries and harsh discordant yells, accompanied by whimsically energetic gestures and convulsive facial distortions, as members of the different gangs recognize each other in the crowd, and search out the places assigned them," the writer reported. The human procession lasted two hours. By the end, the ship had deposited 1,272 "Chinamen" on American shores.

At this point, Chinese inhabitants in California totaled about fifty thousand, just under 10 percent of the state's population. Their numbers fell slightly below those of Irish immigrants, who had streamed into the United States by the hundreds of thousands in the middle of the century and then began making their way west in the aftermath of the Civil War, in search of economic opportunity. They joined other first- or second-generation white immigrants who made up the majority of California's labor force. By the late 1860s, California was burgeoning with new residents, as westward migration to the state reached levels not seen since the gold rush. Many who made the journey had been displaced by the changes wrought by industrialization back east, or were suffering through the effects of the postwar recession. They came in search of prosperity in the West but found instead a stagnating economy. Mining yields had been declining in California for years. Farmers were experiencing a drought. Building construction slowed; factories were shuttered, or workforces slashed. The transcontinental railroad had turned out not to be a boon after all. California businesses suddenly found themselves facing new competition, as merchants in the middle of the country began seeking out suppliers on the East Coast as well. "Instead of bringing them new worlds to conquer, it brought a new world to conquer them," one newspaper account said. Over the next decade, shipload by shipload, Chinese immigration to America would swell. Chinese residents would eventually replace the Irish as the largest foreign-born population in the state. The new Chinese arrivals and their white counterparts were like railcars racing towards the same switch in the track: a collision was inevitable.

Discontented workers increasingly began to focus their ire on Chinese workers. In the fall of 1869, mass meetings began taking place inside Congress Hall, a large theater on Bush Street, organized by Thomas Mooney, a prominent Irish financier who had been involved in efforts to recruit more white European immigrants to California. In

December, Mooney petitioned Congress on behalf of the Anti-Coolie and Anti-Monopoly Association of San Francisco to stop subsidizing the Pacific Mail Steamship Company, declaring that "taxes wrung from the sweat of free American labor" should not be "devoted towards the vile purposes of renewing the slave trade in coolies." In July 1870, thousands of Irish laborers marched through the streets and rallied against the "Mongolian slave"; about 150 men signed on to an armed company. Labor leaders established the Anti-Chinese Convention of the State of California to oppose Chinese immigration and press for the abrogation of the Burlingame Treaty.

The Chinese passengers on Pacific Mail's steamships likely had only the dimmest sense of the unfolding rancor. Upon disembarking, they set out through the city's streets. The blocks to the Chinese quarter were often a gauntlet. On one spring evening in 1870, a reporter witnessed packs of children pelting Chinese arrivals with stones, sticks, old shoes, and clods of dirt. Some of the white drivers of wagons carrying Chinese passengers and their baggage tried to drive the assailants off with whips. Nearby, a crowd of adults urged on other boys and girls who were harassing Chinese arrivals struggling to make their way on foot. A policeman stood idly by. On another occasion, a mob of about fifty boys wielding clubs dragged Chinese men from their wagons. A brief news account described the attacks as an "almost daily occurrence." From a bridge near the dock, gangs of young white men found merriment in dropping stones onto the heads of the Chinese in wagons.

Law enforcement was mostly indifferent to the harassment. George Lem arrived in America in 1875, at the age of eleven or twelve, as part of a group of a half-dozen travelers that included his father and uncle. Lem began working for an American family as a cook. He was walking on Kearney Street one day, wearing a long coat and round cap. A boy knocked off his cap and threw rocks at him. Lem ran home crying. The family Lem was working for bandaged his wounds and gave him a police whistle for his safety. The next time Lem was accosted, he blew it. A policeman on the scene told Lem to "run along home, now" and let his assailant go. Andrew Kan, the son of a poor farmer and merchant in Guangdong province, was fifteen years old when he arrived in San Francisco Bay on a steamer, after a thirty-two-day journey across the

Pacific. "When I first came, Chinese treated worse than dog," he later recalled. "Oh, it was terrible, terrible." Children would pull at his queue, slap him in the face, and throw old vegetables and rotten eggs at Kan and other Chinese. "All you could do was to run and get out of the way," Kan said. "Nobody would ever try to stop them."

The Chinese quarter in San Francisco first emerged during the early 1850s, on Sacramento Street, between Stockton and Kearny Streets. Residents called it Tong Yun Gai, or "street of the people of the Tang Dynasty." Over time, Chinatown grew into a bustling district that encompassed about a dozen square blocks. By 1870, about a quarter of California's Chinese inhabitants lived in San Francisco—just over twelve thousand people. Many Chinese who had once made their livelihoods in the interior had filtered back into the city after placer mines became depleted. They took up new occupations as laborers in factories, or as laundrymen or domestic workers. The completion of the Pacific railroad brought still more Chinese men in search of economic opportunities. The buildings in Chinatown tended to be two or three stories, made of brick; Chinese lanterns dangled from brightly painted balconies; fruit and vegetable peddlers, cobblers, razor-sharpeners, and other sellers of wares crowded the wooden sidewalks. A pair of Chinese theaters sat across from each other on Jackson Street. An aroma of opium, tobacco leaves, dried fish, and vegetables suffused the quarter. Signboards advertised all manner of establishments: wholesalers of rice and tea; silversmiths; tin and sheet-iron shops; factories for shoes, woolens, and women's undergarments; barbershops; gambling halls; and restaurants. Many merchants operated boarding rooms behind or above their storefronts. A half-dozen former hotels became Chinese lodging houses.

As resentment towards Chinese immigrants curdled among the laboring classes in San Francisco, Chinatown became a convenient target. Mooney and other anti-Chinese leaders began pressing city officials to regulate the "sanitary conditions of the Chinese." In the middle of June 1870, they submitted a petition to the city's board of supervisors, demanding that they appoint a committee to visit the Chinese quarter and "ascertain their mode of living and lodging." Several weeks later, during a meeting of the board of health, the group read a statement on the "crowded, filthy, abominable condition of Chinese life in our midst" and urged that health officers "remove the Chinese nuisance." The board members ultimately deflected the association's requests, but the city's health officer incorporated a section on the Chinese into his annual report, describing the living conditions in the Chinese quarter as "the most abject in which it is possible for human beings to exist." He called the Chinese a "moral leper in our community." On July 29, 1870, the board of supervisors enacted Order 939, "Regulating Lodging Houses," which required every "building, house, room, or apartments" used for living or sleeping within the city limits contain at least five hundred cubic feet for each adult in the lodging. Violators of the so-called Cubic Air Ordinance would be charged with a criminal misdemeanor, punishable by a fine of up to five hundred dollars, three months in prison, or both.

For reasons that aren't entirely clear, the first significant effort to enforce the ordinance was not made until May 20, 1873, when police converged, at one o'clock in the morning, upon a large basement room on Jackson Street, where several dozen Chinese men were sleeping. The apartment measured forty-five feet by eighteen feet, with an eight-foot ceiling, which meant that by law it should have held a maximum of a dozen people. Officers sent them to the city jail. In another raid, in June, this time on a lodging house on Clay Street, the police arrested fifty-six men who occupied nine different rooms. In total, more than four hundred Chinese residents were arrested in May and June of 1873. Lon Ci Tat, who had converted the former Globe Hotel into a Chinese lodging house, was among those swept up in the raids. In the Globe, as many as fifteen men occupied an eight-by-ten-foot room, in bunks stacked up to the ceiling. A county judge overturned the verdict against Lon Ci Tat, ruling that the board had exceeded its authority. The police halted their raids but resumed them in earnest after the state legislature passed its own lodging house law in April 1876. The local press avidly reported on the police forays into Chinatown: thirty arrested, on May 1, in a rooming house in Spofford alley in the heart of the Chinese quarter; forty-seven in a house on Clay Street on May 17; another fifty-six on Clay Street, about a month later. One San Francisco police officer alone,

James R. Rogers, arrested eleven hundred Chinese men for violating the cubic-air law. The Chinese-language newspaper *The Oriental* reported incredulously on the ordinance, arguing that Chinese laborers lived in cramped quarters because they could hardly "even get two meals a day."

Many of the Chinese swept up in these raids were subjected to an additional humiliation. The board of supervisors had first tried to enact a "pigtail ordinance" in 1870, requiring that inmates at the county jail have their hair cut or clipped to within one inch of their scalp. The city's mayor, William Alvord, however, vetoed the measure. In the spring of 1876, with the election of a new mayor, James Otis, the board tried again. This time, their proposal passed with no objections. In the spring of 1878, a man named Ho Ah Kow was arrested in one of the cubic-air raids and, upon his admittance to the county jail, had his braid cut off. After his release five days later, Ho enlisted the help of the Six Companies' lawyers and filed a lawsuit. Depriving a Chinese man of his queue was a "mark of disgrace," Ho said in his complaint. He had been "mutilated" and suffered from "mental anguish" and ostracism "from the respectable association of his countrymen." Remarkably, a panel of circuit court judges agreed with him, ruling that the sanitary justification for the law was "mere pretense," and that imposing such a requirement amounted to "wanton cruelty." The law was struck down.

By this point, in the latter 1870s, the city had become a cauldron of idle white workingmen. By one estimate, some fifteen thousand of them were unemployed in the city, perhaps a quarter of the labor force—victims of a prolonged economic depression that had settled over the country during the middle of the decade. Concern grew about the "tramp nuisance" in the city. A reporter visited a homeless encampment and interviewed an elderly man picking through the trash. "All the men here go every day from wharf to wharf and hunt the whole city over for a job at any price," he said. "We can't get anything." Another man, washing himself with a can of water, chimed in and said he had been living at the camp for three months. "I have never let a day go by that I have not walked mile after mile to get a job," he said. "Some weeks I have made a dollar, and weeks I have not made anything. I have offered to work for one-half the price that Chinamen get in any branch of hard labor. But no use. No one would take me."

Chinese laborers were, in fact, usually not directly in competition with most white workers. The two groups mostly existed in different labor pools, with Chinese laborers concentrated in lower-wage, less-skilled work. Competition with eastern factories and the broader shift to mass production were the biggest factors in California's economic travails. Nevertheless, anti-coolie clubs spread in the city; shoemakers and cigar makers introduced labels that proclaimed their goods "Made by White Labor." Groups of angry white workers roamed the city targeting the Chinese. (The term "hoodlum" can be traced, in part, to these disaffected young men.) One group became known as the Telegraph Hill Rollers for their rolling of large stones down the steep slope upon hapless Chinese crossing the street. Huie Kin, who made the journey by steamer to America as a teenager, recalled the fear among the new arrivals. "The Chinese were in a pitiable condition in those days," he said. "We were simply terrified; we kept indoors after dark for fear of being shot in the back. Children spit upon us as we passed by and called us rats."

On April 5, 1876, thousands of people—estimates ran as high as twenty-five thousand—filled the galleries of Union Hall and spilled out onto the streets for a meeting denouncing Chinese immigration. Both the city's mayor, James Otis, a Republican, and the governor, William Irwin, a Democrat, delivered full-throated denunciations of Chinese immigration and urged pressure on officials in Washington to deliver relief. The meeting concluded with a series of resolutions attacking the Chinese as "a distinct race, of a different and peculiar civilization," and a presence that "has a tendency to demoralize society and minister to its worst vices."

Less than a week later, a commission organized by the state senate began a series of hearings in San Francisco on the "social, moral, and political effect of Chinese immigration." As part of the proceedings, several members of the commission toured the Chinese quarter. "We went into places so filthy and dirty I cannot see how these people live there," Edward J. Lewis, a member of the commission, reported. "The fumes of opium, mingled with the odor arising from filth and dirt, made rather a sickening feeling creep over us. I would not go through that quarter again for anything in the world. The whole Chinese quarter is miserably filthy, and I think that the passage of an ordinance removing them from the city, as a nuisance, would be justifiable."

The heads of several of the Chinese companies testified through interpreters, patiently responding to questions about gambling, prostitution, and coolie labor. They explained, again and again, that their members had all come freely. "I don't know what you mean by coolies," Yung Ty, the president of the Hop-wo Company, said. "They are not slaves; they are simply the lower class of men who work for a living." Around this time, representatives of the Six Companies issued an open letter to the American public, reminding them that they had tried to discourage their countrymen from coming to America. They suggested that the government of the United States should simply renegotiate the terms of the Burlingame Treaty and prohibit people in either country from crossing the ocean. "Then shall we Chinese remain at home and enjoy the happiness of fathers, mothers, wives, and children, and no longer remain strangers in a strange land," they said. "Then the white laborers of this country shall no longer be troubled by the competition of the Chinese, and our Chinese people no longer be subjected to the abuses and indignities now daily heaped upon them in the open streets of this so-called Christian land."

The committee issued a report calling on Congress to bring an end to Chinese immigration. It warned that a "profound sense of dissatisfaction" had settled in among white men about the situation. The feeling had been restrained, but the committee predicted there would come a day "when patience may cease." For members of the committee, the problem was the Burlingame Treaty. So long as it remained in place, they believed, citizens of the Chinese empire would continue to cross the Pacific. In the interim, those hostile to the Chinese presence needed a different, more targeted approach. There was one particularly vulnerable class of arrivals: Chinese women. They represented a sliver of the population, but they engendered near-universal opprobrium.

CHAPTER 7

Lewd and Immoral Purposes

Ah Toy was among the most famous of San Francisco's pioneer residents. In 1849, when she was about twenty years old, she arrived in the city, alone. A native of Guangzhou, she had made the journey to America, she later said, for the purpose of "bettering her condition" and hoped to make it her home. She was unusually tall for a Chinese woman, with delicate, bound feet and a "slender body and laughing eyes," as one admirer later put it. He called her "strangely alluring." She was also enterprising. Her first place of business was a shanty in an alley off Clay Street, between Dupont and Kearny Streets. The line of men often stretched down the block. After disembarking their steamboats from the interior, miners would often break into a run to claim a spot. The men paid Ah Toy with an ounce of gold dust, which she carefully weighed. In return, she gave men a chance to "gaze on her countenance," another early San Francisco arrival recalled. This was likely a decorous way to put it. Ah Toy was widely understood to be the city's first Chinese courtesan. Regardless of how she initially earned her living, Ah Toy quickly became a madam and began employing other Chinese women, operating brothels in at least two locations and eventually moving into a brick mansion nearby. In May of 1850, a local newspaper reported that the "well known China woman, named Achoi, from Hong Kong," had married a white man named Pete Conrad in Sonoma. It's unclear how long the union lasted, because subsequent articles about the madam failed to mention him. Ah Toy also soon reportedly had a new lover,

John A. Clark, the leader of a special task force investigating prostitution in the city. Chinese women began arriving regularly on steamships, many of them under Ah Toy's charge. She made frequent appearances at the city's Recorder's Court, testifying with the help of an interpreter but also speaking enough English to be understood. On one visit, she confronted two men she accused of shortchanging her; as evidence, she marched home to fetch a large basin filled with the brass filings that customers had tried to pass off as gold to show the judge. The display drew laughter in the courtroom, but the judge dismissed the case. On another occasion, Ah Toy personally chased a man down for stealing a $300 diamond brooch from her home and rounded up witnesses to testify against him. He was convicted and sentenced to a year in jail. One of her more disturbing courtroom encounters involved a confrontation with Norman Assing, the early leader of the Chinese community. Ah Toy accused Assing of a blackmail scheme, sending cronies to kill her unless she returned to China. The judge ordered Assing and his compatriots to pay a $2,000 bond to keep the peace.

Ah Toy also began to clash with leaders of the fighting tongs, the secret societies that vied for influence in the Chinese immigrant community. (The Assing dispute was likely related to a tong conflict.) Within a few years, the tongs had taken control of the sex trade. In 1857, Ah Toy announced she was returning to China, only to make her way back to the city a few years later. She resumed operating brothels but largely disappeared from public view. (Decades later, in February 1928, a city newspaper published a three-paragraph article reporting that "'Mrs. Ah Toy,' better known as 'China Mary,'" had died in San Jose, a few months shy of her hundredth birthday. The article described her as the widow of a prosperous Chinese merchant and said that she'd sold clams in Alviso, becoming a familiar figure in town. There was no mention of her colorful earlier life.) The sex trade went on without Ah Toy. Tong leaders established an elaborate system to entrap girls in Guangzhou, Hong Kong, and the vicinity and then transport them across the ocean. Agents lured young girls with promises of riches or marriage, and then made them sign oppressive contracts.

The Chinese quarter was overwhelmingly a bachelor society, making prostitution lucrative. The 1852 census tallied a Chinese population of just over 3,000 in San Francisco, only 19 of them women. The imbalance persisted as Chinese migration to America continued to climb. According to the census of 1870, fewer than 4,000 of the roughly 49,000 Chinese residents in California were female. Many of the men who journeyed to Gold Mountain married before they left, or on return trips home, and the couples endured long separations. The Rev. A. W. Loomis, who succeeded the Rev. William Speer as the head of the Presbyterian mission, blamed the reluctance of Chinese women to follow their husbands to America, in part, on patriarchal customs that dictated the women tend to domestic duties back home. He also contended that most Chinese migrants planned to return to China, so it made little sense for wives to make the journey across the Pacific. Economic uncertainty and the dangers facing Chinese emigrants in America, however, were other major deterrents. "It is exceedingly difficult to bring families upon distant journeys over great oceans," a Chinese merchant, Lai Chun-chuen, wrote in a tract published in 1855. "Further, there have been several injunctions warning the people of the Flowery land not to come here, which have fostered doubts; nor have our hearts found peace in regard to bringing our families."

Prostitutes of all nationalities plied their trade in San Francisco. From early on, however, the authorities focused on Chinese prostitutes as a particular scourge. The forces committed to shutting down the Chinese sex trade saw the women as a paramount threat to American family life. Western missionaries in the Far East had long portrayed China as a place of licentiousness. "Girls scarcely twelve-years-old were given up to the beastly passions of men," one missionary said. The image belied the sexual modesty that generally characterized Chinese culture, but it became ingrained in the broader indictment of Chinese immigrants as an alien, heathen people. On March 20, 1854, the city's board of aldermen approved Ordinance No. 546, "To Suppress Houses of Ill-Fame Within the City Limits," which imposed fines and jail time on violators. Several months later, the board convened a special committee to investigate conditions in the Chinese quarter. It found Chinese arrivals living in the "filthiest places that could be imagined" and reported that every female inhabitant was a "degraded" prostitute. The committee recommended that all Chinese residents be expelled. Alarmed, leading

Chinese merchants resolved to do their part to clean up the quarter, proclaiming their own "universal contempt" for the sex trade, but it proved resilient.

In 1866, the state legislature enacted a new measure, designating "houses of ill fame, kept, managed, inhabited, or used by Chinese women for the purposes of common prostitution" to be public nuisances. Landlords and others who consented to the operation of brothels in rooming houses and elsewhere faced misdemeanor charges. When prosecutions threatened to overwhelm the court system, however, brothel operators reached a tacit agreement with the authorities to restrict their businesses to certain buildings and abide by rules imposed by the board of health and police commissioners. Chinese prostitution became less brazen but remained rampant. One evening in 1869, a reporter toured an alley in Chinatown in the company of a police officer. On both sides were dimly lit apartments containing expressionless, elaborately made-up women, just viewable through window sashes. On a second visit, the reporter wound his way through narrow passages and low doorways until he reached a cramped room that he later described as a hospital for dying former prostitutes. He recounted an abject scene: "Here these poor creatures, deserted by both friends and owners, with no one to turn to for help, nor any God to pray to for consolation in their house of distress, terminate their miserable lives."

On October 20, 1871, a police captain ordered that a note be delivered to the Rev. Otis Gibson, the head of the Methodist Episcopal Church's Chinese mission. A young woman had escaped from a brothel on Jackson Street, run down to the waterfront, and thrown herself into San Francisco Bay. A fisherman had hauled her out with a boat hook, and a policeman delivered her to the station. She begged in Chinese not to be taken back and asked to speak instead to a "Jesus man." Gibson, a native of New York and former missionary in Fuzhou, China, had arrived in San Francisco in 1868 and founded the Chinese Domestic Mission. Gibson, sturdily built, with a chinstrap beard and piercing eyes, became a stalwart defender of Chinese immigrants. He later said that he prayed to never have to shoot a man but, if he ever had to do it, he asked the Lord to assist him in shooting straight.

Soon after his arrival in the city, Gibson had turned his attention to the plight of Chinese women. "There is nothing connected with this whole subject of Chinese immigration so objectionable, so revolting, so wicked, as this woman question," he later wrote. In Gibson's view, the degraded condition of Chinese women was the inevitable result of thousands of years of Chinese civilization that "rested upon a heathen idolatrous basis." In August 1870, he and his wife, Eliza, helped to establish the Women's Missionary Society of the Pacific Coast, whose mission it was, according to its constitution, to "elevate and save heathen women on these shores." On Christmas Day 1870, Gibson turned over the third floor of the mission's newly purchased building on Washington Street to the organization as a refuge for rescued Chinese women. For nearly a year, the quarters sat empty, as the small cadre of women who founded the ministry cast about for ways to establish contact with the Chinese women. The society opened a school for the women but got only sporadic attendance and, after eight months, decided to close it. Jin Ho, the wet, bedraggled woman fished from San Francisco Bay, became the first resident. In Gibson's subsequent telling, within six months, Jin Ho was unrecognizable to those at the police station. She ended up staying a year at the home, became a baptized member of the Methodist Church, and married Jee Foke, a Chinese Christian.

The stories of other residents of the home were similarly dramatic. It was close to midnight on a Sunday, in December 1872, when the doorbell to the home rang twice, insistently. Gibson was the only person awake. When he opened the door, a teenage girl, in ragged clothing, darted inside. Gibson stopped her. She explained that she had run away from an abusive mistress. The teenager's name was Sing Kum; she was the oldest of three children in a poor family in China. When she was seven years old, her father decided to sell her. Her mother wept. Her father later visited her and gave her some money, wishing her prosperity. She was passed from one owner to the next and arrived in California at the age of twelve. Her final owner was the cruelest of all, whipping her and pulling her by the hair. A friend had pointed out the mission home, and Sing Kum waited for a moment when she was unattended and snuck away. At the mission, the teenager learned English, arithmetic, geography, and history and eventually became an assistant teacher. "I used to gamble, lie, and steal," she later wrote. "Now I love Jesus."

By January 1873, the home had three residents and the society hired a full-time teacher. That spring, a merchant, Lun Yat Sung, came to the home with a tip about three women being held captive by a brothel owner on Pacific Street. The women managed to smuggle out a letter, identifying the owner as a man named Hon Chan, assisted by an elderly woman, Ah Yee. If they failed to make enough money every night, the women said they were beaten. The three women begged to be rescued. "We would like to lead a more honorable life," they wrote. An investigation led to a basement room, where the women were rescued and brought to the police station; the brothel owners were arrested several days later. Chinese merchants rallied to help the women and suitors were found for them. On June 23, Rev. Gibson presided over a wedding at the mission home between an eighteen-year-old bride, Ah Sing, one of the escaped prostitutes, and the merchant, Yat Sung. A judge convicted Hon Chan and Ah Yee of operating a brothel and fined them $1,000.

Several weeks later, however, henchmen of the Hip Yee Tong society, one of the criminal gangs that controlled the vice trade in Chinatown, summoned Yat Sung. He found himself facing a tribunal of thirty men. Hip Yee Tong had begun in 1852 as a small organization and gradually expanded its operations until it counted over three hundred members. The society imported large numbers of women, stashed them in warehouses, and then turned them over to brothel operators for a fee. The tong leaders demanded that Yat Sung return Ah Sing, or reimburse them for her value, $350; otherwise, they said, they would have him killed. When Yat Sung pleaded poverty, they told him he had two days to raise the funds. The couple fled to the mission home, where Rev. Gibson alerted the authorities.

The police swept into the society's headquarters, located on the second floor of a brick building in an alley off Jackson Street, and arrested eight of its leaders. During the three-day trial, the courtroom was crowded with Chinese spectators. The prosecution's case began to falter, however, after Ah Sing took the stand and delivered a confusing, halting performance, in which she insisted her name was not Ah Sing and that she could not remember when she had married her husband, or even where she came from. After a frustrating exchange, the prosecutor realized what was happening. When pressed by the prosecutor, Ah Sing finally glanced at the eight tong members seated in front of her and bowed her head, admitting that she feared "the people of the Hip Yee Tong." The eight men were acquitted.

The women at the mission home continued their work. Within a few years, several dozen women had found refuge inside, a mix of escaped prostitutes, former *mui tsai*—servants—who had run away from abusive households, and women who had been placed at the mission by Chinese men who hoped to eventually marry them. Initially, stints at the home were of varying lengths. The society's board eventually decided that stays should be at least a year. In the mornings, residents attended school, learning to read and write; they devoted afternoons to sewing and other needlework that helped to defray the costs of the home. On Sunday mornings, there was a prayer meeting and worship service; in the evenings, the women had Bible study. The society's intent was to marry the women off to "Christian Chinamen," and weddings were regular occurrences.

The Methodist women soon had co-laborers in their rescue work. On April 14, 1873, a group of Presbyterian women gathered to establish the California Branch of the Woman's Foreign Missionary Society of the Presbyterian Church. The original intention of the group was to open an orphanage in Shanghai, but during a subsequent meeting inside a plain room at the YMCA, a member from Oakland persuaded the group to change its focus. "I move that we work for the Chinese here," she said. The women decided that they would pour their energies into the establishment of a home in San Francisco that would be "a refuge for Chinese women who may desire to lead lives of respectability and usefulness" and be "rescued from a life of sin." In July 1874, a committee set out to find a suitable home, settling on a four-room apartment on the upper floor of a house on Prospect Place. A matron, Sarah M. N. Cummings, was appointed, and, in the middle of August, two Chinese girls became the first residents of the Mission Home; others quickly followed. Mrs. Cummings did not speak Chinese and relied upon a pair of interpreters, one of them a former enslaved girl named Ching Yuen, to lead residents in worship every morning and conduct lessons in reading, spelling, numbers, and writing; afternoons were devoted to sewing work. As more women arrived, the home became cramped. In her annual report, in 1875, Cummings described her time with the women as pleasant, marred only by her "inability to show to these sin-stricken ones their ruined state and the way of repair."

In their zeal for eradicating the sex trade, leaders of the Protestant missionary movement in California found common cause with opponents of Chinese immigration. Together, they pressed lawmakers to block the arrival of women from Asia. In 1870, a new state law made it illegal for any ship to land any "Mongolian, Chinese, or Japanese females," unless the passengers furnished proof that they were coming to California voluntarily and possessed "correct habits and good character." The measure empowered a new state commissioner of immigration to enforce the legislation. Anti-Chinese politicians considered nearly all women arriving on steamships from Hong Kong to be suspect. The census of 1870 recorded a population of 2,018 Chinese women in San Francisco; 1,426 of them, or just over 70 percent, were counted as prostitutes. There are reasons to believe this might have been an overcount, driven by language difficulties and census takers' biases.

That meant a sizable number of the Chinese female arrivals were, in fact, wives coming to join their husbands. The impetus was often their husbands' achieving a measure of financial success, enough so that they felt comfortable sending for their spouses. Lee Wong Sang, a native of Taishan, had arrived in San Francisco in 1866, at the age of nineteen. He went to work right away for the Central Pacific. His facility with English helped him become a "headman" in his work camp. After the railroad was completed, he opened an import-export store on Dupont Street in San Francisco's Chinatown. Before Lee left for America, his mother had arranged for him to be married to a woman named Chin Shee. She had stayed behind in Lee's village, living with her in-laws. In the early 1870s, however, Lee sent word back home for her to join him. She packed her wedding skirt and a few other belongings and made the voyage to America with two other Gold Mountain wives on a boat with hundreds of men. The seas were so violent that, as the story goes, one of the women lost all of her hair, tossing and turning in her bunk. When they arrived, Chin Shee was able to be reunited with her husband, but the other two women initially went with the wrong men and had to make the switch when they arrived in Chinatown. Lee and his wife took up residence above his store, where they would eventually raise three sons.

Chin Lin Sou was in his early twenties when he sailed from Hong Kong to San Francisco in 1859. He came from a wealthy family in Guangdong province and was well-educated. Unusually, he already spoke English. Chin was also tall for a Chinese man, measuring six feet two inches. He had a broad face and striking blue-gray eyes. He spent his first few years mining for gold in California and then established a trading company in San Francisco. When work on the Pacific railroad got underway, Chin oversaw a crew of Chinese laborers. After Promontory, Chin continued working for the Union Pacific on other railroad lines through Wyoming and Colorado. He eventually moved on to gold mining in Colorado, partnering with a white man who had served as the Chinese interpreter for Sisson, Wallace, and Co., one of the principal suppliers of Chinese laborers for the Pacific railroad. Chin oversaw a contingent of three hundred Chinese men in Gregory Gulch, Colorado, just south of a settlement called Black Hawk. In 1871, Chin's wife, who was known in America as "Miss Ng," joined him. Chin was devoted to her. "Her countenance shone like the moon at midnight," he later said to newspaper reporters. "Her lips were like lotus blossoms, and her fingertips were dripping with honey." In 1873, she gave birth to a daughter, Lily Chin, who was said to be the first Chinese child born in Colorado. The couple went on to raise six children in Colorado. Chin became a celebrated figure in the small Chinese community, but only the barest of details are known about his wife.

How to tell the difference between these "virtuous" women and the debauched? This was the dilemma for officials trying to stem the tide of sexual perversion. On August 24, 1874, the Pacific Mail Steamship *Japan* arrived in San Francisco harbor, carrying 589 Chinese passengers;

more than 90 of them were female, including several children. Rudolph Piotrowski, the state's commissioner of immigration, along with E. B. Vreeland, his deputy, boarded for their inspection. The ship's captain, John Freeman, had found the women to be model passengers during their voyage. The U.S. consul's office in Hong Kong had also examined all and certified all to be of good character, but the two men were there to make their own determination. They spoke no Chinese, so an interpreter, who had been sworn in beforehand, accompanied them. They gathered the female passengers on the upper deck. Inside a smoking room, Piotrowski and Vreeland conducted their interrogations, pressing the women to prove their marital status and for details of when they were married and where; if the women said they were meeting husbands in California, the officials probed their plans for finding them. A contingent of thirty-three women who were on board with their husbands and children sent word to the officials that they wanted to be examined separately. Vreeland questioned them and let them go. But the request made the men suspicious of the remaining women. A few Chinese men who spoke English were allowed aboard to look for their wives and take them away. After three hours of questioning, the officials barred twenty-two of the women, between the ages of seventeen and twenty-eight, from disembarking, unless the shipmaster paid a $500 bond for each of them—a recent provision added to the law. "According to my judgment, they were perfectly improper to come into this community," Piotrowski later said.

With the women confined on board the *Japan,* a writ of habeas corpus was filed on their behalf in the state supreme court, arguing their detention was unconstitutional. The identity of the person who filed the application and his relationship to the women is murky. Court records reference a petitioner named Ah Coo; one newspaper account reported that representatives of two Chinese *huiguan,* the Sam Yup and Sze Yup companies, were involved; another cited "a Chinaman named Ah Lung, who traffics in this kind of business." Whoever it was, the petitioner had the resources to retain a prominent San Francisco attorney, Leander Quint, a former judge and state senator. Pacific Mail Steamship Company, whose business was threatened by the immigration commissioner's intervention, hired its own lawyers from the prestigious firm McAllister

& Bergin to assist in the case. The case was quickly transferred to the Fourth District Court, which had jurisdiction over the city and county of San Francisco. A new petitioner, Chy Lung, became attached to the case. A deputy sheriff boarded the vessel to escort the women to City Hall, which housed the district court, for a hearing. When they arrived at the imposing four-story brick building, across from Portsmouth Plaza, they refused to enter. Someone had apparently informed them that they were headed to their own executions. The women began wailing; some beat their heads against the wall; two of them vomited. The Rev. Otis Gibson and the Rev. Ira Condit, a Presbyterian missionary to the Chinese, who both happened to be nearby, were summoned to defuse the situation. Despite the men's entreaties, the women only grew louder. All other business in City Hall ceased, as a crowd gathered. Judge Robert F. Morrison, a genial but stern Democrat who had served as the district attorney in Sacramento and had been elected to the bench in 1869, decided it would be prudent to delay the hearing. The deputy sheriff and other officers dragged the women to wagons and delivered them to jail.

The next day, spectators crowded the courtroom. The twenty-two women sat in seats on the other side of the railing. John Freeman and Rudolph Piotrowski were the first witnesses to take the stand. A twenty-two-year-old woman named Quong Ling became the first of the accused to testify. She said that she'd previously come to the United States with her mother, at the age of twelve, but returned to China five years later. She had ventured back across the Pacific on the *Japan* because she was engaged to be married. Her mother and sister were living on Jackson Street, and she had been planning to be reunited with them. A parade of women followed Quong Ling to the stand with similar stories. All said they were married or engaged.

In the afternoon, Thomas P. Ryan, San Francisco's district attorney, called Gibson, the Methodist clergyman, as an expert witness. On the stand, Gibson enumerated distinctive characteristics by which a Chinese courtesan or prostitute could be identified, including the silk floral-printed dresses they usually wore, often yellow or purple, though he admitted that he was not "very good at colors." By contrast, he said that wives tended to wear plain clothing. During cross-examination by

Quint, the lawyer for the petitioners, Gibson admitted his information
was anecdotal and conceded that it was entirely possible for some prostitutes to wear drab clothing and for virtuous wives to sometimes favor
gaudy outfits. Quint asked Gibson to review the women in the courtroom and point to any indicators of their lewdness. Gibson singled out
two women on the end who seemed to be wearing clothing underneath
their black outfits. A discussion between the lawyers and Judge Morrison soon ensued over the propriety of examining the women to verify
Gibson's suppositions. The judge suggested that the women's sleeves
were wide and loose-fitting, so there was nothing indecent about peek-
ing underneath. In a pregnant moment, Quint raised the sleeves of
several of the women, revealing colorful outfits underneath. Gibson
seized on this as the "same style you will find in all of these Chinese
bawdry houses."

On the second day of the hearing, the women in the courtroom
suddenly erupted in ululations. They prostrated themselves on the floor,
pounded their breasts, screamed, and wailed. Judge Morrison clapped
his hands over his ears and hurriedly left the bench. A Chinese man,
one of the petitioners, managed to quiet the women escorting them
down the hallway to another room. The women eventually returned to
their seats and the proceedings resumed. As the testimony finished in
the afternoon, Quint introduced to the court a plump, good-natured
Chinese merchant. His wife was allegedly one of the accused. Ryan, the
prosecutor, was skeptical and proposed that they put together a lineup of
several men and ask her to pick him out. When Ah Lin was brought in,
the man seemed to signal her, drawing a protest from Ryan. The judge
agreed that the selection was invalid. "Got any more husbands?" Ryan
asked Quint. He said he hadn't had time to look for more.

The next day, in his closing arguments, the district attorney argued
that the power to enforce the prostitution statute rested upon every
community's right to self-defense. Mr. Quint, however, contended that
the fundamental question in the case was one of fact: "Are these women
prostitutes?" This needed to be established beyond a reasonable doubt,
which the state had failed to do. "You cannot exclude them," he said.
"There is no evidence to show that they are lewd women."

The courtroom was crowded the following morning, at half past ten o'clock, when Judge Morrison issued his decision, upholding the constitutionality of the law and finding that the women had landed for the "purposes of prostitution." He ordered the women be remanded back to China. The courtroom burst into applause. The *Japan* was scheduled to depart in an hour. A prison van and express wagon delivered the women back to the ship. A crowd gathered on the wharf to cheer their banishment, but when ordered to board the ship the women threw themselves down on the ground. Officers carried the women kicking and screaming up the gangplank. The women's lawyers rushed to file a new writ, this time on behalf of Ah Fong, a twenty-year-old woman who was among the detained, with the state Supreme Court. When Chief Justice William Wallace granted it, the city coroner hurried to the wharf, arriving just after noon, when the ship was scheduled to leave. The women came ashore, once again. A week later, the state supreme court ruled against them as well, but the women's lawyers pursued yet another legal option in federal court, with the Ninth Circuit.

In 1869, President Grant had appointed Lorenzo Sawyer, a dignified former judge on the California Supreme Court, to the newly created circuit court. Once every two years, however, justices of the Supreme Court of the United States were required to spend a term on their assigned circuit court. As a result, it was Justice Stephen J. Field, a former chief justice of California's Supreme Court and longtime Democrat, who took the lead during oral arguments on the case, when the parties assembled inside the federal courthouse on September 18. Field focused on the significance of the Fourteenth Amendment, which had been ratified six years earlier. He emphasized the use of the word "person" in the language of the amendment: "Nor shall any state deprive any *person* of life, liberty or property without due process of law, nor deny to any *person* within its jurisdiction the equal protection of the laws." The fact that the word "person" had been invoked, instead of citizen, signaled to Field that the amendment's protections applied to foreigners as well. In his decision, issued on September 25, Justice Field acknowledged the widespread opposition to Chinese immigration and even conceded "there is ground for this feeling." Nevertheless, he wrote that this did not justify discriminatory legislation that treated the Chinese differently from "inhabitants of the most favored nations of the Caucasian race, and of Christian faith." He ruled that the law exceeded the limits of the state's police powers and crossed over into the regulation of immigration, which was the purview of the federal government. Under the free emigration requirements of the Burlingame Treaty, the detention of the women was unlawful. He ordered that Ah Fong be discharged. Quint filed a separate writ for the others. At eleven o'clock in the morning on September 24, twenty women settled into the spectator section of the courtroom, chattering excitedly. (The lawyers deliberately left one woman off the petition, so the Supreme Court of the United States could rule on the matter. More than a year later, the court struck down the statute.) Field declared that the women were free to go. A crowd surrounded them when they reached the sidewalk. A trio of wagons transported them back to the city jail to collect their belongings, before transporting them to the Chinese quarter.

On December 7, 1874, President Ulysses S. Grant delivered his annual Christmas message. For weeks, he had been toiling over the address for several hours a day. Grant was in the middle of his second term and confronting a perilous time in his presidency. He had easily won reelection in 1872, but the financial panic of 1873 and the depression that followed had led to the failure of thousands of businesses and widespread unemployment. Ever since Lincoln's election to the presidency in 1861, the Republicans had been the dominant national party. But Reconstruction had turned the South into a redoubt for the Democratic Party. During the 1874 midterm elections, they capitalized on the frustrations of workingmen and picked up nearly a hundred congressional seats and seized control of the House. It was a stunning humiliation for Grant. To salvage his presidency, Grant needed to find a way to rescue the country from its economic malaise. He settled on a scapegoat: the Chinese. "I call the attention of Congress to a generally conceded fact—that the great proportion of the Chinese immigrants who come to our shores do not come voluntarily, to make their homes with us and their labor productive of general prosperity, but come under contracts with headmen, who own them almost absolutely," Grant said. "In a worse form does this apply to Chinese women. Hardly a perceptible percentage of them pursue any honorable labor, but they are brought for shameful purposes, to the disgrace of the communities where settled and to the great demoralization of the youth of those localities."

It was Rep. Horace Page, a California Republican, who took up Grant's call. In 1872, Page was elected to Congress, representing the state's second congressional district, which included Colfax, Placerville, and other former mining districts. Page had journeyed to California in 1853, at the age of twenty, from western New York. He went on to study law and established a law practice in Placerville, before running unsuccessfully for state senate in 1869. Page became an ardent foe of Chinese immigration, proposing legislation that variously prohibited coolie labor, called upon the president to renegotiate the Burlingame Treaty, and excluded Chinese immigrants from naturalization. He framed his crusade as part of the Republican Party's anti-slavery tradition, but he couldn't help but betray his underlying racist attitudes. "The Chinese are constitutionally and by race an inferior people to any of the nations of Europe," he told his colleagues on the House floor.

None of Page's earlier proposals advanced beyond the committee level, but in February 1875 Page began championing a more circumscribed measure that carried the benign-sounding title "An Act Supplementary to the Acts in Relation to Immigration." The law contained language barring the contracting of the "labor of any cooly" and the transporting of anyone from Asia "without their free and voluntary consent" for "a term of service," but the legislation was mostly aimed at Chinese prostitution. The measure required American consular officials to bar the emigration of anyone traveling for "lewd or immoral purposes," and threatened importers of Chinese prostitutes with a felony, punishable by up to five years in prison and a fine of up to $5,000. Page introduced affidavits from Gibson and Condit, detailing the sex trade. Condit asserted that "certainly nine-tenths" of the Chinese women in San Francisco were prostitutes. Gibson furnished an original bill of sale of $470 for a prostitute, Yut Kum, who had been enslaved under a four-year contract. Page cited the recent circuit court decision and said California lawmakers were powerless to deal with the issue. He urged his colleagues to "send the brazen harlot who openly flaunts her wickedness in the face of our wives and daughters back to her native country." The legislation sailed through the House and Senate, drawing little comment. On March 3, 1875, President Grant signed what became known as the Page Act into law. The legislation largely excluded Chinese women from entering the United States. Like a rock formation blocking a tree's root system, it disrupted any chance for a stable Chinese community to form.

CHAPTER 8

Order of Caucasians

By the middle of the 1870s, the mostly male Chinese population had spread across northern California, migrating from the mining regions into not just San Francisco but other Bay Area counties, along with the Sacramento and San Joaquin Valleys. There were some who welcomed their new neighbors. A farmer's wife in San Joaquin County, who identified herself only as "Martha," wrote a letter to a Stockton newspaper, on October 29, 1876, about how much she had come to rely upon her Chinese help. For years, she had toiled alone, cooking, churning butter to prepare for the market, washing the laundry, and performing all the other chores needed to support a disabled husband, two boys, and three hired hands. She struggled to find people willing to work in her home, even when she offered as much as $50 a month. She went through a series of workers, "every nationality under the sun." Each proved inadequate, or unreliable. Finally, she turned to "Chinamen." Her first worker stayed a year before moving on for better wages. "What a blessing he was," she said. "What bread and coffee and nice broiled steak he gave us, and no fuss nor noise." She continued to hire Chinese servants, seldom finding one she could not trust. "The one I have now has been with me nearly two years, is about 18 years of age, a good plain cook, washer and ironer, churns, takes care of pigs and poultry, harnesses my buggy horse, herds stock, is handy with carpenters' tools, or paint brush, and is in fact very quick to learn anything; can kill and dress a hog and take care of the meat and lard as well as any professional butcher," she wrote. "If I leave my home and there is any money in the house I give it into his charge. I pay him $20 per month. Will anyone tell me how or by whom I can replace him except by one of his countrymen?" She challenged the argument that "the Chinese usurp the place of white labor," arguing they simply satisfied a need that could not otherwise be fulfilled. She characterized "the warfare" made upon the Chinese as "unjust" and said her "China boy" was honest and had "principles that would do credit to a Christian."

George D. Roberts, president of the Tide Land Reclamation Company, employed three or four thousand Chinese laborers for digging ditches, building dikes, and constructing floodgates to reclaim swampland in the Sacramento–San Joaquin River Delta. "They are the best field-men that we have," he told a Senate panel investigating Chinese immigration in 1877. "The Chinaman is the best human labor-machine we have in this country for certain classes of work, and he does a class of work generally that the white men scorn to do, and which the white man will not do if he can possibly avoid it." The Chinese accounted for three-quarters of all agricultural workers in the region. Roberts recounted an experience he had during harvest time with a large wheat field he owned. At first, he dispatched several hundred white men but found that they typically worked a few days and then quit. He was in danger of having to discard much of the wheat that had been reaped, so he contracted several hundred Chinese workers to bundle and stack it all. They got the job done in a matter of hours. "They did the work well and faithfully, and of course we abandoned white labor," he said. Roberts also leased land to Chinese farmers, who grew sweet potatoes and other crops. He explained to the senators that many craved a "quiet life," away from the "excitement of the city."

Peaceful living for the Chinese would prove difficult to attain. In April 1868, anti-Chinese vigilantes claiming affiliation with the Ku Klux Klan, the white supremacist organization better known for its terrorizing of Black Americans in the South, staged a series of raids on ranches employing Chinese workers in Grass Valley. A year later, arsonists linked to the Klan burned down a church in San Jose that had hosted a Chinese Sunday school. They left the church's pastor a letter warning him to stop ministering to the Chinese. In Nevada City, a school for the

Chinese held classes only during the day and on Sundays to avoid the attention of the hate group.

On January 1, 1876, an item appeared in a Santa Cruz newspaper: "The working men of Gilroy have organized a society styled 'The Order of the Caucasians,' with the object of which is to aid all white men and women in securing work at living prices, when such work is needed and the persons are competent, in preference to the employment of Chinese." The organization's ranks quickly swelled to about ten thousand people in California and Nevada, across more than sixty local "camps." Members adhered to a manual of instruction and constitution that aimed to "protect the white man and white civilization" against the Chinese barbarians, as one official put it, and "elevate the white toiler." Anyone who employed Chinese immigrants was considered a "public enemy" and members were sworn to "impede, harass, and destroy" them by every means possible "within the bounds of law." Inevitably, there would be those who would be willing to go further.

Truckee, a bustling town located high on the eastern slope of the Sierra Nevada, north of Lake Tahoe, owed its existence to Chinese labor. In 1863, Joseph Gray, an adventurous, young English immigrant, built a log cabin along a wagon road that served as a stage stop and general store for weary travelers traversing the Sierras. A crude settlement soon sprang up nearby, comprising a handful of saloons and stores, a boardinghouse, and a sawmill. In the summer of 1868, the ramshackle buildings mostly burned down to the ground. It was the conquering of the Donner Summit by Chinese railroad workers that led to the town's rebuilding and rapid expansion. Central Pacific officials rechristened it "Truckee," after the river that ran through it. The town, surrounded by magnificent forests and located just above the crystalline waters of Lake Tahoe, became the first major refueling stop for trains heading east, after they crossed over the Sierra Nevada from Sacramento, and a vital gateway connecting east and west. Within a few months of the devastating fire, more than 250 buildings had been erected, including a theater, a railroad roundhouse, and five new stores. Despite the commerce flowing through it from the railroad, Truckee remained a rugged pioneer town, notorious for its saloons and brothels. Gunfights took place practically nightly. The renowned adventurer and writer Isabella Bird, who stopped in the town overnight in 1873, described clapboard buildings crowded with men drinking and smoking, surrounded by the austere majesty of the Sierra Nevada. Mountains "seemed to wall in the town, and great pines stood out, sharp and clear cut, against a sky in which a moon and stars were shining frostily," she later wrote.

By the middle of the 1870s, several hundred Chinese immigrants had settled in Truckee. They lived in wooden shanties on Front Street, the town's main thoroughfare, as well as on nearby Main Street, alongside white residents. Most of the Chinese residents had arrived after the completion of the Pacific railroad. Soon, they made up about a quarter of the town's population. The census of 1870 records who they were: mostly railroad laborers, woodchoppers, and washmen, as well as grocers and gardeners; there were also three physicians, a butcher, and a woman named Ah Key On, who said her occupation was "keeping house" and appeared to be the wife of a laborer, Ah Look; another woman, Ah Fou, is listed in the same household with a three-month-old son, Colfax. Early in the morning of May 29, 1875, a fire destroyed at least ten Chinese-owned businesses on Front Street. A few white-owned businesses were damaged as well. Afterward, white merchants in Truckee set out to isolate the Chinese population, building roads to separate the quarter from the rest of the town and barring Chinese residents from leasing lots outside the designated zone.

The Order of Caucasians chapter in Truckee, also known as the "Caucasian League," claimed more than three hundred members and included some of the community's most prominent citizens. In the spring of 1876, the organization embarked on a campaign to force local business owners to stop using Chinese workers. Among the targets was Joseph Gray, the early Truckee settler, who owned a lumber mill that supplied timber to the railroad and employed Chinese to cut cordwood in the heavily forested mountains. Gray, who had become a popular community leader known around town as "Uncle Joe," refused to accede to the demand to fire his workers. On the evening of June 17, a meeting of the order took place at Hurd's Hall, a large community gathering place with a stage, upstairs from a popular restaurant and saloon. Leaders of the order called for volunteers to pressure recalcitrant employers. After the meeting adjourned, a small group of men decided to raid an encampment of woodcutters who worked for Gray, at Trout Creek, about three miles outside of the city. They assembled at a nearby cabin and followed an old trail along the banks of the creek to a cabin occupied by four Chinese men. James Reed, a carpenter and a popular leader in the order, carried a double-barreled shotgun; the others armed themselves with rifles and a pistol. While the rest of the group squatted in the brush about fifty yards away, one man doused the cabin with kerosene and set fire to it with a torch. When a Chinese man came out to try to put out the flames, the white men opened fire but missed.

The men crept up to another cabin, about a half mile away, and set it aflame as well. The four Chinese men inside had gone to sleep an hour or two after dark. A forty-five-year-old man named Ah Ling was the first to awaken; he alerted the others. At first, the men tried to put out the fire with cans of water. When that failed, Ah Ling rushed out to the creek a few feet away, where he was shot. Wounded in the abdomen and right arm, Ah Ling stumbled back inside. When the heat and smoke became too much, the men fled the cabin, carrying Ah Ling with them over a bridge and across the creek. They covered him with blankets and hid in the brush. At daylight, they dragged him to town and consulted a Chinese doctor, who applied a poultice of leaves to his wounds. After Gray was alerted about the attack, he sent for the town's physician, William Curless, a member of the Order of Caucasians. Curless dressed Ah Ling's wounds, but he died at about four o'clock in the afternoon.

The authorities struggled at first to gain the cooperation of Chinese witnesses. The *Truckee Republican* insisted that town citizens were outraged "as though the victims had been Americans" and speculated that the crime was committed by "idle dissolute vagabonds who frequent our town." A group of white Truckee citizens offered a reward of $1,275 for information leading to the conviction of the killers; Governor William Irwin promised $300 for the first conviction and $200 for each succeeding one; Chinese merchants of Truckee put up $1,000 as well. Detectives from Nevada City arrived to help. The Central Pacific Railroad, too, dispatched their best investigator.

After several weeks of chasing leads, the lawmen caught two men, who quickly confessed. A grand jury indicted seven defendants for arson and murder. They were far from vagabonds. Several were well-known in the community. E. H. Gaylord, the district attorney for Nevada County, decided to begin by trying one of the defendants, William O'Neal, a timid-looking, twenty-eight-year-old Irishman, with smooth skin and blue eyes. O'Neal was a newcomer to town, having arrived from Pennsylvania in May. He joined the Caucasian League shortly afterward and worked as a track repairer for the Central Pacific. Gaylord called several members of the league to testify, including two men who had taken part in the raid. One of them, G. W. Getchell, told jurors their goal had been to frighten the Chinese. He described pouring coal oil on the cabin and watching it burst immediately into flames. "The Chinamen came out to put it out, and we all fired on them," he said.

O'Neal's defense attorneys included Charles McGlashan, a member of the Order of Caucasians who would go on to become the editor of the *Truckee Republican* newspaper. The defense called fifty witnesses, including various league officials, who insisted that "nothing of any importance transpired that evening." The jury required just nine minutes to acquit O'Neal. News accounts reported that "public opinion sanctions the verdict" and that a guilty verdict was likely impossible in the area, given the pervasiveness of anti-Chinese sentiment. Gaylord decided not to pursue the cases against the others.

On October 30, 1878, Truckee's Chinese quarter burned down again. As three fire engines and a bucket brigade rushed to extinguish the flames, an angry white resident yelled, "The Chinese must go!" Another man threw stones at fleeing Chinese residents. This time, the town's safety committee blocked them from rebuilding and ordered that they leave Truckee and relocate across the river. A ragged line of Chinese immigrants made their way over a bridge, carrying whatever furniture and household goods they could salvage.

Chinese immigrants first arrived in Butte County during the gold rush, when makeshift towns were sprouting up and down the Feather River, a northern tributary of the Sacramento River. Hundreds of Chinese miners began congregating in Oroville, a stagecoach hub on the eastern bank of the Feather River, about twenty-seven miles from Marysville. "I thought that the entire population must be Chinese," one traveler through the town observed. During the early 1860s, the Chinese population continued to increase in the mining districts, even as the returns from placer mining faded. Some began to drift into Chico, a growing agricultural community clustered around a sprawling ranch belonging to John Bidwell, the town's founder. It was at Bidwell's direction, in 1860, that surveyors began laying out a street grid for Chico across from his ranch, on the other side of Big Chico Creek. By 1870, Bidwell's vision had materialized into a thriving hamlet of nearly four thousand inhabitants, the county's largest town. The Chinese population numbered just over five hundred, mostly concentrated on a single block, on Flume Street in the eastern part of town, known as Old Chinatown; a newer, smaller Chinese section, across Chico, by the railroad tracks, also began to emerge. The dwellings were two-story wooden structures, with canopies on the ground level, opening onto stores and restaurants, and residences located above. All of the laundries in town were run by Chinese men, who scrubbed customers' clothes in the creek.

Resentment towards the Chinese accumulated, as their population grew. In the late 1860s, a new proprietor of the *Butte County Press,* a weekly newspaper in Chico, renamed it the *California Caucasian,* hoping to capitalize on burgeoning anti-Chinese sentiment. Organizers established anti-coolie societies in Oroville and other communities. On June 15, 1876, a new chapter of the Order of Caucasians convened inside Chico's Town Hall, drawing about a hundred people. The attendees chose George H. Crosette, a hotelkeeper and the editor of the *Butte Record,* as their chair. According to a subsequent account published in the *Record,* the group's purpose was to "restrain the traffic in Chinese labor" and to restore to "our own citizens the places, rights and privileges usurped by Chinamen." At the group's next meeting, William Armstrong, a lawyer and the county recorder, delivered a rousing forty-five-minute speech, interrupted frequently by applause, about the evils inflicted upon the laboring classes from "the competition of Chinamen." The group continued to meet throughout the summer, drawing up a constitution and bylaws, electing a council, and hearing from speakers, including Patrick Dorney, the statewide leader of the Order of Caucasians. The Chico "camp" grew to two hundred members.

When the operators of a newly built lumber factory located just east of town decided, in December, to hire a crew of Chinese workers, anger in the town spilled over. Several hundred white men, including prominent merchants and other leading Chico citizens, crammed into the town hall on a Saturday evening to discuss what could be done. Two days later, a follow-up meeting drew an even bigger crowd. Organizers circulated a petition criticizing the factory overseers for introducing into Chico "an obnoxious class of people, who claim no affinity with us as American citizens—who never can be taught to read and speak our language, or deal with us in trade, and whose habits are such as to introduce disease and pestilence wherever they are located." The petition appealed to the factory officials to fire their Chinese workers and asserted that "there was a large element of steady laborers, men and boys, who are now, in the dead of Winter, unemployed, and would only be too glad to accept positions at almost any price."

Afterward, several dozen men met, in the rain, in a wooded area near Chico. They believed more drastic steps were needed and decided to form their own hardline anti-Chinese group. They initially called themselves "the Laborer's Union"; then simply "Labor Union." Members swore an oath of secrecy and carried out orders issued by the union's leaders, known as the Council of Nine. The council discussed burning Chinese dwellings and killing Ben True, a constable who had become friendly with the Chinese residents, as well as Bidwell, a major employer of Chinese workers at his ranch. News of the impending violence made its way to members of the Chinese community, and they began arming themselves, buying up revolvers and shotguns and commencing a noisy target practice in late December near the Chinese quarter.

A terrifying campaign against the Chinese soon followed. At a quarter to eight in the evening on February 7, 1877, arsonists used kerosene and bags of hay to set fire to a former soap factory belonging to Bidwell that he had rented to a Chinese man as a slaughterhouse. Less than a month later, at a ranch just outside of Chico, a group of Chinese laborers had just gone to sleep when one man heard a noise, opened the door, and saw a nearby barn on fire. He headed outside with a bucket, only to encounter a white gunman who fired a shot at him. The frightened laborer dove into a ditch; when his companions dashed outside as well, there were more gunshots. One man ran to a house a half mile away to summon help from the ranch owner. When they returned, they discovered the dwelling house on fire too. The house and the barn, which contained six horses, burned to the ground.

About a month later, on March 9, a group of white men set fire to a Chinese lodging house in Chico's old Chinatown. One of the inhabitants awoke at three o'clock in the morning and managed to extinguish the flames. An hour later, a similar attempt was made to set fire to a building in the new Chinatown. The next day, in the nearby town of Nord, a group of men poured kerosene upon a camp where a group of Chinese railroad laborers were living and fired upon them as they fled; the following day, unidentified gunmen shot up the home again. The small Chinese population living in Nord fled.

All of this was just a prelude. At around nine o'clock in the evening on March 15, 1877, six Chinese men were resting in a cabin near Big Chico Creek, about two miles from town, on the property of a rancher, Chris Lemm. A candle sat on the table, illuminating the small room. Six white men clambered over a fence and descended upon the camp, with revolvers in hand. After searching the men and the cabin but finding nothing of value, the assailants opened fire on the inhabitants. Four of the men—Ah Lee, Ah Gow, Shu In, and Ah Quen—were shot in the head; a fifth man, Ah Shung, was shot in the chest. A sixth man, Wo Ah Lin, suffered a flesh wound in his arm but pretended to be dead. The killers tried to cover their tracks by setting fire to a pile of clothes in the middle of the cabin, but Wo Ah Lin managed to put out the blaze with a blanket. Afterward, he helped Ah Shung hide in some shrubs outside and then ran to the Lemm home. Hearing a commotion on the front porch, Lemm opened the door. Wo Ah Lin rushed inside and fell to the floor. "White man come," he said. "Poo', poo' Chinaman, all sleep, sleep." Lemm's wife, Louisa, took a clean sheet and bandaged Wo Ah Lin's arm. He continued on to Chico, about two miles to the west, to raise the alarm. He reached town at about midnight and sought out True, the friendly constable. The following morning, the city marshal and a line of wagons and people on horseback arrived at the ranch. "The first Chinaman we saw was lying partly across the door, dead, with his brains oozing out," one witness later wrote. "We had to step over him to get in. The next two lay on their bunks dead; the fourth had been shot in his head and his brains were oozing out and he lay moaning. He died while the inquest was being held. The fifth Chinaman we found across the slough under a buckeye bush. He was shot in the breast, the bullet ranging downward and lodging in his back." This was Ah Shung. He had used a jackknife to try to cut the bullet out, making several gashes in his skin. A physician later removed the bullet, and he was nursed back to health by a Chinese doctor in Chico.

Notices appeared in the mailboxes of prominent Chico residents, including Bidwell, warning them to get rid of their Chinese labor. Bidwell, who had hired Chinese workers to clear land on his property, made a point of retaining them. Doing otherwise "would have been interpreted as fear on my part," he later said.

The Six Companies offered a reward for information leading to the capture of the killers, as did a citizens committee in Chico. The latter group hired a former county sheriff to investigate the crime. He joined two detectives who had been retained by the Six Companies, along with True, who was conducting his own inquiry. The break in the case came when detectives, at Bidwell's suggestion, began monitoring the post office. They followed a man who had mailed letters that had handwriting matching that of the threatening missives. The suspect, a Labor Union member named Fred Conway, was promptly arrested. He initially insisted he had tagged along with others, not knowing what was planned. Two days later, however, he confessed to the shooting, as well as the other arsons. His admissions led to the arrests of four co-conspirators in the murders and several dozen others believed to have participated in the other attacks. Labor Union members soon filled Chico's small jail. The authorities placed the facility under tight guard. According to news accounts, many of the defendants had been previously "considered good citizens." One suspect had recently been elected a member of Chico's three-man police department. Bidwell personally obtained the bylaws of the organization and had them published in newspapers throughout the state "to show what men could do," he later said.

A jury found five men guilty of the murders; four of them were sentenced to 25 years in prison; a fifth man received a sentence of 27½ years. Five others were found guilty of arson and sentenced to 5 to 25 years in prison. In 1883, Governor George Stoneman acceded to pressure from hundreds of Chico residents and commuted the sentences of three out of four of the convicted murderers to 10 years, and they were released on time served.

Years later, Bidwell reflected on the turbulence in the town he founded. "I have never yielded to any of those bad influences," he said. "I stood my ground." Nevertheless, even he said that he didn't want to be "over-run by Chinese."

CHAPTER 9

The Chinese Must Go!

The trouble began with a rumor. On the morning of September 18, 1873, word spread on Wall Street that Jay Cooke & Co., a venerable investment firm with houses in New York and Philadelphia that had invested heavily in the expansion of the railroad, was suspending payments on its obligations. When the news was confirmed from the rostrum of the stock exchange, stunned brokers and speculators were momentarily silent, then erupted into bedlam as they rushed to sell their securities. A cascading series of crises across the country followed, overwhelming other sectors of the economy. Over the next few years, tens of thousands of businesses across the country defaulted. Half of the railroad companies in America entered receivership. Employers laid off thousands of workers and slashed wages. In the summer of 1877, the fury of working-men and the jobless combusted into violence in cities across the country.

On the night of July 16, 1877, in Martinsburg, West Virginia, a placid town of eight thousand people, workers for the Baltimore & Ohio Railroad, upset about a 10 percent cut in their wages, seized control of a railway roundhouse. Within days, worker uprisings were taking place in several mid-Atlantic cities. In Pittsburgh, on the morning of July 19, a group of railroad employees took over a series of railroad switches near the 28th Street crossing. The crowd of agitated workers and supporters began to swell. For two days, they halted railroad service. On Saturday afternoon, July 21, 1877, a detachment of a thousand federal troops dispatched from Philadelphia, accompanied by a battery of Gatling guns, arrived. Several pistol shots rang out from the crowd, and the soldiers opened fire. Over two days of rioting, forty people were killed.

In California, financial distress was like a woolen blanket over the population, heavy and suffocating. In the spring of 1877, more than four thousand people applied for relief at the office of the San Francisco Benevolent Association, the most in the organization's more than decade-long history. Central Pacific officials had been poised to impose a wage reduction but pulled back as the labor conflagrations spread on the other side of the country. On Monday, July 23, advertisements appeared in the morning newspapers in San Francisco, and handbills went out across the city, calling for a meeting in support of the eastern strikers. It was to be held that evening on the sandlot, a triangular plot of land with ankle-deep sand, encompassing several acres off Market Street, in front of the new City Hall building that was still under construction. One of the chief organizers of the meeting was James F. D'Arcy, a prominent agitator against the Chinese. As the day progressed, rumors spread about plans to set fire to the Pacific Mail Steamship Company's docks and the Chinese quarter. The city's police chief, Henry Ellis, deployed most of his 150-man force around Chinatown. He also requested that three infantry regiments of the California National Guard stand by. By seven o'clock, an unruly crowd of as many as eight thousand men filled the sandlot and the surrounding streets.

A brass band commenced the meeting with a tinny national anthem from a wooden platform in the center of the sandlot. When D'Arcy ascended the rostrum, he insisted the rally was not meant to be an anti-coolie meeting but a way to support their brethren on the East Coast. To this, people in the crowd jeered: "Tell us how to drive out the Chinamen!" "Talk about the Chinamen!" On the outskirts of the rally, a man knocked down a passing Chinese man. When an officer moved to arrest the assailant, a group fell upon him and freed the prisoner. "On to Chinatown, boys," the group cried. A mob of two hundred men rushed up Leavenworth. On Tyler Street, the group attacked a Chinese laundry, smashing windows and doors with stones and brickbats as the occupants fled out the back. Further down the block, they vandalized another laundry. Just after nine o'clock, a crowd of about a hundred men surged towards a two-story, wood-frame building on the corner of Geary and

Leavenworth Streets. In the basement was a Chinese washhouse, Yee Wah; upstairs was a fruit store and a lodging house. The mob descended upon several Chinese men inside. An overturned oil lamp set the building ablaze. The fire department quickly responded, but members of the mob cut their hoses. As the firemen struggled to bring the flames under control, the mob continued down Geary Street, whooping and sacking other washhouses as they went. By then, the crowd had swelled to as many as six hundred. When they reached Dupont Street, on the edge of the Chinese quarters, a phalanx of police with clubs met them, driving the rioters back. The mob diverted to Washington Street, where they smashed the windows of the Chinese Mission House for the Methodist Church. By night's end, more than a dozen Chinese laundries had been destroyed.

The following day, at about two o'clock in the afternoon, the body of a Chinese man was found on Clay Street, in front of the Hop Wo association's building in the Chinese quarter. His name was Yee Hen War, and he had been the proprietor of a laundry on Geary Street that had been burned to the ground. The death was ruled a suicide. A few blocks away, two hundred prominent citizens gathered at the Chamber of Commerce, at the invitation of John McComb, a brigadier general with the California National Guard, to discuss how to preserve order. The group included Charles Crocker, the railroad magnate, and Martin J. Burke, a former San Francisco police chief. They agreed to the creation of a special committee, headed by William T. Coleman, a merchant who had led the "Vigilance Committee" of 1856, a vigilante organization of more than six thousand men who patrolled the streets of San Francisco for several months. Collectively, the group pledged $75,000 to the protection of the city. Telegrams to the War Department in Washington resulted in the Benicia Arsenal, an army ordnance facility, dispatching more than seventeen hundred rifles, five hundred carbines, and ten thousand rounds of ammunition to Coleman.

At around eight o'clock, an unruly crowd began to gather at Fifth and Mission Streets, near the building for the United States Mint, growing to about a thousand people. They started up Mission Street, intending to burn down Mission Woolen Mills, a factory that employed Chinese. The mob attacked several Chinese laundries, before a large force of police caused the rioters to scatter. At about ten thirty, two Chinese men encountered a group of rioters outside a laundry on Greenwich and Devisadero Streets. The Chinese men had been visiting friends at the laundry. The two men rushed back inside, where a half-dozen other Chinese men were gathered. They locked the front door and tried to escape out the back but were turned back by two men with oil cans in hand, preparing to set fire to the building. This time, the Chinese inhabitants fled out the front entrance, ducking bullets fired at them from the crowd. The men crouched under bushes, as the mob entered the building. Inside, the rioters struggled to break into a large chest belonging to the proprietor, Si Sow, who had purchased the laundry six months earlier. The chest contained about $150 in gold and silver coins, earnings from his business. After hiding for about a half hour, the Chinese men outside fled, while the rioters set fire to the building. One of the men, however, Wong Go, turned back to get his clothes. When members of the fire department arrived, they discovered his charred remains. He had died of smoke inhalation. He was twenty-five years old. Several miles away, near the entrance to the Presidio military reservation, firefighters searching the embers of another Chinese laundry that had been burned to the ground found the bodies of two other Chinese men.

Throughout the following day, volunteers arrived at the offices of the Chamber of Commerce, the makeshift headquarters of the Special Committee of Safety. Coleman's plan was to muster a special police force made up of "citizens of all sects and all parties," committed to restoring law and order. In a proclamation, Coleman referred to the Chinese as a "disturbing element" and insisted that committee members were eager for their removal, but he said violence would not hasten a solution. In the evening, about three thousand men filed into Horticultural Hall, a cavernous venue on Stockton Street. They received hickory pickax handles, shortened into police clubs. When Coleman took the stage, he reported that there was an immediate need for a hundred men to report to City Hall. "He can have a thousand" was the roar that came back to him. A member of the committee counted off a contingent in the back, and the volunteers hurried off; shortly afterward, a police officer requested that men be posted to the Pacific Mail Steamship docks. Other members of the Pick-Handle Brigade, as the men came to be called, fanned out for duty across the city.

While the safety committee was getting organized, a crowd of several hundred people gathered in front of the new City Hall. A speaker named N. P. Brock mounted a primitive platform, his face lit by a bonfire. He appeared to be drunk. Brock called for the "extermination of Chinamen." Soon, about two hundred teenage boys and older men were rampaging through the surrounding streets. They headed down Howard Street towards the waterfront, smashing the doors and windows of Chinese laundries as they went. They arrived at No. 1051, a washhouse belonging to a Chinese man named Hong Soon. Two people wielded a piece of timber like a battering ram, destroying the door and window shutters. At another laundry, near the corner of Mary Street, a lone officer, armed with a club, managed to push the crowd back. A drunken rioter at the front exhorted the mob to leave no laundry in the city standing. At Ning Guin's laundry, at 565 Howard Street, a man climbed onto the roof and kicked down the business's large sign. The mob was about to set fire to the washhouse when a woman next door persuaded them to stop. By this point, every washhouse on Howard Street, from Seventh Street to First Street, had been destroyed. The group turned down another street and encountered Wing Sing's laundry, at 247 Minna Street. The rioters tore down the front wall and stormed into the building, tossing laundry everywhere. At another laundry down the block, a gunshot rang out from within, fired by a Chinese man inside. The crowd backed away but charged again, only to be driven back by another pistol shot. At this point, police officers appeared and arrested several of the ringleaders. The rest of the mob melted away.

While these clashes were occurring, a huge blaze burned on the waterfront. At first, the authorities believed the Pacific Mail Steamship Company had been targeted, but it turned out an arsonist had set fire to an adjacent set of docks on Beale Street. The flames climbed a hundred feet high and grew so intense that boats in the harbor had to be towed away. On a bluff above, police confronted about two thousand rioters. About four hundred men arrived from the Horticultural Hall and formed a cordon around the wharf. A contingent from the safety committee charged up the hill, dodging stones raining down on them, while police officers fought the insurrectionists from above. At ten thirty in the evening, the two groups were finally able to drive the rioters over the crest. Firemen used fire hoses to disperse stragglers.

By two o'clock in the morning, the city was mostly quiet, with a large force of safety committee members, armed with rifles, guarding the scene of the fire near the Pacific Mail docks, and others patrolling the rest of the city. "Even the terrified Chinaman, hid away in unsuspected places, heaved a great sigh of relief as he listened to the measured footfalls," one account said.

Overnight, a steamship delivered ten thousand more rifles, carbines, and pistols from the state arsenal. The city turned into an armed encampment: two naval steamships, the *Pensacola* and the *Lackawanna,* patrolled the waterfront, ready to land marines with Gatling guns; two hundred additional marines guarded the Pacific Mail wharf; companies of National Guard stood at the ready throughout the city.

By Friday evening, July 28, five days after the riots began, more than two thousand safety committee men were patrolling the city. The streets were mostly deserted. The Pacific Mail steamship *City of Tokio* arrived overnight, anchoring off the company's wharf. In the late afternoon, a platoon of several dozen policemen established a protective cordon on the wharf. A hundred and thirty-eight Chinese passengers disembarked and clambered aboard a train of express wagons that bore them to Chinatown. Their lives in America were beginning.

Order was restored in the city, but, like the roots of an ugly weed, hatred of the Chinese awaited a new occasion to surface. On July 30, Coleman ordered that the volunteer forces of the safety committee be relieved from duty. Among the discharged was a thirty-year-old Irish drayman named Denis Kearney, who had been among the committee men who charged up Rincon Hill to disperse the rioters during the Beale Street blaze. Kearney was born in Ireland, in the county of Cork, during the height of the potato famine. When Kearney was a child, his father died;

at the age of eleven, Kearney went to sea as a cabin boy to support his mother and six siblings. He was barely able to read when he landed in America in 1868, as a first officer aboard the clipper ship *Shooting Star*. For several years, he worked for a steamship company that operated along the Pacific coast, from Mexico to Vancouver. In 1870, he married Mary Ann Leary and, two years later, purchased a part of a draying business that hauled goods for city merchants. The couple had four children and, in 1876, Kearney became an American citizen. On Sunday afternoons, Kearney attended the Lyceum of Self-Culture at Dashaway Hall, a kind of private debating society whose purpose was to encourage the use of reason. Kearney, diminutive and stout, with a mustache that drooped over his lip, was known at the Lyceum as a loudmouthed attention-seeker. He frequently derided the laziness of workingmen and delivered diatribes from the perspective of a business owner. He also began hanging around the offices of the *Chronicle*, becoming friendly with a reporter there named Chester Hull, who was obsessed with the encroachment of the Chinese on the white race. In the spring of 1877, Kearney was named to a committee representing the city's draymen, who were upset with the way the city was awarding hauling contracts. It marked Kearney's emergence as a public figure. He applied to join the Workingmen's Party of the United States, the Marxist-influenced political organization that would help shape the modern labor movement, but its leaders rejected him, because of his past criticism of workers. In August 1877, he tried to establish his own party, the Workingmen's Trade and Labor Union of San Francisco. The effort foundered, but Kearney soon found another way to build a following.

His debut on the sandlot in front of City Hall was relatively ordinary. On September 16, 1877, an unseasonably warm day in San Francisco, Kearney addressed an audience of several hundred people. It had been less than two months since the riots. Kearney lamented that the workers needed to meet "for self-defense." He called for all the Chinese in the city to be dismissed and for employers to give "the white men a chance." Less than a week later, on a Friday evening, Kearney delivered an incendiary speech before a large crowd gathered at the Union Hall. "We must settle this Chinese question within the next two years, or the system will have settled us," he said. "I say, the people have a right to settle it; and if it becomes necessary every freeman in California has a right to keep a musket in his house, and ammunition to use it." Kearney predicted that within a year they could have twenty thousand men signed up, with twenty thousand muskets. He condemned the business owners who employed the Chinese. "Don't these capitalists know that the Anglo-Saxon spirit is not dead, that the doctrine of the survival of the fittest is hourly growing more salient, and that we are superior to these Mongolians, and will survive them?" Kearney later told a biographer that he had concluded that the survival of "California civilization" depended on stopping Chinese immigration. "I saw in the people the power to enforce that 'must,'" he said.

On October 5, 1877, during a meeting attended by about 150 men at Dashaway Hall, Kearney and other organizers established the Workingmen's Party of California; they elected Kearney as their first president. The party's platform included tenets targeting the "great money power of the rich," but its overriding attention was on the Chinese. "We propose to rid the country of cheap Chinese labor as soon as possible, and by all the means in our power," the party's declaration of principles said. They also pledged to "mark as public enemies" anyone who continued to employ them. Kearney's primary aim was to goad Congress into action during its next session. He began holding rallies every Sunday at the sandlot. He adopted a slogan first invoked by another organizer: "And whatever happens, the Chinese must go!" His audiences steadily grew. On October 28, Kearney stood atop a large wagon and urged a crowd of about four thousand workers to meet the following night on Nob Hill, the neighborhood of fine homes and gorgeous city views where the railroad magnates Leland Stanford, Charlie Crocker, and Mark Hopkins had erected mansions. About three thousand people trudged up the steep hill, braving the stiff wind. As they waited for the evening's speakers, the protesters lit bonfires, feeding them with barrels they found around Crocker's estate, which occupied nearly an entire city block. When it was Kearney's turn to speak, he vowed to organize workingmen to march through the city and compel the leaders of the Central Pacific to "give up their plunder." He gave the company three months to discharge their Chinese workers and urged the men to wait on the docks for the arriving steamships with their holds full of Chinese and throw them overboard.

Kearney's sandlot rallies threatened the city's fragile order. Crocker met with the chief of police to ask for protection. The heads of the Chinese Six Companies, too, became increasingly fearful. On November 3, they issued an appeal for protection to the mayor and warned that the Chinese would not stand idly by if they were attacked: "As a rule, our countrymen are better acquainted with peaceful vocations than with scenes of strife, yet we are not ignorant that self-defense is the common right of all men, and should a riotous attack be made upon the Chinese quarter, we should have neither the power nor disposition to restrain our countrymen from defending themselves to the last extremity and selling their lives as dearly as possible."

Later that evening, Kearney's workingmen held a meeting at the corner of Washington and Kearny Streets. The streets became so packed with people that the police needed to clear a corridor for wagons. Kearney was late. When he finally appeared on a building balcony, he said that he expected to be arrested before the morning. At that moment, a half-dozen policemen emerged into the lantern light. The officers hustled him down the stairs and took Kearney to the city jail, holding him on two misdemeanor charges for inciting violence. The authorities arrested several other leaders of the Workingmen's Party as well. A judge later dismissed the incitement charges against Kearney based on a technicality, but prosecutors added additional charges for the commissioning of a riot. After a brief trial, a judge acquitted Kearney and other party leaders. Vigorous celebrations erupted inside the courtroom and on the street. Kearney was unbowed by his confinement. At a ward meeting afterward, he vowed to drive the Chinese out, "peaceably, if we can, forcibly if we must."

Membership in the Workingmen's Party surged. Kearney visited several ward meetings a night. His attention also turned to a Thanksgiving Day parade, intended as a show of strength for the anti-Chinese movement. The city girded itself for the demonstration, putting the National

Guard on alert and deploying the entire police force. In the Chinese quarter, shopkeepers closed for the day and barricaded windows and doors. The procession began at ten o'clock in the morning, with Kearney riding in front on one of his own horses. More than seven thousand marchers thronged the streets, bearing banners that read "Don't cry, mother; the Chinamen will soon leave" and "Discharge your Chinamen; give us work and you will have no hoodlums." One sign depicted a group of workers on a wharf, waving farewell to the last departing Chinese, accompanied by the words "This Is Our Country."

Support for Kearney soon spread beyond San Francisco, a nimbus of outrage among workingmen, small business owners, middle-class property owners, and rural farmers. In San Jose, Oakland, Sacramento, and elsewhere in the interior of the state, Workingmen's Party organizers established new wards. In mid-December, Kearney and other party leaders ventured south to Los Angeles, addressing in front of the courthouse the largest meeting ever held in the city.

The threat posed by the discontented masses at Kearney's rallies became alarmingly real to San Francisco's leaders one morning, in early January 1878, when Kearney led a crowd of fifteen hundred people to City Hall to demand relief for the unemployed. Only a handful of police officers were on duty at the time; officials inside locked up their valuables and prepared to be overrun. Mayor Andrew Bryant came out to try to placate the crowd. He insisted that he, too, wanted to rid the state of Chinese and said that he was heartened that the number of new arrivals was declining. After the mayor returned to his office, Kearney succeeded in diverting the crowd back to the sandlot. A little more than a week later, on January 15, at a ward meeting at the Irish-American Hall, Kearney asked the crowd: "How many of you have got muskets?" (Many hands went up.) "How many of you have got about ten feet of rope in your pocket?" Kearney said, "Well, you must be ready and arm yourselves." He called for "forty thousand men to march down to the Pacific Mail dock" to blow up the next arriving steamship.

The next day, the authorities arrested Kearney and other Workingmen's Party leaders on a new grand jury indictment, for rioting and conspiring "by threats, intimidation, force, and violence, to compel, without authority of law, a large number of persons lawfully residing in the said

State of California, commonly known as the Chinese and natives of the Empire of China, to leave and depart from the State." As Kearney and his cohort awaited trial, the mayor outlawed public assemblies. National Guard commanders mustered several infantry regiments to quell disturbances. Once again, the U.S. warship *Lackawanna* took up a position off the Pacific Mail's wharf. Police squads broke up Workingmen's Party meetings throughout the city. After a short trial, Kearney and his cohort were acquitted. He was soon back on the sandlot.

For years, lawmakers in California had discussed the shortcomings of California's constitution, written in 1849, when the state was sparsely populated and undeveloped. There had been sporadic efforts to remedy the charter, but public indifference helped to maintain the status quo. Finally, in 1878, the populist grievances that Kearney's movement had stirred—outrage over excessive taxes and the power of corporations, among other issues—helped to force the legislature to authorize a second constitutional convention. Kearney threw himself into campaigning to elect Workingmen's Party of California delegates to the convention. The party's election ballots were printed with the slogan "The Chinese Must Go!" and featured a Chinese man on the run, being kicked in the rear by a boot, labeled W.P.C. On the evening of Saturday, June 15, 1878, four days before the election, an estimated six thousand Kearney supporters held a torchlight procession through the city. The ambitions of the workingmen, however, were hampered by internal squabbling. A coalition of Democrats and Republicans came together to form a "Non-Partisan" slate of candidates, designed to block the sandlot movement. On June 19, the election took place. Among the 152 seats at the convention, 77 Non-Partisans were elected, compared to 51 from the Workingmen's Party; the rest were a scattering of Democratic, Republican, and Independent delegates, who were more closely aligned with the Non-Partisans. The results were still impressive for the nascent party. The Workingmen carried the vote in San Francisco and fared well in certain mining counties but struggled in farming districts in the interior.

Rather than dwell on any disappointment from the election, Kearney announced to his followers that he was heading to the East Coast to attend to the needs of the workers there. He promised to go to Washington to denounce lawmakers who had adjourned without addressing the Chinese question. Thousands of workingmen saw him off at the Oakland ferry. On August 5, Kearney made his East Coast debut, addressing thousands who jammed into Boston's Faneuil Hall. With the gaslight, summer heat, and the crush of humanity, the temperature inside was sweltering. People in the galleries stripped off their clothing. Kearney paced back and forth on the stage, sweating profusely; he doffed his coat and loosened his tie. He spoke deliberately and forcefully, punctuating his points with a raised right hand. He blasted the "capitalistic thief and land pirate of California," who he said had spurned white men and "contracted with a band of leprous Chinese pirates." (Leprosy was an ancient, widely misunderstood disease that had spread around the world and engendered much fear in the nineteenth century.) A few days later, Kearney delivered a profane speech on Boston Common, in front of a boisterous crowd of more than four thousand people, who were not deterred by a rain shower. "Let me caution workingmen not to employ Chinese laundry men," he said. "They are filthy; they spit on clothes, and if they have any disease it is transmitted to men and women through such washed clothing when the body perspires." He again invoked the specter of leprosy. "Do you want leprosy here?" (There were cries of "No.") He promised: "By not employing them you can drive them from the country." Kearney's itinerary over the next few weeks was relentless. In Indianapolis, he addressed more than fifteen hundred people; in Newark, it was three thousand. At noon, on August 28, Kearney visited the White House, where he had a brief audience with President Rutherford B. Hayes. Their exchange was stilted, but Hayes praised Kearney for his work. "You are concentrating the minds of the people on these evils," the president said. The next day, from the Capitol steps, Kearney delivered an oration in front of about five thousand people. On September 6, in New York City, he addressed an audience of about fifteen thousand people from a wooden-plank platform that had been erected in the middle of Union Square.

The accounts of Kearney's speeches in the eastern press were scornful. "He was circus and clown combined," the *Boston Advertiser* reported. "The great agitator delights in epithets, and if his speech did not contain any real argument, it was stuffed full of abuse," *The New York Times* said. Kearney himself later boasted that his trip was "a brilliant success," arguing that he "succeeded in lifting the Chinese from a local to a great national question." On November 26, thousands were on hand to greet Kearney upon his arrival back in San Francisco. A carriage delivered him to the sandlot, where a tangle of bodies carried him to the speakers' stand. While fireworks exploded above him, Kearney told the crowd that he was exhausted from his journey and unable to speak for long, but he reiterated "the cry that in thunder tones has traveled all over this nation: 'The Chinese must go!'" This drew an ovation. He later predicted to a reporter: "The people are in earnest—the Chinese must go. Mark what I tell you. There will be a bloody revolution. And not only here but through the whole United States."

By the time Kearney arrived back on the Pacific coast, the deliberations of the second constitutional convention in Sacramento had already been underway for two months. The delegates had voted overwhelmingly to establish a committee focused on the Chinese question. The issue was the highest priority of the Workingmen delegates, but one of the Non-Partisan delegates, John Franklin Miller, a forty-seven-year-old former brigadier general in the Union army, was selected to head the fifteen-member panel. Miller was a native of Indiana who had come to California at the age of twenty-two during the gold rush. He became a state senator, but after three years in California, he had returned home to fight in the Civil War. He eventually retired from the service and made his way back to San Francisco, where he served as the revenue collector for the city's port. He earned his fortune as the president of a seal-hunting company. During the convention's morning session on December 9, Miller explained that the members of the committee were united in their belief that "Chinese immigration was an evil" and that the flow of Chinese into the country should be halted, but they disagreed about the limits of the state's power to do so. The committee set aside some of the most extreme proposals from Workingmen delegates, such as one that prohibited the granting of licenses to any Chinese operating a business and another that made it a criminal offense to send overseas the disinterred remains of aliens, targeting the Chinese practice of shipping their dead home for burial. But the committee advanced nine measures for debate by the full convention, including one that blocked further immigration of Chinese to the state and another that barred anyone ineligible for citizenship from settling in California.

The only provision that had the entire committee's backing was one that authorized the legislature to pass laws and regulations that protected the state from the burdens of aliens who became "vagrants, paupers, mendicants, criminals, or invalids afflicted with contagions or infectious diseases, and aliens otherwise dangerous or detrimental to the well-being or peace of the State." Miller explained that the theory behind this measure was that the state could regulate the Chinese presence under its police powers as necessary for "self-preservation." Miller delivered a lengthy rationale for opposing the Chinese presence. "It is an unassimilative population, and unfit for assimilation with people of our race," he said. "Were the Chinese to amalgamate at all with our people, it would be the lowest, most vile and degraded of our race, and the result of the amalgamation would be a hybrid of the most despicable, a mongrel of the most detestable that has ever afflicted the earth." Miller argued that the fact that the country's naturalization laws barred Chinese from citizenship made clear that they were unwelcome. "Immigration has been encouraged, but what kind of immigration?" he said. "The truth is that the invitation has been limited to white men, men of our own race and color, men of similar aspirations, hopes, desires, and aims in life." The speakers that followed Miller were equally vitriolic in their denunciations of the Chinese, many of them arguing that the state could go further and exclude the Chinese entirely.

It was during the evening session that a lone delegate arose to defend the Chinese, Charles V. Stuart, a member of the Non-Partisan ticket from Sonoma County, who had not taken the floor since the convention began. Stuart had been a merchant in Ithaca, New York, and journeyed to California during the gold rush with a mule train organized by him and fifty neighbors. He arrived in San Francisco in 1849 and eventually opened a tavern, the Mansion House, which became a fixture in the city. He also became a farmer, acquiring a thousand acres and planting a vineyard. In his speech, Stuart said that he had employed hundreds of men and had never previously been involved in politics. He described himself as unaccustomed to public speaking, but he declared himself opposed to all the anti-Chinese measures that had been introduced. "They are not proper to be placed in any Constitution of the United States, let alone ours," he said. Another delegate interrupted Stuart, pressing him on the makeup of his employees: "Have you not employed hundreds of Chinamen?" Stuart said, "I have, sir, thousands of them, and hundreds of white men and thousands of white men, too." He pressed on, pointing out that the subject of the Chinese had become a hobbyhorse for politicians in recent years, but he remembered that in 1850, when the state celebrated its admission into the union, the Chinese were given "a post of honor, and they followed the officers of the State and city in the parade." Stuart said that he believed the country's naturalization laws should be repealed and scoffed at the idea that the Chinese might overthrow the Anglo-Saxon race. There were forty million people in the United States, after all. "A hundred thousand a month scattered through the United States would not affect it in a hundred years," he said.

When it came time for the convention delegates to vote, they rejected several of the harshest anti-Chinese proposals because of fears about their constitutionality, but they easily passed a slew of others, including the one that Miller had said was needed for "self-preservation," authorizing the legislature to pass laws regulating aliens "dangerous or detrimental to the well-being or peace of the state"; and another that prohibited Chinese from being employed "on any State, county, municipal, or other public work." Separately, under the new constitution, only "foreigners of the white race, or of African descent," eligible for naturalization, were permitted to own and inherit land; and no Chinese, "idiot, insane person, or person convicted of any infamous crime," or person convicted of embezzling public money, could ever serve as an elector in the state.

Kearney had initially criticized the work of the convention but now threw himself into campaigning for the new constitution, delivering 130 speeches across the state. On May 7, 1879, voters in California narrowly approved the new constitution.

· · ·

In June 1879, Kearney was re-elected as president of the Workingmen's Party, but his hold on his followers had already reached its apex. The *Chronicle*, which had once championed Kearney, turned on him. The newspaper urged the establishment of a new party that could attract a broader base of support to carry out the redrawn constitution. During the mayoral election, the newspaper assailed the Workingmen's Party candidate, the Rev. Isaac Kalloch, who pastored the Metropolitan Temple, the city's largest congregation. Kalloch, a former New England abolitionist who once hosted at his church the largest Chinese Sunday school in the city, had initially been a foe of the sandlot movement, castigating them as "incendiaries" and "blatherskites." But he later reversed himself, as the Workingmen's Party movement grew, and began invoking the slogan "The Chinese must go" from the pulpit. He closed his church's Chinese Sunday school and began delivering Tuesday night lectures at his church inveighing against the Chinese. Congregants sang "The Heathen Chinee" and "Don't Put the Workingmen Down" from the pews. Kalloch responded to the *Chronicle*'s attacks with innuendo about the family of Charles de Young, one of the newspaper's owners. The animus culminated in a shocking episode, in which de Young shot and nearly killed Kalloch. He recovered and capitalized on the wave of sympathy for him to win the mayoralty. As a near martyr for the cause, Kalloch's popularity soon eclipsed Kearney's in the party. Several months later, however, on the evening of April 23, 1880, his son, Milton, entered the *Chronicle* offices with a revolver and killed de Young.

When the shooting took place, Kearney was in the middle of serving a six-month jail sentence for libel. A mass meeting to protest Kearney's imprisonment turned celebratory upon news of de Young's death. The horror of the shooting, however, turned public opinion against Kearney, and his party's political fortunes deteriorated. Some in the Workingmen's ranks returned to the Democratic Party; Kearney himself began to sidle closer to the national Greenback-Labor Party, which attracted disenchanted agrarian voters with its anti-monopolist message. By the middle of 1880, the Workingmen's Party had disintegrated. During a sandlot meeting on July 5, Kearney found himself shouted down and had to be rescued from the mob. He soon retreated from the public stage, returning to his hauling business. Kearney made brief returns to politics in the coming years—he later issued warnings about the threat of Japanese immigration—but mostly focused on business ventures.

Even as Kearney's relevance faded, the sandlot movement he created spread. In the early months of 1880, after the new constitution went into effect, mobs of unemployed laborers marched daily on woolen factories, laundries, and other businesses in San Francisco, demanding that they discharge their Chinese workers. The legislature enacted a new law, later ruled unconstitutional, that prohibited any corporation chartered by the state from employing Chinese. Many employers dismissed their Chinese workers. The city board of health condemned the Chinese quarter as a "public nuisance" and declared that the "Chinese cancer must be cut out of the heart of our city, root and branch."

Yet, for all their vigorous efforts, Kearney and his imitators failed to expel the Chinese from America. The size of the Chinese population remained largely unchanged; the number of arrivals in America edged upward again after Kearney's rallies receded. Across the vast ocean, the Gold Mountain still glittered. One of the newcomers was a sixteen-year-old boy named Lee Chew, who grew up in a village on the banks of the Si-Kiang River in Guangdong province. At the age of ten, he had started working on his father's ten-acre farm, harvesting sweet potatoes, rice, beans, and other crops. It was exhausting work, digging and hoeing, without a horse. He lived with other boys from the village, sharing a house with about thirty or forty people. He ate his meals at his parents' house, a one-story structure with four rooms, occupied by the couple, their eldest son and his wife and two young children, and Lee's grandfather. A man from the village who had returned from America inspired Lee to emigrate. The man constructed a palatial estate, with bridges, streams, and walkways, surrounded by a stone wall. When it was completed, he held a lavish banquet in which he served one hundred roasted pigs, chickens, ducks, and geese. "The man had gone away from our village a poor boy," Lee later wrote. "Now he returned with unlimited wealth, which he had obtained in the country of the American wizards." Lee said he became fixated on the idea that he, too, could become a wealthy man in America. His father gave him a hundred dollars, and Lee traveled to Hong Kong with five other boys from his village and bought passage on a steamer to America, arriving in San Francisco during the tumult of 1880. "It was the jealousy of laboring men of other nationalities—especially the Irish—that raised all the outcry against the Chinese," Lee later wrote. "No one would hire an Irishman, German, Englishman or Italian when he could get a Chinese, because our countrymen are so much more honest, industrious, steady, sober and painstaking. Chinese were persecuted, not for their vices, but for their virtues." Lee worked for two years as a servant for a family of four, learning how to cook, clean, make beds, and polish the silverware. He attended Sunday school, where he learned English. Lee diligently saved most of his earnings—the family paid him $3.50 a week—accumulating $50 in his first six months in America and $90 in the second. By the end of two years, he had more than $400, enough to start his own business. He opened a laundry with a partner, working from seven o'clock in the morning to midnight every day. He eventually made his way to Chicago and then New York, where he opened a shop in the Chinese quarter. He concluded that "Americans are not all bad, nor are they wicked wizards."

CHAPTER 10

The Mission

At noon on a fall day in 1850, the freshmen and sophomore classes at Yale College, in New Haven, Connecticut, gathered on a field in front of the State House, opposite the school, for the annual football game. About two hundred young men lined up, preparing for a gladiatorial contest. In those days, the sport had few rules. Games began with a kickoff, and the man receiving it could kick the ball or run with it. The object was to advance the ball to the opposite end of the field and toss it over the line. The freshmen, smaller in stature and still growing into their bodies, were at a disadvantage in a contest of brute force, but on this afternoon, when the ball was kicked to them, they placed it in the hands of one of their strongest members, closed ranks, and began advancing down the field. There was a collision of bodies, and the game collapsed into a heaving mass of limbs and torsos. "The whole field was a melee," one participant later recalled. Slowly, inexorably, the sophomores forced the freshmen backwards, until they were a few yards from their end line. Unnoticed, the ball fell to the ground. Standing off to the side was an exceedingly reserved but affable twenty-year-old student named Yung Wing, the first Chinese student in Yale's history. He wore a straw hat, beneath which was coiled a long braid, secured by a silk tassel and pinned in place. He had only been an observer in the game up to that point, but when the ball rolled to his feet, he snatched it up and—before anyone saw what was happening—dashed downfield. Suddenly, the mass of humanity separated and wheeled. Yung "bounded like a deer," one freshman recalled. "His queue burst from the pins and streamed out behind him like a pump-handle." A speedy sophomore grabbed desperately at Yung, jerking him backwards by his queue, but he had sent the ball over the fence onto Chapel Street. The class of 1854 had an unlikely hero, and the nascent community of Chinese in America had a promising new emissary.

Yung Wing's uncommon journey to the United States began when he was seven years old, living in Nam Ping, a small village on Pedro Island, southwest of Macau, which was then a Portuguese trading colony. His parents were peasants, and he was one of four children. His older brother had been educated in the traditional Confucian manner, but Yung's father happened to be acquainted with a Chinese aide to Mary Gutzlaff, the wife of a Lutheran missionary to China, the Rev. Charles Gutzlaff. In the summer of 1835, she started an English-language school for girls in Macau. Yung's father managed to secure him one of the few spots for boys. For a family like Yung, it was an unusual choice, given that the most prestigious career paths for young men were dictated by the competitive Confucian examination system. Years later, Yung Wing speculated that his parents must have believed that there might be some advantage in him learning English. Their village's proximity to Macau gave its residents an early vantage point on China's first sustained interactions with the West. Yung remembered Gutzlaff as a tall woman, with clear blue eyes, blonde hair, and heavy eyebrows. In their first encounter, she greeted him wearing a flowing white dress with two ballooning mutton sleeves. "I remember vividly I was no less puzzled than stunned," Yung recalled. "I actually trembled all over with fear at her imposing proportions—having never in my life seen such a peculiar and odd fashion." He clung to his father, petrified. Yung was Gutzlaff's youngest pupil. She soon became a mother figure to him. When she departed for the United States and her school closed, in 1839, Yung returned briefly to his village. His father passed away the following year, and he turned to caring for his mother. Gutzlaff, however, had left instructions with a fellow missionary in Macau to summon Yung as soon as a boys' school that had been planned, the Morrison Education Society School, opened. The school, whose name commemorated Robert Morrison, an early missionary to China, was

led by the Rev. Robert Brown, a tall, finely proportioned Yale graduate.
Yung enrolled at the school in 1841, joining five other boys, all older
than him. His classmates included Tong Achick, who would go on to
be instrumental in the early Chinese community in San Francisco. A
year after Yung arrived, the school moved to Hong Kong, occupying a
hilltop overlooking the harbor. In the fall of 1846, Brown announced to
a classroom full of students that he was returning to the United States
because of his health. He hoped to take a few of them with him to finish
their education and asked for anyone who might be interested in joining
him to stand. At first, no one moved. Yung clambered to his feet; two
other students, Wong Shing and Wong Foon, did as well. Yung returned
to his village to seek his mother's permission. She was initially reluctant,
but Yung managed to assuage her. She had three other children who
would take care of her. The ocean journey to New York, via the Cape of
Good Hope, took ninety-eight days. Brown and his pupils then made
their way by boat and railroad to East Windsor, Connecticut. With
support from patrons that Brown had arranged back in Hong Kong,
the three Chinese youths enrolled in Monson Academy, a school for
boys in Massachusetts. They lived with Brown's mother, Phoebe, about
a half mile from the school. Phoebe Brown, a widow and a deeply religious woman, had acquired a degree of renown for authoring a popular
Christian hymn, "I Love to Steal a While Away." They readily took to
Monson's course load, and Brown reported back to the Morrison Society that the boys were keeping up with their peers academically, even
as "they have been objects of great curiosity, and it has been annoying
to them to be gazed at." One of the boys, Wong Shing, was forced to
return to China because of health issues, but the other two graduated
from Monson in the summer of 1850. Under Phoebe Brown's influence,
Yung converted to Christianity. His counterpart, Wong Fooh, accepted
an offer to study medicine at the University of Edinburgh, in Scotland,
while Yung resolved to stay in the United States. He had originally
promised his family that he would return to China after two years. But,
in a letter to Samuel Wells Williams, a Morrison society trustee and
mentor in Hong Kong, Yung explained that he had a "great inclination
to get a liberal education." He successfully passed the entrance examination for Yale and, in the fall of 1850, began his freshman year.

Yung was one of ninety-eight students in the class of 1854. With only a year of Latin and Greek, far less preparation than most of his classmates had, Yung found himself struggling early on to keep up, while also working to help pay his way through school. "I used to sweat over my studies till twelve o'clock every night the whole Freshman year," he later wrote. Without his former companion, Wong Fooh, Yung was often lonely. At the beginning of his sophomore year, his mother informed him in a letter that his older brother had passed away, sending Yung into a deep depression. He confessed in a letter to Williams that at times he contemplated giving up and going home. At one point, after not having heard from his mother in a long while, Yung begged Williams to let him know if she was still alive. Yet Yung also found his Yale classmates invigorating, full of "mental excitement." Remarkably, during his second and third terms of his sophomore year, he won first prize in English composition. On October 30, 1852, during his junior year, he visited the New Haven City Court and became a naturalized American citizen, at the age of twenty-two. At some point, he also cut off his queue. A photograph of him during his senior year shows Yung to be dapper and trim, his hair handsomely coiffed. Even as he became thoroughly westernized, he continued to closely follow events in his homeland, asking in his letters to Williams about whether "the Chinese and the foreigners" were "getting along" and for news of the "revolution," evidently referring to the Taiping Rebellion, the bloody uprising against the Qing government that had begun in southern China. "All through my college course, especially in the closing year, the lamentable condition of China was before my mind constantly and weighed on my spirits," he later wrote. An ambition began to take shape of helping others in China come to America to be educated. His aspiration was "that through western education China might be regenerated, become enlightened and powerful." On November 13, 1854, a bitterly cold day, Yung boarded the clipper ship *Eureka* on the East River in New York City and set off on a 154-day journey back east to Hong Kong.

When Yung returned to China, he initially had to recover his mother tongue. He discovered just how much his command of the language had deteriorated when the *Eureka* entered Hong Kong harbor and a Chinese pilot boarded to guide the ship to shore. Yung found himself unable to interpret for the captain. Later, at his home village, near Macau, he had an emotional reunion with his mother. He recounted his experiences in the United States and tried to explain the meaning of the bachelor of arts degree he had earned at Yale. When she asked if the diploma came with money, he told her: "Knowledge is power, and power is greater than riches." The reality was that Yung's career prospects in China were limited. An American friend of his, the Rev. Joseph Twichell, later said that Yung encountered a "strong prejudice, stronger than we can appreciate against people educated abroad." Without a Confucian education, he was unfit for the most prestigious route for educated young men in China, the imperial service. Instead, he found work at first as a secretary for an American official, apprenticed for a time as an attorney in Hong Kong, and worked as an interpreter and a clerk. For a year or two, he was mostly unemployed. He eventually accumulated a small fortune, after venturing, on behalf of English tea firms, deep into territory controlled by Taiping rebels and retrieving thousands of boxes of green tea and embarking on the business himself. In 1863, he received a surprise invitation from the secretary to the viceroy, Zeng Guofan, commander of the imperial forces, to travel to his headquarters in Anqing for a meeting. Zeng had become one of the most powerful figures in China, leading the effort to crush the Taiping Rebellion. He was also an advocate of the country's self-strengthening movement, a push to modernize China by adopting Western methods and technology. Zeng asked Yung to find a Western manufacturer to outfit an ironworks factory near Shanghai, where the viceroy hoped to manufacture modern munitions. In 1864, Yung returned to the United States, traveling west from Hong Kong and making his way to London, where he caught a steamship bound for New York. The Civil War was in its third year, and most manufacturers in New England were engaged, but he managed to find a company in Fitchburg, Massachusetts, willing to fulfill Zeng's order. While he waited for the machinery to be completed, he attended his tenth reunion at Yale and presented himself in Washington as a volunteer for the Union army to "show my

loyalty and patriotism to my adopted country," he later wrote. A brigadier general, who had years earlier met Yung at Yale, informed him that
his service was not needed, so Yung returned to Massachusetts. When
the machinery order was finished, in the spring of 1865, Yung journeyed
back to China by way of the Isthmus of Panama and San Francisco.
Upon Yung's return to China, Zeng wrote a special memorial to the
emperor praising him and promoted him to a mid-ranking position in
the government. Several years later, in the fall of 1870, Yung was asked
to serve as an aide for a group of imperial commissioners who traveled
to Tianjin to meet with French officials after Chinese rioters killed
more than twenty foreigners in the city. The commissioners included
Zeng and Li Hongzhang, another reformer who favored learning from
the West. It was in Tianjin that Yung was finally able to broach his
education plan. Zeng and Li immediately gravitated to it and decided
to present it to the throne. Over the course of several messages to the
Qing government, the two officials argued that China's humiliations
in the Opium Wars necessitated bold changes. They laid out Yung's
proposal to send 120 students to the United States over the course of
four years. They would live there for fifteen years and attend various
schools, including the country's military and naval academies, before
returning to China, where they would then teach the technical skills
and other knowledge they'd acquired abroad. The Burlingame Treaty of
1868 offered an opening for the scheme in the United States, because
it specifically promised that Chinese subjects would enjoy the same
privileges as other foreign students at public educational institutions in
the United States.

On September 15, 1871—a little over a month before the massacre of
Chinese residents in Los Angeles—the Qing government approved the
plan. They appointed Yung, along with another official, Chen Lanbin, an
ambitious, mid-level bureaucrat who was known for his strict adherence
to Confucian etiquette, to head the mission. A headquarters was established in Shanghai to begin the process of recruiting the students and
preparing them for their stays overseas with teaching in both English
and Chinese. In February 1872, Yung wrote to his former Yale professor,
Noah Porter, to ask for advice about how to organize the program. Yung

explained that it was vitally important that the students maintain their knowledge of Chinese—two teachers were being dispatched with them to help with this—and made clear that the students "are not allowed to become citizens of the United States, nor to settle there permanently." Yung arrived in the United States several months later to begin making preparations for the arrival of the first cohort. His Yale connections led him to Birdsey G. Northrop, the secretary of the state board of education in Connecticut. Northrop, a former Congregational clergyman, had helped to establish Connecticut's free public school system. He suggested the students be placed with host families, who would care for them and work with the boys to improve their English, until they were ready to be enrolled in regular schools. He later issued a circular on Yung's behalf, calling for "cultured families in different parts of Connecticut and Massachusetts" to take in two boys each. In exchange for room and board and private instruction, families would receive $18 a week. "The significance and importance of this noble and comprehensive plan of the Chinese Government, ought to be so appreciated by a Christian people as to secure a welcome for these boys in the homes which illustrate the best phase of American society," he wrote.

On August 12, 1872, thirty students, who ranged in age from ten to sixteen years old, departed Shanghai aboard a small steamship, as their loved ones waved goodbye from the wharf. "Our hearts beat as we saw the last speck of our native shore grow smaller and smaller until it was no longer visible," one student later recalled. The ship needed a little more than a week to reach Yokohama, Japan, where the students disembarked and boarded the *Great Republic*, the majestic wooden vessel that was part of the Pacific Mail Steamship Company's fleet, for the journey to the United States. The students occupied first-class cabins, while 255 other Chinese passengers traveled in steerage. There is no evidence that the two groups mingled together. A menagerie of cows and sheep were aboard as well for their supply of milk and meat. When the seas were rough, the ship groaned alarmingly, and the students mostly stayed in their cabins reading, taking advantage of the ship's well-stocked library. On Sundays, the ship's captain read from the scriptures and a chaplain prayed. Mid-journey, the steamship encountered another ship bound for Japan. The boys hurriedly wrote letters home, and a small boat was dispatched to the ship to deliver the mail. On September 12, the ship arrived in San Francisco, and the students disembarked, wearing their traditional silk gowns, skullcaps, and satin shoes, marking their status as scholars. Newspapers across the country reported on their arrival. "The thirty Chinese students who arrived yesterday are very young," *The New York Times* reported. "They are fine intelligent ladies and gentlemen, and of much fairer complexion than any of their countrymen who have heretofore visited the United States." The boys were accompanied by Chen Lanbin, the co-head of the mission, along with Zeng Laishun, the mission's interpreter, his wife, and their six children. (The couple's three daughters were apparently the "ladies" whom the reporter observed.) Zeng was a native of Singapore, where he had attended an American missionary school. He later spent two years at Hamilton College in the United States. His wife, who went by "Ruth," had grown up on the island of Java, in modern-day Indonesia, also under the influence of Western missionaries. The entire family spoke English fluently. At this point, the boys possessed only the most rudimentary English, a few rote phrases they'd acquired and words of greeting. Zeng served as their primary intermediary with the alien world they were about to encounter. After sightseeing in San Francisco and recuperating for a few days, the students embarked upon a weeklong railroad journey across the country. From a special train car assigned to them, they took in miles of grassy prairies out the window and watched in wonderment herds of buffalo and Native Americans on horseback hunting them with bow and arrow. A few months later, students who arrived in the second cohort experienced a train robbery on their way across the country. They heard gunshots and the screams of other passengers and spotted a man outside, about forty feet away, with a revolver in each hand, pointed at them. The students' teachers told them to crouch down on the floor and hide. After a half hour, a brakeman barreled through and informed them that a group of bandits had robbed the train of gold bricks, ransacked a baggage car, killed the engineer, and disabled the engine. Another engine was eventually dispatched, and the students were back on their way. "One phase of American civilization was thus indelibly fixed upon our minds," a student later wrote.

The first stop on the students' itinerary on the East Coast was

Springfield, Massachusetts, a town of 27,000 people in the Connecticut River Valley, about fifteen miles from where Yung had attended boarding school as an adolescent. It was here that Yung decided to establish a temporary hub for his Chinese Educational Mission, as the program came to be called. The students were lodged at the Haynes Hotel, a five-story, brick, Italianate-style structure on Main Street that was one of the city's finest buildings. As the students awaited their family assignments, they got an initial orientation on American life, touring the town's armory, taking in a theatrical performance, and attending church. "As they are under the conduct of Chinese gentlemen, and represent the highest intelligence and refinement and good-will of their nation, we hope that they will everywhere be received in a manner becoming the confidence with which they are intrusted to us, and as strangers in a strange land will be treated with all civility," an article in the *Springfield Republican* said. Inevitably, however, the students were treated like creatures on display. A band of children took to shouting at the students and peeping at them through the windows of the hotel. The harassment got to the point that the town police had to intervene. When the students went to dinner one evening at their hotel, a curious woman accosted them and peppered the women in the group with questions. She sidled up to the boys and examined their queues before she was finally escorted out. At one point, the Chinese boys seemed to make a game of the town's children staring at them, scattering pennies on the street outside their hotel and watching their white counterparts scramble after them. The local newspaper observed the irony: "Think of it! The 'heathen Chinese' tossing coppers to the children of Puritan and enlightened New England."

The "Chinese question" had only recently begun to stir public feelings beyond the Pacific coast. The Chinese population on the Eastern Seaboard was almost nonexistent. The census of 1870 recorded just two Chinese residents in Connecticut; Rhode Island and Vermont had none; Maine counted just one. A small community—the census tallied twenty-nine—had taken root in New York City, but it would be several years before a discernible Chinatown emerged. One day, in May 1870, however, an exasperated factory owner in North Adams, Massachusetts, a mill town nestled in the picturesque northern Berkshires, about sixty miles northwest of Springfield, ordered one of his men to get on the next train to San Francisco and bring back "seventy-five Chinamen."

The factory owner was Calvin T. Sampson, a bearded, compactly built former farmer who had spent more than a decade as a shoemaker in North Adams. Sampson ran his enterprise with a stern hand, building an operation that produced 300,000 shoes a year. He had been an early adopter of labor-saving machinery, introducing pegging machines that fastened the soles of shoes to their upper portions. By 1870, Sampson employed a workforce of 150 white men and women—mostly Irish and French-Canadian immigrants. The Secret Order of the Knights of St. Crispin, an aggressive trade union that dominated the workforces of shoemakers in Massachusetts, organized a series of strikes at Sampson's factory, advocating for higher wages and an eight-hour workday. They also blocked workers who were not members of the order from taking jobs at the factory. Finally, after yet another work stoppage, Sampson vowed to break the union.

Sampson had read a newspaper account of a shoe manufacturer in San Francisco who employed Chinese workers. He sent a trusted superintendent, George W. Chase, to the West Coast. In San Francisco, Chase found a shoemaker who had recently retained Chinese laborers and raved that they could "imitate anything they see." He directed Chase to the office of Kwong, Chong, Wing & Co., a Chinese labor contracting firm. After investigating Sampson's credit and confirming he was of decent character, the firm agreed to supply him with the men, recruiting them in San Francisco and Sacramento. They ranged in age between eighteen and twenty-eight. Sampson paid a commission of a dollar a man and arranged for two train cars to deliver his workers to Massachusetts for $125 a passenger. The Chinese workers signed three-year contracts, in which they were to be paid $23 a month for the first year and $26 a month for the second and third. An English-speaking interpreter and foreman who called himself Charlie Sing was to be paid $60 a month. Sing was in his early thirties and had arrived in the country as a young boy. He'd scratched out a living in various mining towns and carried a revolver for protection.

On June 13, 1870, the train pulled into the railroad depot in North Adams. The workers, dressed in blue frocks and thick wooden shoes, disembarked. They each carried a roll, containing their bedding and clothing, slung over their shoulder on a bamboo pole. With Sampson and Chase leading the way, the workers marched in pairs to their destination, a three-story brick building on Marshall Street that contained the shoe factory. A force of thirty policemen escorted them through a jeering, hostile crowd of more than two thousand people.

Inside the factory, Sampson's new employees had to be shown every step of the shoemaking process, mostly through pantomime. Within the first two weeks, Sing, the foreman, lost his right thumb in an accident with a pegging machine. Soon, however, the Chinese cobblers were turning out 120 cases of shoes a week, compared to the 110 produced by their white counterparts, and costing Sampson seven dollars a case less. His annual savings amounted to $40,000.

Labor leaders responded with fury. On June 29, less than two weeks after the arrival of the Chinese workers in North Adams, a workingmen's convention, in defense of "free labor," was held at the Tremont Temple in Boston. As it had been in California, the coolie falsehood—that the Chinese were indentured workers, laboring in servitude—was invoked against them. "Are you in favor of freedom, or of slavery?" one speaker asked. The following morning, journalist John Swinton published an editorial on the front page of the *New York Tribune,* beneath a two-word heading: "The Alarm." "Suddenly—by a lightning flash, as it were, the Chinese question has become the living question of the hour," he wrote. Swinton warned of capitalists "introducing tens and hundreds of thousands of Chinese workers into the industrial establishments of the country." He made clear, however, his objection was rooted in more than economics. Swinton, who had briefly attended New York Medical College and frequently written about science for the *Times,* betrayed deep-seated, pseudo-scientific beliefs about white supremacy. "The deepest dividing line between men is that of *race,*" he wrote. "Deeper than politics or religion—deeper than the contemporary differences of laws or manners, are the depths and differences of *race.* It enters into the elements of the blood; establishes itself in the forms of the bones, expresses itself through the material and size of the brain." The same day Swinton published his editorial, another "anti-coolie" meeting was held, this one in Tompkins Square in New York City. Abraham Oakey Hall, the city's mayor, was among the featured speakers. He praised Swinton's editorial. "We object to no kind of voluntary immigration to this country," he said. "But this is forced immigration of a class debased in race, irreligious, and in many respects incapable of free reason."

Despite the agitation from labor and its allies, most of the press accounts about the Chinese workers were generally approving, contending that the Knights of St. Crispin had forced the manufacturer's hand. "What he sought was not men who would work cheaply, but men who would work well—men, in fact, who would work at all," an editorial published next to Swinton's in the *Tribune* said. A writer from *Harper's New Monthly Magazine* visited North Adams to view the Chinese cobblers himself. He passed through the factory's gates and several rooms, before walking up a staircase and entering a brightly lit room with a series of workbenches. Suddenly, he later wrote, "we are in China." The Chinese cobblers were working in teams of three, putting the finished pieces of the shoes together, with the help of pegging machines, whose staccato hammering filled the room. Everyone was intent on their work. "There are about sixty of the Chinese workmen in the room, and there can be nowhere a pleasanter room, nor a busier, more orderly group of workmen," he wrote. Tensions in North Adams, too, seemed to ebb. The Chinese workers were initially locked inside the factory's gates, but several weeks later, they felt comfortable enough to walk to town in small groups.

Other employers took notice of Sampson's experiment. A month after the arrival of the workers in North Adams, James B. Hervey, the owner of the Passaic Steam Laundry in Belleville, New Jersey, journeyed to California to arrange his own supply of Chinese labor. Hervey was a former sea captain who had started his laundry business in 1856. His workers mostly serviced linen shirts that arrived from New York City, washing them by machine and then ironing them by hand. His workforce was primarily comprised of white women, the daughters of German and Irish immigrants, whom he typically paid by the piece. He was having trouble, however, retaining his female workers for longer than a few months. In San Francisco, Hervey met with Ah Yung, the same agent who furnished laborers to Sampson. It was close to midnight, in late September, when two train cars delivered sixty-eight Chinese workers to Belleville under the cover of darkness. Hervey turned a dozen rooms on the second floor of the laundry into living quarters for his new employees. Each man slept on a simple bed consisting of a board covered by a thin straw matting and a light blanket. A washroom was converted into a cafeteria, where the Chinese ate their meals on rude wooden tables. The Chinese workers supplied their own cook, who made simple meals of rice, along with beef, pork, mutton, and fish, as well as vegetables, washed down with tea. Hervey made sure to erect a wooden fence around the laundry grounds to guard his workers from any harassment.

He put the Chinese men to work ironing, as opposed to traditional male tasks, like moving heavy loads of laundry and operating machinery. The Chinese workers proved, once again, to be conscientious imitators, fastidious in their ironing of each shirt. They ironed more slowly than their female co-workers but over the course of a week got through more orders because of their diligence. Hervey paid the men $30 a month; his most productive female workers, working by the piece, could make $60. A small group of Hervey's Irish employees refused to work with the Chinese workers and quit, but most eventually returned. Hervey received a letter from the unnamed chairman of a "committee of five" opposed to the Chinese. "After the first of October if those Chinamen are not off your Premises we will Murder you," the letter said. Hervey ignored the threat. Shortly afterward, local Democratic politicians held a rally attended by about two hundred people denouncing the Chinese influx. Just as in North Adams, however, the Chinese workers had their defenders. The *New York Herald* reported that the invective against them came from "unthinking, low classes in Belleville," but that the "respectable portion of the community take no interest in the matter whatever."

Within a few months of their arrival, the workers were able to go around Belleville unimpeded. Hervey soon felt comfortable enough to increase his Chinese workforce to about a hundred. A year into the experiment, a group of Belleville residents started a Sunday school for the workers, teaching them English. The classes, which averaged about fifty students, opened with the Lord's Prayer, and the students sang hymns every week; a favorite was "Come to Jesus." During a celebration held with a local church, the students presented a banner that they had written in Chinese characters that said, in translation, "The china-boys of Canton accept Jesus the Exalted One." By then, most had learned how to speak, read, and write passable English.

In late June 1872, another contingent of Chinese workers made their way eastward. Their destination was a cutlery factory in Beaver Falls, Pennsylvania, a hamlet of several thousand residents, situated on the banks of the Beaver River, just south of Pittsburgh. The factory belonged to the Harmony Society, a religious community established in 1805 that had invested in land in Beaver Falls and was responsible for much of its development after the Civil War. The factory's operations were overseen by a pair of brothers, John and Henry Reeves, and a trustee of the society. The company employed a workforce of several hundred white laborers and was one of the largest cutlery manufacturers in the country. Earlier in the year, the workers had gone on strike, the latest in a series of labor disruptions at the factory.

It was reportedly a local Methodist minister, interested in evangelizing the Chinese, who first suggested to the company managers that they try recruiting them as laborers. John Reeves, the company's secretary and treasurer, set out for San Francisco, where he sought help from a former Pittsburgh resident who was engaged in missionary work in the Chinese community. Reeves learned of a gang of Chinese railroad workers in Louisiana who were wrapping up grading work east of New Orleans. Reeves traveled back across the country and met with the group. With the help of an interpreter, he persuaded about a hundred of them to make the journey to Beaver Falls.

On June 29, 1872, a throng of angry residents greeted the initial cohort of seventy workers on their arrival into Beaver Falls. With Reeves at the head of the line and the town's lone constable standing guard, the Chinese workers managed to walk the few blocks from the train depot to their lodgings, a wooden structure erected behind the Mansion House, a hotel near the factory, without major incident. For their new employees' safety, Reeves and the company's lawyer, Judge Henry Hice, stayed inside the factory for several weeks. A little more than a month after the workers' arrival, a large meeting of workingmen took place at a Pittsburgh school. An organizing committee was appointed and 127 people signed on to oppose the "importation of Chinese Coolie Labor." Just like at the Passaic Steam Laundry in New Jersey, the managers of the cutlery company retained most of their white workforce, though several white foremen refused to work with their new colleagues and quit. Over the next few months, a contingent of about twenty white men were laid off from the factory's forge room and replaced by Chinese laborers. On December 1, another group of Chinese workers arrived, bringing the total at the factory to about 170. Soon, many of the skilled white workers who had trained the Chinese were reassigned to lower-paying tasks, causing another exodus.

In February 1873, a citizens committee met with the leaders of the Harmony Society, demanding that they discharge the Chinese workers. Several weeks later, the society issued a lengthy statement, explaining that the cutlery business had been sustaining heavy losses for years and that the overseers were faced with either closing the factory entirely or bringing in a Chinese workforce to labor alongside the white employees. In order to help ease tensions, the society committed to sharing the proceeds of the cutlery company's profits with the community for the establishment of religious, educational, and charitable institutions. An uneasy detente took hold.

Lee Ten Poy, a foreman and interpreter, served as the workers' main intermediary with the factory managers and the rest of the community. He distributed their pay and set up a store across the street from the Mansion House, selling supplies and Chinese wares to the workers. He was later replaced by another interpreter, Chow Hung, who brought his wife. She lived in an apartment above the store and wore immaculate silk outfits and jewelry but was rarely seen in public. The workers mostly kept to themselves but occasionally ventured into town. Some developed a taste for American ice cream, often frequenting a local confectionary. They experienced occasional harassment from mischievous boys, who liked to shove the Chinese men off the planks that were laid over muddy streets. But they largely co-existed peacefully with other town residents. "The turbulence which their first appearance caused wore away in time, for they did not strike back when they were struck, except so far as was necessary in the way of defence," one visiting journalist later wrote. "For some time back they have been free from attack, and have been only subjected to an occasional hooting or a few words of contempt from the native population. The trials of this kind which they have undergone prove them to be patient, forbearing and forgiving."

It was amid these first stirrings of anti-Chinese sentiment on the Eastern Seaboard that 122 New England families applied to host students from the Chinese Educational Mission. The number was far more than was required for the first cohort. The students were clearly regarded differently than their countrymen. One account described the boys as belonging to "cultured and polite families" and of "a quite different class" from the Chinese who worked in laundries and elsewhere. Most of the students were placed in towns throughout Connecticut; a smaller contingent stayed in Massachusetts. Birdsey Northrop emphasized to the host families the importance of the mission for the progress of the "oldest and largest nation on the globe" and advised them to maintain for the students a strict regimen of study and recitation, as well as exercise and recreation. "The Chinese justly despise vacillation and effeminacy," he said. "They scorn sloth, love labor, and practice industry and economy."

Northrop suggested Yung establish his headquarters in Hartford, a prosperous city—in the latter half of the nineteenth century, it was the most affluent city in the country—centrally located for visiting the students and their host families. Hartford was also home to some of Yung's closest friends in the United States. They included David and Fannie Bartlett, whom Yung had met through his mentor, Samuel Brown, when he first arrived in America. David Bartlett was a teacher at the American Asylum for Deaf-Mutes in Hartford. He and his wife took in three students from the first cohort. The Bartletts' daughter, Mary, then twenty-one years old, was a stern taskmaster with the boys, admonishing them when they held their knives and forks too low at meals and rigidly enforcing their bedtimes. Every morning and evening, David Bartlett led the boys in prayer.

Other friends in Hartford included Samuel Wells Capron, a Yale classmate of Yung's, and his wife, Eunice, who had attended Monson Academy with Yung. (She was his first-ever date to a formal evening party.) The Caprons and their five children lived in a three-story duplex home on Willard Street. The family turned over the south side of their house to Yung's co-commissioner, Chen Lanbin, and his retinue, which included two teachers, a cook, a laundryman, an interpreter, a tailor, a secretary, and a servant. Clara Capron was then eight years old. She and her siblings would ring at the front door and be ushered into the front parlor, which was decorated with Chinese tapestries; a Confucian shrine occupied one corner of the room. The commissioners, invariably immaculately attired, would always greet the children. Capron often perched, with her friends, on the fence separating her backyard from the one belonging to her new neighbors. When the laundryman brought out tubs of wet clothing from the basement and dried them on the grass, she and her friends would try to teach him rudimentary English. "Our method was to shout each word as loudly as possible to make it sink better into his consciousness, although we were almost near enough to touch him," she said. "His face wreathed in smiles as he repeated each word after us, and when he could not pronounce the letter 'r,' we shouted with laughter."

When Yan Phou Lee, a member of the second contingent of students to arrive, met his host family for the first time, Sarah Vaille, a tall, motherly woman from Springfield, wrapped him in her arms and kissed him, causing him to blush and the other boys to laugh. "I would say nothing to show my embarrassment," he later wrote. "But that was the first kiss I ever had since my infancy." Vaille and her husband, Henry, a physician, were active in the First Congregational Church in Springfield. The first Sunday after the students' arrival, they went to service. Understanding very little English, they thought they were going to school, but as they walked up the steps of the house of worship, it dawned on them what was happening. "It is a church," Lee's companion told him in Chinese. Alarmed, they fled the building together.

In their first few months in America, the boys wore their traditional gowns. This made them objects of curiosity every time they ventured out. Wen Bing Chung, another student in the second cohort, later recalled the students drawing crowds that would follow them around and call them "Chinese girls." The students persuaded the commissioners to let them switch to Western attire. They took to discreetly tucking their long braids into their clothing. The students' English lessons proceeded apace. In the Vaille household, the boys were instructed on the names of various food dishes. At mealtimes, if they couldn't name the food, they couldn't eat it. "Taught by this method, our progress was rapid and surprising," Yan Phou Lee later wrote. The boys initially conversed amongst themselves, entirely in Chinese, but this soon gave way to a mixture of Chinese and English; eventually, Chinese communication all but vanished. This enabled the students to "enter the arena of student life on equal terms with Americans," Yung Kwai, another student in the Vaille household, later recalled.

When it came time for the boys to enter regular schools, they predictably had to deal with their share of adolescent bullying. A satiric poem, "Plain Language from Truthful James," published in the September 1870 issue of the *Overland Monthly* magazine that played on racist stereotypes of the "heathen Chinee," had swept the country. Wen Bing Chung said that the Chinese students "fought their way with the fists in true American style." Nevertheless, their assimilation was remarkably swift. Students from the mission were soon earning some of the top marks in area middle schools. Cai Shaoji, one of the boys living with the Bartletts and a classmate of Clara Capron's at Hartford West Middle School, scored the highest average score in his class in writing. Other students took top prizes in declamation and spelling.

The family of Zeng Laishun, the mission's first interpreter, became active in the life of the South Congregational Church in Springfield, Massachusetts, making an impression every time they ventured down the aisle in their formal silk outfits. According to church records, three of the Zeng children were received into the church; one of the daughters, Annie, became a teacher in the Sunday school. William Lyon Phelps attended West Middle School and then Hartford Public High School with several students from the mission. He later recalled the boys excelling at baseball, football, and even ice hockey. One boy, Se Chung, short and stout but unusually quick, was invariably the first pick during football games. Phelps became closest with Cao Jiaxiang, a serious boy who could recite Julius Caesar in Greek. Every Saturday, Cao and Phelps would go bird hunting together, looking for meadowlarks and yellowhammers. The boys from the mission were popular socially, too. "You should have seen them cutting the double eight and the grapevine!" Phelps later wrote. "Their manner to the girls had a deferential elegance far beyond our possibilities. Whether it was the exotic pleasure of dancing with Orientals, or, what is more probably, the charm of their manners and talk, I do not know; certain it is that at dances and receptions, the fairest and most sought-out belles invariably gave the swains from the Orient the preference. I can remember the pained expression on the faces of some of my American comrades when the girls deliberately passed them by and accepted the attentions of Chinese rivals with a more than yielding grace."

Yung's own integration into American life served as a model for his students. In the winter of 1873, he traveled to Washington, at the request of the imperial government, for some diplomatic meetings. At a formal dinner, organized by the Japanese minister, Yung held forth among the high-society guests, dressed in his traditional silk gown. He seemed to attract particular attention from a gaggle of women in ball gowns. "I managed to be just as agreeable to them as a 'heathen Chinese' knows how, but I had to do an immense amount of talking," he later wrote to a friend. "Of course I had on my long gown and clumsy boots, which made me look as though I had gout for years." But Yung wrote that his "grotesque habiliments" did not deter the women but instead "attracted greater attention."

The Rev. Joseph Twichell was the pastor of the Asylum Hills Congregational Church, located a short walk from the mission's headquarters. Twichell befriended Yung during regular fireside chats. "He is the shyest person almost I ever met, and the least disposed to talk about himself," he told a friend. "It was a slow process getting his story out of him." Twichell became one of the mission's most important supporters. Yung had confided to Twichell and his wife, Julia, his fears about finding a spouse. He told the couple "there was no Chinese woman whom he would marry and no American lady who would marry him," Twichell wrote in his diary. The couple admonished Yung that he had no way of knowing this. "Possibly we helped him venture in the matter," Twichell wrote. On February 24, 1875, Twichell officiated Yung's marriage to Mary L. Kellogg, of Avon, Connecticut. Kellogg had been one of a handful of young, single women who had served as hosts for the mission. The wedding took place in the Kellogg home, which was decorated with garlands and flowers. She wore an elaborate, long-sleeved dress of white crepe, embroidered with silk, and imported from China. The reception featured both Chinese and American dishes. Two officials from the commission appeared in their formal Chinese dress, but Yung wore a Western-style suit. When the festivities were over, the couple left on an evening train to New York for a brief honeymoon.

The Americanization of the students began to cause consternation among some of the mission officials. Tensions had long festered between Yung and his fellow commissioner, Chen Lanbin, over issues like the students' dress, their attendance at church services, and even their participation in athletics. Prior to his arrival in the United States, Chen, who was in his mid-fifties, had never traveled outside of China. He had only begun to study English several years earlier. The transformation occurring in the students alarmed Chen, while Yung celebrated the changes as a flowering of "life, energy and independence, candor, ingenuity and open-heartedness."

In the fall of 1875, the imperial government jointly appointed the two men to be the first Chinese ministers to the United States. Chen was to lead the mission and Yung was to serve as his second in command. While the appointment was ostensibly a promotion for Yung, he was dismayed because his new responsibilities would keep him away from the students. Nevertheless, Yung threw himself into his duties, becoming a persistent voice, pressing American officials to address the growing hostilities directed at the Chinese residents of the West Coast.

In the latter half of 1879, the Qing government dispatched a new commissioner to Hartford to oversee the mission, Wu Zideng, an elderly, classically trained scholar and member of the prestigious Hanlin Academy, reserved for the most exceptional academicians. Wu was fluent in written English and a skilled translator —he later published a dictionary that went through several printings—but, notably, did not speak the language. When he met with the students in Hartford, he became enraged when they balked at prostrating themselves, as was the custom in Confucian circles. He accused them of becoming too accustomed to foreign ways. He later issued a letter to the students, sternly reminding them to not neglect their Chinese studies and customs. The students had previously been required to spend two weeks of every summer back in Hartford, studying Chinese and Confucian texts. Wu tripled this requirement.

Wu's reports back to the Qing government disparaged the students as "undereducated in Confucianism." He declared that "their virtues are not firm," making them prone to picking up "western vices." He recommended that the mission be canceled. In the minds of Qing officials, perhaps the worst of the temptations for the students was the Christian religion. The imperial court decreed that anyone who converted to Christianity was to be "withdrawn immediately." Proselytizing by host families was forbidden in the program, but there is little doubt that the opportunity to model Christian living for the students motivated many of them. The strenuous efforts of Chinese officials to "fortify young minds against Christianity" bemused Yung, who wrote to his friend Twichell at one point that "they might as well keep youngsters from daylight as from truth." Immersed in the daily lives of their host families, the boys prayed before meals, attended Bible studies, and went to church on Sundays. Over time, the exposure to what had previously been an alien faith inevitably had an effect. During the winter of 1877–1878, a group of Chinese pupils who attended Williston Seminary, a boarding school in Easthampton, Massachusetts, approached the minister of a local Congregational church about becoming members. Yung advised the boys in a letter that they were free to hold whatever religious beliefs they wished privately, but they should avoid public professions of faith and church membership. The boys agreed and started amongst themselves the Chinese Christian Home Mission at the school, conducting weekly prayer meetings and meeting on Sunday afternoons for scripture study. Twichell recorded in his diary several occasions in which boys asked him how they might become Christians, marveling that he had once considered becoming a missionary overseas. Instead, "lo, God has brought the work to my very door," he wrote. Twichell admired the shrewdness with which Yung handled the issue among the boys. "Practically and in all essential respects the way is left open for Christian influence and instruction, and numbers of the boys have become Christians, though it is not allowed, for evident prudential reasons that they make a formal public profession of their faith," Twichell wrote to a friend.

It was the conversion of Yung Kwai, a nephew of Yung Wing's, in 1878, and the boy's subsequent decision to cut off his queue, that led to the mission's biggest scandal. Yung Kwai wrote to his family with the news, and his father sent a blistering response, disowning him and threatening to starve and beat him if he didn't abandon his newfound faith. In May 1880, Wu summoned the student back to Hartford and confined him to a room with just bread and water. Yet the boy refused to back down. Only after Twichell intervened did Wu permit Yung Kwai to return to Springfield to graduate from high school as the class salutatorian. In the end, Wu still expelled Yung Kwai from the mission and ordered him to return to China, in the company of another student, Tan Yew Fun, who had been one of the founders of the Chinese Christian Home Mission at Williston Seminary, along with several other students who had been forced out of the program, either for behavior reasons or health problems. In late August, the group proceeded by train to Boston, where they were to set sail for China, but Yung Kwai and Tan Yew Fun slipped away from the group in Springfield and went into hiding. Yung Wing soon came to his nephew's aid and arranged, through Twichell, to pay for his expenses for six months, so he could remain in the United States and continue his education at Yale. Eventually, Wu agreed to let both boys stay. They were safe, but the mission's future was now precarious.

On December 11, 1880, Yung wrote an anguished letter from Washington to Twichell. Wu was visiting from Hartford and had brought gloomy news from Li Hongzhang, Yung's former patron, about the mission. The program would be shut down; the only question seemed to be whether it would be "at once or gradually." Yung blamed Wu's "representations of the students" and "the howl of the Pacific Coast," among other factors. Li had become increasingly skeptical about the mission's value. He was concerned about the deleterious effects of Western customs on the boys and had been urging Yung's counterpart, Chen Lanbin, the Chinese ambassador and the former head of the mission, to do more to manage the situation. The program was also expensive—annual spending far exceeded Yung's original budget. Since the mission was first conceived, the rising enmity in America towards Chinese immigrants had altered the tenor of relations between the two countries. American officials had already notified Chinese officials that students from the mission would not be permitted to enroll at West Point or the U.S. Naval Academy, as had originally been planned. Draconian restrictions on Chinese immigration appeared to be only a matter of time.

Yung and Twichell scrambled to save the mission. Twichell presented a petition to James Angell, the U.S. minister to China, signed by the heads of various educational institutions that had accepted the students, and requested that it be presented to Li. "They have proved themselves eminently worthy of the confidence which has been reposed in them to represent their families and the great Chinese Empire in a land of strangers," the letter said. "As the result of their good conduct, many of the prejudices of ignorant and wicked men towards the Chinese have been removed, and more favorable sentiments have taken their place." Twichell also enlisted his close friend and neighbor Mark Twain to arrange a meeting with the former president, Ulysses S. Grant, in New York City. Grant sent a five-page letter to Li, arguing that the mission should be continued. Yung believed that they had won a temporary reprieve. "General Grant's letter has done its work," Yung wrote to Twichell in early March. Thousands of miles away, Li was vacillating, worrying that an abrupt withdrawal of all of the students would engender "surprise and speculation" in the United States. On June 8, 1881, however, the Chinese foreign office recommended to the Guangxu Emperor that the mission be disbanded immediately, asserting that the mission had lost its "original purpose." The imperial court recorded its approval.

The students had been gathered for a lakeside camping trip in Connecticut. Their mentor, Yung Wing, came and delivered the news. One student later described the order from Beijing as a "bolt from the blue." The camp broke up, and the students returned to their homes to begin preparations for their departure. The Bartlett family hosted a farewell gathering for the students. Mary Bartlett wrote a letter to the mother of Wu Yangzheng, a member of the original cohort of students, who had been with the family for nearly a decade. "You will, I am sure, be glad to see your little boy grow into a man, and feel proud of him," she wrote. "He has been with us during his whole stay in America and we have become much attached to him. He has pursued an upright, steadfast course in his studies as well as in his general character, and we feel that he will be a useful man and serve his country with honour to himself and to his parents." Another student, Sun Kwang Ming, walked to the home of his Sunday school teacher to bid him farewell. William Phelps's dear friend, Cao Jiaxiang, presented his prized hunting rifle to him as a parting gift.

The first departing contingent of students left Hartford at just before five in the evening, on August 8. The group included twenty-two students, laden with forty leather trunks and other boxes, all stenciled with the words "Chinese Commission" in English. As they waited at the train depot, they made for a distinctive party, all dressed in Western attire, their braids running down their backs, with the ends tucked into their pockets. Many of them wore expensive eyeglasses, and they chattered easily amongst themselves in English. They made a brief stop in Niagara Falls, and then headed west to San Francisco, where they would depart by steamer for Shanghai. The next group of students followed three weeks later. In San Francisco, this group was challenged by a team from Oakland to play a game of baseball. Unbeknownst to their opponents, one of the Chinese players, Liang Tun-yen, had played for Yale and possessed a wicked curveball. "The Oakland nine got the shock of their life as they attempted to connect with the deliveries of the Chinese pitcher," Wen Bing Chung, one of the students in the group, later recounted. "The Chinese walloped them, to the great rejoicing of their comrades and fellow countrymen." As their ship departed San Francisco harbor, the group of about fifty boys sang hymns. On September 26, the final group of students, escorted by their commissioner, Wu Zideng, departed Hartford.

After the closure of the mission, Yung Wing resigned his position in the Chinese legation and prepared to make his own return to China to call on officials of the imperial government, as was customary for diplomatic officers at the end of their terms. He fretted about the effects of a prolonged separation from his wife and two young sons, who were to remain in Avon with the Kellogg family, but he was resolved to fulfill his duties. Yung spent a year and a half in China, visiting with various dignitaries. He had a dismaying appointment with the viceroy, Li Hongzhang, who insisted to Yung that he had not meant for the mission to be closed. In the spring of 1883, Yung rushed back to the United States upon hearing that his wife was ailing. "She had lost the use of her voice and greeted me in a hoarse low whisper," Yung later wrote. "I was thankful that I found her still living though much emaciated." Yung's return seemed to revive her, but she fell ill again, in the winter of 1885. She finally died, in June of 1886, from a kidney condition. Yung became a single father to his two sons, who were seven and nine years old. He spent the next few years raising them.

In 1895, the Qing government summoned Yung back into its service, seeking his help in China's war against Japan. He was later involved in various reform efforts, including a venture to build a railroad connecting northern and southern China. In 1898, he sought the help of the United States consulate in Beijing to resolve a dispute over the initiative and presented himself to Charles Denby, the U.S. minister to China. In a perplexing series of events, the State Department deemed Yung's American citizenship to be invalid. "In view of the construction placed upon the naturalization laws of the United States by our highest courts, the Department does not feel that it can properly recognize him as a citizen of the United States," the secretary of state, John Sherman, wrote in a diplomatic cable to Denby. Sherman included a detailed explanation, concluding that it was well established that a "Mongolian is not a 'white person' within the meaning of the term used within the naturalization laws of the United States." Yung sought the help of his influential American friends, writing a letter to Twichell that the minister described as a "cry for help." Twichell enlisted the assistance of Connecticut senator Joseph Hawley, another friend of Yung's, but their efforts went nowhere.

In 1902, at the age of seventy-four, Yung managed to obtain permission to re-enter the United States. He spent his final years in Hartford, living in a series of boardinghouses. At one point, he was forced to leave a house when one of his roommates refused to share a table with a Chinese man. In 1911, he suffered a stroke, and his son Morrison and his wife, a Chinese woman educated in Australia, took him into their home. On April 21, 1912, Yung died at the age of eighty-three. Like other Chinese Americans, he was a man without a country.

Part III

At the Gates

CHAPTER 11

The Chinese Question

The event at the opera house in Chicago's West End, in March of 1879, was billed as a debate on the "much-talked-of Chinese question." The main attraction was an itinerant lecturer named Wong Chin Foo, who called himself America's "first missionary from China." A slight, graceful man, whose queue reached to the floor, Wong had been crisscrossing the United States for several years, delivering lectures in fluent—even elegant, as one observer put it—English on Chinese customs and culture. On this evening, he was to share the stage with a city resident, William E. Lewis, whose chief qualification seemed to be that he had once been a sailor along the China coast. Lewis described himself as merely a "humble citizen of the United States," trying to do his duty for his country. He promised to respond to "fine spun tales with hard, stubborn facts which will take all the cunning of the Celestial to refute."

The clamor over Chinese immigration was getting more vociferous on the Pacific coast. Wong, a Mandarin-speaker from northern China, was an unlikely champion for his countrymen, not least because he was openly dismissive of his Cantonese brethren. He had grown up in Yantai, a coastal town in Shandong province. At the age of thirteen, his elderly, destitute father, who had been raising him alone, handed him over to the care of Landrum and Sallie Holmes, Southern Baptist missionaries, who had arrived in the village. Sallie Holmes described Wong in a letter to a friend as a "pretty bright boy" and obedient but probably one who would "never take the lead." She was doubtful about his principles. "It is but little we can expect in that respect concerning a child brought up in heathenism," she wrote. Several years later, Wong made a brief sojourn to America for schooling, before returning to his homeland. In 1873, he fled his country, under murky circumstances, after becoming involved in a plot against the Manchu government. His appearances in churches and other venues in the United States had a circus-like quality. Wong dressed in the formal attire of a Chinese mandarin and performed "lightning calculations" with an abacus, which some newspapers mistakenly called an "abracadabra." But he also extolled the virtues of Confucianism and made the case "that the Chinaman is as civilized as an American." On April 2, 1874, Wong appeared in front of a judge at the circuit court in Grand Rapids, Michigan, and became an American citizen, an event that was widely covered in newspapers across the country. He falsely proclaimed that he was the first Chinese immigrant to be naturalized.

Wong was a natural showman, by turns charming and acerbic. He explained to his audiences that it was understandable that the Chinese arrivals would be viewed suspiciously in America, but he ticked off the accomplishments of the Chinese empire, including the invention of the art of printing with movable type, the devising of the first mariner's compass, the first cannon, and the first suspension bridge. All of these, he liked to say, came from "the heathens." He poked at Americans for their supposed Christian values. "In all her heathenism, China has in no time surpassed the Christians in their persecution of races," he wrote in a letter to the *Chicago Tribune.* "We persecute people on account of their lawless conduct, and never on account of their nature or birth. The Chinamen here are persecuted for no other reason than because they are Chinamen."

There are scant details about how the idea of a public debate with Lewis, an engineer who worked in a building on Michigan Avenue, came about. Wong had a habit of getting into public scraps. He was arrested in Reading, Pennsylvania, for striking a drunken man who had pulled on his braid and shouted insults at Wong and a Chinese companion. In another incident, just outside of Bethlehem, Pennsylvania, Wong got into a dispute with a hotel proprietor over a bill and kicked in a paneled door with one of his sandaled feet and threatened to shoot the man. In an open letter, published in the *Tribune*, Wong made a show of challenging Lewis to appear for a meeting at the Tribune building, to arrange the terms of a debate. The lecturer signed his brief missive "the benighted heathen."

On the evening of March 23, 150 people paid twenty-five cents each to witness the contest. Each man was allotted a half hour to speak. Wong began by needling Lewis for calling him a liar. "Being a heathen," Wong said, his own religion did not permit him to respond in kind, drawing applause from the audience. He explained that Confucius taught men how to live "happily and economically." That's what enabled the population of the Chinese empire to grow so vast and to last for so many centuries, he said. He made the point that the importation of American technology had hurt the livelihoods of many in China, but he also denied that America was in any danger of being overrun by a "flood of Chinamen to America." Most Chinese citizens, he explained, would never leave their country. He asserted that Chinese laborers had not hurt the income of white Americans, pointing out that the wages in San Francisco, where the vast majority of the Chinese population lived, were the highest in the country. He noted that American missionaries could travel in China unmolested, evidence that "the people were no worse in their morals than any other nation."

When it was Lewis's turn, he delivered a rambling description of Shanghai, talking about its foul smells and a visit to a public bathhouse, where men, women, and children were naked. He contended that a third of Chinese were addicted to opium and mocked Chinese religion with a story about a storm at sea and Chinese passengers bowing to an idol and singing "Ching, ching, ching." He retrod familiar arguments about "degraded" Chinese workers coming to America as slaves. "Did our fathers make this a land of milk and honey for the barbarian hordes to come and take it away from us?" he said, drawing applause. In his closing statement, he said there was only one thing to which he would compare a Chinaman and that was a rat. "He had the same keen eye, the same sinewy form, and the same appendage behind," Lewis said, eliciting roars from the crowd. A *Tribune* reporter later described both men's arguments as "incoherent" but reported that the audience seemed amply entertained. The original conceit of the evening was for the audience to decide the winner of the argument, but no verdict was rendered, which the reporter said was likely for the best, given what they had heard.

On the same evening as Wong's debate, several blocks away, another Chinese immigrant, a decorous Christian convert named Chan Pak Kwai, addressed a large audience that included some of the city's most prominent citizens at the First Methodist Church. An introductory letter on his behalf, written by the Rev. Otis Gibson, the indefatigable minister to the Chinese on the Pacific coast, explained that Chan was visiting the city for a lecture tour on "The Real Chinese Question," and that he was interested in "defending his people against the many false charges so persistently made by anti-Chinese advocates." The *Tribune* described Chan, who had taken to preaching at a Chinese chapel in San Francisco, as a "good type of the Chinaman," who "speaks the President's American quite fluently."

Chan touched on many of the same points as Wong, highlighting the good wages in California and dismissing the possibility of "a vast emigration" of Chinese to the United States. Chan also pointed out that the Chinese residents of San Francisco paid tens of thousands of dollars a year into the city's treasury, yet their children were not allowed to attend public schools. He added that it was absurd to think that the country's institutions could be overthrown by Chinese immigrants without access to the ballot. He ended his message by leading the congregation in a hymn: "Let us gather up the sunbeams, lying all around our path. Let us keep the wheat and roses, casting out the thorns and chaff. Let us find our sweetest comfort, in the blessings of today, with a patient hand, removing all the briars from the way. Then scatter seeds of kindness, then scatter seeds of kindness, then scatter seeds of kindness, for our reaping, by and by."

Kindness stood little chance when confronted by political exigencies. By the mid-1870s, racist violence and intimidation had become endemic in the South and Reconstruction was in tatters. The country's politics were split along sectional lines, with Republicans maintaining their stronghold in the Northeast and Midwest and Democrats dominating the South. Both parties turned to the Pacific coast for advantage. In the presidential election of 1876, the Republican candidate Rutherford B. Hayes defeated his Democratic opponent, Samuel Tilden, by a single electoral vote, the narrowest electoral vote margin in American history. (The election was settled in controversial fashion by a specially appointed commission that awarded twenty disputed electoral votes to Hayes.) Hayes managed to eke out victories in all three Pacific coast states, but the difference between him and Tilden was vanishingly small—several thousand votes in all.

Party supremacy, it seemed increasingly clear, hinged on the Chinese question. Democratic politicians had long been ascendant in the West, having adapted easily to the race-baiting tactics needed to court anti-Chinese voters. (The one dissenting constituency within the party were southern planters, some of whom still hoped that Chinese workers could be the solution to their labor problems after the end of slavery.) A beleaguered Republican Party, consumed by internal dissension and in search of a new rationale after the failure of Reconstruction, began to fall under the thrall of the politics of racial division as well. The Senate debate in early 1879 over the "Fifteen Passenger bill," which limited the number of Chinese arrivals in ocean vessels, demonstrated the degree to which a new vanguard in the party had shed its former commitment to equal rights.

The most critical voice in favor of the legislation was not a senator from the Pacific coast but a forty-nine-year-old Maine Republican, James Blaine, who openly pined for the presidency. Blaine, a heavyset man with a thick neck and round torso, had been the Speaker of the House for six years and was serving his first term in the Senate. He had come close to securing the Republican nomination in 1876 and was one of the frontrunners for the 1880 election. Blaine saw the debate over the Fifteen Passenger bill as his opportunity to become the shrillest voice of all against the heathen Chinese.

In the Senate chamber, on February 14, 1879, Blaine stood beside his desk, one hand resting on some law books; he wore a black frock coat, with a triangle of white from his shirtfront showing. He began speaking without notes. He moved methodically through his argument, contending that China had already abrogated the Burlingame Treaty by failing to take steps to halt migration to the United States by people working under contracts of involuntary servitude—the coolie trope, again—and that it was impractical for the United States to absorb an entire class of people who had been excluded from citizenship and would "forever remain political and social pariahs in a great free Government." He framed the issue of Chinese immigration in apocalyptic terms. "The question lies in my mind thus: either the Anglo-Saxon race will possess the Pacific slope or Mongolians will possess it," he said. "You give them the start today, with the keen thrust of necessity behind them, and with the ease of transportation before them, with the inducements to come, while we are filling up the other portions of the continent, and it is entirely inevitable if not demonstrable that they will occupy that great space of country between the Sierras and the Pacific coast." He asserted that Chinese immigration was fundamentally different from the migration from Europe. "The immigrants that come to us from all portions of the British Isles, from Germany, from Sweden, from Norway, from Denmark, from France, from Spain, from Italy, come here with the idea of the family as much engraven on their minds and in their customs and in their habits as we have it," he said. "The Asiatic cannot go on with our population and make a homogeneous element."

While Blaine spoke, his counterpart from Maine, Hannibal Hamlin, the chamber's elder statesman at the age of sixty-nine and Lincoln's first vice president, sat impassively by his side, clasping his hands and studying his fingers. Hamlin, his hair nearly white and his shoulders stooped, was known in Washington for ambling about town in winter without an overcoat. Several years earlier, he'd collapsed in the Senate cloakroom, after a bout of vertigo. He rarely spoke in the Senate chamber and was not known for his oratory, but he seemed bemused now by his younger colleague's vehemence. When the junior senator asked rhetorically whether any senators wanted the Pacific coast states to be "overridden" by the Chinese population, Hamlin interrupted. "If my colleague wants an answer, I will give him one for myself," he said. "I do," Blaine said. Hamlin told Blaine his fears were overblown. "When the sky falls we shall catch larks," he said. "That is an old adage." Hamlin, who was the chairman of the Foreign Relations Committee, characterized himself as "indifferent" to any threat posed by Chinese immigration, pointing out that it only amounted to a few thousand a year. "Treat them, I will not say like pagans, because Confucius would shame us if we go to his counsel—treat them like Christians, and they will become good American citizens," he said, drawing applause from the galleries.

Hamlin's remarks on the Chinese would turn out to be a kind of parting address to the Senate, his final significant speech before his retirement from the chamber the following year. He seemed conscious of the legacy he was leaving behind. Hamlin had witnessed firsthand the great upheaval of the nineteenth century over race. Both of his sons had been generals in the Union army, and he had personally pushed Lincoln to emancipate enslaved Black Americans. He recognized the threshold the country was about to cross, closing off immigration to an entire class of people on the basis of race. "Where shall it end?" he asked. "Shall it apply to the lazzaroni that swarm the coasts of the Mediterranean, and shall they be excluded from our country and our government? Shall it next enter the theological arena, and shall the Catholic be told that he shall not come here to breathe the free air of this Republic? I know not where it may end." Hamlin declared that the country's deepest principles were at stake. His colleagues were rushing to enact legislation that he predicted would one day be "read with amazement and astonishment."

The following day, Hamlin continued his address, with one of his adult sons by his side. He had an almost embarrassed air, as he rose in a wrinkled black suit, his white dress shirt folded over on his chest. He had asked for the debate on the bill to be extended so he could conclude his remarks. He seemed to be groping for a compromise and pointed out that, during the last session of Congress, he had personally drafted a resolution recommending that the clause on unrestricted emigration in the Burlingame Treaty be modified. He argued that this was the proper approach to the Chinese question, entrusting the matter to the executive branch. Nevertheless, he swung back to lauding the contributions the Chinese had made to America. "I insist that this labor in California of Chinese has advanced that state a century beyond where she would now be had she been deprived of it," he said. Hamlin argued that "the intelligent, the cool, the deliberate, and the Christian portion" of the population would agree that Chinese labor had built their railroads, reclaimed marshlands, and added "uncounted millions of wealth." The elderly senator urged a spirit of hospitality, consonant with the nation's highest ideals, and called his vote against the Fifteen Passenger bill a "last legacy to my children that they may esteem it the brightest act of my life."

Despite Hamlin's plea, the measure passed easily, backed by most of the Democrats in the chamber, along with about half of the Republicans. The legislation awaited the signature of President Hayes. Letters and telegrams on both sides of the issue poured into the White House. Officers of the Supreme Order of Caucasians of the Pacific Coast demanded that the president sign the measure to "save our people." The editor of the *San Francisco Morning Call* warned of a "calamity" if the Chinese question remained unresolved. The faculty at Yale College, led by Yung Wing's former professor Noah Porter, cited the success of the Chinese Educational Mission and urged a veto.

Another notable opponent was the legendary abolitionist William Lloyd Garrison. He castigated Blaine in a pair of letters published by the *New York Tribune,* in February 1879, just three months before his death at the age of seventy-three. Garrison characterized the effort to exclude the Chinese as part of the same "hateful spirit of caste" that he had fought against for a half century. "The Chinese are our fellow-men, and are entitled to every consideration that our common humanity may justly claim," he wrote. Garrison himself had received a two-page handwritten letter, in English, from a Chinese merchant in Boston, Wong Ar Chong, about the legislation. "In your Declaration of Independence it is asserted that all men are born free and equal, and it is understood by the civilized world that the United States of America is a free country, but I fear there is a backward step being taken by the government," Wong wrote. "I claim for my countrymen the right to come to this country as long as other foreigners do. If they make themselves a nuisance, establish proper health laws and enforce them, and if they don't like them let them go back home again, but they must conform to American ideas of law and order if they wish to stay. That is my idea, but you cannot bring it about by such a law as is now awaiting the President's signature. You must do to others as you would have them do to you if you wish to gain their confidence."

A rare public voice of dissent from the Chinese community came from Moy Jin Kee, the former cook for Leland and Jane Stanford. In 1878, Moy had made his way to New York, joining a younger brother,

Jin Fuey, and started working as an assistant to Henry Parke, a dealer of Chinese and Japanese goods. Moy became a Christian and began preaching at various churches in the city. He would soon establish a mission school in the Chinese quarter. A *Tribune* reporter sought him out to ask him about the legislation. "We expected more from this country than any other, because it was a 'nation of freemen,' but we have got less," Moy said. "The treatment we have received here has been shameful; and if the good people of the United States could only realize how we have been hunted and hounded about, our property taken from us by force, and our poor homes burned over our heads, and we stoned and driven from place to place, subject to the gibes of every loafer of an 'Irish fellow-citizen,' I am sure we would not have been so misrepresented by Mr. Blaine and others, and we would find greater protection than we now receive. The Chinamen are patient, and they bear a great deal; but they cannot bear everything."

President Hayes ultimately vetoed the measure but not because he had any quibbles with its aim of restricting Chinese immigration. Instead, Hayes was concerned that the legislation violated the United States' obligations under the Burlingame Treaty. In his veto message, Hayes went to great lengths to explain that abrogating a treaty was a serious step that should only be undertaken under extreme circumstances. But he made clear that he considered the "very grave discontents of the people of the Pacific states" to be a matter deserving "the most serious attention." In his private diary, he wrote that he believed that other measures should be used to deter Chinese emigration. "No doubt a population without women—without wives and mothers—that can't assimilate with us, that underbids our laborers, must be hateful," he wrote. "It should be made certain by proper methods that such an invasion cannot permanently override our people. It cannot safely be admitted into the bosom of our American society." Even the ostensible allies of the Chinese were moving inexorably towards a future in which they would be excluded from America.

Blaine entered the 1880 election campaign as one of the favorites, along with former president Ulysses S. Grant, who had just returned from a world tour that included stops in several Chinese cities and a visit to San Francisco's Chinatown. Both parties' platforms included declarations about ending Chinese emigration. But, because the Republican Party was maneuvering to shore up its position among the laboring classes, its platform dwelled on the issue at greater length. The party called unrestricted immigration from China a matter of "grave concernment," something that should be dealt with by "just, humane and reasonable laws and treaties." The Hayes administration was preparing to send a commission, led by James B. Angell, who had been newly appointed as the United States minister to China, to renegotiate the Burlingame Treaty and amend the provisions that promised Chinese citizens the right to free immigration and travel in the United States. The political intent behind the mission was unmistakable.

On the evening of June 5, 1880, the fourth day of the Republican convention in Chicago, the heat was oppressive under the iron and glass roof of the Interstate Exposition Building, the enormous hall where ten thousand Republicans had gathered to witness the beginning of the selection process. Frank Pixley, the staunchly anti-Chinese former attorney general of California, seconded Blaine's nomination and announced that the Maine senator had the support of all the delegates from the territories of Washington, Idaho, and Arizona, as well as the states of Oregon, Nevada, and California, "composing, together, the magnificent Empire of the Pacific."

The convention paused for a day and reassembled on Monday morning, June 7. After a brief opening prayer, balloting commenced. All day, the 756 delegates went back and forth, but neither Blaine nor Grant was able to reach the 379 votes needed to secure the nomination. Deliberations resumed the following morning, but the delegates were deadlocked. Finally, on the thirty-fourth ballot, a group of Blaine supporters from Wisconsin decided to switch their votes to a new candidate: the Ohio congressman, James A. Garfield. A murmur of surprise went through the hall. Garfield was a member of the Ohio delegation and seemed as shocked as anyone. He rose to question the validity of the votes for him and insisted he was not interested in being a candidate. After two more ballots, however, the nomination was his, with most of Blaine's supporters throwing their support behind him. The nominee sat motionless, with his white delegate badge affixed to his coat, as the cheers of the convention hall washed over him.

Several weeks later, Garfield wrote to Blaine, a close friend, to ask him to draft language on the Chinese question for his letter formally accepting the Republican nomination. "You know the platform is pretty full on that subject—but our Pacific coast friends are anxious, and this side the mountains are suspicious," he wrote. "Please write such a paragraph as you would use." Garfield knew he was vulnerable on the subject. In the House, he had voted against the Fifteen Passenger bill, noting in his diary at the time that he believed "Senator Blaine has made a great mistake in his advocacy of it."

Blaine responded to Garfield's letter several days later, reminding him that the "three Pacific states will be largely, if not entirely, controlled by it." He urged Garfield to make clear that "a servile class—assimilating in all its conditions of labor to chattel slavery—must be excluded from free immigration" but suggested that it would be better for Garfield to use his own language. Garfield also consulted another confidant, William Evarts, the secretary of state. Evarts sent back a detailed response arguing that Chinese immigration "partakes too much of the nature of invasion not to be looked upon with solicitude," but he emphasized the need to wait for the outcome of the treaty negotiations that were expected to take place that summer.

In his acceptance letter, Garfield took pains to explain that the United States had long had a tradition of offering the "widest hospitality to emigrants who seek our shores for new and happier homes" and were intent on assimilating and becoming "an undistinguishable part of our population." The Chinese population in America bore little resemblance to these previous new arrivals, he asserted. "It is too much like an importation to be welcomed without restriction; too much like an invasion to be looked upon without solicitude," Garfield wrote, adopting Evarts's language. Blaine's influence was evident as well. Garfield added: "We cannot consent to allow any form of servile labor to be introduced among us, under the guise of immigration."

.   .   .

The messaging of the Republican National Committee initially focused on the tried-and-true "bloody shirt" strategy of the post–Civil War era, invoking the specter of the Rebellion and accusing the Democratic candidate, Winfield Hancock, of being an avatar of the rebel cause, even though he had been a general in the Union army and a hero of the Battle of Gettysburg. After a shocking Democratic victory in the Maine governor's race on September 13, Garfield and Republican officials switched to emphasizing the issue of tariffs and protecting American manufacturers and workers' wages. But Garfield's potential weakness on the issue of Chinese immigration—and its capacity to incite voters—would prove to be an irresistible target for his Democratic opponents. They were aided by an unexpected turn of events, which would prove incendiary in the campaign's final days.

On October 18, two weeks before Election Day, Joseph Hart, the proprietor of an obscure penny newspaper in New York City that called itself *Truth,* found an envelope on his desk. Inside was a letter, marked "personal and confidential," on the stationery of the House of Representatives. It was dated January 23, 1880, and addressed to one "H.L. Morey," of the "Employers' Union, Lynn, Mass." In neat cursive handwriting, the letter read as follows:

Dear Sir:

Yours in relation to the Chinese problem came duly to hand. I take it that the question of employees is only a question of private and corporate economy, and individuals or companies have the right to buy labor where they can get it cheapest.

We have a treaty with the Chinese Government which should be religiously kept until its provisions are abrogated by the action of the general Government, and I am not prepared to say that it should be abrogated until our great manufacturing and corporate interests are conserved in the matter of labor.

Very truly yours,
J.A. GARFIELD

Hart and two of his colleagues studied the letter, recognizing instantly the implications for the purported signer. The letter demonstrated Garfield's obeisance to corporate interests and his lack of concern for the laboring classes. The newspaper quickly published a teaser in the next morning's edition, promising to "produce positive evidence" that Garfield is a "pronounced advocate of Chinese cheap labor."

Hart later testified that he had compared the letter to another one from Garfield that the newspaper had previously published and consulted with officials at the Democratic National Committee headquarters, satisfying himself the letter was authentic. The following day, under the headline "Garfield's Death Warrant," the newspaper published the text of the entire letter, accompanied by the attestation that it was a "true copy" and that the newspaper was in possession of the original. The article reported that the letter had been mailed by Garfield to Henry L. Morey, "a prominent member of the Employers' Union at Lynn, Mass.," who had recently died. The letter had been found among his effects.

The letter, transmitted by telegraph, appeared in newspapers across the country. Democratic officials sent it to every state committee and encouraged them to disseminate it. In New York City, the *Truth* followed its scoop by printing, a day later, a facsimile copy of the letter. The newspaper furnished the Democratic National Committee with a copy of the letter as well. Party officials printed some two hundred thousand copies and mailed them all over the country; the largest shipment, about a hundred thousand copies, went to California. They also photographed the letter and produced several thousand electroplates, which were forwarded to Democratic papers across the country. They even translated the letter into multiple languages. Democratic workers posted themselves outside of factory gates with the letter and handed out copies to children leaving school. Suddenly, in the closing stages of a previously sedate presidential campaign, the Chinese question was everywhere.

Garfield was at his home in Mentor, Ohio, when he first learned about the letter from a telegram sent by James Simonton, the general manager of the Associated Press and a longtime newspaper proprietor in San Francisco, asking if it was genuine. Garfield was initially cautious and had Simonton wire him the text of the letter. After reviewing it, Garfield assured him that the correspondence was a forgery. The candidate sensed that something was amiss and wrote in his diary that the Democrats might be playing a dirty trick to "seek by this means to take the Pacific Coast."

The following day, a copy of the *Truth* arrived, but Garfield was still slow to understand its gravity. "I can hardly believe a rational and just-minded public would be influenced by such a wicked device," he wrote in his diary. Garfield dispatched one of his assistants by train to Washington to look through his office files that were carefully indexed. That evening, he sent a telegram to Marshall Jewell, the Republican National Committee chairman, authorizing him to denounce the letter as a forgery but not to issue any statement from Garfield himself. "I still hope to get through the campaign without appearing in my own defense against any of the charges," he wrote in his diary.

On the morning of October 23, three days after the publication of the letter in the *Truth*, a lithographic copy of the letter arrived at Garfield's home. Finally, able to study the handwriting firsthand, Garfield no longer harbored any doubts. He described it as a "manifestly bungling attempt to copy my hand and signature" and directed Jewell to release his telegram from the night before. On October 27, Kenward Philp, a reporter from the *Truth*, was arrested for planting the letter and charged with criminal libel. (The charges against him were later dropped, after prosecutors concluded the evidence against him was inconclusive.) But Hancock partisans continued their denunciations. Escalating rhetoric against the Chinese consumed the campaign's final days. Democrats held angry, torchlit rallies; Republicans labored to make the case that their candidate would not tolerate "cheap Chinese labor." Garfield remained sanguine. "We shall see whether this last device of a desperate party will avail them before the people," Garfield wrote. "It may lose us the Pacific States, and possibly some others, but I do not think it can turn the current that now sweeps so strongly in our favor."

As it would turn out, there would be another late development in the election related to anti-Chinese agitation. In Denver, an anti-Chinese demonstration that doubled as a Democratic rally took place on Saturday evening, October 30, in the downtown area. Participants issued a resolution warning of the "Chinese flocking to our young state" and urging workingmen to vote for Hancock, so they could avoid the "ruin that has overtaken California." The next day, a fracas at a saloon involving two Chinese men exploded into an eight-hour-long orgy of violence, in which white mobs, chanting pro-Hancock slogans, hunted down Chinese residents, rampaged through the red-light district in the city's Chinatown, and pillaged Chinese laundries and stores. Some three thousand people thronged the streets, screaming "Kill the Chinese! Kill the damned heathens!" There were continuous whoops for Hancock. A group of rioters dragged Look Young, a twenty-eight-year-old laundryman and a recent arrival in Denver, into the street by a rope around his neck. They cut off his queue and beat him mercilessly, even as a few bystanders tried to protect him. He was finally taken by wagon to a doctor's office, where three doctors treated him. He had a gash on his forehead, and his face was badly swollen; many of his teeth were broken. He had bruises all over his body, as well as strangulation marks around his neck. His feet and hands were cold, and he was drenched in sweat. After an hour and a half, he died. By the time the violence had subsided, nearly every Chinese residence in the city was destroyed. "Chinatown no longer exists," the *Rocky Mountain News* reported, adding that the "dens of infamy" were all in ruins. "Washee, washee is all cleaned out in Denver."

On Election Day, November 2, more than 78 percent of eligible voters cast ballots, which remains among the highest participation rates for a presidential election in American history. By three o'clock in the morning on November 3, Garfield knew he'd swept the northern states, with only New Jersey and the Pacific states still in doubt. The next day, fifty telegrams of congratulations were waiting for Garfield at breakfast; more than five hundred letters arrived throughout the day. His victory in the Electoral College was decisive, but his edge in the popular vote turned out to be less than two thousand votes. Among Garfield's supporters was one Chinese American voter in the fifth ward of Grand Rapids, Michigan, whose support for the Republican candidate was widely reported in the local press: Wong Chin Foo.

For all of Garfield's assurances to voters on the Pacific coast that he would take steps to restrict Chinese immigration, Hancock carried both California and Nevada, important breakthroughs for his party. Several days after the election, as congratulatory letters continued to arrive at Garfield's home in Ohio, Republicans received another boost in the form of a brief, coded telegram from Beijing, sent to the State

Department. The diplomatic delegation that had been dispatched over the summer reported momentous news: "Burlingame treaty modified. China consents United States at discretion regulate, limit, suspend immigration Chinese laborers." The negotiations had been contentious. Early on, a Chinese commissioner had challenged the Americans: "Is it not in accordance with the fundamental principles of your great nation to admit people from all lands who seek asylum on your shores?" Angell, the head of the American delegation, had admitted that it was. But principles could be cast aside.

CHAPTER 12

Beyond Debate

On a frigid February day in 1881, a cluster of Chinese men marched into the criminal courthouse in Chicago. Leading the way was Wong Chin Foo, who had recently returned to Chicago and cut off his queue. He was there as a translator for the other men. Their destination was the office of John Stephens, the clerk of the court. Wong explained to Stephens that his companions—all members of the Moy clan, which had a sizable presence among the nearly two hundred Chinese residents of Chicago—were interested in becoming citizens. He rendered their names for the court as Moy Hong Kee, Moy Yee, and Moy Sam.

The leader of the Moys in the city was Moy Dong Chow, who had arrived in Chicago several years earlier. At the time, the handful of Chinese in the city mostly operated laundries. Moy bought a store at the corner of Clark and Madison and began selling dry goods. He called his new establishment Hip Lung Yee Kee and Company. He was soon urging others he knew in San Francisco, as well as members of his family clan in China, to join him. By 1878, several dozen in Moy's circle had settled in the city. They found the city's residents to be generally welcoming and the atmosphere far more tolerable than that of the Pacific coast. "They never asked me whether or not I ate rats and snakes," Moy later said. "Chicagoans found us a peculiar people, to be sure, but they liked to mix with us." Moy felt like he had found a place he could call home. "I was destined not to return to my fatherland, I thought."

Among the Moys who went to the courthouse that day, Hong Kee had only recently arrived in the country, so he was not yet eligible for naturalization. With Wong's assistance, he filed a formal declaration renouncing his allegiance to China and pledging his intention to become a loyal U.S. citizen, the first step to naturalization. This was relatively straightforward, as there was no law against making such a declaration. The situation for the two others, who had both been in the country for more than ten years, was very different. Wong escorted the men into the courtroom, as others stopped to stare. With Wong interpreting, Judge Thomas A. Moran conducted an examination of the men. They both testified that they had come to the United States at the age of sixteen. When asked for their impressions of the country, one man said he preferred it to China; the other said he "liked America's peculiarities very much," eliciting laughter in the courtroom. Moran said he needed time to research the legalities and took the matter under advisement, asking the men to return in about a week. The issue was not a new one in the city. Several years earlier, a judge had granted naturalization papers to two Chinese residents. In the spring of 1880, in Fond du Lac, Wisconsin, a village about 150 miles north of Chicago, a Chinese man in Western attire named Sing Yan had surprised poll workers when he appeared at a municipal election with his naturalization papers to vote. Chinese men had, in fact, managed to become naturalized in states across the country.

In his decision, issued a week and a half later, Judge Moran recalled the debate on the floor of the Senate in 1870, after Charles Sumner, the Massachusetts Republican, tried to strike the word "white" from the naturalization laws; many had feared that the privilege would then be granted to Chinese immigrants. Moran pointed to an 1878 ruling, by Lorenzo Sawyer, a California circuit court judge, involving the citizenship petition of a Chinese immigrant named Ah Yup. In his decision, Sawyer wrote that "a native of China, of the Mongolian race, is not a white person within the meaning of congress." There had apparently been a period of ambiguity after Congress enacted the statute granting the privilege of naturalization to "aliens of African nativity and to persons of African descent," because the revisers of the statute had inadvertently left out of the law the word "white," an omission that was fixed in 1875. Moran suggested that this might explain how other Chinese immigrants had managed to obtain their citizenship papers, but the judge said he had no choice but to deny the application from Moy Sam and Moy Yee. There is no record of the Moys' response.

The Chinese population in Chicago continued to grow. Moy Dong Chow moved his store to 323 South Clark Street, the heart of the Chinese quarter, and Hip Lung became a vital hub for the community. As new Chinese arrivals continued to settle in the city, Moy grew concerned that their increasingly visible presence could make them a target, just as they had been on the West Coast. "We began to worry about it," he said.

Slowly but surely, Chinese immigrants were beginning to establish themselves in cities beyond the Pacific coast. It was frequently bigotry and violence that drove them east. They came mostly by train but sometimes even on foot. The largest community—by some estimates, numbering nearly two thousand people—took up residence in New York City. One morning, in March 1880, a cross-country train arrived in Jersey City carrying about thirty Chinese men from San Francisco, by way of Chicago. They were clad in their native dress—loose, flowing trousers and blouses, along with wooden-soled slippers. Their possessions were contained in a dozen canvas bags and a solitary carpet bag, which were sent onward to locations in the Chinese quarter, on the southern end of Mott Street in Manhattan. Several of the new arrivals had operated laundries on the West Coast; others were cigar makers and bootmakers. One traveler, a laundryman identified as Wah Ling, told a reporter through an interpreter that San Francisco was "no good place for Chinaman any more." Chinese were getting "pounded with stones" by boys on the street. Ticket prices on the Central Pacific Railroad had been unusually low—$35—so Wah Ling had decided to come east, in hopes of establishing his own shop.

Two days later, the reporter ventured into Chinatown, in search of further evidence of a Chinese influx. He encountered James Baptiste, a Portuguese Chinese man from Macau who had lived in America for nearly two decades. Baptiste, a member of the Roman Catholic Transfiguration Church, spoke fluent English. He told the reporter that "as long as the Kearney agitation is kept up in the West," his countrymen would continue to come, but he doubted that it would become a flood. A different reporter visited a general store on Mott Street operated by Wo Kee, a thirty-four-year-old merchant from Hong Kong. Wo Kee had first opened a store on Mott Street in the early 1870s and was at the time the only Chinese storekeeper in the impoverished, crime-ridden neighborhood. He struggled to turn a profit and almost closed his shop. A Chinese quarter, however, gradually took root around his establishment and business picked up enough for him to buy an entire building at 8 Mott Street, where he moved his store. Wo Kee often greeted new Chinese arrivals in New York and served as a postmaster and hotelkeeper for them, as well as an interlocutor with Westerners. The cramped front parlor of Wo Kee's store was filled with pasteboard boxes bursting with dried roots, herbs, seeds, and other Chinese medicines. There were incense sticks and bracelets; ducks that had been split, flattened, and baked; opium and pipes for smoking. From behind a narrow counter, Wo Kee performed sums with an abacus and recorded transactions in an account book with a calligraphy brush. He kept a pot of tea on a small table near the window, always ready to entertain visitors. The reporter spoke with Quong Lee, a clerk, who told him that many of the new arrivals were skilled workmen who demanded high wages. "We mean to do the best work of which we are capable and to command respect by being well paid for it," he said. He chastised Americans for their animosity towards Chinese residents. "You call your United States a free country, but there are a great many in it who do not like it to be free at all," he said. "Why are they not stopped in their assaults upon the Chinese? We only ask to be allowed to live peaceably and labor honestly. We are not robbers, thieves, drunkards, or paupers, but honest, industrious men. We are invited here by the same invitation upon which the Germans, the Irish, the Italians, and other foreigners come here." Quong Lee revealed that he had been an American citizen for thirteen years. "Consider us without prejudice, and you will have to admit that in all that goes to make good citizens, we are worthy of better regard than is shown to us," he said.

In the city, among the new arrivals was a twenty-one-year-old laundryman named Lee Teep, along with his brother, Lee Leep. The Reformed Presbyterian Church, on West 23rd Street, hosted a Sunday school for Chinese immigrants. In the fall of 1880, Lee Teep started attending the classes. He seldom missed a week. His Sunday school teacher, a young woman he knew as "Miss Smith," also started teaching him the English alphabet. On Sunday afternoon, April 24, 1881, he went to class and then to dinner with his cousin, Kwong Tong, and another laundryman, Ah Sin, who were both new to the city as well. The three men visited a store on Mott Street and ventured back uptown by streetcar. They got off on Spring Street and were walking east towards Marion Street when they encountered a group of four young white men. One of them struck Lee Teep in the head, knocking his hat off. "What did you hit me for," Lee Teep asked, as he bent to pick it back up. The man, who had a pimple on his cheek, pulled out a knife and stabbed Lee Teep in the chest, abdomen, and leg. The white men fled. Lee Teep's companions helped him walk several blocks to a laundry belonging to some friends. There, they helped Lee Teep remove his clothing and saw that he was badly hurt. Kwong Tong rushed to a nearby police station, and an ambulance ferried Lee Teep to St. Vincent's hospital. Several days later, Kwong Tong accompanied a detective on a canvas of Spring Street, when he spotted a boyish-looking man he believed to be his cousin's assailant, sitting on a stoop. He was an express wagon driver named John Corcoran. As the pair approached, Corcoran tried to flee but was caught several blocks away. He cried out to his friends: "Don't say anything up at the house." The next day, the police brought him to St. Vincent's, where Lee Teep identified him from his hospital bed. Several days later, Lee Teep died from his wounds, and Corcoran was charged with first-degree murder.

About thirty Chinese mourners attended Lee Teep's funeral at Reformed Presbyterian Church. They gathered at the front of the sanctuary; the others in attendance were mostly female congregants. Lee Teep's body lay in a plain black coffin; he was dressed in a blue coat; his hat lay across his chest; a white silk handkerchief was tied around his neck. A minister opened the proceedings by reading from the book of Hebrews: "Be not forgetful to entertain strangers: for thereby some have entertained angels unawares."

The speakers told the story of Lee Teep's brief residence in New York City and his untimely death. Lee Teep's Sunday school teacher,

Miss Smith, had visited him in the hospital. He told her that he was going home to "our father who art in heaven" and had recited the Lord's Prayer with him. He seemed unafraid. "These men need friends," the Rev. David Gregg, the church's pastor, said. "Let us be their friends, for Christ's sake." Afterward, a funeral cortege made its way through the city's streets to the Hudson River ferry, which transported the mourners to Weehawken. At the cemetery, a floral cross and bouquet of flowers were placed atop the grave. Kwong Tong lit a small wax candle and ignited strips of brown paper and a package of firecrackers, part of the traditional Chinese practice of keeping the devil away.

Corcoran's trial was held in the Court of General Sessions, a three-story brick building on Chambers Street. Fred K. Smith, the county recorder, postponed the start of the proceedings several times, after prosecutors requested more time to gather evidence. The trial finally opened at the end of June, before a jury of twelve men. It marked the first time in the history of New York County that a white man was being tried for the murder of a Chinese immigrant. Chinese residents crowded the courtroom. The community had raised $2,000 to help with the prosecution of the case. James Baptiste, the Portuguese Chinese merchant, served as a courtroom interpreter. The Chinese legation in the United States had also paid for a private lawyer to assist William C. Beecher, the assistant district attorney, who was the son of the abolitionist Henry Ward Beecher. Private detectives from the Pinkerton agency were also enlisted. Corcoran was represented by Horace Russell, a former judge and prosecutor, and another lawyer. Corcoran's father, a longtime tailor at Devlin & Co., a popular men's clothing store, sat in a corner of the gallery behind him, joined sometimes by John's sisters and his little brother.

At the trial, Lee Teep's friends, Kwong Tong and Ah Sin, both testified, as did Lee Leep, the victim's brother. The defense presented several witnesses who insisted that Corcoran was elsewhere when the murder took place. In his closing statement, Russell was emotional, breaking down in tears at times. He insisted that the case had nothing to do with animosity towards Chinese immigrants. "This is not, let me say, a case of the Irish against the Chinese," Russell said, even though he admitted that he was personally "opposed to giving our heritage over to the heathen." Russell argued that the Chinese eyewitnesses must have been mistaken in their identification of Corcoran, pointing out they were laundrymen. "These are not brain sharpening occupations," he said. The jury deliberated for thirty minutes and returned a verdict of not guilty.

The most pressing priority for advocates of Chinese exclusion was the ratification of the treaty revisions with China. On May 4, 1881, the U.S. Senate met in executive session to consider the agreement negotiated by James Angell and his diplomatic mission in Beijing. California's newly elected senator, John Franklin Miller, introduced the motion. Mass meetings had been taking place all week in California—in Vallejo, Marysville, and San Francisco—denouncing Chinese immigration as "an evil of great magnitude" and calling on the Senate to act without delay on the diplomatic agreement. Miller made the case to his Senate colleagues that the Angell commission could have negotiated further concessions but that the new agreement should be ratified so that new legislation restricting Chinese immigration could advance without a presidential veto.

Miller was deeply familiar with the Chinese question. During California's constitutional convention, he had served as chairman of the Committee on Chinese. He had first traveled to California in 1853 as a young lawyer from Indiana, but returned home and served as a colonel in the 29th Indiana Infantry Regiment, which fought on behalf of the Union during the Civil War. He was twice wounded in battle, the second time nearly fatally, when a musket ball entered his left eye. He recovered and was promoted to brigadier general. In 1865, he resigned from the army and moved with his family to California. He built a successful company that traded in seal furs and owned a sprawling ranch in Napa Valley that grew grapes. He steadfastly refused to employ Chinese laborers in his businesses. In the Senate, he settled into his assigned desk on the far left of the Republican side of the chamber. His neighbor, albeit only for a few days, was Senator Blaine of Maine, who would soon be appointed secretary of state in the Garfield administration. Miller, a dignified figure who carried himself with an athletic bearing, was not an avid speechmaker. In the Senate, he preferred to mostly work in the background. But he would become the leading anti-Chinese voice in the Senate.

The debate over the treaty proposal took only a few hours, over the course of two days. One of the few dissenting voices was Massachusetts senator George Frisbie Hoar, a descendant of Roger Sherman, one of the signers of the Declaration of Independence. Hoar was fifty-five years old, his hair prematurely white, his features round. He had studied law at Harvard, where he first developed an interest in politics. In 1852, at the age of twenty-six, he was elected to the state legislature in Massachusetts as a bitter opponent of slavery. He ascended to the United States House of Representatives in 1869 as a protégé of the Radical Republican firebrand, Charles Sumner, and joined the Senate less than a decade later. Hoar's moral certitude evoked his Puritan ancestors. He was a vigorous advocate of the rights of formerly enslaved Black Americans and an early champion of women's suffrage. Opposing the treaty proposal, Hoar argued that its treatment of the Chinese violated the "brotherhood of man." The Angell Treaty, as it would come to be known, passed nearly unanimously.

President Garfield never got a chance to fulfill his campaign promise to restrict Chinese immigration. At twenty minutes past nine in the morning, on July 2, 1881, Garfield and Blaine, his secretary of state, strode into the Baltimore & Potomac railroad station in Washington together. Garfield had been in office for four months and was planning to travel with his wife and some friends to Long Branch, an oceanside village in New Jersey, where the couple had a vacation cottage. Charles Guiteau, a forty-one-year-old, mentally unstable lawyer, was waiting for him inside a passenger waiting area. Guiteau, who had been plotting to assassinate the president for weeks, approached Garfield from behind and shot him in the back. Garfield survived and lingered for two months, in terrible agony.

Late in the evening, on September 19, 1881, the doorbell rang at the New York City home of Garfield's vice president, Chester A. Arthur. A newspaper reporter informed him that the president had died. "It cannot be true," Arthur said. The vice president, known to his friends as "Chet," was a portly, genial man with refined tastes, whose carefully groomed walrus mustache blended into his thick sideburns. He had risen through the ranks of the Republican Party's machinery in New York and became the collector of tolls for the Port of New York, a lucrative position, only to be ousted over allegations of corruption and mismanagement. He remained a powerful party boss in New York, however, and was added to the Republican ticket at the convention as a way of appeasing the so-called Stalwart faction of the party, made up of supporters of former President Grant. His ascension to the presidency was an improbable political story. The Chinese question was now Arthur's problem to contend with.

On February 27, a memorial service for Garfield was held at the Capitol. Among the notables who crowded into the House gallery were four members of the Chinese legation, dressed in formal regalia. Blaine delivered a soaring remembrance of his friend, alluding only obliquely to the tumult in the closing days of the campaign. "Under it all he was calm and strong and confident; never lost his self-possession, did no unwise act, spoke no hasty or ill-considered word," Blaine said. "The great mass of these unjust imputations passed unnoticed, and with the general debris of the campaign fell into oblivion."

The following afternoon, Senator Miller opened the debate on restricting Chinese immigration. As Miller spoke, his colleagues in the chamber listened intently; a few Democratic senators made their way to the Republican side to make sure they could hear Miller's remarks. In the gallery, several dignitaries from China happened to be present. It seems likely that this was the same group that had attended Garfield's memorial service. They were interested in witnessing Congress in session, but they exited after it became clear what was being debated. Miller's proposed legislation, Senate bill 71, had an innocuous title: "A bill to enforce treaty stipulations relating to Chinese." But its effect was sweeping, barring new Chinese laborers from entering the country for twenty years. (Miller's proposal granted an exception for Chinese laborers who had arrived in the country before the effective date of the Angell Treaty on November 17, 1880.) Violators faced a fine of $100 and imprisonment for up to a year. The Chinese who were still eligible for entry, such as merchants, teachers, and students, as required under the Angell Treaty, would have to obtain a certificate issued by the Chinese government that provided a litany of information, including their residence in the United States, employment, height, physical marks, and other "peculiarities" by which they might be identified. Laborers residing in the country who hoped to leave and return would have to register with the collector of customs at their departure port and then obtain a certificate that attested to their right to reentry. The measure also explicitly prohibited courts from admitting Chinese to citizenship.

Miller began by arguing there was little to debate. "The question of Chinese restriction has passed the stage of argument," he said. He pointed out that both parties' platforms in the election of 1880 recommended that limits be imposed on Chinese immigration. He cited Garfield's words in his acceptance speech, as well as his forceful denunciation of the Morey letter. Seldom in the country's history, Miller argued, had there been such "perfect unanimity" of the two major parties on a government policy. At the heart of his nearly two-hour-long address were his dire warnings of what would transpire if Chinese immigration was allowed to continue unchecked. Miller had an elaborate theory of racial conflict over the course of human history. He offered a series of rhetorical questions: "If we continue to permit the introduction of this strange people, with their peculiar civilization, until they form a considerable part of our population, what is to be the effect upon the American people and Anglo-Saxon civilization? Can these two civilizations endure, side by side, as two distinct and hostile forces? Is American civilization as unimpressible as Chinese civilization? When the end comes for one or the other, which will be found to have survived? Can they meet halfway, and so merge in a mongrel race, half Chinese and half Caucasian, as to produce a civilization half-pagan, half-Christian, semi-Oriental, altogether mixed, and very bad?" Miller's argument was that assimilation was impossible. "Like the mixing of oil and water, neither will absorb the other," he said. He characterized the Chinese as "invaders." The Chinese might seem "inert and pusillanimous," but they were in reality "the most successful conquerors the world has ever known."

He depicted Chinese immigrants as automatons, products of "long training and a heredity which is stamped upon them and ground into them through centuries of time." According to Miller, the result was a class of people who were "machine-like," immune to heat or cold, "wiry, sinewy, with muscles of iron; they are automatic engines of flesh and blood." The white man stood no chance in the face of this competition, Miller reasoned, casting restrictions on Chinese immigration as a matter of a civilization's right to self-preservation.

Miller dismissed objections rooted in the party's historic defense of equal rights, making the case that times had changed. "I believe that the national safety demands an intelligent discrimination, and that it is not only just and wise but human to keep the bad sorts out," he said. "The time for a judicious sifting process has come, and I would sift out the Chinese laborers first; not alone because they are laborers, but because they are unfit, always were and always will be unfit, for American citizenship." Miller contended that the only way to extend the blessings of liberty and free government was to *be discriminating*. "Let us keep pure the blood which circulates through our political system," he said.

The following afternoon, Senator Hoar took to the floor once again to defend the Chinese. Hoar began by returning to the country's first principles. "A hundred years ago, the American people founded a nation upon the moral law," he said. "They overthrew by force the authority of their sovereign, and separated themselves from the country which had planted them, alleging as their justification to mankind certain propositions which they held to be self-evident. They declared—and that declaration is the foremost action of human history—that all men equally derive from their Creator the right to the pursuit of happiness; that equality in the right to that pursuit is the fundamental rule of the divine justice in its application to mankind; that its security is the end for which governments are formed, and its destruction good cause why governments should be overthrown." He emphasized this principle was embedded in California's own constitution. Hoar was aghast that the "foremost of republican nations" was now seeking to inflict upon a class of people "a degradation by reason of their race."

Hoar pointed out that, in 1881, more than 720,000 immigrants had arrived in the United States. Of these, fewer than 21,000 were Chinese. "What an insult to American intelligence to ask leave of China to keep out her people, because this little handful of almond-eyed Asiatics threaten to destroy our boasted civilization," he said. "We go boasting of our democracy, and our superiority, and our strength. The flag bears the stars of hope to all nations. A hundred thousand Chinese land in

California and everything is changed. God has not made of one blood all the nations any longer. The self-evident truth becomes a self-evident lie. The golden rule does not apply to the natives of the continent where it was first uttered." He decried the return of "old race prejudice" that had "so often played its hateful and bloody part in history."

To Hoar, it was hardly surprising that the Chinese had so far remained separate from their white neighbors. "That they do not incline to become Christians or republicans may perhaps be accounted for by the treatment they have received," he said. "They are excluded by statute from the public schools. They have no honest trial by jury." He read to his colleagues the anti-Chinese provisions in California's constitution and described the cubic-air law. Hoar also offered a litany of positive testimonials about Chinese laborers that were presented during the Senate investigation of Chinese immigration in 1876 and took pains to dismantle the argument that Chinese labor lowered the wages of white men. He ended his speech with his own warnings of where the country was heading. "As surely as the path on which our fathers entered a hundred years ago led to safety, to strength, to glory," he said, "so surely will the path on which we now propose to enter bring us to shame, to weakness, and to peril."

Over seven days of debate, Miller and Hoar would go back and forth, in a series of extraordinary exchanges over the meaning of America and its deepest values. The chamber was evenly divided between Republicans and Democrats, but the dispute unfolded along regional lines, with senators from the Pacific coast joined in a race-based compact with their Democratic allies from the South; the dissenting voices were almost entirely New England Republicans. A speech by Senator James Z. George, a Mississippi Democrat who had been a general in the Confederate army and served on his state's board of secession, made clear the incongruity of the coalition backing Miller's legislation. George expressed hope that the "calm and philosophical spirit" that characterized the discussion of "this inferior race" might one day be applied to that of another one. "The Constitution was ordained and established by white men, as they themselves declared in its preamble, to 'secure the blessings of liberty to themselves (ourselves) and their (our) posterity,' and I cannot doubt that this great pledge thus solemnly given will be as fully redeemed in favor of the white people of the South, should occasion for action arise, as I intend on my part and on their behalf to redeem it this day in favor of the white people of the Pacific States, by my vote to protect them against a degrading and destructive association with the inferior race now threatening to overrun them," he said.

Hoar was not entirely alone in his defense of the Chinese. For more than a decade, Senator Joseph Hawley of Connecticut had been outspoken in his defense of the Chinese in America. Hawley had been the editor of the *Hartford Courant* and the governor of Connecticut. Perhaps most importantly, he was a member of Asylum Hill Congregational Church in Hartford, led by the Rev. Joseph Twichell, who had been so involved with Yung Wing's educational mission. On the Senate floor, Hawley invoked the country's republican heritage. Denying entrance to America because an immigrant "is yellow, or because he is black, or because he was born in a certain place" violated America's foundational principles, Hawley said.

Others who opposed the bill took a more pragmatic approach. Senator Orville Platt, a Connecticut Republican, argued that the bill still violated the Angell Treaty. "I cannot consent to the infraction even of the spirit of a treaty, while professing to be bound by it," he said. "The object of the bill is to extirpate the Chinese; it is to exclude them; it is to prohibit them from coming here hereafter." Over the course of the debate, a compromise position had begun to emerge among Republican senators, as they struggled to balance politics and principle: shortening the restriction period from twenty years to ten. Senator George F. Edmunds, of Vermont, the influential chairman of the Judiciary Committee, became the most prominent advocate for this solution. Edmunds had been instrumental in legislation after the Civil War protecting the civil rights of formerly enslaved Black Americans. He commanded respect across party lines for his deep knowledge of constitutional law and had served as head of the bipartisan commission that settled the disputed election of 1876. On the afternoon of March 7, when he spoke on Miller's bill, he insisted that he was not asserting that the Chinese were any better or worse than their Anglo-Saxon counterparts; they were merely *different*. "There is no common ground of assimilation," he said. Edmunds suggested that Chinese immigration be paused to see how the hundred thousand or so who were already in the United States blended in with the rest of the population. "How should that shock humanity?" he said. "How should that touch up the moral sense of any man who loves this Republic or who loves the empire of China? It is a simple coordinated arrangement of these two nations that they will not proceed in what must be considered an experiment, until with the elements we have we are able to see whether it will work or not." Edmunds made the case that a ten-year cessation was an entirely reasonable step. If it turned out that the Chinese were "able to assimilate with our institutions and we with them, it will be very easy to open the door and say 'come in,' but if it should turn out that the nature of the two peoples, their ideas, their habits, their thoughts are incompatible to that firm concord and unity which must characterize a republic, I repeat then we have done no wrong either to them or to ourselves, but good to both," Edmunds said. On the evening of March 9, however, Miller's original bill passed easily, thanks to a coalition of western Republicans and nearly all of their Democratic colleagues: the race-based alliance held.

The question turned to whether it would be signed by the president. Arthur's views on the Chinese question were unknown. During his first annual address to Congress, in December of 1881, Arthur had delivered bland comments on the issue. "The prompt and friendly spirit with which the Chinese government, at the request of the United States, conceded the modification of existing treaties should secure careful regard for the interests and susceptibilities of that Government in the enactment of any laws relating to Chinese immigration," he said. "Legislation is necessary to carry their provisions into effect." Early in his tenure as president, Arthur was mostly focused on civil service reform and addressing issues in the presidential succession process that had been exposed during the two months before Garfield died. The president's reputation was hardly that of a principled crusader for equal rights, though his Baptist minister father had been a fierce opponent of slavery. As a young lawyer, too, Arthur had worked on a high-profile case that resulted in the freeing of eight slaves traveling through New York.

For the Chinese bill, Arthur turned to his cabinet for advice, convening a series of meetings over the course of a week. One meeting, on

March 31, lasted more than three hours. The Chinese legation pressured the president to veto the measure, sending a strongly worded memo that criticized the twenty-year cessation as "unreasonable" and protested other requirements imposed upon Chinese residents and immigrants in the bill as "vexatious discrimination." Reports circulated about the views of members of the cabinet; Arthur's secretary of state, Frederick Frelinghuysen, who had replaced Blaine, was widely understood to be opposed to the bill; the attorney general, Benjamin Brewster, was rumored to be as well.

On the afternoon of April 4, the Senate secretary read aloud Arthur's veto message to Congress. His focus was not on whether the restrictions should be imposed on the Chinese immigration but for how long. Arthur made clear that he believed in the "necessity of some legislation on this subject" and concurred with the "objects which are sought to be accomplished," but he argued that "a shorter experiment" would be better. Arthur had hoped the Pacific coast might be mollified by this compromise, but residents of western states erupted in fury. News of the veto arrived in San Francisco on the bulletin boards outside of the *Chronicle*'s office. All day, crowds jammed the street in front to read the news. A Republican ward in the city quickly held a meeting that evening to denounce Arthur's decision, declaring that he had "insulted the people of the coast by listening to Eastern fanatics who know nothing about the evil of Chinese immigration." In Santa Cruz, flags were lowered to half mast and an angry rally took place on the town plaza; in Watsonville, Republicans set ablaze an effigy of Arthur; in Santa Rosa, a crowd threatened to rampage through the Chinese quarter but eventually dispersed. The protests were not limited to the West Coast. In Philadelphia, ten thousand workers gathered for a torchlit procession and a raucous, open-air meeting to denounce Arthur's decision. In St. Louis, workingmen paraded through the streets bearing banners that read "The Chinese Must Go," and "Down with the Veto."

In Congress, the foes of Chinese immigration quickly introduced a new measure that shortened the ban to ten years. This time, there was little suspense about the outcome. Hoar once again rose to defend the Chinese, denouncing the legislation "as a violation of the ancient policy of the American Republic." The Massachusetts senator seemed to recognize that the law marked a turning point in his party, as well as the country. On May 4, Congress sent the revised anti-Chinese bill to the president. This time, Arthur had no appetite for further deliberations. In a cabinet meeting the following day, the matter was not even raised. Charles Folger, the treasury secretary, explained to a reporter that there had been other pressing issues to discuss. The next day, a British steamer, the *Altonower*, dropped anchor in San Francisco harbor and delivered 829 Chinese immigrants on American shores; another vessel, the *Glamis Castle*, discharged 970. On the morning of May 8, Arthur asked his private secretary to read over the bill to make sure that it had been correctly copied. After confirming there were no errors, Arthur signed into law the Chinese restriction bill, as it was commonly referred to then—though some also used the stronger term "Chinese exclusion"— without any ceremony. (The legislation later became known as the Chinese Exclusion Act.) He initially refrained even from an announcement, because he had planned to craft a brief message explaining his decision, but in the end, he decided to send the legislation back to Congress with no comment.

The language of the law specifically targeted Chinese laborers, but lawmakers' motivations were clear. For the first time in its history, the United States had closed its gates on a people based on their race. "Hereafter, we are to keep our hand on the door-knob, and admit only those whose presence we desire," the *Chicago Times* declared. In San Francisco, Republican officials organized an artillery regiment to drag a pair of ten-pound Parrott rifle cannons onto a hill overlooking Sacramento Street and fire off a hundred-round salute. The deafening reports echoed across the city as American flags that had been hoisted for the occasion rippled in the wind.

Across the ocean, steamships filled with Chinese passengers rushing to enter the United States before the restrictions took effect. In 1882, American immigration officials recorded a quadrupling of Chinese arrivals, nearly forty thousand in all, easily the biggest influx from Asia up to that point. In Hong Kong, a thirteen-year-old boy named Fong Sec boarded the *China*, squeezing into a hold so crowded that he had trouble moving about. Fong had grown up in a small farming village about three miles from Taishan. His family of ten occupied a small plot of land that was not large enough to feed so many mouths. Fong often went hungry. When the family ran out of rice, Fong and his siblings often ate taro, a kind of sweet potato, as a substitute. Fong mostly went barefoot in the village, saving his shoes for special occasions. He attended the village school and tended to the family water buffalo and performed other farming chores. It was his father's idea to send him to America, after seeing many in the village come home flush with money. He entrusted Fong, his second-oldest son, to a neighbor making a return journey to America. The money for Fong's trip came from funds borrowed from relatives and friends. As Fong and others waited in Hong Kong for the ship to take them to America, he saw white women for the first time, with their strange black veils hiding their faces and their odd dress. On board the *China,* stormy weather caused the ship to pitch violently, making Fong seasick and unable to eat. Fong later recalled waves that were a "mountain high." A fellow passenger began to teach him English. Upon arrival in San Francisco, Fong rode atop a wagon loaded with luggage to Chinatown. White onlookers threw trash at him and his fellow passengers. This was his welcome to America.

CHAPTER 13

The Gatekeepers

The closed gate would be tested almost immediately. At eight o'clock in the morning on August 8, 1882, the Pacific Mail steamship *City of Sydney* churned into San Francisco Bay; nearly a hundred first-class passengers were on board and another seventy-two in steerage. The vessel had departed Australia twenty-six days earlier and, on its route across the Pacific, made stopovers in Auckland, New Zealand, and Honolulu in the Hawaiian Kingdom. By the time it arrived in the United States, the restrictions on Chinese immigration had been in effect for four days.

A quarantine officer from the Customs House boarded for his usual inspection. Afterward, the ship's master, William Seabury, guided the vessel along the waterfront towards the Pacific Mail Steamship's dock. Customs officials aboard a revenue barge in the harbor, however, signaled Seabury to turn around. He headed back out into the bay and dropped anchor a mile offshore. A tugboat soon made its appearance and delivered the passengers—all of them white—and its cargo of mail to shore. Negotiations ensued between customs officials and Seabury. He had a problem: his fourteen-member crew, whom he had hired in San Francisco, were all Chinese. At two o'clock in the afternoon, San Francisco's collector of customs, Eugene L. Sullivan, ordered that the men be transferred to an abandoned hulk in the harbor. The imprisoned crew members included a thirty-year-old cabin waiter named Ah Sing, who had come to California six years earlier. He would become the first

Chinese immigrant to fight for his right to remain in the United States during the era of Chinese restriction.

Customs collectors at ports of entry were now the country's gatekeepers. Sullivan, a successful real estate speculator and two-term state senator, had been appointed the collector of the port of San Francisco in 1880. Sullivan, who was sixty-two years old and had a handlebar mustache and a pointed goatee, had a reputation for conscientiousness and principle. He was a former chairman of the Republican state central committee, but his appointment was endorsed by members of both political parties. Like other collectors, Sullivan received limited guidance from Washington on how to administer the new strictures on Chinese immigration, but he believed his job was to be as severe as possible. He noted in a letter to his superiors that "the public is keenly alive to the operation of this law" and would take umbrage with any sign it was not being enforced.

The reality was that the law was filled with ambiguities. Who was a laborer? What evidence was needed to establish merchant status? How should the cases of wives and children be handled? Should a physician be considered a laborer? A fisherman? An opera singer? A preacher? After President Arthur signed the measure on May 6, there was officially a ninety-day grace period until it took effect. After that, if Chinese laborers wanted to leave the country and then re-enter, they would need to produce a certificate that established their identity. The document was to include their name, age, occupation, last place of residence, and a physical description. On May 19, the Treasury Department issued to collectors of customs a circular on the distribution of the certificates. Chinese diplomatic officials quickly recognized that many of their countrymen would struggle with the process because of their lack of English. The Chinese consulate in San Francisco stepped in to facilitate the issuance of the documents. But what to do with people who left before "return certificates," as they were called, became available?

Ah Sing and his fellow crew members had departed San Francisco on May 8, when federal officials had yet to put in place any procedures for departing Chinese. Seabury faced a quandary. Shipmasters who landed Chinese laborers without proper documents were guilty of a misdemeanor and liable for fines of up to $500 for each illegal entrant. But Seabury was also bound, by contract, to return his crew members to San Francisco, their original port of embarkation, and would forfeit a $500 bond if he failed to do so.

A day after the *City of Sydney*'s arrival, another Pacific Mail steamship, the *Oceanic,* arrived from Hong Kong, with seventy-five Chinese crew members. This time, the ship was allowed to dock, but the gangways were closely monitored to ensure that only white passengers were allowed off. A disabled tea merchant named George Oliver tried to disembark with his Chinese servant, only to be told that he'd have to leave his help behind. He protested loudly to no avail. Aboard a nearby bark, the *Wildwood,* a Chinese cook and pantry boy were similarly detained. America's gate was closed to them.

On August 18, the tenth day of detention for the *City of Sydney*'s crew, the law firm of McAllister & Bergin, acting at the behest of the Chinese consulate, filed a writ of habeas corpus in federal court on behalf of Ah Sing, arguing that his imprisonment was unconstitutional. Two days later, at eleven o'clock in the morning, Ah Sing and his lawyer, Hall McAllister, appeared in the federal courthouse, a drab, four-story brick building that ran along Sansome Street, not far from the waterfront. McAllister was an imposing presence in the courtroom: large-framed and vigorous, with a broad, placid face. During hearings, he was a furious notetaker; while making an argument, he had an affection for his own doggerel. He had come to San Francisco as a young man during the gold rush and went on to establish, with his partner Thomas I. Bergin, one of the city's preeminent law firms, representing clients like the Pacific Mail Steamship Company and the Southern Pacific Railroad. In 1858, he published an opinion on behalf of several of the city's merchants arguing that a state law barring Chinese immigration was unconstitutional. (The measure was later struck down.) He was later part of a team of lawyers who successfully challenged legislation in California that sought to prohibit corporations from employing Chinese. Most recently, McAllister had represented Chinese laundrymen in their quest to roll back discriminatory ordinances directed at them.

McAllister's case was carefully calibrated. He argued that the restriction law did not apply to the cabin waiter because he had never disembarked from his ship and, therefore, had never left American territory. Philip Teare, the United States attorney, and his assistant, A. P. Van Duzer, who appeared on behalf of the collector of the port, countered that the case was straightforward: Ah Sing and his crew members were laborers and did not have return certificates, so they should be barred from entering the United States.

The case was decided by a two-person panel on the Ninth Circuit: Lorenzo Sawyer, the circuit court judge, and Stephen J. Field, the United States Supreme Court justice who was serving his required term on the circuit court. Sawyer, a native of New York, had practiced law in Chicago and then Wisconsin before traveling overland in 1850 to California to join the gold rush. He opened a law office in Nevada City, where he witnessed the legions of Chinese streaming to the mines. Sawyer found himself thoroughly impressed by this "interesting class of foreigners," he wrote in a letter at the time. "They are the most sober, honest and industrious people in this country," he said. "Their deportment is grave and dignified. They seem never to meddle or interfere in any manner with the affairs of others." Sawyer typically presided over the court, but Field was the ranking federal judge in the Far West, and, by law, his opinion was controlling when he was on the circuit court.

Field is a contradictory figure in the history of Chinese immigration. He arrived in San Francisco in 1849 with $10 to his name and ascended to the state legislature, the state supreme court, and, finally, the highest court in the land. He was a brilliant jurist, whose forcefulness often tilted towards arrogance. His relationship with Sawyer, as well as with Ogden Hoffman Jr., the longtime district court judge in San Francisco who also shared in circuit court duties, was often tense. Field was dogged in his belief in the existence of certain inalienable rights that needed to be protected but also in the importance of the court's role in preserving social order.

In August 1872, while preparing the members of a circuit court grand jury for their term, Field made a point of addressing the Chinese question, presumably because of the frequency of crimes against Chinese residents. He told the members that there were reasonable differences of opinion about the "wisdom and policy of encouraging the immigration to this country of persons, between whom and our people there is such marked dissimilarity in constitution, habits and manners," but Field emphasized the United States' treaty obligations to protect Chinese citizens and called it "unchristian and inhuman" to mistreat them in the way they so frequently had been in the district. The Chinese community later lauded him for striking down the so-called queue ordinance, which Field excoriated as "unworthy of a brave and manly people," but even in that decision, Field made clear his belief that the Chinese were unassimilable, contending that "thoughtful persons" would look at the "millions which crowd the opposite shores of the Pacific" and consider the possibility of them "pouring over in vast hordes among us."

In Ah Sing's case, Field and Sawyer ruled unanimously that the seaman should be discharged, agreeing with his lawyer that aboard the *City of Sydney* he was "within the jurisdiction of the United States, at all times under their protection and amenable to their laws." The circuit court judges dealt with Ah Sing's crewmates in a separate decision. Unlike Ah Sing, the other crew members had all briefly disembarked the ship, but Field and Sawyer ruled that this should not disqualify them as residents of the United States. Deciding otherwise would lead to an "unjust or absurd conclusion," they wrote. Ultimately, they argued, it was better for the law to be administered in a way that was "less repellant to our sense of justice and right."

In early September, McAllister appeared in court with another habeas corpus petition. This time, McAllister's client was a merchant, Low Chow Yam, who had arrived in San Francisco on August 17, in the late afternoon, with eight other Chinese passengers, all claiming to be merchants, aboard the steamship *Rio de Janeiro* from Panama. Once again, Sullivan, the collector of customs, refused to allow them to land, because they did not have the documents required under the new law— certificates from the Chinese imperial government that established them as merchants. He later acknowledged in correspondence with Treasury Department officials that he had "no doubt" that Low Chow Yam and the other Chinese passengers were merchants, but he was conscious of the potential political ramifications and wanted to "leave all doubtful points to the court to decide."

In the courtroom, Low Chow Yam appeared in a flower-embroidered robe that reached to the floor, a velvet-edged jacket, and silk pants. His hands were pudgy and soft. He had run a business in Peru for a decade before establishing himself in Panama. He'd left Panama on July 31—before the restriction law went into effect—intending to travel to San Francisco to purchase supplies of rice and flour. For the last five years, the merchant had been part of a San Francisco firm, Kwong Sing Lung Chow Kee & Co., an affiliation that was affirmed by a Chinese witness who took the stand. A. P. Van Duzer, the assistant United States attorney, argued that all that mattered was Low Chow Yam's lack of proper documentation. Presiding over the hearing was Ogden Hoffman Jr., the longtime district court judge. Hoffman, whose father and grandfather were both distinguished lawyers in New York City, had arrived in San Francisco in 1850 and set up a law practice in the burgeoning city. A year later, largely through his father's political connections in New York, Hoffman won the nomination to become the first Northern District judge. He was twenty-nine years old. He had sat on the bench ever since, never marrying and dedicating his life wholly to his court. Over the years, he became a fierce defender of judicial independence. Hoffman pressed Van Duzer about the certificate requirement, pointing out that the merchant was never able to obtain one. "That is his misfortune under the law," Van Duzer said, gesturing with his glasses.

Hoffman disagreed with the customs collector's reading of the law, as did Justice Field. Both men issued opinions. The hearing established the facts of the case "beyond doubt or controversy," Hoffman wrote. Low Chow Yam was clearly, as he claimed to be, a merchant in Panama, affiliated with a firm in the city that was "largely engaged in commerce." The petitioner's "dress, appearance, and manners" all corroborated his account, Hoffman said, making clear that he was a member of a class that was explicitly exempted under the law. Hoffman pointed out that it would have been impossible for the merchant to obtain the certificate demanded by the collector of the port. The judge argued that the purpose of the legislation was to curb the "teeming population of China of laborers" who menaced "our interests, our safety, and even our civilization," but that lawmakers were also at pains to avoid impeding the growing commercial interchange with China. Restraining

Chinese merchants from the ability to come and go risked violating the United States' obligations under the Angell Treaty, Hoffman said. The district judge's invocation of the country's diplomatic promises was an important legal precedent, giving Chinese immigrants new standing to press their cases. Hoffman acknowledged the incendiary debate over the restriction law but argued that the measure's backers would be best served if the legislation was given a "reasonable and just construction."

Over the next eight years, Hoffman alone would hear more than seven thousand Chinese habeas corpus cases—a result of opaqueness in the law, overzealousness on the part of customs inspectors, and the initiative of Chinese arrivals. The workload nearly consumed Hoffman. "It would be hard to convince one who has never been in these courts how great is the physical and mental strain caused by a day's conscientious attention to these Chinese cases," he said. "And when the day lengthens out into weeks and months the torture of mind and body is unbearable." Over time, Hoffman's health suffered. He struggled with his appetite. His clerks complained they were getting headaches from the strain. The Chinese cases filled him, he wrote in a letter to Rep. Charles Felton of California, "with dismay and almost with despair."

The arrival of a steamship from Hong Kong three times a month invariably meant days of packed courtrooms. On the afternoon of December 19, 1883, more than two hundred Chinese passengers, who had arrived several days earlier on the *Oceanic,* crowded into the district court, spilling into the corridors on several floors. Hoffman had been hearing cases from the *Oceanic* for several days, including that of Leland Stanford's former cook, Moy Jin Kee, who had spoken out against the restriction law in New York City. Moy had returned to the United States on the *Oceanic* with his wife. His brother, Jin Mun, happened to be Hoffman's courtroom interpreter. Hoffman quickly discharged the couple, but the rest would have to wait as Hoffman worked his way through the cases, one by one.

About a month later, just before the adjournment of an evening session of his court, Hoffman asked his clerk how many Chinese cases remained on his calendar. The clerk consulted his records and responded,

Before the discovery of gold in 1848, fewer than a thousand hardy inhabitants occupied the windswept settlement of San Francisco.

News of California's gold rush spread throughout the Pearl River Delta in China.

As more and more Chinese miners arrived in the goldfields, ugly episodes of racial violence became increasingly common.

During the 1850s, the Reverend William Speer, a Presbyterian missionary in San Francisco, emerged as an important ally of the Chinese arrivals.

Chinese labor became essential for the construction of the western portion of the transcontinental railroad.

In order to scale the Sierra Nevada mountains, Chinese laborers bored fifteen tunnels through solid granite.

The *Great Republic* was the first of four vessels constructed for the Pacific Mail Steamship Company, enabling the establishment, in 1867, of a regular route for passengers and cargo across the Pacific Ocean.

In 1868, Anson Burlingame (center) led a Chinese diplomatic mission to the West. Here he is shown with members of his delegation.

"Nigger Alley" was the site of the Los Angeles Chinese massacre of 1871. In this photograph, taken several years later, the alley is on the right. In the center is the Coronel building, where the violence began.

The morning after the massacre, the bodies of victims were laid out in a courtyard at the county jail.

In the fall of 1872, the first cohort of the Chinese Educational Mission arrived in New England.

The mission was the brainchild of Yung Wing, shown here in 1900. Yung, a graduate of Yale, hoped to help China modernize by bringing students to America to be educated.

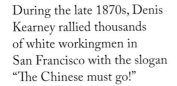

During the late 1870s, Denis Kearney rallied thousands of white workingmen in San Francisco with the slogan "The Chinese must go!"

Wong Chin Foo founded the Chinese Equal Rights League and said his hope was to "influence every Chinaman in America to become American citizens."

Over more than two decades, a Chinese immigrant named Ah Quin kept a diary in English. He became a successful businessman in San Diego. Here he is shown, in 1901, with his wife, Leong Shee, and their children.

His diary is a rare chronicle of Chinese assimilation in America.

The Tape family, shown here in 1883. The year after this portrait was taken, Joseph (left) walked Mamie (center) to Spring Valley Primary School, hoping to enroll her, but the principal turned her away. The family successfully challenged the decision in court. Rather than integrate the city's schools, however, officials established a separate school for Chinese students.

The Chinese quarter in Eureka, California, shown here in 1885. White residents forcibly expelled the town's Chinese residents, in what would become the opening act in a harrowing period in American history known as the "driving out."

On September 2, 1885, in Rock Springs, a coal mining town in Wyoming Territory, a white mob killed at least twenty-eight Chinese people.

A week after the massacre, Chinese laborers returned to Rock Springs and soon resumed coal production.

A photograph taken of the twenty-seven Tacoma citizens charged with organizing the expulsion, in November 1885, of Chinese residents. The case against the men ultimately foundered.

In Seattle, a merchant named Chin Gee Hee tried to sound the alarm about the danger facing Chinese there. In February 1886, hundreds of Chinese residents fled. Chin Gee Hee, shown here in 1903, was among a small contingent who stayed behind.

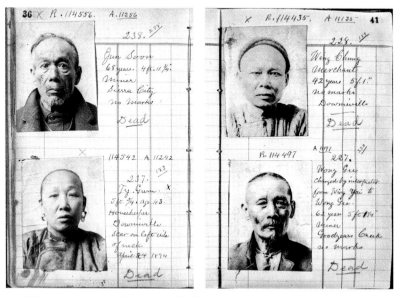

Under the Geary Act of 1892, all Chinese residents in the
United States were required to register and obtain a certificate that established their right to be in the country. After
an initial period of defiance of the law, more than a hundred thousand men, women, and even children registered.

In 1894, a constable in Downieville, California, began maintaining a journal
that tracked the area's Chinese residents over many years. A total of twenty-
one people in the journal are marked as dead.

A scene in San Francisco's Chinatown near the turn of the century

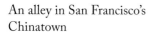

An alley in San Francisco's Chinatown

Pell Street in New York City's Chinatown on a Sunday in 1899

On the morning of April 18, 1906, one of the most devastating earthquakes in recorded history struck San Francisco. By evening, Chinatown was a whirlpool of fire.

In the aftermath of the quake, foes of the Chinese celebrated, believing that they would finally be able to rid the city of its Chinese quarter. But Chinese residents quickly moved to rebuild.

In the early twentieth century, a new voice emerged on behalf of the Chinese in America: Ng Poon Chew, the founder of *Chung Sai Yat Po*, a newspaper modeled after the crusading dailies of the day.

An issue of *Chung Sai Yat Po*, dated May 11, 1906. The article reports the newspaper's printing presses were destroyed during the earthquake.

Over the course of three decades, tens of thousands of Chinese arrivals were held on Angel Island. This photograph from 1923 shows the physical examinations that were part of the intake process.

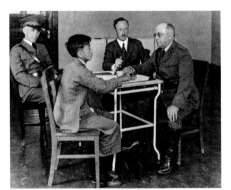

Immigration inspectors conducted lengthy interrogations. "They ask so much, you got tired," one former detainee recalled.

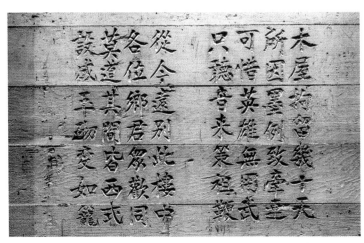

To pass the time, some of the incarcerated Chinese carved poetry on the walls of their barracks, expressing their grief and rage.

Survivors of the Rock Springs massacre continued to work in the mines for years. Finally, in 1925, Union Pacific officials decided to send the remaining survivors back to China. The initial group included a septuagenarian named Lao Chung, third from left, who still carried a bullet in his back from the attack.

In 1926, Mamie Louise Leung became the first Asian American reporter at a major American newspaper when she joined the *Los Angeles Record*. Here she is shown on the left interviewing the actress Anna May Wong.

In February 1928, a delegation of Chinese American men arrived in Washington to lobby for the easing of immigration restrictions to allow for the admission of Chinese wives of American citizens. The leader of the group was Y. C. Hong, shown here on the front step, second from right.

On February 18, 1943, Soong Mayling, the American-educated wife of China's leader, Generalissimo Chiang Kai-shek, became the first private citizen and second-ever woman to address Congress. China's strategic importance to the United States during the Second World War helped lead to the repeal of Chinese exclusion.

On October 3, 1965, President Lyndon Johnson signed into law an overhaul of the country's immigration system. Yet he was careful to emphasize that this was "not a revolutionary bill." He was wrong.

The author (second from left) and his family, around 1980. Their American story was made possible by the 1965 legislation, which finally threw open America's gates for Chinese immigrants.

"One hundred and ninety." Hoffman was despondent. "We try but ten a day," he said. He calculated that the earliest he could clear the backlog was the beginning of March. An assistant United States attorney, Carroll Cook, interjected that this assumed "no more Chinamen come," and pointed out that another steamship had arrived that evening. Hoffman fretted over what to do. "I certainly cannot let drop all other business of this court," he said. On the other hand, he believed these were important decisions and said, "We must try them by all means." Hoffman decided to pause the Chinese habeas corpus cases for two weeks to rush through other matters. "I do not see a better way," he said, and adjourned the court, as lawyers turned to their Chinese clients to inform them about the new delay.

The following day, Hoffman issued a ruling on Chinese petitioners who had been barred from entry but detained for so long that the ships they arrived on had long since departed. There were some two or three hundred of such cases. Hoffman decided that the Chinese could not be held indefinitely and stated that after two months, they should be released unless a "just excuse" could be demonstrated. The judge recognized his decision would be controversial and "possibly attract some public attention." Hoffman delivered a plea to Congress to address the problems in the law. "All ordinary business, public and private, of the court is necessarily suspended, or, if resumed, these passengers, many of whom may be entitled to their discharge, are left, either in custody or on bail, awaiting the determination of their cases," he said. Hoffman wrote that he had been toiling for five or six weeks, even adding night sessions to his court, but unable to make "any great impression" on his backlog of Chinese cases.

The relentless churn of Chinese cases—local newspapers referred derisively to Hoffman's court as a "habeas corpus mill"—turned into a lucrative business for a handful of lawyers. Besides McAllister & Bergin, the Chinese consulate retained Thomas D. Riordan, another prominent San Francisco attorney. The attorney, who also did work for the Chinese Six Companies, eventually handled most of the habeas corpus cases and went on to argue four cases on behalf of the Chinese before the U.S. Supreme Court. Several former federal prosecutors began taking on Chinese cases, too, after they entered private practice. One of the first to do so was Van Duzer, the assistant United States attorney who had argued against both Ah Sing and Low Chow Yam. By the following year, he was advocating on behalf of Chinese clients.

Colonel Frederick A. Bee, the consul at the Chinese consulate in San Francisco and a longtime adviser to the Chinese community, frequently appeared in court alongside the lawyers. Bee was easily recognizable with his mutton chops and bushy eyebrows. Since he spoke no Chinese, Bee was often accompanied by Tsang Hoy, the consulate's vice consul and interpreter. Bee, a native New Yorker who had sailed around Cape Horn and arrived in San Francisco in August 1849 and joined the gold rush, had first aided Chinese miners in their legal claims in El Dorado County. He later became an official spokesman for the Six Companies. In 1876, when a joint congressional committee conducted an investigation of Chinese immigration, Senator Oliver P. Morton asked Bee to represent the Chinese over the course of seven weeks of hearings. In 1878, when Yung Wing and Chen Lanbin established the Chinese legation in Washington, one of their first priorities was to appoint Bee to assist in the San Francisco consulate. When steamships arrived from China, Bee and Huang Zunxian, the consul general in San Francisco, stood on the docks and greeted disembarking passengers. On one occasion, a group of white laborers gathered outside the Customs House to taunt the Chinese arrivals. One of them pointed a pistol at the two men. "If you dare lead the Chinese to enter, I am going to give you this," he said. Bee was nonplussed. He touched the gun he carried in his boot and said, "Do you dare?" Huang, a renowned poet, later wrote of Bee: "When someone's guts are bigger than his body, his spirit is naturally heroic and fearless."

The federal judges handling habeas corpus cases established several broad categories of exceptions to the law. Their decisions enabled laborers who had left the United States after the passage of the Angell Treaty but before certificates of return were available to still enter. The judges also decided that the wives and children of merchants should be allowed to land. In another notable case, in September of 1884, Justice Field ruled that Look Tin Sing, a fourteen-year-old boy born in Mendocino, California, whose parents had sent him back to China in 1879, should be allowed to re-enter the country, because he was an American citizen by birthright under the Fourteenth Amendment. A slew of prominent attorneys made arguments on behalf of the boy, whose father was a merchant in Mendocino. His advocates included Van Duzer and former Nevada senator William Stewart, who had so vociferously opposed naturalization of Chinese immigrants in Congress but now had a law office in San Francisco. Stewart warned that there were "millions" of white children born in the United States whose parents were not yet naturalized. Refusing to recognize Look Tin Sing as a citizen could spur a backlash that would jeopardize the passage of additional Chinese restrictions. Field ordered that the boy be discharged, stating "no citizen can be excluded from this country except in punishment for crime."

Some of the most nettlesome disputes in the courtroom involved the certificates required of merchants. The Qing government had established an office in Whampoa, about ten miles south of Guangzhou, for the issuance of the documents. Customs officials, however, believed many of the certificates presented to them were fraudulent. At American ports of entry, Chinese inspectors labored to identify merchant impostors, looking for callused hands and sunburnt legs. Court hearings regularly featured elaborate cross-examinations of Chinese petitioners about their merchant credentials. Foes of Chinese immigration expressed skepticism that so many of them had "uncles" hoping to start them in business. Hoffman lamented that the task of ferreting out the truth was an "insuperable" one.

Customs collectors across the country grew increasingly agitated, believing that the law was being evaded at every turn. In New York, Chinese inspectors even went so far as to detain Chang Yu Sin, the eight-foot-four-inch Chinese giant who was a performer for the Barnum, Bailey & Hutchinson circus. Only after an agent of the circus produced affidavits certifying that the giant was not a laborer was he released and allowed to proceed to his hotel uptown. Nowhere was the clamor greater than in San Francisco, where Sullivan portrayed himself, in letters to Charles Folger, the secretary of the treasury, as valiantly fulfilling his duty, while constantly dealing with new "vexations and perplexing questions," as well as the subterfuges of a "very cunning" enemy. Despite all his struggles, Sullivan was confident that the law was still having its intended effect and the "influx of Chinese laborers stopped." According to records kept by the Custom House in San Francisco, over the course of the law's first fifteen months, 2,652 Chinese were allowed to land in San Francisco, while more than 12,000 departed. Only 64 of the Chinese permitted to land were admitted directly by habeas corpus petitions; more than 500 others, however, had entered under circumstances that had been opened up by judicial review. In a letter dated October 12, 1883, the Rev. Augustus Loomis, the head of the Presbyterian Church's mission to the Chinese in California, observed: "The Chinese are going home in large numbers and have been for months." He noted that just the day before, a steamer had departed for China carrying 1,150 Chinese passengers and, less than two weeks earlier, another vessel had taken 750. The mission's schools and Sabbath services for the Chinese were half as full as they had been six months earlier. The Chinese population was, indisputably, shrinking. Yet the foes of Chinese immigration remained dissatisfied.

In July 1884, Congress tightened the restriction law further, mandating that it applied to anyone of Chinese descent, even if they were not Chinese subjects, and that only certificates issued by the Chinese government and endorsed by an American consul were acceptable evidence of merchant status or any other exempt category. Similarly, for laborers, the new law stated that only return certificates would be permissible documentation for re-entry. The provision was quickly challenged in court by a Chinese laborer named Chew Heong, who had left the United States for Honolulu in June of 1881, nearly a year before the restriction law was passed. After three years away, Chew Heong was seeking to re-enter the country. Justice Field ruled that Chew Heong should be barred, because he lacked a return certificate; his circuit court colleagues vigorously dissented. Riordan appealed the matter to the U.S. Supreme Court, which overruled Field. In his opinion for the majority, Justice John Marshall Harlan wrote that Chew Heong's right to freely come and go from the United States could not be revoked based "upon a condition impossible to be performed."

Public frustration about the duplicity of "cunning celestials," as one newspaper referred to them, mounted. In December of 1884, the San Francisco Board of Supervisors approved a resolution that urged the creation of a registration system for the Chinese to "protect our people."

Less than a year later, John S. Hager, a former United States senator from California and zealous opponent of Chinese immigration, was appointed the new collector of the port of San Francisco. He made clear that he would not tolerate interference by the judiciary.

The capriciousness of customs officials is conspicuous in the case files of Chinese arrivals. On July 5, 1885, Chong Moy, an eight-year-old girl who wore a baleful expression in her identification document issued in Hong Kong, entered San Francisco harbor aboard the *Oceanic*. Her mother said that she had been born in the city and had left at the age of three. But the girl stopped responding to questions from Chinese inspectors. They stamped her application "Disapproved." The case for Tom Bok Gum, a nineteen-year-old who arrived in the fall of 1885, seemed unassailable. He had been born in California and had returned to China in 1877 with his father, Poy Kee, a prominent San Francisco merchant, his mother, and two brothers. The following year, Poy Kee traveled alone back to the United States. He eventually summoned Tom Bok Gum back to work as a bookkeeper and to one day take over the family business, which consisted of a store on Dupont Street and another on Washington Street. The teenager had four white witnesses vouch for him, including Riordan, but inspectors turned Tom Bok Gum away.

A few years into his tenure, Hager compiled statistics for Congress on the enforcement of the restriction act. They showed that, as of December 31, 1885, fewer than nineteen thousand Chinese had landed since the law took effect and more than forty thousand had departed. Nevertheless, a backlash was brewing.

CHAPTER 14

Transformations

Even in the face of hostile government officials seeking to keep them out, tens of thousands of Chinese immigrants continued to scratch out a place for themselves in the United States. The documents kept on Chinese arrivals are like the blurry images of a pinhole camera, capturing the faint impressions of lives being built. On May 12, 1884, a sixteen-year-old girl, Leong Cum, arrived on the steamship *Oceanic,* along with 768 other Chinese passengers. Chinese inspectors detained Leong Cum for questioning. She furnished affidavits, dated July 9, 1883, from Jerome Mulliard, a Chinese interpreter in San Francisco, along with Leong Unn and Chin Ang Gee, San Francisco residents who had previously lived in Lewiston, a former gold rush town in the Idaho Territory. Their attestations sketched the outlines of her family's American story. Her father, Leng Sing, and her mother, Tye Lane, had come to America and made their way to Lewiston after gold was discovered there in 1860. In 1868, Leong Cum was born. When she was five years old, her mother, Tye Lane, took Leong Cum and her two brothers back to China. Several years later, Tye Lane returned alone to the United States, leaving her children behind. She found work as a seamstress in San Francisco, while her husband remained in Lewiston. Mulliard testified to Tye Lane's "excellent reputation and good character"; both Leong Unn and Chin Ang Gee described her as having "irreproachable character." Two days after Leong Cum's arrival, customs officials granted her permission to re-enter the country of her birth.

On June 15, a thirty-two-year-old merchant named Chow Cheung Lee entered San Francisco harbor aboard the *City of Tokio*. He explained to customs inspectors that he'd been a grocer and tea merchant in New Orleans and had returned to China in February of 1882. Just before he left, he sent $2,000 back home, earnings from his time in America. He also revealed that, in 1878, he'd become a naturalized American citizen. He furnished papers to prove it. Chow said he was a Republican and had previously voted in American elections. He indicated that this election he planned to vote for James Blaine, the ardent foe of Chinese immigration, who had just become the Republican presidential nominee. "He is a good man," Chow said. The next day, a customs official stamped his documents "LANDED."

Several months later, customs officials detained a fourteen-year-old Chinese boy named Yeung Fook Tin, who had arrived from Hong Kong on the steamship *Arabic*. A Chinese physician in San Francisco, Li Po Tai King, provided an affidavit on the boy's behalf. The physician explained that he had been in the country for more than thirty years and had employed the boy's father, Yeung Kan Sing, as an assistant for nearly a decade. In 1864, Yeung had gone back to China and returned with a wife; the couple then raised three sons in the United States; Yeung Fook Tin was their eldest. In late 1873 or early 1874, Yeung Kan Sing had departed for Peru, while his wife took the children back to China with her. Li Po Tai King also helpfully brought with him to the customs house a former patient, a white man named Osgood Hilton, who worked in the United States Appraiser's office. Hilton explained to customs officials that he and other family members had received treatment from the physician, at his office on Sacramento Street, for more than a decade and that their medicine had usually been prepared for them by Yeung Kan Sing. Hilton recalled Yeung always seeming to "take special pride" in referring to his two boys as Americans, because of their place of birth. "I have examined Hilton in person and made other inquiries," the collector of the port wrote on Yeung Fook Tin's file jacket. He pronounced himself satisfied that the boy "was born in this city and, therefore, is entitled to land."

On August 24, 1885, three brothers, Lee Tai Chuen, Lee Bing Quinn, and Lee Bing Hoon, ages eleven, twelve, and thirteen, respectively, arrived aboard the steamship *China*. Customs inspectors detained them together. Their father, Lee Hee Wah, kept a Chinese temple off Sacramento Street in Chinatown. The boys, along with two other siblings, had all been born there. In a letter, Lee described his boys as "native Americans." In June of 1878, Lee had brought all five in his brood back to China, because he feared for their safety during the "Kearney riots." He had returned alone to America a year later. While anti-Chinese sentiment in America had hardly dimmed, he was now seeking for his three sons to join him. "I respectfully ask you to allow them to land," he wrote. Lee's white landlord, who had been collecting rent from Lee for the past nineteen years, testified on his behalf. The family was reunited.

Metamorphoses in America were occasionally possible. Huie Kin was in his late twenties when the Chinese restriction law went into effect. He had arrived in California more than a decade earlier, from a tiny farming village in Taishan, and had been employed for most of that time as a domestic worker inside a stately home in Oakland. Now he resolved to "get an education at all costs." His employers, the Gardiner family, had taught him to read and write. They had also granted Huie permission to leave work to attend Sunday school classes. Huie wound up enrolling in evening classes for Chinese immigrants at three different churches. He also joined a group of a dozen Chinese boys who met regularly at the First Presbyterian Church of Oakland to practice their English. Initially, Huie's motivation was not so much spiritual but educational, to improve his language skills. On a Sunday morning in July 1874, however, the church's pastor, the Rev. James Eells, baptized him into the Presbyterian Church. Eells served as a mentor for Huie, who became active in the church's Chinese Sunday school and then in the establishment of a Chinese congregation. It was Eells's suggestion that Huie consider the ministry. After Eells became a professor at Lane Theological Seminary, in Cincinnati, Ohio, he sent Huie a letter and urged him to enroll at the school. Huie hesitated, because it would mean giving up a steady income, but he had $300 in savings and considered the opportunity a "thrilling adventure."

So on a fall day in 1880, Huie bade farewell to the Gardiners and, with another young Chinese man, Chin Gim, boarded a train bound for the Midwest. Huie was dressed in a traditional Chinese gown and still wore his hair in a queue. When they arrived at the seminary, they were assigned a shared suite in the seminary's dormitory, but the two Chinese men found themselves quickly thrown in among the school's forty American students. Huie later admitted that he was initially hesitant and awkward, but he quickly made friends. During the summer, to earn money for their studies, a fellow seminary student organized a lecture tour for his Chinese classmates through other midwestern towns. Huie entitled his lecture "China, by a Chinaman." He dressed in "full Chinese costume," as one newspaper account put it, describing him as a "real, genuine, simon-pure Chinaman." Another reporter called Huie's lecture "spicy and interesting, containing many humorous allusions to the peculiar customs of that wonderful people." Huie had a heavy Chinese accent, but he delivered his remarks ably. Afterward, he read a chapter from the Bible in Chinese and sang a hymn. "China was then little known among American people and Chinese lecturers were a rarity," Huie later recalled. "So our tour was quite a success." He credited his "Oriental garb" for lending an authentic touch to the events and "filling our pockets in a way beyond our expectations."

The two men were shielded to a degree on campus, but it was impossible to escape the menace of anti-Chinese bigotry. One winter evening, they were attacked by a half-dozen young men, who knocked Huie to the ground. A resident of the neighborhood invited them inside to clean up. In the fall of 1882, several months after the passage of the Chinese restriction bill, the pair transferred to Geneva College, in the bucolic town of Beaver Falls, Pennsylvania, so that they could continue their education. A decade earlier, three hundred Chinese laborers had famously descended on the community from San Francisco to work at the local cutlery factory. By the time Huie and Chin Gim arrived, the workers were gone; the large warehouse that had been built to house them was all that remained to mark their presence. On weekends, Huie and Chin Gim traveled to nearby Pittsburgh to help with the Chinese Sunday school at the First Presbyterian Church. By now, the young men had switched to Western clothing and kept their queues tucked underneath their shirts.

Huie was a burly young man with a garrulous personality who could preach extemporaneously for hours. He wore his hair in a pompadour and sported a full mustache. Chin Gim, who was several years younger, was gentler and more refined, his public prayers tender. He cut off his queue before Huie did. Presbyterian officials thought Chin Gim's judgment might be sounder than Huie's. They decided that the two men would be most effective as ministers to their own countrymen in the United States. In this way, they could also be "an exhibit to Christians in America of what the gospel can do," the Rev. Elliot E. Swift, pastor of the First Presbyterian Church in Allegheny, wrote to church officials. The denomination's Board of Foreign Missions decided to dispatch Chin Gim to Chicago and Huie to New York City.

In Huie's first report to the missions board, in August 1885, he said that he had visited more than a hundred laundries, two cigar factories, as well as the heart of the Chinese quarter on Mott Street. He estimated he'd met three or four hundred of the more than four thousand Chinese immigrants in Manhattan and Brooklyn. He had begun speaking during Chinese services at the Presbyterian church on Fourteenth Street and taught at five different Sunday schools, for both American and Chinese children. He emphasized to the mission board the importance of Chinese ministering to other Chinese in America. "Our people are naturally shy when asked to go among strangers," he wrote. Perhaps the biggest obstacle of all to the spread of the gospel among the Chinese, Huie believed, was the abuses they experienced. "They do not receive the treatment which the Christian religion requires and this one fact deters members from accepting it," he wrote.

On October 11, 1885, in a rented parlor on University Place, Huie held the first meeting of his Chinese mission church, attended by a dozen Chinese immigrants. Within a few years, the number of attendees had grown to several dozen. Crucial to the mission's work was a cadre of women volunteers. Among them was Louise Van Arnam, a former schoolteacher from Troy, New York, who had moved to the city with aspirations of finding a vocation in Christian ministry. From the moment he met Van Arnam, Huie sensed he had found his match. "Even the fact that she was of another race made no difference to me," he later wrote. Acquaintance became friendship, and then "life comradeship." Van Arnam's father, a manufacturer in Troy, objected to her marrying a Chinese man, but her mother reluctantly gave her blessing. On April 4, 1889, the couple married in a small ceremony. They honeymooned in Washington, D.C., where an introduction by the Chinese legation led to a visit to the White House. President Benjamin Harrison presented the bride with a bouquet of flowers from the White House garden. The couple's home at 29 West Ninth Street became the center of mission life. Every Sunday, Huie preached at four Chinese services. The couple then hosted forty or fifty men for dinner, usually a Chinese meal prepared by the couple's German maid. Chinese scrolls hung from the walls; the furniture was a blend of Eastern and Western tastes. The couple went on to raise nine children: three boys and six girls, all American born. They were an American family, even if the patriarch could never become an American.

Chronicles of Chinese assimilation in America in the nineteenth century are almost nonexistent, but on June 12, 1877, a twenty-seven-year-old Chinese immigrant on the Pacific coast began keeping a diary. His name was Tom Chong Kwan, but in the United States he was known as Ah Quin. He was slender and had delicate features; a photograph of him at the time shows him with a serious mien and a look of resoluteness, his queue falling down his shoulder. He usually jotted a few lines per day in an appointment book; notably, he wrote in English. The journal's purpose is unclear. He was likely trying to improve his language skills, though he kept at his journaling over the course of more than two decades, lapsing at times but then picking it back up again. The writing was mostly prosaic, recording the mundanity of daily living. (One early entry: "take walk in the street." Another: "comb my hair.") For modern readers, however, the entries are like pottery shards, glazed with the pathos of the Chinese immigrant experience; piece them together and the entire vase comes into view.

Ah Quin was born in Midong, a rural village in Kaiping county, part of the Siyi. As a child, he moved to Guangzhou and began attending an American missionary school, where he learned English. In 1868, at the age of twenty, he made the journey to America. He initially spent

several years in San Francisco, studying English and working as a household servant, while an uncle helped to support him financially. He later
landed in Santa Barbara and became a merchant. It was around this time
that he became a Christian and helped to organize a Sabbath school for
the small Chinese community in town, becoming its superintendent. A
brief about the school published in the annual report of the American
Missionary Association recounted an evening in which Ah Quin read
the Beatitudes in English and explained them in Chinese to nearly two
dozen students.

His journaling began when he was about to commence a year-long
sojourn in Coal Harbor, a tiny island off the Alaskan peninsula, to work
as a cook in a coal mining camp. His first entry captured the sorrow of
his departure. "See all the Friends and Teachers good by to them they
feel sorry and some cry because they may not see me no more." He went
initially to San Francisco, where his uncle scolded him for signing up for
the trip. In the city, Ah Quin reunited with a cousin and visited friends;
one of them, Ah Tan, was hired for the trip as well. During the ocean
journey, Ah Quin got terribly seasick. Once there, he was consumed by
work, struggling to cook two meals a day for the miners on a tiny stove;
at night, he was plagued by mosquitoes. There were small pleasures: he
saw snow for the first time; he read the Bible and recorded scripture
passages in his diary. He lamented that his parents in China had "no
body take care of them" and cried when he prayed for them. "I may
not see them no more," he writes. On June 1, 1878, he asked his boss,
E. T. Gourley, to cut off his queue, so he "just look like the white people
not like our china any more." Ah Quin gave a few strands to his boss,
who had become a friend, and another white workman. They celebrated
together, before the cook turned to making clam chowder for dinner.

In the summer of 1878, Ah Quin returned to Santa Barbara. Shortly
afterward, he made a brief trip to San Diego to see relatives and friends
and scout for business opportunities. He eventually made his way back
to San Francisco. He took odd jobs, mostly as a cook and servant, and
sent money home regularly. His life was mostly tedium: wake up, work,
and then sleep. When he did have leisure time, he noted in his diary
trips to the Chinese theater, visits with friends, and stops at both Chinese and white "whore houses," even as he continued his devotion to

studying scripture and volunteering with the Chinese mission. The anti-Chinese movement roiling San Francisco makes only occasional appearances in his journal. On February 19, 1880, he woke up, rested and studied the dictionary, and read the newspaper about the "Irish" trying to force factories "discharge all our Chinese." A few days later, he ironed his clothes and read the news in his kitchen about the "trouble Irish Democrat," who "insult our Chinese." On April 4, he stayed in church to hear the minister preach about Denis Kearney. Ah Quin's curtailed existence in America as a Chinese man suffuses the entire diary but seems almost too ordinary for comment. Like the fog that rolled daily into San Francisco, it was simply his reality.

In the fall of 1880, his trajectory in America began to bend upward. Connections he had made in San Diego, through the Presbyterian Church, led to an invitation to join the building of a railroad there as a labor contractor. On October 25, Ah Quin boarded a steamer in San Francisco; he stopped in Santa Barbara and greeted his old friend from the Alaska sojourn, E. T. Gourley, on the wharf, before continuing to San Diego. Soon after his arrival, Ah Quin opened a variety store on Fifth Street, in the heart of the Stingaree district, a neighborhood near the waterfront that was notorious for its saloons, gambling houses, and brothels. It was also where the small Chinese quarter was located. In January 1881, there were about 180 Chinese in San Diego, mostly working as house servants, or laundrymen. An advertisement for Ah Quin's store began appearing in the *San Diego Union,* selling "Chinese and Japanese fancy goods, teas, cigars & notions." He promised new goods with every arriving steamer.

The work on San Diego's railroad connection, which would run northward from the city along the coast and then inland to San Bernardino, accelerated quickly, and with it the demand for labor. In early March, more than a hundred Chinese laborers arrived aboard a steamship from San Francisco. A reporter who ventured out to witness the heavy grading work marveled at a camp of 250 Chinese laborers that had sprung up. Ah Quin was soon dividing his time between his store and working for the railroad, recruiting workers and supplying their provisions. One day, in the fall of 1881 he traveled to San Francisco to marry a twenty-year-old woman named Leong Shee, who was also known as Ah Sue. The *San Diego Union* reported on their "notable wedding," declaring that the couple wished to marry in the manner of "'Mellican' people." There are conflicting accounts of Leong Shee's background. According to the *Union,* she was a member of the Chinese mission church in San Francisco, but descendants believed that Ah Quin purchased her. Another report suggests she was a resident of the Mission Home, the refuge for Chinese prostitutes run by the Woman's Foreign Missionary Society of the Presbyterian Church, after having been brought there by a suitor who later died. Ah Quin makes no mention of the wedding in his journal—it came during a several-year gap in his chronicle—but she makes frequent appearances as "Mrs. Ah Quin" in later volumes. In 1883, the couple had their first child, Annie— reportedly the first Chinese baby born in the city. The following year, Ah Quin's store became among the first in town to have a telephone inside it, an indication of his burgeoning success as a businessman. He began investing in land throughout the region. In 1885, the couple welcomed the arrival of George, heralded by the *Union* as "the first male Chinese child born here." The article noted that Ah Quin had shaved the baby's head for the first time, leaving a small patch on his crown—the beginnings of a queue. The couple would go on to have twelve children, all American born, raising them in a two-story home that Ah Quin had constructed on Third Street in Chinatown. The merchant eventually accumulated a fortune of more than $50,000, the equivalent of well over a million dollars today.

On April 8, 1901, a photograph of the couple and their large brood, seven girls and five boys, appeared in the *Los Angeles Daily Times,* under the headline "How Mr. and Mrs. Ah Quin Have Stuffed the Census of San Diego." Every few years, the article reported, the family sat for a portrait by a local photographer. This was the latest. The oldest in the group was Annie, age eighteen, who was about to attend high school and was described as "intelligent and interesting, as, indeed, are all the children." The youngest, McKinley, was six months old, and had been named for the American president. In the photograph, the children surrounded Ah Quin and his wife. The children are all elegantly coiffed and expressionless, but Ah Quin seems to have the faintest of smiles on his face, a look of contentment.

. . .

The sheets of rain failed to deter the guests making their way to the First Presbyterian Church on Stockton Street in San Francisco. It was November 15, 1875, the fifth successive day of wet weather in northern California. A remarkable wedding of a Chinese couple was taking place inside the vaulted sanctuary that evening. The groom was an ambitious young man named Joseph Tape, who drove a milk wagon for a dairy rancher but was about to start his own hauling business. Tape had arrived in America a little more than a decade earlier, from Taishan, at the age of ten or eleven years old. He was known then as Jeu Dip, and he had worked initially as a household servant. Several years later, Jeu Dip cut off his queue and began wearing Western clothing. At some point, he adopted the Westernized sobriquet Joe Tape, a kind of homophone for his name.

The bride was "Miss Mary McGladery," a native of northern China, near Shanghai. She had arrived in the United States at around the age of eleven, in the late 1860s. She had lived for several months in the Chinese quarter, before winding up at a home for orphans run by the San Francisco Ladies' Protection and Relief Society. The story that Mary later told her children is that her parents had died, but a memoir by the Rev. Otis Gibson about his ministry to the Chinese in San Francisco references his fellow clergyman, the Rev. A. W. Loomis, bringing one or two women who had escaped "cruel servitude"—prostitution—to the home. It seems quite likely that Loomis's rescues included Mary, as she was the first child of Chinese descent to grow up in the home. What is known for certain is that the home's matron, Mary McGladery, adopted the child, and from then onward Mary spoke only English. Her home was an imposing brick building on the corner of Franklin and Geary Streets, where the Chinese girl lived with almost two hundred other orphans. The home's two dozen managers trained their wards in homemaking, sewing, and moral living. Mary was, by all accounts, a precocious child and thrived in the home, so much so that she later became an assistant teacher.

The pair courted for six months, getting to know each other in English, the only language they had in common. The Rev. A. W. Loomis and the Rev. Ira Condit, longtime missionaries to the Chinese in California, presided over their wedding ceremony. Most of the wedding guests were friends from the Ladies' Society home. Patrons helped to set the newlyweds up in a house near the Presidio. A year later, Mary gave birth at home to their daughter, Mamie; a son, Frank, followed two years later. By then, the family had moved to a new home on Green Street. Two more daughters, Emily and Gertrude, later rounded out the first Chinese American generation of Tapes.

In March 1882, on Chinese New Year, a newspaper reporter encountered the family and was astonished to find them "dressed American style" and appearing "quite genteel." Joe Tape had an accordion under his arm and obliged the visitor with some tunes. In the evening, the reporter accompanied Tape on a tour of Chinatown with three women from the Ladies' Society home. Tape served as an interpreter for the group, as they visited merchants and the Chinese Presbyterian mission. The writer had an almost zoological curiosity about his encounter with "heathens," but the Tapes stood out to him as an exception. In their daily lives, in fact, the couple's social circle was mostly made up of white Americans. They lived outside the Chinese quarter. One close family friend was their neighbor, Sarah Eveleth, who stayed overnight with Mary for the birth of each one of the couple's children. The Tape children mostly had white playmates as well. The language barrier made it difficult for them to make Chinese friends. As the Tape children approached school age, Sarah Eveleth's teenage daughter, Florence, began tutoring them, but their options for further schooling were limited because of their Chinese heritage.

Since their earliest days in America, Chinese immigrants had demonstrated an interest in education. In January 1853, the Rev. William Speer, the early champion of the Chinese, started an evening school dedicated to them on the second floor of a rented storeroom. In 1858, as the Chinese population in California edged upward, Andrew J. Moulder, the state superintendent of public instruction, warned in his annual report that continued efforts to "force Africans, Chinese, and Diggers"—invoking a derogatory term for Native Americans—into "our white schools" would result in their ruin. He boasted of his efforts to resist the inclusion of "these inferior races."

Lawmakers made provisions for the establishment of separate schools for Black and Native American children but, notably, took no steps to ensure education for the Chinese. In March 1859, thirty Chinese parents petitioned the board of education in San Francisco to create the first Chinese public school but were told the district lacked the funds. Finally, in September, the board allotted $75 a month for the salary of a single teacher and rented the basement of the Chinese chapel at the corner of Stockton and Sacramento Streets. Several dozen pupils, a blend of children and adults, began attending, only for the board to suspend the enterprise several months later, because of low attendance. After the decision drew criticism in the press, the board reopened the school and operated it in the evenings. In his annual report, James Denman, the city's school superintendent, declared that the "prejudices of caste and religious idolatry" made the task of educating the Chinese "almost hopeless." During the next few years, the Chinese school operated in fits and starts, before closing for good in 1871.

Over the next decade, the Chinese community continued to press for access to education, even as the vitriol towards them grew. In 1877, a coalition of thirty-nine Chinese businesses petitioned the school board to open schools for the Chinese. The following year, thirteen hundred Chinese immigrants, including leading merchants of San Francisco and Sacramento, presented a petition to the state legislature, describing themselves as "law abiding people," taxpayers who "add largely to the prosperity of this state." They reported that there were more than three thousand school-age children of Chinese descent in the state, "anxious to learn the English language," but who were barred from public schools. "We simply ask that our children be placed upon the same footing as the children of other foreigners," they wrote. Their petitions went nowhere. In 1882, a coalition of white clergymen once again called upon the board of education to make public schools available to the growing number of Chinese youths.

One day in September 1884, Joe Tape walked his eight-year-old daughter Mamie a few short blocks from their home to the Spring Valley Primary School, a slightly dilapidated, one-story wooden building on Union Street. The school had five haphazardly arranged rooms; it hadn't been painted in eighteen years and required a new roof. During the 1884–1885 school year, 379 students were enrolled. Tape asked that his daughter be allowed to join them, but the school's longtime principal, Jennie M. A. Hurley, refused. There's no record of Hurley's interaction with the Tape family that day. Decades later, Florence Eveleth recalled in an interview that the principal's decision "broke her mother's and father's heart."

Andrew Moulder, the former state schools superintendent, had taken charge of the city's schools. He consulted with William T. Welcker, the state schools superintendent, who backed Hurley's decision. Public education in the state was intended only for citizens, or those who could become citizens, and the Chinese were ineligible, Welcker said. Mamie later said that it was her father who ultimately decided to fight the decision. "He just made up his mind," she told an interviewer years later. "He just wanted to try to get us educated." Frederick Bee, the Chinese consul, sent a letter to Moulder, arguing that the school board's actions were "inconsistent with the treaties, constitution and laws of the United States," particularly given that Mamie was a native-born citizen. Welcker was unmoved, arguing that the courts could not force schools to educate a group that the state constitution had deemed "dangerous to the well-being of the state." Moulder agreed, telling a reporter that the Chinese "are a nation of perjurers, and if admitted would doubtless soon overrun our schools."

The Tapes hired William Gibson, a Harvard Law School graduate and the son of the Methodist missionary to the Chinese, Otis Gibson, to represent them. They decided to use Mamie as a test case. One day in late October, Mamie showed up again at Spring Valley Primary School, this time accompanied by her mother. Hurley turned her away a second time. Joseph Tape asked a superior court judge to compel Hurley, Moulder, and the city's board of education to allow Mamie to enroll. Tape's lawsuit emphasized the ways his family had assimilated in America, explaining that he had long ago discarded his queue and adopted "the American costume," as had Mamie, and that she had always played with and been "otherwise associated with American children." She spoke English fluently, because it was the language used at home by her family, and they lived far outside of Chinatown. "Both my family and myself have adopted the manners, habits and customs of American people of our station in life, and the only objection that can possibly be made to the admission of said Mamie Tape to the said Spring Valley Primary School was on the ground of race or color," Tape said. The lawyers for Hurley and the board of education were brutal in their assessment of the Chinese people in their response, arguing that they "live together in close, crowded, unventilated, and filthy apartments" and that "fatal, contagious, and infectious diseases" are continually transmitted by them, and that the parents and children of the "Mongolian or Chinese kind" have "filthy and vicious habits." The school officials contended that they had no information that "Mamie Tape is not a child of fidelity or vicious habits, or suffering from any contagious or infectious disease," nor did they have proof that she had "adopted the manners, habits and customs of Caucasian people."

On January 9, the superior court judge, James Maguire, a Democrat, ruled in favor of the Tapes. He made plain that the only reason school officials barred Mamie from admission was because "she was born of Chinese parents" and "descended from the Chinese branch of the Mongolian race." This was a "direct conflict with the Fourteenth Amendment," Maguire ruled. Maguire admitted that there was "great force" in the argument that the "mingling of the Mongolian and Caucasian races in the public schools will be fraught with disastrous consequences for our civilization," but he said that this was not the province of the courts, whose job it was to ensure that the established laws were fairly administered upon every person, "high or low, rich or poor, favored or despised." School officials quickly appealed. On March 3, 1885, the Supreme Court of California unanimously affirmed the decision.

Moulder had already set in motion a new stratagem. The next day, he sent a telegram to W. S. May, a state assemblyman representing San Francisco, asking that the legislature immediately take up a measure to establish separate schools for Chinese students. Otherwise, Moulder warned that some schools for white children would be "inundated by Mongolians." The legislation, Assembly Bill No. 268, was deemed a "matter of urgency" and made its way, in just three days, through the Assembly and Senate, passing overwhelmingly.

To accommodate the Chinese school, the board of education agreed to rent a building on the corner of Jackson and Stone Streets, in Chinatown. Three upstairs rooms would house the school. The board hired Rose Thayer, a well-regarded principal, to lead the school, paying her a salary of $100 a month. On April 6, the Tapes appeared at Spring Valley Primary School, accompanied by their lawyers. Hurley, the school principal, introduced a new obstacle, demanding that the Tapes produce a certificate of vaccination for their daughter. When they were unable to provide one, she turned them away. A week later, the Chinese school opened. Thayer arranged seventeen desks in front of a blackboard and waited to see who would show up. Bee, the Chinese consul, had been trying to encourage Chinese parents to send their children. The first students to arrive were Mamie Tape and her six-year-old brother, Frank, dressed in American clothes. Frank's hair was neatly trimmed. Mamie wore her hair in a braid, tied with a ribbon. They were accompanied by two lawyers and a small gaggle of press. They watched as Frank horsed around in the classroom, taking a while to settle. Mamie was soon bent over her copy of McGuffey's second reader, an elementary school textbook, and doing simple subtraction problems. In the afternoon, the clatter of children climbing the stairs was heard outside the classroom. Four Chinese boys had arrived to enroll in the school as well, two of them twelve years old and two of them ten. They were dressed in Chinese robes and took off their caps when Thayer greeted them. They all spoke English fluently, having studied in missionary schools. They fell easily into the rhythms of school, while the Tape children, unused to the structure of the classroom, seemed restless. At recess, Thayer allowed them to roller-skate in the upstairs playroom.

The Tapes remained stung by their rejection. Mary Tape wrote a letter to the school board, excoriating them for making "all sorts of excuses" to keep Mamie out of school. "Is it a disgrace to be Born a Chinese?" she wrote. "Didn't God make us all!!!" She invited the members of the board to meet her family and judge for themselves if they are "not the same as other Caucasians, except in features. It seems no matter how a Chinese may live and dress so long as you know they Chinese. Then they are hated as one. There is not any right or justice for them."

The Tapes continued to commute to the school "way down in Chinatown," as Mamie Tape later put it, for the rest of the school year. Attendance at the school remained sparse in those early months—the Chinese population seemed suspicious of the school board's intentions. The next year, two dozen students enrolled. The number gradually climbed, and by the end of the century, about a hundred and thirty students were in attendance. In the summer of 1885, a special committee of the board of supervisors in San Francisco issued a report about the condition of the Chinese quarter and devoted a section to the issue of Chinese children and the public schools. The report argued that, with the way they were raised in "filth and degradation," mingling them with white children was out of the question. "And yet something must be done with them, some action must be taken to rid them of their proclivities and habits if we would protect posterity from unlimited evil consequences," the report said. How to deal with this "constantly increasing number of Mongolian children?" The committee mused about separating the children from their parents and scattering them "among our own people" but concluded this was impracticable. The only real remedy, the committee concluded, was stopping Chinese immigration for good, making it "physically impossible for the Chinaman to land upon our shores." It was a belief held by a growing number of residents on the Pacific coast. They would soon decide to take matters into their own hands.

Part IV

———————

Outcasts

CHAPTER 15

Wipe Out the Plague Spots

The Chinese quarter in Eureka, California, was known for its stench. It occupied a single square block in the center of town. The land was low-lying and swampy; a gulch cut through the middle, marking the course of a stream that ended in a nearby marsh. By the mid-1880s, more than two hundred Chinese residents had crowded into crude shanties in the quarter. In the summer, the stream bisecting the quarter turned into a fetid pond, covered in green scum and smelling of rotten vegetables and other refuse, a result of the lack of proper drainage for the neighborhood.

Eureka, a town of about three thousand people at the time, was situated on a plateau, surrounded by redwood trees. The community was rough-hewn and remote, located on the shoreline of Humboldt Bay, about fifty miles south of the Oregon border. Rain and fog enveloped the region. Large sawmills, totems of the region's main industry, dotted the waterfront. The turquoise waters of the bay, a long, narrow estuary separated from the ocean by two spits of land, circumscribed the northern and western boundaries of the town. Until the completion of a railroad that connected the town to the rest of the state in 1914, the most common way to travel to Eureka was by steamship.

The first Chinese arrivals in the region were miners, making their way to the rich diggings along the Trinity River during the gold rush. The Chinese quarter in Eureka, the seat of Humboldt County, did not take shape until the mid-1870s. By then, the placer mines had been depleted. The inhabitants of "China Town," as it was known, occupied a district bounded by E and F Streets and Fourth and Fifth Streets. They mostly worked as laundrymen, cooks, miners, and laborers. They rented their homes for six to eight dollars a month from Casper Ricks, an early arrival in Eureka who had purchased many of the lots that made up the original town site. Relations between Chinese residents and their white counterparts were relatively amicable, but there were signs of the hostility that could be provoked.

On a Monday evening in January 1876, Chinese residents were celebrating the Lunar New Year. A drunken white man barged into a house on the block and got into a skirmish with a man inside. The fracas spilled out into the street. The Chinese man drew a pistol and fired, wounding the intruder—a man named Scotty Foulds—in the abdomen. Foulds staggered away, making his way to First Street. Onlookers summoned a pair of doctors, who examined the injured man and suggested he go to the hospital. His prognosis appeared bleak. (He died several days later.) As word spread of the shooting, a crowd gathered on First Street. "Tomahawk every heathen in the place," one man shouted. The mob turned on a Chinese residence on First Street, hurling rocks that shattered windows and tearing out doors and window sashes. One Chinese resident was struck in the mouth, knocking out his front teeth; another Chinese bystander was struck as well. As the frenzied crowd prepared to head to Fourth Street, the heart of China Town, the city marshal stopped them. Two days later, the *Humboldt Times* chastised members of the mob, calling the attack a disgraceful affair, and argued that "the Chinese are here and cannot be removed." The editorial portrayed the Chinese residents of Eureka as harmless, a people who kept to themselves, and asserted that they deserved protection, just like any other nationality. Prosecutors tried a Chinese resident named Ah Ying for murder, but an initial trial ended in a hung jury; a subsequent jury found him not guilty.

In the late 1870s, the region's economy soured amid the nationwide economic depression. Resentment over the Chinese presence metastasized. Kearney's Workingmen's Party, with its rabidly anti-Chinese platform, rose to prominence in the county. Children made a sport of pelting the houses in China Town with rocks and pulling on the braids of Chinese men they encountered. The mischief grew so prevalent that in January 1876 a grand jury issued a warning to parents and law enforcement that steps should be taken to curb the harassment, because it could "lead to serious results." In March 1880, the residents of Garberville, a small settlement built on a sheltered ridge near the Eel River, in the southern part of the county, expelled their Chinese residents.

Chinese laborers were becoming an increasingly conspicuous presence in railroad construction and in canneries in the area. Alarm grew among white residents that lumber companies were poised to turn to Chinese laborers. On March 4, 1882, Thomas Walsh, Eureka's mayor, convened a mass meeting at Centennial Hall, the town's largest gathering spot, on the Chinese restriction bill. The wooden building looked like a large barn. It had been built in 1876 to mark the country's centenary and stood just outside of China Town. During the meeting, attendees adopted resolutions denouncing "the hordes of Mongolian paupers, criminals and prostitutes flooding our shores" and demanding that "at last it may be taken from us and our institutions and government relieved from this threatening danger."

On April 6, 1882, news of President Chester Alan Arthur's veto of the bill reached the town. A Eureka man, John O'Neil, had been drinking heavily and discussing the issue with other residents when he called out to a passing Chinese man and knocked him to the ground. O'Neil was arrested and brought before a judge. The accused man warned in court that anyone who "stood in" with the heathen should be careful. The judge sentenced him to thirty days in jail.

Soon there was a new complaint about China Town. A pair of rival tongs had made their way to Eureka. During the summer and fall of 1884, their feuding became increasingly public. "They had been fighting among themselves," one town resident later recalled. "I don't know what for. But there were two tongs and each one had a flagpole alongside of the street and the great game was to go chop the other tong's flagpole down." They had also acquired guns. On a Sunday evening in August, a row broke out in the Chinese quarter. A reporter watched a knot of men, "a struggling mass of humanity," armed with knives and pistols, scuffle. A gunshot rang out, leaving a boy prostrate in the street. (It was later discovered that he was uninjured.) Several more shots were fired.

The police arrived and made several arrests. The next day, the judge released the suspects, because it was unclear who had fired the shots, and no real damage had occurred. The skirmishes continued and local authorities struggled to identify the culprits, stymied by language and the lack of cooperation from tong members. The *Times-Telephone*, a newspaper whose offices were across from the Chinese quarter, had previously defended the Chinese residents of Eureka, but now it decided that they were "becoming an intolerable nuisance to our people." The newspaper asserted that "if some means cannot be devised to make them behave they should be made to leave."

In the early morning hours of February 1, 1885, another gun battle broke out, at the corner of Fourth and F Streets, in the Chinese quarter. Two Chinese men were killed and three were wounded; the police took eight men to jail. On February 5, the *Times-Telephone* published a searing editorial with the headline "Wipe Out the Plague Spots." It called the Chinese district a "leprous quarter" in the heart of the city that threatened Eureka's future. The editorial focused on the recent violence, but there were other familiar complaints, about the Chinese threat to the morals of the town's "good citizens," as well as the danger they posed to public health. Like dry kindling, the anger towards Eureka's Chinese inhabitants was accumulating.

It was an errant bullet that was the steel striking flint. Just after six o'clock on Friday evening, February 6, two Chinese men brushed past each other on the sidewalk, on the north side of Fourth Street, in the Chinese quarter. They exchanged words; both men began shooting. They fired nine or ten shots, in rapid succession. David Kendall, a member of the city council and owner of a livery stable, had just eaten dinner and was returning to the stable, heading down E Street. Kendall was fifty-six years old. He had been a resident of Eureka for a dozen years, after previously living in Oregon. He was known as kindhearted and cordial. When Kendall crossed Fourth Street, a stray bullet struck him in the head. He fell face down on the road. A passerby, Willard LaGrange, who knew Kendall from local Republican circles, was quickly by his side. LaGrange carried Kendall to his home, about a block away. Reuben

Gross, a longtime doctor in town who had been trained at the Royal College of Surgeons in Edinburgh, Scotland, was summoned; W. H. Wyman, the publisher of the *Times-Telephone*, also rushed to Kendall's home. The councilman managed to say a few words to them but died shortly afterward. Kendall's wife, Prudence, along with his daughter, Maggie, were nearly catatonic. Lou Ballschmidt, a youth whose father owned a furniture store in Eureka, had also been caught in the crossfire and was struck in the foot. He would walk with a limp for the rest of his life.

Word spread of Kendall's shooting. Several hundred men gathered on the corner of Fourth and F Streets. There were shouts of "Burn them out! Hang them!" The police arrested a Chinese man who they believed had fired the shot that struck Kendall, but they struggled to transport him to the jail through the frenzied mob. Rioters surged around the prisoner, beating him. By the time the police managed to deposit him inside the jail, news that Kendall had died whipped through the crowd. "The town went wild," another resident later said. There were screams to round up the Chinese and drive them into Humboldt Bay. Seemingly every able-bodied man in town had grabbed a lantern and converged on the Chinese quarter.

Town leaders called for a meeting at nearby Centennial Hall. Within twenty minutes, more than six hundred men had assembled in the building; hundreds of others stood outside. It was quickly decided that Mayor Walsh would preside over the meeting. Capt. Hans Buhne, a prominent Eureka citizen who had piloted the first schooner across the bar into Humboldt Bay, was chosen as the meeting's secretary. Frank McGowan, a lawyer who was active in Republican politics, and A. J. Bledsoe, a fellow attorney who would author a book the next year called *The People v. John Chinaman*, rose to deliver vitriolic speeches on the evils of the Chinese presence. Humboldt's sheriff, Thomas M. Brown, an early California settler who had driven an ox team across the Great Plains during the gold rush, stood and told the men in the hall that he agreed with their aims but pleaded for restraint. He had sworn an oath to uphold the law and promised to adhere to it. "If anybody starts anything violating the law," he said, "they've got to reckon with me and my deputies."

The Rev. Charles Andrew Huntington, the seventy-three-year-old pastor of the Congregational church, just down the street from the Chinese quarter, was a lonely voice, defending the Chinese. Huntington, who had snow-white hair and genial eyes, had lived an itinerant life that included stints as a schoolmaster in Illinois, a nurse in the Union army during the Battle of Vicksburg, and an administrator in the Bureau of Indian Affairs in Washington Territory. After he left the Indian service, he had turned to full-time church ministry. In the fall of 1881, he had arrived in Eureka and thrown himself into rebuilding a struggling congregation. He found the "powers of evil" strong in a town that included two dozen saloons. By contrast, he admired the Chinese residents for their work ethic. He established a thriving Sunday school for about a dozen Chinese students.

Before the enraged crowd inside the hall, Huntington argued that Kendall's death was accidental. "The Chinaman who fired the shot is guilty of violating a city ordinance and should be summarily punished," he said. "But the rank and file of the people in Chinatown are as innocent of the death of Mr. Kendall as I am. They pay their rent, they mind their own business, and you have no more right to drive them from their homes, than you have to drive me from my home. If Chinamen have no character, white men ought to have some." The Rev. C. E. Rich, who had taken over the pastorate of the Methodist Episcopal church in Eureka several months earlier, urged the crowd to avoid violence and "do no evil." After heated deliberations, the most extreme measures were set aside, including a proposal to massacre the residents of the Chinese quarter and another to raze the neighborhood. The men in the hall finally approved a resolution to elect a Committee of Fifteen, charged with notifying Chinese residents that they had twenty-four hours to leave town. The committee included McGowan, Bledsoe, and other anti-Chinese zealots; they elected Buhne as the committee's chairman. The city marshal, George Lindsay, assisted by an officer, rounded up three representatives from each warring Chinese faction and brought them before the committee. The *Humboldt*, a steamship from San Francisco, was at the docks and scheduled to depart the following afternoon. (A second ship, the *City of Chester*, arrived the following morning.) All

Chinese residents should gather their belongings, the committee said, and be on board when the ships departed.

Within a half hour, Chinese residents were packing. By morning, there were piles of merchandise and personal belongings on the sidewalk. Several white men erected a gallows on Fourth Street, a visible warning. Some white residents raided Chinese laundries to retrieve their clothing. In many cases, the washers were already gone.

Squads of white men fanned out to ensure that every Chinese resident was informed of the edict. One Chinese gardener, who lived on the outskirts of Eureka and sold vegetables every day in town, had no idea what had transpired. He had ten fat hogs, ready for sale at the market, and a garden full of vegetables. He protested the order. "What have I done?" he said. "You are a Chinaman and you must go," they said. The gardener went to his neighbor, James Gill, a longtime resident of Eureka who maintained the county's hospital for the indigent next door. Gill advised him that the safest option was to simply obey. The gardener left his vegetables and livestock with Gill for safekeeping and headed for the docks. A group of Chinese laborers had been working on railroad branch lines at Warren Creek, northeast of Eureka. Their camp was just below the home of John Warren, an early settler of the area. When news of the turbulence reached the Chinese workers, they were frightened, but they trusted Warren enough to let him escort them into town.

At one o'clock in the afternoon, several hundred people convened inside Centennial Hall to hear a progress report from the committee. They resolved that no Chinese resident would be allowed to return to the city and agreed that the committee would warn any new Chinese arrival to stay away. All property owners would also be encouraged not to rent to Chinese tenants. After the meeting adjourned, the crowd marched through the Chinese quarter, a visible show of force.

Around the same time, a Chinese resident who went by the name Charley Way Lum called upon Rev. Huntington and his family at the church parsonage, next door to Centennial Hall. A year or two after the Huntingtons arrived in Eureka, Lum had showed up at the Congregational church on a Sunday evening. He was neatly dressed and attentive. Afterward, Huntington greeted Lum and learned that he'd been a part of the Chinese mission in San Francisco. He owned a book containing Bible lessons in English and Chinese, published by Rev. Gibson, the Methodist minister. Lum asked Huntington for help continuing his studies of the scriptures. Huntington began meeting with him four nights a week; when Huntington was busy, his wife, Lucretia, or their daughter, carried on the lessons with Lum. Lucretia asked Lum if there were other Chinese residents who might be interested in Bible lessons. Soon, a dozen young Chinese men were meeting regularly at the Huntingtons' kitchen table. When the class got too large, they moved to the basement of the chapel. The men took up a collection of $2.50 a month to defray the costs of the school. Lum became the Huntingtons' interpreter. In November 1884, shortly before the expulsion, the congregation voted unanimously to grant the full rights of church membership to Lum, and Huntington baptized him.

After hearing news about the committee's decree for Chinese residents, Lum had rushed to leave. He hurried over to the Huntingtons to bid them farewell. The minister was not home, so Lucretia Huntington ushered Lum inside. He asked for the family's prayers. Suddenly, the yard in the rear of the church filled with men. Some children had alerted them about a "Chinaman going into that house." The men barged into the parsonage and demanded, "Where's that Chinaman?" Lum cowered behind the women, as they tried to hide him with their skirts. Lucretia Huntington pleaded with the men, explaining that Lum was already on his way to the docks, but they led Lum out by his queue and dragged him to the gallows that had been erected. Someone placed a noose around Lum's neck. Suddenly, a stentorian voice commanded, "Take that rope off that boy's neck." It was Rev. Rich, the Methodist minister. "If you hang him, you'll hang him over my dead body," he said. Writing about the episode later in his memoirs, Rev. Huntington likened Rev. Rich's intervention to "a clap of thunder." The men removed the noose and instead hauled Lum to the warehouses by the docks, where the Chinese were being held until the ships left for San Francisco. When Huntington returned home, he learned from his wife and daughter what had happened. They realized that Lum had left on their kitchen table his Bible, a pair of gloves, and an umbrella. Huntington took the items to the docks and, after much cajoling, persuaded the guards to let him through. He found Lum in a corner, weeping, surrounded by his Bible study class-mates. Huntington tried to comfort him, reminding him of Jesus's words to his followers that they would need to take up their own crosses if they wished to follow him. Huntington said a prayer for Lum and then had to leave. The *Humboldt* had been scheduled to set off for San Francisco at three o'clock in the afternoon, but rough seas delayed its departure. That night, clusters of Chinese residents straggled out of the city on their own, some on the wagon road towards Arcata, a neighboring town to the north, where white residents had also resolved to expel the Chinese; others headed south, in the direction of the Eel River Valley.

The following morning, more than three hundred Chinese residents boarded the two waiting steamships. At least a few of the passengers had resided in Eureka for more than a decade. Between them, the ships carried 150 tons of cargo—the possessions that the Chinese residents had managed to bring with them. Two of the passengers on board the ships had suffered gunshot wounds. They would be treated in San Francisco. The city marshal accompanied the passengers on the *City of Chester,* intending to solicit the help of police in San Francisco in arresting the tong members in the group. After the group arrived, however, it soon became clear there was not enough evidence to keep anyone in custody. (The Chinese suspect arrested on the night of the shooting was also released.)

Word of what had taken place in Eureka filtered quickly through San Francisco's Chinatown. A meeting was held, in which several for-mer Eureka residents recounted what they'd been through. A reporter asked Colonel Bee, of the Chinese consulate, about his feelings on the expulsion. "We intend to wait quietly till the excitement dies down and then seek redress in the courts," he said. He blamed the tumult on "a few highbinders—lawbreakers." But he made clear that most of the expelled were innocent. "Many of them are peaceable merchants, whose business has been broken up by their expulsion," he said. "Somebody will have to pay for the injury done them."

On January 21, 1886, Wing Hing, a Chinese merchant, sued the city of Eureka in federal court on behalf of fifty-six Chinese plaintiffs, for loss of property and loss of business from the "mob of disorderly and riotous persons" that had driven them out. Wing Hing himself claimed $5,559 in lost or damaged merchandise and other goods and another $3,200 in losses from the destruction of his business. In total, the former Eureka residents sought $132,830 in damages. Thomas Riordan, the prominent San Francisco lawyer retained by the Chinese consulate, represented the Chinese plaintiffs before Judge Sawyer in circuit court.

Several weeks after the lawsuit was filed, hundreds of Humboldt County residents assembled again in Centennial Hall to mark the anniversary of the Chinese exodus. It was the largest public meeting ever held in the town. More than three hundred people traveled by boat from Arcata for the gathering. As people filed into the hall, a brass band played outside. The Committee of Fifteen presented their final report and encouraged "eternal vigilance" against Chinese encroachment. By loud ovation, the meeting attendees reappointed the members of the committee to a new term. J. P. Haynes, a lawyer and committee member, paid tribute to David Kendall and declared that the focus had shifted, from "the Chinese must go" to "the Chinese must never return." A Chinese man named Charley Mock had recently tried to purchase a property on Second Street in Eureka, with the help of a white man. A group of Eureka citizens had escorted Mock onto a steamship back to San Francisco. The citizens in the hall unanimously approved a resolution assailing anyone who sold or leased real estate to the Chinese as a "traitor to his race." One speaker compared Kendall's death to the "first shot at Lexington," the beginning of a race war sweeping the state.

In early February, Eureka's city council dispatched S. M. Buck, the city attorney, to San Francisco to undertake its defense. He found the circuit court's calendar overstuffed with cases, making clear that the suit would not be adjudicated quickly. Buck's first task was filing a motion to strike from the lawsuit the damages for loss of business, which Sawyer granted, leaving just the property damage claims. It would be another three years, however, before the case was finally settled. The court record offers little explanation of what transpired. A judgment entered on March 2, 1889, reads: "The court having upon the third call of this cause on the 'General Trial Calendar' of this Court, without answer from either party, ordered that this case be dismissed for want of prosecution." Sawyer ordered that the Chinese plaintiffs pay $15 to cover the city of Eureka's court costs. A brief newspaper account published several weeks later reported the court had "rendered a decision for the defendant against the Chinaman." There would be no redress for the Chinese.

Eureka's example became a model for other towns in the region. In late February 1886, white residents in Ferndale, a town about twenty miles south, built a bonfire in the heart of town. During a mass meeting, they resolved to abolish the "existing evil" of the Chinese immigrants in their midst and pledged to stop employing them. The town's Chinese residents scrambled to leave. A week later, the local press reported that "the Chinamen have left Ferndale," except for two whose departure had been delayed for financial reasons. They, too, would be encouraged to "move to a more healthy and congenial atmosphere." In mid-February, Arcata residents pledged to take steps towards the "total expulsion of the Chinese from our midst." By the end of April, they were also reportedly all gone.

In the years after the expulsion, Humboldt County leaders exulted in what they'd done. A county business directory, published in November 1890, boasted about Humboldt's "natural resources," "delightful climate," "picturesque scenery," and "beautiful homes." In boldface letters, it also proclaimed Humboldt to be "the only county in the state containing no Chinamen." In a more detailed description inside the directory, the author explains "there is not a Chinaman in Humboldt county," except in isolated pockets in the rugged far reaches of the county. "Nature's benefactions to Humboldt county have been many, but we pride ourselves on having, by our own efforts, eradicated a festering, putrescent sore from our vitals," the directory says. In 1931, a longtime resident and newspaper publisher, Will Speegle, who had been a friend of the committee member Frank McGowan, published an article fondly recalling the expulsion. "It is now almost 45 years since the last of the Chinamen left here and the younger generation have during all that time been denied the thrill of throwing rocks at the China houses," he wrote. Yet, for all the vitriol of anti-Chinese zealots, some Chinese residents managed to persist in Humboldt. A houseboy named Lee Wong had been living with the Porter family at their ranch in Hydesville, a tiny agricultural community in the Eel River Valley. The family's patriarch, Robert, was a prominent resident of the county and one of the operators of a railroad that ran through Eel River Valley to Eureka. When members of the Committee of Fifteen visited Porter after the expulsion edict, he had refused to turn Lee Wong over to them, arguing that his wife, Eliza, needed him. Lee Wong, who was known to the family as "Leong," was a good cook and the family's four young children were all attached to him. He stayed on with the family for another year after the expulsion. One evening, the Porters hosted some members of the committee for a meal. Despite entreaties from Eliza, Lee Wong refused to cook for the men. He finally parted ways with the family in early 1886, when his uncle in San Francisco sent word that he was returning to China and that he should come with him. The family devised a plan to sneak him into town. Eliza escorted him to the railroad station and had the conductor lock him inside a baggage car. When the railroad arrived, however, the steamship to San Francisco was not at the dock. A friendly express wagon operator took him to his office and hid him overnight. The next morning, Lee Wong boarded the ship and safely departed Eureka. When he finally returned to his village in China, he continued writing letters to the Porters, affectionately signing off as "Your Chinese maid, Lee Wong."

Another Chinese man survived the expulsion by swimming along the shoreline of Humboldt Bay to Buhne Point, several miles south of Eureka, then stumbling through marshes and hiding out at a ranch on Humboldt Hill, where he later found employment doing odd jobs. Chinese miners persisted in Orleans Bar, a settlement in the northeastern corner of Humboldt County, near the Klamath River. William Lord, a storekeeper, stocked canned lobster, abalone, and shrimp, as well as dried oysters, rice wine, and dried mushrooms, for his Chinese customers. He also sold them opium. His ledgers show the number of Chinese customers declined in the first months after the expulsion, but by the summer they had returned. After the turn of the century, at least three elderly Chinese men who'd married Native American women were still living in other remote communities nearby, along the river. One man, known as "Bow," lived near Marten's Ferry, and had a son, Willie Bow, who went to school with white children. Fong and John Cook lived further down the river, near Capell Creek. Fong had a school-age son as well. The Chinese men had evidently been left alone after the expulsion because the three-day journey by horseback from Eureka, over mountainous terrain, was so arduous.

The best-known survivor of the expulsion was Charley Moon, a wiry man with skin like aged leather, weathered and furrowed. He had come to America in the mid-1870s, at the age of twelve, under the care of an older brother. He would later recall leaving his village and drifting for several days down a wide river, in a boat that was hardly more than a raft, before arriving in Guangzhou, and then sailing to America in the hold of a ship, not knowing for days at a time whether it was night or day. His brother went to work in the Klamath mines. Moon, however, was too young and small for mining, so he was left behind in Arcata. He fell in with a man known as "Old Man Tilly," who put the boy to work collecting nails and other items of value from the ruins of burned-down houses.

It's unclear exactly how Charley came to be the responsibility of Thomas Bair, a swarthy Arkansas native, with a walrus mustache and reserved manner, who had crossed the Great Plains with an uncle in 1855, at the age of eleven. Both of Bair's parents had died when he was nine years old, leaving him an orphan and penniless. Bair's uncle settled in Shasta County, but Bair proved to be uncommonly industrious. He began working for a freighting business, leading mule trains through the mountainous terrain of the Trinity River region. He soon saved up enough money to buy his own mule train, working in Montana and Idaho. He later sold that business and settled in Arcata, working as a packer for a merchant with stores throughout the mining districts. After several years, Bair once again struck out on his own, acquiring the packing business for himself. He also secured a government appointment as a trader at Fort Gaston, where he ran a general store and exchanged goods with the Indigenous people of the Hoopa Valley Reservation. He eventually owned about two hundred mules, which he relied upon to haul goods in trains twenty to fifty animals long. He'd often sleep overnight on the trail with his pack train, ensuring that no other trader passed him in the night, so he could reach the reservation first.

Bair's grandson, Tomas, later wrote that his grandfather took charge of Moon after "some sort of a negotiation," bringing him to Maple Creek, one of his ranches near the Upper Mad River, where he maintained a vast cattle range. Moon helped with chores, learned to cook, and planted a vegetable garden. Tomas Bair said that Moon largely did whatever he wanted and was answerable only to the elder Bair. Around the same time that Moon began working for him, Bair married Alice Boyce, who gave birth to three boys. Their home in Arcata had a neat yard and commanding views of the redwood country and Humboldt Bay in the distance. Charley began working at another of Bair's ranches, near Redwood Creek. Charley became a kind of handyman across Bair's various enterprises, possessing an uncanny ability to fix almost anything. In 1882, Alice died, leaving Charley to manage the Bair household, cooking all meals and helping to raise two young boys. (One of the couple's sons had died as an infant.) He became indispensable to Bair.

In February 1885, when the Chinese expulsion took place, several men from Eureka arrived at the Redwood Creek ranch and told Bair that they had come for his "chink." Bair stood his ground. "Charley is the only mother my boys have, and he is doing a grand job, and you are not going to take him," he said. The men continued to threaten and harangue Bair, but he was unbending. The men rode off, promising that they'd return. Bair posted lookouts on his property. Several days later, a group of vigilantes returned to the ranch. Bair greeted them with a Winchester rifle in his arms. The leader of the posse again demanded that Bair turn Moon over. Bair told the men that his rifle had thirteen shells. "You may get me, but there will be more than one of you fellows who will not ride back to town," Bair said. The men hurled insults and blustered but finally turned around, and Moon became known as "Humboldt's only Chinaman."

A few years after the expulsion, Moon married an Indigenous woman, from the Chilula tribe, known as Minnie, who lived on government-allotted land several miles down the creek. The couple went on to raise a large brood of children. Moon continued to serve as the chief cook at the Bair ranch, which came to include a small hotel for paying guests. He became a familiar figure in the kitchen, greeting visitors with his affable smile and laugh, even if he was busy. Every day, at four o'clock in the afternoon, Moon took a break from his chores to travel by horseback to Minnie's home to cook her dinner. He eventually quit the kitchen to work full-time as a ranch hand, preferring to be outside on the range. Bair switched to raising sheep, and Moon took charge of the Maple Creek ranch, patrolling it on horseback in his signature wide-brimmed hat with high crown. He was invariably among his sheep, no matter the weather. He never learned to read or write but was always a fount of historical information and current events. Unlike other Chinese immigrants, he did not drink tea, preferring instead coffee and whiskey. The Bairs maintained a whiskey still at Maple Creek, and Moon took charge of the distilling. Visitors to the ranch were advised to always bring a quart of whiskey for Moon as a gift. After Tom Bair died, in 1913, Moon went to work for his son, Fred, and his wife, Mabel, shuttling between ranches, as well as a fishing resort belonging to the family on the Klamath River. "We have known Charley for 30 years and go on record right now saying that regardless of race, he is one of the whitest men we have ever known," Don Carr, editor of the *Ferndale Enterprise*, wrote in an article. He went on to describe Moon as a "Chinaman by birth, but a loyal American at heart." Moon died in 1943, survived by three daughters and five sons. His obituary said he was eighty-three years old. The headline read: "Charlie Moon, Only Chinese Resident of the County Dies."

CHAPTER 16

White Men, Fall In

Violence usually has a proximate cause that is relatively straightforward to identify—an insult, a taunt, a source of aggrievement. What is more challenging is tracing the larger patterns, when an individual act, or episode, becomes part of a cycle. "For historians violence is a difficult subject, diffuse and hard to cope with," the historian Richard Hofstadter once wrote. "It is committed by isolated individuals and crowds alike; it is undertaken for a variety of purposes (and at times for no discernible rational purpose at all), and in a variety of ways ranging from assassinations and murders to lynchings, duels, brawls, feuds and riots; it stems from criminal intent and from political idealism, from antagonisms that are entirely personal and from antagonisms of large social consequence." Eureka would turn out to be the opening act of a harrowing period in American history that became known as the "driving out," in which dozens of communities across the western United States expelled their Chinese residents. The Eureka method became a manual of racial terror that guided other town leaders. Yet the wave of Chinese expulsions did not begin immediately. There was an interregnum, when the fury over Chinese immigration seemed to still largely be contained. Then, in September 1885, the fury spilled over. The setting was a coal mining town in southern Wyoming Territory called Rock Springs.

As with so much about the American West, the story of Rock Springs begins with the transcontinental railroad. Previously, the area that would become the Wyoming Territory had been a transitory place, where stagecoaches and covered wagons bumped down rutted paths on their way west. There was little about Wyoming that made it attractive for settlement: the soil was unfriendly to farming; roaming tribes of American Indians also posed an omnipresent threat. The area's fortunes began to change in 1867, as Union Pacific tracklayers worked their way across the plains. Tent cities and then more permanent towns began to spring up along the railroad's path. In the summer of 1868, President Andrew Johnson formally established the territory, carving it out of parts of Idaho, Utah, and Dakota territories. After Promontory Summit, growing numbers of Chinese immigrants began arriving in the territory. Most found work with the Union Pacific, performing maintenance on the iron road. They also began toiling in coal mines the company had opened in Almy, in the Bear River valley. A Chinese settlement grew in the neighboring town of Evanston, across the railroad tracks from where the white residents lived.

The leader of the Chinese community was a refined, slender man, known as Ah Say, who spoke fluent English. Ah Say, whose formal name was Leo Wing Jan, was a native of Taishan. He had arrived in the United States as a teenager in 1857, and worked initially in gold mining. When the Central Pacific began to build the transcontinental railroad, he became a labor contractor for them. In May 1869, he settled in Evanston and established himself as a headman, supplying workers for the Union Pacific and other mining companies. More than a hundred and fifty others from the Leo clan would ultimately join him in southern Wyoming. Ah Say became a frequent presence in the homes of mine officials, always bringing fruits and nuts and other gifts. One day, he shared the news that he was to be married, and his wife, Low Shee, would join him in America. They eventually had three daughters and two sons, all born in Wyoming. He also managed to become a naturalized American citizen.

The railroad's steady advance into new communities and its overriding need for fuel turned coal mining into one of the region's most important industries. Two decades earlier, during a surveying expedition, Captain Howard Stansbury, of the U.S. Army's Corps of Topographical Engineers, had noticed large, black outcroppings amid the surrounding sandstone cliffs and concluded that deposits were abundant. In the late 1860s, a pair of brothers, Archibald and Duncan Blair, established a coal mine near a stagecoach station in southern Wyoming, in a valley that followed the path of a swift stream, about fifty feet wide, known as Bitter Creek. The area was arid and treeless, the home of antelope herds and flocks of sage chicken. There was also, most extraordinarily, a small freshwater spring at the base of a sandstone bluff—a rock spring. Soon after the Blairs set up their camp, another set of brothers, Thomas and Charles Wardell, established a mine east of the Blairs, on a bluff overlooking the south bank of Bitter Creek. It was at this site, about two miles south of the spring, that a town, Rock Springs, was birthed.

The Wardells, who had already opened a mine in the eastern part of the territory, had discovered in their new location a fabulously thick seam of bituminous coal—the fuel most used in steam locomotives. The Rock Springs mine had another asset: its entrance happened to be just a few yards away from the Union Pacific's mainline. By 1875, the population of the settlement had grown to a thousand people, with five hundred men, mostly English, Welsh, Scottish, and Scandinavian immigrants, employed by the Union Pacific across two mines. It was a rude livelihood. The workers toiled in pairs in underground "rooms"— work areas usually five to ten yards wide and forty to sixty yards long. They used picks and black powder to extract the coal, which mules then hauled to the surface. The work was dangerous. In 1869, a fire underground in the Avondale mine, in northeastern Pennsylvania, killed more than a hundred miners.

The miners mostly lived in crude dugouts built into the riverbank. Mine officials constructed wood-frame homes along the railroad tracks and a two-story stone building to house their offices, a post office, and a company-owned general store, where miners bought their tools and other necessities. Workers were paid by the bushel of coal they mined. In early November 1875, the prevailing wage was four cents per bushel, which meant workers made anywhere from two to four dollars a day. With winter approaching, company officials sought to increase production. The exact details of what came next are contested. The official accounts from mine executives blame workers for rebuffing the order to step up their work. A different version of events, from the miners themselves, however, describes a cut in their wages and the company reneging on a promise to reduce prices at the company store. What's clear is that the mine workers walked off the job in early November, and company officials acted swiftly to bring in a new workforce.

On the morning of November 13, with bitterly cold temperatures and snow falling, the striking miners were astonished to discover soldiers from Company A of the U.S. Army's Fourth Infantry Division disembarking train cars, with their bayonets glittering in the frosty air. "Marther alive!" one miner said. "If here ain't the sogars!" The soldiers had been dispatched by John Thayer, the territory's recently appointed governor. Union Pacific officials decided to contract with Beckwith, Quinn and Company, which operated the general store in Rock Springs, to bring in Chinese laborers. Its proprietors, Asa C. Beckwith and Anthony Quinn, had gone into business together as young men, hauling supplies unloaded by freighters on the Platte River in Kansas. One day, they happened upon an abandoned steamboat stuck in the mud, laden with guns, ammunition, and whiskey. They unloaded the goods and transported them to Wyoming Territory, where they knew the Union Pacific Railroad was making its way west. They established a series of trading posts along the route and earned themselves a small fortune. They eventually based themselves in Evanston and embarked upon a variety of business ventures.

In late November, Beckwith arrived in Rock Springs on a train full of Chinese miners. He was accompanied by Ah Say, the Chinese labor agent and interpreter, as well as Governor Thayer and a retinue of Union Pacific officials. Mine officials put the Chinese laborers to work right away and posted a list of names of white miners who would be hired back—only a third of them—and declared there would be no further negotiations. Work in the mines resumed with 150 Chinese miners and 50 white miners. The company erected primitive shelters for their new Chinese employees on a sagebrush flat about a quarter mile north of town. Bitter Creek and the Union Pacific Railroad tracks separated the encampment from the rest of town. White miners derisively referred to the Chinese encampment as "Hong Kong."

The Chinese miners and their white counterparts soon settled into what appeared outwardly to be a peaceful coexistence. Beckwith later testified that "no complaints of a serious nature" had been made about their presence, but he was likely blind to the actual dynamics in the mines, or perhaps he was dissembling. In the summer of 1884, the Knights of Labor began organizing restive Union Pacific workers. The Knights had gotten its start in 1869 as a secretive fraternal organization in Philadelphia. It eventually became a driving force behind the national labor movement and one of the most ardent backers of Chinese exclusion. In 1879, Terence Powderly, a former railroad machinist and the mayor of Scranton, Pennsylvania, was elected Grand Master Workman of the Knights. The following year, he decreed that Chinese laborers were barred from membership in the organization. (By contrast, the Knights actively recruited Black members.) The Knights' executive committee issued an invective-filled resolution that urged members to press their representatives in Congress to abrogate the Burlingame Treaty. The Knights became active in organizing lumber workers in Humboldt County and its members participated in the Chinese expulsion that took place there. Powderly would later seek to distance his organization from the violence in Rock Springs, but he blamed the unrest on Congress's failure to act. "In desperation the people of the Pacific coast have petitioned and demanded of Congress to do something to enforce the law, but the Chinese still continue to come," he wrote.

The Knights' inroads among Union Pacific workers began with the company's shopmen, the workers who built and maintained the company's rolling stock. In August 1884, they walked off the job. Several weeks into the strike, company officials agreed to a series of concessions. Two months later, miners in Colorado, as well as at a mine in Carbon, in the eastern part of the Wyoming Territory, went on strike, protesting a summer wage cut. The labor action lasted three months and was ultimately unsuccessful. Throughout the spring, however, there were other walkouts among Union Pacific workers.

In Rock Springs, white miners approached their Chinese colleagues about joining them in work stoppages, but they repeatedly demurred. Tensions rose, as white miners realized that no strike could succeed without Chinese cooperation. The white miners harbored other grievances against their Chinese co-workers—over who got the most lucrative assignments in the mines and who was hired back first after a mine shutdown. Powderly complained about the Chinese to Beckwith, who pointed out that white miners typically earned a dollar more per day. In the summer of 1885, however, Chinese workers were continuing to stream into the mines, while white miners found themselves idled. Objections to Chinese labor became more pointed. "Hints were thrown out that the Chinese were to be driven out of town," O. C. Smith, the town's postmaster, later recalled. By then, there were about 550 Chinese workers in the mines, compared to just under 300 white workers. Notices were posted in mining towns throughout southern Wyoming demanding the expulsion of Chinese residents. In late August, Dave Thomas, a mine boss whom Chinese workers affectionately called "Davie Tom," met with an acquaintance, who would become one of the leaders of the riot. He warned Thomas that "there would be something doing." The phrase lodged in Thomas's mind, but he did not alert anyone about what he'd heard. On August 28, John L. Lewis, a Knights of Labor leader in Denver, warned Beckwith, Quinn and Company officials in a letter about a "storm that is brewing" over the "Chinese problem at Rock Springs." In a separate letter, mailed on the same day to a Union Pacific mining official, Lewis wrote: "For God's sake do what you can to avoid this calamity." On the evening of September 1, the bell rang in Rock Springs, signaling a union meeting. No record of the proceedings survived, but reportedly among the issues discussed was the continued employment of Chinese labor.

That night, Andrew Bugas, a nineteen-year-old miner who had emigrated from Austria several years earlier with his family, was at home with his cousin, also named Andrew, inside their cabin near Bitter Creek. An acquaintance, Sandy Cooper, who worked in the mines with them, showed up unannounced and asked Bugas's cousin if he had a rifle or shotgun. "I will furnish you with one which you must use tomorrow, for we are all going hunting and shooting all the Chinamen we see," Cooper said. Bugas and his cousin thought Cooper was joking, but he returned a half hour later with a heavy rifle and two boxes of cartridges. Cooper then urged them not to go to work in the morning, because it was important for white miners to be "present." It would only become clear the following day what he meant.

. . .

Leo Qarqwang knew his way around the dark passages of the mines, knew how to handle his pick. Leo had been among the cohort of Chinese miners who arrived in Rock Springs in 1875. On Wednesday morning, September 2, 1885, many Chinese miners had the day off, in observance of a Chinese holiday. Leo, however, was working the early shift at the No. 6 mine. The temperature hovered around freezing. There was a light frost on the ground. Farmers across the territory feared damage to their crops. Before dawn, Leo descended on a pit car into the No. 5 entry, one of the main corridors that ran underground in the mine. Two days earlier, mine bosses had closed the other entrances to the mine and marked off new rooms. James A. Evans, the shift foreman, had assigned Qarqwang the second room. He headed there at the beginning of his shift. According to Leo's subsequent testimony to railroad officials, a gang of about fourteen white miners suddenly barged in on him and his partner, Leo Lung Ming, with spades, picks, and shovels. They demanded to know: "What do you Chinamen mean by working here? You have no business to work here." Leo tried to reason with the men and offered to leave if they were in the wrong place. "We Chinamen do not want any trouble," he said. But the white miners set upon them. A half-dozen men surrounded Leo Qarqwang. One miner bashed him in the head with a shovel, leaving a gash on Leo's forehead that cut straight to the bone. Another man attacked Leo Lung Ming, leaving him with deep wounds in the head, chest, and right knee.

White miners later blamed Evans and Dave Brookman, the pit boss that morning, for the dispute. By their account—contradicted by Chinese witnesses—the supervisors had assigned a room to Chinese miners that had been promised to two white men, Isaiah Whitehouse and William Jenkins. Whitehouse, a forty-five-year-old Englishman, was arguably the most prominent member of the mine's workforce. He had arrived in Rock Springs two years earlier and quickly became a popular figure in the community. In November 1884, he won a seat in the territorial legislature, representing Sweetwater County. Whitehouse was a native of Staffordshire, a region with a long coal mining history, and had emigrated to America as a young man in 1861, accompanying his parents. He had been working in mining ever since. In Whitehouse's version of events, he'd started working the day before in one of the new rooms in the entry and had already drilled holes deep into the vein, in preparation for the setting of his charges. He'd taken the afternoon off, because he felt ill. When he returned on Wednesday morning, he found two Chinese miners occupying his room. In the melee that ensued, Chinese working in other rooms rushed in to defend their friends. When the fighting was over, four Chinese miners were badly wounded, one of whom later died. Several of the white miners sustained cuts and bruises.

It was Ah Kuhn, an interpreter and business manager for the Chinese, who first raised the alarm with mine bosses. Ah Kuhn, who was known for the fur coat he liked to wear around town, hurried to the mine office and asked Evans, the foreman, if he was aware of "the trouble over in No. 6 mine." Evans seemed to take his time heading over. When he finally arrived at the No. 6 mine, he found a cluster of Chinese miners at the top of the slope that led out of the mine. He urged them to return to work with him. When the group reached the bottom of the slope, however, they found the white assailants waiting for pit cars to take them out. They grumbled to Evans that they were "not going to suffer Chinamen." Evans blocked them from taking the cars. One of them called out, "Come on boys; we may as well finish it now," and the men walked out together.

Bugas, the young miner who had had the perplexing encounter the night before, was in his cabin alone that morning. His cousin had ignored the admonition to stay home and went to work as usual at the No. 1 mine. At ten o'clock, Bugas noticed through the window that a group of men and boys were harassing the Chinese dinner carriers—men who delivered meals to miners every day, with poles slung over their shoulders—pelting them with stones and causing them to scatter. Soon after, he watched as a brigade of white men assembled nearby. Bugas later estimated there were some sixty to seventy-five men, most with rifles over their shoulders and the others with pistols. They headed in a pack towards town, marching past Chinatown.

When they reached a bridge crossing over Bitter Creek, a group of town residents met them and persuaded them to leave their weapons in a nearby store. The men continued their march into town. "White men, fall in," they chanted. The group headed towards the Knights of Labor hall. From the Chinese quarter, where Leo Qarqwang and other Chinese miners had managed to limp back and were receiving treatment for their wounds, residents could hear a bell ringing for an emergency meeting. Dave Thomas, the mine boss who was friendly with the Chinese, hurried over to Chinatown to warn them about the trouble brewing. A flag, signaling danger, went up in the quarter.

At noon, there seemed to be a lull as miners ate lunch. Saloon owners closed their doors as a precaution. The miners spilled out onto the streets. A cry went up: "Vengeance on the Chinese!" The mob took a vote and decided that the Chinese residents would be expelled. A group of seventy-five armed men began making their way towards Chinatown. When they encountered a group of Chinese workers along the railroad tracks, the rioters fired wildly at them. The mob then halted just outside the Chinese quarter. A committee of three men delivered an ultimatum that residents had an hour to pack up their belongings. Barely a half hour had elapsed, however, when rioters invaded Chinatown.

They came from two different directions, Chinese witnesses later said. One group crossed a plank bridge over Bitter Creek and another advanced towards Chinatown from the railroad tracks. Squads of men encircled the quarter. A group stationed near a pump house opened fire first. A man named Lor Sun Kit was the first resident struck. A bullet pierced his right arm and lodged in his back. He crumpled to the ground, wounded but still alive.

The rioters shot the fifty-six-year-old miner Leo Dye Bah, who had a wife and two children back home in China, in the chest near the bridge, killing him. Another man, Yip Ah Marn, who was thirty-eight years old and lived in the eastern part of the quarter, was also shot dead. Panic ensued in the dugouts and other buildings. Dozens of men were inside a two-story building at one end of the quarter. The sound of arguing came from inside. As the mob advanced, men jumped out of windows and fled. When the rioters began battering down the door, the occupants came pouring out.

Some five to six hundred people lived in the Chinese encampment. Most of them were home at the time of the attack. They fled in all directions. One witness later described the hills to the east of town "literally blue with the hunted Chinamen." Leo Qarqwang had been getting treatment for his wounds at the No. 3 mine, just beyond the Chinese quarter, when he saw armed men approaching. He ran for the hills. He later compared Chinese residents to a flock of frightened sheep. Leo spent several days wandering through the sagebrush, with nothing to eat. He finally found the railroad tracks and caught a train to Evanston.

Many Chinese tumbled down the steep banks of Bitter Creek, splashing into the muddy water. At least one man was cut down struggling to clamber up the bank on the other side. His body was found later, half submerged in the creek. Another miner, Leo Mauwik, another member of the Leo clan, had also been working in the No. 6 mine that morning. He had returned to the Chinese encampment and was inside his hut when a member of the mob ordered him to step outside. As soon as he emerged, he heard gunshots and set off at a run. While he was fleeing, a bullet went through his right arm. He didn't stop running until about four o'clock in the morning, when he reached the neighboring town of Green River, the county seat and the closest other population center, about fifteen miles to the west.

The violence coursed through town like a river, drawing in men, women, and children. One female resident, whose home was near the plank bridge, pointed a revolver at the terrified Chinese men fleeing past her and fired three shots in quick succession, felling two of them. This was likely "Mrs. Osborn," the owner of a laundry in town, who was later celebrated for killing two Chinese men. Another woman had an infant in her arms, but she still managed to knock down a Chinese man running by. When her baby wailed, she spanked him, before turning to pummel the Chinese man some more.

The rioters began setting fire to the buildings in the Chinese encampment. Dense black smoke billowed over the quarter. Frightened residents dashed outside with blankets covering their heads. The bodies of dead Chinese lay everywhere. Rioters tossed corpses into the burning buildings. The smell of burning flesh was acrid. A gusting wind led to fears that the conflagration would spread to the rest of town. Rioters suspended their torching of the Chinese huts, but more than forty homes burned to the ground. Miners usually stored the black powder they used inside their homes. When the licking flames reached a cache, the sky would flash with a powerful explosion. A group of rioters descended upon a dugout belonging to a laundryman, Ah Lee, who had barricaded himself inside. The members of the mob fired through the window. A single shot rang out from inside the building. He was armed. Attackers broke through the roof and a brief scuffle followed. Afterward, Ah Lee lay dead on the floor, with a gunshot wound to the back of his head. A female rioter stomped on his body; another looted bundles of laundry he had laid out for delivery.

Ah Kuhn took shelter in a cellar. When he emerged at about eight o'clock in the evening, several white men spotted him. When the men opened fire, Ah Kuhn ran. In his panic, he dropped about $1,600 in gold that he had been carrying. He made his way to a railroad section house east of town, where a white resident gave him bread and water and allowed him to rest, before he started walking towards Evanston. Several Chinese residents approached the Rev. Timothy Thirloway, who lived near Chinatown with his wife and two daughters. In the evenings, the Thirloways taught English to Chinese miners. The frightened Chinese residents asked if they could hide inside their home, but the family advised them that it wouldn't be safe and sent them away. One miner, known as China Joe, who worked in the No. 3 mine, hid in a large oven for three days, before sneaking out in the middle of the night and fleeing to Green River. A Chinese clerk who worked in the company's general store survived by hiding in the cellar for a week.

A group of rioters marched on the home of James Evans, the foreman who had been involved in the quarrel at the No. 6 mine. They advised him that it would be best if he left town on the evening train. Evans asked for more time to get his affairs in order, but the men were unyielding. Evans departed that night. Rioters next visited the home of Soo Qui, one of the Chinese headmen, but he was out of town, on a trip to Evanston. His petrified wife greeted them instead. "Soo, he go," she said. "I go to him." After the men left, she packed some belongings and went to stay with some white friends. Two days later, she arrived in Evanston by train, disembarking in a colorful gown and shielding her face with a fan. A newspaper reporter characterized her as the "last of her race" to abandon Rock Springs and "probably the last to set foot in the place for many a long year."

James Tisdale, assistant superintendent of the Union Pacific's coal department, was in Cheyenne when the violence broke out. Late in the afternoon, he sent an urgent telegram to Francis E. Warren, the Wyoming territorial governor, asking for help quelling the riot. Warren, a forty-year-old Massachusetts native who earned a Congressional Medal of Honor for his valor during the Civil War, was a rugged former farmer and railroad man. He had arrived in Cheyenne in 1868, when the town was little more than a collection of tents and cabins, to work for a friend's home goods business, and he went on to become a successful rancher. He became the mayor of Cheyenne and chairman of the territory's Republican central committee. In February, President Chester A. Arthur had appointed Warren to the governorship. Warren quickly recognized the gravity of the situation. Wyoming had no organized militia. He sent a request to the army headquarters in Omaha, Nebraska, asking for two companies of soldiers to be dispatched, and alerted the secretary of war in Washington.

At around seven o'clock in the evening, Dave Thomas visited Chinatown with several other men to inspect the situation. They spotted an elderly Chinese man they knew, lying in agony in the dirt but still alive. They debated whether to end his suffering by shooting him, but they left him to die. They saw the body of another Chinese man who went by "Joe Brown." He'd apparently been one of the first to be killed. Joseph Young, the recently elected sheriff of Sweetwater County, arrived from Green River and deployed deputies around the center of town. He struggled, however, to muster enough men in Rock Springs to form a posse to hunt down the rioters. He sent a request to Warren as well for military aid. Warren's alarm was growing. The dispatches from Union Pacific officials were increasingly urgent. He got on a midnight train from Cheyenne to Rock Springs.

Throughout the night, gunfire continued to pop off. Rioters recrossed the creek to torch the remaining buildings in the Chinese quarter. The fires burned all night, bathing the town in a red glow.

In the morning, the full extent of the atrocity became clear. The flat expanse where the Chinese quarter once stood had been transformed into a smoking ruin—a hellscape of smoldering, blackened walls, broken crockery, and other detritus. The most horrific scenes were found in burned-out cellars, where bodies were discovered, often clustered together. Some of the victims had wrapped wet cloths over their heads and burrowed into the earthen walls, trying to escape the smoke and flames. Hogs feasted on a corpse that they had dragged from the ruins. The bodies of other victims, shot as they were trying to flee, lay splayed on the ground. "Today for the first time in a good many years, there is not a Chinaman in Rock Springs," the *Rock Springs Independent*, the town's newspaper, proclaimed. "The five or six hundred who were working in the mines here have been driven out, and nothing but heaps of smoking ruins mark the spot where Chinatown stood."

Some survivors who had hidden overnight in the hills crept back down to the railroad tracks near town. Union Pacific officials loaded up a freight train with food and water and sent it on a rescue mission along the tracks. Some victims made their way to Green River, where they were picked up. One man who managed to reach the town was chased by a band of forty men, until a female proprietor of a local hotel opened her door and ushered the terrified man inside. "She cowed the mob as effectually as could a whole battery of artillery have done," a newspaper account later said. She was one of the few in the white population willing to help the fleeing Chinese. Several hundred eventually took refuge in Evanston. Some went to a gun store in town and bought out everything in stock, in preparation for another attack.

There was confusion about the sending of federal troops to restore order. Army officials told Warren that he needed to make a formal application to President Grover Cleveland, which the governor promptly did on his way to Rock Springs. The president was on vacation in the Adirondack Mountains, however, hunting and fishing with friends. Studying the statutes governing the deployment of federal troops for insurrections, army officials concluded that Warren's request was insufficient, because he failed to make clear that the territorial legislature—the entity normally authorized to make such requests—was not in session. William Endicott, the secretary of war, was also out of town, leaving his second in command, Adjutant General Richard Drum, to confer with Thomas Bayard, the secretary of state. They decided to send two companies to Rock Springs with orders only to protect the United States mail and other federal property. When Warren arrived in Rock Springs, he found the scene almost too much to bear. "The smell of burning human flesh was sickening and almost unendurable, and was plainly discernible for more than a mile along the railroad both east and west," he later wrote.

Railroad officials feared additional violence. "The local authorities are wholly powerless and the City is in the hands of a mob," one company official said in a telegram to the railroad's headquarters in Boston. Tisdale, the assistant superintendent, had returned to Rock Springs but was forced to flee. Subsequent updates reported that white miners had broken into Beckwith, Quinn and Company's large storehouse of gunpowder; that Chinese miners at another Union Pacific mine in Grass Creek, in the Utah Territory, about a hundred and fifty miles away from Rock Springs, had been given twenty minutes to leave town; and that white miners were organizing in Evanston to drive out the Chinese there. In Green River, white vigilantes told the fifteen or twenty Chinese residents in town—about a half-dozen of them cooks at a hotel belonging to the Union Pacific—that they were no longer welcome. Mine operations had ceased almost entirely. Nevertheless, in Evanston, Ah Say pressed company officials to put his people to work. They had lost everything—he estimated their losses totaled more than $200,000. They needed their wages.

In the afternoon, in Rock Springs, John Ludvigsen, the justice of the peace and the acting coroner, summoned a half-dozen local residents to conduct an inquest on fifteen bodies that had been discovered so far. The jurors concluded that four "Chinamen" had died by gunshot wounds by "some means unknown to the jury" and that the others "came to their death by exposure to fire," though their nationality was uncertain because they'd been "defaced beyond recognition." Several days later, a different group of jurors examined another four burned bodies and, again, concluded only that they had "come to their death by fire." The jurors' inconclusive findings hinted at the difficulties to come in bringing anyone to justice. Over the next few days, more bodies would be discovered. The rooting of hogs in a cellar led to the discovery of five additional corpses. Newspapers reported other ghastly stories. According to one account, a Chinese family of three—a husband and wife and their infant—was found in the hills. The mother and her baby had died of thirst and the father committed suicide. Another report: a group of six men who had fled into the hills during the attack wandered for several days amid the sagebrush and grease wood. Without any food or water, they ate their own excrement. One by one, they died. Coyotes feasted on their bodies. On Saturday, September 5, three days after the riot, a lone survivor crept back into town, hungry and thirsty.

Railroad officials were resolute about returning their Chinese workforce to the mines. "Yield nothing to the rioters," Charles F. Adams, the Union Pacific's president, told one of his lieutenants. The company needed assurances, however, that federal troops would protect its workers. The racial terror was spreading. Threats from white men forced an exodus of four hundred Chinese miners from Almy. On September 6, President Cleveland finally emerged from the wilderness, ending a four-week-long vacation and resuming his duties at the White House. The next day, he received a War Department briefing on the violence in Rock Springs. Afterward, the president ordered that soldiers protect Chinese miners "at all hazards." Army officials dispatched six companies to the territory.

On Wednesday afternoon, September 9, a week after the massacre, a passenger train carrying 200 soldiers arrived in Rock Springs, followed by a freight train carrying 650 Chinese miners. In Rock Springs, a jeering crowd of white miners greeted the returning Chinese. They disembarked to a wrenching tableau. While some of the dead had been buried, bodies remained strewn on the ground, mangled and decomposing. The weather was wet and cool. Many of the Chinese miners wept. "It was a sad and painful sight to see the son crying for the father, the brother for the brother, the uncle for the nephew, and friend for friend," a statement from the Chinese laborers later said. The Chinese arrivals bedded down on the sodden ground along the tracks, their campfires flickering in the night.

Labor leaders pledged to block Chinese workers from entering the mines. Mine officials' first attempt, on September 12, to resume coal production failed miserably, as gangs of white miners stood guard outside mine entrances. "The Chinese are so easily frightened," D. O. Clark, the superintendent of the Union Pacific Coal Company, later reported. "They run as soon as any one says anything to them." They had good reason to be apprehensive. The rioters remained at large; many were in the crowds menacing them. Complicating matters for mine bosses, white engineers, carpenters, and other mine employees also refused to work, making it impossible for coal to be hauled out, weighed, and placed on train cars.

A committee representing the white mine workers demanded that Chinese miners and Beckwith, Quinn and Company be dismissed and promised to assist in finding white miners to take their place. Mine officials viewed the request as untenable if white miners continued to threaten them with work stoppages. The Union Pacific bosses were initially careful to avoid antagonizing the labor leaders, but the railroad soon found itself running out of coal to operate. On Saturday, September 19, mine officials issued an ultimatum to the striking workers: If they did not report to work on Monday morning, they would be fired. The day of the deadline, mine officials managed to restart production in two mines with the help of a hundred Chinese miners. By the end of the month, 250 Chinese laborers were back at work. The company began rebuilding Chinatown. The mines were still operating well below capacity, however. Mine officials arranged to replace the striking white workers with a contingent of Mormon miners, another persecuted group. They also began experimenting with labor-saving drilling equipment that helped increase production.

White residents continued to harass Chinese laborers. In late October, a gang of white men attacked a railroad building, just west of town, and drove a group of Chinese track workers into the woods. Company officials resolved to confine Chinese workers to Rock Springs, so they could be better protected. By December, there were nearly 550 men working in the mines—several hundred fewer than before the massacre. Only 85 of them were white miners; the rest were Chinese. The attack had failed in its ultimate purpose—ejecting the Chinese from Rock Springs.

From the outset, Union Pacific officials recognized that the odds of bringing the riot's ringleaders to justice were slim. Most residents were sympathetic to the grievances that white miners had against the Chinese. There was also the threat of retribution against anyone who testified. "I fancy it will be difficult for us to get any of them punished," Samuel Callaway, the general manager of the Union Pacific, wrote to his bosses two days after the massacre. That same day, Sheriff Joseph Young began making arrests, charging suspects with murder, arson, riot, and grand larceny. By Monday, September 7, he'd taken twenty-two men into custody. He was accommodating to his prisoners, letting some of them stop at a nearby saloon before going to jail. The jailed included Isaiah Whitehouse, who had been involved in the initial brawl in the No. 6 mine, as well as his partner that day, William Jenkins. The others were men of varying ages, mostly without distinction. "They would never be singled out from a crowd as rioters and murderers," one account said. A preliminary court hearing for the men had to be delayed until a judge arrived, but the men seemed to be in good spirits, "with no great anxiety as to the result," inside the jail at Green River.

Prosecutors were hampered by the refusal of white residents in Rock Springs to cooperate with the investigation. Augustus Garland, the United States attorney general, ordered A. C. Campbell, the United States attorney for the Wyoming Territory, to travel to Rock Springs to aid the local authorities, but he found himself with little to do, because "none but Chinamen were being examined and the investigation being conducted in the Chinese language," he later wrote in a memorandum.

The Chinese legation in Washington was initially cautious in its public comments about the violence in Rock Springs. A few days after the massacre, when approached by a reporter, the secretary of the legation said only that Chinese officials were hoping to obtain a full report of what had taken place. The Chinese minister in Washington was Zheng Zaoru, a native of the same district in Guangdong province as Yung Wing and a close ally of the reformer Li Hongzhang. In 1882, Zheng had taken over the leadership of the Chinese legation from Chen Lanbin and Yung Wing and quickly found himself fighting the Chinese restriction legislation in Congress. After the riot, Zheng directed Huang Xiquan, the Chinese consul in New York, and Colonel Bee, his counterpart in San Francisco, to head to Rock Springs. The Cleveland administration arranged for two army officers to meet them in Ogden, Utah. On September 16, the two diplomatic officials, along with an interpreter, arrived in Evanston and met with Isaac Bromley, a senior aide to Adams, the president of the Union Pacific. Bromley, a fifty-five-year-old former newspaper editor and Yale graduate, had been dispatched from the company's headquarters in Boston to conduct the railroad's own investigation into the massacre. Bromley had been taking testimony from white miners but was struggling to obtain any reliable information.

The following morning, the group took the train together from Evanston to Rock Springs, where they held a hearing with a committee of white citizens that had been formed after the massacre and then traveled together to the Chinese camp to conduct interviews with the assistance of the consuls' interpreter, Shang Hoy. The consuls asked that the remains of any Chinese killed in the riot be disinterred. The coroner had buried nineteen victims in cheap wooden boxes; the Union Pacific had buried two others. The Chinese officials found only thirteen bodies to be recognizable; the other remains, many of them just bone fragments, had been wrapped in small bundles for burial. According to the Chinese witnesses interviewed by the consuls, at least twenty-eight people were killed in the riot, though the remains of three of the dead were still missing. They had likely died in the barren wilderness surrounding the town or been burned up completely in the fires. At least fifteen people were injured, including some who appeared close to death and others who would likely be maimed for the rest of their lives.

After Huang issued an initial report back to Washington, Zheng, the Chinese minister, sent a telegram to Beijing, summarizing what he knew. He explained that Rock Springs was roughly six thousand *li*, a Chinese unit of measure that was the equivalent of a third of a mile, from the U.S. capital, and blamed the violence on the fact that "Chinese workers are cheap labor" and "local workers are expensive." Huang's final report on the massacre, issued in early October, contained a litany of the dead, listing their names, ages, where their bodies were found, how they had died, and information on who had survived them. The function of the "List of Killed," as it was called, seemed to be both one of accountability but also one of memory:

- The dead body of Leo Kow Boot was found between Mines Nos. 3 and 4, at the foot of the mountain. The neck was shot through crosswise by a bullet, cutting the windpipe in two. I also ascertained that the deceased was 24 years old. His family connections have not yet been clearly made known.
- The dead body of Yiee See Yen was found near the creek. The left temple was shot by a bullet, and the skull broken. The age of the deceased was 36 years. He had a mother living at home (in China).
- The dead body of Leo Dye Bah was found at the side of the bridge, near the creek, shot in the middle of the chest by a bullet, breaking the breast bone. I also ascertained that the deceased was 56 years old, and had a wife, son and daughter at home.

The list went on like this for all the dead and wounded. Huang also cataloged the financial losses sustained by the survivors of the massacre. They were grouped by camp number and hut. There were 764 claims in all. The losses ranged from as little as $25 to more than $2,000. "Every one of the surviving Chinese has been rendered penniless by the cruel attack," Huang wrote. "Since the riot took place it has been impossible for them to secure even a torn sheet or any article of clothing to protect them from the cold, or even the crumbs from the table to satisfy their hunger, or even a plank or a mat to rest their bodies on. These poor creatures, numbering hundreds, are all hungry and clothed in rags. They look worn out and frightened, and most of them forlorn and absent minded."

In Bromley's inquiry, he ultimately decided that there had been no formal plot by white miners to carry out the massacre—a debatable conclusion—even if many had eventually hoped to expel the Chinese. Nevertheless, Bromley believed that there was something "deliberate and cold-blooded" about the mob's actions. This was no drunken riot—Bromley pointed out that none of the rioters were under the influence of alcohol. In early October, a grand jury of sixteen men met in Green River to consider indictments against the accused rioters. Eleven of the jurors were from Rock Springs. Asbury B. Conaway, a popular longtime resident and the prosecuting attorney for Sweetwater County, called more than two dozen white residents to the stand, but none were willing to implicate any rioters.

The surviving record is contradictory about how vigorously prosecutors tried to find Chinese witnesses willing to testify. Campbell, the United States attorney, attended the proceedings and reported afterward in a memorandum to the attorney general that the local authorities had hoped that Bee, the San Francisco consul, would be able to arrange for Chinese testimony, but nothing had materialized. Bee, however, insisted that he never heard any follow-up from Campbell or anyone else. "There was no attempt on the part of the prosecuting officers to indict," Bee later told a newspaper reporter. "They did not want any indictments returned, thanks to the reign of terror." The grand jury hearing also took an unexpected turn, when the Rev. Timothy Thirloway, the pastor who lived near the Chinese quarter with his family, testified that Chinese residents had set fire to their quarter themselves, a preposterous allegation. Thirloway's daughter, Eleanor, said a Chinese resident named Ah Quong had confided in her that a Chinese boy had set the first house, No. 16, ablaze, because he was afraid that Americans would get ahold of their possessions. On October 7, the grand jury voted to return no indictments and issued a report castigating Union Pacific officials for "abuses" in the mines. The men returned that night to Rock Springs, where a cheering throng of several hundred residents greeted them.

Criminal prosecution of the rioters had reached an end, but Chinese officials believed the victims were entitled to financial damages. In late November, Zheng, the Chinese minister, sent a forceful letter to Thomas Bayard, the secretary of state. He criticized the judicial proceedings as a "burlesque" and asked that the victims of the violence be "fully indemnified for all the losses and injuries they have sustained." Zheng understood that his odds of wresting funds from the U.S. government were also slim. When faced with the same request, after the Denver riot in December 1880, American officials had argued that they were not required by treaty obligations to offer any remedies to Chinese residents victimized by mob violence. Zheng tried to appeal to the Cleveland administration's sense of morality. He made the case for indemnification based on "reciprocal justice and comity" between the two countries and the maxim of "to do to others as they would have others do to them." He pointed out that the Beijing government had paid out more than $700,000 to the United States for losses sustained by American citizens from riots and violence in China. He enclosed in his entreaty Bee's full investigative report and an account of the massacre signed by 559 Chinese laborers from Rock Springs.

It took more than two months for the American government to issue a formal response to Zheng. On February 18, 1886, Secretary of State Thomas Bayard acknowledged receipt of Zheng's "very interesting and important communication" and apologized for the tardiness of his reply. He pointed out that, in December, President Cleveland had unequivocally condemned the violence in Rock Springs during his annual address to Congress. Bayard said he also felt "deep mortification that such a blot should have been cast upon the record of our Government of laws." Even so, Bayard insisted that the American government bore no responsibility for the violence. Bayard chided Zheng's countrymen for venturing to a "community on the outposts of civilization," a place with limited governance and no organized police. Bayard blamed the attack on a "lawless band of about 150 armed men," private individuals, mostly aliens themselves, acting on their own. Nevertheless, Bayard suggested that President Cleveland might recommend that Congress approve compensation for Chinese subjects in Rock Springs, from "a sentiment of generosity and pity to an innocent and unfortunate body of men."

On March 3, President Cleveland requested that the House and Senate consider an indemnity for the Chinese victims. The quest for redress for the victims ground on for months, however, even as attacks against the Chinese spread. Finally, on February 24, 1887, Congress awarded $147,748.74 to the Chinese government for losses sustained by the violence at Rock Springs. Chinese officials in San Francisco were tasked with the distribution of the award to victims. By later summer, the process was completed, but Chinese officials discovered that six claims had been inadvertently repeated. Accordingly, they returned $480.75 to the U.S. Treasury.

.   .   .

Chinese survivors of the massacre continued to work for the Union Pacific in Rock Springs for years, guarded by federal troops. The company rebuilt the Chinese quarter, constructing several dozen barn-like dormitories; miners paid rent of $5 a month. Carpenters also erected barracks to house the soldiers who stayed on in Rock Springs. The military post, known as Camp Pilot Butte, occupied the patch of land between Chinatown and "Whiteman's Town," where most white residents lived.

Racial hostilities still ran through Rock Springs, like a hidden vein. On December 30, 1886, a fire broke out in the Chinese quarter. As Chinese residents struggled to extinguish the blaze, a crowd of white residents began throwing rocks at them and cut the fire hose. A contingent of soldiers drove off the white men and saved the quarter from serious damage. After the fire, First Lieutenant James Brennan, the commanding officer of the troops in Rock Springs, reported to his superiors that there remained a "rough class" in the town who continued to pose a threat to the Chinese. Brennan said that the Chinese leader, Ah Say, remained "anxious about their safety." Army officials decided that troops were no longer needed in Evanston but concluded that "it will not do" to withdraw them from Rock Springs. Ah Say had still been living in Evanston with his wife and children, all American-born. In June, however, he decided to take them back to China. Several months later, he returned to Wyoming alone. There's no record of why he decided to send his family away, but it's likely that he had qualms about their safety. For years, whenever there was talk of withdrawing the troops, Ah Say lobbied against it. In 1891, Chinese residents signed a petition to the War Department asking that they be given plenty of time to prepare if the troops were to be withdrawn, so that they could "make preparations for moving to a place of safety."

In 1894, Ah Say arranged to have a 130-foot ceremonial dragon that cost $3,000 in China delivered to Rock Springs for the community's annual New Year celebration. For several years, he marched proudly at the head of the parade, dressed in a new Western suit and with his cane in hand. On the morning of January 27, 1899, he rose, took a bath, shaved off his mustache, and dressed himself in a formal Chinese gown. He had been suffering from dropsy—the mysterious ailment, common in the nineteenth century, marked by swelling in the limbs. Ah Say sensed his death was near and summoned several close friends, Chinese and American, to his side, including William K. Lee, the town mayor. Ah Say left detailed instructions for who should succeed him in his various functions as the Chinese headman and bid them farewell. Later that evening, Ah Say collapsed and died. He was fifty-eight years old. For the next four days, his body lay in state in Rock Springs, before going by train to San Francisco and then by ship to Hong Kong for burial in China.

Less than two months later, army officials abruptly abolished its post in Rock Springs. The decision caught Union Pacific officials off guard. More than two hundred Chinese miners continued to live and work in Rock Springs. The company boarded up the buildings in Camp Pilot Butte. "The presence of troops has prevented any serious demonstrations against the Chinks, although scarcely a day passed without one or more of them having their cues clipped off or getting a beating," one newspaper account said. "It is feared that, under the influence of drink, a raid may be started against the Chinese quarter, which without the restraining influence of troops may be a serious affair." In June, when it became apparent that the soldiers would not be returning, the Union Pacific converted the barracks into homes for its coal miners.

Over the years, Union Pacific officials had been gradually reducing their reliance on Chinese labor, recognizing that their employment no longer made business sense. "You cannot operate a railroad successfully in the face of an all pervading public sentiment, no matter how wrong it may be," Adams, the company president, had confided to a colleague after the massacre. Yet survivors of the massacre continued on with the company, in some cases well into their sixties and seventies. In 1913, the company demolished Chinatown, subdividing the land into lots for new homes. The company faced a dilemma. Most of the remaining Chinese miners could no longer work underground. Many had become paupers, dependent on charity, often administered with the help of Leo Wing, the owner of the Grand Cafe, a Chinese restaurant in town. George Pryde, the vice president and general manager of the Union Pacific Coal Company, began delivering goods to the men from the company store to help them get by.

In July 1925, Pryde proposed to Eugene McAuliffe, the company president, that the Union Pacific cover the cost of sending the men back to China and furnish them with a lump sum payout for their "years of faithful service." He pointed out that the few who could still work were extremely limited in what they could do but were still drawing high wages. Many of the men had visited China over the years and taken on wives, before traveling back to Rock Springs to resume working in the mines. Pryde reasoned it would be better for the men to return to China. He researched the cost of rail transportation to San Francisco and a third-class steamship ticket to China, finding it would total about a hundred dollars. At the time, China was experiencing widespread unrest and political turmoil, driving inflation. Pryde believed that $400 should be the minimum stipend for the departing men. (The company later settled on $800.) In September, Pryde interviewed a dozen of the aging miners and concluded many were "anxious to go home." At least two men, however, Ah Jin and Ah Bow, who had sixty-five years of service to the company between them, were hesitant. Ah Jin, who was sixty-three years old and had a wife and son in China, was one of the company's longest-serving Chinese miners. He had arrived in Rock Springs in 1882 and had survived the massacre while working in the No. 3 mine. In 1917, a coal car rolled over his arm, but he continued to work underground. In January 1924, his service for the Union Pacific finally came to an end, at the age of sixty-one, due to the lingering effects of his wrist injury. Ah Bow, who was also in his sixties, had started working for the company in 1892, working in five different mines, before quitting in 1917 because of illness.

On an evening in November 1925, a banquet honoring nine longtime Chinese employees of the Union Pacific was held at the Grand Cafe. The town band performed; Dave Thomas delivered a speech. Afterward, the group boarded a train bound for San Francisco, accompanied by two company officials. In the end, Ah Jin and Ah Bow could not be per-suaded to leave. A third miner, Leo Wah, decided at the last moment to stay in Rock Springs as well, telling Pryde that he owed debts in China. On November 14, limousines delivered the returning men to the docks, where they boarded the SS *President Taft*, bound for Asia. The longest-serving member of the group was Ah Chung, who was in his seventies and put in forty-six years with the company. Another septuagenarian in the group, Lao Chung, had been shot during the 1885 attack and still carried the bullet in his back. In January 1927, he became the first of the old-timers to pass away in China.

Later that year, a second contingent of "China boys," this time including Ah Jin and Ah Bow, readied themselves to leave Rock Springs. Once again, the company threw the four men a farewell banquet and outfitted them with new suits. Ah Jin appeared in a formal portrait with his bow tie slightly askew, his jacket and pants wrinkled. The men spent several days in San Francisco sightseeing, before setting sail for Hong Kong. In a letter dated November 18, 1927, the four men expressed their gratitude to McAuliffe, the company president. "We regret very much to leave you," they wrote. "Our appreciations cannot be expressed by words."

The company magazine, *Employes'*, occasionally posted cheerful updates about the returnees. One article, from the July 1926 issue, celebrated the marriage of Joe Bow, a sixty-four-year-old massacre survivor who had been in the original group, to a young woman who was a "wonderful cook"; she had an eleven-year-old son who promised to work for Bow in his retirement years. The former miner enclosed a photograph of his new family and sent his appreciation for the "kind treatment" he had received from his former employer. Bow's fortunes, however, began to deteriorate. He was forced to take a job on a farm; then locusts destroyed the rice crop. "I am ashame to ask you help," he wrote to Pryde, in December 1928. "Here I am now very poor as a beggar." Two months later, Pryde wrote a sympathetic letter back and enclosed $100 in Hong Kong currency. "Was very glad to hear from you, Joe, and hope that conditions will improve for you," Pryde wrote. In April 1929, Bow wrote again, explaining that his family was enduring "great sickness" and his home had fallen into disrepair. Pryde continued to send small amounts to Bow and other returnees. Company officials eventually agreed to issue quarterly payments of $30 each to the surviving workers.

In May 1932, McAuliffe wrote to Pryde that the company's financial overseers in New York would no longer sanction payments to the former employees. An exception was made for Leo Chee, a popular former mine foreman and keeper of the company's stables, who had been awarded a company pension before returning to China. Leo Chee had also been serving as an intermediary between Union Pacific officials and his fellow old-timers, traveling great distances to reach their villages to see how they were faring and to disburse checks intended for them. He sent regular updates on the men back to Pryde. No one informed the former miners about the company's decision to cut them off. Leo Chee wrote back to Rock Springs, explaining that the men were begging for help "before they starve to death."

In August 1932, the *Employes'* magazine reported that the last three of the company's "Old Time Chinese," Leo Ong, Leo You, and Leo Yick, were departing, leaving a single Chinese employee, a man named Yee Litt, who worked in the No. 4 mine. "The good wishes of their many Rock Springs friends will be with them on this long journey home," the magazine said. The article went on to imagine them "talking often of Rock Springs and the friends they have left behind." A photograph showed the three men in three-piece suits and fedoras, their skin weathered and their expressions neutral.

CHAPTER 17

Driven Out

On September 5, 1885, a group of thirty-seven Chinese laborers arrived in a pristine, forested valley about fifteen miles east of Seattle. The massacre in Rock Springs had taken place three days earlier. It's unknown if the travelers knew anything about the horror nine hundred miles away. Chin Lan Chong, the headman of Quong Chong Company, a Seattle firm that supplied workers for all manner of jobs in the region, had sent seventy men eastward in two groups. Their destination was a hops farm in a bucolic region that earlier settlers had called "Squak," apparently a reference to a word of the indigenous Lushootseed tribe for the "sound of water birds." The laborers walked laden with tents, bedding, and whatever possessions they could carry. At least one man carried a gun.

The workers had been hired by Lars and Ingebright Wold, brothers from Trondheim, an ancient village in Norway. In the late 1860s, the Wolds had ventured by canoe into the valley, accompanied by a Native American guide, looking for suitable land for farming. Lars, who was in his mid-thirties at the time, was a logger; his brother, about a decade younger, worked in the shoe business in Seattle. They had explored other river valleys in the region but found the most promising locations were already taken. Squak Valley was dense with cedar, hemlock, and maple trees, but its soil was fertile. The Wolds purchased 160 acres for $500. In 1868, they planted half an acre of hop plants, the climbing vine whose flowers are used to brew beer. They steadily cleared more land for hops and eventually built a two-story farmhouse, where they lived together. By the middle of the 1880s, the Wolds had become the largest hops growers in the valley.

In years past, when it came time for the harvest, the Wolds had hired white and Native American pickers. This season, however, the Wolds had decided to experiment with Chinese labor. The idea was originally Ingebright's; Lars was against it. Chin Lan Chong later said that the Wolds told him they couldn't find anyone else to do the work. This was likely only a partial explanation. In the fall of 1885, the market rate for hops had fallen. As a result, some farmers had decided to skip the harvest entirely. The Wolds might have been looking for a way to keep costs down. In late August, Ingebright Wold traveled to Seattle, the bustling commercial hub on the eastern shore of Elliott Bay in Puget Sound. Several hundred Chinese immigrants occupied a densely packed ghetto a few blocks from the waterfront. The Quong Chong Company operated a store in the quarter and performed labor contracting. Wold struck a deal with Lan Chong, as they called him, who agreed to pay the Wolds $1,000 if he was unable to come up with enough men. For his part, Lan Chong got the Wolds to agree to pay him $1,800 if he supplied the men but they were no longer needed. He was looking for insurance, in case something went wrong.

The first group of the Wolds' workers set up camp on a spit of land that curved out into a creek in their orchard. They occupied sixteen small tents. Word traveled quickly through the valley about their arrival. The Wolds had an influential neighbor: George W. Tibbetts, a forty-year-old Maine native who was the area's postmaster and justice of the peace. He was also an anti-Chinese zealot. Tibbetts had a thick mustache and genial eyes. Valley residents called him "General Tibbetts," because he had served for two years as the territory's brigadier general. In Squak Valley, Tibbetts dabbled in a variety of enterprises, including a dairy farm and a stage line. He had recently opened a store and lodging house on his property. He also grew hops, and for the fall harvest season he had hired his usual collection of white and Native American men pickers. He loathed the use of Chinese labor. It was "well known," he later said, that "money paid to the whites and Indians was kept at home while nearly everything paid to the Chinese was taken out of the country by them."

Tibbetts went next door and demanded that the Wolds discharge the workers but was rebuffed. The following afternoon, the second group of Chinese workers sent by Lan Chong entered the valley. About a mile from the Wolds' farm, a group of angry white and Native American pickers confronted them. The Chinese workers fled back into the woods. That evening, at about nine o'clock, nearly thirty men on horseback descended on the Wolds' farm. In the darkness, Lars Wold recognized many of them. They included Henry Tibbetts, George's brother, and others who worked for George Tibbetts. The group again insisted that the Wolds discharge their Chinese pickers. The Wolds told the men that they'd let their workers go when they were done with the job. The group headed in the direction of the Chinese camp. The Wolds trailed after them. Near the orchard, Henry Tibbetts swung a revolver around, pointing it at Lars and his wife, Henrietta. "I shall either die, or the Chinamen shall go," Tibbetts said. His young son tugged at him, urging his father to leave. Eventually, the Wolds succeeded in persuading Tibbetts and the other men to stand down until morning. The group vowed to return. "We are going to be back tomorrow and take the Chinamen camp," one man said.

After being turned away at the Wolds' farm, the second contingent of Chinese hop pickers had set up camp in nearby Coal Creek. The next day, the Wolds visited General Tibbetts and demanded that he, in his capacity as the justice of the peace, escort the pickers to their farm. Tibbetts said that he'd only be willing to help ensure that the Chinese workers in the Wolds' orchard departed the valley safely. After a heated exchange, the Wolds left. Ingebright traveled to Seattle to consult with law enforcement officials. On Sunday morning, he returned with letters from J. T. Ronald, the district attorney of King County, and Sheriff John H. McGraw, ordering that the Chinese workers be left alone. That night, the brothers had a guard watch over the Chinese camp. After the evening passed uneventfully, the Wolds reassured the Chinese pickers that they would be safe.

The following evening, the Wolds elected not to post a watchman again. A group of men gathered at Tibbetts's store. It was Monday, September 7. They included many of the men who had confronted the Wolds over the weekend, including Perry Bayne, a blacksmith; Daniel Hughes, a rancher; and several of Tibbetts's employees. There were two Native American hops pickers as well—one known as Johnny the Indian and the other as Curley the Indian. The white men had intimidated them into joining them. Tibbetts furnished ammunition to the men who didn't have any and loaned one man a Winchester rifle. At the last moment, he decided not to accompany them, explaining that he had a family and would probably slow them down. The group made their way through the meadows to the Wolds' property and stole up on the Chinese camp from the south. After clambering through a gap in the fence, they found themselves in front of their tents. It was just after ten o'clock in the evening. Bayne, armed with a revolver, gave the order to fire. The group fired twenty or thirty shots in all. Gong Heng, a laborer who had learned English while attending church-organized classes for Chinese, was inside his tent. He later compared the din to firecrackers on Chinese New Year. "So much firing," he said. Gong Heng stumbled out of his tent and saw seven men in the darkness. After several minutes of shooting, one of the tents caught fire. "Kill the son of [a] bitch," one man said. Gong Heng fled into the woods. The Wolds were asleep in bed. When they heard the gunfire, they rushed out to the fence enclosing the orchard and saw a group of men running away and the flames of the burning camp.

When Gong Heng snuck back to the camp, he found a horrific scene. Fung Woey, who was thirty-five years old, was dead outside his tent. He had suffered a gunshot wound to the left side of his chest. Another man, Mong Goat, age thirty-two, lay dying on the bank of the creek, having been shot in the belly. He had brought a pistol with him to Squak Valley for self-defense, but he had turned it over to the Wolds the night before. Gong Heng dragged him from the side of the creek and tried to make him comfortable on some blankets. After moaning for fifteen minutes, he died. Three others were wounded. Yeng Son, a thirty-year-old man with a wife and son back home in China, was the worst off. He had been appointed by the Chinese to act as a night watchman and was shot while trying to flee. He yelped in pain throughout the night. He told the other survivors that he knew he was dying and lamented that he'd no longer be able to support his family. By morning, he was dead. Gong Heng and other survivors made their way through the woods to the town of Newcastle, several miles away. The next day, they boarded a train to Seattle. A large crowd of Chinese residents greeted them upon their arrival. Lan Chong summoned a Chinese doctor from Portland to treat the three wounded men.

In the morning, the Wolds notified Tibbetts, as the justice of the peace, about the attack. He organized a perfunctory investigation that concluded the Chinese men had died of gunshot wounds "from the hands of unknown persons." When King County officials arrived from Seattle, they conducted a new inquest, interviewing about two dozen witnesses, including Gong Heng, Tibbetts, and several men who had participated in the attack. Sheriff McGraw arrested seven men for the killings. Ronald, the district attorney, initially tried two defendants: Perry Bayne, the blacksmith who had ordered the men to commence shooting, and Daniel Hughes, the rancher, for first-degree murder. The accused men said they acted in self-defense. During separate trials, juries acquitted both men. Another participant, Dewitt Rumsey, a foreman on Tibbetts's farm, was convicted of riot, a relatively minor offense, with a maximum sentence of one year in jail. A grand jury indicted Tibbetts on the charges of first-degree murder and riot, but after he spent a month in jail, the court released him on bail. "Mr. Tibbetts has extensive business interests which needed his attention," one newspaper account said. He was never prosecuted. Several months later, he had started a new venture: a steamboat and stagecoach route between Seattle and a scenic waterfall east of Squak Valley. In the summer of 1889, residents selected him as one of the members of the state's first constitutional convention in Olympia.

Lan Chong filed a claim of $1,910 with the United States govern-ment for his expenses incurred while caring for the wounded men, along with other costs, including attorney's fees and room and board for the workers driven out of Squak Valley. The three wounded men filed their own claims. Lum Seung, who was shot in the side and needed months to recover, requested $5,730. Ah Chow, who was shot in the left hip, asked only for $40 for doctors' fees and medicine. Mon Gee, who was shot twice and lost his tent to fire, itemized $203 in losses, including two blankets, a pillow, a pair of boots, pants, and a shirt. The United States government would later pay out an indemnity to the Chinese government for losses sustained by their subjects from violence directed at them, but it's unclear if the victims of the Squak Valley attack ever saw this money.

The violence spread quickly, as if all white workingmen across the territory had been roused. In Newcastle, several miles from Squak Valley, about fifty Chinese men worked in a coal mine owned by the Oregon Improvement Company. The Newcastle mine produced more than half of the coal produced in the territory. For about three years, the Chinese miners had been working in the mine with little incident. Most of the Chinese laborers worked as pickers, sifting piles of rock for coal pieces. The company paid them $1.25 per day, a wage that white men would generally not countenance. Mine officials insisted that foreign competition in their primary market, San Francisco, and slim profit margins meant they couldn't pay more. Newcastle's white miners, mostly immigrants themselves, turned increasingly restive.

Close to midnight, on September 11—four days after the rampage in the Wolds' orchard—a gang of more than a dozen masked white men, armed with pistols, surrounded the Chinese quarter in Coal Creek, a town next door to the mine. Most of the Chinese workers were asleep in their lodging house. A handful of others were working the night shift in the mine. The masked men kicked in the door. The noise awoke Chin Poy Hug, the headman for the group. The men hustled him and the other workers, most of whom were only partially clothed, outside. A few minutes later, as the workers hid in the woods, their lodgings and the cookhouse next door erupted into flames. W. J. Watkins, the superintendent of the mine, rushed to the scene and found it deserted, except for a few white men trying to put out the flames. He called out to Poy, who emerged from his hiding place. Together, they rounded up the terrified Chinese workers—about forty in all—and took them to the railroad tracks. Watkins assigned men to escort the group to Newcastle and put them up in an old mine quarters. A few days later, most of the

Chinese workers fled to Tacoma by train. A reporter interviewed one of the arrivals and rendered his responses in pidgin English. "Me no go back," the worker said. There's no record of what became of most of these laborers. Chin Poy Hug eventually made his way to San Francisco, where he wrote to Watkins that he had decided to return to China.

It seems likely that some workers decided to stay in Tacoma, where several hundred Chinese residents lived, mostly in ramshackle shelters along the waterfront. Tacoma was another western frontier town built by the railroad. In July 1873, officials for the Northern Pacific railroad selected Tacoma over its Puget Sound rival, Seattle, as the railway's terminus. At the time, Seattle was the undisputed commercial center of the Northwest, owing largely to its central location on the sound. Its population of about two thousand inhabitants dwarfed that of Tacoma, which was then little more than a village, with a single sawmill, located thirty miles to the south. Tacoma, however, possessed a deep, wide harbor on Commencement Bay, not unlike Seattle's, and could offer the railroad plenty of land along the waterfront. The Northern Pacific's ambition was to establish a transcontinental railroad that began in the Upper Midwest, crossed the northern Plains, and continued onto the tidewaters of Puget Sound. Tacoma's leaders harbored fantasies of their town becoming the primary conduit of American trade with the Far East, perhaps even surpassing San Francisco.

The Northern Pacific employed hundreds of Chinese laborers to perform the arduous work of grading and laying down tracks. The company enlisted the prominent financiers Jay Cooke & Co. to procure the funds to build the railroad, but the banking house's failure in September 1873 imperiled construction. Nevertheless, the Northern Pacific managed to complete the connection from the town of Kalama on the Columbia River to the shoreline by year's end. Land fever seized residents of the area, and a frenzy of construction followed. The economic depression and the halting progress of the Northern Pacific's mainline beyond the Columbia River slowed the town's expansion, but, by 1885, Tacoma had a population of nearly seven thousand people.

On August 7, 1885, a month before the arrival of the Chinese miners from Newcastle, Tacoma residents celebrated an auspicious moment in their history: the arrival of the bark-rigged sailing ship *Isabel*, carrying more than twenty-two thousand chests of tea from Japan. The *Tacoma Daily Ledger* declared that the shipment signaled the "dawning of a new era in the commercial history of this place." The waterfront buzzed with activity as workers passed the cargo, hand over hand, from the vessel's hold and onto the wharf, where it was transported to warehouses and later loaded onto train cars. It took eight days and four hours for the first freight train carrying the tea to speed its way across the country and arrive in New York. The vision that Tacoma leaders had long harbored of their town becoming a gateway to the Far East seemed to be materializing.

Chinese migrants first arrived in the Tacoma area in significant numbers in the early 1870s, as railroad laborers. An early history of Tacoma identified the first Chinese laundryman in town as Lung Fat. He is described as "a man of rather unusual acumen," who charged just seventy-five cents for as much laundry as could be stuffed in a bag. Most Chinese residents were laborers, drawn to Tacoma, the "city of destiny," as it became known, as it expanded. They worked in sawmills and hotels, tended vegetable gardens, and served as cooks and servants in white households.

A Chinese merchant class made its way to Tacoma as well, recognizing that there were profits to be made in the growing city. They sold wares to the nascent Chinese community but also filled a role as liaisons for their countrymen with the white population. Over time, the most prominent merchants became trusted figures in the community. Kwok Sue was among the earliest Chinese arrivals, making his way to Tacoma in 1873. He worked for a time at the Blackwell, the town's first hotel, before setting himself up as a shopkeeper and labor contractor. Mow Lung came two years later and occupied a building near the wharf, where he sold a variety of goods to Chinese residents. He was also a landlord, obtaining permission from the Northern Pacific to build crude shelters on the company's land and rent them out to tenants. Lum Way, who went by Sam Hing in his interactions with white residents, arrived in Tacoma around the same time and opened a business with a partner, Tak Nam, selling dry goods, medicine, and other provisions, and also

acting as a go-between between Chinese workers and white employers. They called their business Sam Hing and Company. Sing Lee, an
enterprising labor contractor, supplied workers to the first lumber plant
that opened in what was then known as New Tacoma, near the railroad
terminus. Chinese laborers earned a dollar a day, while their white counterparts were paid a dollar and seventy-five cents. His business ventures
eventually included a 160-acre farm outside the city, a vegetable garden,
a brickyard, a store on the wharf, and a pair of chartered vessels to China
for the shipment of lumber.

On August 22, 1883, crews of track layers coming from the east and
west met at a junction in western Montana, completing the Northern
Pacific's mainline. A slowdown in railroad construction drove a nationwide economic contraction that would persist for two years. Thousands
of Chinese railroad laborers whose services were no longer needed
drifted back into communities throughout the Pacific Northwest. (At
its peak, the Northern Pacific employed some fifteen thousand Chinese
workers.) Meanwhile, idled white workers, as well as shopkeepers and
small proprietors whose businesses were suffering amid the rippling
economic anxiety, were becoming restive.

On a Thursday evening in January 1884, the first snow of the year fell
on Tacoma, leaving patches of snow on the surrounding hillsides. Mischievous boys pelted passing Chinese men with snowballs. A gloomy
year was dawning on the town. In March, the city council passed an
ordinance forbidding the employment of Chinese laborers on public
works projects. A city councilman, John E. Burns, who still employed
Chinese workers in his pipe-laying company, came under withering criticism from white workingmen, who christened him "Wing Lee Burns."
The episode was an impetus for the establishment of the Workingmen's
Union in Tacoma. During the union's inaugural meeting, attended by
nearly two hundred people, members declared themselves "opposed to
Chinese labor" and pledged to only support candidates in upcoming
municipal elections who would "advance the interests of white labor."
Burns replaced his Chinese workers with Native American laborers,
who were still cheaper than white laborers but were less loathsome to
his constituents.

The daily morning and evening spectacle of Chinese residents carrying stinking buckets of hotel refuse, dangling from poles slung over their shoulders, back to their homes on the wharf, where they fed the slop to their hogs, became a growing irritant in town. The publisher of the *Daily Ledger*, Randolph Foster Radebaugh, and its editor, J. A. Comerford, a frequently drunk, itinerant newsman, were virulently anti-Chinese. The newspaper repeatedly editorialized that something needed to be done about these "insolent Chinamen." The city council finally passed an ordinance barring the slop carriers from sidewalks. Town constables began arresting and fining violators. As Chinese residents began establishing themselves beyond the waterfront, town elders fretted that they were encroaching upon the most desirable locations in the city. A *Daily Ledger* article likened them to "a cancer that is daily eating more deeply into the vitality of each and every municipality."

In the summer of 1884 and then into 1885, several of Tacoma's sawmills suspended their operations, or cut back on shifts. In early February 1885, William Christie, a carpenter who was also a member of the Tacoma school board and a political ally of the town's mayor, Jacob Weisbach, happened to be visiting the town of Eureka, in the northern reaches of California, when white residents rounded up the Chinese in the town and forced them to leave. The *Ledger* published an account of the episode on its front page. Shortly afterward, Christie returned to Tacoma and met with Weisbach, James Wickersham, who was Pierce County's probate judge, and several other opponents of the Chinese above Weisbach's grocery store on the south end of Pacific Avenue, near the railroad terminus. Talk of taking direct action against the Chinese began to circulate in town.

The meeting above Weisbach's grocery was notable, because it establishes a thread between the events in Eureka and what would later transpire in Tacoma and elsewhere. Weisbach, Christie, and Wickersham would all become key figures in the rapidly accelerating anti-Chinese movement. Another participant in the Eureka expulsion, Daniel Cronin, an organizer for the Knights of Labor, also eventually made his way to Tacoma and then Seattle, where he also joined the agitation against the Chinese.

On February 19, shortly after the meeting at Weisbach's grocery, the *Daily Ledger* published a lengthy article headlined "Chinese Invasion of Tacoma." The article declared that the time had come to "crush out this insidious attack on the growth of our city." A notice appeared in the local press, signed by more than two dozen men, calling on Weisbach to convene a mass meeting on the Chinese question. The signatories were mostly small businessmen in town: Francis Tarbell, a real estate and insurance agent; Harry Baher, a cigar store owner; Calvin Barlow, a merchant and hotel proprietor; and others. Weisbach quickly assented, proclaiming that a "speedy and final solution" of the Chinese question was needed. He urged the citizens of Tacoma to assemble at the town's opera house on Saturday evening.

Weisbach, a fifty-two-year-old German immigrant, had been elected mayor the year before, backed by the nascent labor movement in Tacoma. His gray hair, long beard, and erect bearing gave him a distinguished appearance. He was a plain, forceful speaker and a popular figure in Tacoma. His fortunes as a businessman had been mixed. Previously, he'd operated a general store in Frankfort, Kansas, which he was forced at one point to close because of accumulated debts. In Tacoma, just before his election, his grocery business had, again, defaulted. The local sheriff appointed a temporary receiver to manage his business, before Weisbach finally managed to settle with his creditors and reopen.

Weisbach's interest in politics had begun in his native Germany, when he had been an active participant in the Forty-Eighter movement that had pressed for liberal reforms across Europe. When the insurrections petered out, many German Forty-Eighters, including Weisbach, emigrated to the United States. He wound up in Kansas, where he became active in Republican politics, ascending to postmaster of the town of Marysville and later to the state legislature. In the 1870s, however, when his business foundered, Weisbach's politics began drifting towards the Greenback Party, with its labor orientation and opposition to monopolies. In 1881, Weisbach made the move west to Washington Territory. In a letter that he wrote to the *Kansas Liberal,* a weekly free-thought newspaper, he urged others to join him in establishing a colony under "a cooperative system, as a safeguard against aggressive greed and monopolies." Weisbach set up shop anew in a store several blocks from the waterfront. In 1883, voters elected him to the city council and then to the mayor's office the following year. Weisbach's election was a signal of the labor movement's growing clout. Their priority was clear: to rid the town of Chinese.

About a thousand men, one of the largest audiences ever assembled in Tacoma, crowded into the opera house for the anti-Chinese meeting. After Weisbach called the gathering to order, a succession of speakers addressed the audience. At the end of the evening, the crowd pressed to hear from their mayor. When Weisbach rose, he argued that the Chinese had been brought to the United States by "the great soulless corporations" to "degrade white labor." Weisbach insisted he was not endorsing violence but said that white men needed to fight for their own self-preservation. The Chinese presence was encircling the city and "gnawing at its vitals," he said. The meeting ended with the unanimous adoption of a resolution to exclude Chinese from the city and another that said it was the duty of every citizen to discourage their employment. A committee, made up of members from each of the city's three wards, would be appointed to carry out the resolutions.

After the mass meeting, a remarkable letter appeared in the *Tacoma Daily News,* signed by a pair of English-speaking Chinese residents, Un Gow and Mark Ten Suie, addressed to "all rational citizens of Tacoma." They offered to meet with white Tacomans and to "do all in our power to remedy any and all the wrongs and grievances incurred by China-men, and will try to make them good, clean, respectable citizens." The two men tried to ingratiate themselves with their critics, explaining that "some of us have embraced the Christian religion"—Ten Suie managed the Methodist Mission School in Tacoma and Un Gow was a believer as well—and were doing all they could to encourage their countrymen to do the same. Every evening, Ten Suie's school hosted twenty-two students in a tidy room at the mission outfitted with books and other supplies. "We are sorry that so many of us are so bad as to be liable to be driven away by the citizens," they wrote.

There's no record of any meeting taking place. Several weeks later, Weisbach encountered Ten Suie during an inspection of Chinese busi-nesses and abodes conducted by a newly established committee on "Chinese habits and their mode of living." Ten Suie was deferential and pleaded for toleration. Weisbach, who was accompanied by the Rev. J. A. Ward, the pastor of Tacoma's Methodist Episcopal church, later described Ten Suie as a "nice young man with very good manners slick like an eel." The mayor conceded the school suggested that the "younger generation are susceptible of improvement." Nevertheless, anti-Chinese leaders gathered signatures calling for the "speedy and final banishment" of Chinese residents from both the city and the territory. The city council enacted a series of ordinances targeting the Chinese, including requiring that washhouses be connected to a sewer and that living quarters contain at least five hundred feet of cubic air for every occupant.

On September 3, news of the massacre in Rock Springs appeared on the front page of the *Tacoma Daily News* under the headline "The Chinese Go." Racial violence had accomplished its end. Four days later, on the same evening as the attack on hops workers in nearby Squak Valley, Daniel Cronin, the labor organizer who had been present at the events in Eureka, presided over a boisterous meeting in a large hall in Tacoma to establish a Knights of Labor chapter. Weisbach delivered brief remarks and about sixty men signed up.

Several weeks later, Cronin addressed an anti-Chinese meeting in Seattle, where he explicitly invoked Eureka as a model. "I was in Eureka, California, when the edict went forth that the Chinese must go," he said. "There are two million five hundred thousand men here without employment, and seventy thousand right here on this coast. If we take action in this matter at once we will solve this question." Cronin promised that there could be "no Chinamen on Puget Sound in two weeks." The meeting ended with the resolution to convene an anti-Chinese congress for the five counties on Puget Sound at Yesler's hall, the town's largest gathering spot, at the end of the month.

On Sunday evening, September 27, a delegation from Tacoma, led by Weisbach, arrived in Seattle by steamer. A welcoming party and brass band escorted them by torchlight through the streets to the Occidental hotel. The following afternoon, delegates crowded inside the hall. The largest contingent came from Tacoma. The delegates appointed Weisbach as their president. He made clear to the assembled what he believed had driven them to this point. "When the laws fail to afford the people protection, the people are in duty bound to protect themselves," he said. The delegates called for the immediate discharge of all Chinese workers and agreed to return to their respective localities to hold mass meetings on October 3 to appoint committees to notify the Chinese to leave on or before November 1, 1885.

News of the meeting spread swiftly in the Chinese community on the Pacific coast. Frederick Bee, the Chinese consul in San Francisco, who had just returned to San Francisco from Rock Springs, sent a telegram to Watson Squire, the governor of the Washington Territory, expressing alarm about the rapidly unfolding events: "Will you please inform me if the local authorities can afford the Chinese protection under the law and the treaty, in event that those designs are carried out?" Squire, the son of an itinerant Methodist preacher in northern New York and a former judge advocate in the Union army, had made his fortune as an executive at E. Remington & Sons, the arms manufacturer. He eventually married Ida Remington, a daughter of the company's head, Philo Remington. In 1879, he'd made his way west to Washington Territory and became a major landholder in Seattle. In 1884, President Arthur had appointed him governor of the territory. Squire, a gifted raconteur with a stocky build and walrus mustache, found himself in a vulnerable political position, as the resentment against the Chinese in the territory climbed. In his annual report to the secretary of interior, he would make a point of criticizing the "failure on the part of the Government to adequately enforce the restriction act." But Squire was also aware that it was his responsibility to maintain order and had alerted his superiors in Washington about the growing anti-Chinese agitation. He confirmed to Bee that a movement was underway to discharge Chinese laborers throughout the territory, but the governor said he did not believe violence was imminent.

Even before the mass meeting in Seattle, some Chinese residents of Tacoma had already begun preparing to leave. On a Friday evening in late September, Sun Chong, a prominent merchant in the community, visited E. W. Taylor, the deputy prosecuting attorney in the county. The merchant wanted to know if he and his fellow Chinese had any legal options available to them. Taylor told him that the time for negotiation had likely passed. His best advice was for the Chinese to leave without making a fuss to "avert any trouble." Sun Chong was clear-eyed about the situation and agreed with Taylor's assessment, but he pressed for financial remuneration for him and his countrymen. While no Chinese residents in Tacoma owned real estate, he said, they would still be leaving behind personal property. He proposed a payment of $2,500 for each resident, in exchange for their safe passage. "We will go, rather than take the chances of being mobbed," he said.

After the delegates returned from the congress, Sun Chong followed up in a meeting with Weisbach, who assured the merchant that the Chinese would be treated in a "fair manner." He promised to present Sun Chong's proposal to the city council. During the meeting the following day, however, Weisbach failed to bring up the matter. He later said that Sun Chong had admitted that he was not speaking for all of his countrymen, making the negotiations moot.

The movement to expel the Chinese continued to march forward. At nine o'clock in the evening on October 3, several hundred men and boys gathered in front of the opera house and proceeded through the streets of Tacoma, their torches bobbing in the night. The members of the town fire department bore a sign that drew some of the biggest cheers from the throngs: "Will you go?" It depicted the chief of the department directing his hose at a fleeing Chinese man. During a meeting inside the opera house, Tacoma's anti-Chinese leaders officially endorsed the platform laid out at the Seattle congress and insisted that their goal was to carry out the expulsion without resorting to violence. The attendees established the Committee of Fifteen, whose responsibility it was to ensure the removal of the Chinese. The committee included both William Christie and James Wickersham, who had been part of the original anti-Chinese meeting above Weisbach's store. The members of the committee went door to door to notify Chinese residents of the November 1 deadline and circulated a manifesto addressed to the white residents of Tacoma that asked that they discharge any Chinese employees. By the middle of October, the exodus of Chinese from Tacoma was well underway. Train cars full of Chinese departed for Portland; others left on foot or by stagecoach.

.   .   .

There was still a faction of white residents who believed they could stop the escalating movement against their Chinese neighbors. "You meet a great many fools on the anti-Chinese subject," John C. Weatherred, a thirty-nine-year-old Kentucky native, wrote in his diary several days after the congress. Weatherred had served as a sergeant in the Confederate army before journeying after the war to California and then Oregon, where he was a wheat farmer. In 1883, Weatherred settled in Tacoma and built a real estate business. He was skeptical that ridding the community of the Chinese would be beneficial: "I rather feel like taking up the underdog in the fight—the Chinaman sets some examples that is worthy of immitation [sic] by white laborers, such as industry, economy, & sobriety."

General John W. Sprague, the chairman of Tacoma's Chamber of Commerce, emerged as a prominent voice of restraint. Sprague was sixty-eight years old, with white hair, a walrus mustache, and a stern mien. During the Civil War, he had joined the Ohio Volunteers and had served as a brigadier general under Major General William T. Sherman during his famed "march to the sea" in Georgia. He later became a prosperous railroad man as an executive with the Northern Pacific. He was influential in the selection of Tacoma as the railroad's terminus and later became the city's mayor. In early October, Sprague convened a special meeting of the chamber, made up of 150 of the town's most influential businessmen, to consider the Chinese question. The group found itself split. Ezra Meeker, another prominent early settler—he was the one who sold the Wolds their first hops plants—tried to broker a compromise that included the establishment of a committee to study the ways in which Chinese migrants were evading the restriction law to enter the territory and an endorsement of stepped-up enforcement, but the anti-Chinese members easily carried the debate.

Meeker was a hale fifty-five-year-old whose white hair, long beard, and intense gaze gave him the appearance of a barely tamed wilderness man. In 1852, he made the trip west across the Plains by ox team on the Oregon Trail and later built a hops business in the Puyallup Valley, southeast of Tacoma, that employed several hundred men, including twenty-eight Chinese laborers. In a column in the *Daily Ledger*, Meeker argued that the effort to expel the Chinese crossed over into lawlessness and called out Weisbach in particular for inciting town residents; he beseeched the mayor and his followers to "respect our laws" and to "place ourselves aright in the eyes of our nation and of the civilized world."

A handful of Protestant clergymen in Tacoma used their pulpits to speak out against the clamor. The Rev. W. D. McFarland had previously run a school for deaf and mute children in Portland. In August, he was appointed to assume the pulpit of Tacoma's Presbyterian church. After the mass meeting in Seattle, anti-Chinese zealots spied on his home and visited one evening to see if he employed any Chinese help. McFarland was absent at the time, but when the pastor learned what happened, he vowed to preach on the Chinese question that Sunday. His fiery sermon, denouncing the anti-Chinese movement, caused some members to walk out. "Go! Go! I will preach on till the benches are empty," McFarland called after them. Afterward, McFarland armed himself with a pair of revolvers. He and seven other pastors, members of the Ministerial Union of Tacoma, issued a lengthy statement on the "anti-Chinese question," arguing that it was incumbent on them to weigh in on it as a moral issue. The ministers conceded that the Chinese presence was perhaps, "all things considered, undesirable," but they argued that their expulsion was a "worse evil." They decried the "reign of terrorism" on the Pacific Slope against the Chinese. The statement offered a harrowing portrait of the daily existence of Chinese residents. "Stones are hurled against their houses, in mass, of which the windows are riddled as by a hailstorm daily, by the time the sun has fairly set, they, with boarded windows and barred doors, sit in silence and fear in their houses," they wrote. The committee submitted the statement to the *Ledger* for publication, but the newspaper refused to print it.

As the tensions in Tacoma grew, Squire, the governor of the territory, became increasingly concerned. In a telegram on October 14, Squire pressed Lewis Byrd, the sheriff of Pierce County, on whether he had the manpower to keep the peace. Byrd assured Squire that "so far no disturbance of any kind has taken place here" and that "there seems to be no disposition to harm the Chinamen." He insisted that there was a "sufficient number of good, substantial citizens among the business men of Tacoma" who stood ready to assist him. Byrd proceeded to swear in more than fifty men in Tacoma as deputy sheriffs. General Sprague, the chairman of the Chamber of Commerce, wrote to Squire, praising the sheriff's efforts and announcing that he would himself soon become a deputy sheriff, "an honor that I never expected to attain." Sprague continued to believe that, even though most of Tacoma's white residents wanted the Chinese to leave, they would refuse to "countenance unlawful acts." On October 27, Squire visited Tacoma and addressed a meeting of the chamber at the grand, recently opened Tacoma Hotel. Squire insisted that he was "heart and soul" with those who desired to see the Chinese depart the territory, but he counseled "self control."

On the eve of the deadline for the Chinese to leave, a delegation of about two hundred anti-Chinese demonstrators from Seattle arrived in Tacoma in the middle of a driving rain. They attended a lavish banquet held for them at the Grand Army hall and then joined in a half-mile-long procession down Pacific Avenue, before ending up inside a packed opera house. Several members of Tacoma's Committee of Fifteen, along with Mayor Weisbach, delivered remarks. The gathering issued a series of resolutions, establishing the committee as a "permanent organization" to lead an "anti-Chinese movement over the entire American Pacific coast." It was also decided that on Tuesday, November 3, a "thorough investigation" would be conducted to determine how many Chinese residents remained in Tacoma. If necessary, the Committee of Fifteen was meant to call another meeting to decide what to do next.

The day of the deadline, November 1, passed quietly. The next day was rainy and chilly. Weatherred recorded in his diary: "The laboring men say the Chinese shall go tomorrow." He had little doubt that the outcome would be ugly. "This is one terrible town at present." Hundreds of Chinese residents remained in Tacoma, clinging to assurances from General Sprague and others that law and order would prevail. Rumors coursed through the Chinese community that their homes would be bombed. Some barricaded their doors.

Mayor Weisbach had been personally visiting Chinese merchants and telling them they had to go. A final meeting of the Committee of Fifteen took place in the evening at the Tacoma Hotel. At the time, a separate anti-Chinese organization, whose members called themselves the "committee of nine," met in secret. Theirs was a dissident organization, whose members doubted the commitment of the Committee of Fifteen to force the Chinese out. They included William Christie, the carpenter who had been in Eureka. Each member in the committee of nine had been assigned to organize nine others; these members were then supposed to do the same. In this way, the committee of nine had the ability to summon an army. The members decided to set their plan in motion that evening.

Early in the morning on November 3, Lewis Byrd, the sheriff, met with Weisbach, who assured him that there would be no trouble. Before they parted ways, Byrd reminded Weisbach that they shared the same obligations to the citizenry to maintain law and order. The mayor told Byrd he could rest easy.

At half past nine, the steam whistle from the town's iron foundry sounded, and then from other machine shops. Some residents thought the cacophony was a fire alarm, but it was evidently the signal for the mob to gather. On Pacific Avenue, several hundred men formed a phalanx and headed first to the southern end of C Street, which ran parallel to the waterfront, and began rapping on doors belonging to Chinese residents. At every stop, one man stood guard in front, while two or three others went to the back to corral anyone escaping. The main party went inside to order the occupants to pack up and leave. Some in the crowd had clubs and poles; others had pistols and rifles. They pressed into service an English-speaking Chinese resident, who translated their instructions for them. N. W. Gow, a thirty-two-year-old merchant, maintained a business on the west side of C Street, above South Eleventh Street, near the *Ledger*'s office. Gow had arrived in the city a year earlier and joined the First Baptist Church, where he was a regular at worship services and Sunday school. Others at the store had already left, but Gow had stayed behind to try to protect his goods. The invading men tossed his wares on the street and seized a trunk containing valuables, including a watch, several rings, and $2,800.

Kwok Sue, an early Chinese arrival in Tacoma, had a shanty on the waterfront. Rioters arrived by boat and barged into his home, looting his belongings. On Railroad Street nearby, Tak Nam was inside Sam

Hing and Company, the store he operated with his partner, Lum Way, when the mob descended. Theirs was the largest Chinese store and labor-contracting concern in Tacoma. The two men paid $30 a month to rent the location, which extended back some fifty feet from the front entrance. They had recently spent some $1,400 on renovations. The men shoved one of the store's employees out the door. Tak Nam, who had arrived in America in 1852, at the age of sixteen, recognized some of the angry men, including Jacob Ralph, a member of the Committee of Fifteen who owned a wagon manufacturing and repair business and served as Tacoma's fire chief. Tak Nam begged for more time. They gave him until two o'clock in the afternoon and promised to return.

By late morning, the mob, which included Weisbach, Wickersham, and other members of the Committee of Fifteen, had completed a sweep through the southern end of town. The rioters decided to proceed north to "Old Town," the original settlement. The committee also dispatched teams of men to aid the Chinese in their packing. Once the canvas was complete, the rioters returned to the wharf to conduct a more careful search, ransacking homes and dragging out anyone they found hiding inside. Drays and other wagons arrived to help transport luggage and goods.

In the afternoon, as Chinese merchants were rushing to pack what they could, Weisbach stopped by Gow's store on C Street. The mayor told Gow that he should have been prepared long ago. "You had plenty of time," Weisbach said. Gow's pastor, Barnabas MacLafferty, happened to be in the store at the time and admonished the mayor that Gow had done nothing wrong, but Weisbach insisted that Gow had to "go with the rest." Later, Gow went to Weisbach's grocery to ask for more time. At first Weisbach refused, but after Gow protested and a white merchant whose store was near Gow's pressed Weisbach as well, the mayor furnished Gow with a pass that said he should be protected.

Rioters descended on a stately home on A Street belonging to Ezra Bowen, a Philadelphia financier who had made sizable investments in Tacoma and purchased the residence the year before. Bowen's wife stood at her doorway with a broom, protecting her Chinese servant. "Put him out," the rioters chanted. "Put him out, nothing," she said, charging at the crowd. The agitators elected to move on. Isaac W. Anderson, general manager of the Tacoma Land Company and a critic of the anti-Chinese movement, placed two guards outside his home and offered $500 if they wounded a rioter and $1,000 if they killed one.

Chinese residents sent urgent telegrams to Squire in Olympia. "Mob driving Chinamen out of town. Will you not protect us!" Ten Sin Yee Lee wrote. "People driving Chinamen from Tacoma. Why sheriff no protect. Answer," Goon Gau wrote. Squire responded that he had alerted his superiors in Washington, D.C. He also contacted Sheriff Byrd, demanding to know the situation. After his early morning meeting with the mayor, Byrd had heard the commotion on C Street and watched the crowd proceed door to door to the "China houses," as he later put it. He had rushed ahead to Old Town to warn the superintendent of the Tacoma Mill, a major employer of Chinese laborers, but most had already left the day before. Byrd watched the city's Chinese residents pack up their belongings. He later characterized the rioters as "orderly," insisting that he had only seen a single plank knocked off the end of one Chinese building, the only instance of violence he observed. He repeatedly urged the crowd to "keep the peace." At half past two, he conferred with Fremont Campbell, Pierce County's prosecuting attorney, and they decided that it was too late to telegraph for federal troops to be sent. There was no use calling up all of the deputy sheriffs whom Byrd had sworn in because it was unclear how many they could even trust to be on their side. The two men decided that "any attempt to do anything" would be not just fruitless but would likely "lead to a collision in which many, both of the Chinese and whites, would lose their lives." Byrd spent most of the rest of his day in his office.

In the afternoon, the rioters returned as promised to Sam Hing and Company, bringing wagons and drays. Tak Nam and Lum Way readied boxes to take to the freight depot, where they hoped to send them on to Portland. Afterward, in a driving rain, they joined the Chinese residents streaming out of the city, herded by men on horseback. Bearing whatever possessions they could carry, the Chinese trudged towards the railroad station at Lake View, several miles outside the city limits. Two seriously ill Chinese residents, pulled from their homes by rioters, died of exposure on the way to the station. Lum Way's wife had refused to leave, but several men dragged her outside. Lum Way later said that the traumatic episode drove his wife mad. "From the excitement, the fright, and losses we sustained through the riot, she lost her reason, and has ever since been hopelessly insane," he said in an affidavit. "She threatens to kill people with a hatchet or with any other weapon she can get hold of."

At around five o'clock in the evening, the first bedraggled Chinese residents began arriving at the railroad station. Over the next two hours, about two hundred people, including women and children, streamed into the station. They were wet and cold, and frightened. Some took shelter in the station house and in another building that had once been occupied by Chinese section hands who worked on the railroad. There was an open shed and a nearby stable that also offered meager protection against the elements. Some of the refugees warmed themselves over fires. Several dozen white men stood guard over the group.

N. W. Gow, one of the shopkeepers who had been granted permission to stay behind to wrap up his affairs, hired a carriage and delivered bread to some of his relatives at the station. Weisbach later asserted that he personally arranged to send 150 loaves of bread and 140 boxes of crackers to the station. "I never expected to receive payment for these articles," he said. W. H. Elder, the Lake View ticket agent for the Northern Pacific, sold seventy-seven passenger tickets, some for a group rate of $130 for forty tickets, and the rest at $6 apiece. At about three o'clock in the morning, a passing freight train bound for Portland stopped at the station. "Load 'em aboard, I'll haul 'em," the engineer said. The bulk of the refugees, who could not afford to buy tickets, crowded into the box cars. Others simply began walking along the tracks in the same direction. At half past seven in the morning, the remainder of the refugees boarded a passenger train heading for Portland as well.

The next day, members of the Committee of Fifteen visited the roughly thirty merchants who had been granted reprieves and reminded them that they needed to finish their packing and leave. John Arthur, a lawyer who had been one of the most ardent anti-Chinese voices in the Chamber of Commerce, boasted in a letter to Squire that Tacoma would soon be "*sans* Chinese, *sans* pigtails, *sans* moon-eye, *sans* wash-house, *sans* joss-house, *sans* everything Mongolian." Arthur exulted about the "peaceful victory."

On the morning of November 5, at the request of anti-Chinese leaders, the city's health officer visited the Chinese quarter to decide whether to condemn the buildings on sanitary grounds. At ten thirty, however, steam whistles and the clanging of bells startled residents and smoke was seen rising from the Chinese building near the wharf. The origins of the fire were unknown. By noon, the quarter was a smoking ruin. Jacob Ralph, the fire chief who had been part of the anti-Chinese mob the day before, later said that he had ordered hose carts down to the wharf, but the hoses were not long enough to connect to a water source and reach the Chinese buildings. He formed a bucket brigade, but it was too late. "The citizens," he later said, "did all they could to assist." The next day, the *Daily News* reported, "the Chinese are gone from the city of Tacoma."

CHAPTER 18

Contagion

It turned into a contagion of hate. Up and down the Pacific coast, white residents began expelling their Chinese neighbors. Other Puget Sound communities endeavored to follow Tacoma's example. In Sumner, an agricultural community east of Tacoma, a committee of several dozen men went door to door on November 5, ensuring that about a dozen Chinese residents left town. A similar scene took place in Whatcom, about a hundred miles to the north, near the border with British Columbia.

The movement soon spread beyond the Washington Territory. On November 13, in Lorenzo and Boulder Creek, tiny lumber communities in northern California, agitators gave Chinese laundrymen and woodcutters twenty-four hours to clear out. That same evening, in Pasadena, a few miles north of Los Angeles, a fire broke out at a Chinese washhouse and spread to a meat market next door, owned by a white proprietor. Afterward, a mob of about a hundred men marched to the Chinese quarter, home to about a hundred residents. A committee met with Chinese leaders and gave them a day to vacate the town.

In Truckee, on November 28, throngs at an anti-Chinese meeting adopted a resolution declaring that the Chinese represented "an unmitigated curse to the Pacific Coast" and a "direct menace to the bread and butter of the working classes." The assembly vowed to "use every means in our power, lawfully, to drive the Chinese from our midst." An estimated seven hundred Chinese laborers were living in the area. A violent confrontation seemed inevitable. Charles F. McGlashan, an influential lawyer and the editor of the *Truckee Republican,* helped to establish a citizens "safety committee" whose purpose was to channel the anger towards "peaceful, law-abiding" ends. McGlashan led what would later be called the "Truckee Method," a methodical effort to drive out the Chinese by boycotting anyone who employed them. The committee also issued edicts closing gambling and opium houses and met with cigar dealers to ensure that they sold no Chinese-made cigars. In an important victory, the committee persuaded Sisson, Crocker and Co., which supplied cordwood for the Central Pacific Railroad, to rescind its woodcutting contracts that relied on Chinese laborers. By the end of January, much of Truckee's Chinese quarter was deserted.

In the New Year, the expulsions across the American West accelerated. At nine o'clock in the morning on January 24, in Redding, a town of several hundred people in northern California, a Committee of Forty went door to door to carry out an expulsion order. Washhouses were given five days to close up; vegetable peddlers had a week to sell their goods in town. The committee set up a guard in Chinatown to prevent anyone from returning. On January 30, the former lumber town of Blue Canyon, in Placer County, reported that its population of ten to fifteen Chinese in town had dwindled to just two, both hotel cooks. Three days later, the citizens of Gold Run, a former mining town nearby, reported that all of their Chinese residents had been expelled.

At first, it appeared that the Chinese in Tacoma's Puget Sound rival, Seattle, would be driven out as well. On November 5, a cloudy, windy day, the opposing sides on the Chinese question in Seattle met for a summit. At two o'clock in the afternoon, the Knights of Labor sent a committee of three men to the ornate, three-story brick building at the corner of Mill Street and Front Street, where John Leary, a leading businessman and the city's former mayor, kept his office. Leary was joined by Bailey Gatzert, a former mayor himself and the founder of one of the city's earliest hardware and general stores; and the sitting mayor, Henry Yesler. Collectively, the three men represented the city's conservative establishment. For weeks, anti-Chinese demonstrations had consumed the city.

Unlike in Tacoma, however, a fully fledged opposition movement had taken shape, led by distinguished figures in the city's business and civic communities. Many had forged cooperative, even friendly, relationships with Chinese merchants. Nevertheless, most publicly insisted that they believed the Chinese presence was bad for the country and argued for tighter restrictions on immigration. Their priority was on preserving law and order. In Leary's office, the city leaders concluded that the situation had become untenable for the Chinese. They decided to summon their representatives for a conference.

The most prominent Chinese resident to join the meeting was Chin Gee Hee, a forty-one-year-old merchant who was a personal friend of the mayor's. Gee Hee, as he was known to the white men, had a wiry frame; weathered, pitted skin; and mirthful eyes. He stood about five feet six inches tall. He had grown up in a tiny village in the southern part of Taishan. His father had made a living selling soy sauce crockery. Beginning as a young child, Chin would go to market every day, carrying a pole over his shoulders, loaded with wares. One day, an old man in the village who had recently returned from America approached him. He'd watched the way Chin handled himself at the market and been impressed. He asked, "Young man, how would you like to go to the mountain of gold?" Chin told him that he couldn't afford to make the journey, but the man assured him that he would make it possible. "There is a way and don't worry," he said. A short while later, Chin was on a ship to America. It was the year 1862. He was eighteen years old.

He arrived in San Francisco and made his way to mining towns in the Sierra Nevada, where he worked for several years as a miner and then joined a firm supplying provisions. After a few years in California, the lure of better wages and more reliable income drew him north to Washington Territory. He landed at a lumber mill in Port Gamble, on the northern end of Puget Sound, and became a cook for other workers. He also became friendly with Yesler, a carpenter who had established Seattle's first steam-powered sawmill and often visited the area on business. It was at Yesler's urging that Chin eventually made his way to Seattle, where a small Chinese population had taken root.

In 1873, Chin became a partner in Wa Chong & Co., one of the first Chinese-owned commercial establishments in Seattle. Chin Chun

Hock, one of Seattle's earliest Chinese residents, founded the business, in 1868, as a small store on wooden stilts over a duck-filled marsh. He later moved the store to Washington Street and expanded; other Chinese merchants soon followed him, shifting the locus of the Chinese quarter inland. The two men were the same age and from the same region in China. Chin Gee Hee purchased a quarter share in Wa Chong & Co. At the time, the Chinese population in Seattle had grown to about a hundred people. Wa Chong was the only general store catering to the Chinese customers, selling tea and other Chinese goods. The clientele included area residents, as well as Chinese laborers who dropped in from throughout the Puget Sound region. The store offered them a variety of services. There was a dormitory upstairs for lodgers and a kitchen in a back room. Many laborers utilized the store as their mailing address. Wa Chong even offered letter-writing services for a fee.

Chin Gee Hee's facility with English made him an asset to the firm, enabling him to serve as an intermediary with white businessmen. He threw himself into the business of labor contracting, supplying Chinese laborers to employers across the Puget Sound region. An account book for Wa Chong, which Chin maintained, lists the names of dozens of towns, in English and Chinese, where the firm did business, ranging from San Francisco to Springfield, Massachusetts. Wa Chong often intervened in the legal system on behalf of Chinese residents, posting bonds, vouching for them in court, and securing white lawyers. (In Chin's early years with Wa Chong, Leary's law firm, McNaught & Leary, did most of Wa Chong's legal work.) In the account book, Chin wrote out in neat cursive a page and a half of legal terms, such as "plaintiff," "defendant," "attorney," "treaty," "affidavit," and "deposition."

On November 4, Chin had sent a telegram to the Chinese consul in San Francisco, alerting him that the Chinese residents in Tacoma had been "forcibly driven out." Chin was concerned about what might happen in Seattle, where he said Chinese residents were in "imminent danger." In the summit at Leary's office, the civic leaders told Chin and several other merchants who had assembled that they feared the authorities would no longer be able to protect them and advised them to leave. Lue King, who was the lead partner of Tong Ye Chong & Co. and frequently called upon to act as a Chinese interpreter in court, protested that he had lived in Seattle for thirteen years and invested his life's savings into his business holdings. He hoped that someone could buy out his real estate and leases. "I never saw such a world as this," he said later. "If the people were going to drive us out, they should have said so before we invested our money here. A great many white men owe me money and won't pay. What are we to do? I don't think this is right." Chin told Leary and the other civic leaders that Wa Chong & Co. had more than $100,000 worth of property in the city and was owed more than $30,000 for repair work its laborers had done on Seattle's streets. Nevertheless, the Chinese representatives said they understood and asked only for some time to settle their affairs.

That evening, at a mass meeting at the city's opera house, Thomas Burke, a prominent lawyer and businessman and former probate judge, arose to address the audience. Burke insisted that people of the city were largely in accord. "We are all agreed that the time has come when a new treaty should be made with China restricting Chinese immigration to this country," he said. "But by the lawless action of irresponsible persons from outside, the people of this city are called upon to decide whether this shall be brought about in a lawful and orderly manner or by defiantly trampling on the law, treaties and constitution of our country." He suggested that the choice was whether Seattle's citizens would act as "law-abiding and justice-loving Americans or as turbulent and lawless foreigners." Burke said he favored "the American method." Burke said he had, personally, made the decision to no longer employ Chinese help at his home, even though that meant paying a white woman five dollars more per month than he would typically pay a Chinese houseboy. "It is a matter of principle with me, and I felt it my duty," he said. It was when Burke began criticizing his fellow Irishmen for their persecution of the Chinese and assailing Mayor Weisbach as "a foreigner" who could "hardly speak the English language" that the crowd began to hiss. Burke derided the mob in Tacoma and urged Seattle to set a better example. As the crowd threatened to tip into chaos, Burke was indignant. "In the future," he said, "the blackest page in the history of Washington Territory will be that on which it is recorded that two hundred human beings were driven out of Tacoma like dogs."

The next day, a reporter dropped in on several Chinese merchants to see what they were planning to do. He visited the firm of Quong Chong & Co., which had supplied the workers who had been attacked in Squak Valley. "Lots of boys are getting ready to go tonight," a representative there said. Those who could afford it would take the train; those who couldn't would walk. At Wa Chong, Chin complained that leaving the city would be costly for him and his partners. During the violence at the Coal Creek mines, the firm had already suffered losses for provisions that the firm had supplied to the workers. Chin said that he had been assured that he would have time to sell the firm's real estate holdings before being forced to leave. "We only want to stay long enough to get our money out," he said.

It was the intervention of the federal government that halted the Chinese expulsion in Seattle, at least temporarily. In the early morning hours of November 8, nearly 350 federal troops, comprising ten companies from the Fourteenth Infantry, arrived in Seattle. President Cleveland issued a proclamation that warned "insurgents" in Seattle to "disperse and retire peaceably" to their homes. White residents seemed to want to make a show of their hospitality, surrounding the soldiers' quarters and chatting with them late into the night. Many soldiers clearly sympathized with the anti-Chinese movement. Drunken soldiers got into scrapes with stray Chinese residents they encountered, throwing one man into the mud and another down some stairs. One evening, a group of enlisted men went through the Chinese quarter demanding a "special tax" of twenty-five cents a person. They netted $150 that they split amongst themselves. After a week, the troops departed.

Federal authorities were determined to prosecute the leaders of the anti-Chinese movement. Rumors about pending arrests caused excitement in Tacoma. "They're much worried because they know they are guilty of violating the law," John C. Weatherred wrote in his diary. On November 9, backed by the arrival of federal troops in Tacoma, a United States marshal placed under arrest more than two dozen men who had led the expulsion, including Mayor Weisbach, Wickersham, Jacob Ralph, and William Christie. A grand jury indictment accused them of conspiring to deprive "persons of the Chinese race" of their rights and to "make insurrection against the laws of the United States of America." A trial date was set for April. In a twenty-two-page report on the "recent Chinese troubles," dated November 23, 1885, William H. White, the United States attorney for the territory, wrote that he believed "no greater outrage was ever committed against the laws and government of the United States."

While White focused on the leaders of the Tacoma expulsion, his assistant, Cornelius Hanford, who was one of the founders of a citizens' "Home Guard" that had been established to maintain law and order, was pursuing charges against the Seattle agitators. The day after the Tacoma arrests, a grand jury in Seattle indicted fifteen men—the most prominent defendant was the Knights of Labor organizer Daniel Cronin—for threatening, intimidating, and harassing the Chinese residents of Seattle and seeking to drive them out of the county. Chin Gee Hee was among several Chinese witnesses who testified before the grand jury. The defendants insisted they were merely exercising their right to free speech. In a letter to his superiors in Washington, Hanford promised to pursue the case with "great vigor." In January, however, after an eleven-day trial, a jury needed just ten minutes to render a verdict of not guilty, setting off celebrations in the streets; one reveler fired a shot through a front window of Hanford's home.

The final advance on Seattle's Chinese quarter began in secret. At dawn on Sunday, February 7, 1886, a cloudy, slightly hazy day, squads of five or six men, dressed in overalls, went house to house, under the guise of enforcing a cubic-air ordinance that had recently been enacted by the city. Most of the residents were still sleeping. The inspections soon gave way to orders to pack up. Teams of white men helped Chinese residents with their possessions. Express wagons arrived to transport baggage. The work took place quietly at first, in the morning chill. John H. McGraw, the King County sheriff, had sworn in four hundred deputies to help maintain order in Seattle; an eighty-member force of Home Guards, armed with breech-loading guns, had also been assembled. As the anti-Chinese committees went about their task, however, no alarm was raised initially. W. P. Murphy, the city's acting police chief, arrived on the scene in uniform but made no arrests. "I thought it unwise to do so," he later said.

At nine o'clock in the morning, a messenger alerted McGraw that something was amiss in Chinatown. He hurried over and saw groups of Chinese residents headed to the wharf on Main Street. Watson Squire and his wife, Ida, happened to be in town at the time. She came down for breakfast at their hotel and overheard someone say: "They are moving out the Chinese." She looked out the window just in time to see an express wagon go by. Shortly afterward, a bell from the fire engine house began to ring. Church bells throughout the town clanged as well. It was the signal for McGraw's forces to muster.

The bells awoke Squire, who dressed and hurried to the law office of Thomas Burke, the former probate judge. That morning, a frightened Chinese resident had alerted Burke, while he was sitting down for breakfast, of what was happening. He summoned other leaders of the conservative faction and turned his offices into an impromptu military headquarters. Squire issued a proclamation urging residents to retire to their homes and anyone interested in preserving law and order to present themselves to the sheriff. Messengers delivered the governor's message to church services, summoning deputies to arms. Squire ordered the city's militia, the Seattle Rifles, to report for duty. He also sent an urgent telegram to military officials warning of an "immense mob forcing Chinese to leave" and requesting federal troops.

It would take several hours for McGraw to get his forces organized. McGraw later estimated that the agitators numbered about fifteen hundred men. An orderly process soon gave way to pandemonium, as men swarmed into Chinese dwellings. At Chin Gee Hee's home, rioters went up to the second floor and dragged his pregnant wife out by her hair onto the street. Members of the Home Guard rescued the couple from the mob. Three days later, however, she had a miscarriage. A twenty-three-year-old cigar factory manager barricaded himself inside his building, armed with an ax and a gun. Out his window, he watched William H. White, the prosecuting attorney for the territory, beseeching the rioters to disperse. They ignored him.

After their sweep of the Chinese quarter, the rioters began visiting households that employed Chinese servants and demanding that they be turned over to them. A cook employed by Mayor Yesler and his wife, Sarah, had ventured down to the Chinese quarter to check on his washhouse when he encountered a pack of rioters. He hopped a fence and fled, but they chased him all the way back to the Yesler home on the corner of Front and James Streets. He arrived at their back door, panting for breath. Sarah Yesler let him in and locked the door. Soon after, she heard a rapping. There were six or seven men outside her kitchen. "We want your Chinaman," the rioters said. "You have two in here and we want them." Yesler blocked them from entering. "My husband is mayor of this city and must stand by the law, and I am his wife, I must stand by the law too," she said. "This is my house, and I will protect it." The men blustered and threatened to blow up her house. The confrontation finally ended when several of McGraw's deputies arrived and arrested the men.

The rioters herded several hundred Chinese residents to the wharf, where the *Queen of the Pacific,* a 336-foot steamship, was scheduled to leave for San Francisco at one o'clock in the afternoon. Anti-Chinese leaders faced a dilemma: John Alexander, the ship's captain, refused to accept any passengers who did not pay the seven-dollar fare; few had the means to pay. Alexander connected a hose with the hot water steam pump and threatened to scald anyone who tried to board. The crowd on the dock began raising the funds amongst themselves. They collected about $600, enough for several dozen passengers, who filed onto the ship with their luggage, joining the other ticketed passengers. More than two hundred Chinese residents remained on the docks. McGraw boarded and told the passengers that if they wanted to stay in Seattle, they could. Most, however, seemed to believe that leaving was their best option. Just before the ship was set to depart, there was a new development. An injunction arrived from Judge Roger Greene, who presided over the district court. Addressed to Alexander, it commanded that his ship's Chinese passengers appear before the court for a habeas corpus hearing the following morning. The writ had been filed by Burke and White on behalf of Gee Lee, a laundryman, and "a great number of other Chinese persons" who were "restrained of their liberty" on board the ship. Judge Greene ordered that the sheriff deliver the Chinese passengers to his courtroom. Late in the afternoon, a light rain began to fall; the Chinese still left on the wharf, guarded by white vigilantes, moved to a warehouse. Around midnight, anti-Chinese leaders attempted to escort some of the Chinese residents to the train station, so they could be shipped out of the city that way, but a detachment of the Seattle Rifles, as well as a company from the territorial militia, blocked them. The Chinese on the wharf spread out blankets and settled in for a fitful night, guarded by a Knights of Labor committee.

By morning, the territorial militia members, along with volunteers from the Home Guard and a corps of cadet members from the University of Washington, had secured the two main approaches to the dock, blocking rioters who had begun to gather again. The authorities arrested several of the most prominent anti-Chinese agitators. At a quarter past seven, the members of the Home Guard escorted the Chinese who had been on board the ship to the courthouse. Lue King, the merchant who had attended the summit at Leary's office, was sworn in as an interpreter. Judge Greene was a devout Baptist who had started an English-language school for Chinese at his church with his wife. He called a roll of the ninety-seven residents included on the writ and instructed King to tell them that the law protected them if they wished to stay in Seattle. "The Court is willing if they desire that they shall go as passengers, but no man or set of men has a right to compel them to go," he said. "So if they wish to stay, they must let the Court know it now." He went through the names again. Only twenty-two indicated that they wished to remain. Greene, however, wanted them to be sure. He told King to tell his fellow countrymen that the "government is strong and will do all in its power to protect them." Those who had said they wished to remain conferred amongst themselves and a half-dozen changed their minds. Upon return to the wharf, a new collection took place for the additional tickets needed. The Chinese who had agreed to depart filed onto the ship with their luggage. Finally, Alexander announced that the ship had reached capacity. The remaining Chinese on the dock—about two hundred in all—would need to wait until the following week for the next ship to San Francisco. At noon, crew members of the *Queen of the Pacific* finally cast off the ship's lines. A hundred and ninety-six passengers were on board.

Those left behind gathered their belongings and formed a bedraggled column. With the Home Guards in front, and the cadets and territorial militia members bringing up the rear, the Chinese moved tentatively back down Main Street. Their destination was the Chinese quarter, less than a mile away. Initially, the maelstrom of angry men gave way, but at the intersection of Commercial Street, near the New England Hotel, a group of agitators descended upon the Guards in front. A melee ensued. Several in the crowd reportedly tried to wrest guns away from the citizen volunteers. Shots were fired. Several men in the crowd fell to the ground. (Charles Stewart, a thirty-four-year-old logger, later died from his injuries.) One of the special police officers on the scene was also injured. Some of the Chinese panicked, abandoned their possessions, and ran. Others cowered as their guards struggled to hold off the angry crowd. After a half-hour-long standoff, an infantry company arrived. A captain mounted a box and urged the crowd to disperse, assuring them that the rest of the Chinese would be departing on the next steamer. By then, Judge Burke was also on the scene, clutching a shotgun. Several in the crowd shouted for him to be turned over to them. (Anti-Chinese leaders later demanded—unsuccessfully—that he and other citizen volunteers be arrested for the shootings.) Finally, the crowd began melting away. The frightened Chinese returned home.

Kee Low, a fifty-nine-year-old laundryman who had been in the country for a decade, had managed to evade the mob uptown. Upon hearing the gunshots, he fled into the woods with several friends. Later, they snuck back down to the wharf, hoping to steal aboard the next steamer leaving for Victoria, Canada. While the other men hid amid bales of hops on the wharf, Kee Low flagged down a night watchman, who told him that no ships were leaving that evening. He hailed a passing militia member to help the frightened Chinese men. The soldier took them to a restaurant to find something to eat, only to be turned away. He bought some sandwiches for the Chinese men. Squire had declared martial law, so the streets were deserted. The remainder of the evening passed quietly.

Finally, on February 10, eight companies of federal troops arrived in Seattle, relieving the exhausted citizen volunteers. Brigadier General John Gibbons, the troops' commander, reported that he found the city "perfectly quiet and peaceful." Four days later, more than a hundred Chinese made their way to the wharf and boarded the *Elder*, bound for San Francisco. Several dozen more wanted to go, but the ship could accommodate no more.

A small contingent of Chinese residents chose to remain in Seattle. Chin Gee Hee, the labor contractor from Wa Chong & Co., as well as his partner, Chin Chun Hock, were among them. They likely benefited from Chin's close ties with civic leaders. He spent the next several months cataloging the losses sustained by the Chinese community. Wa Chong's tally alone totaled nearly $200,000, including the destruction of more than a dozen buildings, the interruption of their labor contracting business, and labor and capital invested in eight farms. In April, Zheng Zaoru, the Chinese ambassador in Washington, reported to a government official in Guangdong province that "the fierce fire is fading, and things are turning around." Chinese residents, however, still felt uneasy. On May 5, Wa Chong's owners alerted Chinese officials that "US Soldiers are withdrawing," and warned that "the natives" were "still going to drive out" the remaining Chinese residents. In July, the People's Party, which represented the anti-Chinese movement, dominated Seattle's municipal elections. On August 19, federal troops finally departed. The following month, William White, the prosecuting attorney, brought conspiracy charges against a half-dozen anti-Chinese agitators. The defense submitted no arguments in their case. On September 28, the jury acquitted the men. The case against the organizers of the Tacoma expulsion ultimately foundered as well.

In 1888, Chin struck out on his own, establishing the Quong Tuck Company, a block away from Wa Chong. During the Seattle fire of 1889, his store was burned to the ground, along with the rest of the city's business district. He became the first merchant downtown to rebuild, constructing a new store out of brick. In 1905, Chin returned to China, where he became a pioneering railroad builder. When he died, in 1929, the *Seattle Daily Times* published a laudatory obituary on its front page. The article quoted Judge Burke, who had died several years earlier, on Chin. "Seattle can point to no business career of higher honor, and few of more value to it, than that of Chin Gee Hee. He never ceased to spread the gospel of Seattle throughout the Orient."

CHAPTER 19

No Return

The ghetto became a sanctuary. In the fall of 1885 and the ensuing winter, the Chinese quarter in San Francisco, already dense with humanity, grew even more constricted, as refugees driven out from the interior arrived. Yet violence still attended them. Arsonists repeatedly set fire to buildings in Chinatown; more than a dozen Chinese residents died amid unrest in the city. On the afternoon of February 11, 1886, the *Queen of Pacific* arrived in San Francisco Bay, bearing the exiles from Seattle. Throngs gathered at the wharf to await their disembarkation, while a line of policemen stood guard. A long train of drays and express wagons was soon piled high with luggage, furniture, boxes, bedding, and clothing, and began wending its way to Chinatown.

Widespread unemployment and the boycotts targeting the Chinese made for a grim future for the new arrivals. One day in February, a newspaper reporter visited several factories in Chinatown. Representatives at Quang Sing & Co., one of the largest boot and shoe manufacturers in the city, reported that they were losing at least a thousand dollars a month. At another location, the reporter met a melancholy merchant named Quong Chuen Hing, whose two factories had once made him one of the biggest cigar manufacturers in the city. He told the reporter that his business was beginning to fail. White customers were refusing to buy his cigars; Chinese customers couldn't pay, because they had lost their livelihoods. "Our business is falling off alarmingly," he said. He predicted that within a few months most smaller cigar-making firms would close entirely. Quong said that there was no work for new arrivals, but he pointed out that "they have no other place to go." On the day of the *Queen of the Pacific*'s landing, the heads of two Chinese mercantile firms sent a telegram to the Chinese minister in Washington, Zheng Zaoru, warning that the merchants of the city were on the verge of being "absolutely ruined." Two days later, Lee Kim Wah, the president of the Chinese Six Companies, which was struggling to cope with the numbers streaming into the city, wrote his own concerned telegram to Zheng. "Our people are absolutely terrorized, and are flocking to San Francisco, where great destitution now exists among them," he wrote.

News had made its way back to China of the seriousness of the situation. In December, a newspaper in Hong Kong published a telegram from the Six Companies discouraging further emigration to America: "Those who don't come to California will be benefited greatly; those who discourage their countrymen to California will have endless happiness."

Zhang Zhidong, the governor general of Guangdong province, feared unrest in Guangzhou against Westerners and urged the Zongli Yamen, the Chinese foreign office, to adopt protective measures. Nearly two hundred merchants sent Zhang a joint letter detailing the daily litany of attacks and injustices that they experienced. The letter described "ten bitternesses" experienced by Chinese residents, including the cubic-air law, their fear of random violence, and frequent police raids. The document also listed "six unreasonablenesses" inflicted upon Chinese laundrymen, including arbitrary arrests and fines. Finally, it cited "seven hardships" faced by all laborers and merchants, such as the difficulties of finding work and their defenselessness against criminals. In May, Zhang forwarded the petition to the Guangxu Emperor, and wrote a detailed report, in which he explained that the Chinese in America faced an impossible situation. "They cannot stay if they want to stay," he said, but they lacked the means to return home. "They seek protection, but there is none."

Chinese officials, in China and the United States, were increasingly questioning the wisdom of emigration to America. The Chinese Six Companies began advertising offers to send residents of the Pacific coast back to China at dramatically reduced rates, blaming "the harsh treatment a number of our countrymen have received from the hands of a class of unprincipled white men." Anyone able to show proof of "extreme poverty" would be given free passage and a gift of $10. The departure from San Francisco, on February 10, 1886, of the steamer *City of New York* marked the debut of the discounted offer. In anticipation of a crush of interest, crew members rushed to add hundreds of additional bunks. The scene at the Pacific Mail dock was bustling, as Chinese gathered to bid farewell to friends. When the ship finally sailed, however, it carried just 166 Chinese passengers, far short of the ship's capacity of nearly 800. Most of the passengers, too, carried red-colored return certificates, issued by customs officials, authorizing their re-entry to the United States.

Overall, the Chinese were, in fact, departing in greater numbers. By the end of June, in 1885 and 1886, the San Francisco Customs House had recorded the greatest number of departures—more than fifteen thousand a year—since the Chinese migration to America began. Yet Chinese immigrants continued to stream into the country. In the year ending June 30, 1886, more than eleven thousand arrived. The vast majority gained re-entry through return certificates. On June 9 there was a commotion at the Pacific Mail company's wharf, with the arrival of the steamship *Oceanic,* carrying nearly seven hundred Chinese steerage passengers disembarking in San Francisco. It took much of the day to transport the passengers and their possessions to Chinatown. The landing, the largest in months, seemed to signal that the migration to America from the Far East was far from over, after all.

Hostile crowds began loitering around the home of the Chinese minister, Zheng Zaoru, in Washington, harassing him when he stepped out. He was the first to suggest that the Qing government take the unilateral step of limiting immigration of laborers to the United States. "If we don't do it, they will exclude us nonetheless," he wrote to the Zongli Yamen. Ouyang Ming, the consul general at San Francisco, made a similar proposal. Other prominent officials, including Chen Lanbin, the first Chinese minister in Washington, who had served alongside Yung Wing, agreed. On August 3, 1886, the foreign office sent a letter to Charles Denby, the United States minister in China, detailing the outrages perpetrated against Chinese subjects in America, including "the expulsion of the Chinese, burning and destroying their property, and killing them." The foreign office criticized the local authorities for failing to take steps to prevent the attacks and pointed out that the offenders had not been punished, clear violations of treaty stipulations. As a result, the letter continued, the Chinese government was considering "a plan for adopting prohibitory measures herself." Under its provisions, Chinese laborers who had never been to the United States would be "strenuously prohibited" from emigrating; only returning laborers who still had families or property in the country would be permitted to travel.

The foreign office's proposal was intended, ultimately, for the consideration of President Grover Cleveland. In the fall of 1884, Cleveland had become the first Democrat to win the presidency since the Civil War, defeating his Republican opponent, James Blaine, in an invective-filled contest. Republicans, however, managed to maintain control of the Senate, thanks in part to President Chester Arthur's passage of the Chinese restriction legislation. The support of the Pacific coast remained a coveted prize, making the potential resolution of the Chinese question a boon for the Cleveland administration. For reasons that are unclear, news of the Chinese proposal failed to reach Cleveland's secretary of state, Thomas F. Bayard, until January 1887, when the recently installed Chinese minister, Zhang Yinhuan, a middle-aged Cantonese official, brought it up to him in a meeting. Bayard, a descendant of a distinguished French family and a former Democratic senator from Delaware, was a realist on the issue of Chinese immigration. In 1879, as a member of the Senate, he had voted in favor of Blaine's Fifteen Passenger bill, which President Rutherford B. Hayes later vetoed. Bayard also viewed the Burlingame Treaty skeptically and believed additional restrictions on the flow of Chinese into the country were inevitable. He blamed the "peculiar characteristics and habits of the Chinese immigrants" that caused them to refuse to "mingle with the mass of population" for the "race prejudice" that had been aroused against them. When he learned of the openness of Chinese officials to self-prohibition, he wrote to Zhang less than a week later, enclosing a draft of a new convention, in which he suggested that Chinese laborers be "absolutely prohibited" from entering the United States for thirty years.

Zhang was a native of Foshan, a village west of Guangzhou that had long been a trading center. He had been a highly regarded local administrator who came to the attention of the Chinese ruler, the Empress Dowager, because of his expertise in foreign affairs. She appointed him to a probationary position in the Zongli Yamen, and he had risen rapidly through the ranks. Just over a year after his appointment, he became the third Chinese minister to the United States. When he arrived in San Francisco, in April 1886, to take his post, customs officials blocked him from landing, demanding that he present his credentials. After "considerable detention," according to a telegram by the consul general at San Francisco, he was finally permitted to come ashore. It was an ignominious introduction to America. Zhang's familiarity with English was limited—he depended on staff for translation help—but he was an assiduous worker and a zealous defender of Chinese character and morals. He was wary of Western influences, once recording in his diary that "Jesus Christ would be ashamed of the way Christians treat Chinese in Rock Springs." Yet he also came to enjoy Washington's social scene, throwing elaborate parties and often enjoying a box at the theater, and praised aspects of America, including its business methods and the transcontinental railroad. In this way, he presented an ideal negotiating partner for Bayard, open and reflective, even as China was newly assertive in its interactions with the West.

By the time Bayard was ready to engage on the Chinese proposal for self-prohibition, Zhang was preoccupied with securing compensation for victims of the Rock Springs massacre. On February 24, 1887, President Cleveland finally signed the indemnity bill, awarding nearly $150,000 to the victims. Several weeks later, Zhang commenced discussions for a new treaty, leaving a lengthy memo at the State Department, in which he began by highlighting the "numberless cases in which Chinese were outrageously treated." He pointed out that treaty stipulations required that the United States take steps to protect Chinese subjects, but the residents of western territories had "made the ill treatment of the Chinese a constant practise and have looked upon the acts of expelling and burning out the Chinese as sources of pleasure."

An immediate point of contention was the duration of any prohibition. Zhang argued that a fixed period was unnecessary, because China was proposing to adopt the prohibition on its own accord and would do so "from time to time, in such manner as may be required by circumstances." Zhang also pressed for a public proclamation from President Cleveland that Chinese subjects were to be protected from persecution and asked that a federal officer be appointed in San Francisco to deal with cases of violence or potential violence against the Chinese on the Pacific coast. Zhang requested that anyone found guilty of "assailing and killing the Chinese with fire arms" be punished "by hanging as a warning to others." The specifics of Zhang's proposals showed he was struggling to understand the American system of governance. Zhang later admitted that he had not been entirely certain whether his requests conformed to the "usual practices in the United States" but was hoping for guidance from Bayard on ways the United States could honor its treaty obligations under its existing laws.

A month later, Bayard responded with a new draft, in which he reduced the proposed ban to twenty years but, notably, included no new mechanisms for protecting existing Chinese residents in America. Bayard was privately incredulous at some of Zhang's requests. "It seems almost impossible for them to comprehend the limitations upon the power of officials under our system," he wrote to Denby. Several months elapsed in the correspondence between Bayard and Zhang, as the Chinese minister traveled to Spain. (His diplomatic remit included that country and Peru.) When Zhang resumed the negotiations, in August, he raised anew the issue of protections for Chinese residents. He pointed out that "not a single American has lost his life by mob violence" in China and that any cases of property damage and other injury were dealt with promptly. Zhang emphasized that he was simply asking for the "same measure of protection as is extended to Americans in China." Zhang also pressed for another indemnity payment from the United States in response to the dozens of other cases of mob violence against the Chinese.

Consternation over the waves of Chinese returning to America was growing. In a letter about the enforcement of Chinese restrictions, dated November 28, 1887, Judge Lorenzo Sawyer, of San Francisco's circuit court, reported that "a much larger number have returned within the last few months than ever before." He attributed the influx to apprehensions that they soon would be blocked completely from returning. With the corresponding onslaught of habeas corpus cases, Sawyer pronounced the burden upon the courts to be "little short of intolerable." Bayard was slow to respond to Zhang's latest missive, perhaps an indication of his irritation at the Chinese minister's forthrightness. On December 28, 1887, Bayard wrote to Zhang, arguing that "systematic evasion" of the Chinese restriction law was taking place, and urged the Chinese minister to negotiate with him a "just and wise convention." Once again, however, he pointedly ignored Zhang's entreaties for greater protections.

Meanwhile, the Republican majority in the Senate was eager to assert itself on the Chinese question. On January 12, John H. Mitchell, an Oregon Republican, introduced legislation abrogating existing treaties with China and "absolutely prohibiting the coming of Chinese to the United States." Mitchell was a fifty-two-year-old former railroad attorney with piercing eyes and an unruly beard. He had ascended to the Senate in 1873, at the age of thirty-eight, overcoming revelations that, as a schoolteacher in Pennsylvania, he had impregnated a fifteen-year-old student, married her, and then abandoned her and changed his name to remake himself out west. Mitchell assailed the Cleveland administration for failing to renegotiate the country's treaty stipulations with the Chinese empire and allowing "this oriental octopus to fasten its disgusting and poisonous tentacles upon us." William Stewart, the Nevada Republican who had led the fight a decade and a half earlier against Chinese naturalization, made his own case against the Chinese presence in America. "I have no feeling of resentment against the Chinese," Stewart said. "I have always been in favor of treating them kindly while they are here. I have met the opposition of my own people in defending the Chinese from violence which naturally arises from race hatred and prejudice. But I have long since seen that we can not live with the Chinese." The Senate agreed to refer Mitchell's bill to the Committee on Foreign Relations, as well as a resolution introduced by Stewart that urged the president to negotiate "at the earliest practical moment" a treaty that excluded all Chinese.

Once again, an atrocity became a matter of foreign relations. One day, in October 1886, a group of Chinese men set out from the Chinese quarter in Lewiston, in the northwestern corner of Idaho Territory, to prospect for gold in Oregon. They set up camp in Snake River Canyon, a deep slash in the earth named after the swift-moving tributary that carved through it. For several months, the men sifted for gold on the riverbank and gravel bars. They moved to a cove, near the junction of the Imnaha River, surrounded by rugged, basalt cliffs. The accounts of what happened next, sometime in late May or June of 1887, are sketchy but generally point to the actions of a band of horse-rustling outlaws in the canyon. In one version of the events, the men hatched a plan to rob the Chinese men of their gold dust; in another, the incident was merely a chance encounter, as the gang of men schemed for a way to ford the river with their horses. Whatever the motivation, the result was a massacre. One account, published years later in the memoirs of an early Oregon settler, described bullets raining down on the miners, and "one by one the Chinamen were shot down like sheep-killing dogs." The outlaws chased after a lone survivor and "finished him off" with a rock. Afterward, the white assailants threw the mangled bodies into the river.

It took some time for news of the attack to filter out. The Chinese miners were members of the Sam Yup Company, which hired an English-speaking interpreter named Lee Loi to investigate the murders. On February 16, 1888, Zhang wrote to Bayard to bring to his attention "another case of outrage inflicted upon my countrymen." The letter listed ten victims, including eight from the same clan: Chea Po, Chea Sun, Chea You, Chea Shun, Chea Cheong, Chea Ling, Chea Chow, and Chea Lin-Chung, as well as Kong Mun-kow, and Kong Ngan. All the men came from the Punju district, near Guangzhou. (Subsequent reports suggested more than thirty Chinese miners were killed. For years, their corpses washed up along the banks of the river.) Zhang highlighted the brutality of the murders—one man had been shot in the back and struck in the head with an ax; another had been shot in the back twice and his head and left arm severed; and still another was found with multiple ax wounds in the head. Zhang enclosed a report by Joseph K. Vincent, a Lewiston official who had been retained by Lee Loi to help investigate the murders. Vincent had struggled to reach the remote location where the attack took place, but he said the evidence suggested "white men were the murderers." Zhang emphasized that the killings were different from the usual homicide, because of the racial animus that inspired them. He expressed concern that others, "from their hatred of the Chinese," might draw inspiration from the crimes.

Bayard's response to Zhang, dated February 23, was hardly sympathetic. He highlighted the contradictory aspects of Zhang's account, suggesting that the legal authorities had little to go on. Nevertheless, Bayard promised to send copies of Zhang's note to officials in Oregon and Idaho Territory. (A grand jury later indicted six men for the murders; prosecutors brought three men to trial, but a jury found them not guilty.) The following day, Bayard nudged Zhang again about their negotiations and invited him to come to the State Department for a meeting. By this point, Bayard realized that they needed to move quickly. When the two men met, on February 29, Bayard said that, if they failed to come to an agreement, Congress was poised to enact draconian restrictions without them. Bayard's latest draft convention included a clause specifying that existing Chinese residents had all the rights given by law to "citizens of the most favored nation," as well as one awarding an additional indemnity payment for Chinese subjects victimized by incidents of mob violence. The next day, the Senate approved by a voice vote Stewart's resolution calling for a new treaty with China that barred Chinese laborers altogether from entering the country.

The negotiations between Bayard and Zhang finally began to progress. Zhang pressed for some additional changes, before pronouncing himself satisfied. On March 3, the Chinese minister presented to Bayard a final statement of claims. It included property losses suffered by Chinese citizens at Eureka, Squak Valley, Coal Creek, Tacoma, and Seattle, as well as a lengthy list of other locations of anti-Chinese violence. (Zhang's list was hardly comprehensive. According to a tally, published in 2018 by the historian Beth Lew-Williams, in 1885 and 1886, at least 168 communities across the American West forced their Chinese to leave.) In his statement of claims, the Chinese minister asserted that "near 100,000 Chinese had been driven from their homes." The itemized property losses totaled $246,619.75. Zhang also presented a tally of forty lives lost—not including the Snake River murders, since the details remained uncertain—and asked for compensation of $2,500 each, for a total of $100,000.

Zhang included a separate note about Chin Gee Hee's losses, specifically, evidence of his influential place in the Chinese community. The claim of his firm, Wa Chong and Company, was easily the largest on the list. Zhang explained that the original amount of his claim was nearly $190,000, but he had subtracted losses that were "not clearly sustained by international law," as well as another portion that reflected uncollected debts owed to the firm, resulting in a final claim of just under $50,000. On March 12, 1888, Bayard and Zhang finally signed the treaty. The indemnity payment included in the treaty totaled nearly $300,000. The treaty's centerpiece was a twenty-year prohibition on Chinese laborers entering the United States, with an exception granted for those who had a wife, child, or parent in the country, or property or debts owed to them that amounted to at least $1,000.

Months of negotiations had culminated in exactly what the anti-Chinese movement wanted: a near-total ban. Nevertheless, the Republican-led Senate remained bent on showcasing its anti-Chinese bona fides. Republican senators insisted on adding two amendments that ostensibly toughened the requirements but amounted to nothing more than some additional ornamental language. President Cleveland recognized the Republicans' political maneuvering and urgently wrote to Bayard, anxious to know how the Chinese might respond. The president reminded Bayard that their best strategy was to swiftly approve the treaty. Bayard tried to make clear the superfluousness of the amendments to Zhang, explaining that "they only repeat what the Treaty itself was intended to express." During a lengthy meeting, Zhang complained the changes were "very unnecessary" but agreed. On May 12, after carefully studying the amendments, he telegraphed them to the Zongli Yamen for ratification.

Unbeknownst to American officials, across the Pacific, Chinese officials were becoming uneasy with the treaty. The merchant community on the Pacific coast and in Hong Kong and Guangdong province was beginning to agitate against it. They feared a twenty-year ban on Chinese laborers—the main customers for imported goods from China—would be devastating for their businesses. They also warned that thousands of laborers returning to China in search of work could pose problems for the empire. They petitioned the foreign office to press for a shorter prohibition and less onerous terms on the return requirements. A mob smashed the windows of Zhang's home in Guangzhou during a protest. Worried about unrest, Zhang Zhidong, the provincial official in Guangdong, recommended that the Qing government decline to ratify the treaty.

Late in the evening on August 31, word came by cable from newspapers in London—apparently reporting on rumors—that the Qing government had rejected the treaty. Three days later, the State Department still had not received confirmation from Chinese officials. At noon, when the House convened, Rep. William L. Scott, a Pennsylvania Democrat and a trusted friend of President Cleveland's, obtained the unanimous consent of the chamber to introduce a bill that outlawed all Chinese laborers who had departed the country from re-entering and voided all return certificates. Scott was the chairman of the Democratic National Campaign Committee and had a reputation as a pugnacious politician. With the election fast approaching, he recognized that the Democrats could not squander the opportunity to settle the Chinese question. He told his colleagues that if the Chinese government had indeed rejected the treaty, the bill was "the only possible way by which Chinese laborers can be kept out of the United States." After a brief discussion, the bill passed the House by a voice vote.

On September 5, Denby sent a telegram to Bayard from Beijing: "Believe treaty has been rejected." The following day, he cabled that the treaty had been "postponed for further deliberation." In the Republican-controlled Senate, the Scott bill stalled, as senators sought clarification of the Qing government's intentions. For two weeks, Democratic and Republican senators jousted over the propriety of acting unilaterally on the issue. On September 21, the Scott bill finally went to the White House for the president's signature. On the same day, Denby cabled Bayard to relay that the imperial government had refused to ratify the treaty unless the twenty-year ban was shortened and the provisions for the return of laborers loosened. Bayard had been urging Cleveland to veto the bill, because it represented a gross departure from the "decorum essential to international proceedings." Political considerations, however, trumped diplomatic protocols.

On October 1, Cleveland signed the legislation into law and used the occasion to deliver a special message to Congress. "The experiment of blending the social habits and mutual race idiosyncracies of the Chinese laboring classes with those of the great body of the people of the United States has been proved by the experience of 20 years, and ever since the Burlingame Treaty of 1868, to be in every sense unwise, impolitic, and injurious to both nations," he wrote. He asserted that the "object and intent" of the Chinese restriction law, approved in 1882, had been thwarted by widespread fraud. The problems with the law and the earlier Angell Treaty had, in turn, led to "deep-seated and increasing discontent among the people of the United States," he said. Cleveland portrayed himself as being left with little choice but to "answer the popular demand for the absolute exclusion of Chinese laborers." Cleveland also sought to enshrine the principle that it was the "paramount right and duty" of the government to "exclude from its borders all elements of foreign population which for any reason retard its prosperity or are detrimental to the moral and physical health of its people." Cleveland's language eliminated any remaining ambiguity about lawmakers' intentions: Chinese restriction was, unequivocally, becoming Chinese exclusion.

In conclusion, Cleveland extended the tiniest of consolations to the Chinese government, urging Congress to indemnify Chinese subjects who had "suffered damage through violence in the remote and comparatively unsettled portions of our country at the hands of lawless men." Cleveland was careful to add the caveat that the United States was not acknowledging liability but simply offering the sum "in a spirit of humanity befitting our Nation." Several weeks later, Congress approved the appropriation. On January 11, 1889, at the State Department, Bayard delivered the sum of $276,619.75 to Zhang, who acknowledged in his receipt payment "for all losses and injuries sustained by Chinese subjects within the United States at the hands of residents thereof."

On the Pacific coast, residents exulted, as if a bloody, stalemated war had finally come to an end. When news of the Scott Act becoming law reached San Francisco, on October 1, both the Democratic and Republican state central committees ordered hundred-gun salutes.

Bands of revelers spilled onto the streets. In Oakland, crowds gathered around the *San Francisco Examiner*'s bulletin board to read the news from a telegram that said "Bid all ye Californians rejoice." That evening, Democratic supporters crammed into the Metropolitan Hall to celebrate, while bonfires blazed throughout the city. In San Jose, Denis Kearney was among the speakers at a triumphant anti-Chinese meeting; Democrats in Los Angeles fired off their own cannon salute. The *Alta California* heralded it as "California's day of jubilee."

Records at the San Francisco Customs House showed that more than twenty-three thousand return certificates were outstanding. Most of these former residents of the United States would be barred from returning to their property, businesses, and families. Existing residents would also find themselves cut off, unable to visit ailing parents or be reunited with wives and children in their native land, if they hoped to return to the United States. Letters would pour into the Treasury Department from lawyers, seeking clarification on this question. Some wrote that their clients would be willing to become citizens, "if acceptable." A more pressing legal question, however, immediately presented itself. Hundreds of Chinese former residents had been refused entry while the Scott Act was being considered and were awaiting hearings in federal court. On Saturday, the day before President Cleveland signed the legislation, the steamship *City of New York* had arrived into port, bearing eighty-eight Chinese passengers. Customs officials had blocked all of them from landing. The *Belgic*, a British vessel belonging to the Occidental and Oriental Steamship Company, was en route across the Pacific and due in San Francisco in a matter of days. In Hong Kong, where the ship had originated, the *Belgic* initially had a manifest of nearly a thousand Chinese passengers, but most had decided to wait to see the outcome of the Scott Act. A hundred and seventy-six Chinese passengers, including two women and a child, nearly all carrying return certificates, had decided to risk the passage. Another steamship, the *Duke of Westminster*, had eased into the harbor in Vancouver, British Columbia, that very day, with 252 Chinese passengers on board, most of whom planned to continue to San Francisco.

On October 3, John Hager, the seventy-year-old, fanatically anti-Chinese collector of the port of San Francisco, posted a notice in the

Custom House and at the entrance to the Chinese Registration Bureau in the city Appraisers' Building: "No Chinese return certificates will hereafter be issued." Around noon, someone who wished to drive home the point that the bureau was closed to Chinese applicants draped white cloth and crepe paper across the door. A sign was also later added in Chinese. Throughout the day, customs officials turned away several dozen people who had hoped to obtain a certificate. Hager sent a telegram to his superiors at the Treasury Department in Washington, asking for instructions about how to handle the passengers on the arriving ships. They cabled back that the exclusion act was in full force and return certificates were to be "declared void." Hager posted this decision on the Custom House doors as well.

The *Belgic* finally arrived in port on Sunday, October 7, nearly a month after it had first departed Hong Kong. Delayed by rough seas, the ship was several days overdue. The *Duke of Westminster* slipped into the harbor not far behind. Customs officials ordered that the Chinese passengers on both ships stay on board for questioning. The standard protocol for arriving ships was for an inspector to embark with a Customs House interpreter, Carleton Rickards, a man in his early twenties who had been studying Chinese since he was a teenager and spoke multiple dialects. On Monday morning, Rickards and his colleagues began interviewing *Belgic* passengers. A half-dozen said that they were born in the United States and claimed American citizenship. Several others carried merchant certificates; another passenger, a man named Sue Sung Seng, said he was an actor. The rest of the remaining passengers were returning laborers, almost all with return certificates. Normally, the certificates would be brought ashore and compared with a register of departures kept at the Customs House; Hager would then stamp them as "registered." With the arrival of the *Belgic*, however, Hager deemed the certificates to be no longer valid, prompting a confrontation between the collector and the Chinese consul general, who had arrived at the dock and lobbied for the passengers to be landed.

The next day, Judge Hoffman ordered that about two dozen passengers from the *City of New York* be permitted to come ashore based on their claims of prior residency. The ship had arrived just ahead of the new law. The passengers of the other two ships would have to litigate their right to return in court. On the morning of October 11, Lorenzo Sawyer, the dignified circuit court judge who had assiduously protected the civil rights of Chinese immigrants over the years, issued two writs of habeas corpus for passengers aboard the *Belgic* and the *Duke of Westminster*. These would be the first test cases for the constitutionality of the Scott Act and whether its provisions applied to Chinese who had been in transit to the United States when it became law. The following afternoon, the corridors of the courthouse were crowded with Chinese men, waiting for the case to begin. Sawyer summoned Hoffman to appear on the bench with him. Thomas Riordan, the San Francisco attorney who had been representing the Six Companies for several years, appeared in court to make the case for the two Chinese men in the custody of the U.S. Marshals Service. Riordan was joined by two other lawyers who frequently represented the Chinese: Lyman Mowry, a veteran lawyer who was said to have tried more homicide cases than anyone else in the state, and Alfred Ricketts, a prominent mining lawyer.

The gallery was filled with spectators. They included several dozen Chinese observers, who had arrived early to take their seats; others milled about outside. The Chinese consul, Frederick Bee, occupied another seat in the courtroom. On the opposite corner from Bee was C. C. O'Donnell, a political gadfly and former coroner who had been involved in the establishment of the state's Workingmen's Party. O'Donnell was waging a quixotic bid to become mayor of San Francisco on a platform that would have "coolies removed outside the city limits." Garret McEnerney, a lawyer from Napa who had been selected in August as counsel to a citizens' anti-Chinese committee, also listened attentively. Appearing on behalf of the federal government was General John T. Carey, a Sacramento lawyer who was prominent in Democratic politics and had been appointed to be the district attorney for the northern district by President Cleveland.

The lawyers agreed to first take up the case of a thirty-four-year-old laborer, identified in his habeas corpus petition as Gi Chow, because his case for landing was the strongest. The man had arrived in San Francisco in 1875 and departed for China on June 2, 1887, aboard the steamship *Gaelic*. Before he left, he had obtained a certificate from the Custom House, no. 53778, signed by a deputy collector, that attested he was permitted to "return to and re-enter the United States upon producing and delivering this certificate to the collector of customs." In the courtroom, Sawyer asked for the man's certificate, which a customs inspector drew from his pocket. Sawyer chided customs officials for confiscating the document, saying they had no legal reason for doing so. There was some confusion, however, because the name on the certificate, Chae Chan Ping, was different from that of the habeas corpus petition. Riordan explained that Chinese names were impossible to spell in English; Sawyer agreed to amend the petition. The case would henceforth be known as *Chae Chan Ping v. United States.*

Riordan began his argument by citing the Angell Treaty of 1880 and its provisions stipulating that Chinese residents in the United States at the time would be allowed to leave and return at will. He then traced the developments in the "Restriction Act of 1882," which had first established the certificate requirement for returning Chinese, the amendments to the law made in 1884, and then finally "the Act of 1888, known as the Exclusion bill," which had declared that the certificates were no longer valid. Riordan argued the Scott Act violated constitutional protections that bar the depriving of life, liberty, or property without due process of law. Riordan's argument was, essentially, that the certificates were the equivalent of contracts from the federal government that could not be arbitrarily revoked. Carey countered that the certificates were a form of "personal privilege given to an alien, subject to revocation at any given moment." Riordan went on to criticize the retroactive nature of the Scott Act, arguing that Chae Chan Ping could not be subjected to a law whose existence he would have had no way of knowing about. The judges appeared skeptical. Sawyer had once been thoroughly impressed by the Chinese as a people, but his views on their presence in America had evolved considerably. He would later explain that his issue was "very different from the population objection" but one of the "distinction of races." He characterized the Chinese as "vastly superior to the negro, but they are a race entirely different from ours and never can assimilate."

On the morning of October 15, the day of the verdict, the courtroom was once again "crowded almost to suffocation," as one observer put it. When Sawyer took his seat on the bench, the room quieted. Sawyer told the assembled that he and Judge Hoffman were satisfied that the law was constitutional. As a result, the petitioners should be remanded back to China. In his decision, Sawyer wrote that the language of the law was clear that it would take effect immediately. Sawyer dismissed the argument that it would be "a great hardship" for the law to affect people who were on their way to America at the time of the president's signing, arguing this was "not the concern of the Courts." He characterized the "going and coming from one country to another" as a "privilege" that could be superseded by an act of Congress.

Chae Chan Ping's lawyers immediately filed an appeal to the Supreme Court of the United States. The *Duke of Westminster,* which had been anchored in the harbor, was scheduled to depart that afternoon. There was a flurry of activity at the courthouse, however, as more than a dozen passengers filed new habeas corpus petitions, claiming citizenship or merchant status. A deputy U.S. marshal came aboard to remove a small group whose writs had been granted by Judge Sawyer. Finally, at half past four, the ship weighed anchor, setting sail for Vancouver. On October 18, just before the departure of the *Belgic,* the marshal's service removed fifty-two passengers by court order. Most asserted that they were merchants; thirteen said they were citizens, born in California; four passengers said they were in transit to Panama or Cuba. Newspaper accounts later jeered these last-minute petitions as obviously fraudulent. In the late afternoon, the ship finally sailed, bearing just under a hundred of its original Chinese passengers. The passengers who had been taken off arrived at the Appraisers' Building and huddled at the end of the corridor, waiting to have their cases heard. Carey, the district attorney, argued that the petitioners were "committing wholesale perjury" and said he would not force his assistants to work late to accommodate them. He later confided in a memo that he believed that the Chinese in America were all "entirely regardless of the truth" and had "no appreciation of an oath." Judge Sawyer finally ordered that the group be taken to the county jail. Carey spent the weekend interrogating petitioners, finishing at three o'clock in the morning on Monday. Over the next week, most would be remanded back to China, the largest group returning to the dock on four wagons, on the afternoon of October 27, as people on the streets cheered. The thirty-eight remanded Chinese quickly boarded the waiting steamship *Arabic* for their voyage to Hong Kong.

To argue Chae Chan Ping's appeal before the Supreme Court, the Six Companies retained an accomplished legal team. George Hoadly, the former Democratic governor of Ohio, and James C. Carter, a leading New York litigator, prepared the main brief on his behalf. On March 28, inside the half-domed, semicircular chamber on the second floor of the capitol building that housed the Supreme Court, Hoadly made his opening remarks in front of eight justices. One chair on the dais was vacant, marking the absence of the late Justice Stanley Matthews, who had died from illness less than a week earlier. Presenting the case for the United States were George Jenks, the solicitor general, and three lawyers retained by the state of California, including John F. Swift, who had helped to negotiate the Angell Treaty. The court's gallery was crowded with spectators, including William Stewart, the Nevada senator, and John Mitchell, the Oregon senator, who had proposed the absolute pro-hibition on Chinese immigration the year before. The oral arguments for Chae Chan Ping's case took place over two days. Based on the justices' questions, however, there seemed to be little doubt how they would rule. "Chae Chan Ping and his brethren will have to be content to remain out of the United States," the *Chronicle* predicted. On May 13, 1889, the Court handed down its unanimous decision, in an opinion written by Justice Stephen Field, the former chief justice of the Cali-fornia Supreme Court, who had once been lauded by the Chinese for his favorable decisions on their behalf. After the passage of the restric-tion bill, in 1882, however, Field's views on the Chinese question had evolved. While presiding over the circuit court in northern California, he increasingly found himself at odds with Sawyer and Hoffman over the interpretation of the law.

Field, whose bald head, fringed with long gray hair, and pointed gray beard gave him the look of an ascetic, began his opinion by offering a history of Chinese immigration to America and an explanation for the rising tensions over their presence. He cited economic competition with white laborers but blamed "the differences of race" for adding "greatly to the difficulties." According to Field, the Chinese "remained strangers in the land, residing apart by themselves, and adhering to the customs and usages of their own country." Field explained that, as a result, "it seemed impossible for them to assimilate with our people." The heart of Field's opinion was his assertion that the federal government had broad authority to "exclude foreigners from the country whenever, in its judgment, the public interests require such exclusion." According to Field, the ability to exclude certain immigrants came with the government's duty to protect the country "against foreign aggression and encroachment." He explained: "It matters not in what form such aggression and encroachment come, whether from the foreign nation acting its national character or from vast hordes of its people crowding in upon us." He likened the situation to that of a war with a foreign power. If the government, through Congress, "considers the presence of foreigners of a different race in this country, who will not assimilate with us, to be dangerous to its peace and security, their exclusion is not to be stayed because at the time there are no actual hostilities with the nation of which the foreigners are subject," he wrote.

In mid-June, the clerk of the circuit court in San Francisco formally entered the Supreme Court's decision into the record and issued a new order for Chae Chan Ping's bondsmen to turn him over, so he could be remanded back to China. The *San Francisco Examiner* published an article headlined "Where Is Chae Chan Ping?," reporting that he had lately "not appeared so regularly at his old haunts." His lawyers said there was no need for trepidation. "I saw Ping a few days ago," Mowry said. "He can be had at any moment by his attorneys, who will turn him over to the Marshal as usual in such cases." Several weeks later, the marshal's office reported that it had the paperwork in hand for Ping's remanding and that his bondsmen were ready to surrender him.

At one thirty in the afternoon on August 22, Chae Chan Ping appeared in the U.S. marshal's office. A deputy marshal locked him inside a stateroom and placed a guard outside. Just before three o'clock, the deputy marshal escorted him aboard the *Arabic,* bound for Hong Kong. On board was about $100,000 in American goods for trade in the Far East, along with the new United States consul in Hong Kong, Oliver H. Simons, and his wife, as well as two Chinese diplomatic officials. The ship's captain stopped Chae Chan Ping and asked if he had money for passage. Newspaper accounts rendered his response differently, but the *Examiner* likely captured the essence: "I do not wish to return to China, but your courts have ordered you to take me back, and I am here in compliance with their order. I have not bought a ticket. I paid my fare to come here, and as I cannot land, you have to take me back." The marshal turned him over to the ship's officers, and the *Arabic* left the dock. Chae Chan Ping's American odyssey was over.

Newspapers across the country celebrated his departure. In the Petaluma *Courier*, a Sonoma County newspaper, "Peggy's Pencilings," a social column noting comings and goings in the area, reported: "Chae Chan Ping started on an ocean voyage Thursday for the good of his health."

Part V

———

Belonging

CHAPTER 20

The Resistance

Representative Herman Lehlbach was a sturdy, bearded forty-four-year-old who had the rugged look of a western frontiersman. Before he was elected to Congress, he had worked as a land surveyor and real estate agent in the industrial hub of Newark, New Jersey. He was himself an immigrant, born in Germany, the son of a pastor who had opposed the monarchy and fled to America. Perhaps that is how Lehlbach, a New Jersey Republican in his third term in Congress, ended up on a joint congressional committee investigating federal immigration laws. The committee had begun its work by holding hearings in cities along the Eastern Seaboard; then, in the middle of November in 1890, Lehlbach and a colleague, Representative Herman Stump, a Maryland Democrat, set out by train from Chicago for Washington state, as part of a subcommittee conducting a six-week fact-finding tour of the Pacific coast. The trip had the quality of a junket. A nephew of Stump's tagged along on the trip; the Senate's assistant sergeant at arms, a clerk, and a stenographer rounded out the delegation. They made the nearly two-thousand-mile journey west in a private car furnished by the Union Pacific's president, Charles F. Adams. In Spokane Falls, Lehlbach and Stump joined up with Senator Watson Squire, who was to serve as the subcommittee chairman. Squire, the former governor of Washington Territory, had been elected to the Senate in 1889, after Washington achieved statehood. Although Squire had been instrumental in protecting the Chinese residents of Seattle during the riots, as a senator he made clear that he believed in restrictions that "protect our country against the Chinese." He insisted that he had "nothing against the Chinese themselves" but wished that "American citizens should have the preference always."

The subcommittee began its Pacific coast tour with hearings in four towns in Washington, where much of the focus was on the number of Chinese coming illegally over the border from British Columbia. The panel headed south to Portland, Oregon, and then on to San Francisco, where the lawmakers, along with Squire's wife, Ida, and others in the delegation, spent several hours touring Chinatown. They heard from a parade of witnesses, including Denis Kearney, who lauded the Scott Act. He used the opportunity, however, to warn about the growing threat of Japanese immigration. "They will create a bigger agitation in ten years than the Chinese did," he said. After the hearings in San Francisco, Squire headed back to Washington, D.C., leaving Lehlbach and Stump to handle the southern California leg of the trip on their own.

On the morning of December 17, 1890, Lehlbach occupied the chair at the subcommittee's final stop, the Hotel del Coronado, a mammoth recently opened Queen Anne–style beachfront resort in San Diego. Before the trip began, Lehlbach had generally harbored no objections to Chinese immigration, but his views had shifted as he listened to witness after witness testify about their refusal to assimilate, their deviousness in entering the country, and the debasing influences that were rife in Chinatowns. The subcommittee had heard from only a few Chinese residents. Most testified before the panel with the help of an interpreter. In San Diego, however, the subcommittee summoned Ah Quin, the journal-keeping merchant who had become a leader of the city's Chinese community. He stood nearly six feet tall, had close-cropped hair, and was dressed in Western clothing. He addressed the two congressmen in fluent, assured English.

Lehlbach appeared perplexed as he quizzed Ah Quin, who was roughly the same age as the congressman, on the details of his life. The slender merchant explained that he had lived in the United States for more than two decades and in San Diego for about half of that time. He operated a store that sold Chinese, Japanese, and French merchandise and regularly attended a church on Eighth Street. Ah Quin said he had learned English in San Francisco and Santa Barbara and suggested that two-thirds of the roughly five hundred Chinese residents in San Diego spoke at least some English, an assertion that seemed to startle Lehlbach. "Two-thirds speak English?" he asked. "A little," Ah Quin said. When it was his turn to question Ah Quin, Stump observed that he had "adopted the American habit of dress" and wondered when he had begun doing so. "You mean the clothes I am wearing now?" Ah Quin said. "I always dressed this way in this town." Stump wanted to know more, wondering if Ah Quin had changed his "mode of dress" after he had become a Christian, but Ah Quin said that his faith had nothing to do with his decision. He said that he simply dressed this way because he "felt like it."

Lehlbach asked if Ah Quin had "adopted this country as your home and the home of your children." Ah Quin confirmed that he had. "Of course I have my property here." This interested the congressman, too. "Do you own property?" Ah Quin said he did, in Los Angeles, San Bernardino, and San Diego. The congressmen pressed Ah Quin about the "lottery business" in Chinatown and opium smoking, but the merchant had little to offer, other than to say that he had nothing to do with either and insisted that most Chinese residents didn't use opium. At one point, Stump asked him whether he was an American citizen. "No sir," Ah Quin said. "I wish I was."

On March 2, 1891, Lehlbach submitted the subcommittee's report, which ran nearly six hundred pages. The subcommittee had found that the Chinese population in the country was decreasing but "not as rapidly as in the opinion of your committee is desirable." The committee recommended that more resources be allocated for the enforcement of the law. "The Chinaman is very shrewd and cunning and will resort to all practices in order to obtain admission to the country," the report said. It went on to pronounce that the "universal sentiment of all testimony taken at the different places mentioned is that the Chinese should be excluded." The committee's opinion was that "the Chinamen never assimilates with our people, knows nothing of the institutions of this country, and in nine cases out of ten of those who attend our Sunday schools and make pretense of religious belief, do it in order to learn our language, and thereby be better able to acquire comparative wealth."

Yet the committee didn't believe any additional legislation was necessary, other than a renewal of the Chinese exclusion law and making it permanent. As long as the law was strictly enforced, the report said, "it will not be many years before the race will, in all probability, be extinct in this country."

Nevertheless, the following year, when it came time for renewal of the law, Congress extended the restrictions for another ten years but also imposed additional harsh requirements. Under provisions introduced by Representative Thomas J. Geary, a California Democrat, all Chinese laborers in the United States were given a year to obtain a certificate of residence that established their right to be in the country. Afterward, anyone found without one was presumed to be in the country illegally and subject to immediate arrest and deportation. Chinese defendants seeking to establish their right to remain in the country needed to produce at least one credible white witness on their behalf. Chinese petitioners filing writs of habeas corpus were also denied bail.

The Chinese legation in the United States had followed the congressional proceedings with alarm, repeatedly pressing James Blaine, who was serving his second stint as secretary of state, this time under President Benjamin Harrison, about their misgivings. Chinese officials pointed to figures that showed Chinese immigrants were departing at far greater rates than they were arriving, arguing the additional restrictions were unnecessary. Cui Guoyin, Zhang Yinhuan's successor as the Chinese minister plenipotentiary, was a Confucian scholar and a keen observer of the United States. Cui wrote a series of missives to Blaine about the Geary Act, all unfailingly polite. On May 5, 1892, a day after passage of the legislation in Congress, Cui implored Blaine to use his influence to prevent the "enlightened Chief Magistrate of this great country" from approving the bill. As usual, however, political exigencies were paramount. The Harrison administration was in a hurry, fearing the consequences if restrictions imposed on Chinese immigration expired the following day. One San Francisco newspaper reported rumors that Chinese were "waiting along the Canadian border for the golden opportunity." Just after noon, President Harrison signed the legislation into law.

.   .   .

The response from the Chinese community in America to the Geary Act initially seemed restrained. The rules for the implementation of the law had yet to be worked out. On May 7, two days after Harrison signed the bill, a Treasury Department official sent a telegram to John C. Quinn, the collector of customs in San Francisco, and requested for him to furnish "without delay" his views on regulations for the certificate requirement. Quinn, the former assistant postmaster of San Francisco, had been appointed to his position only a year earlier, at the age of thirty-three. At the time, he was the youngest man to ever occupy the position. His office prepared a form that listed the name, age, occupation, height, color of eyes, complexion, and "physical marks or peculiarities" of the certificate holder. Applicants were required to furnish three photographs that depicted the head "not less than 1½ inches from base of the hair to base of the chin." The commissioner of internal revenue adopted the form and, on July 8, disseminated detailed regulations to collectors across the country. They included a requirement for affidavits from "two credible witnesses of good character," who were also required to appear before the collector or his deputy for questioning.

Quietly, leaders of the Chinese community on both coasts began meeting to consider ways to resist the law. Yung Wing, the former commissioner of the Chinese Educational Mission, wrote a letter to the Rev. E. R. Donohue, a Presbyterian pastor in Pittsburgh who was active in evangelistic work with the Chinese, outlining a three-pronged strategy, involving diplomatic pressure, a legal challenge, and, most unusually for the Chinese in America, a public lobbying campaign. At this point, the Chinese population in the New York area was becoming its own thriving locus of influence in the community. Some ten thousand Chinese immigrants lived in either New York or Brooklyn. The most popular vocation was operating a laundry—by one estimate, in 1885, there were 4,500 Chinese laundrymen across the region alone. The community was primarily centered on Mott Street, where there were restaurants that served meals of rice and chicken and fish for twenty-five cents; general stores crammed with dried mushrooms, ginseng teas, incense sticks, and other bric-a-brac; and a three-story brick building, known to outsiders as the Joss House, that contained the headquarters of the Six Companies in New York.

In August, deputy collectors of internal revenue began undertaking a census of the Chinese population and distributing application forms, encouraging registration. An assertive Chinese physician, Joseph Chak Thoms, approached Foster L. Backus, one of Brooklyn's leading Republican attorneys, about legal options. Thoms, whose Chinese name was Tom Ah Jo, was unusually well connected in the city. He had arrived in the country as a teenager and quickly mastered English. He became an active member at the Washington Avenue Baptist Church and was at the forefront of their efforts to minister to Chinese immigrants. For several years, he and Huie Kin, the Presbyterian missionary to the Chinese in the city, waged a campaign against gambling in Chinatown. Through his church, Thoms met a prominent Brooklyn physician, Nelson B. Sizer, whose wife, Georgina, was the superintendent of the Chinese Sunday school. Thoms began apprenticing with Sizer at his Brooklyn medical practice. In March 1890, at the age of twenty-five Thoms became the first Chinese graduate of an American medical school, Long Island College Hospital. Three months later, he married Ethel Wright, an Englishwoman who taught Sunday school at an Episcopal church in the city. In January 1891, several churches in Brooklyn and New York decided to establish a hospital for the Chinese in a brownstone building on Hicks Street in Brooklyn. Thoms became the resident physician. The hospital was meant to attend to both physical and spiritual needs. For the latter, Huie Kin made regular visits to minister to patients. Thoms and his wife lived in the same building as the hospital and, several months later, welcomed their first child, Ethel.

On August 17, 1892, a Brooklyn newspaper broke the news that there was "no doubt" that the "Chinamen of this city" would challenge the Geary law and identified Thoms as a leading figure in the movement. A week later, Thoms disclosed that Chinese merchants across the country were organizing and raising funds to fight the law. "That Chinamen living in peace in the community and respecting the laws of the land should be compelled to be registered like dogs and be subjected to severe penalties without the rights of habeas corpus, is undemocratic and un-American," he said.

In early September, the Six Companies issued a proclamation that directed Chinese residents across the country not to register and asked them to each contribute a dollar towards the campaign against the law. The organization hoped to raise at least $100,000 to mount a legal challenge. Seeking comment from a Chinese resident, a reporter visited Yung Hen, a portly poultry dealer on Dupont Street. He said the law "gives me excruciating pains in the neck" and complained that "for some reason you people persist in pestering the Chinaman." He asked: "Why do they not legislate against Swedes, Germans, Italians, Turks and others? There are no strings on those people. Your Declaration of Independence, in defense of which oceans of blood were spilled, says that all men are equal in the pursuit of life, liberty and happiness."

Quinn, the city's collector of internal revenue, wrote to the Six Companies, notifying them he was ready to begin registrations. He also sought confirmation that they had indeed instructed members to flout the law. The Six Companies sent a lengthy response, detailing point by point what they found objectionable in the law. "It is in violation of every principle of justice, equity and fair dealing between two friendly powers," the letter said.

In New York, a kind of professional class of English-speaking Chinese began to coalesce under the leadership of Wong Chin Foo, the former peripatetic lecturer who had become an important figure in New York's Chinatown. (*The New York Times* referred to him as the "high priest of the Chinese colony.") In February 1883, Wong had founded the first Chinese-language newspaper on the East Coast, the *Chinese American,* likely marking the first time that the term had ever been used. He only managed to sustain the concern for several months before shutting it down. Wong began to acquire renown, however, writing for mainstream American periodicals. In 1887, he published an essay in *The North American* with the provocative headline "Why Am I a Heathen?" It shrewdly filleted white Americans for their hypocrisies. "Though we may differ from the Christian in appearance, manners, and general ideas of civilization, we do not organize into cowardly mobs under the guise of social or political reform, to plunder and murder with impunity; and we are so advanced in our heathenism as to no longer tolerate popular feeling or religious prejudice to defeat justice or cause injustice," he wrote.

On September 1, Wong and several associates convened the first meeting of what would become the Chinese Equal Rights League. According to a pamphlet later published by the organization, it counted 150 members. Most had been in the United States since they were children. Sam Ping Lee, a Philadelphia merchant who wore a carefully styled mustache, spoke English fluently, and liked to carry cards with his name neatly engraved on them, was installed as president; Tom Yuen, a merchant in New York City, was the treasurer; and Wong served as secretary. The leaders organized the organization's first major event for the Great Hall at Cooper Union, where Lincoln had delivered his watershed speech rejecting slavery's advance that cemented his candidacy for president.

On the evening of September 22, the meeting at Cooper Union began inauspiciously. At half past seven, barely a hundred people occupied seats inside the hall. By eight o'clock, however, about five hundred people had arrived, filling about two-thirds of the hall. The vast majority in the audience were white Americans, many of them women. They were Sunday school teachers, pastors, and other supporters of Chinese immigrants. The roughly hundred Chinese men in attendance all dressed in Western clothing; many wore patent-leather shoes and white neckties. One observer said they "looked like mercantile clerks, students and professional men." Wong opened the gathering and introduced Thoms, who wore glasses, a high collar, and tie, as the chairman of the evening's proceedings. "The torture that we have endured in the last few years would not be permitted in any other civilized nation," Thoms said. "I have lived for many years under the despotism of the Chinese government, but I have never seen personal liberties interfered with as ours have been here." Wong followed Thoms's address with a warning. "You have known the Irish to kick, the Italian to kick, the Jew to kick, even the American, but the Chinese never until now," he said. In the corridors, counter-protesters handed out tracts from an anti-Chinese journal. Afterward, a member of the Anti-Chinese League of New York called the civil rights organization a "fraud."

Two months later, the Equal Rights League held another public gathering, this time in Boston's Tremont Temple, the historic downtown church that had long been associated with the abolitionist movement. Sam Ping Lee, the organization's president, was the evening's first featured speaker. He was a smallish man, dark-complexioned, with a thick mustache and handsome features. He spoke hesitantly, in accented English, but was forceful and clear, calling the Geary Act a "brand new slavery system" and describing the protests of the measure as the "first attempt of the Chinese to defend themselves against cruel outrages in any country." Wong was stouter than Lee and clean-shaven. He wore a formal frock coat and striped trousers, giving him the air of wealth. He spoke rapidly and with a grandiloquence. "On the 5th of May next, a hundred and fifty thousand law-abiding and industrious citizens and residents of the United States will be made state criminals, and every one of them will have his picture taken for the national rogues' gallery," he said. William Lloyd Garrison Jr., the son of the legendary abolitionist, connected Chinese immigrants' quest for justice with the long struggle for equality for Black Americans, pointing out that nearly three decades had passed "since the great war fought for the rights of a despised race was ended." And yet, he said, once again, a public meeting was taking place in Boston, in 1892, to "take measures for the protection of another persecuted and abused people within our gates." Garrison read from letters of support for the Chinese that he had received and circulated a petition in the hall calling for the repeal of the Geary Act. By the end of the meeting, hundreds had signed.

Garrison spearheaded a lobbying campaign to repeal the law, forwarding dozens of letters to Representative John Forrester Andrew, a Massachusetts Republican, who laid them on the clerk's desk in the House in a single, great roll. They included appeals from hundreds of clergymen and religious societies, as well as prominent businessmen and trade associations in Massachusetts, New Hampshire, New York, and Pennsylvania.

In mid-January, Wong arrived in Washington with an armful of literature to buttonhole lawmakers himself. He stayed at the Willard Hotel, the elegantly appointed, five-story hotel near the White House that was a favored haunt of both Lincoln and Grant. Geary happened to stay there as well when he was in town. It doesn't appear that they ever encountered each other. On the morning of January 26, Wong appeared before the House Committee on Foreign Affairs, along with Tom Yuen, his fellow officer in the Chinese Equal Rights League. The occasion was a hearing on a measure, introduced by Rep. Andrew, to repeal the Geary law. Wong opened his remarks by making the case that his demands were quite limited. "We represent, and speak for the hundred and fifty thousand Chinamen of this country who are no longer emigrants, but bona fide residents of the United States; Chinamen who have resided here ten, twenty and thirty years," he said. (Wong was likely exaggerating—the 1890 census recorded a total Chinese population in the United States of less than a hundred and ten thousand.) The Geary law would now require these longtime residents to be "photographed precisely like criminals," Wong said. He was at pains to make clear that he was not advocating for additional Chinese immigration but speaking "only for those already residing here." He said his members might be "classified as Chinese by birth," but they were "truly Americans by adoption in their ideas, habits, mode of living, and education." Geary tried to interrupt Wong but was told by the committee's chairman, James Henderson Blount, a Georgia Democrat, to let him proceed. Wong concluded with a question: "Is it a crime, punishable by law, to be a Chinaman?"

When it was Geary's turn to question Wong, the congressman pressed him on what he contended was widespread evasion of immigration restrictions. "Your people are not law-abiding," he said. Despite Geary's broadsides, when Wong concluded his testimony, several members shook his hand and congratulated him on his address. The repeal effort went nowhere.

By the middle of March, the Six Companies had raised $60,000 and retained a legal team led by Joseph H. Choate, one of the country's most prominent trial lawyers, whose law partners in New York City included William Evarts, the secretary of state in the Hayes administration who had dispatched James B. Angell to China to negotiate changes to the Burlingame Treaty. The Six Companies also retained Evarts's son, Maxwell, for the case, along with James C. Carter, an influential legal theorist. The United States attorney general agreed to cooperate in the

Six Companies' motion to the Supreme Court to take up the case as soon as possible. As the one-year mark of the passage of the legislation and the deadline for registering approached, the Six Companies issued another admonition to "all Chinese in America," urging them to continue to defy the law.

The resistance to the registration law, and the realization that deporting tens of thousands of Chinese who had failed to register would be prohibitively expensive, seemed to have some effect. On April 8, 1893, collectors across the country received a telegram from Washington, signed by John W. Mason, the commissioner of internal revenue: "Chinese regulations modified today, dispensing with photos and requiring only one credible witness. Follow this course hereafter and give such publicity to this change as you can." On the Pacific coast, newspapers reported that the law had been "emasculated" and was now "open to Chinese cunning." Quinn, the collector in San Francisco, attacked the change, describing the photographs as "the very best safeguard against fraud." In Washington, however, treasury officials pointed out that the Geary law had not expressly required the photographs. "Our first regulations required the Chinese to be photographed, but as their principal objection seemed to be to this, we decided to dispense with this mode of identification," one official said.

Simple math made plain the Treasury Department had nowhere near the funds needed to enforce the law. The most recent census had tallied 106,688 Chinese people in the United States. Assuming about 10 percent of them were exempt from registration, because they were merchants, students, and others, that would leave about 85,000 people subject to deportation. The lowest cost for transportation from San Francisco to Hong Kong was $35 a person, meaning the total cost of deportation would be about $6 million. Congress had only allocated $100,000 for the enforcement of the Geary Act. During a cabinet meeting, John G. Carlisle, the secretary of the treasury, revealed that less than $35,000 remained in his department's coffers to carry out the law.

On May 4, the day before the registration deadline, Carlisle issued instructions to customs officials across the country to refrain from making arrests under the Geary Act. Richard Olney, the United States attorney general, sent word to United States attorneys across the country that they should defer proceedings "until necessary arrangements for the arrest, imprisonment, and deportation of persons accused can be perfected."

With prosecutions under the Geary Act on pause, the long-awaited test case unfolded by careful arrangement. On the morning of May 6, the first day that unregistered Chinese residents were subject to arrest, three laundrymen, Fong Yue Ting, Lee Joe, and Wong Quan, walked into the office of the United States marshal for the Southern District of New York, and surrendered themselves. They were each unregistered, but their cases tested different aspects of the law. Fong Yue Ting and Wong Quan had simply refused to register; Lee Joe had applied several weeks earlier but revenue officials had rejected his application, because the witness he offered was a Chinese interpreter, who was deemed not credible because of his race. Choate and Evarts, on the Six Companies' legal team, were on hand to apply for writs of habeas corpus on their behalf; officials from the Chinese legation also attended the hearings. The circuit court judges rejected the applications; the Six Companies posted $500 bail for each of the men; their lawyers immediately appealed.

On May 10, Choate and an associate, Joseph Hubley Ashton, who had served as the assistant attorney general in the Lincoln and Johnson administrations and was a founder of the American Bar Association, argued the case before the Supreme Court. In his legal brief, Choate pointed out that the laundrymen had all been legally living in the United States for more than ten years. "The expulsion or banishment of such a class or of members of such a class of unoffending resident aliens in time of peace has never, so far as we can learn, been attempted by the government of any civilized nation in history," Choate wrote. The Constitution did not vest in Congress the "power to expel friendly alien residents" in a time of peace, he argued. What's more, Choate said, the Chinese were more than just friendly alien residents—they were "denizens," occupying a privileged status in between alien and native. They were unable to vote, in the way native-born subjects could, but they were also more than ordinary aliens. Expelling them from the country would amount to a violation of the Fifth Amendment, which guarantees that no person can be deprived of "life, liberty, or property, without due process of law." At noon on May 15, inside the dim room of the court, a crowd of spectators gathered to await the decision. No one from the Chinese legation was present, but Riordan and Ashton were there on behalf of the Six Companies. The justices went through a series of other decisions, before Associate Justice Horace Gray arrived at the Chinese exclusion cases, naming the Chinese appellants. Instantly, the spectators in the room leaned forward. Speaking rapidly, in an even, neutral tone, Gray pronounced the court's five-to-three decision, affirming the constitutionality of the law. Gray would go on to write the opinion for the majority, but for the moment he delivered his remarks on the case without notes. He explained that the power of the government to bar certain people from entering the country, based upon the public interest, had already been established in the case of Chae Chan Ping. "The right of a nation to expel or deport foreigners, who have not been naturalized or taken any steps towards becoming citizens of the country, rests upon the same grounds, and is as absolute and unqualified as the right to prohibit and prevent their entrance into the country," Gray later wrote.

Notably, Justice Field, who had written the Chae Chan Ping decision, wrote a forceful dissent that he read aloud in the courtroom. Field argued that there was a "wide and essential difference" between exclusion of immigrants and deportation of existing residents. He asserted that the "deportation of friendly aliens in time of peace" amounted to a "dangerous and despotic power" and urged his colleagues in the majority to consider how far their ruling might extend. If Congress was permitted to set aside constitutional protections for "the unnaturalized resident" today, Field reasoned there was nothing to prevent it from doing the same to naturalized citizens in the future.

News of the decision reached San Francisco at about ten o'clock in the morning on the West Coast. Thomas Riordan, the Six Companies' lawyer, notified a clerk in his office by telegram. "Decision against us. Five to three," Riordan said, and asked his colleague to notify the Chinese consulate and the Six Companies. Newspaper editors scrawled the news on their bulletin boards. At noon, C. C. O'Donnell, the political gadfly, and Denis Kearney held an impromptu open-air meeting atop a wagon, in front of a small crowd, near the city's stock exchange. Kearney crowed that the sandlot had finally prevailed and the "Chinese must go."

A short walk away, Chinatown itself remained quiet. In the bright morning sunshine, a procession of elementary-age Chinese boys, students at the school on Stockton Street, made their way noisily down the street, escorted by their teachers. The doors of the Six Companies' headquarters remained locked for much of the day. In the afternoon, a reporter from the *Call* found Gee Chong Tone, the secretary of the Six Companies, inside his office, surrounded by stacks of telegrams from concerned immigrants across the state and country. Tone, who spoke English fluently, admitted that he was shocked by the decision. "It's like a man feeling safe being hit between the eyes in the dark," he said. "He don't know what to do."

In New York, at the headquarters of the Six Companies at 16 Mott Street, knots of men crowded inside a room, where the decision was posted in Chinese on three walls. Dr. Thoms, who had helped to orchestrate the movement against the act, was reached at his office on Doyers Street. He called the law an "act of barbarity" but said that Chinese residents were awaiting information from the Chinese minister in Washington. He struck back against accusations that the Chinese kept themselves apart from Americans. "Let me tell you that we would gladly make ourselves one of your great community, but whenever a Chinaman tries to make friends with an American he is rebuffed and insulted."

Revenue collectors across the country were still awaiting instructions from Washington. Only a fraction of the Chinese population had registered. (The Treasury Department's annual report later showed that, by the end of the year, customs officials had issued only 13,292 certificates.) A few days after the decision, Walter Gresham, who had been appointed secretary of state several months earlier by President Cleveland, reassured Cui Guoyin, the Chinese minister, in a meeting that enforcement of the Geary law would be "attended with some delay," likely until the next Congress convened. Several days later, Carlisle ordered customs officers to continue to refrain from enforcing the Geary law until further notice.

.   .   .

Wong Chin Foo, the leader of the Chinese Equal Rights League, remained unbowed in his quixotic crusade on behalf of his countrymen. In conjunction with the World's Fair of 1893, an elaborate exposition held in Chicago celebrating the four hundredth anniversary of Christopher Columbus's voyage to America, Wong began planning another foray as a newspaper publisher. In Chicago, with some American partners, Wong incorporated *The Chinese Weekly News* and told reporters that his hope was "to influence every Chinaman in this country to become an American citizen, to speak the English language, to wear American dress and to enter into politics the same as any other Irishman." On June 24, the newspaper made its debut. Instead of the original name the publication had incorporated under, the moniker on the masthead was *The Chinese American,* a callback to Wong's earlier publishing venture. The first issue, published in Chinese and English, featured a front-page illustration of a fearsome Chinese dragon, with its back feet in China and its front feet in the United States, wringing the neck of a bald eagle that had the Geary bill stuffed down its throat.

In a rambling article, Wong laid out his aims. "The Chinese American is published in the interest of all Chinese in the United States, but more especially it will appeal to the members of the Americanized Chinese of this country who understand the English language and love the institution of America, and are willing to cast their lots with us here instead of with the people of China." He asked readers "willing to become American citizens" to send him their addresses, because he was organizing a national conference to "discuss matters of vital importance concerning their own welfare as residents of the United States, and as reputable citizens we must demand an equal recognition of manhood, franchise and the ballot." Wong's blend of braggadocio and impudence was on full display. "We must show them that even the Chinamen can kick when driven to the wall," he wrote. Nevertheless, by the end of the year, his newspaper had folded.

During the spring and summer of 1893, financial hysteria beset the country. On April 22, the Treasury Department announced that its gold reserves had fallen below $100 million, the minimum threshold required by law. In the beginning of May, stock prices began collapsing amid a panicked sell-off. A run on deposits at banks across the country followed. Hundreds of banks and thousands of businesses across the country failed. Unemployment soared, as mills, factories, mines, and other employers cast off their workers.

The result, once again, was hordes of restive white laborers. This time, the trouble for Chinese residents began in rural California, in the Central Valley, where it was fruit-packing season. In the town of Selma, an agricultural community of just over a thousand people, a group of white citizens met with the manager of the Earl Fruit Company and demanded that he employ only white labor. He insisted, however, that his Chinese employees were essential, because of their dexterity with packing. He offered to have them train white women in the task. On August 12, a Saturday, a train full of Chinese workers arrived from Fresno. In the afternoon, some two hundred unemployed white laborers, businessmen, and farmers agreed in a mass meeting to form the White Labor Protective Association. Afterward, a group marched to the packing company and forced the newly arrived Chinese back to Fresno. The leaders of the organization also notified Chinese restaurant owners and laundrymen in Selma that they had five days to leave town.

On the same evening, about thirty miles away, a mob of thirty white men descended upon the Paige orchard, a fruit ranch and vineyard in Tulare that stretched over a thousand acres and employed dozens of Chinese and Japanese laborers. Pistol-wielding members of the mob shot up a tent encampment where the workers were sleeping; no one was hurt. The orchard's superintendent promised to discharge most of his Chinese employees but said he needed to retain a contingent of fruit packers. Dissatisfied, an even larger contingent returned the following night and demanded that all be let go. In the morning, several dozen frightened Chinese and Japanese workers piled aboard the first train out of town. In the evening on August 15, about two hundred white men marched through Tulare's Chinatown and began forcibly evicting residents who did not have certificates of registration under the Geary Act. Within a few days, only a handful of Chinese residents—mostly merchants who owned property in town—remained. By then, the anti-Chinese agitation had spread to Fresno, Vacaville, Stockton, and Bakersfield.

It was in Redlands, a newly incorporated town about sixty miles east of Los Angeles, that the Geary Act was weaponized for the first time in a concerted way. Redlands, partially encircled by the snow-capped San Bernardino Mountains, boasted a temperate climate and rich, loamy soil. When the town's plat was filed in 1887, it comprised just several dozen homes and a hundred acres of newly planted navel orange trees. The town would prosper alongside its booming citrus industry. The anti-Chinese violence began on a Sunday night, August 27, when a mob of white men visited a ranch near Mentone, a few miles from Redlands, and told two Chinese employees that they had twenty-four hours to leave. The following evening, a marauding band of white men kidnapped a group of Chinese men and robbed them. They later refused to allow a Chinese train passenger arriving from Santa Fe, New Mexico, to disembark in Mentone. Finally, at eight o'clock in the evening on Wednesday, August 30, a mass meeting of more than six hundred white workingmen took place at the town square, culminating in a resolution to "use all means at our command that is consistent with reason and good judgment," in order to "relieve the country of this hideous curse." Just before the meeting adjourned, however, two men rose and proposed setting a forty-eight-hour deadline for Chinese residents to leave town. About two hundred and fifty men proceeded to Chinatown, where they delivered their ultimatum. The city marshal arrived on the scene and dispersed the mob.

Town leaders took on an emergency footing. Rumors circulated that the Chinese were arming themselves. Newsboys hawked copies of newspapers with shouts of "All about the Chinese agitation." On Thursday evening, E. G. Judson, one of the town's founders and its first mayor, chaired a "law and order" meeting of concerned citizens. They passed resolutions denouncing the "lawless persons" fomenting acts of violence, but speakers also criticized Chinese residents and their defiance of the Geary law. It was James P. Booth, the sheriff, who first proposed what would become known as the Redlands Plan. The day before, Erskine Ross, the district court judge in Los Angeles, had issued a significant ruling on a case brought by an association of white farmers in the Cahuenga valley who were worried about Chinese competition, affirming that any private citizen could swear out a complaint against a Chinese resident for violating the Geary Act. Booth suggested employing the Geary Act as a "legal method" for dealing with the Chinese question.

The following evening, a citizen brigade of some seventy-five men patrolled Chinatown and the surrounding streets. In the morning, National Guard soldiers, activated by Governor Henry Markham, relieved the volunteers. Unbeknownst to Chinese residents, however, local civic leaders were simultaneously drawing up a list of the town's unregistered Chinese and drafting legal complaints against them.

On Monday, September 4, a committee of three Redlands businessmen traveled to Los Angeles to meet with George J. Denis, the United States attorney for the Southern District of California. Denis had received instructions from the attorney general in Washington that there were no funds to enforce the Geary law and any violators in custody should be discharged. Nevertheless, Denis agreed to facilitate warrants for twelve Chinese residents of Redlands as a test. The next day, Judge Ross ruled that Chun Shang Yuen, a Chinese farmer who leased a small parcel of land in Cahuenga to grow vegetables and was unregistered, should still be deported. In his ruling, Ross dismissed the attorney general's guidance as legally immaterial. On Thursday morning, James Faris, the deputy United States marshal for San Bernardino County, arrived in Redlands, armed with arrest warrants for a dozen Chinese residents. Faris and a committee of Redlands citizens first visited a Victorian mansion belonging to James S. Edwards, a wealthy citrus grower. His two Chinese employees had fled the night before. (They were later found in Chinatown.) Faris moved on to another home, where he arrested a Chinese cook. At yet another residence, a white man on horseback apparently alerted the Chinese laborers, who fled. By late morning, Faris had rounded up three men on the list from ranches in the southern part of the city. Two of the men were stoic as they rode into town on a carriage, bound for the city jail; a third man broke down, weeping. By day's end, nine out of the twelve unregistered Chinese had been found and were sent off to Los Angeles for trial. Three days later, the remaining three were taken into custody. Just before noon on Monday, September 11, the trial for the first eight men took place before Judge Ross, in a courtroom crowded with white and Chinese spectators. The proceeding lasted only an hour. Ross ordered seven of the men to be deported; he suspended judgment in one case to give the accused time to gather evidence that he was not a laborer. By day's end on Wednesday, however, Ross had ordered that eleven of the twelve arrested men be deported. The lone exception was a man named Louie Tom, who managed to establish, with the help of several supporting witnesses, that he was born in the United States. In Redlands, a petition circulated for the city to pay for another committee to travel to Los Angeles to swear out additional warrants. The legal terror was having its intended effect. By one estimate, there were just fifty Chinese residents left in Redlands, down from two hundred before the arrests.

Other communities sought to implement their own versions of the Redlands Plan. In Riverside, Faris started by making his way down Magnolia Avenue, the town's picturesque main thoroughfare, lined with elegant homes. The deputy marshal rounded up five Chinese servants, including a youthful cook named Wong Sing who spoke fluent English and was born in the United States to parents who leased land on an area orchard. (Judge Ross later ordered that Wong be discharged.) Faris eventually took into custody a total of ten Chinese laborers. He traveled next to San Bernardino, where an exodus of Chinese residents was underway, and Fresno, where he made fifteen more arrests. Ross continued to conduct deportation proceedings in Los Angeles, sometimes requiring just a few minutes to issue an order. On September 15, George Gard, the United States marshal for the Southern District of California, reported to the Treasury Department that sixty-two arrest warrants had been issued under the Geary Act; forty-five arrests had been made; and twenty Chinese residents had been slated for deportation.

The crackdown finally eased as it became clear that congressional action was coming on the Geary law. On October 11, James B. McCreary, a Kentucky Democrat who was the chairman of the House Committee on Foreign Affairs, introduced a bill that extended the registration period by six months. McCreary argued to his House colleagues that Chinese residents who had failed to register were simply following the advice of their lawyer and cited a new Treasury Department estimate that it would cost more than $7 million to deport the country's Chinese laborers. Geary later introduced several modifications of his own—most significantly, adding the requirement that certificates be accompanied

by photographs. "You can not make a verbal description of a Chinaman such as you can make of a white man, and have it definite," Geary
said. "All Chinamen look alike, all dress alike, all have the same kind of
eyes, all are beardless, all wear their hair in the same manner. Now, you
sit down and write out a description of a Chinaman, give his height,
weight, the color of his skin and the shape of his eyes, and after you
have done it, what have you got? You have a description that will fit any
other Chinaman you happen to run up against." McCreary's bill, along
with Geary's amendments, sailed through the House and Senate. On
November 3, President Cleveland signed the extension of the Geary
Act into law.

Ultimately, it appears that none of the Redlands Chinese, or anyone else
sentenced by Judge Ross, were ever actually deported back to China. On
the afternoon of October 27, the *City of New York* pulled away from the
Pacific Mail Steamship Company wharf, carrying the first four Chinese
deportees under the Geary Act. Less than an hour after departure, a bar
pilot guided the ship through the land strait that marked the entrance
of the San Francisco Bay and then found himself in a thick fog shroud-
ing Point Bonita, a rocky promontory that extended into the Pacific.
Suddenly, passengers felt a shudder and then a violent wrenching. The
ship had foundered on the rocks; the collision had torn a gash on its
starboard side. A compartment in the heart of the ship immediately
began taking on water. The pilot sounded its distress signal, a sonorous,
deep-toned steam whistle that could be heard over the ocean breakers.
The fog was so dense that even the keeper of the lighthouse on Point
Bonita nearby could not make out the vessel. Later, six tugboats tried to
pull the steamer down from its perch, but it would not budge.

There were 128 passengers traveling in steerage. Ten were Japanese;
the rest were Chinese, including the group of deportees. After tugboats
delivered the passengers back to the Pacific Mail dock, the deportees
were taken back into custody. A week later, with the extension of the
Geary Act, they were suddenly free to go. Tens of thousands of Chinese
residents prepared to register with the federal government.

CHAPTER 21

Native Sons

The town of Downieville, California, is situated at the junction of two tributaries of the North Fork of the Yuba River, about seventy-five miles northeast of Sacramento. It began as one of the gold rush's earliest mining camps and became a place where miners could restock their tools and provisions, take advantage of the mail service, and find amusement away from the diggings. Gambling saloons, restaurants, hotels, and even a small theater all occupied a single street, wedged between a mountain slope and the river. Long trains of pack mules crowded the steep trail that descended into town. For miles above Downieville, miners toiled on riverbeds and banks, building elaborate wing dams and flumes. It was rugged living, and a frontier justice prevailed. In July 1851, Downieville became notorious for the hanging of a Mexican woman named Josefa, who was accused of killing a white miner. By 1852, Downieville's population had swelled to five thousand people, making it one of the largest cities in the state. Chinese miners flocked to the region, at times outnumbering their white counterparts on the diggings. They tended to work in small, organized companies and were known for their patient toil. Mining persisted in the area for decades, long after the gold rush had faded. A newspaper article from May 1883 observed that "seven or eight Chinamen" had built flumes and a dam, and erected a derrick in a creek; it noted, "It is quite interesting to watch the heathens hunt for gold." As the mining boom faded, the town shrank to just a few hundred residents. Yet the Chinese remained a sizable presence, working as

cooks and servants in white households, operating laundries, and ped-
dling vegetables. Others continued to work the mines for themselves.
During the turbulence of the mid-1880s, anti-Chinese rallies were rife
throughout the region.

The town's newspaper, the *Mountain Messenger*, avidly reported the
latest developments with "Geary's law." When the Supreme Court
upheld the statute, the newspaper urged its strict enforcement. "The
Chinese should be given to understand in a way not to be mistaken,
that they must not stand on the order of their going, but go at once,
and the sooner the better for the people of the whole coast, and especially Californians," an article published in the newspaper on May 20,
1893, said. The constable in Downieville was John T. Mason, a longtime
resident who had made the overland trip to California with his family
in 1851, at the age of two. In the mid-1870s, Mason and his wife, Laura,
settled in Downieville. In 1884, at the age of thirty-five, Mason was
made constable, and shortly afterward, he became a deputy sheriff as
well. One of his first tasks was to rid the town of hogs that were clog-
ging the streets. A book published in 1930 about Mason's adventures
in the mining country characterized Mason as being "friendly with the
Celestials," adding that he "could handle the chop-sticks to perfection."
But any purported friendliness between law enforcement and Chinese
residents is contradicted by the realities of the period.

In the spring of 1889, Mason began recording notes about his activities as constable in a small red ledger. Ephemera consumed the first few
pages: instructions for treating varicose veins, an entry about a letter sent
to a detective bureau in Cincinnati, a list of legal summonses served. On
April 8, 1890, Mason wrote his name on a blank, unlined page, inside
the cover, along with the date, seeming to inaugurate a new period of
his commitment to the ledger. About a month later, Mason jotted down
information about an arrest warrant and six subpoenas he had served.
Afterward, the list peters out.

Nearly four years later, the ledger book took on a new purpose. On
February 17, 1894, a few months after President Cleveland signed into
law the extension of the registration period of the Geary Act and the
new photography requirement, Mason's son-in-law, Decatur Dudley
Beatty, a photographer, arrived in Downieville on a stagecoach with

his wife, Lillian, who was Mason's daughter. The couple had traveled from Grass Valley, in Nevada County, where Beatty had a studio. Over the course of the next week and a half, Downieville was crowded with Chinese people from across the county, "all anxious to have their pictures taken in readiness for the registering officer," the *Mountain Messenger* reported. According to the newspaper, "these photographs must be paid for by these heathens." Beatty took portraits of more than 150 Chinese residents before he departed, on February 28, for a neighboring town to fulfill the same duties there. At the end of March, Thomas P. Ford, a deputy internal revenue collector, conducted the registration of Downieville's Chinese.

On page 4 of his red ledger, Mason began inscribing a list of names. These were, as Mason scrawled at the top of the index, "Chinese Photographed by DD Beaty at Downieville." A catalog of Chinese residents of Downieville and the surrounding area, their photographs pasted two to a page, followed. Mason added notations for each subject's name, age, height, occupation, place of residence, and selected physical characteristics: "little finger of right hand crooked," "mole under right ear," "pockmarked." At the end of the ledger, a handful of additional photographs are included, taken years later.

Mason's maintenance of the book was anomalous. Local officials like him were not required to track the Chinese as he so avidly did. The intention behind the ledger seems to be a kind of surveillance. It is a record of the oppressed, authored by the powerful. Yet, viewed more than a century later, the pages also furnish valuable details of the lives led by Chinese people in the Downieville area. Multiple generations are represented in the document. On page 23, Mason identified Yup Gee, age fifty-six, a resident of the mining town of Alleghany, as the mother of "Ah Moon"; roughly thirty pages later, there is an entry for Quok Moon, a twenty-two-year-old miner who was born in the same town. Census records point to them being mother and son. The youngest subject in the ledger, a round-cheeked teenager named Eva Yee Chung, was born on the other side of the country, in New York City, making her an American citizen. The last few photographs of the ledger, taken well into the twentieth century, show their subjects dressed mostly in elegant Western attire, perhaps indicating a degree of affluence. Quong

Dong Bing, age twenty-six, is in a suit and tie, his hair neatly combed back; Tong Ka Jou, age twenty-three, wears a polka-dot bow tie.

Mason made handwritten addenda to the entries over many years, revealing a grim attention to the movement of Chinese people in his jurisdiction. On page 27, for example, Mason noted details about Ung Gook, otherwise known as "China Susie"—a petite, fifty-five-year-old housekeeper with hoop earrings and a brooch pinned to her blouse. Scrawled at the bottom of the entry is an abrupt epilogue: "Gone to China for good 1900." Nung Owen, a sixty-two-year-old man with a widow's peak and a defiant expression, "went to China Sep 1906" and was "told never to come back." The photographer caught Jung Chung, a genial-looking sixty-three-year-old miner, in what appears to be the beginnings of a wry smile: he is listed as "gone to China to never return" in December of 1894. In total, the ledger records that eleven of the Chinese residents of the Downieville area returned to their country of origin.

Even more foreboding is the tally of twenty-one people who are marked as dead. Yung Jung, a fifty-eight-year-old miner, who was nearly six feet tall, "froze to death on Lost Creek" in February of 1895. Wong Sang, a sixty-one-year-old miner with stubble on his chin and mournful eyes, was "killed" in 1905. For most of the dead, there is no explanation: Jo Jung, miner, age sixty-seven; Lock Yan, miner, age sixty-three; Chin Foo, cook, age sixty-five. The entry for Wong Fun, a fifty-two-year-old miner, contains only the frightening observation "Burned."

Across the country, during the spring of 1894, Chinese men, women, and even children crowded into the offices of internal revenue collectors to register. In New York City, eight clerks worked full-time, registering as many as two hundred Chinese residents a day at their office on Nassau Street. In San Francisco, there were thirty-two clerks, processing some two thousand applications a day. By the end of the day on May 3, the registration deadline, internal revenue collectors had issued 106,811 certificates, including nearly 70,000 in California and Nevada, more than 11,000 in Oregon, Washington, and Alaska Territory, and more than 6,000 in New York.

A generational shift was beginning to take place in the Chinese community. A native-born population was slowly coming of age. In 1870, the census enumerated just 518 Chinese residents born in the United States, less than one percent of the total population. Three decades later, according to the census, there were 9,010, representing a tenth of all Chinese residents. By 1920, native-born Chinese Americans would account for nearly a third of the Chinese population. In May 1895, officers of an organization calling itself the "United Parlor of the Native Sons of the Golden State" filed articles of incorporation with the office of the secretary of state, with the intention of promoting "social and friendly intercourse, mental improvement and mutual benefit" among naturalized and native-born Americans. Within two months, the Native Sons had about fifty members. On July 4, the Native Sons celebrated Independence Day at their headquarters on Clay Street, in the heart of Chinatown, draping the building with bunting and American flags. Inside, men with long queues and wearing traditional Chinese attire mingled, speaking to each other in fluent English. The organization's leaders estimated there were at least a thousand native-born Chinese in the city, and as many as a hundred American-born Chinese residents were reaching voting age every year. Kong You, a member of the group who lived nearby on Dupont Street, boasted to a reporter that many in the group had voted previously and that "we expect to drop a good many more ballots in the box at the next election."

Among the members of the Native Sons was a young man named Robert Leon Park. He had been born in 1876 in Bartlett Alley, a notorious, brothel-filled section of San Francisco's Chinatown that ran between Jackson and Pacific Streets. He was part of a family of three boys and two girls, all born in the United States. His father had been a sailor and later became a teamster. As a boy, Park worked as a servant for Frederick Bee, the celebrated official in the Chinese consulate, who took an interest in him and made sure he was educated. Park stood out as the rare Chinese boy who eschewed the queue. In 1892, he became the first Chinese pupil to graduate from the Lincoln School, a storied public grammar school on Fifth Street, south of Chinatown. (Principals of neighborhood schools would occasionally quietly admit Chinese students if no parents objected.) Park went on to Lowell High School and then became a student at the University of California at Berkeley. He stood about five feet, four inches tall. He wore his hair neatly parted and was a sharp dresser, one of the few in the Native Sons who wore Western clothing. He taught English at a nearby Chinese school and later became a translator in the municipal and superior courts for the city and managing editor at *Chinese World*, a Chinese-language newspaper that became an important institution for the community. Park was comfortable moving between worlds and, by 1896, had taken over as the organization's president. "We are Americans, and we shall all claim the right of franchise," he told a reporter. Park suggested that these votes would be used, principally, to oppose the exclusion laws. "We cannot see why our father's countrymen should be the victims of such unfair discrimination that they are made by the laws a sort of debased race."

In Chicago, in early 1897, Wong Chin Foo inaugurated a new chapter of the Chinese Equal Rights League, establishing a headquarters on Clark Street in Chinatown and declaring that his aim was to "organize the better class of the Chinamen of this country—those who expect and intend to make the United States their home—and then demand a franchise for this class of American citizens." In late January, the secretary of state's office in Springfield approved Wong's articles of incorporation in Springfield. Wong's new group already had a membership of two hundred "American-Chinamen," as one article put it. In May, Wong issued a circular appealing for financial support and elaborating on the group's purpose—to "restore to the Americanized and American-born Chinese of the United States their rights to citizenship." Notably, Wong sought to distance the group from Chinese residents "who persist in their own civilization." He emphasized: "We are for the Americanized and American-born Chinese only."

On November 27, inside the Central Music Hall, a cavernous space renowned for its wondrous acoustics, Wong convened a mass meeting, marking the public debut of his new chapter. A racially mixed audience of about two hundred people joined him, a modest turnout, given the size of the theater, but it included the entire executive committee of the Chicago Republican club, who promised their support. In his remarks, Wong cast the league's mission in the same tradition as the abolishment of slavery. "Forty years ago this nation denied a large class of its citizens civil rights because they were black," he said. "But let us thank God for Grant and Lincoln and the great federal army, which at length set them free and gave them their rights. Today the same question confronts us. A new wound has taken the place of the old. A new color line has sprung up. Instead of black, we have substituted yellow." The meeting quickly devolved when a white interloper, E. W. McGann, a physician from Louisiana, who happened to be passing through Chicago, mounted the stage and asserted that "no Chinamen can be a citizen of the Republic." Nevertheless, on December 16, Rep. George Washington Smith, an Illinois Republican, introduced a bill in Congress to "permit the naturalization of Americanized Chinese," under which "all male persons of Chinese birth or descent who are of good character and repute, and who have been lawfully within the United States for ten years or more; who have discarded the characteristic dress of the Chinese peoples, including the queue; who have adopted the dress of the people of the United States and who speak the English language" would be eligible to become citizens. Smith also presented a petition in support of the measure from the league. The House Committee on Immigration and Naturalization held a hearing on the bill, but it went nowhere.

Opponents of the Chinese recognized the threat posed by the American-born Chinese population. Habeas corpus petitions filed by Chinese arrivals had plummeted, after changes in the law and court decisions curtailed the ability of Chinese arrivals to claim merchant status. Lawmakers had also moved to limit judicial authority on exclusion cases. As part of a general appropriations bill, in 1894, Congress approved a provision that made the denial decisions of immigration and customs officials final and reversible upon appeal only to the secretary of treasury, as opposed to the courts. The intention behind the provision was to shutter the so-called habeas corpus mills in the federal courts. The following year, the Supreme Court upheld the law, in a case brought by a wholesale and retail druggist, Lem Moon Sing, who had returned to China in late January 1894 and tried to re-enter the United States less than a year later.

Yet Chinese who claimed that they were American citizens on arrival still had an opening. In November 1894, William Morrow, the federal district court judge in San Francisco who had ruled against Lem Moon

Sing, denied a motion by the United States attorney in San Francisco to quash a habeas corpus petition filed by another arriving passenger, Tom Yum. The difference in the cases lay in Yum's assertion that he had been born in San Francisco in 1879. Morrow said the collector in San Francisco, John H. Wise, who was known for his fiercely anti-Chinese views, had "undoubted and complete jurisdiction" over Yum's fate if he was an alien, but he did not have the authority to render a final decision on Yum's right to enter the country if he was indeed a citizen. Wise warned his superiors at the Treasury Department of a "great influx of youngsters from China, who will claim to be born in the United States." The decision would help set the stage for what would become a land-mark Supreme Court case, brought by another native son.

In the fall of 1870, on the southeast corner of Sacramento and Dupont Streets, the merchant Wong Si Pong operated a store, known as Quong Sing, and lived upstairs with his pregnant wife, Wee Lee. In the early 1850s, Sacramento Street had been where the Chinese quarter first began to take shape. It's unclear when the couple first arrived in the neighborhood. Records suggest that by the time Wee Lee was about to give birth, the couple had been living there for more than a year, enduring the mounting pique among the white laboring classes over the Chinese presence. On October 1, in a middle room on the second floor, Wee Lee delivered the couple's first child. They named him Wong Kim Ark.

Wong's early childhood unfolded in America, but soon after rioters rampaged through San Francisco's Chinatown, in the summer of 1877, the couple decided to take their son back to their home village, Ong Sing, a cluster of fewer than two dozen homes, in Taishan. Several years later, Wong returned to Gold Mountain in the company of two uncles. His parents stayed behind. He "went to the country" with one uncle, he later told an immigration inspector, winding up in the "Sierra," likely referring to the Sierra Nevada. Wong initially helped in his uncle's store and then worked as a dishwasher and eventually as a cook. In the fall of 1889, as a nineteen-year-old, Wong returned to China with several friends. Before his departure, Wong made sure to obtain an attestation from four white witnesses that he was born in the city. In the photo-graph pasted onto the document, the hair atop Wong's head is tousled; his teenage face is unsmiling but confident. In China, at his family's village, he married a seventeen-year-old girl with bound feet named Yee Shee. Wong's stay in China, however, was brief. He was eager to return to the United States to earn a living. On July 8, 1890, he arrived back in San Francisco, planning to rent a room and find work. Frederick Bee, the Chinese consul, assisted Wong in collecting affidavits vouching that he had been born in the city. The collector of customs in San Francisco at the time, Timothy Phelps, granted him entry.

In November 1894, Wong embarked on another trip to China to see his family. Shortly after his last visit, his wife had given birth to a son, Yook Fun, whom he'd never met. Before his departure, once again Wong made sure to obtain a document signed by three white witnesses, certifying that he was "well known" to them and had been born in the city and county of San Francisco, and that his father was a merchant and member of the firm Quong Sing & Co. Just like his prior visit, Wong stayed in China less than a year. Yee Shee became pregnant with their second son. Nevertheless, Wong made the weeklong journey by wagon and boat from his village to Hong Kong and, in early August 1895, boarded the SS *Coptic*, a stately, four-masted ship belonging to the Occidental and Oriental Company, to return to his home country.

The *Coptic* was one of the largest and fastest vessels traversing the Pacific. On August 18, the ship departed Yokohama, Japan, bound for San Francisco. The cabin passengers included James Parmelee and Ralph King, bankers from New York who had been on holiday in Asia; H. J. Hunt, a wealthy English tea merchant; and Pao Tie, a Chinese dip-lomat headed for Washington, D.C. A hundred and eighteen Chinese and fifteen Japanese passengers traveled in the steerage compartment. During warm days, an orphan orangutan from Borneo, the charge of a trader who had captured him in the jungle, cavorted on deck and entertained the ship's passengers. On August 30, the ship entered San Francisco Bay, a day ahead of schedule, but a dense fog forced it to cast its anchor offshore. The following day, a quarantine officer cleared the ship for landing, and the cabin passengers disembarked.

The Chinese in steerage waited to be examined by immigration officials. During Wong's interrogation, he seemed to do some dissembling, saying that he'd only been back to China once before. He responded to questions in short, clipped sentences. When asked if any white men could vouch for him, he mentioned a "Mr. Selinger," one of the men who had signed the affidavit attesting to his American birth. "He knew me when I was little," Wong said. The examiner pressed Wong, "You are sure you were born here?" He said he was.

Notes added to Wong's arrival case file suggest that customs officials came to question aspects of his story. They visited Wong's old address, 751 Sacramento Street, and found no trace of his father's firm. They concluded that he had merely been a vegetable peddler. They also seemed to have trouble locating the witnesses who had attested to Wong's citizenship. On September 7, Wise, the collector of the port, and his recently appointed "Chinese inspector," a former prosecutor named Charles Weller, denied Wong permission to land. Wise had continued to raise the alarm about the number of Chinese arrivals claiming to be "native born citizens" and had recently alerted treasury officials about the existence of a new "Native Sons" organization that "proposes to demand rights for its members as citizens, to vote at elections, and take part in the politics of this country." Wise and Weller considered seventy-five cases that day and only landed twenty passengers. Over the next few weeks, customs officials detained Wong aboard a number of Occidental and Oriental vessels.

Customs officials' decision to turn away Wong Kim Ark was likely done in consultation with the Justice Department. Judson Harmon, an Ohio judge whom President Cleveland had appointed as United States attorney general several months earlier, was eager to bring a test case on the citizenship question. In 1884, a circuit court had ruled in the case of Look Tin Sing, a fourteen-year-old boy born in Mendocino, California, that his American birth made him a citizen. The Fourteenth Amendment stipulates that "all persons born or naturalized in the United States, and subject to the jurisdiction thereof, are citizens of the United States." For years, however, George D. Collins, a San Francisco lawyer, had been pressing a legal theory that the children of Chinese immigrants were "at the moment of birth subject to a foreign power," because their parents were Chinese subjects. In June 1895, Collins made his argument anew in an article in the *American Law Review*. He also personally lobbied Justice Department officials to hire him to take on the citizenship case; he even conferred with Wise, who urged that Collins be retained. The United States attorney in San Francisco, Henry Foote, cautioned his superiors that Collins had a "bad reputation" for professional ethics, but Collins became an adviser on the case. On October 2, Judge Morrow, of the district court, granted a petition filed on Wong's behalf by Hoo Lung Suey, a San Francisco merchant and friend, for a writ of habeas corpus. Once again, it was the Chinese Six Companies who retained lawyers, Thomas Riordan and Joseph Naphtaly, to argue Wong's case.

A little over a month later, Morrow convened a hearing for Wong's lawyers and the government to make their arguments. Foote acknowledged that Wong was born in San Francisco but asserted that he has been "at all times, by reason of his race, language, color and dress, a Chinese person" and not an American citizen. After the hearing, Foote made clear that if Morrow ruled in Wong's favor, his instructions from the Justice Department were to appeal the case to the Supreme Court. "It is a very important question and should be settled for all time," Foote said.

On January 3, 1896, in a twenty-four-page opinion, Morrow ruled that Wong's detention was illegal. After holding Wong for more than four months, the authorities released him, once he'd paid a $250 bond. It would be another two years before Wong's case was finally settled by the Supreme Court. In a 6–2 decision, the court affirmed Wong's claim to American citizenship. Justice Horace Gray's opinion for the majority was dense with explication of common-law doctrine and legal precedents, but he pointed to another important factor: "To hold that the Fourteenth Amendment of the Constitution excludes from citizenship the children, born in United States, of citizens or subjects of other countries would be to deny citizenship to thousands of persons of English, Scotch, Irish, German or other European parentage who have always been considered and treated as citizens of the United States." In other words, the citizenship status of hundreds of thousands of first-generation white Americans would be endangered, an unacceptable outcome. Gray concluded that the amendment, "in clear words and manifest intent, includes the children born within the territory of the

United States, of all other persons, of whatever race or color, domiciled within the United States."

The decision enshrined Wong's place in America, but it did not end his troubles with immigration officials. In late October 1901, he came to the attention of Charles Mehan, the Chinese immigration inspector in El Paso, Texas. Mehan, a solidly built, mustachioed veteran of the Treasury Department's immigration bureau, was heralded as "one of the most celebrated Chinese capturers in the United States." He had started in the customs service, in 1894, in Nogales, Arizona, before being promoted three years later to the position of Chinese immigration inspector in El Paso. He was briefly sent to the Canadian border, before being transferred back to help with an influx of Chinese crossing the border from Mexico. Wong had been living just across the border in Juarez, Mexico. Economic opportunity likely drew Wong to the area. Hundreds of Chinese workers had first made their way to El Paso in the early 1880s, when they helped to build the Southern Pacific railroad to Los Angeles. At the turn of the century, it was still home to some three hundred Chinese residents. The Mexican border, west of town, had become a popular entry point for Chinese immigrants. Immigration officials later reported that the Chinese population in the town had "banded together as one man for the purpose of concealing and conveying into the interior of the country those Chinese coolies who have crossed the line," secreting them away in cellars and attics.

On October 29, Mehan arrested Wong in El Paso for illegally entering the United States and remaining there "in violation of the 'Chinese exclusion acts.'" It appears that Mehan and other immigration officials understood who it was that they'd taken into custody. On the day of Wong's arrest, the *El Paso Times* reported the news and explained his connection to the famous Supreme Court case. Nevertheless, the authorities insisted on holding Wong until he posted a bond of $300. It took more than three months before a commissioner finally dismissed the case against Wong, at the request of an assistant United States district attorney. After his release, Wong appears to have remained in Texas. Nearly a decade later, in October 1910, Wong was in El Paso working as a cook at Wing Wah Hing, a general store, when his eldest son, Wong Yook Fun, tried to enter the United States as an American citizen. (Under the Naturalization Act of 1790, the children of U.S. citizens born abroad are considered natural-born citizens, unless the father has never been a resident of the United States.) Immigration officials in San Francisco barred Yook Fun, who was twenty years old, from landing. He wrote to his father: "Now I am in the detention shed. I am well. Please do not worry and buy me some clothes, ½ doz. socks and a cap, also some money." The authorities later moved Yook Fun to a new immigration station on Angel Island, where they questioned him at length about Ong Sing village, his family, and other details of his life in China. They then sought out Yook Fun's father for questioning. Wong, who was apparently unaware that his son had planned to come to America, didn't have the money to make the journey to San Francisco. Immigration officials instead interviewed him in El Paso. The responses of father and son seemed to diverge over details like the exact location of the family's homes in the village, Yook Fun's occupation in China, and his schooling there. On January 9, 1911, immigration officials deported Yook Fun back to China aboard the SS *Mongolia*.

Wong Kim Ark eventually returned to San Francisco and resumed living, once again, on Sacramento Street, not far from where he'd been born. He later helped three other sons resettle in America. Immigration officials detained all of them on Angel Island and subjected them to tedious interrogations, including his youngest son, Yook Jim, who crossed the Pacific as an eleven-year-old.

In the summer of 1931, Wong made another trip back to China, his sixth visit during his lifetime. He was in his early sixties, but in the photograph he took before his departure, he appeared older. His hair had grown wispy and turned gray; his face was weathered and mottled; white appeared in his stubble. He never returned to America. On August 26, 1936, he died in Ong Sing village. The country to which he ostensibly belonged never stopped treating him with suspicion.

CHAPTER 22

Ruin and Rebirth

His was a lonely voice of dissent. On April 16, 1902, George F. Hoar, the senior senator from Massachusetts, took the floor to address his colleagues on the Chinese question. At the age of seventy-five, his hair a shock of white and his face ruddy and round, Hoar was nearing the end of a more-than-three-decade-long career as a Republican lawmaker in Congress. When he was first elected to Congress, in 1869, the championing of equal rights had been the cornerstone of his party. By the end of the nineteenth century, however, that commitment had long been abandoned.

For two weeks, the Republican-led Senate had been jousting over the details of another renewal of the exclusion law. The debate had long since moved past the wisdom of the policy. As Senator John Mitchell, an Oregon Republican and ardent foe of Chinese immigration, observed, when he introduced his renewal proposal in early April, the policy had "become one of the great policies of the country, as firmly supported and almost as thoroughly acquiesced in by all political parties as the Monroe Doctrine." Under a new diplomatic agreement, the Gresham-Yang treaty, ratified in 1894, the Qing government had acceded to a complete bar on the immigration of Chinese laborers to the United States for ten years. A narrow exception had been agreed upon by the two countries for the return of registered Chinese laborers with a wife, child, or parents in the United States, or property worth a thousand dollars or more. Mitchell was seeking to make the ban on Chinese laborers permanent, as well as to extend the law to U.S. territories, including the recently annexed Hawaii and the Philippines. His measure also proposed more restrictive definitions for each of the exempted classes, narrowing who was qualified to enter as a teacher, student, or merchant. Some of Mitchell's colleagues in the Senate objected to Mitchell's lengthy bill as overreach. Senator Orville Platt, a Connecticut Republican, introduced a vastly simplified measure that extended the existing exclusion laws until the expiration of the Gresham-Yang treaty in December of 1904, or as long as the treaty remained in force. As a freshman senator two decades earlier, Platt had joined Hoar in opposing the original Chinese restriction bill. Since then, he had become one of the Senate's most influential voices, known for his pragmatism. Platt's priority was honoring the country's treaty commitments. Wu Tingfang, the Chinese minister to the United States, had sent a series of missives to the State Department, protesting "the unwarranted and unjust provisions of the bill."

It was Platt's substitute bill that finally advanced to a floor vote. Passage in the Senate was a foregone conclusion, but Hoar asked to be recognized before the votes were cast. In Hoar's old age, he was comfortable with solitude. He lived simply in Washington and did little socializing, preferring a good book late into the night. He remained one of the Senate's great orators. When he took the podium, he told his colleagues that he felt duty-bound to register his disagreement. "I believe that everything in the way of Chinese exclusion can be accomplished by reasonable, practical, and wise measures which will not involve the principle of striking at labor because it is labor, and will not involve the principle of striking at any class of human beings merely because of race, without regard to the personal and individual worth of the man struck at," he said. "I hold that every human soul has its rights, dependent upon its individual personal worth and not dependent upon color or race, and that all races, all colors, all nationalities contain persons entitled to be recognized everywhere they go on the face of this earth as the equals of every other man."

William P. Frye, a Maine Republican who was the Senate's president pro tempore, rapped his gavel. The patrician senator was confused and asked to finish his remarks. Frye informed him that he had used up his five minutes. The secretary of the Senate called the roll. The tally was seventy-six to one. Hoar's vote against the renewal of Chinese exclusion would turn out to be the only one in either the House or the Senate. He later defended his decision in his autobiography, noting that "every man's conscience is given to him as a lamp for his path. He cannot walk by another light."

The congressional debate over the terms of the renewal, however, was not yet at an end. The House had passed a far more draconian version of the legislation, sponsored by Rep. Julius Kahn, a California Republican. A conference committee met to reconcile the House and Senate bills. The debate was "strenuous," as Pratt later put it. The committee ultimately adopted the Senate bill but with a significant change: the exclusion laws would continue, provided they did not contravene treaty obligations, "until otherwise provided by law." On April 28, both chambers approved the measure. The following day, wielding a pen given to him for the occasion by Kahn, President Theodore Roosevelt signed the bill into law. Chinese exclusion was permanent.

Two years later, in January 1904, Chinese diplomatic officials notified their American counterparts that they planned to terminate the Gresham-Yang treaty when it expired at the end of the year. Democratic lawmakers warned that America's gates would be thrown open to the "Chinese hordes." The cabinet of President Theodore Roosevelt met, in April, to consider the administration's options. Philander Knox, the United States attorney general, issued an opinion that the exclusion laws would be unaffected by the treaty lapsing. Nevertheless, Congress scrambled, just before adjourning in late April, to add language to an appropriations bill that would, as Senator Shelby Cullom, the Illinois Republican who introduced the amendment, put it, "remove any possible doubts" that Chinese exclusion remained the law of the land.

By at least one measure, the exclusionists could claim victory. The total Chinese population in the United States was shrinking. In 1890, census takers had recorded more than 107,000 Chinese people in America. Three decades later, the number in the mainland of the United States had declined to less than 62,000, even as the country's overall population swelled. The drop-off was even more pronounced in California, where the Chinese population had decreased by more than half, falling below 30,000. An article published in 1904 in *The World's Work*, a monthly national affairs magazine, predicted that in fifty years the "Chinese population of the United States will become practically extinct," pointing out that adult residents were overwhelmingly male; unmarried, or, at least, without a wife in America; and aging. The writer concluded: "Yesterday they were a menace; today they are out of the race; tomorrow they will be a memory."

The shrinking population was, in large measure, the handiwork of an increasingly emboldened federal bureaucracy that guarded America's gates. In 1891, Congress had established the nation's first permanent immigration agency within the Treasury Department, but the collectors of the various ports still administered the Chinese exclusion laws. In 1900, Congress centralized that overall responsibility in the office of the commissioner general of immigration, headed by Terence V. Powderly, the fiercely anti-Chinese former leader of the Knights of Labor. Powderly, who had a drooping walrus mustache and a dignified bearing, embarked on a personal crusade to block all Chinese from entering America, except for diplomats. He filled his ranks of inspectors with allies of labor and issued onerous new regulations curtailing Chinese admissions. On January 1, 1902, as part of a collection of New Year's greetings from public officials, a Washington newspaper published Powderly's aspirations for the coming year: "It is my wish that during the new year only such foreigners will come to this country as will make good citizens. To these we always extend our welcome, but the others we must exclude for our own good. I wish that the day when there came here those sturdy men of Scotland, Germany, Ireland, and Scandinavia, who built up the great Northwest and other regions of this country would return, and that whatever is done, the Chinese will be kept out."

In the spring of 1902, Frank P. Sargent, another former labor leader who believed that Chinese immigration was "a threat to our very civilization," succeeded Powderly as the country's immigration overseer. Sargent directed his inspectors to begin photographing all Chinese arrivals and subjecting them to physical examinations, as dictated by a system of criminal identification established by Alphonse Bertillon, a French police official. Chinese arrivals were required to strip naked and subject themselves to a battery of measurements, including the width of their skull, the lengths of their hands and feet, and the distances between their eyes, nose, and mouth. Immigration officials looked for telltale physical markers, such as calluses, sunburnt legs, and pronounced musculature to ferret out laborers trying to enter the country. The primary effect of the screening measures was to treat all arriving Chinese as objects of suspicion. Liang Qichao, a renowned Chinese intellectual, toured North America in 1903 and later published a memoir of his travels, in which he observed: "The Chinese immigrants coming to America have not yet committed any crimes, but they are treated as criminals."

Officials in Washington gave inspectors in the field vast discretion. Irascible officers refused landings on the narrowest of grounds. Chinese arrivals often languished for weeks or even months as their cases were adjudicated, before finally being deported. In 1898, the Pacific Mail company converted the second story of a wooden office building on its pier into a detention shed to house them. A customs officer stood guard at the foot of a narrow stairway. Above him, hundreds of Chinese squeezed into a space about a hundred feet long and fifty feet wide, no larger than a small cottage. Sanitation was nonexistent; the stench was often overpowering. Ira Condit, a Presbyterian missionary to the Chinese, complained that Chinese arrivals were "penned up, like a flock of sheep."

On September 17, 1899, Ho Mun, a merchant and a native of Macau, arrived in San Francisco aboard the steamer *Coptic*. He presented documents issued to him by Portuguese authorities in Macau and approved by the United States consul general at Hong Kong, but inspectors barred him from landing, because he had failed to state how long he had been working as a merchant in Macau. They ordered him confined to the detention shed, pending his deportation, but he soon fell ill. The head of San Francisco's Chinese bureau, James R. Dunn, was reviled in the Chinese community for his harsh tactics. (Immigration officials once investigated an alleged plot to assassinate him with a poisonous white nut.) Dunn refused to allow a physician to treat Ho Mun. Two months later, his friends filed a writ of habeas corpus, which was granted, and the authorities finally transferred Ho Mun out of the shed, but he died shortly after.

There were other outrages attributed to Dunn. One day, in early 1899, a young boy named Lew Lin Gin arrived on a steamship from China with his stepmother. The boy's father was a merchant in the interior and a native of California. His American birth meant his son was also a citizen, even though the boy had been born in China. Lew Lin Gin's mother had died when he was young, and his father had remarried and returned to the United States alone. When Lew Lin Gin was around three years old, his father sent for him and his stepmother. When they arrived, immigration officials permitted the stepmother to land, presumably as the wife of a merchant, but rejected Lew Lin Gin because of his Chinese birth. The collector of the port placed the boy at the Chinese Presbyterian Mission Home, while his father pursued legal options. After a year, Dunn ordered that the boy be deported on a steamship scheduled to depart on January 26, 1900. While delivering some clothes to Lew Lin Gin at the mission home, his stepmother discovered that he was missing. A frantic search ensued. Just before the ship was supposed to cast off, an agent of the Pacific Mail company received a writ of habeas corpus, demanding that the boy be turned over to a judge. The agent scoured the ship but failed to turn up the boy. The following year, a lawyer for the Chinese community lodged a formal complaint against Dunn, asserting that the parents had been unable to locate their child and he was "now supposed to be lost to them forever." According to an account of the episode published by the sociologist Mary Coolidge in 1909, Dunn had ordered the boy hidden in a stateroom in a section of the ship reserved for white passengers. It was later reported that a Chinese boy dressed in American clothes disembarked the ship in Shanghai. Seven years later, Coolidge reported, Lew Lin Gin's parents were still searching for him.

Immigration officers began conducting regular raids on Chinese businesses, schools, and other establishments. The most notorious operation took place in Boston on a Sunday evening in October 1903. More than a dozen immigration officials from the city, joined by four inspectors dispatched from New York, gathered outside Boston's Chinese quarter. Four United States marshals and more than fifty city patrolmen and officers were also on hand to assist. The shops and restaurants in Chinatown were crowded. The immigration inspectors approached the quarter in pairs to avoid raising any alarm. Patrolmen set up a skirmish line, encircling the quarter and sealing off escape routes. At the appointed moment, officers swarmed in and dragged frightened residents from underneath beds and from behind boxes and doors and other hiding spots and tossed them onto overloaded wagons. A large horse-drawn wagon, filled to capacity, overturned while making a sharp turn en route to the district courthouse, injuring several Chinese prisoners, at least two severely. Some 234 Chinese men were held overnight in the city's federal building. About twenty were locked into a thirty-by-twelve-foot cage on the third floor; more than a hundred others were crammed together into a fourth-floor room that was normally reserved for pensioner examinations. By noon the following day, the authorities had released nearly half of the prisoners. Court commissioners held hearings right away for five men and ordered that they be deported. Several days after the raid, William Lloyd Garrison Jr. led a mass meeting at Faneuil Hall to condemn the arrests and helped to establish a legal defense committee for the prisoners that raised $4,000. Over the course of months, the court proceedings dragged on, eventually exhausting the defense fund; several dozen more were ordered deported.

For the Chinese in America, the constant harassment made for a punishing, demeaning existence. A new voice emerged on behalf of the community, a newspaper editor named Ng Poon Chew, who had journeyed to the United States from Taishan, in 1880, as a teenager. He had come dreaming of riches, having seen an uncle return from America a wealthy man. After he arrived in California, he began working as a domestic servant for a family in San Jose. In his evenings, he studied English at a Presbyterian mission school. The experience proved transformative. Ng's parents had once aspired for him to join the Daoist priesthood. Instead, in America, he converted to Christianity and, in 1884, moved to the mission home in San Francisco, with the goal of studying for the ministry. Ng went on to graduate from the San Francisco Theological Seminary and then became an assistant pastor at the Chinese Presbyterian mission in San Francisco and later the head of the church's Chinese missions in Los Angeles, Santa Barbara, and San Diego.

In 1898, while still a pastor, he started a newspaper in Los Angeles. It was around then that Ng, who wore oval spectacles with thin metal frames and had a neatly groomed handlebar mustache, decided to cut off his queue with a pair of scissors. When he went to an American barber to get a fresh haircut, he was rebuked: "We don't cut hair for Chinks." As his convictions about the injustices suffered by the Chinese in America mounted, Ng began to find ministry too limiting. "The paper gave me a lever with which to elevate the Chinese," he later said. In 1900, Ng returned to San Francisco to found *Chung Sai Yat Po*, a daily newspaper for the Chinese community.

The newspaper's offices were located on the second floor of a building on Sacramento Street, up a narrow stairway. Ng modeled *Chung Sai Yat Po* on the crusading American dailies of the day. In the newspaper's early days, Ng held the roles of managing editor, editorial writer, business manager, city editor, and news editor simultaneously. In order to cover the news affecting Chinese residents, Ng assigned one of his reporters to the police courts and the other to the federal courts; a photographer rounded out the editorial staff. *Chung Sai Yat Po* also employed six typesetters, who laboriously manipulated several thousand pounds of type that rendered eleven thousand Chinese characters. The entire staff slept in apartments in the back of the pressroom.

Ng saw the *Chung Sai Yat Po* as a voice for the community and a bridge between China and the West. (Its name translates literally as "China West Daily Newspaper.") Several of his Chinese employees had, like him, attended American schools. Ng also hired John Fryer, a professor of Chinese literature at the University of California, as an adviser. One early account of the *Chung Sai Yat Po* described it as "an influential organ of what might be termed the Americanized Chinese, or the New Chinaman." An early advertisement in the newspaper encouraged readers to "debunk the myth that we are unassimilable." In the fall of 1901, Ng embarked on a lecture tour of eastern cities, lobbying against the renewal of the exclusion laws. Presbyterian church officials underwrote the trip, and congregations across the country hosted the former pastor. Ng, who spoke fluent English, as well as the Sze Yup and Sam Yup dialects, had a penetrating voice and a warmth and wit that made him a lively public speaker. During Ng's trip, *Chung Sai Yat Po* published a series of articles forcefully rebutting exclusionists' arguments. The following year, Ng argued for the easing of Chinese immigration restrictions in *The Independent,* a weekly magazine that had built its reputation during the Civil War era campaigning against slavery. The magazine's editors described Ng to readers as "an Americanized Chinaman" who had "made a study of the Chinese question" as a journalist and a clergyman. In his essay, Ng sought to allay Americans' fears that the country would be overrun by Chinese immigrants and pushed back against the criticism that the Chinese lived only amongst their own, pointing out that they had little choice in the matter. Like Wong Chin Foo, Ng tried to make the case for a "better class of Chinese," who he suggested would be open to certain reasonable restrictions, such as requiring everyone entering the country be able to read and write English.

In the spring of 1905, the distress of the Chinese community in the United States over the exclusion policy, as well as a rising sense of nationalism among the merchant class in China, along with students and other educated elites, grew increasingly pronounced. In Shanghai, Guangzhou, and other cities in southern China, a roiling protest movement, calling for the boycott of American imported goods, began to spread. In the United States, *Chung Sai Yat Po* and other Chinese newspapers took up the cause with vigor. Ng became one of the boycott movement's principal spokesmen, embarking on another East Coast tour and even traveling to Washington to meet with President Theodore Roosevelt. Alarmed by the potential cost to American trade interests, the president issued instructions to the secretary of commerce and labor that the exclusion law "must be enforced without harshness" and that "all unnecessary inconvenience or annoyance" towards members of exempt classes should be "scrupulously avoided." Roosevelt warned that abuses by Bureau of Immigration officials would "be cause for immediate dismissal from the service."

On the afternoon of July 16, 1905, a man in his twenties, dressed in a kimono, appeared on Whangpoo Road, in Shanghai, across the street from the United States consulate, drank from a bottle of muriatic acid—a corrosive, industrial chemical—and collapsed. Several men inside the consulate helped to carry his body into the shade. A physician who was summoned concluded that he had been poisoned. Later, at the hospital, the man recovered enough to converse in Spanish with a priest. He gave his name as Fernando Ruiz and said he was a sailor from the Philippines. The next day, he died.

Mystified American officials arranged for his burial at the foreigners' cemetery in Shanghai. A month later, imperial officials in Shanghai contacted the consulate and informed them that an acquaintance of the man who had committed suicide was seeking to have his body disinterred and reburied at his home. The man claiming the body identified the deceased as Feng Xiawei, a native of Nanhai, in Guangdong province, who had gone to America to study. He had been turned away and was sent back on the same ship he had arrived on. His suicide had been intended as a protest against the mistreatment of the Chinese in America. The consul general in Shanghai quickly relinquished his body. Two notes left behind by Feng were later published in the Chinese press, one addressed to the U.S. consul that criticized the exclusion laws and the other urging his countrymen to boycott American goods. "Blessings will come for those who fight," he said. On October 15, 1905, Feng's body arrived in Guangzhou. His portrait was put on display at a local temple. Tens of thousands took to the streets to hail his sacrifice and vent their anger towards the United States.

In November 1905, Ng and Patrick J. Healy, a San Francisco journalist who was sympathetic to the plight of the Chinese in America, jointly published "A Statement for Non-Exclusion," a 250-page catalog of atrocities inflicted upon Chinese immigrants. Soon after, Ng went back east as a delegate to a gathering at Madison Square Garden in New York City, convened by the National Civic Federation, a Republican-leaning organization that brought together representatives of business and labor, for what was billed as the first-ever national conference on immigration. On the morning of December 8, the conference's final day, delegates debated a series of resolutions on the "Asiatic question." Ng was the morning's first speaker. His acerbic wit was on full display. "I am here to plead the cause of the yellow people, not a yellow cause," he said. "Some people have a great fashion of calling things they do not like yellow. You exclude the yellow man. You fear the yellow peril. I edit a white paper turned out by yellow men, and many white men turn out yellow papers." Ng's address drew laughter and applause. *The New*

York Times later reported that he "made the hit of the day." A series of anti-Chinese speakers, however, followed Ng to the podium, including Powderly, the former immigration commissioner, who denounced the Chinese as "morally unfit for association with the American people." The conference ultimately approved a resolution that endorsed the principle of exclusion, with narrow exceptions for "Chinese students" and "business and professional men," as well as travelers.

In the end, the boycott of American goods proved to be relatively short-lived, even as it marked a signal moment of nationalistic fervor in China and political consciousness for the Chinese in America. From the movement's inception, Qing officials had been divided about its wisdom. Under pressure from American officials, they began to take steps, tentatively at first and then with increasing firmness, to bring the boycott to an end. Support in the merchant community in China splintered, even as boycott leaders in the United States continued to press for the complete overhaul of the exclusion policy. By the end of the year, the protests had largely been exhausted. The attention of the Chinese community in the United States, including Ng's, was about to shift to a more immediate crisis.

Just past five o'clock in the morning on April 18, 1906, the earth beneath the city of San Francisco murmured. At first, the sound seemed distant, but within moments the volume was like a train in the tunnel. The ground was jerking, swaying, and writhing. There was a brief lull, perhaps ten seconds, before the oscillations resumed, with even more violence. The tumult lasted about a minute. Across the city, hundreds of buildings collapsed in heaps of rubble; cobblestone streets lay like rumpled rugs; water poured out of broken mains; and ominous columns of smoke began to climb the dawn sky. One of the most devastating earthquakes in recorded history had struck a ribbon of land along the coast, about fifty miles wide and nearly three hundred miles long, with its epicenter just offshore from San Francisco.

In Chinatown, residents rushed outside in their night garments. The bell of St. Mary's church, on the edge of the quarter, pealed in an unending distress signal. Hugh Liang, a fifteen-year-old Chinese American boy, was sleeping in the back room of his family's grocery store. "Suddenly, I was rocking from side to side in my bed," he later wrote in an unpublished memoir. "The debris from the cracked ceiling was pouring down on me. I thought I was in a boat about to drown with water all over me." In 1889, Liang's parents had sailed to America together from Hong Kong. Soon after their arrival in San Francisco, Liang's father, Kai Hee, used winnings from a lottery game in Chinatown to lease the building at 823 Washington Street. The family occupied the top floor and rented out the other rooms. They also opened a grocery store in the basement. Hugh was their firstborn; the couple went on to have four more sons and a daughter. In 1900, his mother had returned to China with the rest of the children, believing that "the American people did not want us here," Liang wrote. Hugh stayed behind to help his father with the grocery business, only for him to suddenly pass away, in 1905, from pneumonia, leaving Hugh alone at the age of fourteen. A cousin of his father's, Lung Tin, who had helped in the store for years, lived with Hugh behind the store.

On the morning of the earthquake, Lung Tin awoke Liang with cries of "*dey long jun, dey long jun!*" Earthquake! He ran to the front door and saw the entire front of the building across the street had crumbled. Liang hurriedly packed his belongings inside an old wooden trunk that once belonged to his father. Liang lugged it outside, where he found the cobblestone street cracked open. "It seemed that the whole population of Chinatown was out on the streets," he recalled.

A fire alarm operator stationed nearby was startled to see hundreds of Chinese residents stream into Portsmouth Square, "jabbering and gesticulating in excited terror." Once the initial tremor had subsided, some residents returned to their homes. Smoke and fire, however, were consuming the city. Panic began to spread in Chinatown. Merchants threw together their merchandise and hired wagons to take them out of the city. Lung Tin paid fifty dollars to hop on one and apologized to his young charge that he didn't have enough money for him. Liang dragged his father's trunk alone towards Nob Hill, as the flames drew closer.

Firefighters had no water to fight the flames. They resorted to using dynamite and then black powder to clear entire city blocks, including parts of Chinatown, to try to create firebreaks. By noon, however, fires raged north and south of Market Street. It advanced block by block until it reached the Chinese quarter in late afternoon. By evening, Chinatown had become a "whirlpool of fire," as one witness later put it. It would be another day and a half before the flames were finally extinguished. Chinatown lay in ruins.

Desperate Chinese refugees, with large bundles containing the possessions they could carry, joined the throngs making their way towards Golden Gate Park. Women with bound feet tottered, struggling amid the rubble. Liang fell in with the slow procession. At one point, he looked back and saw all of Chinatown in flames, including the building on Washington Street where he was born and had grown up. "A feeling of true sadness and awe came over me," he later wrote.

Chung Sai Yat Po was about to go to press when the earthquake struck. The fire destroyed its offices and the thousands of blocks of Chinese type required for printing the newspaper. It took more than a week for the staff to resume publishing, borrowing the facilities of the *Oakland Herald,* across the bay. The newspaper's first article on the quake, written by hand with a Chinese ink brush, described a wrenching tableau of people in the cold, walking away from Chinatown, "some pensive, and some crying."

Many Chinese fled the city, climbing aboard ferries and junks to escape the firestorm. Oakland absorbed thousands of Chinese refugees. In the middle of the night, with the flames still encroaching, Liang snuck aboard a boat he found along the waterfront and wound up in Napa. The refugees who stayed behind in the city filled vacant lots and parks and wandered from camp to camp, prodded by soldiers with bayonets. The initial relief efforts, organized by military authorities, mostly bypassed the Chinese. Most were too frightened to join the bread lines where white residents queued. For the first three days after the quake, the Chinese survivors were largely left hungry and drifting. Many huddled in tents and makeshift shelters on the north shore of the bay, drawing complaints from other refugees about their presence. Branches of the Chinese Six Companies along the Pacific coast rushed to send provisions to the city by railcar. On April 23, the *San Francisco Examiner* reported that the Chinese were in "grave danger," because most of them were "absolutely penniless and destitute." Alarmed by what he was hearing, Roosevelt ordered his secretary of war to ensure that relief was administered "wholly without regard to persons and be as much for Chinese as for any others." The military authorities prepared an encampment for the Chinese on a vacant plot of land at the foot of Van Ness Avenue, not far from the old Chinatown site, but residents in the area feared that it might become a permanent Chinese quarter. Officials designated a new location, a golf course on the Presidio, on the theory that the refugees would be unable to put down roots there. But when a delegation of homeowners protested that the summer winds would blow odors from the Chinese camp into their homes, the authorities scrambled to relocate the refugees yet again to a parade ground at the eastern edge of the Presidio.

In the aftermath of the quake, anti-Chinese zealots celebrated the destruction of Chinatown, believing that they could finally cleanse the Chinese stain from the city. The *Oakland Enquirer* suggested that every town in the region could seize the opportunity to "do away with the huddling together of Chinese in districts where it is undesirable." *Chung Sai Yat Po,* which continued to publish from Oakland, was instrumental in the Chinese campaign to retain their place in the heart of San Francisco. The newspaper suggested that the community hire "famous attorneys" and urged Chinese landlords to rebuild right away, without waiting for permission from the city. The newspaper pointed out that "Americans and foreigners in the United States are protected by the provisions of the constitution" and were free to choose where they wanted to live, without interference. By early June, a dozen Chinese businesses had reopened in Chinatown, erecting temporary wooden structures over the ruins. A rebirth was coming. Once again, the Chinese had held fast to their place in America.

CHAPTER 23

The Station

The first Chinese prisoner to emerge into the morning sun stood at the top of the stairway, blinking in confusion. Throngs of his countrymen were gathered below. Their murmuring rose to a clamor. Immigration inspectors nudged the crowd back, while the driver of a large dray maneuvered into position at the foot of the stairs. The men descended one by one and stepped onto the rear. When the wagon was full, the driver headed down the pier, protected by a gaggle of officers. He deposited his cargo aboard a tugboat moored nearby, the *Arab,* retraced his path, loaded up again, and repeated the process, until the boat reached capacity. The *Arab* then churned its way across San Francisco Bay to a cove on the northern side of an irregularly shaped patch of land, about a mile offshore. The tugboat made two trips to the island; during one, it towed a barge laden with the belongings of the incarcerated men. By the end of the day, all the men had been transferred. More than a hundred Chinese arrivals in the United States occupied new quarters on the island. It was January 22, 1910. A dozen years after it first opened, the detention shed on the Pacific Mail Steamship dock was finally empty.

For years, immigration officials had acknowledged that the conditions at the shed were shameful. In 1902, Frank P. Sargent, the commissioner general of immigration, had inspected the facility and pronounced it a "serious evil." The commissioner of immigration in San Francisco, Hart Hyatt North, proposed that a new immigration station be constructed on Angel Island. For immigration officials, the island's isolation was its principal attraction. With the shed, they had constantly fretted about the "coaching" of prisoners, by other Chinese residents, through the barred windows. On the island, the detainees would be cut off—from potential co-conspirators and escape. The remoteness of the island was also helpful in containing diseases that immigration officials believed were "peculiarly prevalent among aliens from oriental countries." In March 1905, Congress appropriated $200,000 for construction of the station. Several months later, Sargent approved the plans of architect W. J. Mathews for the station. It would later turn out that Mathews's preparation for the project apparently consisted mostly of a visit to the immigration station at Ellis Island and reading through the agency's annual report. Mathews's designs included a large, two-story administration building on the leeward side of the island, sheltered somewhat from the harsh winds; an "Oriental quarters" located up the hill; a hospital with separate wards for European and Oriental patients, divided by gender; and a power station. The building materials were to be the "cheapest material obtainable," a report later said. Three years later, Congress allocated another $300,000 for the station. Workers finally completed the bulk of the work on the main buildings in October 1908, but it sat unused for more than a year after federal officials estimated it would cost another $50,000 a year to operate it. As one official noted in a report, the station was "delightfully located, so far as scenic, climatic, and health conditions are concerned," but it took forty-five minutes "wharf to wharf" to reach it by boat. Immigration officials decided that it would be better to wait a few years, until the completion of the Panama Canal, which was expected to bring an influx of European immigrants, to open the station.

During a visit to San Francisco in October 1909, President William Howard Taft went on a tour of San Francisco Bay, and city officials briefed him on the deplorable conditions at the shed. Afterward, the president announced that he supported the immediate opening of the station, telling immigration officials he feared that the treatment of Chinese in San Francisco would lead to another boycott. Immigration officials scrambled to purchase furniture, transport records to the island, and make other final preparations to get the station ready. They warned that it'd take six months to complete the electric lighting on the island and make other repairs, but administration officials ordered that they make do with lanterns. A lone inspector remained in the city to hear evidence from local witnesses in the applications of European immigrants for entry. All the examinations for Chinese arrivals would take place on Angel Island.

On the day of the station's opening, immigration officials herded the 354 people in their custody, most of them Chinese, into the barracks, which was ringed by barbed wire. They occupied canvas bunks that were triple-stacked to the ceiling. Besides the longer-standing prisoners in the shed, there were more recent arrivals: ninety-two passengers, all but a handful Chinese, from the ocean liner *Siberia,* which had pulled into the harbor more than a week earlier but had been delayed after inspectors discovered dozens of tins of opium on board; and more than 150 Chinese passengers, along with 75 South Asians—inspectors called them "Hindoos"—from the ocean liner SS *China,* which had arrived in the harbor late in the evening on January 21, just in time for the opening of the station the next day. Upon arrival, inspectors deposited passengers' luggage in a shed on the dock and herded them into a large examination area filled with wooden benches, where they waited, separated by race—European and "Asiatic"—and gender. When it was their turn, they traveled down long stalls where inspectors interviewed them and then directed them to the next room for physical examinations that required them to strip naked.

On January 24, an inspector named Lauritz Lorenzen, who would later draw complaints from the Chinese consul general for his harshness, interviewed Wong Chung Hong, a thirty-year-old arrival on the *China.* Wong was five feet six inches tall and had a wife and four young children back home. Lorenzen interrogated him at length about the schools he had attended as a child, the nature of his business interests, and the makeup of his family. Several years earlier, Wong had used money inherited from his father and, with two partners, started a dried fruit business in Guangzhou. For his trip to the United States, he had brought with him $500 in U.S. currency to invest in a new business and was planning to join Sang Wo & Co., a butcher and grocery store on Dupont Street. He presented a "section six" certificate signed by the American consul general in Guangzhou, attesting to his exempt status.

A photograph attached to his arrival file showed him in an elegant Chinese robe. Lorenzen noted that Wong "presents a good appearance." The following day, Wong retained a lawyer. Perhaps not coincidentally, on that same day, the inspector recommended Wong for admission, certifying that his documents appeared "regular" and emphasizing that "the appearance of applicant is such as to show conclusively that he has not been a laborer." Wong became the first passenger held on Angel Island admitted to the United States.

The other cases from the *China* went less smoothly. Only thirty-one case files from the ship's passengers can still be found in the arrival records at the National Archives office in San Bruno, California. In more than half the cases from the *China* that remain on file, immigration officials denied the passenger permission to land; the average length of detention in the cases was thirty-seven days. One passenger, a man named Liu Poy, who said he was the son of a merchant, was detained for ninety-four days, before his application for landing was finally rejected. Lau Tsan Tung, a twenty-year-old from a prosperous mercantile family in Hong Kong, was held on the island for three months while he pressed his case. Lau told inspectors that he was planning to study English and agriculture and return to China to become a farmer. Several witnesses, including a white freight clerk on the *China,* vouched for him, but officials identified discrepancies in Lau's testimony. Finally, Daniel Keefe, the commissioner general of immigration in Washington, sustained Lau's appeal and allowed him to land. "On most carefully reviewing the record and scrutinizing its minutest detail, the Bureau cannot escape the impression that appellant is what he claims to be," Keefe wrote.

Chinese leaders in San Francisco protested the treatment of arrivals at the new immigration station right away. They had tried unsuccessfully to block its opening by threatening a boycott of American goods. The prospect of having wives and children stranded on the island for weeks or months was appalling. The island's remoteness would also make it harder to persuade white witnesses to come and vouch for Chinese arrivals. Within days of the station's opening, those incarcerated on the island sent a petition to the Six Companies, the Chinese Chamber of Commerce, and the Chinese consul general, complaining about the food, the lack of bedding, and inspectors' surliness. About a fifth of the individuals being held were sick, complaining of coughs, colds, and stomach ailments. The Chinese on the island said that the barracks resembled a dungeon, with poor light and ventilation. In early February, the Chinese Six Companies sent cables to Hong Kong, Guangzhou, and Shanghai, urging that Chinese emigrants boycott San Francisco and instead head to other ports in Oregon and Washington. They distributed circulars throughout Chinatown, urging that witnesses not appear for their scheduled examinations and that residents protest "with one accord." In March, Ng Poon Chew and Look Tin Eli, a prominent Chinese American merchant, traveled to Washington to meet with Department of Commerce and Labor officials to explain the "difficult situation for Chinese people on Angel Island," as Ng later put it. Over the course of several days and multiple meetings, the two men pressed for the closure of the station but got nowhere. The federal government had invested heavily in the station, so immigration officials were not about to abandon it. The Chinese delegation managed to secure some minor concessions relating to the way certain arrivals were treated. Those who simply needed to retrieve their passports, for instance, would be interviewed in San Francisco; arrivals from exempt classes, such as merchants and students, whose cases were clear-cut, could be landed directly from their steamships. Before Ng and Look departed Washington, they met with President Taft, who told them that he had vigorously supported the opening of the station. He promised if there were complaints about the new station, he would order department officials to address them. He described the station as a "kind gesture" for the Chinese people.

The station was at capacity almost immediately. By the end of January, there were 556 detained passengers on the island. The station included seven hundred sleeping berths but not all could be utilized because of the way inspectors segregated the detainees by gender and nationality. In April, fearing that they were on the verge of running out of space, station officials requested two hundred more berths but were told there were no available funds. It did not take long for federal officials to realize that the design and construction of the station verged on negligence. On November 21, 1910, less than a year into the station's operation, Dr.

M. W. Glover, the head of the island's medical division, wrote to his superiors that ventilation in the barracks was "totally inadequate." He also criticized the walls and ceilings, which were unpainted and made of soft wood. "Nothing could be worse from a sanitary point of view, to say nothing of the added fire risk," he wrote. In a subsequent letter, he reported that the hospital building where he worked was settling after every rain, causing cracking in the plaster and doorframes to shift; the roof was also not draining properly. In late December, Luther Steward, the acting commissioner of immigration at San Francisco, issued his own damning evaluation, calling the construction of the buildings "defective, in many respects." He reported that the toilet facilities were "grossly inadequate" and lacked proper drainage. The slurry on the floor was often an inch and a half deep. By the early 1920s, immigration officials were calling the station's ramshackle frame buildings "fire traps."

According to Pacific Mail Steamship Company records from the station's early years, between 1913 and 1919, Chinese passengers accounted for 70 percent of arrivals who spent any time on the island. Most white passengers managed to avoid Angel Island altogether, or endured stays of a few days or less. By contrast, immigration officials permitted less than a quarter of Chinese arrivals to go directly ashore. Among those who wound up on the island, the average length of detention of Chinese passengers varied. Those claiming to be the son of either a merchant or a native-born American had the longest detentions, with a median of two or three weeks, respectively; the cases of passengers claiming to be merchants were more straightforward, typically lasting a few days. About a fifth of Chinese prisoners were detained for more than two weeks. In later years, officials began allowing more Chinese arrivals to bypass the island. According to information compiled from lists of Chinese applying for admission in San Francisco, in the 1930s as many as three-quarters went directly ashore, but the time that detainees spent on the island began to creep upwards—in 1940, the median detention was forty-two days.

The crucible of the admissions process was a hearing before a Board of Special Inquiry, which consisted of an inspector, a stenographer, and an interpreter. Inspectors fixated on small differences in the testimonies of applicants and the witnesses vouching for them. "The inspector, to whom the case was assigned, was handed the file with any related files of that person's family," Emery Sims, a former inspector, recalled years after his retirement. "And then it was up to him to review these old files and start questioning the applicant about his birth, family, home, and in the course of the testimony, it would develop that the applicant was either very much in accord with the old files or there were rather serious discrepancies between him and the others." John Birge Sawyer, a newly appointed inspector who began working at the station in January 1917, despaired about the "wastefulness of the methods of Angel Island," complaining in his diary of the volume of his caseload and the manner in which he had to constantly switch between investigations.

Several months after the station opened, a joint investigation by the San Francisco Chamber of Commerce and a Chinese merchants' organization criticized the lengthy interrogations, concluding that it was "almost an impossibility to answer the question correctly," and found that cases were often taking weeks to be resolved. "They ask so much, you got tired," one former detainee later recalled. In June 1911, the *Chinese Defender,* an English-language newspaper in San Francisco endorsed by an organization of merchants and other community leaders calling itself the Chinese League of Justice of America, reported on the ordeal of a Chinese boy who had spent five months on Angel Island, before finally being permitted to land. "With all due respect to proper formalities of the law and necessary procedure thereunder, we would hate to have a boy—or even a friend—of ours kept there five days," the editorial said. "Would you, gentle reader, like your boy to be held captive five months simply because he was applying for admittance into the country? Would you stand it for five weeks, even?"

Some detentions stretched on far longer. On September 1, 1916, a twenty-year-old woman from Hong Kong named Quok Shee arrived in San Francisco Bay aboard the *Nippon Maru.* Quok Shee was petite and almost childlike in appearance. She arrived in the company of her "alleged husband," as immigration officials referred to him, a returning merchant more than twice her age named Chew Hoy Quong. J. B. Warner, the inspector on the case, appeared dubious of their relationship. Chew was a partner in a Chinese herb company in the city. He had lived in the United States for more than three decades. He left for China in

May 1915, his first return visit to his homeland, with the intent of finding a bride. He told Warner that Quok Shee's father had died, so her uncle had arranged their marriage, which took place in Hong Kong in February 1916. In separate interviews, Warner grilled the couple about the minutiae of their purported lives together. What time did Quok Shee arrive on their wedding day? How was their bedroom and parlor furnished? Where were the electric lights? The inspector's suspicion was that Quok Shee was a prostitute. "Are you positive you are not bringing this woman to the United States for an immoral purpose?" Warner asked. Chew assured him that he was not.

Four days after the couple's arrival, immigration officials admitted Chew. Warner recommended that Quok Shee be admitted as well. W. H. Wilkinson, the chief inspector of the bureau's law section, however, decided to detain her. A week later, inspectors summoned Quok Shee's "alleged husband" back to the island for further interrogation. There would be another important development in the case. On September 15, Wilkinson met with an informant, whom he described in a confidential memorandum as a "woman of refinement and culture, and one in whom full confidence could be placed." She told him that a friend of hers had confided to her that Chew had admitted that Quok Shee was not his wife but that he had brought her to the United States for "immoral purposes," in return for a fee of $3,000. The following day, Edward White, the commissioner of immigration at the port of San Francisco, formally notified Quok Shee that he had denied her application to land.

Chew immediately hired lawyers to appeal his wife's case. Immigration officials, however, refused to let them meet with Quok Shee. They also, crucially, failed to say anything about the role of the informant's testimony in her case. In November, the secretary of labor dismissed the appeal and ordered that Quok Shee be deported. Chew's lawyers took the case to federal court, filing a writ of habeas corpus. In December, a district court judge denied the writ. Her lawyers appealed once again, this time to the circuit court of appeals. As her time on the island stretched on, Quok Shee's desperation grew. Seven months into her detention, an anonymous note in her case file reported that she "had no money" and was "wearing shoes and stockings that have been given to her by American friends." The note said that she "desires earnestly to be sent back to China." On September 14, 1917, she told inspectors: "Since I have had to stay here so long at the island I think it would be better for me to go back to China." Two months later, she asked again. On December 13, 1917, her lawyer, Dion Holm, wrote an urgent letter to immigration officials, asking them not to oppose a request he was planning to make to the court to release her on bail. "Quok Shee is in a highly nervous state and I really believe that she will undergo great physical suffering, as well as mental if confined at Angel Island any longer," he wrote. "I have been told that she has on many occasions threatened to commit suicide if not released." Yet she remained imprisoned. In the end, however, it was immigration officials' imperiousness that gave Quok Shee a legal opening. On April 1, 1918, the circuit court of appeals ruled that Quok Shee had not received a fair hearing, pointing to both the lack of disclosure of the informant's testimony and the fact that her lawyers were barred from interviewing her while her appeal was pending. A district court judge subsequently ordered immigration officials to turn her over for a hearing at ten o'clock in the morning on May 11, when she was finally freed. She had been detained on Angel Island for nearly two years.

The inspectors on Angel Island were even willing to go so far as to separate children from their parents. On January 15, 1924, the SS *President Cleveland,* a steamship originally built during the First World War as a fast troop transport ship, entered San Francisco Bay. On board was Wong Shee, a forty-two-year-old widow, who stood five feet tall and had bound feet; in her charge were six of her children. The four girls ranged in age from twelve to eighteen years old; all had been born in the United States. The boys, who were just seven and ten, had been born in China, but they were also American citizens through their father, Lee Yoke Suey, a native-born American. Their eldest sister awaited them in San Francisco. As the ship passed through the Golden Gate, the older girls jumped up and down on the ship's deck. They were home.

The family's roots in America dated back to the mid-1860s, when Lee's father, Lee Wong Sang, had at the age of nineteen journeyed with several cousins from Suen Chuen village in Taishan to San Francisco. Lee had gone to work on the Pacific railroad and later became a partner in an import-export firm in San Francisco's Chinatown. In the early 1870s, he sent for his wife, Chin Shee, to join him in the United States. The couple raised three American-born sons. A few years after the earthquake, Lee Wong Sang decided to return to China, leaving his interest in the trading business with his middle son, Lee Yoke Suey. In 1912, Lee Yoke Suey returned to China as well with his wife, Wong Shee, and their five youngest children—all under the age of eight. The couple wanted them to be educated in China. Lee himself traveled back and forth, tending to his business. His family continued to grow—the couple had twelve children in all. In 1922, Lee Yoke Suey became ill with cancer. On a trip back to China, he unexpectedly died on board the ship. Wong Shee received a telegram in Shanghai, where the family was living. After mourning her husband for a year, Wong resolved to return to America with her children.

Immigration officials quickly admitted the six children but detained their mother. A medical examination found Wong Shee had clonorchiasis, more commonly known as liver fluke disease. The ailment, caused by parasitic flatworms, was prevalent in Asia, typically triggered by consuming undercooked fish. The disease does not spread person to person, but it became a common reason for denying admission to Chinese arrivals. The island's surgeon issued a certificate that diagnosed Wong Shee with a "dangerous contagious disease." The Chinese Chamber of Commerce quickly came to her aid, petitioning the commissioner of immigration to land Wong Shee, so that "this mother may be restored to her American born and citizen children." Immigration officials ruled, however, that Wong Shee had lost her legal status for entering the country after her husband's death. On February 8, immigration officials ordered that she be deported. A pair of lawyers retained by the family filed a habeas corpus petition in federal district court, halting her deportation.

Her oldest daughter, Mary, visited her three times a week, taking the government ferry from San Francisco, even though it made her seasick. She often brought rice and salted eggs to her mother to supplement the rations she ate in the barracks. "Each month felt like a year," she later recalled. "We waited in agony for the news, afraid that the decision would be to deport my mother." In June, five months into her detention, a judge approved Wong Shee's release on bail, so she could report for treatment at a hospital in the city. Afterward, she returned to Angel Island. On February 20, 1925, a board of special inquiry on the island convened again to consider her case. Wong Shee struggled to understand the proceedings. "I can read and write a little Chinese," she said, speaking through a translator in the Sze Yip dialect. "I can talk a little English." She told the board that she planned to take over her husband's interest in the trading firm. "I would like to land as a merchant and stay here so I could take care of my children," she said. "I don't know the law so I don't know what is required of me." The board concluded there was "no ground for this applicant's admission under the Chinese Exclusion Law." Wong Shee's lawyers appealed the decision anew, arguing that denying her landing would be "unjust and inhumane," and cited a recent case similar to Wong Shee's in which a widow was landed in Seattle. Finally, on May 1, 1925, more than fifteen months after she and her children arrived, immigration officials granted Wong Shee indefinite parole, and she was reunited with her children. Connie Young Yu, Wong Shee's granddaughter, later described the emotional toll inflicted upon the Lee family as "incalculable."

Sometimes despair on the island proved overwhelming. On October 7, 1919, a brief article in the *San Francisco Chronicle* reported that a thirty-two-year-old Chinese man, Fong Fook, who had arrived on Angel Island several days earlier aboard the *Persia Maru*, intending to travel onward to the town of Mexicali, Mexico, had hanged himself with a towel tied to a gas fixture. There were other tragedies. The Rev. Edwar Lee, a Chinese American pastor, began working at Angel Island in 1927 as an interpreter. Years later, he recalled one woman who realized she was about to be deported. "She couldn't face the people back home," he said. "So she committed suicide by sharpening chopsticks and plunged that chopstick through her ears to her brain. And she practically died right there and then."

On the island, women were allowed outside two or three times a week to stroll the station's grounds, but guards confined the male detainees to their barracks. After meals, a small courtyard, about thirty yards long, was available for exercise. Some read newspapers and books; others wrote letters. Mostly, they stared out at the scenes beyond the barbed wire fence. "Besides listening to the birds outside the fence, we could listen to records and talk to old-timers in the barracks," one former detainee recalled. "Some, due to faulty responses during the interrogation and lengthy appeal procedures, had been there for years. They poured out their sorrow unceasingly." To pass the time, some of the prisoners began scribbling poetry on the wall, using a brush or a knife, deriding their American tormentors and lamenting their imprisonment. In 1916, an official on the island observed in a letter to the commissioner of immigration that the walls of the station had "been considerably marred by the aliens writing on them" and suggested signs be posted, "under glass, and framed," warning that defacing the walls was prohibited.

On August 11, 1931, Jann Mon Fong, an eighteen-year-old from Muey Duck village in the Zhongshan district in Guangdong province, arrived in San Francisco Bay aboard the steamship *President McKinley* and transferred to a smaller boat that transported him to Angel Island. "The Americans treated us like cattle," he later recalled. "Those green-eyed people must have thought Chinese were the offspring of pigs and goats. Carrying a cloth bundle on my back and a suitcase in my hand, I was herded into the detention center under their wolf-like authority. Tears flowed down my face." The next day, a physician ordered Jann and other detainees to disrobe and stand in the damp chill for hours. "He felt our chest and spine, and ordered us to jump around like monkeys," he later said. "I was not sure if this was a physical examination, or, rather, an act of insult." Jann joined the island's Self-Governing Association, established by male detainees to offer mutual support and maintain order. Idle, inside the locked barracks, he noticed the writings on the wall. He began to record them in a notebook.

It is indeed pitiable, the harsh treatment of our fellow countrymen.
The doctor extracting blood caused us greatest anguish.
Our stomachs are full of grievances, but to whom can we tell them?

We can but pace to and fro, scratch our heads, and question the blue
heavens.

This unworthy one with the group is grief-stricken.
Who will transmit the news of death back to the village?
I mourn your having ridden the crane to return to the dark regions.
A traveler arrived in America on a ship.
Tears enveloped the lonely soul as the cuckoo uttered its mournful cry.

Sadly, I listen to the sounds of insects and angry surf.
The harsh laws pile layer upon layer; how can I dissipate my hatred?
Drifting in as a traveller, I met with this calamity.
It is more miserable than owning only a flute in the marketplace
of Wu.

Over the course of twenty days in detention, Jann copied dozens of poems. His interrogation by immigration inspectors took place over three days. He told them that his father was a native-born American citizen living in San Francisco. His alleged father and an alleged sister both came to the island to testify on his behalf. Finally, on August 31, the chief inspector on Jann's case pronounced that the "claimed relationship has been reasonably established." He was free to go. "I finally landed in this place erroneously called since my childhood years the heavenly 'Gold Mountain,'" he later wrote.

Jann fumed at his treatment on the island, but he had succeeded in an elaborate ruse. Jann was a "paper son," entering the country with faked legal documents that established for him an American lineage. The tactic had soared in popularity after the 1906 earthquake and fire destroyed San Francisco City Hall and the Hall of Records, containing the city's vital records. A Department of Commerce and Labor report published a month later warned about the growing prevalence of citizenship claims among Chinese arrivals and its potential consequences. "The Chinaman, having been declared an American citizen, is then privileged to bring his wife and children to this country; and as these men belong almost without exception to the laborer or cooly class (for it is a singular fact that very few members of the other classes, according to the claims advanced, were ever born in America), the objection of the exclusion laws is thus being defeated to a great extent," the report said.

After decades of decline, beginning in the 1920s the Chinese population in the United States began to rise again, driven by Chinese claiming American citizenship, as well as those able to establish themselves as merchants or as part of some other category exempted under the exclusion laws. The fearsome bureaucracy built to keep the Chinese out was no match for the determination of a people seeking to better their lives.

CHAPTER 24

Becoming Chinese American

It was a plaintive plea. On November 4, 1934, page 3 of the *Los Angeles Times Sunday Magazine,* a weekly insert in the newspaper, featured a pair of photographs, arranged opposite each other, of the same Asian woman. One depicted her in a traditional Chinese gown; the other in a plaid blazer, a long skirt, and pumps. Running down the middle of the page were the words: "*Please, What Am I?* Chinese or American?" The author was a journalist, Mamie Louise Leung. In 1899, Leung's father, Tom Cherng How, had left his home village, Gum Jook—translated in English as "Sweet Bamboo"—and made his way to Los Angeles, where he had an offer to join a cousin's herb company. He was twenty-four years old, recently married, and with a child on the way. When he bid farewell to his wife, Wong Bing Woo, in order to remember her, he took from her finger a gold ring she had worn since she was a child. He left her a supply of writing brushes and paper to keep in touch.

In Los Angeles, he began working as a cashier at his cousin's business, Foo and Wing Herb Company. He soon took the name Tom Leung. In early 1901, he learned that his eighteen-month-old son, born in his absence, had died of pneumonia. Several months later, Leung returned home and persuaded his wife to join him in America. She entered the United States as the wife of a merchant. Their plan was to stay a few years, until he had accumulated some savings. Aside from a return visit, in 1921, they never left.

Tom Leung went on to become one of the wealthiest Chinese merchants in Los Angeles, running a successful herbal medicine business that catered to an almost entirely white clientele. He built a grand, three-story home on West Pico Street, an upscale white neighborhood, with eighteen rooms and a library of nearly thirty thousand classical Chinese works. He always dressed impeccably, wearing finely tailored $200 suits and favoring tie pins adorned with pearls. He kept his mustache neatly groomed and his hair carefully combed. (Early in his time in America, he wore a wig to cover up his queue, before he finally went to a barber to cut it off.) His customers called him Dr. Leung. The state medical board repeatedly targeted Leung and other Chinese herbalists for practicing medicine without a license. The police arrested Leung more than a hundred times on misdemeanor charges. He paid about $5,000 in fines, before finally agreeing to drop "doctor" from his title. Leung had a knack for publicity, advertising widely in newspapers and publishing a twelve-chapter booklet, "Chinese Herbal Science: How to Get Well and Keep Well." Every year, he sent Christmas cards to current and former patients. He later opened branch offices in San Diego and San Bernardino and began attracting mail-order patients from as far away as Canada. The couple raised eight American-born children. Mamie, born in 1905, was the second eldest.

It was in elementary school that Mamie first sensed she was different from her peers. She started out in kindergarten at Grand Avenue School, a redbrick building a few blocks from her home. All of her classmates were white. Sometimes schoolboys called her and her older sister, Lillie, "Chink." In Mamie's telling, however, it was in junior high that she had her first real encounter with racism, when some of her classmates threw a party and tried to prevent her from attending. A girl who Mamie thought was a friend took her aside and warned her not to come. "She didn't say why, nor did she speak in an unfriendly way, but acted as though I should have known I wasn't wanted," she later wrote. In high school, Mamie "chummed with white girls," as she later put it, and chafed at her parents' conservative attitudes, rooted in the old country. She rebelled against learning Chinese and even eating Chinese food, because "being Chinese meant being different."

She excelled in school and went on to the University of Southern California, where she majored in English. During her junior year, she had a gap in her schedule and decided to take an evening class on news-writing. She discovered that she had an affinity for reporting and started writing for the student newspaper, the *Daily Trojan*. She managed to sell several feature stories to the *Los Angeles Times*, including one about foreign students on campus and another on a Chinatown theater. For days afterward, she walked around in a state of euphoria, treasuring the check she received. After college, she initially considered going to China to teach, thinking the opportunities would be better there, but a few weeks after graduation she walked into the newsroom at the Los Angeles *Record* and offered her services. The *Record*, an afternoon news-paper, was the smallest of the city's half-dozen daily newspapers and had a crusading, progressive reputation. The city editor asked her to come back the next day with a story. She delivered a lighthearted account of her nephew's one-month-old birthday, explaining to American readers the traditional Chinese celebration her family held. On July 15, 1926, the *Record* published the story on its front page and offered her a job that paid $20 a week. Leung became the first Asian American reporter at a major American newspaper and was soon covering the sheriff's office, the district attorney's office, the county supervisors, and the municipal courts by herself. "I kept thinking, well, this won't last," she later said. "I didn't think I could ever make it 'cause they'd find out that I was completely inexperienced."

She went on to work for the San Francisco *News* and the Chicago *Daily Times*, where she covered the Al Capone tax evasion trial. Over time, she came to embrace her Chinese American identity as an asset. The novelty of being interviewed by a Chinese woman was helpful in persuading press-shy subjects to open up; editors often hired her, she believed, because they were looking for "something new." Her accent-less English always surprised people. "They exclaim, 'Why, she speaks perfect English,' and are quite certain that proves I am an exceptional person," she said in an interview. In 1930, she married Arnold Larson, a white reporter, with blond hair and blue eyes, who worked for United Press International. At the time, interracial marriages were rare. When the couple looked for a place to live together, they found many landlords turned them away after seeing Mamie. She kept the marriage secret from her family, because she feared her parents' reaction.

On a sweltering day in June 1931, she was at her desk in the newsroom in Chicago when a telegram arrived, informing her that her father
had died. He was only fifty-seven years old. She took a train home to
Los Angeles, grieving that she had never really known her father. She
blamed the distance of language and culture. "Papa succeeded at being
both Chinese and American," she later wrote. "His great disappointment was that his children were so American that they did not appreciate their Chinese heritage." In a letter written to her older sister, in April
1932, she finally broke the news of her marriage and the fact that she
had a seventeen-month-old son, Stanley. She enclosed a photograph,
hoping that her mother would be assuaged by the fact "he looks like a
Leung." Soon after, she moved back to Los Angeles.

In her *Los Angeles Times Sunday Magazine* article, she invited readers
to experience the discordance of her bicultural existence. "When my
parents came to this country thirty-five years ago, it was their intention
to return soon to China to raise their family," she wrote. "Years passed,
the family grew to five boys and three girls, events piled on each other.
Three times arrangements were made to go 'home,' even to passport
photos and luggage, but each time something occurred to delay the
return. Meanwhile, what has America done to us? Step into our home
and in nearly all phases of our everyday life you will see the inevitable
conflict of two cultures." Her mother's English had never progressed
beyond rudimentary. Even with years of tutoring, Mamie only spoke
a halting, pidgin Chinese. Mamie rued the anguish that her parents
endured and concluded that they would have been more content if
they had reared their children in China. "Then there would be between
us only the bridge between generations, not the vast chasm that exists
between opposing standards and cultures," she wrote. "As for us, life
would have been much simpler. We would not have to decide—each
one for himself—that question, 'What am I—Chinese or American?'"

It was around the time that Mamie caught on at the *Record* that her family became close with Kit King Louis, a graduate student from China
who moved in next door to them. Louis's family had roots in Taishan.
Her grandfather had come to America during the gold rush and became

a successful businessman. She grew up in China in an affluent, scholarly family and came to the United States in 1924, at the age of nineteen, and initially studied chemistry at Stanford before deciding to pursue a master's degree in sociology at the University of Southern California. To earn money for school, she taught Chinese-language classes, mostly to the American-born offspring of Chinese immigrants. In January 1931, Louis completed her thesis, "A Study of American-born and American-reared Chinese in Los Angeles." She returned to China several months later to take a faculty position. (She would go on to become a prominent activist and civic leader, serving as a delegate to the National Peoples' Congress and the vice mayor of Beijing.) The focus of Louis's thesis was the growing native-born Chinese population, which in the 1920 census accounted for 30 percent of the total Chinese population in the United States. After conducting nearly a hundred interviews, Louis concluded that American-born Chinese experienced "a problem of maladjustment of a group in the American community." The culture and values of their parents collided with that of the country of their birth, a conflict familiar to European immigrants, but for Chinese Americans there was the added complication of race. "The American-born Chinese, at least most of them, are legally and qualitatively American citizens," Louis wrote. "But on account of the physical ear-marks of their ancestry, the average American reacts to them in the same way as to their parents and classifies them with the foreign-born Chinese. They are treated to all intents and purposes as if they were aliens." The result was a kind of psychic homelessness. "Although American education has successfully made Americans of them, the American-born Chinese are not accepted as Americans," she wrote.

In an article published by the *Chinese Times,* a Chinese-language newspaper, one native-born Chinese American addressed the struggle to belong. "Legally we are American citizens," he wrote. "In name, we have all the citizens' rights, but in fact we are the men without a country." He asserted, "There is discrimination everywhere." Yet it was difficult for Chinese Americans to find work in their own community, because "there is a barrier between us and the old Chinese." Louis's dissertation is full of similar accounts, drawn from her interviews, of Chinese Americans confronting their circumscribed existences. One college student went to a local pool to fulfill his school's swimming requirement and was told that "orientals" were not allowed. Another woman recalled going to Venice Beach with classmates and lining up for a ticket, only to be turned away because of her race. Many of her interview subjects described their travails trying to rent outside of Chinatown. "When I looked for a house I went through more than a hundred houses," one American-born Chinese told her. "Most of the owners will not rent to the Chinese." Recent college graduates told her of the prejudice they faced in the job market. "If I were a member of the white race I would have a job by this time," one recent graduate said. "I was recommended to several firms after I graduated from college. But when the manager saw that I was Chinese, he usually told me that the firm did not need anybody or found other alibis to refuse giving me any position." Louis concluded that there was "discrimination against them in almost every field." As part of her research, Kit King interviewed Mamie at length. "I feel that I am neither American nor Chinese," Mamie told her. "I don't seem to belong entirely to either one or the other. Those with whom I feel most at home are the American-born Chinese, like myself. I do not feel at home with the old-fashioned Chinese because I speak Chinese poorly and we seem to have nothing in common. Then, on the other hand, I do not feel perfectly at ease with all Americans because all of them do not accept me as one of them."

Four of the five sons in the Leung clan went on to serve in the armed services during the Second World War. One of them, William, was an army infantry machine gunner in the Pacific, fighting in a half-dozen major battles, including the storming of the island of Okinawa. Mamie went on to raise three children; two of them married white spouses. In 1976, she visited China for the first time as part of a "friendship" tour that included Beijing and Guangzhou. The following year, she returned with her adult daughter, Jane. An interpreter helped them locate her parents' ancestral village, Gum Jook, and they discovered that a hydraulic power plant had been built there. A driver took them to the plant, wending his way through a countryside of terraced green fields; for the final few miles, they bounced down an unpaved road. A member of the plant's revolutionary committee greeted them. After a brief tour, Mamie and her daughter stood outside, overlooking the river, and watched a

man below fishing and, on the opposite bank, some workers harvesting rice; several boys carried vegetables with poles slung across their
shoulders. She wondered if these were relatives and tried to conjure in
her imagination the place where her parents grew up. She scooped up
some yellow dirt and deposited it into a bag to take home.

During the early twentieth century, a mushrooming movement of nativ-
ists and eugenicists had become increasingly fixated on the racial and
ethnic stock of the immigrants entering the United States, believing the
Anglo-Saxon character of the country was endangered. Chinese exclusion offered them a mason's mold for accomplishing their ends. With
the Chinese question largely settled, politicians, journalists, and other
xenophobes turned to refashioning the language of the anti-Chinese
movement to target other immigrant groups. On the Pacific coast,
attention quickly focused on Japanese immigrants, whose population
was surging. The *San Francisco Chronicle* published a series of editorials
on the "Japanese invasion," arguing "the Japanese is no more assimilable
than the Chinese." In 1907, President Theodore Roosevelt secured a
"Gentlemen's Agreement" with the Empire of Japan, in which government leaders pledged to curb the migration of laborers from the country
to the United States. In 1917, Congress established an "Asiatic Barred
Zone" that stretched from the Middle East to Southeast Asia and
imposed a literacy test on immigrants. During the 1920s, the Ku Klux
Klan re-emerged, this time as a nativist force targeting Catholics, Jews,
Black Americans, and other racial minorities. Eugenics-based arguments declaring the inferiority of Jews, Italians, and other immigrants
from Southern and Eastern Europe began gaining widespread credence.
The Immigration Act of 1924 imposed strict quotas on immigration
from those regions; lawmakers also added a clause excluding "aliens
ineligible for citizenship," a measure that effectively closed off Asian
immigration entirely.

It was amid this atmosphere of rising racial and ethnic animus that a
delegation of Chinese American men arrived in Washington in February 1928. A photograph taken of the group, standing on some marble
steps, shows them clad in Western suits; most of them wear their hair

in combed pompadours. They appear confident and at ease. Standing in the front row is a boyish-looking man in an ill-fitting suit, who is a head shorter than the rest of the group. His name is You Chung Hong. He owed his small stature to a spinal deformity, caused when he was dropped as a baby. At the age of twenty-nine, he was the president of the Los Angeles chapter of what would become known as the Chinese American Citizens Alliance. The group had begun in San Francisco in 1895 as the Native Sons of the Golden State, but its leaders had decided to adopt a new name, as they sought to evolve it into a national organization. Hong's life embodied the new possibilities for native-born Chinese. His father had been a laborer who helped to build the transcontinental railroad. He died when Hong was just five years old, leaving his mother, Lee Shee, to raise a son and a daughter alone, working as a cigar roller and seamstress. Hong attended the Oriental Public School in San Francisco and later Lowell High School and Berkeley High School. After graduation, he moved to Los Angeles, where he taught English to Chinese immigrants and worked as a bookkeeper in Chinese restaurants. In 1918, he became an interpreter in the immigration service. Two years later, he started night classes at the University of Southern California Law School, borrowing textbooks from classmates. In 1923, he became the first Chinese attorney to pass the California state bar exam and launched an immigration law practice.

On the morning of February 7, 1928, Hong testified before the House Committee on Immigration and Naturalization, lobbying for a modification to the 1924 Immigration Act to allow for the admission of Chinese wives of American citizens. Prior to the passage of the act, American-born Chinese had been able to bring over wives from China, but the clause in the act barring entrance of aliens ineligible for citizenship now made the practice impossible. The citizens' alliance had appointed Hong to lead the campaign to amend the law. In a "Plea for Relief," a pamphlet written by Hong, he argued that "a law permanently separating a husband from his wife is an unnatural law, contrary to common humanity and the institutions of civilized society."

During his testimony before the committee, Hong explained that the only available options for a Chinese American man hoping to be married was to go to a state where interracial marriages were legal—

eleven states, including California, Arizona, and Virginia, prohibited it—or travel abroad to marry a white woman who was eligible for citizenship; a third option was to go to China and marry a woman and leave her behind. He characterized the first two choices as "undesirable and inadvisable"—shrewdly playing into fears of miscegenation. The third option, he said, involved "considerable hardship." Two years passed before Congress finally settled on a compromise measure that allowed alien wives married before the Immigration Act went into effect to enter the United States. It was a modest victory, at best, for Hong and his colleagues. Hong seemed to understand, however, the need to calibrate the alliance's goals. In a letter written in 1929 to his future wife, Mabel Chin Quong, an American-born Chinese student at Portland State University, Hong said that he did not believe there was going to be "any great changes" in the Chinese exclusion laws. What he failed to anticipate was a shift in geopolitics.

On December 7, 1941, the Empire of Japan made what would prove to be a profound miscalculation, launching a sneak attack on the United States' naval station at Pearl Harbor. For several years, Japanese leaders had been waging a brutal campaign of military expansion in Asia, first invading China and then occupying northern Indochina. These were strategic conquests, aimed at helping the country achieve economic self-sufficiency. The Roosevelt administration had moved cautiously to try to rein in Japanese aggression, initially imposing economic sanctions and then blocking exports to the country of American-made war material. The steps failed to deter a Japanese incursion into southern Indochina, which then prompted the United States to freeze Japanese assets in the United States and impose an embargo on oil. At Pearl Harbor, Japanese leaders had hoped to scuttle the American Pacific fleet, giving them time to consolidate their territorial gains. Their attack was a stunning success, but they underestimated American fury and resolve. A day after the attack, President Franklin D. Roosevelt addressed a joint session of Congress and declared that the date would "live in infamy"; he promised "absolute victory." An hour later, Congress approved a declaration of war. Four days later, Nazi Germany declared war against the United

States. The outbreak of the Second World War suddenly catapulted China, an impoverished nation-state that was still struggling to modernize, into a vital actor on the international stage.

The latter half of the nineteenth century had been a humiliating period for China, as the Qing empire contended with foreign incursions, internal rebellion, and financial crises. During the early part of the twentieth century, the weakened imperial regime undertook a series of reforms, including upgrading its military and abolishing the examination system that determined who got government positions. On October 10, 1911, a revolt began in central China that eventually led to the overthrow of the Qing court and the establishment of a republican government, under the visionary leadership of Sun Yat-sen. The years that followed were chaotic, as warlords took advantage of the power vacuum and carved out rival fiefdoms. In 1927, the Kuomintang, the Nationalist Party, led by Chiang Kai-shek, managed to unify China but struggled to govern effectively. It soon confronted a dual threat in the form of Communist insurgents, led by Mao Zedong, along with Japan's militaristic advance. In 1937, China's full-scale war of resistance against Japan commenced. Over the next eight years, some fourteen million to twenty million Chinese would die in the conflict.

Several weeks after the attack on Pearl Harbor, the United States, the United Kingdom, and the Soviet Union, along with twenty-two other nations, entered a mutual pact, known as the Joint Declaration of the United Nations. Roosevelt envisioned a postwar order in which the "Four Policemen" would protect "four essential freedoms"—freedom of speech, freedom of worship, freedom from want, and freedom from fear—in their respective spheres of influence. The Roosevelt administration's strategy was to focus first on the war in Europe, while the United States' new ally, China, occupied Japanese troops in the Pacific. Confronting Allied forces, Japanese leaders began to cast the conflict in the Pacific as one of liberation of the Asian people "from Anglo-Saxon imperialists."

Yet the repeal of Chinese exclusion did not take place right away. Racial hysteria swept the West Coast, as suspicion fell on Japanese Americans. On February 19, 1942, President Roosevelt issued Executive Order 9066, commencing a process of forcibly removing tens of thousands of Japanese residents, many of them American citizens, and incarcerating them in concentration camps. Leaders in the Chinese community in San Francisco and Oakland distributed thousands of badges that read, "I am Chinese," or just "China." Business owners posted signs that announced "This is a Chinese Shop." *Time* magazine published "How to Tell Your Friends from the Japs," an article featuring side-by-side photographs of Chinese and Japanese men. The bullet points included: "Japanese are hesitant, nervous in conversation, laugh loudly at the wrong time"; "the Chinese expression is likely to be more placid, kindly, open." The prism of wartime suddenly bifurcated Americans' views of "Asiatics."

In February 1942, *Asia,* a monthly magazine focused on the region, published an article by Charles Nelson Spinks, an East Asia scholar, that called for dealing with the Chinese people "upon a basis of equality." The publishers of *Asia* were Richard J. Walsh, the former editor of *Collier's* magazine and the president of a book publishing company, and his wife, the author Pearl S. Buck, who had won the 1938 Nobel Prize in Literature for *The Good Earth,* her historical novel set in rural China. The couple ran the magazine together from their home in eastern Pennsylvania. Walsh was officially the magazine's editor, but Buck waded through most manuscripts that arrived. Walsh had commissioned the article by Spinks, asking him to elaborate on a memorandum that Walsh had received from Donald Dunham, a former American consular officer in Hong Kong, about the effect of the exclusion laws in China.

In his article, Spinks argued that the United States was waging a war to "build a new world where freedom, justice and equality can survive," yet the country was violating its own fundamental principles. That same month, Buck delivered an address on China at a literary luncheon at the Astor Hotel in New York, warning that Japan was using "our racial prejudice, as her weapon." Buck, who had been born and raised in China by missionary parents and had served as a missionary herself, was an unflinching advocate for racial equality in the United States and believed that these principles needed to be reflected in the war effort. In March, Buck and Walsh traveled to Washington to meet with members of Congress about repealing Chinese exclusion, but came away uncertain about the path forward. "I myself do not know my way around in politics," Walsh confided to a friend. Several weeks later, Walsh and H. J. Timperley, a former Australian newspaperman in China and a public relations adviser to the Nationalist government, met with labor officials to sound them out on the possibility of repeal. Some were openly hostile, but others seemed more amenable, if repeal was beneficial to the war effort. The two men believed a public campaign was necessary. In May, Walsh and Buck joined a small contingent of others eager to dismantle the exclusion laws at a meeting in New York. The group assigned Walsh the task of publicity; several members in California were put in charge of exploring political options. Yet the group moved cautiously. On the eve of Chinese Independence Day, October 10, marking the establishment of the Republic of China, Walsh published an essay in *The New Republic* in which he proposed a "revision of those laws which continue to insult the Chinese," but the members of the group decided it would be unwise to press the matter further ahead of the midterm elections in November. Meanwhile, Japanese war propagandists continued to seize upon the United States' mistreatment of Asian immigrants. A widely distributed leaflet read: "America is China's ally. Americans say they love and admire the Chinese. But can you go to America, can you become citizens? No. Americans do not want you. They just want you to do their fighting."

By the late summer of 1942, Chiang was growing frustrated with his American allies. Despite repeated promises, the military aid arriving in China from the United States had been limited, as the Roosevelt administration pursued a Europe-first approach to the war. Chiang also bristled at the condescension he sensed in his American counterparts during their interactions. Roosevelt had sent a series of envoys to China to mollify Chiang but was also confronting growing isolationism at home. He realized he needed a more direct channel to Chiang and a way to revive support for his internationalist postwar vision.

In September 1942, the first lady, Eleanor Roosevelt, extended an official invitation from the White House to Chiang's Western-educated wife, Soong Mayling, to visit the United States. Madame Chiang, as she was known, was already a celebrated figure in the United States. Clare Boothe Luce, the wife of Henry Luce, the publisher of *Time, Life,* and *Fortune,* had recently hailed her as the "greatest living woman." Her father, Charlie, was born on the island of Hainan in southern China and grew up as an illiterate, impoverished peasant boy. In 1878, at the age of seventeen, he made his way to the United States, in the company of an uncle, a shopkeeper in Boston. Soong converted to Christianity and, with the help of Christian patrons, went on to attend Vanderbilt University, before eventually returning to Shanghai as a Methodist missionary. He married a fellow believer, Ni Kwei-tseng, who belonged to one of the most prominent Christian families in the city. Soong was suddenly part of the city's elite. He quit the ministry and became a wealthy industrialist. The couple reared their three daughters and three sons in China, but Charlie was determined that they be educated in the United States. All three daughters attended the Wesleyan Female College, affiliated with the Methodist Episcopal Church, in Macon, Georgia. Ching-ling, the middle daughter, and Mayling, the youngest, followed their older sister, Eling, to America, in 1907. Mayling was just nine years old at the time. At Wesleyan, a pair of older students tutored Mayling, because the public schools barred Chinese children. She went on to attend Wellesley College in Massachusetts, where she studied English and philosophy. In 1917, she returned to China, where she had to work with tutors to reacquire her fluency in Chinese. In 1926, she met the Generalissimo, as he was known, Chiang Kai-shek, the commander in chief of the Nationalist Army, through her eldest sister. The following year, the couple married in Shanghai, in an opulent wedding attended by more than a thousand guests. During China's war with Japan, she quickly became the country's public face to the Western world.

In late November 1942, Madame Chiang arrived in the United States and checked into a hospital in New York. News accounts reported that she was seeking treatment for an injury she had suffered several years earlier during a car crash on a visit to the front. This was apparently a gilding of her story. She was fatigued and struggling with a variety of health issues. After convalescing for nearly three months, she embarked on a national tour, in which she would captivate Americans with her refined bearing, ivory skin, and fluent English, spoken with a faint Georgia lilt. In Washington, D.C., the first stop on her itinerary, crowds lined Constitution Avenue to catch a glimpse of Madame Chiang as she made her way to the White House, escorted by Eleanor Roosevelt.

On February 18, 1943, she became the first Chinese person and the second woman to ever address Congress. Clad in a slim black dress, with a high collar, and wearing jade earrings, she spoke first, extemporaneously, inside the Senate chamber. "I came to your country as a little girl," she said. "I know your people. I have lived with them. I spent the formative years of my life among your people. I speak your language, not only the language of your hearts, but also your tongue. So coming here today I feel like I am also coming home." Her speech in the House chamber was broadcast nationally. She spoke at the lectern in a lilting, formal cadence. She praised the way in which "devotion to common principles eliminates differences in race" in America and argued that "identity of ideals is the strongest possible solvent of racial dissimilarities." She promised that China would do its part to build "a sane and progressive world society." After her stint in Washington, she returned to New York, where she addressed tens of thousands who had waited for her in freezing temperatures at City Hall Park and then visited Mott Street in Chinatown. The following evening, she spoke in front of seventeen thousand people in Madison Square Garden. Stops in Boston, Chicago, and San Francisco, all before rapturous crowds, followed. On April 4, she culminated her public tour in front of thirty thousand people inside the Hollywood Bowl in Los Angeles.

During her national tour, Madame Chiang was careful to never explicitly criticize the United States for its discriminatory immigration laws. Shortly after her speech at the Hollywood Bowl, however, she met with Wei Tao-ming, China's ambassador to the United States, and urged him to do whatever he could to facilitate legislation repealing Chinese exclusion. In the middle of May, she had dinner with a handful of congressmen on the House Immigration and Naturalization Committee and emphasized the meaningful effect repealing the exclusion laws would have on Chinese morale.

By the spring of 1943, a variety of measures relating to repeal were under consideration in Congress. They included a proposal to strike down all racial restrictions in naturalization; another measure that repealed the Chinese exclusion laws themselves and added China to the broader "Asiatic Barred Zone"; and still another that assigned the Chinese an immigration quota under the 1924 law, conforming their treatment to that of immigrants from Europe. Rep. Walter Judd, a recently elected Minnesota Republican and former medical missionary to China, had called on his colleagues to dismantle the entire regime of discriminatory laws on Asian immigration and naturalization, but he set the legislation aside to focus on winning support for a narrower measure. The House Committee on Immigration and Naturalization announced it would hold hearings in late May on two bills focused solely on Chinese exclusion. Walsh, Buck, and their fellow agitators against Chinese exclusion sprang into action, helping to organize witnesses and gathering names for the establishment of a citizens committee to press for repeal.

When Buck testified before the House committee, on May 20, she emphasized the importance of repeal for the war effort and focused on China's strategic importance. "It is going to be very hard for our men, when they go to China, to feel like friends and act like friends to Chinese," she said. "The wall of this injustice is going to rise higher and higher between our two peoples. Our men will be continually embarrassed by the Chinese questions. 'Why,' the Chinese will ask, 'why are we altogether excluded from your country if you are our friends and allies?'"

The hearings featured fulsome praise from witnesses and supportive congressmen on Chinese valor in their war against Japan, but racism remained a powerful element in the opposition. Rep. A. Leonard Allen, a Louisiana Democrat and staunch segregationist, argued that rolling back Chinese exclusion would open the door to hordes of other Asian immigrants. "Other groups are watching this and if this passes, then before this very session is over, we are going to be confronted with the same demand for the 400,000,000 Hindus or Indians, or whatever you please to call them, and other groups." He explained that Southerners had long had to contend with a "serious minority problem" and warned that letting "orientals generally come into this country" would result in the country having "not one minority problem, but perhaps several minority problems." James L. Wilmeth, national secretary of the national council of the Junior Order of American Mechanics, a nativist organization in Philadelphia, warned of "a great flood" of Chinese immigration that would be "ruinous to our people."

Over the course of a half-dozen hearings in May and June of 1943, the committee heard from fifty-one witnesses; just two of them were people of Chinese descent. On May 27, Paul Yee, an electronics engineer with the War Department, testified briefly in front of the committee. He emphasized that he was not there as a representative of any Chinese organization and, in fact, did not belong to any Chinese organization. He had three brothers and a brother-in-law serving in the American military and was a third-generation American citizen. "Probably not all Americans have met, or are acquainted with an American Chinese who is actually living here and who has become assimilated, and I like to be here just to show you," he said.

Shortly after Yee's testimony, Min Hin Li, a Chinese American physician from Hawaii, recited his own American credentials: born in Hawaii, where he had attended the public schools; college at the University of North Dakota; and medical school at the Jefferson Medical College of Philadelphia. He had also served as commander of the American Legion chapter in Hawaii. He told the committee that he believed he could be most helpful by highlighting the Chinese contributions to the development of Hawaii, "based on the fundamentals of the Chinese character which America esteems—wisdom, loyalty to the adopted land, adaptability, courage, intelligence, perseverance, integrity, social responsibility, and a sense of humor." He pointed out that Chinese from Hawaii had gone on to Harvard, Yale, Princeton, and Tulane, among other elite universities. Both Li and Yee knew the stories they needed to tell of the Chinese in America—not of the cost they'd borne from exclusion but of their triumphs despite it.

During the Second World War, there were nearly eighty thousand Chinese residents in the United States, more than half of whom were American born. It was a transformational moment for many, affording them a chance to assert their Americanness. On the evening of March 17, 1942, as an entire nation tuned into a radio broadcast of the first wartime draft lottery since 1918, Secretary of War Henry Stimson, wearing a blindfold in the auditorium of the Department of Labor, selected from a bowl No. T-3485. In New York City, the number matched just two draft registrants, a Greek-born chef named Anthony Stephen Douris and Chin Fong Ho, a twenty-year-old waiter who lived with three roommates on Bayard Street in Chinatown. Chin, a native of Guangzhou who had only been in the country for three years, was an American citizen through his father. When his number was called, he was at work at a Brooklyn Chinese restaurant. "I'm glad to get a chance to get a crack at the Japs," he said, when interviewed by reporters. "The sooner the better for me." Chin posed for photographs alongside portraits of Chiang Kai-shek and General Douglas MacArthur; another image depicted him in a suit and tie, holding a bowl and chopsticks, accompanied by the crisscrossing flags of the United States and China. As many as fifteen thousand Chinese Americans would go on to join the armed services.

Thousands of Chinese Americans also found work in the country's defense industries. In an article for the magazine *The Survey Graphic,* published in October 1942, Rose Hum Lee, a pioneering Chinese American lecturer from Butte, Montana, reported that Chinatowns across the country were experiencing labor shortages from the absorption of Chinese into American industry. In Lee's community of Butte, there were eleven Chinese Americans of draft age. All had enlisted or found another way to serve the war effort. Lee was at pains to emphasize how assimilated many Chinese Americans already were. She argued the war was another "stepping stone" along that path. "The crisis of December 7 has emancipated the Chinese in the United States," she wrote. "It is up to the American people to effect the emancipation by law."

At the end of the House hearings, the committee was divided. A majority of the committee, which consisted of eleven Democrats and ten Republicans, supported repealing the Chinese exclusion laws, but the members disagreed over the issue of allocating an annual immigration quota to Chinese immigrants. The national-origins quota system, established under the 1924 law, permitted annual immigration by nation at two percent of population levels in the United States during the 1890 census. Labor officials feared that legions of Chinese would slip into the country by way of Latin America or Hong Kong, which fell under the expansive British annual quota. To address these concerns, repeal supporters crafted a race-based formula, in which all Chinese immigrants, no matter where they were born, would be placed under a single quota. Nevertheless, the committee tabled the matter until after the Congress's summer recess.

The newly organized Citizens Committee for the Repeal of Chinese Exclusion, which elected Richard Walsh as its chairman, suggested to its members that the recess would give them time to step up pressure on congressmen in their home districts. By the middle of August, the committee had 223 members from thirty-two states. The committee produced a pamphlet, "Our Chinese Wall," outlining the case for repeal, and distributed over twenty thousand copies to libraries, labor unions, religious organizations, and others.

The Citizens Committee, notably, lacked visible involvement by anyone of Chinese descent. The committee decided, for strategic reasons, that membership should be restricted to non-Asians. This way, it would be easier to make the case that it was *Americans* who wanted to change the law. The committee's files contain hints of Chinese American involvement behind the scenes. A Chinese American optometrist in Lansing, Michigan, asked for a hundred copies of "Our Chinese Wall" to distribute. Dai-Ming Lee, the editor of a Chinese newspaper in Hawaii, sent regular reader contributions to the committee. In all, Chinese in Hawaii donated $1,100, accounting for more than a quarter of the committee's total. A report to members dated September 20, 1943, also noted that Donald Dunham, the former member of the consular service in Hong Kong whose memo had helped to launch the committee's work, was helping to organize Chinese Americans "to support repeal in the most effective way possible," but the effort was later abandoned.

On October 7, the House immigration committee reconvened and voted to advance the measure introduced by Representative Warren Magnuson, a Washington state Democrat, that repealed the exclusion laws, made Chinese eligible for naturalization, and imposed a single racial quota for Chinese immigration. The committee's report made clear that China was not being placed on a "full quota parity basis" with

European immigrants. Under the bill's formulation, only 105 Chinese persons would be permitted to enter the country every year. The report also suggested that the number of Chinese who would be eligible for naturalization was "negligible," because most Chinese in the United States had never been admitted for lawful permanent residence, which precluded them from gaining citizenship.

The *Chinese Press,* a weekly English-language tabloid in San Francisco, covered the repeal issue closely. Most Chinese Americans, however, seemed to recognize that the legislation was largely symbolic. Gilbert Woo, a columnist for the *Chinese Times,* the organ of the Chinese American Citizens Alliance, published a satirical column in the fall of 1943 that poked fun at objections to the admitting of such a limited number of Chinese immigrants. "In number there are not enough of you to make up a full set of mahjong tiles; yet in power you can scoop up the moon's reflection in the water," he wrote. "Do you know that an American boxer claims he can take on 100 men? So actually, they can summon a boxer and he alone can beat you black and blue in the face. And yet, believe it or not, just hearing about you strikes terror into the hearts of millions of Americans."

On October 11, President Roosevelt issued a message to Congress urging the passage of the bill. He framed the measure "as important in the cause of winning the war and establishing a secure peace" and cast it as an opportunity to "correct a historic mistake and silence the distorted Japanese propaganda." The measure sailed through the House and Senate. On December 3, a cablegram of appreciation from Madame Chiang was read on the House floor. Two weeks later, after returning from a meeting in Cairo about the Pacific war with Generalissimo Chiang and his wife, along with British prime minister Winston Churchill, President Roosevelt signed the bill into law. The reaction from the Chinese community was muted. Some Chinese American groups issued statements of appreciation; in Hawaii, Chinese Americans purchased more than a million dollars in war bonds "to give concrete evidence of their thanks to America." Fifty years later, the Chinese American historian Him Mark Lai, who was in San Francisco at the time, recalled that there were no public celebrations marking the milestone.

CHAPTER 25

Confession

Suspicion has a way of departing reluctantly. After the war, a booming American economy propelled a small cohort of educated, second-
generation Chinese Americans into the middle class. Many found jobs
in science and technical fields; some even joined the managerial ranks.
The newly affluent also began to move out of Chinatowns and settle
in suburban neighborhoods, even as some white homeowners tried to
repel them. Yet legal progress for Chinese Americans came haltingly.
In late 1945, Congress approved the so-called War Brides Act, a measure written primarily to benefit European spouses of American service
members. The bill was designed to be temporary, speeding the screening
process for military spouses seeking to enter the United States under
existing immigration laws. The following year, leaders from the Chinese
community lobbied for equitable treatment of the Chinese wives of
American citizens, pressing lawmakers for legislation admitting them to
the country beyond the tiny quota allocation for Chinese immigration.
During the hearings on the bill, lawmakers fretted about the number
of Chinese bachelors who might return to China to marry and bring
their wives over. In the end, Senator William F. Knowland, a California
Republican and ardent supporter of Nationalist China during the war,
offered reassurance in his report on the bill: "It is not anticipated that
many Chinese wives will be involved." On August 11, 1946, President
Truman signed the legislation into law. A year later, Congress expanded

the War Brides Act to cover other racially ineligible spouses, primarily from other countries in Asia.

Over the next few years, tens of thousands of European spouses would arrive in the United States, but immigration officials would fixate on a much smaller influx from China. Between 1946 and 1950, more than seven thousand Chinese wives entered the country, beginning a metamorphosis of the Chinese community from a bachelor society into one anchored by families. Most of these arrivals were not young brides but women who had been living alone for years, waiting for their husbands who had gone to Gold Mountain. Upon landing in the United States, many endured prolonged detentions as skeptical immigration inspectors and interpreters struggled to keep up with the onslaught of cases. A fire in 1940, believed to have been caused by an overloaded circuit, had forced the closure of the immigration station at Angel Island. Immigration officials in San Francisco had subsequently moved their detention quarters to a new building on Sansome Street, which it shared with a dozen other federal agencies. The building was sixteen stories tall, towering over the rest of the neighborhood; the terra cotta exterior gave it the austere look of a standard office building. The Immigration and Naturalization Service occupied the uppermost floors. Women and children were housed together on the thirteenth floor; male prisoners over the age of twelve were assigned to the floor below. There were bars on the windows and guards posted everywhere. With the backlog of wives' cases, the accommodations quickly became overcrowded. I. F. Wixon, the district director of immigration, later complained to his superiors that the facility was "ill-adapted in every respect for the lengthy detention of persons." As early as January 1947, veterans and civil liberties organizations complained that Chinese wives were being held incommunicado for weeks at a time. Some detentions lasted more than a year. Immigration officials blamed the delays on the limited number of interpreters and the fact that the wives lacked proper documents. With five or six hundred Chinese arrivals every month, most of them women, the delays persisted. The despair inside rose, like stormwater in a cistern.

Around three o'clock in the afternoon on June 1, 1948, a distraught forty-one-year-old woman, Wong Loy, clad in tattered black pajamas and barefoot, edged out onto a narrow ledge, fourteen stories above Sansome Street. Wong had been in federal custody for nearly six months. She had journeyed to America to join her husband, Gin Hop, an herbal medicine doctor in Aberdeen, Washington. A pair of Chinese attorneys, along with immigration officials, speaking through interpreters, tried to coax Wong back to safety. On a lower floor, firemen rigged a makeshift net. Hundreds of onlookers gathered on the street, transfixed by the drama above. Finally, John Breen, a police inspector, wriggled out on the ledge on his stomach and managed to grab Wong. Afterward, he waved to the throngs. "I had a dinner date and got tired of waiting," he told a reporter. Several days later, immigration officials paroled Wong and allowed her to join her husband.

At the end of June, a thirty-two-year-old Chinese woman from Tai-shan, Leong Bick Ha, arrived in the Sansome building, accompanied by her fourteen-year-old son, Eng Lung Tuck. Inspectors quickly separated mother and child. Leong was hoping to be reunited with her husband, Eng Bak Teung, a former army sergeant who was working at a Chinese restaurant in Atlantic City. The couple had married sixteen years earlier. After interviewing Leong and taking a statement from her husband in New York, however, inspectors began to doubt aspects of their story. On Friday, September 17, Leong appeared before the Board of Special Inquiry. She had not eaten for several days and told her examiner that she was too weak to testify. The board recalled her on Monday, but she once again begged off, saying she could not swallow food. The chairman of the board told her that her husband was due to arrive by plane the next day and dismissed her. A doctor prescribed sedatives and assigned her to a semi-private room with several other female prisoners. A security officer checked on her every fifteen to twenty minutes, but just before two o'clock in the morning Leong's roommates alerted the officer that something was wrong. Leong had barricaded herself inside a bathroom. When guards kicked in the door, they found Leong had hanged herself with a rope from a shower rod. More than a hundred other Chinese women who were being held inside the building waged a brief hunger strike to protest her treatment. "These things never last long," Wixon later told reporters. "Usually they get pretty hungry after one day." Immigration officials promptly paroled Leong Bick Ha's son, pending the adjudication of his case. In 1951, a district court finally declared him an American citizen. The outcry over his mother's death helped to pressure immigration officials into ending the lengthy detentions of Chinese brides.

A new era of apprehension was beginning. In the aftermath of the Second World War, American foreign policy shifted to a global contest for influence with the Soviet Union. The policy of Communist containment reshaped American priorities, at home and abroad. On October 1, 1949, Mao Zedong, the leader of the Chinese Communist Party, proclaimed the establishment of the People's Republic of China, ending nearly two decades of internecine warfare between Communist insurgents and the Kuomintang army. Chiang Kai-shek and his Nationalist government retreated to Taiwan. The Truman administration refused to recognize Mao's government and withdrew its diplomatic personnel. A year later, the two countries went to war, after Mao decided to enter the conflict on the Korean peninsula and dispatched Chinese forces to join the Soviet-backed North Korean army in repelling "American imperialists."

After the Communist takeover in China, only the American consulate in Hong Kong remained open, because the island was a British territory. Its primary mission was to serve as a listening post, gleaning intelligence on the intentions of Mao's government. It was here, far away from any oversight of concerned citizens in the United States, that a new exclusion regime would take shape. This time the imperative was national security.

During the Second World War, the State Department had required that in China, Chinese claiming American citizenship who were seeking to emigrate first apply for passports at American consulates. In the late 1940s, as the Communists advanced southward, thousands had descended upon consulates in Shanghai and Guangzhou, swamping consular officials. A backlog of several thousand passport applications wound up the responsibility of a single vice consul in Hong Kong. The consulate processed applications at a sluggish rate, about two a day.

On February 9, 1950, a relatively unknown junior senator from Wisconsin named Joseph McCarthy delivered a speech at a Lincoln Day dinner in Wheeling, West Virginia. McCarthy warned that the country was engaged in an apocalyptic struggle, a "final, all-out battle" with "communistic atheism." In McCarthy's telling, the biggest threat was from within. "Here in my hand," he proclaimed, was a list of 205 members of the Communist Party inside the State Department. Paranoia about Communist infiltration would soon consume the country.

In August 1950, the State Department, in consultation with immigration officials and the Department of Justice, implemented onerous new requirements for passport applicants in Hong Kong. Those claiming citizenship through an American father needed to provide affidavits in triplicate from him, another set of affidavits in triplicate by a "reputable United States citizen," and then conclusive evidence of the father's citizenship. Types of evidence suggested by the State Department included an identifying witness, "preferably an American citizen, who is well and favorably known to the consular office"; letters from parents or relatives in the United States; and a birth certificate issued by local authorities or a reputable hospital. The result was a kind of double jeopardy, specific to Chinese American immigrants, in which they endured scrutiny on both sides of the Pacific. The consulate introduced a blood-testing protocol, using applicants' blood types to evaluate paternity claims, and took X-rays of bones and joints to verify applicants' age. "These indignities are not inflicted on persons of any other race than Chinese," an immigration lawyer said during a congressional hearing.

The applicants typically hailed from rural villages in the interior of China; they were required to travel to the consulate to register in person. Unless they possessed incontrovertible documentation—very few did— their names were placed on a waiting list, and they were sent away. Usually, it would be several years before consular officials contacted them for an interview; afterward, the applicant would have to wait another few months, as consular officials consulted with immigration authorities in the United States and investigated their case further.

The number of consular officers processing applications quickly grew to ten, then twenty, then fifty, and continued to climb. In May 1952, the consulate established an investigative unit that specialized in exhaustive, "full field" investigations. Edward Ingraham, a young consular officer who had joined the Foreign Service after serving in the army during the Second World War, arrived in Hong Kong in 1950. He sympathized with the Chinese applicants he spent his days interviewing, thinking many "would make damn good citizens," he later recalled. Nevertheless, it was his responsibility to puncture the elaborate fictions that many had constructed to claim American citizenship. "Our job was to try to trip them up and prove that their claim was false," he said. "Now they knew the claim was false, we knew that they knew the claim was false, and they knew that we knew that the claim was false. So it was the sort of game that went on and on and on. Sometimes you won and sometimes they won." The workload was punishing. Jerome Holloway, a political officer who joined the consulate in 1952, later recalled about his overburdened colleagues in the consular section: "You had twenty-five thousand Chinese claiming American citizenship, that they had to deal with."

In July 1953, the United States, North and South Korea, and China signed an armistice ending the Korean War. The following year, Everett F. Drumright, a longtime China hand whose first posting in the country was in 1932, became the American consul general in Hong Kong. Drumright, an imposing, aloof presence with steel-blue eyes, was a political survivor. After China fell to the Communists, many in the American diplomatic corps in China came under attack during the recriminations of the McCarthy era. Drumright's staunchly conservative views—he was known to colleagues as "Drum," but some joked that the other half of his surname was a better descriptor—helped him continue his ascent through the diplomatic ranks. He was an exacting boss, stubborn about protocol. On December 9, 1955, he sent an eighty-nine-page dispatch to Washington, "Report on the Problem of Fraud at Hong Kong," which characterized the "'immigration family' racket" among Chinese emigrants as a vast criminal conspiracy that posed "a serious problem of national security." Drumright estimated that more than 80 percent of passport applicants in Hong Kong were lying in their citizenship claims and charged that almost any Chinese with financial means could purchase entrance into the United States for as little as $3,000. His assessment was filled with familiar racist tropes about Chinese people, suggesting that they were by nature deceptive because they lacked the "concept of an oath." He called for denials of virtually all applications.

In a series of columns, Dai-Ming Lee, who had taken over as the publisher and managing editor of *Chinese World* in San Francisco's Chinatown at the end of the Second World War, excoriated Drumright's report as based on a "deep-seated anti-Chinese attitude." Lee argued there was scant evidence of wholesale fraud. The report "should provide Hollywood with scores of melodramatic plots," Lee wrote. Drumright's report would circulate widely in the federal government and have profound consequences on Chinese emigration and on the Chinese population in the United States. Congress earmarked $500,000 to expand the investigative unit in Hong Kong, which ultimately employed more than a hundred investigators, many of them former FBI agents or people with investigative experience from other federal agencies. The unit was brazen in its tactics, conducting surprise, pre-dawn raids of residences. "Members of this Fraud Unit did things and went places in a way which would have raised the hair on the neck of civil libertarians," William Andreas Brown, a commercial officer who arrived in the consulate in 1956, later recalled. The fraud unit assembled an extensive library of family records from the districts in Guangdong province where most of the emigration to America originated and cultivated a far-flung network of paid informants.

On February 14, 1956, federal prosecutors in New York announced that a special grand jury had been impaneled to hear evidence on a nationwide, "million-dollar-a-year" passport fraud racket that had smuggled some two thousand Chinese immigrants a year into the country since 1950. The scheme allegedly involved rings operating in San Francisco, New York, Boston, and Baltimore. Paul W. Williams, the United States attorney in New York, said investigators had evidence that some were Communist agents with "concealed skills," planted by the Chinese government. Around the same time, prosecutors in San Francisco convened their own grand jury to investigate a different citizenship scheme in their city. Their probe began with an unprecedented legal incursion.

On March 1, more than two dozen leaders of San Francisco's Chinatown family associations assembled outside the jury room on the fourth floor of the ornate United States Post Office and Courthouse building on Mission Street in San Francisco. They had been ordered to appear by government subpoena. Some of the men carried leather-bound volumes that resembled business ledgers; others bore thick packets of rice paper, or pasteboard boxes full of records. Prosecutors believed the family association membership rolls contained information that would be helpful in disrupting a fraud ring that had been going on for years. Chow Lip Sing, secretary of the Gee Tuck Sam Tuck family association, was the first to be escorted into the grand jury room. Overnight, the Chinese Six Companies had retained lawyers for the associations. On their advice, Chow Lip Sing refused to surrender his records, contending the subpoena he'd received was overly broad. A recess was called, and the parties appeared before a federal judge, who ordered the records be impounded. Several days later, the grand jury summoned the owners of a half-dozen photography studios in Chinatown and ordered them to relinquish all group photographs they'd taken over the past fifteen years. Fear settled over Chinatowns on both coasts. Restaurants and businesses emptied; many organizations canceled their Chinese New Year parties; in New York, a group of Chinatown businessmen met with Williams and told him they were losing a hundred thousand dollars in revenue a week. The Chinese Six Companies told reporters that the sole purpose behind the subpoenas was "oppressing and intimidating the entire Chinese-American community in San Francisco." Chinese leaders in New York sent telegrams to the White House, the State Department, and congressional leaders. In late March, after hearing legal arguments, the judge granted the associations' motion to quash the subpoenas, calling them a "mass inquisition." Yet prosecutors continued to pursue their probes, in concert with investigators from the immigration service.

Over the coming months, prosecutors would bring charges against nearly sixty defendants: a group of laundrymen in New York, accused of making false statements on their passport applications; a sixty-five-year-old dishwasher in Oregon, who prosecutors said had pretended to be the father of four children in China, creating immigration slots for them; a cook and his wife, who both worked for a State Department legal adviser, charged in a similar scheme involving one son. None approached the vast conspiracy that prosecutors had trumpeted. The most high-profile case involved a fifty-seven-year-old businessman and civic leader in Chinatown, Sing Kee, as he was known, who prosecutors said was the largest broker of fictitious immigration slots on the East Coast. Lau Sing Kee was born in January 1896, in Saratoga, California. His grandfather had come to America during the gold rush; Sing Kee's father worked as a labor agent, supplying workers to ranches and mines. The family later moved to San Jose, where his father operated a cigar store. Sing Kee went to China and married; he and his wife had a son. He returned to America alone and settled in New York's Chinatown. When war broke out in Europe, Sing Kee enlisted in the army in 1917, becoming one of more than a hundred Chinatown residents who would serve. Sing Kee joined G Company, 306th Infantry, assigned to the 77th Division. The division endured brutal, unrelenting combat in northern France. In the middle of August 1918, Sing Kee's company was stationed in the village of Mont Notre Dame, when it began experiencing heavy bombardment from a German counteroffensive. Sing Kee's commanding officer ordered the company to withdraw, but Sing Kee refused to abandon his post at a regimental message center and single-handedly held out in the town for hours, as German mustard gas and explosive shells rained down. He hurtled back and forth, dodging machine-gun fire and artillery shells, to deliver messages. A few days later, a mustard gas attack left him severely wounded. For his bravery, Sing Kee received the distinguished service cross. He came home to a hero's welcome in San Jose. After the war, he took a job as an interpreter for the Immigration and Naturalization Service in Cleveland and then on Ellis Island. He later opened a thriving business on Mott Street as an immigration broker and travel agent. He also became active in Democratic politics in Chinatown and served on Chinatown's draft board. He and his wife, Ina Chan, raised five children. Prosecutors accused him of using his travel agency to orchestrate hundreds of fraudulent passport applications, clearing at least $23,000 in two years in the scheme—hardly the million-dollar-a-year bonanza they'd first announced. Sing Kee was found guilty and sentenced to two and a half years in prison. He appealed his case all the way to the U.S. Supreme Court, which declined to take up his case. He served his time in a federal prison in Danbury, Connecticut, and died in 1967. Several years later, a longtime Chinese journalist, Y. K. Chu, asserted that witnesses against Sing Kee had made up their testimony in exchange for having their citizenship statuses adjusted. In 1997, Sing Kee's remains, along with those of his wife, were interred at Arlington National Cemetery.

With every arrest, prosecutors boasted of closing fraudulent "slots." These were the holes in the fence, the apparent vulnerabilities in America's defenses. In 1956, immigration officials began reaching out to the Chinese community, suggesting that if individuals came forward and acknowledged their illegal status, they might be eligible for naturalization, based on military service, or some other form of "discretionary relief." Notices materialized all over Chinatown in San Francisco. An immigration official announced details of the program at a banquet in New York's Chinatown. No promises were made, so many "paper sons" remained wary, but the idea was that they could have their legal status adjusted and immigration officials could close more immigration slots. In the immigration service's annual reports, officials boasted of their "great strides" in overcoming the "Chinese fraud problem" through the confession program, as it became known.

The opportunity to finally emerge from behind the invented identities that many immigrants had constructed was a relief to some families. In April 1984, an elderly man who asked that he only be identified by his last name, "Mock," sat for an oral history interview for a documentary on Angel Island and described his experience as a paper son. He'd arrived in the United States in May 1937, at the age of eighteen, harboring grand visions of wealth. His father had agreed to pay $1,600 for a falsified passport and birth certificate that established American ancestry for his son. The family had paid a third of the fee up front, borrowing money against land they owned in China. The rest was due upon landing. Mock's father raised most of the funds from relatives and friends. Before the trip, Mock's paper father—the man whose name was on the identity papers the family had purchased—gave him a coaching book to memorize. Immigration officials detained Mock for ten months on Angel Island, before finally landing him. During the Second World War, Mock joined the army and had the chance to correct his papers, but he didn't think his legal status posed a problem. He finally grew worried during the terror that came with the 1950s probes. "They search everywhere," he recalled. In 1964, a paper brother who had come to America with Mock told him that he was planning to enter the confession program and urged him to join him. By then, Mock had children. They would have to come forward too. In the end, Mock described a great burden being lifted. "Before I was always worried about some immigration officer will come to my house and start to ask me questions," he said. "Now we are being truthful and honest."

Since so many paper-son stories were interlocking, each confession carried the potential of implicating dozens of others. They were like hidden grenades. Both paper and actual families could fall within their lethal radius. The confession of a single eighty-year-old man, Huey Bing Dai, led to an entire clan, some two hundred and fifty people from a single village, Sai Kee, in Taishan, coming forward. Then there were stories like that of the Cheung family. Cheung Tong Wai was the son of a rice farmer in a coastal village. In 1921, at the age of twenty-five, he sailed across the Pacific under a new identity: Jung Tong, the second son of Jung Chong, an American citizen. In America, Jung Tong made a living harvesting asparagus and then became a family cook. He later returned to China and married a woman from Zhuhai, Chuck Yook King. The couple had a daughter and three sons. After the war, the family was reunited in America, bound together by a chain of falsehoods. In 1961, the chain broke when an immigration officer tricked Jung's elder paper brother into a confession. "Afterwards, he called my father, but by then, it was too late," Jung's daughter, Laura Lai, later recalled. "Everything was out." Her father fled to Hong Kong, hoping to protect the citizenship status of his children. Lai lost her citizenship for ten years; her brothers went through similar ordeals. Her mother, ailing from diabetes, stayed in the United States but later decided to go back to Hong Kong to join her husband. She passed away shortly afterward. Lai's father was then struck by liver cancer. He negotiated with immigration authorities for permission to re-enter the country to see his family for a final time. He died on April 5, 1963, a week after his arrival back in the United States.

The confession program formally ended in 1966. Immigration officials reported nearly fourteen thousand Chinese confessions, implicating more than twenty-two thousand other Chinese who'd entered the country without proper documents, enabling the closure of more than eleven thousand immigration slots. This was how success was measured, by the number of future aliens kept out. Exclusion was at an end, but its legacy lingered.

Epilogue

The door opened almost by accident. In 1952, restrictionist law-makers overcame President Harry S. Truman's veto and enacted the McCarran-Walter Act, retaining the immigration quota system. The measure included some liberalizing provisions, such as the introduction of modest allowances for the "Asia-Pacific triangle" and the elimination of racial barriers on naturalization, but Truman castigated the bill as a "slur on the patriotism, the capacity, and the decency of a large part of our citizenry." Among the lawmakers who opposed the measure was a slender, tousle-haired congressman named John F. Kennedy, who represented a working-class, predominantly Italian district in Boston. Throughout his time in public life, Kennedy, the great-grandson of Irish Catholic immigrants, would nurse a commitment to reforming the country's immigration laws. In 1958, after becoming Massachusetts's junior senator, he wrote an essay entitled "A Nation of Immigrants," which praised their contributions to America and called for a "generous," "fair," and "flexible" immigration policy. On July 23, 1963, as president of the United States, he sent a detailed proposal to Congress for a new immigration system that "serves the national interest and reflects in every detail the principles of equality and human dignity to which our nation subscribes." The measure faced a difficult path in Congress. Four months later, Kennedy was assassinated.

His successor, Lyndon Johnson, grew up amid the grinding poverty and isolation of the Texas Hill Country. He had never demonstrated particular interest in overhauling the immigration system. As a senator, in fact, he had voted to override Truman's veto of the McCarran-Walter Act. Nevertheless, he saw himself as a steward of Kennedy's agenda and was determined to muscle it through Congress. In the Senate, Johnson had been a transformational majority leader, a master at the horse trading, ruthlessness, and flattery that it took to pass legislation. During his first State of the Union speech, delivered seven weeks after Kennedy was killed, Johnson identified a series of priorities, including the passage of civil rights legislation, an "all-out war on human poverty," and lifting the "bars of discrimination" in the nation's immigration preferences.

In the spring and summer of 1964, an epic legislative struggle culminated with the enactment of the most comprehensive civil rights law since Reconstruction. The following year, the Johnson administration turned to the immigration overhaul. On the surface, the effort carried the same moral valence: it was no longer acceptable to use race, ethnicity, or national origin as the criteria for deciding who should be admitted to the United States. Yet a crucial argument made by supporters of the legislation—one that would prove essential for its passage—was that it would not upend the country's racial status quo. The message they sought to convey was that this was an essential change, one that was consonant with the nation's values and necessary for advancing the country's interests abroad, but one that would not dramatically alter the American fabric.

The Immigration and Nationality Act of 1965, as the measure became known, proposed to abolish the national-origins quota system and prioritize the relatives of U.S. citizens and permanent residents, as well as immigrants with skills and "exceptional ability" in various fields. "The bill will not flood our cities with immigrants," Senator Edward Kennedy, who presided over Senate hearings on the legislation, reassured his colleagues. "It will not upset the ethnic mix of our society." Representative Emanuel Celler, the bill's House sponsor and chairman of the Judiciary Committee, explained that the need to compete "quantitatively and qualitatively" for immigration preference and the math underlying the family reunification system meant little would change. "There will not be, comparatively, many Asians or Africans entering this country," he said. "Since the people of Africa and Asia have very few relatives here, comparatively few could immigrate from those countries because they have no family ties in the U.S."

Representative Michael Feighan, the chairman of the House immigration subcommittee, was a staunch anti-Communist and an abrasive personality who enjoyed support from nativist groups that still supported the quota system. Feighan, an Ohio Democrat, had held up the administration's bill in his subcommittee for months, while engaged in a power struggle with Celler over control of immigration policy. Under heavy pressure from officials in the Johnson administration, including the president himself, Feighan finally allowed the legislation to proceed, but he secured from the Johnson administration an agreement to tilt the preference system towards family reunification, believing that this would help ensure that the country's existing racial and ethnic composition was preserved.

On October 3, 1965, President Johnson signed the immigration overhaul into law on Liberty Island in New York Harbor. The ceremony took place about seventy-five yards from the Statue of Liberty, whose raised torch offered welcome to "the huddled masses yearning to breathe free." Yet the president opened his remarks by emphasizing that this was "not a revolutionary bill. It does not affect the lives of millions. It will not reshape the structure of our daily lives." Johnson proclaimed that the new law fixed "a deep and painful flaw in the fabric of American justice." He also summoned the American mythology around immigration: "Today we can all believe that the lamp of this grand old lady is brighter today—and the golden door she guards gleams more brilliantly in the light of an increased liberty for people from all countries."

President Johnson and others would turn out to be wrong about who would come through the door. The law—actually, a series of amendments to the McCarran-Walter Act—would unleash a tide of immigration from Asia, Africa, and Latin America, and set in motion a demographic transformation of the country that is still unfolding today. By 1970, the Chinese population in the United States would grow to more than 430,000 people, almost double what it had been a decade earlier. The number would continue to double every ten years until the end of the century. Since 1965, about a quarter of immigrants to the United States have been Asian. They have become the country's fastest-growing ethnic population. Today, there are more than five million Chinese Americans in the United States.

I owe my American story to this accident of history. My dad came to America in 1967 as a doctoral student in electrical engineering at Northwestern University in suburban Chicago. My mother, who arrived a few years later, studied for a master's degree in accounting at Western Illinois University, a several-hour drive away. They met at a party in Evanston for Chinese students. Their emigration stories trace a similar path. Ancestors on both sides of my family hailed from Hunan province, in central China. Both of my parents fled the mainland as children during the Communist revolution. My paternal grandfather was a general in the Kuomintang army and disappeared in 1948, while fighting Communist forces in a mountainous region in Yunnan province. His body was never found. My grandmother raised my father and his five siblings in Tainan, a small city in the southern part of Taiwan, relying on the meager income and food rations provided by the Nationalist government. My mother's side of the family experienced their own wartime traumas. My maternal grandmother lost two babies in infancy during the war with Japan, before she gave birth to my mother and uncle. The family never spoke of the loss. In Taiwan, my grandfather was a mid-level official in the forest service. When my mother and uncle were old enough to stay home alone, my grandmother went back to work, eventually becoming a telephone operator at Taiwan's first television broadcasting company, where she stayed until she retired. She then joined her offspring in the United States.

When I asked my parents about their decision to venture to a strange land as young adults, neither recalled it as much of a choice. In the late 1960s, the island of Taiwan was still underdeveloped. Its emergence as one of Asia's economic dragons was still years away. Job opportunities for educated young people were limited. Many of my parents' classmates were going to the United States. (The exodus would become known as Taiwan's "brain drain.") They went, too.

Around the time both of my parents arrived in Illinois, *The New York Times* published an article with the headline "Orientals Find Bias

Is Down Sharply in U.S." The article's main protagonist was a balding, fifty-one-year-old corporate executive, Jeffrey Chuan Chu. He was born in Tienjin, China, into a family of scholars. At the end of the Second World War, he came to the United States to study engineering at the University of Minnesota. At the time, he had trouble finding a place to live, because of his Chinese background, but the article touted the turnaround in Chu's life. He had since become a vice president at Honeywell Information Systems and lived in the affluent suburb of Wellesley, Massachusetts. "If you have ability and can adapt to the American way of speaking, dressing, and doing things," Chu told the reporter, "then it doesn't matter any more if you are Chinese." The article proclaimed the "almost total disappearance of discrimination" against both the Chinese and Japanese American populations in the United States and their seamless "assimilation into the mainstream of American life." Yet there were signs that this tale of transformation was not necessarily what it seemed. The article noted that Chu had been denied admission to the Wellesley Country Club. A spokesman for the club denied any discrimination but conceded that "the club at present had no members of oriental ancestry."

The article makes for a useful artifact, capturing mythmaking in the middle of its manufacture. During the Cold War years, a narrative of Asian American ascent began to take hold in the country. The historian Ellen D. Wu traces its origins to the contest of moral suasion taking place around the globe with Soviet totalitarianism. The turbulence over the civil rights of Black Americans had complicated efforts by American policymakers to portray the United States as a beacon of freedom and opportunity for all. The story of a different minority group freeing itself of discrimination's shackles presented an opportunity to renovate the country's image. While the status of Asian Americans had improved, progress had hardly proceeded in a straight line and the community remained beset by problems like poverty and racial discrimination. In 1974, the sociologist Stanford Lyman highlighted an array of studies that suggested Chinese Americans still encountered "considerable discrimination in both private and public sectors." Lyman described a "bipolar" situation facing the Chinese community. A highly visible contingent of mostly American-born and college-educated Chinese had found success in select fields, even as most in the community continued to work in menial jobs.

Many who have been part of the modern wave of Asian immigration have been highly educated or skilled. Their economic success has shaped perceptions of Asian Americans as the "model minority," proof of the possibilities of assimilation and racial progress. It's a misleading characterization, one that obscures other realities. In New York City, where I live, nearly one in four Asian Americans lives below the poverty line. The surge in harassment, violence, and other racist attacks against Asian Americans during the COVID-19 pandemic was merely the latest evidence of the brittleness of the model minority narrative.

The complicated racial dynamics resulting from Asian immigration to the Western world have not gone away. The years from the California gold rush to Congress's decision to make Chinese exclusion permanent coincided with a humbling period for China, as it contended with foreign incursions, internal rebellions, and financial crises. Today, by contrast, China is an economic, political, and military juggernaut, vying with the United States for global influence. This has raised anew the bugbear of the unassimilable Other in our midst. In 2023, Florida enacted a law prohibiting many Chinese citizens from buying property in the state. Lawmakers in dozens of other states weighed similar measures or imposed their own anti-Chinese restrictions. The echoes of Senator John Franklin Miller's warnings about the "oriental invader" are unmistakable.

Our family's immigration story has been one of upward mobility. What does it mean, then, that our existence in America still sometimes feels conditional? That the precarity of the Asian American experience still seems never far away? Once we begin to understand what anti-Asian racism has looked like throughout American history, the contradictions start to become less perplexing. Overt discrimination against Chinese and other Asian immigrants is no longer legally sanctioned, and violent expulsions of Chinese are a matter of history, but for many Asian Americans a sense of belonging remains elusive.

Acknowledgments

For thirteen years, my journalistic home was *The New York Times*. Towards the end of my tenure there, I was part of an initiative that brought together reporters and editors across the newsroom to cover race in America. It was Marc Lacey, then the national editor, and Rachel Swarns, a talented reporter and historian herself, who encouraged me in the fall of 2016 to write "An Open Letter to the Woman Who Told My Family to Go Back to China," which was initially published online and then on the front page of the newspaper, generating an enormous reader response. I'm grateful to Matt Purdy and Dean Baquet, for their unusual decision to put the letter on A-1, and Marc and Rachel, because that short reflection was what set me on the path to writing this book.

Yet it was not until the spring of 2021, when reports of anti-Asian violence were surging across the country, that I began to think of writing a narrative history. Drawing on several books, I wrote an essay for *The New Yorker* about the bigotry and violence experienced by the Chinese in America during the nineteenth century. It marked the beginning of the intellectual journey that became *Strangers in the Land*. Over the course of more than three years of research and writing, my collection of books on Chinese immigration to the United States and the Chinese American experience—by scholars like Him Mark Lai, Mae Ngai, Erika Lee, Gordon Chang, Beth Lew-Williams, Judy Yung, Liping Zhu, Yong Chen, Sucheng Chan, Charles J. McClain, Andrew Gyory, Lucy E. Salyer, Madeline Hsu, Haiming Liu, Paul C. P. Siu, John Kuo Wei Tchen, Xiaojian Zhao, K. Scott Wong, Henry Tsai Shih-shan, Jane H. Hong, and many others—came to fill an entire closet in my bedroom. One day, midway into this project, I discovered the weight of the books had caused the closet floor to buckle. I mention this, because I owe the greatest debt to the many historians who labored for decades to make these events known.

The following is just a partial list of works that were helpful as I immersed myself in different aspects of this history: on the historical origins of anti-Asian hate, *The Chinese Question* by Mae Ngai; on the Pacific railroad, *Ghosts of Gold Mountain* by Gordon H. Chang; on the Los Angeles Chinese massacre, *The Chinatown War* by Scott Zesch; on the treatment of Chinese prostitutes, *Unsubmissive Women* by Benson Tong; on Yung Wing and the Chinese Educational Mission, *Stepping Forth into the World* by Edward J. M. Rhoads; on the debate over Chinese exclusion, *Closing the Gate* by Andrew Gyory, and *The Road to Chinese Exclusion,* by Liping Zhu; on the enforcement of the exclusion laws, *At America's Gates* by Erika Lee and *Laws Harsh as Tigers* by Lucy E. Salyer; on the Chinese legal fight against discrimination, *In Search of Equality* by Charles J. McClain; on the Chinese diplomatic response to the anti-Chinese movement, *China and the Overseas Chinese in the United States, 1868–1911* by Shih-shan Henry Tsai; on *Tape v. Hurley* and the extraordinary Tape family, *The Lucky Ones* by Mae Ngai; on the anti-Chinese violence that swept the American West, *The Chinese Must Go* by Beth Lew-Williams and *Driven Out* by Jean Pfaelzer; on the life of Wong Chin Foo, *The First Chinese American* by Scott D. Seligman; on the immigration station at Angel Island, *Angel Island* by Erika Lee and Judy Yung; on the fight for Chinese wives and the repeal of Chinese exclusion, *Opening the Gates to Asia* by Jane H. Hong; on the postwar years of suspicion, *Remaking Chinese America* by Xiaojian Zhao. Finally, I should mention that Iris Chang's sweeping book, *The Chinese in America,* which starts in mid-nineteenth-century China and ends in early-twenty-first-century America, was a source of inspiration for me from the beginning.

The scenes and characters in this book are constructed almost entirely from primary documents—historical newspaper accounts, manuscript collections, court records, and government archives. I'm grateful for the invaluable assistance provided by staff and volunteers at the Bancroft Library and the Ethnic Studies Library at UC Berkeley; the Searls Historical Library; the Truckee-Donner Historical Society; the California Historical Society; the California State Library; the California State Archives; the San Francisco Theological Seminary; the Huntington Library; the UCLA Library Special Collections; the Chinese Historical Society of America; the Chinese Historical Society of Southern California; the Presbyterian Historical Society of America; the San Diego History Center; the Issaquah History Museums; the National Archives in San Bruno, Seattle, Boston, and Washington, D.C.; the Washington State Archives; the Tacoma Historical Society; the Pearl S. Buck House; the University of Washington Libraries, special collections; the Immigration History Research Center Archives at the University of Minnesota; the Waterman Research Center at the Connecticut Museum of Culture and History; the Yale University Library, manuscripts and archives; the Stephen H. Hart Research Center at History Colorado; the Nebraska State Historical Society; the Washington State University Libraries; the Wallowa History Center; the University of Oregon Libraries, special collections and university archives; the New-York Historical Society; the Library of Congress; the Museum of Chinese in America; the American Heritage Center; and other repositories I consulted. Thanks, especially, to Sine Hwang Jensen, Frances Kaplan, Theresa Salazar, Jenny Barr, Sean Heyliger, William Creesh, Pat Chestnut, Li Wei Yang, Stephanie Arias, Gene Moy, Midori Okazaki, Karen Gath, Cassandra Hartnett, Stephanie Miller, Katy Phillips, Nancy Ng Tam, and Samantha Freise. The staff of the New York Public Library and the Rose Main Reading Room, my home on many weekends, deserve special thanks. I could not have written this book without the miracles of Interlibrary Loan.

In recent years, digitization of historical records has advanced rapidly, including at many of these archives. For this reason, the timing of my project was fortuitous. (I'm an evangelist for websites like Newspapers.com, Ancestry.com, and GenealogyBank.com.) I benefited tremendously from initiatives like the HathiTrust Digital Library; the California Digital Newspaper Collection at the University of California, Riverside; the National Digital Newspaper Program; the digital materials of the Chinese Railroad Workers in North America Project; and the bounties of the Chinese in California Virtual Collection.

Thanks also to Scott Seligman for sharing his vast knowledge of the archives and helpful documents; Connie Young Yu, a pioneering historian and author, for her advice and counsel throughout this project; Sue Lee, a former president of the Chinese Historical Society of America who threw herself into helping me in every way she could; Julia Flynn Siler, the author of *The White Devil's Daughters,* and David Lei, a longtime community historian in San Francisco, who pointed me to various archives; John R. Wunder and Michael Traynor for help puzzling through the details of *People v. Hall;*

Tian Atlas Xu for sharing his expertise on the attorneys who advocated for Chinese immigrants; Susie Lan Cassel, of California State University, San Marcos, for sharing her insights on Ah Quin and his diary; Jane Leung Larson for being so helpful with details about her mother, Louise Leung Larson; Jia Lynn Yang, the author of *One Mighty and Irresistible Tide,* for engaging with me about the Immigration and Nationality Act of 1965; and Laura Ng, a historical archaeologist at Grinnell College, who answered all manner of questions from me. I am also grateful to Chisa Hughes, of the Eureka Chinatown Project, and Robert Cliver, of Cal Poly Humboldt, for sharing their trove of documents with me. In Rock Springs, I was aided immeasurably by Dudley Gardner, of Western Wyoming Community College, who turned over hundreds of files and shaped my understanding of the massacre. Thanks to Amanda Frost, of the University of Virginia School of Law, and Hardeep Dhillon, of the University of Pennsylvania, for helping me grasp the intricacies of the Wong Kim Ark case and its aftermath. Numerous descendants of early Chinese arrivals in America told me their families' stories. They all helped shape this project, even ones that did not make it into the final manuscript. Gratitude especially to Libby Lok for passing along details about the life and legacy of Loke Kee and other valuable research and contacts.

I am grateful, too, to scholars who read all or parts of my manuscript, including some I have already mentioned: Mae Ngai, Gordon Chang, Jane Hong, Laura Ng, Dudley Gardner, Robert Cliver, Connie Young Yu, Erika Lee, and Beth Lew-Williams. I couldn't have written this book without the help of a cadre of researchers across the country—especially Yinuo Shi, Serena Lin, and Zhiwei Feng, all promising young journalists themselves. Elizabeth Eames, my photo researcher, stuck with this project for months, tracking down images from dozens of sources. Susanna Sturgis did a wonderful job copy editing the manuscript and caught many blunders from me.

Deep appreciation to the Long Family Foundation and the Asian Pacific Community Fund, for their support of this project. Thanks to my friend Josh Kwan, for connecting me to them. I am especially grateful to Marilyn and Vivian Long for their belief in me.

This book would not exist without David Black, my agent, who helped me imagine what was possible. I am delighted that this book landed in the deft hands of Kris Puopolo, at Doubleday, who believed in the importance of this book from the start and was probing and perceptive at every stage. Much thanks as well to Bill Thomas, Elena Hershey, Anne Jaconette, Faith

Griffiths, Ana Espinoza, Rita Madrigal, Betty Lew, Kathryn Ricigliano, and the entire team at Doubleday for their care in shepherding this book into the world.

I am beyond fortunate to work at *The New Yorker*, a place that celebrates books and authors. Thanks to David Remnick, for his unflagging support and enthusiasm. Virginia Cannon, Henry Finder, and Marella Gayla each edited pieces I wrote on the events covered in this book, portions of which are included in this manuscript. I am grateful to colleagues at the magazine who offered encouragement and advice along the way, including Jonathan Blitzer, Evan Osnos, Eliza Griswold, Jay Caspian Kang, Patrick Keefe, Hua Hsu, David Rohde, Josh Rothman, Rob Fischer, Pam McCarthy, Maraithe Thomas, Sigrid Dilley, Sharan Shetty, Leily Kleinbard, Monica Racic, Joanna Milter, and Nicholas Blechman.

The support of friends from far-flung parts of my life as I worked on this project helped buoy me. Thanks to Kim Barker, Mike Schwirtz, Kurt Streeter, Damien Cave, Fernanda Santos, Andrea Elliott, Jenny Lee, Min Jin Lee, Tom Kim, Julia Cho, Will and Julie Chun, Jason and Jeannie Lee, Alex and Nancy Zhang, and Phil and Jessica Kim.

Finally, thanks to my family. My parents, Fan and Marlinda Luo, willingly submitted to my questions about their own immigrant experience. My dad was the first to read a full draft of this book. My brother, Chris, was another early reader and champion. My sister-in-law, Lynn, offered wise feedback. My wife, Wenny, has had to live with this book for more than three years, through many early mornings, late nights, weekends, and vacations. I am lucky to have her as a partner in life and am bolstered every day by her patience and fortitude. I wrote this book for our daughters, Madeleine and Vivienne. May they find belonging.

Notes

Abbreviations

AC Alta California

ACF Arrival Investigation Case Files, Between 1884–1944, Records of the Immigration and Naturalization Service, RG 85, National Archives, San Bruno, CA

AIOHP Angel Island Oral History Project, Ethnic Studies Library, UC Berkeley

BL UC Berkeley, Bancroft Library

BOFMS Record Group 31, Box 45, Presbyterian Church in the U.S.A. Board of Foreign Missions Secretaries' files, Presbyterian Historical Society

CCF Segregated Chinese Records, Entry 134: Custom Case File No. 3358D, Related to Chinese Immigration, 1887–1891, Records of the Immigration Naturalization Service, RG 85, National Archives, Washington, DC

CEACF Chinese Exclusion Act Case Files, Record Group 85, Records of the Immigration and Naturalization Service

CIC Chinese in California Virtual Collection, Bancroft Library, UC Berkeley

CT Chicago Tribune

GRDOJ General Records of the Department of Justice, 1872–1896, Chronological Files: Washington, Government Publications, Maps, Microforms & Newspapers Department, Suzzallo Library, University of Washington, Seattle, WA

HT Hartford Courant

HFP Hong Family Papers, Huntington Library

HHB Hubert Howe Bancroft collection

HMLRFA Him Mark Lai research files, additions, 1834–2009 (bulk 1870–2009), AAS ARC 2010/1, Ethnic Studies Library, UC Berkeley

IACF Immigration Arrival Investigation Case Files, 1884–1944, Records of the Immigration and Naturalization Service, RG 85, National Archives, San Bruno, CA

JHT Joseph Hopkins Twichell Papers, Yale Collection of American Literature, Beinecke Rare Book and Manuscript Library

LAACR Los Angeles Area Court Records, Huntington Library

LADN *Los Angeles Daily News*
LAS *Los Angeles Star*
LAT *Los Angeles Times*
MLDS Miscellaneous Letters of the
  Department of State, 1789–1906, M179,
  General Records of the Department
  of State, RG59, National Archives,
  Washington, D.C.
NFCL Notes from the Chinese Legation
  in the United States to the Depart-
  ment of State, 1868–1906, M98, Notes
  from Foreign Missions, General
  Records of the Department of State,
  Record Group 59, National Archives,
  College Park, MD
NTFM Notes to Foreign Missions,
  China, June 3, 1868, to January 4, 1899,
  M98, General Records of the Depart-
  ment of State, Record Group 59,
  National Archives, College Park, MD
NYT *New York Times*
NYTr *New York Tribune*
PRFRUS Papers Relating to the Foreign
  Relations of the United States, Trans-
  mitted to Congress, with the Annual
  Message of the President
RJWP Papers of Pearl S. Buck and

Richard J. Walsh, Archives of the
  Pearl S. Buck House, Perkasie, PA
SB *Sacramento Bee*
SDU *Sacramento Daily Union*
SFB *San Francisco Evening Bulletin*
SFCa *San Francisco Call*
SFCh *San Francisco Chronicle*
SFE *San Francisco Examiner*
SFTS San Francisco Theological Semi-
  nary Branch Library of the GTU
  Library
SPFINS Subject and Policy Files, 1894–
  1957, Records of the U.S. Immigration
  and Naturalization Service, RG 85,
  National Archives, Washington, D.C.
SRR Survey of Race Relations records,
  1924–1927, Hoover Institution Library
  & Archives
TCF Territorial Court case files, Wash-
  ington State Archives, Puget Sound
  Regional Branch, Bellevue, WA
UPCC Union Pacific Coal Company
  Collection, Western Wyoming Com-
  munity College
UPR Union Pacific Railroad records, His-
  tory of Nebraska, Lincoln, NE

Introduction

3 The Founding Fathers celebrated: John
  Higham, *Send These to Me: Immigrants
  in Urban America*, rev. ed. (Baltimore:
  Johns Hopkins University, 1984), 31;
  Roger Daniels, *Guarding the Golden
  Door: American Immigration Policy and
  Immigrants Since 1882* (New York: Hill
  and Wang, 2004), 6; Robbie Totten,
  "National Security and U.S. Immigration Policy, 1776–1790," *Journal of Interdisciplinary History* 39, no. 1 (Summer
  2008): 49–51.
3 "The present desire": Thomas Jefferson,
  Notes on the State of Virginia (Philadelphia, 1787), 92.
3 In the 1840s, some states: See Hidetaka

Hirota, *Expelling the Poor: Atlantic Sea-
  board States and the 19th-Century Origins
  of American Immigration Policy* (New
  York: Oxford University Press, 2017).
3 Only a few hundred: Theodore Hittell,
  History of California (San Francisco,
  1898), 2:469; Ralph J. Roske, *Everyman's
  Eden: A History of California* (New York:
  Macmillan, 1968), 193. Parts of this
  introduction were drawn from Michael
  Luo, "America was Eager for Chinese
  Immigrants. What Happened?" *New
  Yorker*, August 23, 2021, https://www
  .newyorker.com/magazine/2021/08
  /30/america-was-eager-for-chinese
  -immigrants-what-happened, and

Michael Luo, "The Forgotten History of the Purging of Chinese from America," *New Yorker,* April 22, 2021, https://www.newyorker.com/news/daily-comment/the-forgotten-history-of-the-purging-of-chinese-from-america.

3 In 1844, James K. Polk: Amy S. Greenberg, *A Wicked War: Polk, Clay, Lincoln, and the 1846 U.S. Invasion of Mexico* (New York: Vintage Books, 2012), 62–63; Reginald Horsman, *Race and Manifest Destiny: The Origins of American Anglo-Saxonism* (Cambridge, MA: Harvard University Press, 1991), 10–16.

4 The fledgling town: Bancroft, *The Works of Hubert Howe Bancroft,* vol. 23, *History of California,* vol. 6, *1848–1859,* 6–10; Rand Richards, *Mud, Blood and Gold: San Francisco in 1849* (San Francisco: Heritage House Publishers, 2009), 26–28; Hittell, *History of California,* 2:593–594.

4 He spotted some glints: "The Discovery of Gold in California," *Hutchings' Illustrated California Magazine* (November 1857), 199–202, in Rodman W. Paul, *The California Gold Discovery* (Georgetown, CA: Talisman Press, 1947), 116–120; Bancroft, *The Works of Hubert Howe Bancroft,* vol. 23, *History of California,* vol. 6, *1848–1859,* 56, 60; Edward Dunbar, *The Romance of the Age* (New York, 1867), 108–109; Malcolm E. Barker, *San Francisco Memoirs, 1835–1851: Eyewitness Accounts of the Birth of a City* (San Francisco: Londonborn, 1994), 45.

4 According to Chinese lore: *SFCh,* July 21, 1878, 5; Kil Young Zo, "Chinese Emigration into the United States, 1850–1880" (PhD diss., Columbia University, 1971), 89.

4 a ship carrying: Mae Ngai, *The Chinese Question* (New York: W. W. Norton, 2021), 19.

5 "Americans are the richest": Wu Shang-Ying, *Meiguo hua qiao bai ian ji shi: Jianada fu, One Hundred Years of Chinese in the United States and Canada* (Hong Kong, 1954), 10–13.

5 By 1860, Chinese immigrants: U.S. Census Bureau, "Population of the United States in 1860: California," Table No. 2—Population by Color and Condition, 28.

6 They twisted the principle: Ngai, *The Chinese Question,* 86.

6 It also excluded: Mae M. Ngai, "The Architecture of Race in Immigration Law: A Reexamination of the Immigration Act of 1924," *Journal of American History* 86, no. 1 (June 1999), 72–73; Erika Lee, *America for Americans: A History of Xenophobia in the United States* (New York: Basic Books, 2019), 80–81.

6 A population of Chinese Americans: See James W. Loewen, *The Mississippi Chinese: Between Black and White,* 2nd ed. (Long Grove, IL: Waveland Press, 1987).

7 a crucial period of formation: On the threads connecting the failure of Reconstruction and the condition of immigrants, Native Americans, and others, see Manisha Sinha, *The Rise and Fall of the Second American Republic: Reconstruction, 1860–1920* (New York: Liveright, 2024).

8 I was standing in the rain: Michael Luo, "An Open Letter to the Woman Who Told Us: Go Back to China," *NYT,* October 9, 2016, https://www.nytimes.com/2016/10/10/nyregion/to-the-woman-who-told-my-family-to-go-back-to-china.html.

8 Today, there are: "U.S. Census Bureau Releases Key Stats in Honor of 2023 Asian American, Native Hawaiian, and Pacific Islander Heritage Month," *U.S. Department of Commerce* (blog), May 1, 2023, https://www.commerce.gov/news/blog/2023/05/us-census-bureau-releases-key-stats-honor-2023-asian-american-native-hawaiian-and/; "Modern Immigration Wave Brings 59 Million to U.S., Driving Population Growth and Change Through 2065," Pew Research Center, September 28, 2015, https://www.pewresearch.org/race-and-ethnicity/2015/09/28/modern

-immigration-wave-brings-59-million
-to-u-s-driving-population-growth
-and-change-through-2065.

Chapter 1: Gold Mountain

13 Huie Kin grew up: Huie Kin, *Remi-niscences* (Peiping: San Yu Press, 1932), 16–23. Taishan was previously known as Xinning, or Sunning in Cantonese.

14 A decisive factor: Yong Chen, "The Internal Origins of Chinese Emigration to California Reconsidered," *Western Historical Quarterly* 28, no. 4 (1997): 521–546, https://doi.org/10.2307/969884.

15 In 1854, a ship arrived: Gunther Barth, *Bitter Strength: A History of the Chinese in the United States, 1850–1870* (Cambridge, MA: Harvard University Press, 1964), 72.

15 One captain contracted: Joseph Splivalo, "Captain Stephen Splivalo," typescript, n.d., BANC MSS 73/122 c, CIC, BL, 7–8.

15 "There can be no excuse": William Speer, *The Oldest and the Newest Empire: China and the United States* (Hartford, CT: S. S. Scranton and Company, 1870), 490.

15 During Huie Kin's trip: Huie Kin, *Reminiscences*, 23.

15 In 1878, a reporter: *SFCh*, July 21, 1878, 5.

16 On February 2, 1848: Charles V. Gillespie, "Vigilance Committee," 1875, BANC MSS C-D 190, HHB, BL, 1; Elizabeth Sinn, *Pacific Crossing* (Hong Kong: Hong Kong University Press, 2013), 50–51; Judy Yung, *Chinese Women of America: A Pictorial History* (Seattle: University of Washington Press, 1986), 14; Hua Liang, "Living Between the Worlds: Chinese American Women and Their Experiences in San Francisco and New York City" (PhD diss., University of Connecticut, 1996), 53.

16 In July 1849, the manifest: Mae Ngai, *The Chinese Question: The Gold Rushes, Chinese Migration, and Global Politics* (New York: W. W. Norton, 2021), 20; Sinn, *Pacific Crossing,* 66; James

O'Meara, "The Chinese in Early Days," *Overland Monthly* 3, no. 5 (May 1884).

16 about eight hundred Chinese: Bancroft, *Works of Hubert Howe Bancroft,* vol. 24, *History of California,* vol. 7, *1860–1890* (San Francisco, 1890), 336.

17 "strangers as we are": *AC*, December 10, 1849.

17 In 1850, a Chinese merchant: "Chinese Letters," trans. Quelp, *The Pioneer,* March 1855.

17 "the pleasure shared": Albert Williams, *A Pioneer Pastorate and Times Embodying Local Transactions and Events* (San Francisco, 1879), 122–123; *AC*, August 29, 1850.

18 At eleven in the morning: *AC*, August 30, 1850.

18 The next day, Assing delivered: *AC*, September 1, 1850.

18 McDougal, a Democrat: *Report of the Debates in the Convention of California, on the Formation of the Station Constitution, in September and October, 1849* (Washington, 1850), 142.

18 "one of the most worthy": John McDougal, "State of the State Address, January 7, 1852," https://governors.library.ca.gov/addresses/s_02-McDougall.html.

18 A few months after McDougal's address: *AC*, May 23, 1852.

19 Soon, a Chinese quarter: J. D. Borthwick, *Three Years in California* (Edinburgh, London, 1857), 76–77; William Perkins, "El Campo de los Sonoraenses or: Three Years Residence in California," unpublished manuscript, CIC, BL, 217–218.

19 In a journal entry: Timothy Coffin Osborn, journal entry, December 26, 1851, CIC, BL.

19 "flock of black birds": Ezra Gregg letter to "Distant Brothers and Sisters," May 9, 1863, CIC, BL.

20 "They did not venture": Borthwick, *Three Years in California,* 144–145.

20 Nevertheless, some Chinese stumbled: Bancroft, *Works of Hubert Howe Bancroft,* vol. 24, *History of California,* vol. 7, *1860–1890,* 655.

20 The first mass expulsion: Theodore H. Hittell, *History of California* (San Francisco, 1897), 4:102.

21 In 1852, the number of Chinese: Mary Roberts Coolidge, *Chinese Immigration* (New York, 1907), 498.

21 "Chinamen are getting": Chauncey L. Canfield, ed., *The Diary of a Forty-Niner* (Boston: Houghton Mifflin, 1920), 222.

21 In April, the State: Report of the Committee on Mines and Mining Interests, California State Assembly Journals, 1852 Session, Appendix, 830–831.

21 Governor John Bigler, a Democrat: Mae Ngai, *The Chinese Question*, 85–87.

21 On April 23, 1852: *Journal of the Third Session of the Legislature of the State of California* (San Francisco, 1852), 373–378.

21 Anti-coolieism became: Ngai, *The Chinese Question*, 88.

22 Tong had been: Carl T. Smith, *Chinese Christians: Elites, Middlemen, and the Church in Hong Kong* (Hong Kong: Oxford University Press, 1985), 36–49.

22 "The poor Chinaman": *SDU*, May 8, 1852.

22 Norman Assing, the merchant: Ngai, *The Chinese Question*, 93; *AC*, May 5, 1852; Hab Wa and Tong Achick, "Letter of the Chinamen to His Excellency, Gov. Bigler," in "An Analysis of the Chinese Question. Consisting of a Special Message of the Governor and, in reply thereto, Two Letters of the Chinamen and a Memorial of the Citizens of San Francisco" (San Francisco, 1852), Huntington Library.

23 In early May, Tong Achick went: Chun Aching and Tong Achick, "To His Excellency, Gov. Bigler, from the Chinamen," in "An Analysis of the Chinese Question. Consisting of a Special Message of the Governor and, in reply thereto, Two Letters of the Chinamen and a Memorial of the Citizens of San Francisco."

23 In the town of Columbia: *SDU*, April 14, 1852.

23 A similar meeting: *SDU*, May 31, 1852.

23 In El Dorado County: Charles Caldwell Dobie, *San Francisco's Chinatown* (New York: Appleton-Century, 1936), 51; *AC*, May 15, 1852.

24 A clipper ship: *San Francisco Herald*, May 28, 1852.

Chapter 2: Indian, Negro, or Chinaman

25 The committee was led: J. P. Munro-Fraser, *History of Marin County, California* (San Francisco, 1880), 481.

25 Others on the committee: *Sacramento Daily Bee*, August 22, 1882; *Sacramento Evening Bee*, December 7, 1897; J. Roy Jones, *Saddle Bags in Siskiyou* (Yreka, CA: News-Journal Print Shop, 1953), 344–347, in Him Mark Lai Papers, 1778– (bulk 1970–1995), Collection Number AAS ARC 2000/80, carton 22, folder 10, UC Berkeley, Ethnic Studies Library.

25 The *huiguan*, essentially: Him Mark Lai, *Becoming Chinese American: A History of Communities and Institutions* (Walnut Creek, CA: AltaMira Press, 2004), 40–43; Thomas W. Chinn, *Bridging the Pacific: San Francisco Chinatown and Its People* (San Francisco: Chinese Historical Society of America, 1989), 3–7; William Hoy, *The Chinese Six Companies: A Short, General Historical Resume of Its Origin, Function, and Importance in the Life of the California Chinese* (San Francisco: Chinese Consolidated Benevolent Association, 1942); "The Chinese Companies," in "Remarks of the Chinese Merchants of San Francisco upon Governor Bigler's Message, and Some Common Objections" (San Francisco, 1855), 6–15, CIC, California Historical Society. The pinyin romanization of Yeong Wo Association is Yanghe Huiguan.

26 He was replaced: William Speer to Walter Lowrie, November 30, 1852, BOFMS.

26 In the meeting with the lawmakers: Report of the Committee on Mines and Mining Interests, *Journal Fourth Session of the Legislature of the State of Califor-*

nia (San Francisco, 1853), Appendix to Regular Session, Document No. 28.

26 The houses had been keeping: Speer, *The Oldest and the Newest Empire,* 595–596.

26 In his subsequent report: Report of the Committee on Mines and Mining Interests, 9.

26 The law was part: Najia Aarim-Heriot, *Chinese Immigrants, African Americans, and Racial Anxiety in the United States, 1848–82* (Urbana: University of Illinois Press, 2003), 21–23.

27 Mexican American residents: Ibid., 28–29; D. Michael Bottoms, *An Aristocracy of Color: Race and Reconstruction in California and the West, 1850–1890* (Norman: University of Oklahoma Press, 2013), 26; Richard L. Nostrand, "Mexican Americans Circa 1850," *Annals of the Association of American Geographers* 65, no. 3 (September 1975): 384.

27 "without the desired effect": Report of the Committee on Mines and Mining Interests, 2.

27 "We have no authority": Ibid., 12.

28 The resulting infusion: Mae Ngai, *The Chinese Question: The Gold Rushes, Chinese Migration, and Global Politics* (New York: W. W. Norton, 2021), 100.

28 In a letter to his parents: Robert W. Pitkins, letter to his parents, August 16, 1852, CIC, BL.

28 One sheriff's deputy: Charles E. De Long and Carl I. Wheat, eds., "'California's Bantam Cock': The Journals of Charles E. De Long, 1854–1863 (Continued)," *California Historical Society Quarterly* 8, no. 4 (December 1929): 338, 341, 346.

29 The Chinese asked Speer: William Speer to Walter Lowrie, March 15, 1853, BOFMS.

29 His first wife, Cornelia: *The Eleventh Annual Report of the Board of Foreign Missions of the Presbyterian Church of the United States of America* (New York, 1848), 33–34.

29 As the numbers of Chinese: Albert Williams, *A Pioneer Pastorate and Times Embodying Local Transactions and Events* (San Francisco, 1879), 127–128.

29 After a difficult voyage: William Speer to Walter Lowrie, November 15, 1852, BOFMS.

29 Soon after their arrival: William Speer to Walter Lowrie, November 30, 1852, BOFMS.

30 Speer began a series: William Speer, "China and California; Their Relations, Past and Present. A Lecture, in Conclusion of a Series in Relation to the Chinese People," delivered in the Stockton Street Presbyterian Church, San Francisco, June 28, 1853 (San Francisco, 1853); Williams, *A Pioneer Pastorate,* 219.

30 Within a year, the settlement: *History of Nevada County, California; with Illustrations Descriptive of Its Scenery, Residences, Public Buildings, Fine Blocks, and Manufactories.* (Oakland, CA, 1880), 78–80.

30 By 1852: U.S. Census Bureau, Census of 1850, Table I.—Population—Whites, Colored, Indians Domesticated, and Foreigners—1852, 982.

30 On the night of August 9: The exact details of what happened that night are difficult to reconstruct. I relied upon the account in William Speer to Walter Lowrie, October 15, 1853, BOFMS. See also *Nevada Journal,* August 12, 1853; *People v. George W. Hall,* WPA 7158, California State Archives; *SDU,* October 13, 1853. For more on the case, see John R. Wunder, *Gold Mountain Turned to Dust: Essays on the Legal History of the Chinese in the Nineteenth-Century American West* (Albuquerque: University of New Mexico Press, 2018), 59–91.

31 After ranging across the region: William M. Stewart, *Reminiscences of Senator William M. Stewart of Nevada,* ed. George Rothwell Brown (New York: Neale Publishing Company, 1908), 56–76.

31 When McConnell resigned: Ibid., 76.

31 Stewart interviewed: Ibid., 78.

31 According to a letter: Speer to Lowrie, October 15, 1853.

31 Barbour, a native: *History of Nevada County, California*, 94.

31 "upright and intelligent gentleman": Speer to Lowrie, October 15, 1853.

31 Before departing San Francisco: Stewart, *Reminiscences*, 78.

31 On October 4: Entries for October 4–5, 1853, *People v. George W. Hall*, WPA 7158.

32 Stewart called at least: Entries for October 5–7, 1853, *People v. George W. Hall*, WPA 7158; Speer to Lowrie, October 15, 1853; Wunder, *Gold Mountain Turned to Dust*, 70–71.

32 the jury began their deliberations: *SDU*, October 13, 1853; *Nevada Journal*, October 14, 1853.

32 the mutilated body: *Nevada Journal*, October 28, 1853.

32 "It seems hard": *Nevada Journal*, November 25, 1853.

32 A petition began: *Nevada Journal*, August 4, 1854.

32 During the hearing: Stewart, *Reminiscences*, 79.

32 But Chief Justice Hugh Campbell Murray: Michael Traynor, "The Infamous Case of *People v. Hall* (1854)," *California Supreme Court Historical Society Newsletter*, Spring/Summer 2017.

33 Murray wrote the majority: *People v. Hall*, 4 Ca. 399 (1854).

33 One of the principal: *Nevada Journal*, October 6, 1854.

33 Without the Chinese: Stewart, *Reminiscences*, 79.

33 Speer later wrote: William Speer, "An Answer to the Common Objections to Chinese Testimony; and an Earnest Appeal to the Legislature of California for Their Protection by Our Law" (San Francisco, 1857).

33 the state legislature finally: *The Statutes of California, Passed at the Fourteenth Session of the Legislature, 1863* (Sacramento, 1863), 69.

34 he opened a chapel: Speer to Lowrie, January 31 and September 13, 1853,

BOFMS; Speer, "Annual Report of the Mission to the Chinese in California" (1854), BOFMS; Ira M. Condit, *The Chinaman as We See Him* (Chicago, 1900), 92–96.

34 While his superiors: Speer to Lowrie, October 13, 1854, BOFMS; Speer, "Annual Report of the Mission to the Chinese in California" (1854), BOFMS; Speer, *The Oldest and the Newest Empire*, 660.

34 He viewed the English-language section: "Prospectus of The Oriental, or Tung-Ngai San-Luk; A California Newspaper in China and English," BOFMS.

34 In the first issue: *The Oriental*, January 4, 1855.

34 Speer's most tangible accomplishment: Michael L. Stahler, "William Speer: Champion of California's Chinese, 1852–1857," *Journal of Presbyterian History* 38, no. 2 (Summer 1970): 123–124.

35 "Scarce any persons": Speer to Lowrie, March 5 and July 1, 1856, Record Group 31, Box 45, Folder 2, BOFMS.

35 His letters record: William Speer, "Third Annual Report of the Mission to the Chinese in California," December 31, 1855, BOFMS.

35 In the spring of 1856: Speer to Lowrie, May 2 and September 27, 1856, February 5, 1857, BOFMS.

35 the Presbytery in California ordered: Letter to Speer from Presbytery of California, March 4, 1857; Speer to Lowrie, March 5 and March 19, 1857, BOFMS.

36 In a concluding letter: Speer to Lowrie, March 13, 1858, BOFMS.

36 On February 5, 1859: *Shasta Courier*, February 5 and 12, 1859.

36 an armed mob: *Shasta Courier*, March 5, 1859; *Sacramento Daily Bee*, February 26, 1859.

36 In the following days: *Shasta Courier*, March 5, 1859; *Placer Herald*, March 5, 1859.

36 "There is at present": *Shasta Courier*, March 26, 1859; Journal of the House

Assembly of California at the Tenth
Session of the Legislature (Sacramento,
1859), 401–406.

37 "Quiet once more reigns": *Placer Herald*,
March 19, 1859.

37 Miners in Colville: *SFB*, December 2,
1862.

37 In San Francisco: *SFB*, July 12, 1862.

37 "John Chinaman must leave": *SDU*,
March 10, 1859.

Chapter 3: The Great Army and the Iron Road

38 Shortly after noon: *SDU*, January 9,
1863.

39 Sailing from New York: Hubert Howe
Bancroft, *The Works of Hubert Howe
Bancroft: Volume XXIII, History of California, Vol. VI, 1848–1859* (San Francisco, 1888), 126–163.

39 When Stanford himself: Norman
Tuturow, *The Governor: The Life and
Legacy of Leland Stanford, a California
Colossus*, vol. 1 (Spokane, WA: Arthur
H. Company, 2004), 42; Hubert Howe
Bancroft, *History of the Life of Leland
Stanford: A Character Study* (Oakland,
CA: Biobooks, 1952), 13.

39 where white miners' resentment:
Charles Caldwell Dobie, *San Francis-
co's Chinatown* (New York: Appleton-
Century, 1936), 51; *AC*, May 15, 1852.

39 "This store always": Julie A. Cain, "The
Chinese and the Stanfords: Immigra-
tion Rhetoric in Nineteenth-Century
California" (master's thesis, California
State University, East Bay, 2011), 11;
Gordon H. Chang, "The Chinese and
the Stanfords: Nineteenth-Century
America's Fraught Relationship with
Chinese Men," in *The Chinese and the
Iron Road: Building the Transcontinen-
tal Railroad*, ed. Gordon H. Chang
and Shelley Fisher Fishkin (Stanford,
CA: Stanford University Press, 2019),
347. The sign in Chinese said, *bendian
changyou tangshan zahuo*, which can also
be translated as, "This store often has
Chinese goods."

39 Stanford tried again: Tuturow, *The

Life and Legacy of Leland Stanford, 51;
Hubert Howe Bancroft, *History of the
Life of Leland Stanford: A Character
Study* (Oakland, CA: Biobooks, 1952),
14; Oscar Lewis, *The Big Four: The Story
of Huntington, Stanford, Hopkins, and
Crocker, and of the Building of the Central Pacific* (New York: Alfred A. Knopf,
1938), 164–165.

39 He hurried back across the country:
Norman Tuturow, *Norman E. Leland
Stanford: Man of Many Careers* (Menlo
Park, CA: Pacific Coast Publishers), 23;
Tuturow, *The Governor*, 56–57; Gunther
Nagel, *Iron Will: The Life and Letters of
Jane Stanford* (Stanford, CA: Stanford
Alumni Association, 1985), 20.

40 some fortuitous mining investments:
Bancroft, *History of the Life of Leland
Stanford*, 14; Tuturow, *Norman E. Leland
Stanford*, 24; Tuturow, *The Governor*,
74–79.

40 He also began getting involved: Tuto-
row, *The Governor*, 90–95.

40 a young railroad engineer: Carl I.
Wheat, "A Sketch of the Life of Theo-
dore D. Judah," *California Historical
Society Quarterly* 4, no. 3 (1925): 240–245.

40 "If you want to come": Collis Potter
Huntington, typescript, biographical
material for H. H. Bancroft's *Chronicles
of the Builders of the Commonwealth,
1887–1890*, 1887, BANC MSS C-D 773,
folder 1, HHB, BL, 8–9.

40 His proposed path: Theodore D. Judah,
"Report of the Chief Engineer on the
Preliminary Survey, Cost of Construction, and Estimated Revenue of the
Central Pacific Railroad of California, Across the Sierra Nevada Mountains, from Sacramento to the Eastern
Boundary of California, October 22,
1862" (Sacramento, 1862), 2–15, 32.

41 Finally, on June 28, 1861: Wheat, "A
Sketch of the Life of Theodore D.
Judah," 246.

41 Stanford called the union's: Cain, "The
Chinese and the Stanfords," 24.

41 "I prefer the white man": Ibid., 20.

41 During his inauguration: Leland Stan-

ford, Inaugural Address, January 10, 1862, https://governors.library.ca.gov /addresses/08-Stanford.html. See also Chang, "The Chinese and the Stanfords," 347–348; Cain, "The Chinese and the Stanfords," 24–25.

41 Stanford signed a measure: 1862 Cal. Stat. 462, 1; Cain, "The Chinese and the Stanfords," 26.

41 Soon after, they hired: William Hoy, "Moy Jin Mun—Pioneer," *Chinese Digest*, May 1936, 12; *Indianapolis News*, March 1, 1900; Chang, "The Chinese and the Stanfords," 348–349. On Moy Jin Mun, see Montgomery Hom, "Discovering My Great-Grandfather Moy Jin Mun," in *Voices from the Railroad: Stories by Descendants of Chinese Railroad Workers*, ed. Sue Lee and Connie Young Yu (San Francisco: Chinese Historical Society of America, 2019), 17–25. For a comprehensive account of the Moy family, see Scott Seligman, *Three Tough Chinamen* (Hong Kong: Earnshaw Books, 2012).

42 In 1862, Jane Stanford became: Cain, "The Chinese and the Stanfords," 28–29; Chang, "The Chinese and the Stanfords," 349; *SB*, January 18, 1998.

43 He later talked about the insomnia: Charles Crocker, "Facts Gathered from the Lips of Charles Crocker Regarding His Identification with the Central Pacific Railroad and Other Roads Growing Out of It," typescript, BANC MSS C-D 764, typescript, folder 1, HHB, BL, 58.

43 "I used to go": Ibid., 49.

43 The directors of the railroad: Ibid., 29; Charles Nordhoff, "California. II.—What to See There, and How to See It," *Harper's New Monthly Magazine* 45, no. 265 (June 1872): 68–71.

43 Many of the desultory workers: Lewis Clement testimony, in *Testimony Taken by the United States Pacific Railway Commission*, vol. 6 (Washington, DC: Government Publishing Office, 1887), 3225–3226.

43 "If you want to jubilate": Collis P Hun-

tington, "Collis Potter Huntington Biographical Material for H. H. Bancroft's Chronicles of the Builders of the Commonwealth, 1887–1890," BANC MSS C-D 773, typescript, folder 1, HHB, BL, 13.

43 It was around this time: For a detailed account of Hung Wah's life, see Gordon H. Chang, *Ghosts of Gold Mountain: The Epic Story of the Chinese Who Built the Transcontinental Railroad* (Boston: Houghton Mifflin Harcourt, 2019).

43 Hung Wah's life: Chang, *Ghosts of Gold Mountain*, 68–69; *Mountain Democrat*, April 17, 1931; *LAT*, April 15, 1931; *SB*, April 14, 1931; *Marysville Appeal-Democrat*, April 14, 1931.

44 Hung Wah's advertisement: *Placer Herald*, August 29, September 5, September 12, 1863.

44 Hung Wah began working: CPRR payroll, no. 26, for month of January 1864, Payroll Records Gallery, Chinese Railroad Workers Project, Stanford University; William F. Chew, *Nameless Builders of the Transcontinental Railroad* (Victoria, BC: Trafford, 2004), 37.

44 Later that month, the company: *SDU*, January 7, 1865.

44 "as near as brutes": Crocker, "Facts Gathered from the Lips," 51.

44 Strobridge found himself: Charles Crocker testimony, in *Report of the Joint Special Committee to Investigate Chinese Immigration*, 44th Cong., 2nd sess. (Washington, DC: GPO, 1877), 667.

45 "I will not boss Chinese": Frederick Low testimony, in ibid., 65.

45 "You can get Chinamen": Charles Crocker, in *Testimony Taken by the United States Pacific Railway Commission*, vol. 7 (Washington, DC: GPO, 1887), 3660.

45 At first, Strobridge: Frederick Low testimony, in *Report of the Joint Special Committee to Investigate Chinese Immigration*, 78.

45 "Did they not build": Crocker, in *Testimony Taken by the United States Pacific Railway Commission*, vol. 7, 3660.

45 In his report: Samuel S. Montague, *Report of the Chief Engineer upon Recent Surveys, Progress of Construction, and an Approximate Estimate of Receipts of the Central Pacific Railroad of California* (N.p., October 8, 1864), 17.

45 Crocker arranged: Crocker testimony, in *Report of the Joint Special Committee to Investigate Chinese Immigration*, 674; Yong Chen, "Uncovering and Understanding the Experiences of Chinese Railroad Workers in Broader Socioeconomic Contexts," web exclusive essay, Chinese Railroad Workers in North America Project (2020): 13.

45 Most of the Chinese workers: Ping Chiu, *Chinese Labor in California: An Economic Study* (Madison: State Historical Society of Wisconsin, 1963), 45–46.

46 "We have now about": Cornelius Cole, *Memoirs of Cornelius Cole, Ex-Senator of the United States from California* (New York: McLoughlin Brothers, 1908), 183.

46 "Without them, it would be": Mark Hopkins to Collis P. Huntington, May 31, 1865, Incoming Correspondence, Collis P. Huntington Papers, 1856–1901, Microfilming Corporation of America, Sanford, NC.

46 a dollar a day: Crocker, in *Testimony Taken by the United States Pacific Railway Commission*, vol. 7, 3660–3661.

46 "We cannot keep the names": Crocker testimony, in *Report of the Joint Special Committee to Investigate Chinese Immigration*, 674–675.

46 "found to be good": Leland Stanford, "To the Stockholders of the Central Pacific Railroad Company," *Railroad Record*, August 24, 1865, 323.

47 Stanford led a contingent: Albert D. Richardson, *Beyond the Mississippi: From the Great River to the Great Ocean. Life and Adventure on the Prairies, Mountains, and Pacific Coast* (Hartford, CT, 1867), 461–462.

47 One traveler through: *Berkshire County Eagle*, December 3, 1868. There has been much debate about whether Chinese

workers deployed baskets in railroad construction. For a careful examination that concludes it did happen, see Chang, *Ghosts of Gold Mountain*, 87–92.

47 In October, Stanford issued: Leland Stanford, *Statement Made to the President of the United States and the Secretary of the Interior, of the Progress of the Work, October 10, 1865* (Sacramento. CA: H. S. Crocker & Co., 1865), 7–8.

48 Chinese workers would need: John R. Gillis, "Tunnels of the Pacific Railroad," A Paper Read Before the Society January 5, 1870, in *Transactions, American Society of Civil Engineers* 1, no. 1 (1872): 168.

48 a spectacular explosion killed: *SDU*, April 18, 1866; *Sacramento Daily Bee*, April 18, 1866.

48 "We measured the work": Crocker testimony, in *Report of the Joint Special Committee to Investigative Chinese Immigration*, 667.

49 Railroad engineers kept: Gillis, "Tunnels of the Pacific Railroad," 169.

49 In late February: Gillis, "Tunnels of the Pacific Railroad," 155.

49 "The snow slides": James H. Strobridge testimony, in *Testimony Taken by the United States Pacific Railway Commission*, vol. 6., 3150.

49 At night, the mountain: Gillis, "Tunnels of the Pacific Railroad," 154–155.

49 "the Chinamen have all": Hopkins to Huntington, June 26, 1867, Incoming Correspondence, Collis P. Huntington Papers.

49 It was a remarkable: See Gordon H. Chang, Shelley Fisher Fishkin, and Hilton Obenzinger, "Introduction," in *The Chinese and the Iron Road*, ed. Gordon H. Chang and Shelley Fisher Fishkin, 14–15; and Chang, *Ghosts of Gold Mountain*, 151–157.

49 "The question of whether": E. B. Crocker to Huntington, May 27, 1867, Incoming Correspondence, Collis P. Huntington Papers.

49 Charles Crocker, however: E. B. Crocker to Huntington, July 2, 1867, Incoming

Correspondence, Collis P. Huntington Papers.

50 "All have gone": Hopkins to Huntington, July 2, 1867, Incoming Correspondence, Collis P. Huntington Papers.

50 "If there had been": Crocker testimony, in *Report of the Joint Special Committee to Investigate Chinese Immigration*, 669.

50 "I like your idea": Huntington to Charles Crocker, October 3, 1867, Personal Papers, 1862–1901, Collis P. Huntington Papers.

50 On June 17, 1868: *AC*, June 20, 1868.

51 A horse-drawn flatcar: George Kraus, *High Road to Promontory: Building the Central Pacific Across the High Sierra* (New York: Castle Books, 1969), 210–211; J. D. B. Stillman, "The Last Tie," *Overland Monthly* 3, no. 1 (July 1869): 81.

51 "We must take off": Crocker, "Facts Gathered from the Lips," 55–57.

51 Two weeks later: *New York Herald*, May 12, 1869; *NYT*, May 12, 1869.

52 He made a point: *CT*, May 12, 1869; Chang, *Ghosts of Gold Mountain*, 1.

52 In Camp No. 15: CPRR payroll, for month of June 1866, Payroll Records Gallery, Chinese Railroad Workers Project, Stanford University.

52 One name: Ibid.

52 Ah Chuck, whose real name: Vicki Tong Young, "Mock Chuck: A Golden Treasure," in Lee and Young Yu, *Voices from the Railroad*, 46–50; Vicki Tong Young interview, in Chinese Railroad Workers Oral History Project, 2013–2018, May 13, 2015, Department of Special Collections and University Archives, Stanford University, https://purl.stanford.edu/bm287pw9541.

53 Towards the bottom: CPRR payroll, for month of June 1866.

53 Jow Kee, a twenty-seven-year-old: Gene O. Chan with Connie Young Yu, "Jim King, Foreman of the Central Pacific: A Descendant's Story," in Lee and Young Yu, *Voices from the Railroad*, 33–37.

53 The vast majority: Sucheng Chan, *This Bittersweet Soil: The Chinese in California*

Agriculture, 1860–1910 (Berkeley: University of California Press, 1986), 59.

53 Hundreds of others: Shelley Fisher Fishkin, "The Chinese as Railroad Builders After Promontory," in *The Chinese and the Iron Road*, ed. Gordon H. Chang and Shelley Fisher Fishkin, 278.

54 On February 12, 1867: *AC*, February 13, 1867.

54 Hung Wah, the great: Chang, *Ghosts of Gold Mountain*, 238–239.

54 Obituaries described: *SB*, April 14, 1931; *Placerville Mountain Democrat*, April 17, 1931; *LAT*, April 15, 1931; *Marysville Appeal Democrat*, April 14, 1931.

Chapter 4: Colorblind

55 For nearly a century: Jill Lepore, *These Truths: A History of the United States* (New York: W. W. Norton, 2018), 311–324; James H. Kettner, *The Development of American Citizenship, 1608–1870* (Chapel Hill: University of North Carolina Press, 1978), 10.

55 "warp and bias": Thomas Jefferson, *Notes on the State of Virginia* (Philadelphia, 1787), 93.

55 remarkably expansive and shockingly narrow: Erika Lee, *America for Americans: A History of Xenophobia in the United States* (New York: Basic Books, 2019), 36.

55 Congress later adjusted: Kettner, *Development of American Citizenship*, 236–342.

56 "Chinese of the Pacific states": Andrew Johnson, veto message, March 27, 1866, The American Presidency Project, UC Santa Barbara, https://www.presidency.ucsb.edu/documents/veto-message-438.

56 "The child of an Asiatic": Cong. Globe, 39th Cong., 1st sess. 498 (1866).

56 Two years later: Eric Foner, *The Second Founding: How the Civil War and Reconstruction Remade the Constitution* (New York: W.W. Norton & Company, 2019), 72–73.

57 "Every ship that comes": Cong. Globe, 40th Cong., 3rd sess. 901 (1869).

57 "I presume no": Cong. Globe, 40th Cong., 3rd sess. 1008 (1869).

57 In late 1854: Corinne K. Hoekstra, *From Canton to California: The Epic of Chinese Immigration* (N.p.: Four Winds Press, 1976), 44.

57 at least some managed: John Kuo Wei Tchen, *New York Before Chinatown: Orientalism and the Shaping of American Culture, 1776–1882* (Baltimore: Johns Hopkins University Press, 2001), 232; Sucheng Chan, *Asian Californians* (San Francisco: MTL/Boyd & Fraser, 1991), 43.

57 According to naturalization: New York, U.S., State, and Federal Naturalization Records, 1794–1943, Court of Common Pleas for the City and County of New York, on Ancestry.com. For more on these citizenship petitions and the early Chinese community in New York, see Tchen, *New York Before Chinatown*, 225–232.

58 In the census of 1870: 1870 U.S. census, New York County, New York, 7th District of the 6th Ward, Schedule 1, on Ancestry.com.

58 Frederick Douglass, the former: Edlie L. Wong, *Racial Reconstruction: Black Inclusion, Chinese Exclusion, and the Fictions of Citizenship* (New York: New York University Press, 2015), 84.

58 In 1867: Frederick Douglass, *Frederick Douglass Papers: Speech, Article, and Book File, 1846–1894; Speeches and Articles by Douglass, 1846–1894; 1867, "Composite Nation," lecture in the Parker Fraternity Course, Boston, Mass.*, 2 of 3, https://www.loc.gov/item/mss11879004o7/; *Boston Daily Evening Transcript*, December 2, 1869; *Rutland Daily Herald*, December 2, 1869; *New York Daily Herald*, December 9, 1869.

60 Sumner had introduced: Cong. Globe, 40th Cong., 3rd sess. 1031 (1869).

60 He had tried again: Cong. Globe, 41st Cong., 2nd sess. 5123 (1870).

60 He proposed a new: Cong. Globe, 41st Cong., 2nd sess. 5121 (1870).

60 "But this act": Ibid., 5121.

61 he had always "stood by" them: Cong. Globe, 41st Cong., 2nd sess. 5173 (1870).

61 he had helped: Cong. Globe, 41st Cong., 2nd sess. 3807 (1870); Lucas Guttentag, "The Forgotten Equality Norm in Immigration Preemption: Discrimination, Harassment, and the Civil Rights Act of 1870," *Duke Journal of Constitutional Law & Public Policy* 8, no. 1 (2013): 15, https://scholarship.law.duke.edu/djclpp/vol8/iss2/2.

61 Stewart had been at pains: William Gillette, *The Right to Vote: Politics and the Passage of the Fifteenth Amendment* (Baltimore: Johns Hopkins University Press, 2019), 156–157.

61 He had insisted: Cong. Globe, 40th Cong., 3rd sess. 1035 (1869).

61 "Do not put it": Cong. Globe, 41st Cong., 2nd sess. 5122 (1870).

61 Senator Oliver Morton: Cong. Globe, 41st Cong., 2nd sess. 5122, 5123 (1870).

62 He launched into a disquisition: Cong. Globe, 41st Cong., 2nd sess. 5125 (1870).

62 "They are a pagan": Cong. Globe, 41st Cong., 2nd sess. 5151 (1870).

62 "I ask the Senator": Cong. Globe, 41st Cong., 2nd sess. 5155–5156 (1870).

63 "When foreigners come": Cong. Globe, 41st Cong., 2nd sess. 5164 (1870).

63 Trumbull made one last: Cong. Globe, 41st Cong., 2nd sess. 5177 (1870).

64 "Every precinct officer": Cong. Globe, 41st Cong., 2nd sess. 5151 (1870).

Chapter 5: Rope! More Rope!

65 On January 15, 1851, John R. Evertsen: Maurice H. Newmark and Marco R. Newmark, *Census of the City and County of Los Angeles for the Year 1850: Together with an Analysis and Appendix* (Los Angeles: Times-Mirror Press, 1929), 21, 23, 30.

65 Joseph Newmark: Harris Newmark, Maurice Harris Newmark, and Marco Ross Newmark, *Sixty Years of Southern California, 1853–1913: containing the reminiscences of Harris Newmark* (New

York: Knickerbocker Press, 1916), 123, https://www.loc.gov/item/16017932/.

65 By 1870, the Chinese population: U.S. Census Bureau, 1870 Census, vol. 1, "The Statistics of the Population of the United States," Table 2, "Population of Each State and Territory, (By Counties), in the Aggregate, and as White, Free Colored, Slave, Chinese, and Indian, at all Censuses." Parts of this chapter were drawn from Michael Luo, "Remembering a Victim of an Anti-Asian Attack, a Hundred and Fifty Years Later," *New Yorker*, May 11, 2022, https://www.newyorker.com/news/daily-comment/remembering-a-victim-of-an-anti-asian-attack-a-hundred-and-fifty-years-later.

65 Its streets, lined: Remi A. Nadeau, *City-Makers: The Men Who Transformed Los Angeles from Village to Metropolis During the First Great Boom, 1868–76* (Garden City, NY: Doubleday & Company, 1948), 5–6.

66 The name apparently originated: César López, "Lost in Translation: From *Calle de Los Negros* to Nigger Alley to North Los Angeles Street to Place Erasure, Los Angeles 1855–1951," *Southern California Quarterly* 94, no. 1 (2012): 34, https:///www.jstor.org/stable/10.1525/scq.2012.94.1.25.

66 It was a narrow: Ibid., 36–38, 42; *LADN*, March 23, 1896; *LADN*, August 24, 1870; J. M. Guinn, "The Story of a Plaza," *Annual Publication of the Historical Society of Southern California and Pioneer Register, Los Angeles* 4, no. 3 (1899): 255, https://www.jstor.org/stable/41167736.

66 Coronel divided: López, "Lost in Translation," 27; *LADN*, November 7, 1871.

66 Tong was in his twenties or thirties: 1870 U.S. Census, Los Angeles Township and City, Los Angeles County, Schedule 1, 129, on Ancestry.com; Joseph Mesmer, "Massacre of Chinese," box 2, folder 6, Joseph Mesmer Papers, 1860–1914, Department of Special Collections, Charles E. Young Research Library, University of California, Los Angeles, 2. Mesmer, "Massacre of Chinamen in 1871," box 2, folder 6, Mesmer Papers, 2.

66 He had previously operated: *LADN*, July 23, 1870; *Los Angeles Daily Star*, October 27, 1871.

67 In Los Angeles, acrimony: *LADN*, May 28, 1870, June 7, 1870, June 21, 1870, and July 14, 1870. On the hostilities between the rival factions, see also Scott Zesch, *The Chinatown War: Chinese Los Angeles and the Massacre of 1871* (Oxford: Oxford University Press), 109–121.

67 Yo Hing was a former: *LAS*, March 15, 1871; *Los Angeles Semi-Weekly News*, May 15, 1868; *LAS*, October 30, 1871; J. A. Graves, *My Seventy Years in California, 1857–1927* (Los Angeles: Times-Mirror Press, 1927), 275.

67 San Bernardino, a town: 1870 U.S. Census, *A Compendium of the Ninth Census (June 1, 1870), Compiled Pursuant to a Concurrent Resolution of Congress, and Under the Direction of the Secretary of Interior by Francis A. Walker, Superintendent of Census*, Table 9, Population of Minor Civil Divisions, California (Washington, DC, 1872), 128.

67 The woman had been: *The Guardian*, November 5, 1870, and November 26, 1870.

68 A jury convicted: *The Guardian*, December 10, 1871, and December 30, 1871.

68 He targeted: *LAS*, March 10, 1871; *SFB*, March 11, 1871; *LAS*, March 8, 1871.

68 A legal skirmish: County Court Minutes, March 7, 1871, "In the Matter of the Habeas Corpus of Ut How a Chinawoman."

68 The press delighted: *LAS*, March 8, 1871.

68 In a letter addressed: *LAS*, March 10, 1871.

68 Yo Hing responded: *LAS*, March 15, 1871.

68 Sing Lee had returned: *LAS*, October 26, 1871.

68 Coronel announced plans: *LADN*, May 4, 1871.

69 gun dealers in Los Angeles: *LAS*, October 25, 1871.

69 several hired killers: *SFB*, October 26, 1871.

69 Yo Hing was standing: *LAS*, October 24, 1871, and October 30, 1871.

69 Yuen offered to act: *LADN*, October 26, 1871; *Wing Chung Co. v. City of Los Angeles*, Case No. 1941, June 22, 1872, 17th Judicial District Court, Civil Cases, LAACR.

69 According to Yuen's: *LAS*, October 31, 1871; *LADN*, February 15, 1872.

69 Bilderrain was one of a handful: Paul De Falla, "Lantern in the Western Sky," *Historical Society of Southern California Quarterly* 42, no. 1 (1960): 79, https://doi.org/10.2307/41169431.

70 He later said: *LADN*, February 15, 1872; *LADN*, October 26, 1871.

70 He hurried over on horseback: *LAS*, October 25, 1871; *LADN*, October 26, 1871; *LADN*, April 2, 1872; R. M. Widney, "Chinese Riot and Massacre in Los Angeles," *The Grizzly Bear* 28, no. 165 (January 1921): 3.

70 the county sheriff: James Franklin Burns, "James Franklin Burns, Pioneer: An Autobiographical Sketch," *Historical Society of Southern California Quarterly* 32, no. 1 (1950): 64; Horace Bell, *On the Old West Coast: Being Further Reminiscences of a Ranger—Major Horace Bell*, ed. Lanier Bartlett (Rahway, NJ: William Morrow, 1930), 171.

70 "I'm killed": *LADN*, March 31, 1872.

70 Onlookers dragged: *LAS*, October 25, 1871; Mesmer, "Massacre of Chinese," 4.

70 He had a pregnant wife: *In the Matter of the Estate of Robert Thompson*, No. 474, Probate Court, LAACR.

71 Packs of men: Mesmer, "Massacre of Chinese," 5; P. S. Dorney, "A Prophecy Partly Verified," *Overland Monthly*, March 1886, in *The Overland Monthly: Devoted to the Development of the Country*, vol. 7, 2nd series (San Francisco, 1886), 230–234.

71 Some began chanting: *San Diego Weekly Bulletin*, November 4, 1871.

71 Frank Baker, the city marshal: *People v. Richard Kerren*, Case No. 1101, Los Angeles County Court, January 5, 1872, LAACR; *Los Angeles Daily Star*, October 26, 1871.

71 Harris, a German Jewish immigrant: Norton B. Stern and William M. Kramer, "Emil Harris: Los Angeles Jewish Police Chief," *Southern California Quarterly* 55, no. 2 (Summer 1973): 163; *LADN*, October 25, 1871, and October 26, 1871.

71 In subsequent accounts: Zesch, *The Chinatown War*, 247, n. 17.

71 At Temple and New High: De Falla, "Lantern in the Western Sky," 77; *LADN*, October 25, 1871.

71 A. R. Johnston, a shoemaker: *LADN*, October 27, 1871; Dorney, "A Prophecy Partly Verified," 232. Newspaper accounts referred to Johnston as Johnson, but court records identified him as Johnston.

71 The Chinese prisoner: *San Diego Weekly Bulletin*, November 4, 1871; *LADN*, October 25, 1871.

72 Johnston was later: *LADN*, October 29, 1871.

72 A group of men: *LADN*, February 18, 1872; *LAS*, October 25 and 28, 1871.

72 A member of the mob: *LADN*, October 25 and 28, 1871; *LADN*, February 17, 1872; Mesmer, "Massacre of Chinamen in 1871," 2; De Falla, "Lantern in the Western Sky," part 1, 76.

72 A Chinese man came running out: *Los Angeles Star*, October 25, 1871.

72 When they reached the doorway: *LADN*, February 18, 1872; *San Diego Weekly Bulletin*, November 4, 1871.

73 Tong told the men: There are varying accounts of Tong's death in *San Diego Weekly Bulletin*, November 4, 1871; Mesmer, "Massacre of Chinese"; Dorney, "A Prophecy Partly Verified"; and Michael M. Rice, as told to Arthur La Vove, "I Saw the Wild West Tamed," *LAT Sunday Magazine*, May 13, 1934. In some accounts, it appears that witnesses misidentified Tong. This account

is assembled from the author's judgment of the most reliable sources.

73 He had money: *San Diego Weekly Bulletin,* November 4, 1871; Mesmer, "Massacre of Chinese," 8.

73 "like the breaking": Mesmer, "Massacre of Chinese," 2.

73 "All right, pull away": *San Diego Weekly Bulletin,* November 4, 1871.

73 At one point, two women came: *LADN,* October 28, 1871.

73 Michael Rice, an employee: Rice, "I Saw the Wild West Tamed."

73 Rioters pulled: Mesmer, "Massacre of Chinese," 7.

74 The awning in front: Dorney, "A Prophecy Partly Verified," 233.

74 The store's owner: Boyle Workman, as told to Caroline Walker, *Boyle Workman's The City That Grew* (Los Angeles: Southland Publishing Co., 1936), 146.

74 "They are killing": Widney, "Chinese Riot and Massacre in Los Angeles," 3–4.

75 There were others: *San Diego Bulletin,* November 4, 1871; Bell, *On the Old West Coast,* 323, note 3.

75 Sheriff Burns: *LAS,* October 25 and 27, 1871; C. P. Dorland, "Chinese Massacre at Los Angeles in 1871," *Annual Publication of the Historical Society of Southern California, Los Angeles* 3, no. 2 (1894): 24.

75 The Wing Chung store: *Los Angeles Star,* October 27, 1871; *Wing Chung Co. v. City of Los Angeles;* Stern and Kramer, "Emil Harris: Los Angeles Jewish Police Chief," 166.

75 Members of the mob: *LAS,* October 27, 1871.

76 "I have killed some": *LADN,* October 27, 1871.

76 the victims of the massacre: *LADN,* October 26, 1871.

76 The headline: *LAS,* October 25, 1871.

76 The *Daily News: LADN,* October 25, 1871.

76 the county coroner: *LADN,* October 26, 1871; *LAS,* October 26, 1871.

77 Afterwards, the bodies: *LAS,* October 26, 1871.

77 the jury heard from: John Albert Wilson, *History of Los Angeles County, With Illustrations Descriptive of Its Scenery, Residences, Fine Blocks and Manufactories* (Oakland, 1880), 85.

78 "We find the mob": *LADN,* October 29, 1871.

78 He urged the group: *LADN,* November 9, 1871.

78 The grand jury deliberated: *LADN,* December 3, 1871.

78 Cameron E. Thom: *LAT,* February 3, 1915; "Thom, Cameron Erskine," California Biography File, Municipal Reference Collection, Los Angeles Public Library.

79 Thom had climbed: Joseph Newmark, *Sixty Years of Southern California, 1853–1913,* 434.

79 The first case: *People v. Richard Kerren,* Case No. 1101, Los Angeles County Court, January 5, 1872, LAACR; *LADN,* October 28, 1871; *LAS,* January 6, 1872.

79 Thom decided the best strategy: De Falla, "Lantern in the Western Sky," Part 2, *Historical Society of Southern California Quarterly* 42 (June 1960): 177; Zesch, *The Chinatown War,* 188.

79 first to go to trial: *AC,* February 19, 1872.

79 "His favorite resort": *LADN,* February 20, 1872.

79 Thom's case: *LADN,* February 17 and 18, 1872; Paul R. Spitzzeri, "The Retirement of Judge Lynch: Justice in 1870s Los Angeles" (master's thesis, California State University, Fullerton, 1999), 169–172.

80 the jury deliberated: *LADN,* February 18 and 20, 1872.

80 agreeing to a request: *LADN,* February 27, 1872; Spitzzeri, "The Retirement of Judge Lynch," 174–176.

80 Selecting an impartial: *LADN,* February 22, 24, March 6, 17, 1872.

80 The trial finally: *LADN,* March 19, 22, 23, 26, and 28, *People v. L.M. Mendel,* Case No. 1084, December 2, 1871, 17th Judicial District, Criminal Cases, LAACR; Minutes, 17th Judicial Dis-

trict, March 30, 1872, LAACR; *LAS,* March 22, April 1, 1872.

80 "It has been the universal": *LADN,* March 28, 1872.

80 During the sentencing: *AC,* March 31, 1872.

81 "make known of my accounts": *People v. L. M. Mendel,* LAACR, quoted in Zesch, *The Chinatown War,* 202.

81 Other legal proceedings: Minutes, Justice of the Peace (Gray), November 2, 1871, LAACR; *People v. Sam Yuen,* Case No. 1164, November 19, 1872, LAACR.

81 observed *tachiu: AC,* August 6 and 8, 1872; *LAS,* August 6, 1872; *LADN,* August 6, 7, and 8, 1872.

81 "This morning winds up": *LADN,* August 8, 1872.

82 Based on this technicality: *People v. L. M. Mendel,* LAACR.

82 He asked a white man: *Pajaronian,* November 9, 1871.

82 "The more I see": *Pajaronian,* November 16, 1871.

Chapter 6: The Cauldron

87 "Certainty and rapidity": Thomas Butler King, "Steam Communication with China, and the Sandwich Islands," 30th Cong., 1st Sess., H. Rep. No. 596 (1848), 10.

87 Cole told his Senate: Cong. Globe, 38th Cong., 2nd sess. 831 (1865).

87 Less than two years later: "Launch of the Steamer 'Great Republic,'" *Harper's Weekly,* November 24, 1866; *NYT,* November 10, 1866; Andrew P. Roberts, *"Great Republic:* A Historical and Archaeological Analysis of a Pacific Mail Steamship" (master's thesis, Texas A&M University, 2008), 65–66.

88 On September 3, 1867: *AC,* September 4, 1867.

88 In January 1861, an imperial edict: Earl Swisher, "Chinese Representation in the United States, 1861–1912," in *Early Sino-American Relations, 1841–1912: The Collected Articles of Earl Swisher,* ed. Kenneth W. Rea (New York: Routledge,

2018), 168–170. First published in 1977 by Westview Press.

88 Burlingame had grown up: Frederick Wells Williams, *Anson Burlingame and the First Chinese Mission to Foreign Powers* (New York: Charles Scribner's Sons, 1912), 4–7.

88 Burlingame refused to treat: Ibid., 65–66.

89 Wenxiang, a reform-minded: Swisher, *Early Sino-American Relations,* 167; Burlingame letter to Seward, December 14, 1867, Despatches from U.S. Ministers to China, 1843–1906, M92, General Records of the Department of State, Record Group 59, National Archives, College Park, MD; Jane Burlingame to Ned Burlingame, November 23, 1867, in Warren B. Walsh, "The Beginnings of the Burlingame Mission," *Far Eastern Quarterly* 4, no. 3 (1945): 275–277.

89 On March 31, 1868: *AC,* April 1, 1868; Williams, *Anson Burlingame and the First Chinese Mission to Foreign Powers,* 117.

89 "For centuries this people": *AC,* April 29, 1868.

90 "From him we received": Carl Schurz, *The Reminiscences of Carl Schurz,* vol. 2 (New York: Doubleday, Page & Company, 1908), 174.

90 Seward was a fervent: Tyler Dennett, "Seward's Far Eastern Policy," *American Historical Review* 28, no. 1 (1922): 46–47; Henry Tsai Shih-shan, *China and the Overseas Chinese in the United States, 1868–1911* (Fayetteville: University of Arkansas Press, 1983), 26–27; Williams, *Anson Burlingame and the First Chinese Mission to Foreign Powers,* 144.

90 In the middle of July: *NYT,* July 15, 1868.

90 "thoroughly advantageous": Prince Kung to Burlingame, June 7, 1869, enclosure in Burlingame to Seward, September 3, 1869, NFCL.

91 It was a provision: Williams, *Anson Burlingame and the First Chinese Mission to Foreign Powers,* 156; William Alexander Parsons Martin, *A Cycle of Cathay: Or, China, South and North* (New York:

Fleming H. Revell Company, 1900), 376.

91 He was also convinced: *NYT,* February 25, 1871.

91 The San Francisco Custom House had begun: Mary Roberts Coolidge, *Chinese Immigration* (New York, 1907), 498.

91 One day in 1869: Albert S. Evans, "From the Orient Direct," *Atlantic Monthly,* November 1869.

92 Chinese inhabitants in California: U.S. Census Bureau, 1870 Census, vol. 1, "The Statistics of the Population of the United States," Table 2, "Population of Each State and Territory (By Counties) in the Aggregate, and as White, Free Colored, Slave, Chinese, and Indian, at all Censuses"; 1870 Census, Table 14, "The Foreign-born Population, Distributed According to Place of Birth Among the Principal Foreign Countries—1870."

92 They joined other: Alexander Saxton, *The Indispensable Enemy: Labor and the Anti-Chinese Movement in California* (Berkeley: University of California Press, 1971), 11; Ira B. Cross, *A History of the Labor Movement in California* (Berkeley: University of California Press, 1935), 61.

92 Many who made the journey: Saxton, *The Indispensable Enemy,* 5, 13.

92 a stagnating economy: Cross, *A History of the Labor Movement in California,* 62–63.

92 "Instead of bringing": *Springfield (MA) Republican,* February 12, 1870.

92 Over the next decade: Coolidge, *Chinese Immigration,* 498; *Annual Report of the Commissioner-General of Immigration for the Fiscal Year Ended June 30, 1903* (Washington, DC: Government Printing Office, 1903), 34–35.

92 In the fall of 1869: *SFE,* November 25, 28, 29, December 2, 1869; Robert Arthur, *The San Francisco Irish, 1848–1880* (Berkeley: University of California Press, 1980), 102–104; *Golden Era,* March 13, 1870; *AC,* February 14, 1867.

92 In December, Mooney petitioned: "Memorial of the Anti-Coolie and Anti-Monopoly Association of San Francisco, California," Senate Misc. Doc. No. 34, *Index to the Miscellaneous Documents of the Senate of the United States for the Second Session of the Forty-First Congress, 1869–1870* (Washington, DC, 1870).

93 In July 1870, thousands: *AC,* July 9, 16, 1870; *SFE,* July 12, 16, 1870.

93 a reporter witnessed: *SFB,* June 15, 1870.

93 On another occasion: *Washington Standard* (Olympia, WA), July 19, 1873.

93 From a bridge: Kevin J. Mullen, *The Toughest Gang in Town: Police Stories from Old San Francisco* (Novato, CA: Noir Publications, 2005), 133.

93 George Lem arrived: "Interview with Mr. George Lem," August 4, 1924, by Catherine Holt, in "A Group of 13 Interviews with Individuals of Los Angeles Chinatown," box 30, folder 298, SRR, https://purl.stanford.edu/dk495pg9531.

94 "When I first came": "Life History and Social Document of Andrew Kan," August 22, 1924, by C. H. Burnett, Major Document 178, box 27, SRR, https://purl.stanford.edu/bj914bp6148.

94 By 1870, about a quarter: Sucheng Chan, *Bittersweet Soil: The Chinese in California Agriculture, 1860–1910* (Berkeley: University of California Press, 1986), 44.

94 They took up new occupations: Saxton, *The Indispensable Enemy,* 4–5; Ping Chiu, *Chinese Labor in California: An Economic Study* (Madison: State Historical Society of Wisconsin, 1963), x–xii; Thomas W. Chinn and Philip P. Choy, eds., *A History of the Chinese in California* (San Francisco: Chinese Historical Society of America, 1969), 49–64.

94 The buildings in Chinatown: Otis Gibson, *The Chinese in America* (Cincinnati, 1877), 63–94.

94 they submitted a petition: *SFB,* June 14, 1870; *SFCh,* July 6, 1870.

95 The board members ultimately: *SFCh,* July 13, 1870; *San Francisco Municipal Reports for the Fiscal Year 1869–1870,*

Ending June 30, 1870 (San Francisco, 1870), 233.

95 the board of supervisors enacted: *San Francisco Municipal Reports for the Fiscal Year 1872–1873, Ending June 30th, 1873* (San Francisco, 1873), 592.

95 the first significant effort to enforce: *SFB*, May 20, 1873.

95 In total, more: *San Francisco Municipal Reports for the Fiscal Year 1872–73, Ending June 30th, 1873* (San Francisco, 1873), 154.

95 Lon Ci Tat, who had: *SFB*, August 15, September 9, 1873.

95 The police halted: *San Francisco Municipal Reports for the Fiscal Year 1873–1874*, 122–124; *San Francisco Municipal Reports for the Fiscal Year 1874–1875*, 504–506; *San Francisco Municipal Reports for the Fiscal Year 1875–1876*, 108; "An Act concerning lodging-houses and sleeping apartments within the limits of incorporated cities," *The Statutes of California Passed at the Twenty-First Session of the Legislature, 1875–6* (San Francisco, 1876), 759.

95 The local press avidly: *SFB*, May 2, 18, June 15, 1876.

95 One San Francisco police officer: *Report of the Joint Special Committee to Investigate Chinese Immigration*, 44th Cong., 2nd sess. (Washington, DC: GPO, 1877), 234.

96 The Chinese-language newspaper: *The Oriental (Tang Fan Kung Pao)*, May 13, 1876.

96 some fifteen thousand: *SFCh*, February 10, 1878; Saxton, *The Indispensable Enemy*, 106.

96 "tramp nuisance": *AC*, March 18, 1876.

96 "All the men here": *Irish World and Industrial Liberator*, January 12, 1878, quoted in Philip S. Foner, *History of the Labor Movement in the United States*, vol. 1, *From Colonial Times to the American Federation of Labor* (New York: International Publishers, 1947), 443.

97 The two groups: Chiu, *Chinese Labor in California: An Economic Study*, xi–xii.

97 shoemakers and cigar makers: Cross, *A History of the Labor Movement in California*, 136.

97 The term "hoodlum": Peter Tamony, "Hoodlums and Folk Etymology," *Western Folkore* 28, no. 1 (January 1969): 45.

97 One group became: Mullen, *The Toughest Gang in Town*, 133.

97 "The Chinese were in": Huie Kin, *Reminiscences* (Peiping: San Yu Press, 1932), 27.

97 On April 5, 1876: *NYT*, April 14, 1876; *SFCh*, April 6, 1876.

97 "We went into places": Lewis testimony, in Special Committee on Chinese Immigration, *Chinese Immigration; Its Social, Moral, and Political Effect* (Sacramento, CA, 1878), 110.

98 "I don't know": Yung Ty testimony, in *Chinese Immigration*, 160.

98 "Then shall we": Six Chinese Companies, "To the American public," in Bee testimony, in *Report of the Joint Special Committee to Investigate Chinese Immigration*, 38.

98 The committee issued: "An Address to the People of the United States Upon the Evils of Chinese Immigration," *Chinese Immigration*, 49.

Chapter 7: Lewd and Immoral Purposes

99 when she was about twenty: An obituary for Ah Toy, published in the *SFE* on February 2, 1928, described her as a few months shy of her hundredth birthday.

99 "bettering her condition": *AC*, March 8, 1851.

99 "slender body": Albert Benard de Russailh, trans. Clarkson Crane, *Last Adventure, San Francisco in 1851. Translated from the Original Journal of Albert Benard de Russailh* (San Francisco: Westgate Press, 1931), 89.

99 Her first place of business: Charles Caldwell Dobie, *San Francisco's Chinatown* (New York: Appleton-Century, 1936), 29.

99 The men paid: *SFE*, January 23, 1881.

99 Ah Toy was widely understood: Charles Albro Baker, ed., *Memoirs of Elisha Oscar Crosby: Reminiscences of California and Guatemala from 1849 to 1864* (San Marino, CA: Huntington Library, 1945), 109.

99 Ah Toy quickly became: Curt Gentry, *The Madams of San Francisco: An Irreverent History of the City by the Golden Gate* (New York: Ballantine Books, 1971), 53; Benson Tong, *Unsubmissive Women: Chinese Prostitutes in Nineteenth-Century San Francisco* (Norman: University of Oklahoma Press, 1994), 8.

99 "well known China woman": *AC*, May 22, 1850.

100 many of them under: *Nevada Journal*, June 19, 1852.

100 On one visit: *SFE*, January 23, 1881.

100 On another occasion: *AC*, December 11, 12, 14, 16, 24, 1851, and January 9, 1852.

100 One of her more disturbing: *AC*, March 8, 1851.

100 In 1857, Ah Toy: Gentry, *The Madams of San Francisco*, 58.

100 a city newspaper published: *SFE*, February 2, 1928.

100 The 1852 census: Tong, *Unsubmissive Women*, 3; U.S. Census Bureau, 1870 Census, vol. 1, "The Statistics of the Population of the United States," Table 22, "The Table of Sex," 609.

101 blamed the reluctance: A. W. Loomis, "Chinese Women in California," *Overland Monthly*, April 1869, in the digital collection *Making of America Journal Articles*, University of Michigan Library Digital Collections, 345, https://name.umdl.umich.edu/ahj1472.1-02.004.

101 "It is exceedingly difficult": Lai Chunchuen, *Remarks of the Chinese Merchants of San Francisco upon Governor Bigler's Message, and Some Common Objections; with Some Explanations of the Character of the Chinese Companies, and the Laboring Class of California* (San Francisco, 1855), 3, CIC, California Historical Society.

101 From early on: On the treatment of Chinese women in the nineteenth century, see also Tong, *Unsubmissive Women;* Sucheng Chan, "Exclusion of Chinese Women," in *Entry Denied: Exclusion and the Chinese Community in America, 1882–1943*, ed. Sucheng Chan (Philadelphia: Temple University Press, 1991), 94–146.

101 "Girls scarcely": Stuart Creighton Miller, *The Unwelcome Immigrant: The American Image of the Chinese, 1785–1882* (Berkeley: University of California Press, 1969), 62.

101 On March 20, 1854: Ordinance No. 546, *Ordinances and Joint Resolutions of the City of San Francisco; Together with a List of the Officers of the City and County, and Rules and Orders of the Common Council* (San Francisco, 1854), 264–265.

101 It found Chinese arrivals: *AC*, August 22, 1854.

101 leading Chinese merchants resolved: *AC*, August 22 and 30, 1854; Chunchuen Lai, *Remarks of the Chinese Merchants*, 4.

102 the state legislature enacted: "An Act for the Suppression of Chinese Houses of Ill Fame," *The Statutes of California Passed at the Sixteenth Session of the Legislature, 1865–6* (Sacramento, 1866), 641–642.

102 brothel operators reached: *AC*, June 22, 1866.

102 On both sides were: *SFCh*, May 12, 1869.

102 a police captain ordered: Otis Gibson, *The Chinese in America* (Cincinnati, 1877), 204.

102 he prayed to never: *Harper's Weekly*, October 20, 1877.

103 "There is nothing": Gibson, *The Chinese in America*, 127, 134.

103 In August 1870: *History of the Mission of the Methodist Episcopal Church to the Chinese in California* (San Francisco, 1877), 10–11.

103 She ended up staying: Gibson, *The Chinese in America*, 205.

104 "I used to gamble": Ibid., 221.

104 a merchant, Lun Yat Sung: *SFB,* August 22, 1873.

104 The women managed: *SFB,* July 30, 1873.

104 He found himself: *New York Herald,* August 9, 1873.

104 Hip Yee Tong had begun: *SFB,* August 4, 1873.

104 The police swept: *SFB,* July 30, 1873.

104 The prosecution's case began: *SFCh,* August 12, 1873.

105 The women at the mission: *History of the Mission,* 12–13; Gibson, *The Chinese in America,* 206.

105 "I move that we work": Mrs. I. M. Condit, *A Quarter of a Century* (pamphlet accompanying *Women's Occidental Board of Foreign Missions, Twenty-Fifth Annual Report,* 1898), San Francisco Theological Seminary Branch Library of the GTU Library. (This repository will hereafter be cited as SF Seminary.)

105 "a refuge for Chinese women": California Branch of the Woman's Foreign Missionary Society of the Presbyterian Church of San Francisco, *First Annual Report* (San Francisco, 1874), SF Seminary, 8; Mrs. I. M. Condit, *A Quarter of a Century,* 10.

105 In July 1874: Woman's Foreign Missionary Society, *Third Annual Report* (1876), SF Seminar, 20; *Second Annual Report* (1875), 16. On the Mission Home and its history, see Julia Flynn Siler, *The White Devil's Daughters: The Women Who Fought Slavery in San Francisco's Chinatown* (New York: Knopf, 2019).

106 In her annual report: Woman's Foreign Missionary Society, *Third Annual Report* (1875), SF Seminary, 20.

106 In 1870, a new state law: "An Act to prevent the kidnapping and importation of Mongolian, Chinese, and Japanese females, for criminal or demoralizing purposes," *Statutes of California Passed at the Eighteenth Session of the Legislature, 1869–1870* (Sacramento, 1870), 331.

106 The census of 1870: Benson Tong, *Unsubmissive Women,* 97.

106 Lee Wong Sang: Connie Young Yu, *Voices from the Railroad: Stories by Descendants of Chinese Railroad Workers,* ed. Sue Lee and Connie Young Yu (San Francisco: Chinese Historical Society of America, 2019), 77–89.

107 Chin Lin Sou was in his: This account of Chin's life is drawn from William "Tim" Jung (great-grandson of Chin Lin Sou) interview, in Chinese Railroad Workers Oral History Project, 2013–2018, Department of Special Collections and University Archives, Stanford University, https://purl.stanford.edu /tz584cr6121; Ruth Chin, "The Story of a Colorado Pioneer," undated essay, in *Biography of Chin Lin Sou,* Chin Lin Sou Collection, MSS.113, Stephen H. Hart Research Center at History Colorado; Carolyn and Linda Jew, "Chin Lin Sou," in *Biography of Chin Lin Sou; Colorado Springs Gazette,* November 7, 1874; and Carolyn G. Kuhn, "Chin Lin Sou: Colorado Pioneer," in *Voices from the Railroad,* 27–31.

107 "Her countenance shone": Forbes Parkhill, *The Wildest of the West: A Bold and Lusty Gallery of Colorado's Most Famous Characters in the Nineties* (New York: Henry Holt, 1951), 108.

107 carrying 589 Chinese passengers: The records differ slightly on the exact number of passengers and their breakdown. See the certification of the U.S. consulate in Hong Kong, the emigration officer's certificate, and the passenger manifest in Ex parte Ah Fook case file, No. 10114, California Supreme Court, WPA 107161, California State Archives.

108 The ship's captain: Testimony of John Freeman, Ah Fook case file, 8–9, 21–22.

108 Inside a smoking room: Ah Fook case file, trial transcript, 96, 98.

108 "According to my judgment": Testimony of Rudolph Piotrowski, trial transcript, Ah Fook case file, 18.

108 Court records reference: Ah Fook case file; *SFE,* August 25, 1874; *AC,* August 26, 1874.

109 A new petitioner: Transcript of Record, Chy Lung v. Freeman, 92 U.S. 275, January 8, 1875, 50.

109 The women began wailing: Gibson, *The Chinese in America*, 146–147; *SFE*, August 25, 1874; *SFCh*, August 26, 1874; *AC*, August 26, 1874.

109 The twenty-two women: *SFCh*, August 28, 1874.

109 the first of the accused: *SFE*, August 27, 1874; *AC*, August 27, 1874.

109 On the stand, Gibson: Gibson testimony, trial transcript, Ah Fook case file, 49–50, 57.

110 Quint asked Gibson: *SFCh*, August 27, 1874; Gibson testimony, trial transcript, Ah Fook case file, 59–60.

110 the women in the courtroom: *SFCh*, August 28, 1874; *SFE*, August 28, 1874.

110 Quint introduced: *SFCh*, August 28, 1874; *SFE*, August 28, 1874; *AC*, August 28, 1874; trial transcript, Ah Fook case file, 144. There exists some confusion about whether the woman correctly identified her husband. The news accounts reported that she did; the transcript said she did not.

110 "Are these women": *SFCh*, August 29, 1874.

110 The courtroom was crowded: *SFCh*, August 30, 1874; *AC*, August 30, 1874.

111 the state supreme court ruled: *AC*, September 8, 1874.

111 Field focused on: *SFCh*, September 19, 1874.

111 In his decision: *In re* Ah Fong, 1 F. Cas. 213 (C.C.D. Cal. 1874) (no. 102), 217.

112 More than a year later: See *Chy Lung v. Freeman*.

112 A crowd surrounded: *SFB*, September 25, 1874.

112 he had been toiling: Ron Chernow, *Grant* (New York: Penguin Press, 2017), 785.

112 "I call the attention": Grant, Sixth Annual Message, December 7, 1874, American Presidency Project, UC Santa Barbara, https://www.presidency.ucsb.edu/documents/sixth-annual-message-3.

113 "The Chinese are": 2 Cong. Rec. 4537 (1874).

113 "An Act Supplementary": 3 Cong. Rec. 1599 (1875).

113 Page introduced: 3 Cong. Rec. Appendix 40–42, 44 (1875).

114 President Grant signed: "An act supplementary to the acts in relation to immigration," *Statutes of the United States of America, Passed at the Second Session of the Forty-Third Congress, 1874–75* (Washington, DC, 1875), 477.

Chapter 8: Order of Caucasians

115 the mostly male Chinese population: Sucheng Chan, *This Bittersweet Soil: The Chinese in California Agriculture, 1860–1910* (Berkeley: University of California Press, 1986), 50.

115 A farmer's wife: *Stockton Independent*, October 23, 1876, in Bancroft reference notes, vol. 7, BANC MSS 97/31 c, BL, 31.

116 "They are the best": *Report of the Joint Special Committee to Investigate Chinese Immigration*, 44th Cong., 2nd sess. (Washington, DC: GPO, 1877), 439–440.

116 a series of raids: *SDU*, April 16, 1868.

116 arsonists linked to the Klan: *Christian Advocate*, April 8, 1869.

117 "The working men of Gilroy": *Santa Cruz Weekly Sentinel*, January 1, 1876.

117 The organization's ranks: *Territorial Enterprise*, August 24, 1876.

117 Members adhered: *SFCh*, February 11, 1877.

117 Anyone who employed: Hubert Howe Bancroft, *Inter Pocula: A Review of Some Classical Abnormities* (San Francisco, 1888), 571.

118 "seemed to wall in": Isabella L. Bird, *A Lady's Life in the Rocky Mountains* (New York, 1879), 7.

118 they made up about a quarter: Michael Andrew Goldstein, "Truckee's Chinese Community: From Coexistence to Disintegration, 1870–1890" (master's thesis, University of California, Los Angeles, 1988), 13. On the Chinese community in

Truckee, see also Jean Pfaelzer, *Driven Out: The Forgotten War on Chinese Americans* (Berkeley: University of Cailfornia Press, 2008), 171–196.

118 The census of 1870: U.S. Census Bureau, 1870 Census, Schedule 1, Inhabitants in Meadow Lake Township, Nevada County, California.

118 Early in the morning: *Truckee Republican,* May 29, 1875.

118 white merchants in Truckee: *Truckee Republican,* June 2, 5, 1875; Goldstein, "Truckee's Chinese Community," 30–31; Calvin Cheung-Miaw and Roland Hsu, "Before the 'Truckee Method': Race, Space, and Capital in Truckee's Chinese Community, 1870–1880," *Amerasia Journal* 45, no. 1 (2019): 75, https://doi.org/10.1080/00447471.2019 .1605712.

118 more than three hundred: Guy H. Coates, "The Trout Creek Outrage: 19th Century Racial Violence Targeted Truckee's Sizeable Chinese Population," July 2000, Truckee Donner Historical Society newsletter, in Truckee #2 folder, Hagaman Chinese Collection, Searls Historical Library, Nevada County Historical Society; Wallace R. Hagaman with Steve F. Cottrell, *The Chinese Must Go! The Anti-Chinese Boycott, Truckee, California, 1886: "Peacefully, Orderly, Lawfully"* (Nevada City, CA: Cowboy Press, 2004), 9.

118 Among the targets: Joanne Meschery, *An Illustrated History of the Town and Its Surroundings* (Truckee, CA: Rocking Stone Press, 1978), 71; Guy Coates, "History: Joseph Gray—Early Pioneer and Leader in Truckee," *Sierra Sun,* July 11, 2021, https://www.sierrasun .com/news/history-joseph-gray-early -pioneer-and-leader-in-truckee/.

118 On the evening of June 17: *SDU,* September 27 and 28, 1876; *AC,* September 28, 1876; *Truckee Republican,* June 21 and September 30, 1876.

119 "as though the victims": *Truckee Republican,* June 21, 1876.

119 A group of white Truckee: *SDU,* September 27, 1876; Coates, "The Trout Creek Outrage," TDHS newsletter.

120 A grand jury indicted: *The People v. G.W. Getchell, F. Wilbert, James Reed, G.W. Mershon, Frank Wilson, Calvin McCullough and Wm O'Neal* case file, No. 4263, October 4, 1876, Nevada County District Court records, Searls Historical Library, Nevada County Historical Society.

120 William O'Neal: *Truckee Republican,* September 27, 1876; *SDU,* September 27 and October 3, 1876.

120 Gaylord called: *Truckee Republican,* September 30, 1876.

120 The defense called: *History of Nevada County with Illustrations Descriptive of Its Scenery, Residences, Public Buildings, Fine Blocks, and Manufactories* (Oakland, 1880), 114; *Truckee Republican,* September 30, 1876.

120 The jury required: *AC,* October 4 and 5, 1876; *SDU,* October 6, 1876.

120 Truckee's Chinese quarter: *SDU,* October 31, 1876; *Grass Valley Daily Union,* November 3, 1878.

120 the town's safety committee: *SDU,* November 22, 23, 26, 1878; *Grass Valley Daily Union,* November 26, 1878.

120 Chinese immigrants first arrived: Susan W. Book, *The Chinese in Butte County, California, 1860–1920* (San Francisco: R and E Research Associates, 1976), 9; George C. Mansfield, *Butte: The Story of a California County* (Oroville, CA, 1919), 13.

121 "I thought that the entire": George C. Mansfield, *The History of Butte County California with Biographical Sketches of the Leading Men and Women of the County Who Have Been Identified with Its Growth and Development from the Early Days to the Present* (Los Angeles: Historic Record Company, 1918), 251.

121 It was at Bidwell's: Mansfield, *The History of Butte County California,* 240.

121 hamlet of nearly four thousand: *A Compendium of the Ninth Census (June 1,*

1870), Table 9, Population of Minor Civil Divisions, California, 125; Book, *The Chinese in Butte County*, 30–31.

121 The dwellings were: George C. Orberg, "Chinese in Chico," *Butte County Historical Society Diggin's* 4, no. 3 (Fall 1960): 13.

121 renamed it the *California Caucasian:* Harry L. Wells and W. L. Chambers, *The History of Butte County California in Two Volumes* (San Francisco, 1882), 196.

121 On June 15, 1876: *The Weekly Butte Record*, June 17, 1876; Roger Aylworth, "Enterprise-Record's History as Colorful as It Is Long," *Chico Enterprise-Record*, November 2, 2011. On the anti-Chinese movement in Chico, see also Michele Shover, *Chico's Lemm Ranch Murders and Anti-Chinese Campaign of 1877* (Chico, CA: Association for Northern California Records and Research, 1998), and Pfaelzer, *Driven Out*, 61–74.

121 At the group's next meeting: *The Weekly Butte Record*, July 1, 15, August 26, 1876.

122 The Chico "camp": Shover, *Chico's Lemm Ranch Murders*, 13.

122 Several hundred white men: *People v. John Slaughter* case file, No. 1301, Second District Court, Butte County, B. B. Baker testimony, Meriam Library, California State University, Chico; *Chico Enterprise*, December 15, 1876.

122 several dozen men: Hubert Howe Bancroft, *Inter Pocula: A Review of Some Classical Abnormities* (San Francisco, 1888), 568.

122 The council discussed: *SDU*, March 31, 1877; *SFCh*, April 2, 1877.

122 they began arming themselves: *The Weekly Butte Record*, December 23, 1876.

122 arsonists used kerosene: *SDU*, April 19 and 20, 1877; February 7, 1877, John Bidwell Diaries, 1864–1900, vol. 12, 1877, California State Library.

122 at a ranch just outside of Chico: *Chico Enterprise*, March 2, 1877.

123 a group of white men: *SDU*, April 24, 1877, *Chico Enterprise*, March 30, 1877.

123 nearby town of Nord: *Chico Enterprise*, March 9, 1877; Book, *The Chinese in Butte County*, 43.

123 At around nine o'clock: *The Weekly Butte Record*, March 17 and June 2, 1877; Beulah Lemm Balmer, *Heart of the Family Tree: Darge, Lemm, Kidwell, Schoen, Moak, Mann* (Seattle, WA: Homestead Press, 1979), 26–27.

124 "The first Chinaman": Sim Moak, *The Last of the Mill Creeks, and Early Life in Northern California* (Chico, CA, 1923), 29.

124 Notices appeared: *The Weekly Butte Record*, March 23, 1877; Moak, *The Last of the Mill Creeks, and Early Life in Northern California*, 27.

124 "would have been interpreted": John Bidwell, *Dictation from John Bidwell: An Autobiography*, typescript, BANC MSS C-D 802, HHB, BL, 51.

124 The break in the case: *SFCh*, March 30, 1877.

124 He initially insisted: *SDU*, March 27, 1877; *The Weekly Butte Record*, March 31, 1877; John Bidwell, *Dictation from John Bidwell*, 51.

124 The authorities placed: *SDU*, March 29, 1877.

124 "considered good citizens": *SFCh*, March 30, 1877.

125 "to show what men": John Bidwell, *Dictation from John Bidwell*, 51.

125 A jury found: *Chico Enterprise*, June 1, 1877.

125 In 1883, Governor George Stoneman: *Chico Enterprise*, November 30, 1883.

125 "I have never yielded": John Bidwell, *Dictation from John Bidwell*, 52, 54.

Chapter 9: The Chinese Must Go!

126 On the morning of: *NYT*, September 19, 1873; *Philadelphia Inquirer*, September 19, 1873; *Brooklyn Daily Eagle*, September 19, 1873.

126 A cascading series of crises: Samuel Bernstein, "American Labor in the Long Depression, 1873–1878," *Science & Society* 20, no. 1 (Winter 1956): 61,

https://www.jstor.org/stable/40400385; *First Annual Report of the Commissioner of Labor* (Washington, DC, 1886), 67.

126 On the night of July 16: F. Vernon Aler, *Aler's History of Martinsburg and Berkeley County, West Virginia* (Hagerstown, MD, 1888), 300–304.

126 In Pittsburgh: *Report of the Committee Appointed to Investigate the Railroad Riots in July, 1877* (Harrisburg, PA, 1878), 9.

127 more than four thousand: Ira B. Cross, *A History of the Labor Movement in California* (Berkeley: University of California Press, 1935), 61.

127 Central Pacific officials: Henry George, "The Kearney Agitation in California," August 1880, in *The Popular Science Monthly, Conducted by E.L. and W.J. Youmans*, vol. 17, *May to October 1880*, 437; Cross, *A History of the Labor Movement in California*, 89.

127 On Monday, July 23: *AC*, July 24, 1877; *SFCh*, July 24, 1877.

127 a triangular plot of land: *SFCh*, November 30, 1877.

127 rumors spread about plans: George, "The Kearney Agitation in California," 437.

127 A brass band: *AC*, July 24, 1877.

127 "On to Chinatown": *SFB*, July 24, 1877.

127 Just after nine o'clock: *SFCh*, July 24, 1877; *AC*, July 24, 1877; *NYT*, July 25, 1877.

128 the body of a Chinese man: *SFB*, July 25, 1877; *SFCh*, July 25, 1877.

128 A few blocks away: *SFCh*, July 25, 1877; Hubert Howe Bancroft, *Chronicles of the Builders of the Commonwealth: Historical Character Study*, vol. 1 (San Francisco, 1891), 352–354; Philip J. Ethington, "Vigilantes and the Police: The Creation of a Professional Police Bureaucracy in San Francisco, 1847–1900," *Journal of Social History* 21, no. 2 (Winter 1877): 207, https://www.jstor.org/stable/3788141.

128 Telegrams to the War Department: Major General McDowell to Commanding Officer, Benicia Arsenal, telegram, June 25, 1877, in Henry H. Ellis letters and notes: San Francisco, CA, 1870–1877, MS 657, California Historical Society; Bancroft, *Chronicles of the Builders of the Commonwealth*, 366.

128 At around eight o'clock: *SFB*, July 25, 1877.

129 At about ten thirty: *SFB*, July 25, 1877; *AC*, July 26, 1877; *SFCh*, July 26, 1877; *San Francisco Mail*, July 26, 1877.

129 Several miles away: *SFCh*, July 25, 1877.

129 Throughout the following day: Bancroft, *Chronicles of the Builders of the Commonwealth*, 355, 358; *SFCh*, July 26, 1877; *AC*, July 26, 1877; *NYT*, July 27, 1877.

130 A speaker named N. P. Brock: *SFB*, July 26, 1877; *San Francisco Mail*, July 26, 1877.

130 Soon, about two hundred: *SFCh*, July 26, 1877; *SFB*, July 26, 1877; *San Francisco Mail*, July 26, 1877.

130 a huge blaze burned: *SFCh*, July 27, 1877; *AC*, July 26, 1877; Thomas W. Wells to M. J. Harrington, July 29, 1877, Thomas W. Wells letters, BANC MSS 2004/435 c, BL.

131 "Even the terrified": *SFCh*, July 27, 1877.

131 Overnight, a steamship delivered: *SFCh*, July 26, 1877.

131 The city turned into: *SFCh*, July 27, 1877; *NYT*, July 28, 1877.

131 more than two thousand: *SFB*, July 27, 1877; *NYT*, July 28, 1877; *SFCh*, July 28, 1877; *SFB*, July 28, 1877.

131 The Pacific Mail steamship: *SFCh*, July 28, 1877; *SFE*, July 30, 1877.

131 Coleman ordered: *SFE*, July 31, 1877.

131 charged up Rincon Hill: *SFCh*, November 20, 1877.

131 Kearney was born: Cross, *A History of the Labor Movement in California*, 93; Hubert Howe Bancroft, *The Works of Hubert Howe Bancroft*, vol. 37: *Popular Tribunals*, vol. 2 (San Francisco, 1887), 713; J. C. Stedman and R. A. Leonard, *The Workingmen's Party of California: An Epitome of Its Rise and Progress* (San Francisco, 1878), 95.

132 He also began hanging: John P. Young, *San Francisco: A History of the Pacific Coast Metropolis*, vol. 2 (San Francisco: S. J. Clarke Publishing Co., 1912), 534.

132 Kearney was named: *SFCh*, June 24, 1878.

132 He applied to join: Cross, *A History of the Labor Movement in California*, 93.

132 On September 16, 1877: *SFCh*, September 17, 1877; Stedman and Leonard, *The Workingmen's Party of California*, 18.

132 "We must settle": Stedman and Leonard, *The Workingmen's Party of California*, 18–19.

133 Kearney later told: Denis Kearney to James Bryce, letter, in James Bryce, *The American Commonwealth*, vol. 2 (Chicago, 1891), 748.

133 On October 5, 1877: Cross, *A History of the Labor Movement in California*, 96.

133 Kearney's primary aim: Bryce, *The American Commonwealth*, 748.

133 He adopted a slogan: Frank Roney, *Frank Roney, Irish Rebel and California Labor Leader: An Autobiography*, ed. Ira B. Cross (Berkeley: University of California Press, 1931), 270.

133 On October 28: *SFCh*, October 29, 1877.

133 About three thousand: *SFCh*, October 30, 1877; Stedman and Leonard, *The Workingmen's Party of California*, 26; Bancroft, *Popular Tribunals*, 715.

134 Crocker met with: *SFB*, October 30, 1877.

134 "As a rule": *SFCh*, November 4, 1877.

134 When he finally appeared: Stedman and Leonard, *The Workingmen's Party of California*, 27.

134 At a ward meeting: Frank Michael Fahey, "Denis Kearney, a Study in Demagoguery" (PhD diss., Stanford University, 1956), 82.

134 The city girded itself: *SFCh*, November 29, 1877.

135 The procession began: *SFCh*, November 30, 1877; *SFE*, November 29, 1877; Alexander Saxton, *The Indispensable Enemy: Labor and the Anti-Chinese Movement in California* (Berkeley: University of California Press, 1971), 119.

135 bearing banners that read: Cited in "Denis Kearney, a Study in Demagoguery," by Frank Michael Fahey, 86.

135 In San Jose, Oakland, Sacramento: Fahey, "Denis Kearney, a Study in Demagoguery," 122–123.

135 In mid-December: *SFCh*, December 20, 1877.

135 Kearney led a crowd: *SFCh*, January 4, 1878.

135 "How many of you": *SFCh*, January 16, 1878.

135 new grand jury indictment: *SFE*, January 7, 1878.

136 As Kearney and his cohort: *SFCh*, January 18, 1878; *SFB*, January 18, 1878.

136 the populist grievances: Hubert Howe Bancroft, *The Works of Hubert Howe Bancroft*, vol. 24: *History of California*, vol. 7, *1860–1890* (San Francisco, 1890), 374; Noel Sargent, "The California Constitutional Convention of 1878-9," *California Law Review* 6, no. 1 (November 1917): 1–4, https://www.jstor.org/stable/3474812.

136 The party's election ballots: Workingmen's Party election ballot ticket, Scrapbook of Political Broadsides, 1860s–1890s, MS 5097, California Historical Society.

136 an estimated six thousand: *SFCh*, June 16, 1878.

137 On August 5: Dennis Kearney, *Speeches of Dennis Kearney, Labor Champion* (New York, 1878), 4, 7, 8; *NYT*, August 6, 1878; Fahey, "Denis Kearney, a Study in Demagoguery," 232–234.

137 profane speech on Boston Common: *NYT*, August 10, 1878; Kearney, *Speeches of Dennis Kearney*, 13.

137 Kearney's itinerary: *NYT*, August 18, September 3, 1878.

137 "You are concentrating": *NYT*, August 29, 1878.

137 from the Capitol steps: *NYT*, August 30, 1878.

137 On September 6: *NYT*, September 7, 1878.

137 "He was circus": *NYT*, August 10, 1878.

137 "The great agitator": *NYT*, July 28, 1878.

138 "a brilliant success": Bryce, *The American Commonwealth*, 749.

138 thousands were on hand: *SFCh*, November 27, 1878.

138 The delegates had voted: *Debates and Proceedings of the Constitutional Convention of the State of California, Convened at the City of Sacramental, Saturday, September 28, 1878*, vol. 1 (Sacramento, 1880), 59.

138 John Franklin Miller: T. J. Vivian and D. G. Waldron, ed. and pub., *Biographical Sketches of the Delegates to the Convention to Frame a New Constitution for the State of California, 1878* (San Francisco, 1878), 149; *NYTr*, March 9, 1886.

138 "Chinese immigration was an evil": *Debates and Proceedings of the Constitutional Convention of the State of California*, vol. 2 (San Francisco, 1878), 709.

138 The committee set aside: Elmer Clarence Sandmeyer, *The Anti-Chinese Movement in California* (1939; Urbana: University of Illinois Press, 1991), 68–69.

139 "It is an unassimilative": *Debates and Proceedings of the Constitutional Convention of the State of California*, vol. 2, 631–632.

139 Charles V. Stuart: Timothy Sandefur, "Charles V. Stuart: A Solitary Voice at California's Constitutional Convention," January 29, 2008, 6–10, https://ssrn.com/abstract=1088544.

140 "They are not proper": *Debates and Proceedings of the Constitutional Convention of the State of California*, vol. 2, 642.

140 When it came time: Sandmeyer, *The Anti-Chinese Movement in California*, 71–72.

140 delivering 130 speeches: Fahey, "Denis Kearney, a Study in Demagoguery," 244.

141 foe of the sandlot movement: *SFE*, August 30, 1879.

141 But he later reversed: M. M. Marberry, *The Golden Voice: A Biography of Isaac Kalloch* (New York: Farrar, Straus and Company, 1947), 234–239; George, "The Kearney Agitation in California," 447.

141 Kalloch's popularity: Mary Frances McKinney, "Denis Kearney, Organizer of the Workingmen's Party of California" (master's thesis, graduate division of the University of California, 1938), BL, 78; Fahey, "Denis Kearney: A Study in Demagoguery," 254.

141 killed de Young: *SFCh*, April 24, 1880.

141 A mass meeting: Roney, *Frank Roney*, 306–307.

141 Some in the Workingmen's: Fahey, "Denis Kearney, a Study in Demagoguery," 259–260; Cross, *A History of the Labor Movement in California*, 127.

141 During a sandlot meeting: *SFCh*, July 5, 1880.

142 He soon retreated: Fahey, "Denis Kearney, a Study in Demagoguery," 268; McKinney, "Denis Kearney, Organizer of the Workingmen's Party of California," 85.

142 mobs of unemployed: Cross, *A History of the Labor Movement in California*, 123–124.

142 One of the newcomers: Lee Chew, "The Biography of a Chinaman," *New York Independent*, February 19, 1903.

Chapter 10: The Mission

144 "The whole field was a melee": Charles Hallock, letter to the editor, *NYT*, December 8, 1889.

144 "bounded like a deer": B. J. F. Scott, *Hartford (CT) Daily Times*, November 17, 1922.

145 Yung Wing's uncommon journey: Yung Wing, *My Life in China and America* (New York: Henry Holt and Company, 1909), 1.

145 In the summer of 1835: Thomas E. La Fargue, *China's First Hundred* (Pullman: State College of Washington Press, 1942), 18.

145 Yung's father: Yung, *My Life*, 7.

145 "I remember vividly": Yung, *My Life*, 4.

146 His classmates included: La Fargue, *China's First Hundred*, 19; Carl Smith, "A Sense of History (Part 1)," *Journal of the Hong Kong Branch of the Royal Asiatic Society* 26 (1986): 180, https://www.jstor.org/stable/23887127.

146 Brown announced: Yung Wing, *My Life*, 18–19.

146 Yung returned: Ibid., 19.

146 "they have been": *Morrison Education Society Annual Report*, quoted in Edmund H. Worthy Jr., "Yung Wing in America," *Pacific Historical Review* 34, no. 3 (August 1965): 267, https://www.jstor.org/stable/3636523.

146 Under Phoebe Brown's: *Hartford (CT) Daily Courant*, December 14, 1874.

146 "great inclination": Yung Wing to S. W. Williams, April 15, 1849, MS 602, box 1, folder 10, Yung Wing Papers, MS 602, Manuscripts and Archives, Yale University Library. (This archive will hereafter be cited as Yung Wing papers.)

147 "I used to sweat": Yung, *My Life*, 37.

147 He confessed: Yung Wing to S. W. Williams, December 25, 1850, box 1, folder 10, Yung Wing Papers.

147 Yung begged: Yung Wing to S. W. Williams, July 27, 1853, series 1, box 18, folder 40, Samuel Wells Williams Family Papers, MS 547, Manuscripts and Archives, Yale University Library.

147 On October 30, 1852: Charles Denby to John Sherman, February 28, 1898, No. 2880, Despatches from U.S. Ministers to China, 1843–1906, M92, General Records of the Department of State, Record Group 59, National Archives, Washington, DC.

147 he continued to closely follow: Yung Wing to S. W. Williams, December 25, 1850, box 1, folder 10, Yung Wing Papers; Worthy, "Yung Wing in America," 273–274.

147 "All through my college": Yung, *My Life*, 40–41.

147 Yung found himself: Yung, *My Life*, 48.

148 "strong prejudice": Joseph Hopkins Twichell, Dec. 13, 1874, Journals, volume 1, JHT; *Hartford Daily Courant*, December 14, 1874.

148 Instead, he found work: Yung, *My Life*, 58–78, 123–134; Worthy, "Yung Wing in America," 274–275.

148 "show my loyalty": Yung, *My Life*, 159.

149 They laid out: Yung, *My Life*, 180–182; William Hung, "Huang Tsun-Hsien's Poem 'The Closure of the Educational Mission in America,'" *Harvard Journal of Asiatic Studies* 18, no. 1/2 (June 1955): 58; La Fargue, *China's First Hundred*, 30–33.

149 Chen Lanbin, an ambitious: Hung, "Huang Tsun-Hsien's Poem," 60.

149 A headquarters was established: Yung Kwai, handwritten memoir about the mission (1884), box 1, folder 8, Yung Kwai Papers, Manuscripts and Archives, Yale University Library. (This archive will hereafter be cited as Yung Kwai Papers.)

149 Yung wrote to his: Yung to Noah Porter, February 17, 1872, box 1, folder 5, Yung Wing Papers.

150 He later issued a circular: B. G. Northrop, circular, quoted in "Arrival of Thirty Chinese Boys," *Spirit of Missions* 37 (1872): 700–701.

150 ranged in age: Chris Robyn, "Building the Bridge: The Chinese Educational Mission to the United States: A Sino-American Historico-Cultural Synthesis, 1872–1881," master's thesis, Chinese University of Hong Kong, 1996, 132.

150 "Our hearts beat": *The Exonian*, May 29, 1880.

150 A menagerie of cows: Yung Shang Him, *The Chinese Educational Mission and Its Influence* (Shanghai: Kelly & Walsh, 1939), 7, 42.

150 On Sundays: *The Exonian*, May 29, 1880.

151 On September 12, the ship arrived: *NYT*, September 15, 1872.

151 Zeng was a native: Edward J. M. Rhoads, "In the Shadow of Yung Wing: Zeng Laishun and the Chinese Educational Mission to the United States," *Pacific Historical Review* 74, no. 1 (February 2005): 22–26, 28. In the United States, Zeng was known as Chan Laisun.

151 a few rote phrases: Yung Kwai, handwritten memoir about the mission (1884), box 1, folder 8, Yung Kwai Papers.

151 From a special train car: Yung Shang Him, *The Chinese Education Mission and Its Influence*, 7, 42.

151 They heard gunshots: Yan Phou Lee, *When I Was a Boy in China* (Boston, 1887), 106–111.

152 a town of 27,000 people: Census Bulletin, No. 13, November 18, 1900, "Population of Massachusetts by Counties and Minor Civil Divisions," Table 6, *Twelfth Census of the United States*.

152 touring the town's: *Springfield (MA) Republican*, September 25, 1872

153 an exasperated factory owner: *Springfield (MA) Republican*, June 7, 1870; C. T. Sampson testimony, Senate No. 150, *Report of the Bureau of Statistics of Labor, Embracing the Account of Its Operations and Inquiries From March 1, 1870, to March 1, 1871* (Boston, 1871), 104.

153 early adopter of labor-saving: Wm. F. G. Shanks, "Chinese Skilled Labor," *Scribner's Monthly* 2, no. 5 (September 1871): 495.

153 "imitate anything": Shanks, "Chinese Skilled Labor," 496.

153 After investigating: Sampson testimony, *Report of the Bureau of Statistics of Labor*, 104–105; Shanks, "Chinese Skilled Labor," 496.

153 An English-speaking interpreter: *Springfield (MA) Republican*, June 13, 1870; Sampson testimony, *Report of the Bureau of Statistics of Labor*, 106.

154 On June 13, 1870: *Springfield (MA) Republican*, June 15, 1870; Sampson testimony, *Report of the Statistics of Labor*, 105.

154 Within the first two weeks: *Springfield (MA) Republican*, June 28, 1870; Shanks, "Chinese Skilled Labor," 496.

154 "Are you in favor": *Boston Herald*, June 30, 1870.

154 journalist John Swinton: *NYTr*, June 30, 1870.

155 The same day Swinton: *Springfield (MA) Republican*, July 1, 1870.

155 "What he sought": *NYTr*, June 30, 1870.

155 "we are in China": *Harper's New Monthly Magazine*, December 1870, 138.

155 they felt comfortable: *Springfield (MA) Republican*, July 6, 1870.

155 Other employers took: Shanks, "Chinese Skilled Labor," 497–498; *New York Herald*, September 23, 1870; *Newark Advertiser and Register*, September 22, 1870.

156 Hervey received a letter: *New York Herald*, September 23, 1870.

156 a group of Belleville: E. M. Colie, "The Chinese School at Belleville, New Jersey," *New York Evangelist*, September 12, 1872.

157 The factory belonged: Charles Reeves May, "Beaver County's Chinatown," read at a meeting of Beaver County Historical Society, May 15, 1925, typescript, Old Economy Village museum, Ambridge, PA, 5–7.

157 It was reportedly: May, "Beaver County's Chinatown," 8.

157 On June 29, 1872: May, "Beaver County's Chinatown," 10–11.

158 a large meeting: *Pittsburgh Daily Post*, August 17, 1872.

158 Over the next few months: *Pittsburgh Post*, December 14, 1872.

158 the society issued: *Pittsburgh Daily Post*, March 4, 1873.

158 Lee Ten Poy, a foreman: May, "Beaver County's Chinatown," 12; Albert Rhodes, "The Chinese at Beaver Falls," *Lippincott's Magazine*, June 1877, 710.

158 The workers mostly kept: May, "Beaver County's Chinatown," 11, 15.

159 "The turbulence which": Rhodes, "The Chinese at Beaver Falls," 708.

159 One account described: CHS Social Scrapbooks, volume 6, 106–107, Phyllis Kihn research collection, Connecticut Museum of Culture and History. (This archive will hereafter be cited as Kihn Collection.)

159 Birdsey Northrop emphasized: *HC*, October 11, 1872.

159 The Bartletts' daughter: La Fargue, *China's First Hundred*, 35.

160 The family turned over: Clara D. Capron, "Yung Wing and His Chinese Mission," typescript, Clara D. Capron Papers, Connecticut Museum of Culture and History, 4.

160 When Yan Phou Lee: Lee, *When I Was a Boy in China*, 109.

160 "It is a church": Ibid., 110.

161 scored the highest: Robyn, "Building the Bridge," 41.

161 According to church records: "The Chan Laisun Family," typescript, Kihn Collection.

161 He later recalled: William Lyon Phelps, *Autobiography, with Letters* (New York: Oxford University Press, 1939), 84–85.

162 "I managed to be": Yung Wing to Louise Bartlett, February 12, 1873, cage 255, box 1, folder 4, Thomas La Fargue Papers, Manuscripts, Archives, and Special Collections, Washington State University Libraries. (This archive will hereafter be cited as La Fargue Papers.)

162 "He is the shyest": Joseph Hopkins Twichell to Robert Stiles, April 23, 1878, Charles Ives Papers, MSS 14, box 33, folder 3, Irving Gilmore Music Library, Yale University. (This archive will hereafter be cited as Ives Papers.)

163 "Possibly we helped": Joseph Hopkins Twichell, February 24, 1875, Journals, volume 1, JHT. The historian Edward J. M. Rhoads found that Yung was previously married in China but presumes he was divorced by the time he married Kellogg. See Rhoads, *Stepping Forth into the World: The Chinese Educational Mission to the United States, 1872–81* (Hong Kong: Hong Kong University Press, 2011), 23, 61.

163 Kellogg had been: J. M. Rhoads, *Stepping Forth into the World*, 60–61.

163 Tensions had long: Yung, *My Life*, 202.

163 Prior to his arrival: Shishan Henry Tsai, *China and the Overseas Chinese in the United States, 1868–1911* (Fayetteville: University of Arkansas Press, 1983), 39.

163 "life, energy": Yung, *My Life*, 202.

163 Wu Zideng, an elderly: Hung, "Huang

Tsun-Hsien's Poem," 64; Patricia Cline Higgins, "The Chinese Education Mission 1872–1881: A Study of the Circumstances Affecting Its Establishment, Operation, and Recall" (master's thesis, May 15, 1974, City College of the City University of New York), 119; Anpei Qian, "Finding Their Way Home: A Lifelong Journey of the Chinese Educational Mission Students in China" (honors thesis, April 2019, Wesleyan University), 20.

164 He accused them: "A Short History of Chinese Student Organizations in America," *Oriental Magazine* 14, no. 12 (1917): 173.

164 He later issued: *Hartford Daily Courant*, April 27, 1880.

164 Wu's reports: Qian, "Finding Their Way Home," 17.

164 He recommended: Li Hongzhang letter to the Foreign Office, March 29, 1881, quoted in Hung, "Huang Tsun-Hsien's Poem," 68.

164 The imperial court decreed: *Qing De Zong Shi Lu*, volume 124, Guangxu 6th year, 11th month.

164 The strenuous efforts: Yung to Twichell, February 4, 1874, box 9, JHT.

164 Williston Seminary: *The Independent*, July 5, 1894.

164 "lo, God has brought": Twichell, May 8, 1877, Journals, volume 2, JHT.

165 "Practically and in all": Twichell to Robert Stiles, April 23, 1878, Ives Papers.

165 Yung Kwai wrote: Twichell, May 1, 1880, Journals, volume 4, JHT; *Springfield (MA) Republican*, August 27, 1880.

165 Only after Twichell: Twichell, May 1, 1880, Journals, volume 4, JHT.

165 Yung wrote: Twichell, December 11, 1880, Journals, volume 4, JHT.

165 Li had become: La Fargue, *China First Hundred*: 48–49; Li to Chen, August 6, 1879, Li Hung-chang's collected letters, *P'eng-liao han-kao*, quoted in Hung, "Huang Tsun-Hsien's Poem," 66.

166 The program was: Yingxia Yao, "Exile in

One's Homeland: Yung Wing and the Chinese Educational Mission" (master's thesis, Oregon State University, March 18, 2014), 50–51.

166 American officials had: John L. Cadwalader to George F. Seward, February 20, 1875, No. 68, Diplomatic Instructions, 1785–1906, RG 59, General Records of the Department of State.

166 "They have proved": Yung, *My Life*, 212.

166 "General Grant's letter": Wing to Twichell, March 10, 1881, in Journals, volume 4, JHT.

166 "surprise and speculation": Li Hongzhang letter to the Foreign Office, March 29, 1881, Li Hung-chang's Correspondence with the Foreign Office, in *Li Wen-chung-kung ch'uan-chi*, quoted in Hung, "Huang Tsun-Hsien's Poem," 69.

166 On June 8, 1881: Memorial to the emperor from Yi Xin et al., of the Foreign Ministry, June 8 1881, *Zhongguo jindaishi ziliao congkan-yangwuyundong*, volume 2, 166.

166 The imperial court: Hung, "Huang Tsun-Hsien's Poem," 70; Lian Xi, "Returning to the Middle Kingdom: Yung Wing and the Recalled Students of the Chinese Educational Mission to the United States," *Modern Asian Studies* 49, no. 1 (January 2015): 160; La Fargue, *China's First Hundred*, 49; Yao, "Exile in One's Homeland: Yung Wing and the Chinese Educational Mission," 51.

166 One student later described: Yung Shang Him, *The Chinese Educational Mission and Its Influence*, 12.

167 Mary Bartlett wrote: Bartlett to Mrs. Woo, August 21, 1881, quoted in Arthur G. Robinson, *The Senior Returned Students: A Brief Account of the Chinese Educational Commission (1872–1881) Under Yung Wing* (Tientsin: Tientsin Press, 1932), 19.

167 Another student, Sun: Letter from Annie F. Smith, Lee, Massachusetts, to [unknown], January 23, 1929, cage 255, box 1, folder 1, La Fargue Papers.

167 William Phelps's dear friend: Phelps, *Autobiography, with Letters*, 85.

167 Unbeknownst to their: La Fargue, *China's First Hundred*, 53; Wen Bing Chung, "Reminiscence of a Pioneer Student," December 23, 1923, typescript, box 1, folder 10, La Fargue Papers, 9.

168 He fretted about: Yung to Twichell, December 16, 1881, in Journals, volume 4, JHT.

168 He had a dismaying: Yung, *My Life*, 218.

168 "She had lost": Ibid., 221.

168 "In view of": John Sherman to Charles Denby, April 14, 1898, No. 1567, Diplomatic Instructions, 1785–1906, RG 59, General Records of the Department of State.

168 Yung sought the help: Worthy, "Yung Wing in America," 284.

168 Yung managed to obtain: Yung Wing, June 6 and 12, 1902, *Diary of Yung Wing, Hartford Connecticut 1902* (Hartford: Connecticut State Library, 1924); Worthy, "Yung Wing in America," 285.

168 He spent his final years: Capron, "Yung Wing and His Chinese Mission," 6.

169 his son Morrison: Robyn, "Building the Bridge," 95.

169 On April 21, 1912: *HC*, April 22, 1912.

Chapter 11: The Chinese Question

173 "first missionary from China": *Boston Globe*, September 28, 1874.

173 Lewis described himself: *CT*, March 15, 1879.

173 Sallie Holmes described: Sallie Little Holmes to Anna Kennedy Davis, July 8, 1861, *Bonds of Friendship Love & Truth: Letters from Sallie Little Holmes to Anna Kennedy Davis, 1857–1879* (n.p.: n.p., 1987).

174 In 1873, he fled: Scott D. Seligman, *The First Chinese American: The Remarkable Life of Wong Chin Foo* (Hong Kong: Hong Kong University Press, 2013), 29–32.

174 Wong dressed: *Lebanon (PA) Daily News*, February 22, 1876.

174 On April 2, 1874: *Times Herald* (Port Huron, MI), April 6, 1874; *True Northerner* (Paw Paw, MI), April 10, 1874.

174 "In all her heathenism": *CT,* March 11, 1879.

174 He was arrested: *Daily Evening Express* (Lancaster, PA), February 12, 1876.

175 In an open letter: *CT,* March 16, 1879.

175 On the evening of March 23: *CT,* March 24, 1879.

176 another Chinese immigrant: *CT,* March 24, 1879.

177 Party supremacy: Andrew Gyory, *Closing the Gate: Race, Politics, and the Chinese Exclusion Act* (Chapel Hill: University of North Carolina Press, 1998), 167; Liping Zhu, *The Road to Chinese Exclusion: The Denver Riot, 1880 Election, and Rise of the West* (Lawrence: University Press of Kansas, 2013), 6–10.

177 The one dissenting: Zhu, *The Road to Chinese Exclusion,* 119–120.

177 The Senate debate in early 1879: Gyory, *Closing the Gate,* 15–16; Zhu, *The Road to Chinese Exclusion,* 51.

177 Blaine saw the debate: Gyory, *Closing the Gate,* 3–6.

177 Blaine stood beside: *SFCh,* February 15, 1879.

177 He moved methodically: 8 Cong. Rec. 1301 (1879).

178 clasping his hands: *SFCh,* February 15, 1879.

178 was known in Washington: H. Draper Hunt, *Hannibal Hamlin of Maine: Lincoln's First Vice President* (Syracuse, NY: Syracuse University Press, 1969), 214.

178 He rarely spoke: *SFCh,* February 16, 1879.

178 Hamlin interrupted: 8 Cong. Rec. 1301–1302 (1879).

179 "Where shall it end?": 8 Cong. Rec. 1315 (1879). "Lazzaroni" is a reference to beggars crowding cities in southern Italy and impoverished Italian migrants making their way to the United States.

179 Hamlin continued his: *SFCh,* February 16, 1879.

179 "I insist that": 8 Cong. Rec. 1386–1387 (1879).

180 Officers of the Supreme Order: W. B. G. Keller to Rutherford B. Hayes, February 24, 1879, telegram, Incoming Correspondence, microfilm series 4, roll 89, Rutherford B. Hayes Papers, Rutherford B. Hayes Presidential Library & Museums. (This archive will hereafter be cited as Hayes Papers.)

180 warned of a "calamity": Loring Pickering to A. A. Sargent, February 25, 1879, enclosed in Sargent to Hayes, February 25, 1879, Hayes Papers.

180 The faculty at Yale: Yale College faculty to Rutherford B. Hayes, February 21, 1879, Incoming Correspondence, Hayes Papers.

180 Garrison characterized the effort: *NYTr,* February 27, 1879.

180 "In your Declaration": Wong Ar Chong to Garrison, February 28, 1879, Immigration Restriction—Chinese: Correspondence, Miscellaneous, 1879–1908, reel 8, Garrison Family Papers, Series 6: Subject Files, 1831–1978, microfilm edition, a UPA Collection from Lexis-Nexis, 2008.

180 In 1878, Moy: Scott D. Seligman, *Three Tough Chinamen* (Hong Kong: Earnshaw Books, 2012), 33–34; *NYTr,* May 5, 1879.

181 A *Tribune* reporter: *NYTr,* February 27, 1879.

181 In his veto message: *AC,* March 2, 1879.

181 In his private diary: Hayes, February 28, 1879, *Diary and Letters of Rutherford Birchard Hayes, Nineteenth President of the United States,* vol. 3, ed. Charles Richard Williams (N.p.: Ohio State Archaeological and Historical Society, 1924), 526.

182 The party called: Republican Party Platform of 1880, American Presidency Project, UC Santa Barbara, https://www.presidency.ucsb.edu/documents/republican-party-platform-1880.

182 The political intent: Zhu, *The Road to Chinese Exclusion,* 117–118.

182 On the evening of June 5: *NYTr*, June 6, 1880; *Proceedings of the Republican National Convention, Held at Chicago, Illinois, Wednesday, Thursday, Friday, Saturday, Monday, and Tuesday, June 2nd, 3rd, 4th, 5th, 7th, and 8th, 1880* (Chicago, 1881), 177.

183 "You know the platform": Blaine to Garfield, June 29, 1880, quoted in Gail Hamilton, *Biography of James G. Blaine* (Norwich, CT, 1895), 486.

183 "Senator Blaine has made": Garfield, February 24, 1879, James A. Garfield Papers, Series 1, Diaries, 1848–1881, vols. 13–19, January 1874–September 1979, https://www.loc.gov/item/mss219560002/. (This archive will hereafter be cited as Garfield Papers.)

183 Blaine responded: Blaine to Garfield, July 4, 1880, quoted in Hamilton, *Biography of James Blaine*, 487.

183 Evarts sent back: Evarts to Garfield, July 5, 1880, quoted in Gyory, *Closing the Gate*, 200.

183 In his acceptance letter: James Garfield, Letter Accepting the Republican Presidential Nomination, July 12, 1880, American Presidency Project, UC Santa Barbara, https://www.presidency.ucsb.edu/documents/letter-accepting-the-republican-presidential-nomination.

184 The messaging of the Republican: Herbert J. Clancy, S.J., *The Presidential Election of 1880* (Chicago: Loyola University Press, 1958), 175–181.

184 After a shocking: Clancy, *The Presidential Election of 1880*, 196–197.

184 On October 18: John I. Davenport, *History of the Forged "Morey Letter": A Narrative of the Discovered Facts Respecting This Great Political Forgery, Its Inception, Growth, Authorship, Publication, Endorsement and Support, with Copies and Fac-similes of Original Telegrams, Letters, orders and Receipts Connected Therewith, Its Fraudulent Character Exposed, and the False Swearing, Perjuries, and Additional Forgeries, Perpetrated in the Effort to Sustain the Original Forgery, Made Clear* (New York, 1884), 8, 16. On the Morey letter and its consequences on the 1880 election, see also Gyory, *Closing the Gate*, 204–211; Zhu, *The Road to Chinese Exclusion*, 147–162.

185 newspapers across the country: See *St. Louis Post-Dispatch*, October 20, 1880; *Boston Globe*, October 21, 1880; *SFE*, October 21, 1880.

185 Democratic officials: Davenport, *History of the Forged "Morey Letter*," 11; *SFCh*, October 23, 1880.

185 They even translated: Ted C. Hinckley, "The Politics of Sinophobia: Garfield, the Morey Letter, and the Presidential Election of 1880," *Ohio History Journal* 89, no. 4 (Autumn 1980): 392; *SFCh*, October 29, 1880.

185 Garfield was at his home: Garfield, October 20, 1880, Series 1, Diaries, Vols. 19–21, October 1879–July 1881, Garfield Papers, https://www.loc.gov/item/mss219560003/.

185 The following day: Garfield, October 21 and 22, 1880, diaries, Garfield Papers.

186 He described it: Garfield, October 23, 1880, diaries, Garfield Papers.

186 On October 27: *NYTr*, October 28, 1880; *NYT*, October 31, 1880.

186 The charges against him: Davenport, *History of the "Morey Letter*," 24–25.

186 Escalating rhetoric against: Zhu, *The Road to Chinese Exclusion*, 165–166; Gyory, *Closing the Gate*, 208; *NYTr*, October 30, 1880.

186 "We shall see": Garfield, October 23, 1880, diaries, Garfield Papers.

186 In Denver, an anti-Chinese: *NYTr*, November 1, 1880; *The Sun* (New York), November 1, 1880.

187 "Kill the Chinese!": Statement of M. M. Pomeroy, Inclosure No. 5, Chen Lan Pin to Mr. Evarts, January 21, 1881, Document No. 190, PRFRUS, 1881.

187 A group of rioters: F. A. Bee to the Chinese ministers, Inclosure No. 2, Chen Lan Pin to Mr. Evarts, January 21, 1881, Document No. 190, PRFRUS, 1881;

Testimony of Dr. O. G. Cranston, Dr. C. C. Bradbury, Geo. C. Hickey, George Milligan before the coroner's jury sitting on the body of Sing Lee, Inclosure No. 4, Chen Lan Pin to Mr. Evarts, January 21, 1881, Document No. 190, PRFRUS, 1881.

187 "Chinatown no longer exists": *Rocky Mountain News,* November 1, 1880.

187 On Election Day: Clancy, *The Presidential Election of 1880,* 242.

187 By three o'clock: Garfield, November 2 and 3, 1880, diaries, Garfield Papers.

187 Among Garfield's supporters: *Kalamazoo (MI) Gazette,* November 2, 1880.

188 The diplomatic delegation: Angell, Swift, Trescot to Evarts, telegram, November 9, 1880, M92, General Records of the Department of State, Record Group 59, National Archives, Washington, DC.

188 a Chinese commissioner: S. L. Baldwin, "Revision of Our Treaties with China," *The Independent* (New York), August 26, 1880, 1.

Chapter 12: Beyond Debate

189 On a frigid February day: *CT,* February 18, 1881.

189 returned to Chicago: Scott D. Seligman, *The Chinese American: The Remarkable Life of Wong Chin Foo* (Hong Kong: Hong Kong University Press, 2013), 86; *The Inter Ocean* (Chicago), February 10, 1881.

189 The leader of the Moys: Ting C. Fan, "Chinese Residents in Chicago" (PhD diss., University of Chicago, 1926, reprinted in 1974 by R and E Research Associates), 13–14.

189 "They never asked": Ibid., 13.

189 Among the Moys: *The Inter Ocean,* February 18, 1881.

190 When asked for: *CT,* February 18, 1881.

190 Several years earlier: *CT,* February 18, 1881.

190 in Fond du Lac: *Chattanooga Daily Times,* April 9, 1880.

190 Chinese men had, in fact: Beth Lew

Williams, "Chinese Naturalization, Voting, and Other Impossible Acts," *The Journal of the Civil War Era* 13, no. 4 (December 2023): 522.

190 Judge Moran recalled: *CT,* March 1, 1881.

190 In his decision, Sawyer wrote: *In re* Ah Yup, 1 F. Cas. 223, 5 Sawy. 155.

191 "We began to worry": Fan, "Chinese Residents in Chicago," 14.

191 numbering nearly two thousand: *NYT,* March 6, 1880.

191 a cross-country train: *NYT,* March 4, 1880.

191 the reporter ventured: *NYT,* March 6, 1880.

192 Wo Kee had first: *NYTr,* June 21, 1885.

192 Wo Kee often greeted: For a description of Wo Kee's store, see *NYTr,* June 21, 1885; *The Sun* (New York), June 29, 1879; *NYT,* March 21, 1879; John Kuo Wei Tchen, *New York Before Chinatown: Orientalism and the Shaping of American Culture, 1776–1882* (Baltimore: Johns Hopkins University Press, 1999), 236–237.

192 The reporter spoke with: *The Sun* (New York), March 7, 1880.

193 Lee Teep started attending: *New York Herald,* May 7, 1881, published in *CT,* May 9, 1881; *NYT,* May 7, 1881.

193 On Sunday afternoon: *NYT,* June 30, 1881; Ah Sin and Kwong Tong testimony, in *The Murder of Lee Teep: The Trial and Acquittal of John J. Corcoran, Charged with the Murder. Summing Up of Horace Russell, for the Defence; With a Prefatory Note Giving the Substance of the Testimony* (New York, 1881), 3–5.

193 Kwong Tong accompanied: Kwong Tong and Jacob Cruger testimony, in *The Murder of Lee Teep,* 4–5, 9.

193 Lee Teep identified: James J. Hart testimony, in *The Murder of Lee Teep,* 5.

193 About thirty Chinese: *NYT,* May 7, 1882; *New York Herald,* May 7, 1881, published in *CT,* May 9, 1881.

194 prosecutors requested more: *The Murder of Lee Teep,* 16.

194 The trial finally: Ibid., 2–3; *NYT,* June 30, July 2 and 8, 1881.

194 "This is not": *The Murder of Lee Teep,* 31, 46; *NYT,* July 8, 1881.

195 Mass meetings had been: *SFCh,* May 4, 1881.

195 Miller made the case: *SFCh,* May 5, 1881.

195 He had first traveled: *SFCh,* March 9, 1886.

195 He steadfastly refused: *NYTr,* March 9, 1886.

195 His neighbor: *AC,* February 18, 1881.

195 a dignified figure: *NYTr,* March 9, 1886.

196 The debate over the treaty: *Chicago Daily Tribune,* May 5, 1881; *NYT,* May 6, 1881.

196 One of the few dissenting: Richard E. Welch Jr., *George Frisbie Hoar and the Half-Breed Republicans* (Cambridge, MA: Harvard University Press, 1971), 5–30; George F. Hoar, John H. Mitchell, Angus Cameron, *Woman Suffrage in the U.S. Senate: Argument for a Sixteenth Amendment* (Washington, 1879), https://www.loc.gov/item/93838360/.

196 Opposing the treaty: *SFE,* May 5, 1881.

196 At twenty minutes past nine: Mrs. Blaine to M, July 3, 1881, quoted in Hamilton, *Biography of James G. Blaine,* 538–539; *NYTr,* July 3, 1881; H. H. Alexander and Edward D. Easton, stenographers, *Report of the Proceedings in the Case of the* United States v. Charles L. Guiteau (Washington, 1882), 115 and 118–120.

196 the doorbell rang: *St. Louis Globe-Democrat,* September 20, 1881.

196 He had risen: George F. Howe, *Chester A. Arthur: A Quarter-Century of Machine Politics* (New York: Frederick Ungar Publishing, 1935; republished 1957), 61–93, 107–108; Sybil Schwartz, "In Defense of Chester Arthur," *Wilson Quarterly* 2, no. 4 (Autumn 1978): 182.

197 Among the notables: *NYT,* February 28, 1882.

197 Blaine delivered: *NYT,* February 28, 1882.

197 Senator Miller opened: *SFCh,* March 2, 1882.

197 In the gallery: *NYTr,* March 1, 1882.

197 Miller's proposed legislation: 13 Cong. Rec. 1480–1481 (1882).

198 "The question of Chinese": 13 Cong. Rec. 1481–1482 (1882).

198 his nearly two-hour-long: *NYTr,* March 1, 1882.

198 "If we continue": 13 Cong. Rec. 1483 (1882).

198 He depicted: 13 Cong. Rec. 1484 (1882).

199 Miller dismissed: 13 Cong. Rec. 1486–1487 (1882).

199 "A hundred years ago": 13 Cong. Rec. 1515 (1882).

199 Hoar was aghast: 13 Cong. Rec. 1516 (1882).

199 "What an insult": 13 Cong. Rec. 1518 (1882).

200 "That they do not": 13 Cong. Rec. 1521 (1882).

200 He ended his speech: 13 Cong. Rec. 1523 (1882).

200 George expressed hope: 13 Cong. Rec. 1637 (1882).

201 Denying entrance: 13 Cong. Rec. 1740 (1882).

201 Senator Orville Platt: 13 Cong. Rec. 1702 (1882).

201 "There is no common": 13 Cong. Rec. 1674–1675 (1882).

202 "The prompt and friendly": Chester A. Arthur, "First Annual Message," December 6, 1881, American Presidency Project, UC Santa Barbara, https://www.presidency.ucsb.edu/documents/first-annual-message-13.

202 Early in his tenure: Howe, *Chester A. Arthur,* 168.

202 The president's reputation: Howe, *Chester A. Arthur,* 7, 13.

202 For the Chinese bill: *NYTr,* March 29, 30, and April 1, 1882.

203 The Chinese legation: Chinese legation, memorandum, April 1, 1882, NFCL.

203 Reports circulated about: *NYTr,* March 30, 1882; *SFCh,* March 30 and April 1, 1882; *Washington Post,* April 2, 1882; *New York Herald,* March 29, 1882.

203 On the afternoon of April 4: *NYTr,* April 5, 1882; Chester Arthur, Veto

Message, April 4, 1882, American Presidency Project, UC Santa Barbara, https://www.presidency.ucsb.edu/documents/veto-message-335.

203 News of the veto: *SFCh*, April 5, 1882.

203 In Philadelphia: *The Sun* (New York), April 16, 1882; *The Times* (Philadelphia), April 16, 1882.

203 In St. Louis: *St. Louis Globe-Democrat*, April 28, 1882.

203 Hoar once again: 13 Cong. Rec. 3265 (1882).

204 Charles Folger, the treasury secretary: *SFCh*, May 6, 1882.

204 a British steamer: *SFCh*, May 7, 1882.

204 On the morning of May 8: *SFCh*, May 9 and 10, 1882; Beth Lew-Williams, "Before Restriction Became Exclusion: America's Experiment in Diplomatic Immigration Control," *Pacific Historical Review* 83, no. 1 (February 2014): 26; *SFCh*, May 10, 1882. References to "Chinese restriction" include *Sacramento Union*, May 9, 1882; *CT*, May 9, 1882; *Ferndale Enterprise*, May 12, 1882. References to "Chinese exclusion" include *HC*, May 9, 1882; *Brooklyn Union*, May 9, 1882; *SFB*, July 24, 1882.

204 "Hereafter, we are": *Chicago Times*, April 25, 1882, quoted in Gyory, *Closing the Gate*, 254.

204 In San Francisco: *SFCh*, May 9, 1882.

204 American immigration officials recorded: Mary Roberts Coolidge, *Chinese Immigration* (New York: Henry Holt and Company, 1909), 498.

204 In Hong Kong: Fong F. Sec, "A Living Lesson to the New Youth," in *In Memory of Fong F. Sec* (Hong Kong: Caritas Printing Training Centre, 1966), 1–4.

Chapter 13: The Gatekeepers

206 At eight o'clock: *SFE*, August 9 and 10, 1882; *SFCh*, August, 9, 1882; *SDU*, August 9, 1882.

207 a successful real estate: *Daily Graphic* (New York), July 21, 1880.

207 He noted in a letter: Sullivan, August 8, 1882, box 3, folder 2, CCF.

207 On May 19, the Treasury: Department No. 53, Secretary's Office, Circular, Chinese Laborers, "Letter from the Secretary of Treasury, transmitting in compliance with Senate resolution of the 7th instant, copies of all papers relating to the subject of the extension of the act of May 6, 1882, to execute certain treaty stipulations relating to Chinese" (hereafter cited as Treasury Letter), Senate Ex. Doc. No. 62, 48th Congress, 1st Sess., 1884, 1–2.

207 Chinese diplomatic officials: Tsu Shau Pang to Secretary of State, June 1, 1882, NFCL.

208 another Pacific Mail steamship: *SFCh*, August 10, 1882.

208 McAllister was an imposing: Oscar Tully, ed., *History of the Bench and Bar of California Being Biographies of Many Remarkable Men, a Store of Humorous and Pathetic Recollections, Accounts of Important Legislation and Extraordinary Cases, Comprehending the Judicial History of the State* (Los Angeles, 1901), 419; *SFE*, May 2, 1937.

208 McAllister's case: *AC*, August 22, 1882; *SFB*, August 21, 1882; *AC*, July 28, 1858; Charles J. McClain, *In Search of Equality: The Chinese Struggle Against Discrimination in Nineteenth-Century America* (Berkeley: University of California Press, 1994), 87–89, 104.

209 "interesting class of foreigners": Lorenzo Sawyer, *Way Sketches Containing Incidents of Travel Across the Plans from St. Joseph to California in 1850 with Letters Describing Life and Conditions in the Gold Region* (New York: Edward Eberstadt, 1926), 125.

209 Field is a contradictory figure: *Sketch of the Life of Stephen J. Field of the U.S. Supreme Court, Published in the N.Y. Sun of April 25, 1880* (N.p., 1880), 4, https://hdl.handle.net/2027/yale.39002013270880; Carl Brent Swisher, *Stephen J. Field: Craftsman of the Law* (Hamden, CT: Archon Books, 1963), 205–239; Richard Cahan, Pia Hinckle, and Jessica Royer Ocken, *The Court That Tamed the West: From the Gold Rush to*

the Tech Boom (Berkeley, CA: Heyday, 2013), 87–88.

209 He told the members: Stephen J. Field, Charge to the Grand Jury, August 22, 1872, in *Reports of Cases Decided in the Circuit and District Courts of the United States for the Nine Circuit,* vol. 2 (San Francisco, 1875), 681.

210 which Field excoriated: *Ho Ah Kow v. Nunan,* 5 Sawyer 552 (July 7, 1879).

210 In Ah Sing's case: Case of the Chinese Cabin Waiter (*In re* Ah Sing), 13 F. 286 (C.C.D. Cal. 1882).

210 The circuit court judges: Case of the Chinese Laborers on Shipboard (*In re* Ah Tie and Others), 13 F. 291 (C.C.D. Cal. 1882).

210 a merchant, Low Chow Yam: *AC,* August 18, 1882.

210 He later acknowledged: Sullivan to Charles Folger, August 28, 1882, in Treasury Letter.

211 In the courtroom: *SFCh,* September 3, 1882; Christian G. Fritz, *Federal Justice in California: The Court of Ogden Hoffman, 1851–1891* (Lincoln: University of Nebraska Press, 1991), 1, 10, 18–21, 250–256.

211 Hoffman disagreed: *In re* Low Yam Chow, The Case of the Chinese Merchant, 13 F. 605 (C.C.D. Cal. 1882).

212 Hoffman alone would hear: Fritz, *Federal Justice in California,* 228.

212 "It would be hard": *AC,* March 8, 1888.

212 The arrival of a steamship: Hoffman to Rep. Felton, January 10, 1888, in 19 Cong. Rec. 6569 (1888).

212 On the afternoon of December 19, 1883: *SFCh,* December 20, 1883; Entries December 15–19, 1883, Memorandum Book Habeas Corpus Cases, From October 18, 1882, to June 16, 1887, U.S. District Court for the Northern District of California, San Francisco, http://www.frederickbee.com/memorandum.html; *SFCh,* December 16, 1883.

212 Hoffman asked his clerk: *SFCh,* January 25, 1884.

213 Hoffman issued a ruling: *In re* Chow Goo Pooi 25 F. 77 (D.Cal. 1884).

213 the Chinese consulate retained: Tian Atlas Xu, "Immigration Attorneys and Chinese Exclusion Law Enforcement: The Case of San Francisco, 1882–193)," *Journal of American Ethnic History* 41, no. 1 (Fall 2021): 57; *SFCa,* June 18, 1905.

213 Several former federal: Tian Atlas Xu, "Navigating Worthiness in America: White Attorneys, Black Civil War Pensioners, and Chinese Immigrants, 1862–1930" (PhD diss., Catholic University of America, 2021), 165.

214 Colonel Frederick A. Bee: *SFB,* October 29, 1883; *SFE,* May 27, 1892; *SFCa,* May 27, 1892; Bee testimony, House Report No. 4048, 41st Cong., 2nd sess., Congressional Serial Set 2890, 374.

214 stood on the docks: Huang Zunxian, *Renjinglu shicao jianzhu,* ed. and annot. Qian Zhonglian (Shanghai: Gudian Wenxu Chubanshe, 1981), http://www.frederickbee.com/huangpoem.html, 584–586. The Wade-Giles romanization of Huang Zunxian is Huang Tsun-hsien.

214 In another notable case: *SFB,* September 29, 1884; *In re* Look Tin Sing, 21 F. 905 (C.C.D. Cal. 1884).

215 The Qing government: *Evening Post* (New York), February 28, 1884.

215 Chinese inspectors labored: Kitty Calavita, "The Paradoxes of Race, Class, Identity, and 'Passing': Enforcing the Chinese Exclusion Acts, 1882–1910," *Law & Social Inquiry* 25, no. 1 (Winter 2000): 25.

215 Foes of Chinese immigration: *SFCh,* December 1, 1883.

215 Hoffman lamented: *In re* Tung Yeong, 19 F. 184 (D.C.D.Ca. 1884).

215 In New York, Chinese inspectors: *NYT,* November 11, 1883.

215 Sullivan portrayed himself: Sullivan to Folger, August 13, 1883, box 3, folder 1, CCF.

215 According to records: Sullivan to Folger, December 3 1883, in Treasury Letter, 73; Hudson Janisch, "The Chinese, the Courts, and the Constitution: A Study of the Legal Issues Raised by

Chinese Immigration to the United States, 1850–1902" (JD diss., University of Chicago, 1938), 495–496.

216 "The Chinese are going": Loomis to Ellenwood, October 12, 1883, BOFMS.

216 In July 1884: "An act to amend an act entitled "An act to execute certain treaty stipulations relating to Chinese approved May sixth eighteen hundred and eighty-two," ch. 220, 23 Stat. 115, *U.S. Statutes at Large, Volume 23 (1884–1885), 48th Congress.*

216 Justice Field ruled: *In re* Chew Heong, 21 F. 791 (C.C.D. Cal. 1884).

216 In his opinion for the majority: *Chew Heong v. United States,* 112 U.S. 536 (1884).

216 "protect our people": Erika Lee, *At America's Gates: Chinese Immigration During the Exclusion Era, 1882–1943* (Chapel Hill: University of North Carolina Press, 2003), 44.

217 He made clear: *SFCh,* September 24, 1885.

217 On July 5, 1885: Moy Chong, case no. 313, *Oceanic,* arrival date July 5, 1885, ACF.

217 The case for Tom Bok Gum: Tom Bok Gum, case no. 186, *Oceanic,* arrival date October 3, 1885, ACF.

217 Hager compiled statistics: Letter of Hon. J. S. Hager, Giving Statistics of Number of Arrivals and Departures of Chinese at the Port of San Francisco, February 23, 1888, Senate Misc. Doc. No. 90, 50th Cong., 1st Sess., Congressional Serial Set 2516.

Chapter 14: Transformations

218 On May 12, 1884: Leong Cum, case no. 1630, *Oceanic,* arrival date May 12, 1884, ACF.

219 On June 15: Chung Lee, case no. 1792, *City of Tokio,* arrival date June 15, 1884, ACF.

219 customs officials detained: Yeung Fook Tin, case no. 2120, *Arabic,* arrival date October 31, 1884, ACF.

219 On August 24, 1885: Lee Die Chuern, case no. 353, *City of New York,* arrival

date August 24, 1885, ACF. The boys' names are rendered variously in the case file. I have relied on the spellings in Lee Hee Wah's affidavit.

220 "get an education": Huie Kin, *Reminiscences* (Peiping, China: San Yu Press, 1932), 36.

220 a "thrilling adventure": Ibid., 37.

221 Huie entitled his lecture: *Jackson Standard* (Jackson, OH), May 12 and 26, 1881; *Highland Weekly News* (Hillsboro, OH), May 19, 1881.

221 "China was then little known": Huie, *Reminiscences,* 39.

221 One winter evening: *Jackson Standard,* December 1, 1881.

221 In the fall of 1882: Huie, *Reminiscences,* 40–42.

222 Huie was a burly: Elliot Swift to Dr. Ellenwood, August 18, 1885, BOFMS; *Pittsburgh Daily Post,* June 26, 1883; Huie, *Reminiscences,* 45.

222 In Huie's first report: Huie Kin, "Report to the Presbyterian Board of Foreign Mission on the Summer Work," September 4, 1885, BOFMS.

222 On October 11, 1885: Huie, *Reminiscences,* 48–49.

222 From the moment he met: Huie, *Reminiscences,* 56–58; "The American Wife of a Chinese Missionary," *Literary Digest,* June 1, 1907.

223 on June 12, 1877: June 12, 1877, Photocopy of Diary 1, box 3, folder 4, Ah Quin Diary Collection, MS 209, San Diego History Center Document Collection. (This archive will hereafter be cited as Ah Quin Collection.)

223 His name was: Will Bowen, "Ah Quin: A San Diego Founding Father," March 2, 2014, SDNEWS, https://sdnews.com/ah-quin-a-san-diego-founding-father/. See also tombstone photograph, Tom Ah Quin, Find a Grave website, https://www.findagrave.com/memorial/80581145/tom_ah-quin.

223 One early entry: Diary 1, box 1, folder 1, Ah Quin Collection.

223 Ah Quin was born: Yong Chen, "Remembering Ah Quin: A Century of

Social Memory in a Chinese American Family," *Oral History Review* 27, no. 1 (Winter-Spring 2000): 64, https://www.jstor.org/stable/3675506.

224 His first entry: June 12, 1877, Photocopy of Diary 1, Ah Quin Collection.

224 Once there, he was consumed: July 21, 22, 24, 25, August 21, 1877.

224 There were small pleasures: September 21, October 27, November 25, December 2, 16, January 20, 1877, February 9, July 13, August 26, 1878, Photocopy of Diary 1, Ah Quin Collection.

224 He lamented: December 10, 1877, January 29, 1878, Diary 1, Ah Quin Collection.

224 On June 1, 1878: June 1, 1878, Photocopy Diary 2, box 3, folder 5, Ah Quin Collection.

224 In the summer of 1878: Andrew R. Griego, "Mayor of Chinatown: The Life of Ah Quin, Chinese Merchant and Railroad Builder of San Diego" (master's thesis, San Diego State University, 1979), 49–56.

224 "whore houses": October 31, November 27, 1879, Photocopy of Diary 4, folder 7, Ah Quin Collection.

225 The anti-Chinese movement: February 19, 24, April 4, 1880, Photocopy of Diary 4, Ah Quin Collection. Thanks to Susie Lan Cassel, of Cal State University, San Marcos, for pointing me to these passages.

225 Ah Quin boarded a steamer: October 25 and 26, 1880, Photocopy of Diary 4, Ah Quin Collection.

225 there were about 180: *San Diego Union*, January 28, 1881.

225 An advertisement: *San Diego Union*, February 17, 1881.

225 more than a hundred: *San Diego Union*, March 5, 1881.

225 A reporter who ventured: *San Diego Union*, March 19, 1881.

225 he traveled to San Francisco: *San Diego Union*, November 29, 1881; Yong Chen, *Chinese San Francisco, 1850–1943: A Trans-Pacific Community* (Stanford,

CA: Stanford University Press, 2000), 301–302.

226 There are conflicting: *San Diego Union*, November 29, 1881; Chen, "Remembering Ah Quin," 66; Peggy Pascoe, *Relations of Rescue: The Search for Female Moral Authority in the American West, 1874–1839* (New York: Oxford University Press, 1991), 164.

226 the couple had their first: *San Diego Union*, April 21, 1883.

226 first in town: *San Diego Union*, July 16, 1884.

226 He began investing: Griego, "Mayor of Chinatown," 101.

226 "the first male Chinese child": *San Diego Union*, February 10, 1885.

226 The couple would go on: Walter Bellon, "Walter Bellon Manuscript," box 1, folder 1, Walter Bellon Papers, MS 10, San Diego History Center Document Collection, 105.

226 On April 8, 1901: *LAT*, April 8, 1901.

227 The sheets of rain: *SFB*, November 17, 1875.

227 A remarkable wedding: For a comprehensive account of the Tape family, see Mae Ngai, *The Lucky Ones: One Family and the Extraordinary Invention of Chinese America*, expanded paperback ed. (Princeton, NJ: Princeton University Press, 2010).

227 Tape had arrived: Joseph Tape interview, case of Robert Leon Park, file 12016/1898, CEACF, National Archives, San Bruno, CA; Ngai, *The Lucky Ones*, 3–4, 10; Emily Lowe and Mamie Tape interview, July 29, 1972, box 25: 18–19, HMLRFA; Ruby Tape interview, August 9, 1970, carton 93:8, HMLRFA.

227 Jeu Dip cut off: Joseph Tape, transcript on appeal, affidavit for a writ of mandate, *Tape v. Hurley* case file, California Supreme Court, No. 9916, February 12, 1885, WPA 18443, California State Archives.

227 The story that Mary: Lowe and Tape interview, HMLRFA; Otis Gibson,

Chinese in America (Cincinnati, 1877), 201; *SFB*, November 17, 1875.

227 The pair courted: Ngai, *The Lucky Ones,* 21, 24.

228 presided over their wedding: *SFB,* November 17, 1875.

228 a newspaper reporter encountered: *Cambridge Jeffersonian* (Cambridge, OH), April 6, 1882.

228 One close family friend: Florence Fontecilla interview, case of Gertrude E. Chan, File 120016/8690, CEACF, National Archives, San Bruno, CA.

228 Since their earliest days: On the Chinese community's quest for access to education in San Francisco, see also Victor Low, *The Unimpressible Race: A Century of Educational Struggle by the Chinese in San Francisco* (San Francisco: East/West Publishing, 1982).

228 an evening school dedicated: Speer to Walter Lowrie, January 14 and 31, 1853, BOFMS.

228 warned in his annual report: Andrew Moulder, annual report of 1858, quoted in Low, *The Unimpressible Race,* Appendix A.

229 thirty Chinese parents petitioned: *SFB,* March 3, August 24, 31, 1859; *AC,* September 13, 1859; *SFB,* December 31, 1859; *AC,* May 23, 1861; Low, *The Unimpressible Race,* Appendix B.

229 operated in fits and starts: Low, *The Unimpressible Race,* 22–27.

229 a coalition of thirty-nine: *SFB,* August 22, 1877.

229 thirteen hundred Chinese: "To the Honorable the Senate and the Assembly of the State of California," 1878, trans. J. G. Kerr, CIC, BL.

229 a coalition of white clergymen: *SFB,* July 8, 1882.

229 The school had: *Department of Public Schools, City and County of San Francisco, Twenty-Second Annual Report of the Superintendent of Public Schools for the School Year Ending June 30, 1875* (San Francisco, 1875), 127; *Department of Public Schools, City and County of San*

Francisco, Thirty-Second Annual Report of the Superintendent of Public Schools for the School Year Ending June 30, 1885, 102.

230 Florence Eveleth recalled: Florence Fontecilla interview, case of Gertrude E. Chan, File 120016/8690.

230 He consulted with: *SFB,* September 16, 1884; *SFCh,* September 17, 1884.

230 Mamie later said: Emily Lowe and Mamie Tape interview, July 29, 1972, box 25: 18–19, HMLRFA.

230 Frederick Bee, the Chinese: *SFB,* October 22, 1884; *SFB,* October 11, 1884.

230 Moulder agreed: *SFCh,* October 11, 1884.

230 Mamie showed up: Joseph Tape, affidavit for a writ of mandate, October 28, 1884, Tape case file.

231 The lawyers for Hurley: Young, Platt & Dunn, attorneys for respondents, answer, November 19, 1884, Tape case file.

231 the superior court judge: *SFCh,* January 10, 1885; *AC,* January 10, 1885.

231 On March 3, 1885: *Tape v. Hurley,* Supreme Court of California, No. 9916, 66 Cal. 473.

231 Moulder had already set: *SFB,* March 4, 1885; *Sacramento Daily Record,* March 5, 1885; *The Journal of the Assembly During the Twenty-Sixth Session of the Legislature of the State of California, 1885* (Sacramento, 1885), 543; *The Journal of the Senate During the Twenty-Sixth Session of the Legislature of the State of California* (Sacramento, 1885), 523–524.

231 To accommodate the Chinese school: *SFB,* April 2 and 14, 1885.

232 On April 6, the Tapes: *SFB,* April 7, 1885.

232 the Chinese school opened: *SFB,* April 14, 1885; *SFCh,* April 14, 1885; *AC,* April 14, 1885.

232 Mary Tape wrote: *AC,* April 16, 1885.

232 "way down in Chinatown": Emily Lowe and Mamie Tape interview, July 29, 1972, box 25: 18–19, HMLRFA.

233 The next year: Victor Low, "The Chinese in the San Francisco Public School

System: An Historical Study of One Minority Group's Response to Educational Discrimination, 1859–1959," (PhD diss., University of San Francisco, 1981), 159.

233 by the end of the century: H. M. Lai, "The Chinese in Public School," *East/West*, September 1, 1971, 5.

233 The report argued: *Report of the Special Committee of the Board of Supervisors of San Francisco on the Condition of the Chinese Quarter and the Chinese in San Francisco, July 1885* (San Francisco, 1885), 58–62.

Chapter 15: Wipe Out the Plague Spots

237 was known for its stench: Delmar Thornbury, *California's Redwood Wonderland: Humboldt County* (San Francisco, Sunset Press, 1923), 65; Will N. Speegle, "Orientals Ordered from County in 1885 After Tong War Outbreak Here," November 1, 1931, Chinese in Humboldt County, Humboldt County Pamphlet File, Special Collections, Cal Poly Humboldt Library. (This archive will hereafter be cited as Chinese in Humboldt.)

237 Eureka, a town: "Population of California by Minor Civil Divisions," Census Bulletin, No. 134, November 2, 1891; Thornbury, *California's Redwood Wonderland*, 2, 9; Charles Andrew Huntington, "Incidents in the life of Rev. C. A. Huntington: written at the request of his children," typescript, 1898, WA MSS S-1751, Yale Collection of Western Americana, Beinecke Rare Book and Manuscript Library, 213; *SFB*, October 16, 1914.

237 The first Chinese arrivals: Andrew M. Genzoli and Wallace E. Martin, *Redwood Bonanza . . . a Frontier's Reward: A Lively Incident in the Life of a New Empire* (Eureka, CA: Schooner Features, 1967), 34; Thornbury, *California's Redwood Wonderland*, 64.

237 The Chinese quarter in Eureka: Lynwood Carranco, *Redwood Country*

(Belmont, CA: Star Publishing, 1986), 39; Ronald J. Perry, "'Wipe Out the Plague Spots': The Expulsion of Chinese from Humboldt County" (master's thesis, Humboldt State University, May 2005), 1, 24; Speegle, Chinese in Humboldt; Sanborn Fire Insurance Map from Eureka, Humboldt County, California, May 1886, Library of Congress Geography and Map Division, http://hdl.loc.gov/loc.gmd/g4364em .g4364em_g005331886; Daniel A. Cornford, *Workers and Dissent in the Redwood Empire* (Philadelphia: Temple University Press, 1987), 42; Timothy James Springer, "The Forgotten Pioneer: The Story of C. S. Ricks and His Influence on the Town of Eureka, California" (master's thesis, California State University, Fresno, May 1996), 3–5.

238 A drunken white man: *Humboldt (CA) Times*, January 26 and 27, 1876.

238 Prosecutors tried a Chinese resident: *Humboldt (CA) Times*, March 26, 28, 29, 30, September 27 and 29, 1876.

238 the region's economy: Conford, *Workers and Dissent in the Redwood Empire*, 38, 41–47.

238 Children made a sport: Speegle, "Orientals Ordered from County," Chinese in Humboldt; Peter Rutledge, "Chinese in Humboldt County," talk given at Humboldt County Historical Society, March 23, 1954, typescript, Humboldt County Historical Society; *Humboldt (CA) Times*, January 28, 1876.

239 residents of Garberville: *Democratic Standard* (Eureka, CA), March 27, 1880.

239 Chinese laborers were becoming: Conford, *Workers and Dissent in the Redwood Empire*, 58.

239 Thomas Walsh, Eureka's mayor: *Humboldt Times*, March 5, 1882, January 3, 1877.

239 John O'Neil, had been: *Humboldt Times*, April 7, 1882.

239 "They had been fighting": Sam Kelsey, interviewed by Martha Roscoe, Sep-

tember 16, 1961, Humboldt County Historical Society Meeting at Mattole Grange, typescript, Special Collections and Archives, Cal Poly Humboldt University Library, 5.

239 a row broke: *Humboldt Times,* August 26, 1884.

240 The *Times-Telephone: Times-Telephone* (Eureka, CA), February 20 and September 24, 1884.

240 another gun battle broke out: *Times-Telephone,* February 1, 1885.

240 published a searing editorial: *Times-Telephone,* February 5, 1885.

240 Just after six o'clock: *Times-Telephone,* February 7 and 8, 1885; Thornbury, *California's Redwood Wonderland,* 65; Rutledge, "Chinese in Humboldt County," 3; Speegle, "Orientals Ordered from County," Chinese in Humboldt.

241 Several hundred men gathered: *Times-Telephone,* February 7, 1885; F. T. Onstine, "Hang All the Chinese! Humboldt's Expulsion of the Chinese," unidentified news clipping, circa 1968, Chinese in Humboldt.

241 "The town went wild": Rutledge, "Chinese in Humboldt County," 3; Kelsey interview, 4.

241 Within twenty minutes: *Times-Telephone,* February 7, 1885; Marvin Shepherd, *The Sea Captain's Odyssey: A Biography of Captain H. H. Buhne, 1822–1894* (Walnut Creek, CA: Georgie Press), 49; *Times-Telephone,* January 8, 1886.

241 "If anybody starts anything": Kelsey interview, 6.

242 He found the "powers of evil": Huntington, "Incidents in the Life," 214–215, 222–223.

242 "The Chinaman who fired": Ibid., 225–226.

242 a proposal to massacre: Huntington, "Incidents in the Life," 225.

242 The city marshal: Rutledge, "Chinese in Humboldt County," 4.

243 Within a half hour: *Times-Telephone,* February 8, 1885; Huntington, "Inci-

dents in the Life," 226; Speegle, "Orientals Ordered from County," Chinese in Humboldt.

243 One Chinese gardener: Huntington, "Incidents in the Life," 226.

243 Their camp was just below: *Blue Lake (CA) Advocate,* February 21, 1957.

243 At one o'clock in the afternoon: *Times-Telephone,* February 14, 1885.

243 Lum had showed up: Huntington, "Incidents in the Life," 222–224.

244 He hurried over to the Huntingtons: Ibid., 227–228.

244 "Chinaman going into": Kelsey interview, 7. Kelsey apparently participated in the invasion of the Huntington home and was asked about it decades later in this interview. His recollections, however, differed in certain aspects from Huntington's. Kelsey said, for example, the group "smashed in the door," while Huntington described a "loud rap at the back door."

244 "Take that rope off": Huntington, "Incidents in the Life," 228. Kelsey also said in his interview that he was the one who intervened at the gallows, but this seems less plausible than Huntington's recollection.

245 The *Humboldt* had been scheduled: *Humboldt Standard,* February 7, 1885.

245 clusters of Chinese residents: *Times-Telephone,* February 8, 1885.

245 more than three hundred: *Times-Telephone,* February 13, 1885.

245 "We intend to wait": *Times-Telephone,* February 13, 1885.

245 On January 21, 1886: *Wing Hing v. The City of Eureka,* complaint, File No. 3948 (hereafter cited as Wing Hing case), U.S. Circuit Court, District of California, National Archives, San Bruno, CA.

246 hundreds of Humboldt County residents: *Times-Telephone,* February 7, 1886.

246 A Chinese man named Charley Mock: *Times-Telephone,* January 12 and 24, 1886.

246 Eureka's city council dispatched: *Times-*

Telephone, February 9 and March 13, 1886; *SFCh,* March 24, 1886.

246 The court record offers: Sawyer, judgment, March 2, 1889, Wing Hing case; *Times-Telephone,* March 28, 1889.

247 Eureka's example became: *Ferndale Enterprise,* February 20, 1886; *Times-Telephone,* February 21 and 28, 1886; Thornbury, *Redwood Wonderland,* 68. On the "Eureka Method," see also Jean Pfaelzer, *Driven Out: The Forgotten War Against Chinese Americans* (Berkeley: University of California Press, 2008), 121–166.

247 "there is not a Chinaman": Lillie E. Hamm, *History and Business Directory of Humboldt County* (Eureka, CA, 1890), 91.

247 "It is now almost 45 years": Speegle, "Orientals Ordered from County," Chinese in Humboldt.

248 Lee Wong, who was known: Edith Porter, daughter of Robert Porter, notes from conversation October 16, 1963, Humboldt County Historical Society.

248 Another Chinese man survived: Mildred Hansen, excerpt from letter, July–August 1963, Humboldt County Historical Society.

248 Chinese miners persisted: Laura and Phil Sanders, "The Quiet Rebellion: Chinese Miners Accepted in Orleans Despite 1885 Expulsion," *Humboldt Historian,* Summer 1998, 14–17.

248 One man, known as "Bow": Brenda Harmon Catanich to Wally Lee, February 29, 1955, Humboldt County Historical Society.

249 The best-known survivor: *Blue Lake Advocate,* February 6, 1943; Tomas Bair to Marie Bair, December 5, 1994, Humboldt County Historical Society (hereafter cited as Moon letter).

249 Thomas Bair, a swarthy Arkansas native: *Blue Lake Advocate,* June 17, 1916; "Some History of Redwood Creek Ranch," compiled by Evelyn McComb Deike, 1999, https://www.waterboards.ca.gov/water_issues/programs/tmdl/records/region_1/2003/ref2086.pdf; Jan Olsen, "Tom Bair—Humboldt Developer," *Humboldt Historian,* May–June 1985.

250 "some sort of a negotiation": Moon letter, 2.

250 several men from Eureka: Charlie Blake, "The Winter of 1889 and 1890," *Blue Lake Advocate,* June 21, 1956.

250 A few years after the expulsion: Moon letter; Don Carr, "Charley Moon, Humboldt's Only Chinaman," *Ferndale Enterprise,* n.d., quoted in "Some History of Redwood Creek."

251 "We have known Charley": Carr, "Charley Moon, Humboldt's Only Chinaman."

251 Moon died: *Blue Lake Advocate,* February 6, 1943.

Chapter 16: White Men, Fall In

252 "For historians violence": Richard Hofstadter, "Reflections on Violence in the United States," in *American Violence: A Documentary History,* ed. Richard Hofstadter and Michael Wallace (New York: Knopf, 1970), 4.

253 After Promontory Summit: A. Dudley Gardner, "The Chinese in Wyoming: Life in the Core and Peripheral Communities," *South Dakota History* 33, no. 4 (Winter 2003): 380, 384; Arlen Ray Wilson, "The Rock Springs, Wyoming, Chinese Massacre, 1885" (master's thesis, University of Wyoming, Laramie, 1967), 23; Henry T. Williams, *The Pacific Tourist* (New York, 1877), 112.

253 The leader of the Chinese community: *Rock Springs Miner,* February 2, 1899; *History of the Union Pacific Coal Mines: 1868 to 1940* (Omaha, NE: Colonial Press, 1940), 92; Williams, *The Pacific Tourist,* 112; Ricky Leo and Grace Leo, "From Rock Springs to Ventura," *Gum Saan Journal* 22, 2022, https://gumsaan journal.com/resisting-racism-we-are-in-this-together/from-rock-springs-to-ventura/; Nancy Fillmore Brown, "Girlhood Recollections in Laramie in 1870 and 1871," *Annals of Wyoming* 34,

no. 1 (April 1962): 86; Hong Quon Lew interview, May 14, 1904, File 9999/3445, CEACF, National Archives, San Bruno, CA; *Salt Lake Tribune*, February 1, 1899.

253 noticed large, black outcroppings: Howard Stansbury, *An Expedition to the Valley of the Great Salt Lake of Utah*, University Microfilms, 1966 (Philadelphia, 1852), 234, 236.

253 In the late 1860s: *History of the Union Pacific Coal Mines*, 46; Robert Bartlett Rhode, *Booms and Busts on Bitter Creek* (Boulder, CO: Pruett Publishing, 1987), 30.

254 The workers toiled: Isaac Bromley, *The Chinese Massacre at Rock Springs, Wyoming Territory, September 2, 1885* (Boston, 1886), 28; Rhode, *Booms and Busts on Bitter Creek*, 33–34.

254 a fire underground: *Philadelphia Inquirer*, September 10, 1869.

254 The miners mostly lived: Rhode, *Booms and Busts on Bitter Creek*, 35–36.

254 the prevailing wage: *Laramie (WY) Daily Sun*, November 17, 1875.

254 The official accounts: Bromley, *The Chinese Massacre at Rock Springs*, 39.

254 A different version of events: T. A. Larson, *History of Wyoming*, 2nd ed., rev. (Lincoln: University of Nebraska Press, 1978), 114.

255 "Marther alive!": *Laramie (WY) Daily Sun*, November 15, 1875.

255 Its proprietors, Asa C. Beckwith: Charles Kelly, "A Steamboat in the Desert," unpublished manuscript, box 11, folder 21, Charles Kelly papers, MS 0100, University of Utah Libraries, Special Collections, Salt Lake City, Utah, 2–4; David Hales, "The Renaissance Man of Delta: Frank Asahel Beckwith, Milard County Chronicle Publisher, Scientist, and Scholar, 1875–1951," *Utah Historical Quarterly* 81, no. 2 (2013).

255 Beckwith arrived in Rock Springs: *Laramie Daily Sentinel*, November 25, 1875; Bromley, *The Chinese Massacre of Rock Springs*, 45.

255 White miners derisively: Bromley, *The*

Chinese Massacre at Rock Springs, 12; *Laramie Daily Boomerang*, September 5, 1885; *Democratic Leader* (Cheyenne, WY), September 4, 1885.

255 Beckwith later testified: A. C. Beckwith statement, U.S. Congress, House, Committee on Foreign Relations, *Providing Indemnity to Certain Chinese Subjects*, 49th Cong., 1st Sess., 1885–1886, H. Rep. 2044 (hereafter cited as House Report 2044), 13.

256 Chinese laborers were barred: Philip S. Foner, *History of the Labor Movement in the United States*, vol. 2, *From the Founding of the A.F. of L. to the Emergence of American Imperialism*, 2nd ed. (New York: International Publishers, 1975), 58–59.

256 By contrast, the Knights: Sidney H. Kessler, "The Organization of Negroes in the Knights of Labor," *Journal of Negro History* 37, no. 3 (July 1952): 257–260.

256 invective-filled resolution: "Chinese Labor," *Journal of United Labor* 1, no. 4 (August 15, 1880).

256 "In desperation the people": T. W. Powderly, *Thirty Years of Labor. 1858 to 1889. In Which the History of the Attempts to Form Organizations of Workingmen for the Discussion of Political, Social, and Economic Questions Is Traded. The National Labor Union of 1866, the Industrial Brotherhood of 1874, and the Order of the Knights of Labor of America and the World. The Chief and Most Important Principles in the Preamble of the Knights of Labor Discussed and Explained, with Views of the Author and Land, Labor, and Transportation* (Columbus, OH, 1889), 420.

256 Tensions rose: Beckwith statement, House Report 2044, 13–14; "Memorial of Chinese Laborers," Cheng Tsao Ju to T. F. Bayard, November 30, 1885, Enclosure No. 2, NFCL; Bromley, *The Chinese Massacre at Rock Springs*, 22–32. On the tensions between the Knights of Labor and the Union Pacific, see also

Craig Storti, *Incident at Bitter Creek: The Story of the Rock Springs Chinese Massacre* (Ames, IA: Iowa State University Press, 1991), 99–109.

256 Powderly complained: Beckwith to Powderly, June 5, 1885, Letter file, March–June 1885, quoted in Nicholas Somma, "The Knights of Labor and Chinese Immigration" (master's diss., June 1952, Catholic University of America), 46.

257 "Hints were thrown out": O. C. Smith testimony, House Report 2044, 12.

257 about 550 Chinese: *History of Union Pacific Coal Mines*, 90.

257 Notices were posted: "Memorial of Chinese Laborers," NFCL.

257 the continued employment: *Laramie (WY) Daily Boomerang*, September 3, 1885.

257 That night, Andrew Bugas: Andrew P. Bugas, April 16, 1933, "The Chinee Riot at R.S. in 1885," John S. Bugas Papers, American Heritage Center, University of Wyoming, 2.

258 Leo Qarqwang knew his way: Leo Qarqwang testimony, *The Chinese Massacre at Rock Springs*, 55–59; Callaway to Adams, September 5, 1885, General Manager's report for week ending September 5th, 1885, box 18, folder 20, Series 1, incoming correspondence, Subgroup 2, Office of the President, UPR; *Laramie (WY) Daily Boomerang*, September 5, 1885; "List of Wounded," Enclosure No. 2, Cheng Tsao Ju to T. F. Bayard, November 30, 1885, NFCL.

258 By their account: Bromley, *The Chinese Massacre at Rock Springs*, 26; *Deseret (UT) Evening News*, September 26, 1885; *Laramie (WY) Daily Boomerang*, September 5, 1885.

259 In the melee that ensued: *Rock Springs (WY) Independent*, September 3, 1885.

259 It was Ah Kuhn, an interpreter: Ah Kuhn testimony, *The Chinese Massacre at Rock Springs*, 54; J. H. Goodnough, "David G. Thomas' Memories of the Chinese Riot," *Annals of Wyoming* 19, no. 2 (July 1947): 110.

259 He urged them to return: Evans testimony, *The Chinese Massacre at Rock Springs*, 49.

259 Bugas, the young miner: Bugas, "The Chinee Riot at R.S. in 1885," 3–4; *Laramie (WY) Daily Boomerang*, September 5, 1885.

259 When they reached a bridge: Ralph Zwicky statement, House Report 2044, 14.

259 The group headed towards: "Memorial of Chinese Laborers," NFCL; Zwicky statement, House Report 2044, 14.

260 Dave Thomas, the mine boss: Goodnough, "David G. Thomas' Memories of the Chinese Riot," 108; *Rock Springs (WY) Independent*, September 3, 1885.

260 Saloon owners closed: *Laramie (WY) Daily Boomerang*, September 5, 1885.

260 "Vengeance on the Chinese!": Bromley, *The Chinese Massacre at Rock Springs*, 51.

260 A committee of three men: *Laramie (WY) Daily Boomerang*, September 5, 1885; *Rock Springs (WY) Independent*, September 3, 1885; Wilson, "The Rock Springs, Wyoming, Chinese Massacre, 1885," 30.

260 They came from two: "Memorial of Chinese Laborers," "List of Killed," NFCL.

260 Dozens of men were: Bugas, "The Chinee Riot at R.S. in 1885," 4.

260 One witness later: Zwicky statement, House Report 2044, 14.

261 Many Chinese tumbled: *Laramie (WY) Daily Boomerang*, September 5, 1885.

261 Another miner, Leo Mauwik: Mauwik testimony in Bromley, *The Chinese Massacre at Rock Springs*, 59–60.

261 One female resident: Lee Fang testimony in Bromley, *The Chinese Massacre at Rock Springs*, 59; *New York Evening Post*, September 15, 1885; *Laramie (WY) Daily Boomerang*, September 5, 1885.

261 The rioters began setting fire: *New York Evening Post*, September 15, 1885; *Rock Springs (WY) Independent*, September 3, 1885; *Laramie (WY) Daily Boomerang*, September 5, 1885.

261 A group of rioters descended: *Laramie*

(WY) Daily Boomerang, September 5, 1885; Goodnough, "David G. Thomas' Memories of the Chinese Riot," 108.

262 Ah Kuhn took shelter: Ah Kuhn testimony in Bromley, *The Chinese Massacre at Rock Springs,* 55.

262 Several Chinese residents approached: *Cheyenne (WY) Daily Sun,* October 6, 1885.

262 One miner, known as China Joe: *Wyoming Press* (Evanston, WY), February 24, 1924.

262 A group of rioters marched: *Laramie (WY) Daily Boomerang,* September 3, 1885.

262 Rioters next visited: *Laramie (WY) Daily Boomerang,* September 5, 1885.

262 James Tisdale, assistant superintendent: Wyoming Territory, Governor, "Special Report of the Governor of Wyoming to the Secretary of the Interior Concerning Chinese Labor Troubles, 1885" (hereafter cited as Warren Report), 109–110; Hubert Howe Bancroft, *Chronicles of the Builders of the Commonwealth: Historical Character Study,* vol. 7 (San Francisco, 1892), 25–30.

263 At around seven o'clock: Goodnough, "David G. Thomas' Memories of the Chinese Riot," 109.

263 Joseph Young, the recently: *Laramie (WY) Daily Boomerang,* September 5, 1885; Warren Report, 110.

263 Throughout the night: *Laramie (WY) Daily Boomerang,* September 5, 1885; *Rock Springs (WY) Independent,* September 3, 1885; Zwicky statement, House Report 2044.

263 The flat expanse: Bromley, *The Chinese Massacre at Rock Springs,* 52; Goodnough, "David G. Thomas' Memories of the Chinese Riot," 109; *Laramie (WY) Daily Boomerang,* September 3, 1885.

264 "Today for the first time": *Rock Springs (WY) Independent,* September 3, 1885.

264 Union Pacific officials: Warren Report, 111.

264 "She cowed the mob": *Laramie (WY) Daily Boomerang,* September 5, 1885

264 Several hundred eventually took:

Bromley, *The Chinese Massacre at Rock Springs,* 52.

264 There was confusion: Warren Report, 113–114.

265 "The smell of burning": Warren Report, 111.

265 Railroad officials feared: S. R. Callaway to C. F. Adams Jr., September 3, 4, 5, 8, 1885, box 23, folder 13, UPR; *Laramie (WY) Daily Boomerang,* September 5, 1885; *Tacoma (WA) Daily News,* September 5, 1885.

265 Ah Say pressed: Bromley, *The Chinese Massacre at Rock Springs,* 50; Callaway to Adams, September 5, 1885, "General Manager's report for week ending September 5th, 1885," box 18, folder 20, UPR.

265 Newspapers reported other ghastly: *Laramie (WY) Daily Boomerang,* September 7, 1885.

266 "Yield nothing": Adams to Callaway, September 4, 1885, film roll 27, UPR.

266 Threats from white men: *Laramie (WY) Daily Boomerang,* September 7, 1885; *New York Herald,* September 8, 1885.

266 President Cleveland finally emerged: *NYT,* September 6, 1885; *New York Herald,* September 8, 1885; Callaway to Adams, September 8, 1885, box 23, folder 18, UPR; House Report 2044, 18.

266 On Wednesday afternoon: House Report 2044, 23; *New York Evening Post,* September 15, 1885; Memo for Weekly Report—week ending Sept. 12, box 18, folder 20, UPR; "Memorial of Chinese Laborers," NFCL.

266 Mine officials' first attempt: Clark to Callaway, September 16, 1885, box 23, folder 13, UPR.

267 A committee representing: Thomas Neasham to the General Manager and the President of the Union Pacific Railway, September 19, 1885, box 18, folder 20, UPR.

267 the railroad soon found itself: Callaway to Adams, September 15, 1885, box 23, folder 13, UPR.

267 By the end of the month: Callaway to Adams, September 29, 1885, box 23,

484   Notes

folder 13, UPR; *Democratic Leader* (Cheyenne, WY), September 26, 1885; Clark to Callaway, September 23, 1885, box 23, folder 13, UPR; *History of the Union Pacific Coal Mines,* 90–91.

267 White residents continued: Callaway to Adams, October 24, 1885, "General Manager's report for week ending October 24th, 1885," box 18, folder 22, UPR; *History of the Union Pacific Coal Mines,* 90.

268 "I fancy it will be": Callaway to Adams, September 5, 1885, "General Manager's report for week ending September 5th, 1885," box 18, folder 20, UPR.

268 Sheriff Joseph Young began making arrests: *Laramie (WY) Daily Boomerang,* September 7, 1885; *NYT,* September 8, 1885; *Cheyenne (WY) Daily Sun,* September 10, 1885.

268 "none but Chinamen": Campbell to Garland, October 21, 1885, GRDOJ.

268 the secretary of the legation: *NYT,* September 8, 1885.

268 The Chinese minister in Washington: The Wade-Giles romanizations of Zheng Zaoru, Li Hongzhang, and Huang Xiquan are Cheng Tsao Ju, Li Hung Chang, and Huang Sih Chuen, respectively.

268 The Cleveland administration arranged: House Report 2044, 19; Callaway to Adams, September 16, 1885, box 23, folder 13, UPR; "Obituary Record of Graduates of Yale University, Deceased During the Academical Year Ending in June, 1899, Including the Record of a Few Who Died Previously, Hitherto Unreported," presented at the meeting of the Alumni, June 27th, 1899, 616; Bromley to Adams, September 26, 1885, box 23, folder 13, UPR.

269 The following morning: Bromley to Adams, September 26, 1885, box 23, folder 13, UPR; Huang Sih Chuen to Cheng Tsao Ju, October 5, 1885, "Report of the Chinese Consul at New York and Accompanying Documents," Enclosure 2, NFCL.

269 He explained that: Hansheng Chen, *Hua gong chu guo shi liao hui bian* (Collection of Historical Documents Concern in Emigration of Chinese Laborers), vol. 6 (Beijing: Zhonghua shu ju, 1980), 1333.

269 The function of the "List of Killed": Huang Sih Chuen to Cheng Tsao Ju, October 5, 1885, "Report of the Chinese Consul at New York and Accompanying Documents," Enclosure 2, NFCL.

270 In Bromley's inquiry: Bromley to Adams, September 26, 1885, box 23, folder 13, UPR.

270 a grand jury of sixteen men: Campbell to Garland, October 21, 1885, GRDOJ; *Salt Lake Tribune,* September 20, 1885; Rebecca Wunder Thomson, "History of Territorial Federal Judges for the Territory of Wyoming: 1869–1890," *Land & Water Law Review* 17, no. 2 (1982): 610; *Cheyenne (WY) Daily Sun,* October 6 and 7, 1885.

271 The surviving record: Campbell to Garland, October 21, 1885, GRDOJ; *AC,* October 10, 1885.

271 The grand jury hearing: *Laramie (WY) Daily Boomerang,* October 7, 1885; *Santa Cruz (CA) Sentinel,* October 8, 1885.

271 the grand jury voted: *Cheyenne (WY) Daily Sun,* October 7, 1885; Warren Report, 117; *Galveston (TX) Daily News,* October 7, 1885; *The Nation,* October 15, 1885; House Report 2044, 25.

271 a forceful letter to Thomas Bayard: Cheng Tsao Ju to Bayard, November 30, 1885, NFCL.

272 It took more than two months: Bayard to Cheng Tsao Ju, February 18, 1886, Document 71, No. 67, PRFRUS, 1886.

272 President Cleveland requested: House Report 2044, 1.

272 Congress awarded: Chapter 253, "An act to indemnify certain subjects of the Chinese Empire for losses sustained by the violence of a mob at Rock Springs, in the Territory of Wyoming, in September, eighteen hundred and eight-five," *Statutes of the United States*

of America. Passed at the First Session of the Forty-Ninth Congress, 1885–1886 (Washington, 1886), 418.

272 Chinese officials in San Francisco: Chang Yen Soon to Bayard, October 24, 1887, No. 197, PRFRUS, 1888.

273 Chinese survivors of the massacre: Bugas, "The Chinee Riot at R.S. in 1885," 5; Rhode, *Booms and Busts on Bitter Creek,* 58–59; *Democratic Leader,* September 26, 1885.

273 Racial hostilities still ran: First Lieutenant James Brennan to Adjutant General, Department of the Platte, February 9, 1887, box 2, folder 16, Robert B. Rhode Papers, Collection No. 10453, American Heritage Center. (This archive will hereafter be cited as Rhode Papers.) Major General Alfred Terry to Adjutant General, U.S. Army, September 29, 1886, Rhode Papers; Adjutant General, U.S. Army to Commanding General, Division of the Missouri, January 12, 1887, Rhode Papers.

273 he decided to take them back: There are contradictory accounts of how many children Ah Say had. In an immigration interview, Ah Say's son Hong Quon Lew said he had just one brother; other articles reported Ah Say had as many as five children. Hong Quon Lew interview and Leo Tom testimony, File 9999/3445, CEACF; *Salt Lake Tribune,* February 1, 1899; *Morning World-Herald* (Omaha, NE), February 2, 1899.

273 Chinese residents signed: Rhode, *Booms and Busts on Bitter Creek,* 83.

273 Ah Say arranged: *Rock Springs Miner,* May 27, 1897; *History of the Union Pacific Coal Mines,* 92.

273 On the morning of January 27, 1899: *Rock Spring Miner,* January 26 and February 2, 1899; *History of the Union Pacific Coal Mines,* 93.

274 army officials abruptly: *Cheyenne Daily Sun Leader,* March 27, 1899; *Semi-Weekly Tribune* (La Junta, CO), April 1, 1899; *Morning World-Herald,* June 6, 1899.

274 "You cannot operate a railroad": Adams to Callaway, September 25, 1885, quoted in Storti, *Incident at Bitter Creek,* 171.

274 the company demolished Chinatown: *Rock Springs Rocket,* May 16, 1913.

275 In July 1925: Pryde to McAuliffe, July 24, 1925, box 3, UPCC.

275 Pryde interviewed a dozen: Pryde to McAuliffe, September 30, 1925, UPCC; Ah Jin narrative, Ah Bow notes, UPCC.

275 a banquet honoring: Pryde to McAuliffe, November 12, 1925, UPCC; *Greybull (WY) Standard and Tribune,* November 13, 1925.

275 limousines delivered the returning men: *SFE,* November 15, 1925.

275 The longest-serving member: "Old Retired Chinese Employes who have been paid Gratuities to," June 30, 1932, UPCC; *Salt Lake Tribune,* November 11, 1925.

276 Another septuagenarian: "Lao Chung Dead," *Employes' Magazine,* September 1927, American Heritage Center, 306.

276 a second contingent: Frank Tallmire and H. J. Harrington, "Homeward Bound," *Employes' Magazine,* December 1927, 423–426, American Heritage Center; Ah Jim photograph, November 5, 1827, box 3, UPCC.

276 "We regret very much": "Our 'China Boys' Heard From," *Employes' Magazine,* November 1927, American Heritage Center.

276 celebrated the marriage: "Joe Bow Marries in China," *Employes' Magazine,* July 1926, 208.

276 "I am ashame": Bow to Pryde, December 5, 1928, UPCC.

276 "Was very glad to hear": Pryde to Bow, February 1, 1929, UPCC.

276 "great sickness": Bow to Pryde, April 18, 1929, UPCC.

276 Pryde continued to send: Pryde to Ah Bow, September 18, 1929, Frank Tallmire to Jas. R. Dewar, January 31, 1929, Pryde to Ah Fun, June 21, 1929, Pryde to McAuliffe, January 17, 1930, Tallmire

to Pryde, June 11, 1930, UPCC; Dudley Gardner, "Jade Snow," chapter 7, unpublished manuscript.

276 In May 1932, McAuliffe: McAuliffe to Pryde, May 24, 1932, UPCC.

276 An exception was made: Pryde to Tallmire, May 26, 1932, Leo Chee to Pryde, March 13, 1930, Leo Chee to Quong Chong & Co., June 16, 1931, Leo Chee to Leo Hung, March 3, 1933, UPCC; Dudley Gardner, "Jade Snow," chapter 7, unpublished manuscript.

277 last three of the company's: "Last Chinese Old Timers Go Home," *Employes' Magazine,* August 1932, American Heritage Center.

Chapter 17: Driven Out

278 On September 5, 1885: Ingebright Wold statement, June 7, 1886, Chin Lan Chong statement, May 22, 1886, in Watson Squire to Thomas Bayard (and enclosed documents), July 17, 1886, MLDS; *Seattle Post-Intelligencer,* September 10, 1885.

278 "sound of water birds": Issaquah Historical Society, *Issaquah, Washington* (Charleston, SC: Arcadia Publishing, 2002), 1.

278 At least one man: *Seattle Post-Intelligencer,* October 28, 1885.

278 The workers had been hired: Floyd Bush, Jim and Myrtle Gregory, Roy Pickering, and Andy Wold, oral history interview, November 28, 1965, 88.1.9, Issaquah History Museums (hereafter cited as Bush oral history), 2; *Seattle Times,* January 15, 1961; Harriet and Edwards Fish, Andy Wold, oral presentation, April 27, 1966, 88.1.2C, Issaquah History Museums, 3–4; Clarence B. Bagley, *History of King County Washington,* vol. 1 (Chicago: S. J. Clarke Publishing, 1929), 765.

279 The idea was originally: Bush oral history, 58; *Seattle Post-Intelligencer,* September 10, 1885; Dictation from George Washington Tibbetts, manuscript, 1887, HHB, BL, 7. Ingebright Wold state-

ment, in Squire to Bayard, July 17, 1886, MLDS.

279 Several hundred Chinese: Lorraine Barker Hildebrand, *Straw Hats, Sandals, and Steel: The Chinese in Washington State* (Tacoma: Washington State American Revolution Bicentennial Commission, 1977), 24.

279 The Quong Chong Company: *Seattle Daily Post-Intelligencer,* September 10, 1885; Chin Lan Chong statement, in Squire to Bayard, July 17, 1886, MLDS.

279 The first group: Squire to Bayard, July 17, 1886, MLDS; Tim Greyhavens, "Finding the Site of the Attack on Chinese Laborers in Squak Valley, September 7, 1885," 2010, Issaquah History Museums.

279 The Wolds had an influential: Tibbetts Dictation, HBC, 5; Bagley, *History of King County,* 768; *Seattle Post-Intelligencer,* August 1, 1882.

279 It was "well known": Tibbetts Dictation, 7, HBC.

280 Tibbetts went next door: *Tacoma Daily News,* September 10, 1885; Tibbetts Dictation, HBC.

280 That evening, at about nine o'clock: Ingebright Wold statement, Squire to Bayard, July 17, 1886, MLDS; *Seattle Daily Post-Intelligencer,* September 11, 1885; Lars and Ingebright Wold testimony, *Territory v. Perry Bayne et al.,* case file no. 4600 (King County, 1886), TCF. Ingebright Wold statement, Squire to Bayard, July 17, 1886, MLDS.

280 the Wolds visited General Tibbetts: Ingebright Wold statement, in Squire to Bayard, July 17, 1886, MLDS.

281 A group of men gathered: *Seattle Daily Post-Intelligencer,* October 28 and 29, 1885.

281 "So much firing": Gong Heng testimony, *Territory v. Perry Bayne et al.,* case file no. 4600, TCF.

281 The Wolds were asleep: Ingebright Wold statement, Squire to Bayard, July 17, 1886, MLDS; Lars and Ingebright Wold testimony, *Territory vs.*

Perry Bayne et al., case file no. 4600, TCF.

281 When Gong Heng snuck back: *Seattle Post-Intelligencer,* October 28, 1885; Gong Heng testimony, *Territory v. Perry Bayne et al.,* case file no. 4600, TCF; Squire to Bayard, July 17, 1886, MLDS.

282 they boarded a train: *Seattle Post-Intelligencer,* September 10, 1885; *Tacoma Daily Ledger,* September 10, 1885; Chin Lan Chong statement, in Squire to Bayard, July 17, 1886, MLDS.

282 He organized a perfunctory: *Seattle Post-Intelligencer,* September 10, 1885.

282 they conducted a new inquest: *Seattle Post-Intelligencer,* September 11, 1885; Squire to Bayard, July 17, 1886, MLDS; Coroner's report, *Territory v. Perry Bayne et al.,* case file no. 4600 (King County, 1886), Territorial District Court, TCF.

282 Ronald, the district attorney: *Seattle Post-Intelligencer,* October 29, November 3, 12, 24, 1885; *SFE,* November 15, 1885.

282 Another participant: *Seattle Post-Intelligencer,* September 11, 1885; *SFE,* November 25, 1885.

282 A grand jury indicted Tibbetts: *Territory v. George W. Tibbetts,* case file no. 4632 and 4633 (King County, 1885).

282 "Mr. Tibbetts has extensive": *Tacoma Daily Ledger,* November 15, 1885; *Washington Standard,* April 2, 1886.

282 residents selected him: *Tacoma Daily News,* July 5, 1889.

282 Lan Chong filed a claim: Squire to Bayard, July 17, 1886, MLDS; Mon Gee and Ah Show statements, "Murder and Arson at Squak Valley, Washington Territory," in Cheng Tsao Ju to Thomas Bayard, April 5, 1886, NFCL.

282 The United States government: U.S. Congress, House, *An Account of the Receipts and Expenditures of the United States for the Fiscal Year Ending June 30, 1889,* 52nd Cong., 2nd sess., Ex. Doc. No. 228 (Washington, 1893), 81; Bayard

to Denby, December 10, 1888, Document 58, No. 376, PRFRUS, 1889; Edward Wood statement, in Squire to Bayard, July 11, 1886, MLDS.

283 In Newcastle: *Tacoma Daily Ledger,* September 15, 1885; Marilyn Tharp, "Story of Coal at Newcastle," *Pacific Northwest Quarterly* 48, no. 4 (October 1957): 124–125.

283 The noise awoke: Chin Poy Hug statement, in Squire to Bayard, July 11, 1886, MLDS.

283 W. J. Watkins, the superintendent: Watkins statement, in Squire to Bayard, July 11, 1886, MLDS.

284 "Me no go back": *Tacoma Daily Ledger,* September 15, 1885.

284 made his way to San Francisco: Watkins statement, in Squire to Bayard, July 11, 1886, MLDS.

284 In July 1873: Herbert Hunt, *Tacoma: Its History and Its Builders; A Half Century of Activity,* vol. 1 (Chicago: S. J. Clarke Publishing, 1916), 175–176, 186–187; Murray Morgan, *Puget's Sound: A Narrative of Early Tacoma and the Southern Sound* (Seattle: University of Washington Press, 1979), 164; Neil T. Loehlein, "Rivers of Steel: The Economic Development of Seattle During the Rail Age, 1870–1920" (master's thesis, Portland State University, 2014), 15.

284 The Northern Pacific's ambition: Eugene V. Smalley, *History of the Northern Pacific Railroad* (New York: G. P. Putnam's Sons, 1883), 128; Morgan, *Puget's Sound,* 161; Hildebrand, *Straw Hats, Sandals, and Steel,* 20.

284 the banking house's failure: Smalley, *History of the Northern Pacific Railroad,* 427; Julian Hawthorne, ed., *History of Washington: The Evergreen State; From Early Dawn to Daylight,* vol. 2 (New York, 1893), 383.

284 The economic depression: *Tacoma Daily Ledger,* January 1, 1886; Morgan, *Puget's Sound,* 180; Hunt, *Tacoma: Its History and Its Builders,* 263; Jules Karlin, "The Anti-Chinese Outbreak in Tacoma,

1885," *Pacific Historical Review* 23, no. 3 (August 1954): 271, https://www.jstor.org/stable/3635568.

285 "dawning of a new era": *Tacoma Daily Ledger,* August 9, 1885.

285 It took eight days: *Tacoma Daily Ledger,* August 29, 1885.

285 Chinese migrants first arrived: Hunt, *Tacoma: Its History and Its Builders,* 356.

285 Kwok Sue was among: J. H. Houghton and Kwok Sue statements, in Squire to Bayard, July 17, 1886, MLDS.

285 Mow Lung came: Mow Lung statement, Squire to Bayard, July 17, 1886, MLDS.

285 Lum Way, who: J. H. Houghton and Sam Hing statements, Squire to Bayard, July 17, 1886, MLDS.

286 Sing Lee, an enterprising: J. H. Houghton, Clifton Young, and Sing Lee statements, Squire to Bayard, July 17, 1886, MLDS; Hunt, *Tacoma: Its History and Its Builders,* 240.

286 On August 22, 1883: *Independent-Record* (Helena, MT), August 23, 1884; Rendig Fels, "The American Business Cycle of 1879–85," *Journal of Political Economy* 60, no. 1 (February 1952): 70, https://www.jstor.org/stable/1826297.

286 At its peak: Henry Villard, *Memoirs of Henry Villard: Journalist and Financier, 1835–1900,* vol. 2 (Boston: Houghton, Mifflin, 1904), 348.

286 Mischievous boys pelted: *Tacoma Daily Ledger,* January 27, 1884.

286 A city councilman: *Tacoma Daily Ledger,* March 7 and 25, 1884; Ottilie Markholt, "The Concern of All: Tacoma Working People and Their Unions, 1883–1895," typescript, 1984, Ottilie Markholt Papers, University of Washington Libraries, Special Collections.

286 The daily morning and evening: *Tacoma Daily Ledger,* January 16, March 8, 1884, February 4, 1885, January 18, 1886; Morgan, *Puget's Sound,* 221; Hunt, *Tacoma: Its History and Its Builders,* 358.

287 "a cancer that is daily": *Tacoma Daily Ledger,* August 22, 1884.

287 several of Tacoma's sawmills: Markholt,

"The Concern of All," 27; *Tacoma Daily Ledger,* January 1, 1886.

287 In early February 1885: Hunt, *Tacoma: Its History and Its Builders,* 359; *Tacoma Daily Ledger,* November 6, 1884, February 8, 1885; Markholt, "The Concern of All," 28, 270; Morgan, *Puget's Sound,* 222.

287 The meeting above: Alexander Saxton, *The Indispensable Enemy: Labor and the Anti-Chinese Movement in California* (Berkeley: University of California Press, 1971), 201–202.

287 Another participant: *Seattle Post-Intelligencer,* September 22, 1885; Daniel A. Cornford, *Workers and Dissent in the Redwood Empire* (Philadelphia: Temple University Press, 1987), 73–75; Ronald J. Perry, "'Wipe Out the Plague Spots': The Expulsion of Chinese from Humboldt County" (master's thesis, Humboldt State University, May 2005), 39–40.

288 On February 19: *Tacoma Daily Ledger,* February 19, 1885; *Tacoma Daily News,* February 21, 1885.

288 Weisbach, a fifty-two-year-old: *Tacoma Daily Ledger,* May 6, 1884; Markholt, "The Concern of All," 12; *Tacoma Daily Ledger,* October 22, 1885.

288 His fortunes as a businessman: *Marshall County News,* December 11, 1875; *Tacoma Daily Ledger,* April 19, 1884.

288 Weisbach's interest in politics: *Marshall County News,* September 20, 1879; Charles Williams, "Labor Radicalism and the Local Politics of Chinese Exclusion: Mayor Jacob Weisbach and the Tacoma Chinese Expulsion of 1885," *Labor History* 60, no. 6 (2019): 688–689; E. J. Dallas, "Kansas Postal History," in *Transactions of the Kansas State Historical Society* (Topeka, 1881), 256.

288 In a letter that he wrote: *Kansas Liberal,* December 1881, as quoted in Williams, "Labor Radicalism and the Local Politics of Chinese Exclusion," 694.

289 Weisbach's election: Williams, "Labor Radicalism and the Local Politics of Chinese Exclusion," 692.

289 About a thousand men: *Daily Tacoma News*, February 23, 1885.

289 a remarkable letter: *Daily Tacoma News*, February 26, 1885; Hunt, *Tacoma: Its History and Its Builders*, 364.

289 Several weeks later, Weisbach: *Tacoma Daily Ledger*, June 4, 1885.

289 a newly established committee: *Tacoma Daily News*, March 11, 1885.

289 The city council: Morgan, *Puget's Sound*, 226; *Tacoma Daily Ledger*, May 22, 27, 28, 1885; Hildebrand, *Straw Hats, Sandals, and Steel*, 39; *Tacoma Daily Ledger*, April 2, 1885.

290 On September 3: *Tacoma Daily News*, September 3, 1885. On the anti-Chinese movement turning violent in Tacoma and elsewhere, see also Beth Lew-Williams, *The Chinese Must Go: Violence, Exclusion, and the Making of the Alien in America* (Cambridge, MA: Harvard University Press, 2018), 113–136.

290 presided over a boisterous: *Tacoma Daily Ledger*, September 8, 1885.

290 Cronin addressed an anti-Chinese: *Seattle Post-Intelligencer*, September 22, 1885.

290 On Sunday evening: *Seattle Post-Intelligencer*, September 29, 1885.

291 "Will you please inform": Bee to Squire, September 30, 1885, as quoted in "Report of the Governor of Washington Territory," H.R. Exec. Doc. No. 1, 49th Cong., 2nd Sess. (1886), 866.

291 the son of an itinerant Methodist preacher: Watson Squire, typescript dictation, 1889–1890, HHB, BL, 2, 11–13; *Courier-Journal* (Louisville, KY), December 8, 1889.

291 "failure on the part": "Report of the Governor of Washington Territory," H.R. Exec. Doc. No. 1, 49th Cong., 1st sess. (1885), 1118.

291 alerted his superiors: Squire to Secretary of the Interior, October 12, 1885, in "Report of the Governor of Washington Territory" (1886), 866; *Tacoma Daily Ledger*, October 22, 1885.

291 He confirmed to Bee: Squire to Bee, September 30, 1885, in "Report of the

Governor of Washington Territory" (1886), 876.

291 some Chinese residents: *Tacoma Daily Ledger*, October 3 and 4, 1885.

292 At nine o'clock in the evening: *Tacoma Daily News*, October 5, 1885.

292 circulated a manifesto: Committee of Fifteen, "To the Citizens of Tacoma," GRDOJ.

292 the exodus of Chinese: *Tacoma Daily Ledger*, October 10, 1885.

293 "You meet a great many": John C. Weatherred diary, October 1, 1885, Weatherred Family collection, Tacoma Historical Society. (This archive will hereafter be cited as Weatherred Collection.) *Tacoma Daily Ledger*, April 18, 1930.

293 General John W. Sprague: *Tacoma Daily Ledger*, December 26, 1893, February 24, 1894.

293 Sprague convened a special meeting: *Tacoma Daily Ledger*, October 7 and 9, 1885; *Tacoma Daily News*, October 9, 1885; Clarence Bagley, *History of King County Washington*, vol. 1 (Seattle: S. J. Clarke Publishing, 1929), 766.

293 built a hops business: Morgan, *Puget's Sound*, 233; *NYT*, December 4, 1928.

293 In a column: *Tacoma Daily Ledger*, October 6, 1885.

294 The Rev. W. D. McFarland: *Tacoma Daily Ledger*, June 24, August 25, October 13, 1885; Hunt, *Tacoma: Its History and Its Builders*, 369–370; Lew-Williams, *The Chinese Must Go*, 152–153.

294 issued a lengthy statement: "Sentiments of the Ministerial-Union of Tacoma Respecting the Present Anti-Chinese Question," October 26, 1885, Washington State Historical Society; Minutes for October 25 and November 2, 1885, Minutes of Tacoma Minister's Union from June 1883 to October 1888, Tacoma Ministerial Alliance records, Northwest Room, Tacoma Public Library.

294 In a telegram on October 14: Squire to Byrd, October 14, 1885, in "Report of the Governor of Washington Territory" (1886), 868–869.

294 Byrd proceeded to swear in: Lewis Byrd statement, in Squire to Bayard, July 17, 1886, MLDS.

295 General Sprague, the chairman: Sprague to Squire, in "Report of the Governor of Washington Territory" (1886), 872–873.

295 On October 27, Squire visited: *Tacoma Daily Ledger,* October 28, 1885; Hunt, *Tacoma: Its History and Its Builders,* 328.

295 On the eve of the deadline: *Tacoma Daily News,* November 2 and 3, 1885.

295 Weatherred recorded: John C. Weatherred diary, November 2, 1885, Weatherred Collection.

295 Hundreds of Chinese residents: Kwok Sue and Lum Way statements, in Squire to Bayard, July 17, 1886, MLDS.

295 Rumors coursed: W. H. White to U.S. Attorney General, November 23, 1885, GRDOJ, 14; Lum Way statement, Squire to Bayard, July 17, 1886, MLDS.

295 A final meeting: Hunt, *Tacoma: Its History and Its Builders,* 372–373.

296 met with Weisbach: Lewis Byrd statement, in Squire to Bayard, July 17, 1886, MLDS.

296 At half past nine, the steam whistle: "Expulsion at Tacoma, Washington Territory," Squire to Bayard, July 17, 1886, MLDS; *Tacoma Daily Ledger,* November 4, 1885.

296 Some in the crowd: Tak Nam statement, in Squire to Bayard, July 17, 1886, MLDS.

296 They pressed into service: *Seattle Daily Call,* November 4, 1885.

296 N. W. Gow, a thirty-two-year-old: N. W. Gow and Barnabas S. MacLafferty statements, in Squire to Bayard, April 17, 1886, MLDS.

296 Kwok Sue, an early: Kwok Sue statement, in Squire to Bayard, April 17, 1886, MLDS.

296 On Railroad Street: Tak Nam and William Blackwell statements, in Squire to Bayard, April 17, 1886, MLDS.

297 The rioters decided: Lewis Byrd statement, in Squire to Bayard, April 17, 1886, MLDS; *Tacoma Daily Ledger,* November 4, 1885.

297 Weisbach stopped by: McLafferty statement, in Squire to Bayard, April 17, 1886, MLDS.

297 Later, Gow went to Weisbach's: N. W. Gow statement, in Squire to Bayard, April 17, 1886, MLDS.

297 Bowen's wife stood: Hunt, *Tacoma: Its History and Its Builders,* 375; Thomas Emerson Ripley, *Green Timber: On the Flood Tide to Fortune in the Great Northwest* (New York: Ballantine Books, 1968), 42.

298 Chinese residents sent urgent: "Report of the Governor of Washington Territory" (1886), 877.

298 Byrd had heard: Byrd statement, in Squire to Bayard, April 17, 1886, MLDS.

298 Tak Nam and Lum Way readied: Josephus Howell statement, in Squire to Bayard, April 17, 1886, MLDS.

298 Bearing whatever possessions: "Expulsion at Tacoma, Washington Territory," Kwok Sue statement, in Squire to Bayard, April 17, 1886, MLDS.

298 Lum Way's wife: Lum Way statement, in Squire to Bayard, April 17, 1886, MLDS.

299 At around five o'clock: W. H. Smith statement, in Squire to Bayard, April 17, 1886, MLDS.

299 Some took shelter: B. R. Everetts, in Squire to Bayard, April 17, 1886, MLDS.

299 There was an open shed: W. H. Smith affidavit, in Squire to Bayard, April 17, 1886, MLDS.

299 hired a carriage: N. W. Gow statement, in Squire to Bayard, April 17, 1886, MLDS.

299 Weisbach later asserted: Weisbach statement, in Squire to Bayard, April 17, 1886, MLDS.

299 W. H. Elder, the Lake View: W. H. Elder statement, in Squire to Bayard, April 17, 1886, MLDS; Morgan, *Puget's Sound,* 243.

299 Others simply began walking: "Expulsion at Tacoma, Washington Territory," Squire to Bayard, April 17, 1886, MLDS.

299 boasted in a letter: Arthur to Squire, November 4, 1885, "Report of the Gov-

ernor of Washington Territory" (1886), 875.

300 On the morning of November 5: *Tacoma Daily News,* November 5, 1885; *Tacoma Daily Ledger,* November 6, 1885.

300 Jacob Ralph, the fire chief: Jacob Ralph statement, in Squire to Bayard, April 17, 1886, MLDS.

300 "The Chinese are gone": *Tacoma Daily News,* November 6, 1885.

Chapter 18: Contagion

301 Other Puget Sound communities: *Tacoma Daily Ledger,* November 6, 1885; Jeffrey Dettman, "Anti-Chinese Violence in the American Northwest: From Community Politics to International Diplomacy, 1885–1888" (PhD diss., University of Texas at Austin, May 2002), 91.

301 in Lorenzo and Boulder Creek: *NYT,* November 14, 1885; *LAT,* November 15, 1885.

301 That same evening, in Pasadena: *Los Angeles Mirror,* November 14, 1885.

301 In Truckee: *Truckee Republican,* December 2, 1885.

302 In an important victory: *Truckee Republican,* January 30, 1886.

302 in Redding: *Republican Free Press,* January 30, 1886.

302 lumber town of Blue Canyon: *SFCh,* January 31, 1886.

302 citizens of Gold Run: *SFB,* February 2, 1886.

302 On November 5: Granville O'Haller, November 5, 1885, diaries 1885–1887, box 4, folder 2, Granville O'Haller Papers, University of Washington Libraries, Special Collections. (This archive will hereafter be cited as O'Haller Papers.) *Seattle Post-Intelligencer,* November 6, 1885; *Tacoma Daily News,* November 6, 1885; *Seattle Daily Call,* November 5, 1885.

303 The most prominent Chinese resident: Willard Jue, "Chinese Pioneer Entrepreneur in Seattle and Toishan," *The Annals of the Chinese Historical Society of the Pacific Northwest,* 1983, 32; Chin Gee

Hee statement, March 16, 1905, File 148 (hereafter cited as Chin file), CEACF, National Archives, Seattle.

303 He arrived in San Francisco: Chin Gee Hee interview, March 23, 1905, Chin file; Jue, "Chinese Pioneer Entrepreneur in Seattle and Toishan," 32; Clarence Bagley, *History of Seattle: From the Earliest Settlement to the Present Time,* vol. 2 (Chicago: S. J. Clarke Publishing, 1916), 709.

304 one of Seattle's earliest Chinese: *Seattle Daily Times,* September 11, 1955; Todd Stevens, "Brokers Between Worlds: Chinese Merchants and Legal Culture, 1852–1925" (PhD diss., Princeton University, June 2003), 27–28.

304 An account book: Account and Letterbook, Chin Gee Hee Papers, in Willard G. Jue Papers, microfilm A13191, Microforms/Newspaper collection, Suzzallo Library, University of Washington, 4–9. (This source will hereafter be cited as Letterbook.)

304 Wa Chong often intervened: Stevens, "Brokers Between Worlds," 50–53.

304 Chin wrote out: Letterbook, 23.

304 "imminent danger": Letterbook, microfilm frame 0030.

304 In the summit: *Seattle Post-Intelligencer,* November 6 and 7, 1885; Stevens, "Brokers Between Worlds," 250, footnote 103.

305 That evening, at a mass meeting: *Seattle Post-Intelligencer,* November 6, 1885; Thomas Burke, "Burke's Speech at the Mass Meeting Held at Frye's Opera House, November 5, 1885," box 32, folder 2, Thomas Burke Papers, University of Washington Libraries, Special Collections.

305 a reporter dropped in: *Seattle Post-Intelligencer,* November 7, 1885.

306 In the early morning hours of November 8: "Report of the Governor of Washington Territory" (1886), 883–884; Clayton D. Laurie, "The Chinese Must Go": The United States Army and the Anti-Chinese Riots in Washington Territory, 1885–1886," *Pacific-Northwest Quarterly* 81, no. 1 (January 1990): 25.

306 White residents seemed: *Seattle Daily Call,* November 9, 1885.

306 Drunken soldiers: *Seattle Post-Intelligencer,* November 10, 1885.

306 demanding a "special tax": *Seattle Daily Call,* November 10, 1885.

306 "They're much worried": Weatherred diary, November 7, 1885, Weatherred Collection.

306 On November 9: *Tacoma Daily Ledger,* November 10, 1885; *United States v. Jacob Weisbach and others,* indictment for conspiracy and insurrection against the laws of the United States of America, no. 1786, Second Judicial District of Washington Territory, November 7, 1885, in GRDOJ.

307 "recent Chinese troubles": W. H. White to U.S. Attorney General, November 23, 1885, GRDOJ, 15.

307 one of the founders: Robert D. Wynne, "Reaction to the Chinese in the Pacific Northwest and British Columbia, 1850 to 1910" (PhD diss., University of Washington, 1964), 228.

307 a grand jury in Seattle indicted: Hanford to Garland, November 11, 1885, GRDOJ; *Seattle Daily Call,* November 14, 1885.

307 "great vigor": Hanford to Garland, November 11, 1885, GRDOJ.

307 a jury needed just ten minutes: *Seattle Daily Call,* January 16, 1886; George Kinnear, *Anti-Chinese Riots at Seattle, Wn., February 8th, 1886* (Seattle, 1911), 4.

307 "The final advance: *Seattle Daily Call,* February 8, 1886; *Seattle Post-Intelligencer,* February 19 and 20, 1886; Ordinance No. 694, "An Ordinance for the Regulation of Sleeping Apartments and for the Preservation of Good Health," November 24, 1885, Seattle City Council Bills and Ordinances, https://clerk.seattle.gov/search /ordinances/694.

307 to help maintain order: John H. McGraw, "The Anti-Chinese Riots of 1885," *Washington State Historical Society Publications,* vol. 2 (Olympia: Washing-

ton State Historical Society, 1915), 390; Kinnear, *Anti-Chinese Riots at Seattle,* 5.

307 "I thought it unwise": *Seattle Post-Intelligencer,* February 19, 1886.

308 messenger alerted McGraw: "Report of the Governor of Washington Territory" (1886), 913; *Seattle Post-Intelligencer,* February 19, 1886.

308 "They are moving out the Chinese": Ida Remington Squire, account of Chinese riots, February 1886, box 1, folder 22, Watson C. Squire Papers, University of Washington Libraries, Special Collections, 1. (This archive will hereafter be cited as Squire Papers.)

308 a bell from the fire engine house: Squire, account of Chinese riots, Squire Papers; *Seattle Post-Intelligencer,* February 19, 1886.

308 a frightened Chinese resident: Thomas Burke to Louise Ackerson, February 21, 1886, letterpress copybook, box 33, Thomas Burke Papers, University of Washington Libraries, special collections.

308 Squire issued a proclamation: Kinnear, *Anti-Chinese Riots at Seattle,* 6; "Report of the Governor of Washington Territory" (1886), 886; Granville O'Haller, February 7, 1886, O'Haller Papers; Clayton D. Laurie, "'The Chinese Must Go': The United States Army and the Anti-Chinese Riots in Washington Territory, 1885–1886," *Pacific Northwest Quarterly* 81, no. 1 (January 1990): 27.

308 "immense mob forcing Chinese": Squire to General John Gibbon, telegram, February 7, 1886, box 1, folder 63, Squire Papers.

308 McGraw later estimated: "Report of the Governor of Washington Territory" (1886), 913.

308 At Chin Gee Hee's home: Chang Yen Hoon to Bayard, March 3, 1888, [Document 255], No. 254, PRFRUS, 1888.

308 A twenty-three-year-old: "Life History of Woo Gen," box 27, folder 38, SRR, https://purl.stanford.edu/cb68rcm3403.

308 A cook employed: *Seattle Post-Intelligencer,* February 19, 1886.

309 Anti-Chinese leaders faced: *Seattle Post-Intelligencer*, February 9, 20, and 21, 1886; Kinnear, *Anti-Chinese Riots at Seattle*, 6.

309 The crowd on the dock: "Report of the Governor of Washington Territory" (1886), 913–914; *Seattle Daily Call*, February 8, 1886.

309 An injunction arrived: *In re* Gee Lee and 75 other Unnamed Chinese, case file no. 4819, King County, Washington Territory District Court, in Seattle (1886), TCF.

309 Late in the afternoon: *Seattle Daily Call*, February 8, 1886.

309 anti-Chinese leaders attempted: Kinnear, *Anti-Chinese Riots at Seattle*, 7.

310 The Chinese on the wharf: *Seattle Post-Intelligencer*, February 9, 1886.

310 By morning: Kinnear, *Anti-Chinese Riots at Seattle*, 7.

310 At a quarter past seven, the members: *Seattle Post-Intelligencer*, February 9, 1886; Stevens, "Brokers Between Worlds," 243; "Report of the Governor of Washington Territory" (1886), 914; *Seattle Daily Call*, February 8, 1886.

310 Those left behind: *Seattle Post-Intelligencer*, February 9 and 10, 1886; *Seattle Daily Call*, February 8, 1886; "Report of the Governor of Washington Territory" (1886), 914; Kinnear, *Anti-Chinese Riots at Seattle*, 8–9; "Life History of Woo Gen," box 27, folder 38, SRR.

311 Kee Low, a fifty-nine-year-old laundryman: "Life History of Kee Low," box 27, folder 34, SRR.

311 Squire had declared martial law: *Seattle Post-Intelligencer*, February 10, 1886.

311 Finally, on February 10: Lieut. Colonel De Russy to Squire, telegram, February 10, 1886, in "Report of the Governor of Washington Territory" (1886), 892.

311 "perfectly quiet and peaceful": Gibbons to Squire, February 12, 1886, box 1, folder 28, WSP.

311 more than a hundred Chinese: There are differing accounts of how many Chinese departed aboard the *Elder*. Ida

Remington Squire recalled a hundred and twenty, in her "account of Chinese riots," February 14, 1886, box 1, folder 22, Squire Papers, 7; *Seattle Post-Intelligencer*, February 16, 1886, reported a hundred and ten.

312 Wa Chong's tally alone: "Memorandum of losses and damages sustained by the Chinese at Seattle, in Washington Territory, due to their expulsion thereupon," in Chang Yen Hoon to Thomas Bayard, February 14, 1887, NCFL.

312 "the fierce fire": Cheng to Zhang Zhidong, telegram, April 3, 1886, in Hangsheng Chen, *Hua gong chu guo shi liao hui bian*, vol. 6 (Beijing: Zhonghua shu ju, 1980), 1341–1342.

312 Wa Chong's owners: Zhang Yinhuan diary, May 2, 1886, *San Zhou Ri Ji*, vol. 1 (Changsha, China: Yue Lu Shu She, 2016), 30–31.

312 the People's Party: Jules Alexander Karlin, "The Anti-Chinese Outbreaks in Seattle, 1885–1886," *Pacific Northwest Quarterly* 39, no. 2 (April 1948): 128, https://www.jstor.org/stable/20698169.

312 brought conspiracy charges: Karlin, "The Anti-Chinese Outbreaks in Seattle," 129; *Seattle Post-Intelligencer*, September 28, 1886; Jury verdict, September 28, 1886, in *United States v. M. McMillan and five others*, case file no. 4901 (King County, WA, 1886), TCF.

312 case against the organizers: *Tacoma Daily Ledger*, March 5, 1887; *United States v. R. Jacob Weisbach and others*, case file no. 1878 (Pierce County, WA, 1887), TCF; Karlin, "The Anti-Chinese Outbreak in Tacoma," 283.

312 In 1888, Chin: Jue, "Chinese Pioneer Entrepreneur in Seattle and Toishan," 33.

312 "Seattle can point": *Seattle Daily Times*, July 1, 1929.

Chapter 19: No Return

313 more than a dozen Chinese residents: Tin-yee Kuo, ed., *Chin-tai Chung-juo shi-shi jih-chih* (Taipei: Chung-hua Shu-chü, 1963), 1:785.

313 the *Queen of Pacific* arrived: *SFE,* February 12, 1886.

313 a newspaper reporter visited: *AC,* February 10, 1886.

314 the heads of two Chinese mercantile: Kwong Lun Hing & Co. to Cheng Tsao Ju, telegram, February 11, 1886, Document 67, No. 66, PRFRUS, 1886.

314 "Our people are absolutely terrorized": Lee Kim Wah to Cheng Tsau Ju, telegram, February 13, 1886, Document 68, PFRUS, 1886.

314 News had made its way: Denby to Bayard, February 9, 1886, Document 47, No. 46, PRFRUS, 1886.

314 "Those who don't come": *Hong Kong Xunhuan Daily,* December 8, 10, 12, 13, 14, 1885, as quoted in Yucheng Qin, *The Diplomacy of Nationalism: The Six Companies and China's Policy Towards Exclusion* (Honolulu: University of Hawaii Press, 2009), 110.

314 feared unrest in Guangzhou: Zhang to Tsung-li Yamen, telegram, 1886, in Chen Hansheng, *Hua gong chu guo shi liao hui bian,* vol. 6 (Beijing: Zhonghua shu ju, 1980), 1339.

314 "They cannot stay": Zhang Zhidong, "Report on Handling the Situation of the Killing of Chinese People in San Francisco," May 19, 1886, in Chen, *Hua gong chu guo shi liao hui bian,* 1345–1349.

314 advertising offers to send: *SFCh,* February 7, 1886.

315 The departure from San Francisco: *SFCh,* February 11, 1886.

315 By the end of June: "Letter from the Secretary of Treasury, transmitting in response to Senate resolution of March 28, 1890, statement of arrivals of Chinese at the port of San Francisco," Senate Ex. Doc. No. 97, 51st Congress, 1st Sess., 1890, 3.

315 arrival of the steamship *Oceanic: SFCh,* June 18, 1886.

315 Hostile crowds began loitering: Senator George Edmunds to Thomas Bayard, May 25, 1886, box 88, Thomas F. Bayard Papers, Library of Congress. (This archive will be cited hereafter as Bayard Papers.)

315 "If we don't do it": Zhang Yinhuan diary, July 25, 1888, *San Zhou Ri Ji,* vol. 2 (Changsha, China: Yue Lu Shu She, 2016), 398.

315 Other prominent officials: Shih-Shan Henry Tsai, *China and the Overseas Chinese in the United States, 1868–1911* (Fayetteville: University of Arkansas Press, 1983), 84. Ouyang Ming is the pinyin romanization for Ow-yang Ming.

315 the foreign office sent a letter: Tsungli Yamen to Charles Denby, in Denby to Bayard, August 11, 1886, Despatches from U.S. Ministers to China, 1843–1906, M92, General Records of the Department of State, Record Group 59, National Archives, College Park, MD.

316 news of the Chinese proposal failed: Thomas F. Bayard, memorandum, January 7, 1887, box 101, Bayard Papers. The Wade-Giles romanization of Zhang Yinhuan is Chang Yin-huan; in Cantonese, he is known as Chang Yen Hoon.

316 descendant of a distinguished: *NYT,* September 29, 1898.

316 "peculiar characteristics": Bayard to Chen Tsao-ju, February 18, 1886, Document 71, No. 67, PRFRUS, 1886. On Bayard and his handling of the Chinese question, see also Charles Callan Tansill, *The Foreign Policy of Thomas F. Bayar* (New York: Fordham University Press 1940), 123–181.

316 enclosing a draft of a new convention: Bayard to Cheng Tsao-ju, April 11, 1887, NTFM.

316 Zhang was a native of Foshan: Arthur W. Hummel, ed., *Eminent Chinese of the Ch'ing Period (1604–1912),* vol. 1 (Washington, DC: General Printing Office, 1943), 60–61.

317 "considerable detention": Cheng Tsao-ju to Bayard, April 7, 1886, NFCL.

317 Zhang's familiarity with English: Earl Swisher, "Chinese Representation in

the United States, 1861–1912," in *Early Sino-American Relations, 1841–1912: The Collected Articles of Earl Swisher,* Kenneth W. Rea, ed. (Boulder, CO: Westview Press, 1977), 189; Tsai, *China and the Overseas Chinese,* 81–82.

317 leaving a lengthy memo: Chang Yen Hoon, "Negotiations for the protection of Chinese in the United States," March 18, 1887, NFCL.

318 Zhang later admitted: Chang Yen Hoon to Bayard, August 16, 1887, NFCL.

318 "It seems almost impossible": Bayard to Denby, April 18, 1887, box 197, Bayard Papers.

318 raised anew the issue of protections: Chang Yen Hoon to Bayard, August 16, 1887, NFCL.

318 "a much larger number": *SFE,* December 6, 1887.

319 "systematic evasion": Bayard to Chang, December 28, 1887, NTFM.

319 "absolutely prohibiting the coming": 19 Cong. Rec. 406 (1888).

319 overcoming revelations: *The Oregonian* (Portland, OR), June 16, 1873, November 7, 1874.

319 "I have no feeling": 19 Cong. Rec. 422 (1888).

319 in October 1886: Chang Yen Hoon to Bayard, February 16, 1888, NFCL; R. Gregory Nokes, "A Most Daring Outrage: Murders at Chinese Massacre Cove, 1887," *Oregon Historical Quarterly* 107, no. 3: 328–330.

320 The accounts of what happened next: H. R. Findley, "The Sky Beyond the Mountains: The Life and Times of an Oregon Pioneer Family: The Findleys of Wallowa County," ed. John Gaterud, annot. David Weaver (Wallowa, OR: Wallowa History Center, 2023), 169. The manuscript was first serialized and published as "Memoirs of Alexander B. and Sarah Jane Findley: A True Story of the West When the West Was Young," *Joseph Weekly Herald* and *Wallowa County Chieftain,* October 31, 1957, to February 4, 1960; *The Oregonian,* April 27,

1888; *NYT,* April 29, 1888; *Oregon Scout* (Union, OR), April 20, 1888; John Harland Horner, "Wallowa River and Valley," typescript, 1953, 1210; Nokes, "A Most Daring Outrage," 335–336; Notes taken from a stenographic report taken during an interview with George Craig, March 2, 1936, box 35, folder 3, W.P.A. Oregon Historical Records Survey records, County Records Inventory Survey, Wallowa County, University of Oregon Libraries, Special Collections and University Archives. (This archive will be cited hereafter as WPA Records.)

320 "finished him off": Findley, "The Sky Beyond the Mountains," 170.

320 "another case of outrage": Chang Yen Hoon to Bayard, February 16, 1888, NFCL.

320 corpses washed up: George Craig interview, box 35, folder 3, WPA Records.

321 Bayard's response to Zhang: Bayard to Chang, February 23, 1888, NTFM.

321 A grand jury: Bob Sincock, "Case Is Closed. Fifty Years Snake River Flowed Blood and International Complications Lingered Long," *Oregon Journal* (Portland, OR), September 18, 1938, typescript copy, box 35, folder 1, WPA Records; Nokes, "A Most Daring Outrage," 346.

321 When the two men met: Charles Callan Tansill, *The Foreign Policy of Thomas F. Bayard* (New York: Fordham University Press, 1940), 157.

321 Bayard's latest draft convention: Bayard to Chang, February 29, 1888, NTFM.

321 the Senate approved: 19 Cong. Rec. 1621 (1888).

321 final statement of claims: Chang to Bayard, March 3, 1888, NFCL.

321 at least 168 communities: Beth Lew-Williams, *The Chinese Must Go: Violence, Exclusion, and the Making of the Alien in America* (Cambridge, MA: Harvard University Press, 2018), 253–254. See also Jean Pfaelzer, *Driven Out: The Forgotten War Against Chinese Ameri-*

cans (Berkeley: University of California Press, 2008), 256–290.

322 insisted on adding two amendments: Bayard to Denby, June 7, 1888, no. 214, PRFRUS, 1888.

322 urgently wrote to Bayard: Tansil, *The Foreign Policy of Thomas F. Bayard,* 162.

322 "they only repeat what the Treaty": Bayard to Chang Yen Hoon, May 8, 1888, NTFM.

322 "very unnecessary": Bayard memo, May 11, 1888, box 125, Bayard Papers.

322 he telegraphed them: Chang Yen Hoon to Bayard, May 12, 1888, NFCL.

322 The merchant community: Zhang Yin-huan diary, July 25, 1888, *San Zhou Ri Ji,* vol. 2 (Changsha, China: Yue Lu Shu She, 2016), 398.

323 A mob smashed: Denby to Bayard, September 6, 1888, box 129, Bayard Papers.

323 recommended that the Qing government decline: Tsai, *China and the Overseas Chinese,* 90; Lew-Williams, *The Chinese Must Go,* 184–185; Ching-Hwang Yen, *Coolies and Mandarins: China's Protection of Overseas Chinese During the Late Ch'ing Period (1851–1911)* (Singapore University Press, 1985), 238.

323 word came by cable: *LAT,* September 1, 1888.

323 Rep. William L. Scott, a Pennsylvania Democrat: *Black Hills Daily Times,* March 7, 1888; *Boston Weekly Globe,* July 18, 1888; *Saint Paul Daily Globe,* June 5, 1888; Chap. 1064, An act and supplement to an act entitled "An act to execute certain treaty stipulations relating to Chinese," approved the sixth day of May eighteen hundred and eighty-two, *The Statutes at Large of the United States of America, from December, 1887, to March, 1889* (Washington, DC, 1889), 504.

323 He told his colleagues: 19 Cong. Rec. (1888), 8226–8227.

323 "Believe treaty has been rejected": Denby to Bayard, September 5, 1888, No. 234, PRFRUS, 1888.

323 "postponed for further deliberation":

Denby to Bayard, September 6, 1888, No. 235, PRFRUS.

323 On September 21: *NYT,* September 22, 1888; Denby to Bayard, September 21, 1888, No. 238, PRFRUS.

323 Bayard had been urging: Bayard to Cleveland, September 18, 1888, box 130, Bayard Papers.

324 "The experiment of blending": Cleveland, "Special Message," October 1, 1888, American Presidency Project, UC Santa Barbara, https://www.presidency.ucsb.edu/documents/special-message-1066.

324 Cleveland's language: Beth Lew-Williams, "Before Restriction Became Exclusion," *Pacific Historical Review* 83, No. 1 (February 2014): 26.

324 "for all losses and injuries sustained": Chang Yen Hoon, "Receipt for the Indemnity," January 11, 1889, PRFRUS, 1889.

324 residents exulted: *SFE,* October 2, 1888.

325 "California's day of jubilee": *AC,* October 2, 1888.

325 Records at the San Francisco Customs House: Frederick A. Bee statement, U.S. Congress, House, Select Committee on Immigration and Naturalization, Investigation of Chinese Immigration, 51st Cong., 2nd sess., 1890, H. Rept. 4048 (hereafter cited as Chinese Immigration report), 380. See also *SFE,* October 3, 1888, which reported more than thirty thousand outstanding certificates.

325 "if acceptable": Alfred E. Turner to Secretary of State, on behalf of Lew Long, July 7, 1890, box 6, folder 10, CCF.

325 *City of New York* had arrived: *SFE,* October 4, 1888.

325 the *Belgic* initially had: *SFCh,* October 8, 1888; *Washington Post,* October 9, 1888; *SFE,* October 9, 1888; *AC,* October 19, 1888.

325 Another steamship, the *Duke of Westminster: Victoria Daily Times* (Victoria, BC), October 3, 1888.

325 On October 3: *SFE,* October 4 and 9, 1888.

326 Hager sent a telegram: *SFCh*, October 5, 1888.

326 The *Belgic* finally arrived: *CT,* October 8, 1888.

326 Customs officials ordered: *SFE*, October 9, 1888.

326 The standard protocol: Chinese Immigration Report, 279, 296.

326 On Monday morning, Rickards: *SFE*, October 9, 1888; Shu Cheou Pon to Bayard, October 10, 1888, NFCL.

326 Judge Hoffman ordered: *SFCh*, October 10, 1888.

327 issued two writs of habeas corpus: *Morning Tribune* (San Luis Obispo, CA), October 12, 1888; *AC*, October 12, 1888.

327 corridors of the courthouse: *SFE*, October 13, 1888; *SFB*, October 13, 1888.

327 tried more homicide cases: *The Bay of San Francisco: The Metropolis of the Pacific Coast and its Suburban Cities; A History, vol. 2* (Chicago, 1892), 267.

327 The gallery was filled: *SFB*, October 13, 1888; *SFCa*, May 27, 1912; *SFE*, October 21, 1888; *SFE*, November 21, 1886; *SB*, February 16, 1931.

327 The lawyers agreed: *SFB*, October 13, 1888; Transcript of Record, Appeal from the Circuit Court of the United States for the Northern District, *Chae Chan Ping v. United States,* Supreme Court of the United States, October 1888 Term, No. 1446, In the Matter of Chae Chan Ping on Habeas Corpus, 6; *AC*, October 13, 1888.

328 Riordan began his argument: *SFE,* October 14, 1888; *AC,* October 13 and 14, 1888.

328 "very different from the population": Lorenzo Sawyer dictations, transcription, fol. 1, BANC MSS C-D 321, CIC, BL.

328 "crowded almost to suffocation": *SFB*, October 15, 1888.

329 Sawyer wrote that the language: *In re Chae Chan Ping*, 36 F. 431 (C.C.N.D. Cal. 1888), 432, 434.

329 The *Duke of Westminster: SFE*, October 16, 1888.

329 On October 18: *AC*, October 19, 1888.

329 "committing wholesale perjury": John T. Carey to the Attorney General, October 27, 1888, box 5, folder 1, CCF.

329 Over the next week: *Morning Tribune,* October 23 and 25, 1888; *SFE,* October 28, 1888.

330 On March 28: *SFCh*, March 29, 1889.

330 The oral arguments for: *SFCh*, March 30, 1889.

330 opinion written by Justice Stephen Field: Chinese Exclusion Case, *Chae Chan Ping v. United States,* 130 U.S. 581 (1889), 595, 606.

331 "Where Is Chae Chan Ping?": *SFE*, June 23, 1889.

331 the marshal's office reported: *SFE,* July 17, 1889.

331 At one thirty in the afternoon: *NYT,* September 2, 1889; *SFE,* August 23, 1889.

332 "Peggy's Pencilings": *Petaluma (CA) Courier,* August 28, 1889.

Chapter 20: The Resistance

335 Representative Herman Lehlbach: A. M. Holbrook, *Holbrook's Newark City Business Directory* (Newark, 1885), 577; *St. Joseph Herald,* January 2, 1890; *Montclair Times,* September 13, 1884.

335 set out by train from Chicago: *Evening Star* (Washington, DC), November 17, 1890; *Aegis and Intelligencer* (Bel Air, MD), November 14, 1890; *Cheyenne Daily Leader,* November 21, 1890; *SFCa,* December 5, 1890.

336 "protect our country": Watson Squire, typescript dictation, 1889–1890, HHB, BL, 43.

336 touring Chinatown: *SFCh*, December 6, 1890.

336 "They will create a bigger": U.S. Congress, House, Select Committee on Immigration and Naturalization, Investigation of Chinese Immigration, 51st Cong., 2nd sess., 1890, H. Rept. 4048 (hereafter cited as Chinese Immigration report), 495.

336 Squire headed back: *Seattle Post-Intelligencer,* November 30, 1890.

336 mammoth recently opened Queen

Anne–style beachfront: *Los Angeles Herald*, December 1, 1887.

336 Lehlbach had generally harbored: *Jersey City News*, January 12, 1891.

336 subcommittee summoned Ah Quin: *San Diego Union*, December 18, 1890; Chinese Immigration Report, 554–561.

337 The subcommittee had found: Chinese Immigration Report, I–IV.

338 imposed additional harsh requirements: "An act to prohibit the coming of Chinese persons into the United States," *The Statutes at Large of the United States of America, From December, 1891, to March, 1893* (Washington, DC, 1893), 25.

338 Chinese officials pointed to figures: Tsui Kwo Yin to James Blaine, April 12, 1892, NFCL.

338 Cui Guoyin, Zhang Yinhuan's successor: The Wade-Giles romanization of Cui Guoyin is Tsui Kwo Yin.

338 "enlightened Chief Magistrate": Tsui Kwo Yin to Blaine, May 5, 1892, NFCL.

338 "waiting along the Canadian border": *SFCa*, May 6, 1892.

338 Just after noon: *Washington Post*, May 6, 1892.

339 "without delay": Lorenzo Crounse to Collector of Customs, telegram, May 7, 1892, Letters received from the Office of the Secretary of Treasury, 1895–1912, Records of the United States Customs Service, RG 36, National Archives, San Bruno, CA.

339 His office prepared: U.S. Congress, House, *Enforcement of the Geary Law*, 53rd Cong., 1st sess., 1893, H. Exec. Doc. 10, serial 3150, 11–12; *SFCa*, August 9, 1892.

339 outlining a three-pronged strategy: *NYT*, December 17, 1892; *Pittsburgh Press*, April 8, 1900.

339 thriving locus of influence: *NYTr*, June 21, 1885; *Daily Evening News* (Modesto, CA), July 6, 1892.

340 undertaking a census: *The Evening World* (New York), August 25, 1892.

340 An assertive Chinese physician: *NYTr*, July 7, 1902; *NYTr*, December 21 and 28,

1886; *New York Sun*, January 18, 1891; *Daily Evening News*, July 6, 1892.

340 "no doubt": *Brooklyn Daily Eagle*, August 17, 1892.

340 "That Chinamen living in peace": *The Evening World*, August 25, 1892.

341 the Six Companies issued a proclamation: *SFCa*, September 11, 1892.

341 "gives me excruciating pains": *SFCa*, September 14, 1892.

341 Quinn, the city's collector of internal revenue: Quinn to Six Companies, September 15, 1892, as quoted in 25 Cong. Rec. (1893), 2443.

341 "It is in violation": *SFCa*, September 21, 1892.

341 "high priest of the Chinese colony": *NYT*, November 23, 1891.

341 In February 1883: Qingsong Zhang, "The Origins of the Chinese Americanization Movement: Wong Chin Foo and the Chinese Equal Rights League," in *Claiming America: Constructing Chinese American Identities During the Exclusion Era*, ed. K. Scott Wong and Sucheng Chan (Philadelphia: Temple University Press, 1998), 49; Scott D. Seligman, *The First Chinese American: The Remarkable Life of Wong Chin Foo* (Hong Kong: Hong Kong University Press, 2013), 90, 99.

341 "Though we may differ": Wong Chin Foo, "Why Am I a Heathen?," *North American Review* 145, no. 369 (August 1887): 175.

342 On September 1: *Appeal of the Chinese Equal Rights League to the People of the United States for Equality of Manhood* (New York, 1893), 1; *NYT*, September 15, 1892, and January 15, 1898.

342 the meeting at Cooper Union: *Boston Evening Transcript*, September 23, 1892; *NYT*, September 23, 1892; *NYTr*, September 23, 1892; *SFCa*, September 23, 1892.

343 another public gathering: *Boston Globe*, November 18, 1892.

343 laid them on the clerk's desk: 24 Cong. Rec. (1893), 500–501; *NYT*, January 11, 1893.

343 He stayed at the Willard Hotel: *SFCa*, January 14, 1893.

344 Wong appeared before: *SFCa*, January 27, 1893; *The Chinese American*, June 24, 1893; *Baltimore Sun*, January 27, 1893.

344 When it was Geary's turn: The extent to which Chinese arrivals were resorting to subterfuge is almost unknowable. While there is little doubt that fraud was common—fake partnerships in Chinese companies, for instance, could be purchased with relative ease—there are also clues that fears of illegal Chinese entry were often grossly exaggerated. Anti-Chinese partisans were adamant, for instance, that Chinese migrants were streaming across a porous border in Washington Territory from British Columbia, but Lehlbach's committee estimated that the number did not exceed three hundred annually. See Erika Lee, *At America's Gates: Chinese Immigration During the Exclusion Era, 1882–1943* (Chapel Hill: University of North Carolina Press, 2003), 200–201; Chinese Immigration Report, 1; Lucy E. Salyer, *Laws as Harsh as Tigers: Chinese Immigrants and the Shaping of Modern Immigration Law* (Chapel Hill: University of North Carolina Press, 1995), 45.

344 By the middle of March: *NYT*, March 18, 1893; W. Q. Gresham to Tsui Kwo Yin, March 21, 1893, Document 252, PRFRUS, 1893.

345 the Six Companies issued another admonition: *SFCa*, April 1, 1893.

345 "Chinese regulations modified": *Marysville Daily Appeal*, April 9, 1893; *SFCh*, April 9, 1893; *SFE*, April 9, 1893.

345 "open to Chinese cunning": *SFCa*, April 9, 1893.

345 "Our first regulations required": *SFCa*, April 15, 1893.

345 total cost of deportation: U.S. Congress, House, *Amendment to the Chinese Exclusion Act*, 53rd Cong., 1st sess., 1893, H. Rep. No. 70, serial 3157, 2.

345 Congress had only allocated: *SFE*, May 21, 1893; *SFCa*, May 17, 1893; *Charlotte (NC) Observer*, May 17, 1893.

346 "until necessary arrangements": U.S. Congress, House, *Chinese Exclusion Act*, 53rd Cong., 1st sess., 1893, H. Exec. Doc. 9, serial 3150, 3.

346 tested different aspects of the law: *NYT*, May 7, 1893; Joseph Choate and Maxwell Evarts, Appellant's Brief, *Fong Yue Ting v. United States* 149 U.S. 698 (1893), U.S. Supreme Court Records and Briefs, 1–5.

346 On May 10: *NYT*, May 11, 1893; Choate and Evarts, Appellant's Brief, *Fong Yue Ting v. United States*, 15, 28, 55.

347 At noon on May 15: *SFE*, May 16, 1893; Justice Gray, Opinion of the Court, *Fong Yue Ting v. United States*, 707.

347 Field argued: Justice Field, Dissenting Opinion, *Fong Yue Ting v. United States*, 750, 761.

347 News of the decision: *SFCa*, May 16, 1893.

347 impromptu open-air meeting: *Fresno Morning Republican*, May 16, 1893.

348 Chinatown itself remained: *SFCh*, May 16, 1893.

348 "It's like a man feeling safe": *SFCa*, May 16, 1893.

348 In New York: *NYTr*, May 17, 1893.

348 The Treasury Department's annual report: U.S. Congress, House, *Annual Report of the Secretary of the Treasury on the State of the Finances of the Year 1893*, 53rd Cong., 2nd Sess., 1893, Ex. Doc. No. 2, serial 3219, 563.

348 "attended with some": Memorandum of a conversation between the Secretary of State and the Chinese minister, Gresham to Tsui Kwo Yin, May 19, 1893, Document 267, PRFRUS, 1893; Carlisle, Treasury Department circular, May 24, 1893, H. Exec. Doc. 9, 3–4.

349 Wong incorporated: *Lebanon (PA) Daily News*, April 24, 1893.

349 Wong laid out his aims: *The Chinese American*, June 24, 1893.

349 newspaper had folded: Seligman, *The First Chinese American*, 235.

349 financial hysteria beset: W. Jett Lauck,

The Causes of the Panic of 1893 (Boston: Houghton, Mifflin and Company, 1907), 95–102; Samuel Rezneck, "Unemployment, Unrest, and Relief in the United States During the Depression of 1893–97," *Journal of Political Economy* 61, no. 4 (August 1953): 324–325.

350 In the town of Selma: *SFE*, August 13, 1893.

350 descended upon the Paige orchard: *Tulare Advance Register*, August 14, 1893; *Visalia Daily Times*, August 16, 1893; *SFE*, August 15 and 16, 1893; *The Weekly Bee* (Sacramento, CA), August 9, 1893.

350 anti-Chinese agitation had spread: *Fresno Morning Republican*, August 15, 1894; *San Luis Obispo Tribune*, August 20, 1893.

351 When the town's plat: Henry L. Graham, *Redlands: A Perfect Climate, the Finest Oranges Groves in the State, Beautiful Parks and Fine Residences* (Redlands, CA: Board of Trade, 1906).

351 a mob of white men visited a ranch: *The Daily Facts* (Redlands, CA), August 28, 1893.

351 kidnapped a group of Chinese men: *The Daily Facts*, August 29, 1893.

351 Rumors circulated: *The Daily Facts*, August 31, September 1, 1893.

351 become known as the Redlands Plan: *The Daily Facts*, September 1, 1893; *LAT*, August 31, 1893. On the Redlands Plan, see also Jean Pfaelzer, *Driven Out: The Forgotten War Against Chinese Americans* (Berkeley: University of California Press, 2008), 312–316; Michael Several, "The Chinese and the 'Redlands Plan': Ethnic Cleansing, the Rule of Law, Economic Self-Interest, and Financial Restraint," *Southern California Quarterly* 93, no. 4 (Winter 2011-2012): 407–458.

352 National Guard soldiers: *The Daily Facts*, September 2, 1893.

352 local civic leaders: *The Daily Facts*, September 2, 1893; *LAT*, September 3, 1893.

352 Denis had received instructions: *The*

Evening Express (Los Angeles), September 4, 1893.

352 Judge Ross ruled: *LAT*, September 6, 1893; *Los Angeles Herald*, September 6, 1893.

352 James Faris, the deputy United States marshal: *LAT*, September 8, 1893.

352 nine out of the twelve unregistered Chinese: *The Citrograph* (Redlands, CA), September 9, 1893.

352 the trial for the first eight men: *The Evening Express*, September 11, 1893; *The Evening Bee* (Sacramento, CA), September 11, 1893.

353 The lone exception: Several, "The Chinese and the 'Redlands Plan': Ethnic Cleansing, the Rule of Law, Economic Self-Interest, and Financial Restraint," 447.

353 there were just fifty Chinese residents: *The Citrograph*, September 16, 1893.

353 In Riverside, Faris started: *SFCh*, September 14, 1893; *LAT*, September 2, 1893.

353 He traveled next: *The Evening Express*, September 14, 1893; *SFCh*, September 14, 1893.

353 sometimes requiring just a few minutes: *The Evening Express*, September 15, 1893.

353 sixty-two arrest warrants: H. Exec. Doc. 9, serial 3150, 2.

353 introduced a bill: 25 Cong. Rec. 2565 (1893).

353 Geary later introduced: 25 Cong. Rec., appendix 230 (1893); Anna Pegler-Gordon, *In Sight of America: Photography and the Development of U.S. Immigration Policy* (Berkeley: University of California Press, 2009), 34–41; *NYT*, November 3, 1893; *LAT*, November 4, 1893.

354 the *City of New York* pulled away: *SFCh*, October 27, 1893; *SFCh*, October 27, 1893.

354 they were suddenly free to go: *SFCh*, November 5, 1893.

Chapter 21: Native Sons

355 The town of Downieville: James J. Sinnott, *Downieville, Gold Town on*

the Yuba, 3rd ed. (Nevada City, CA: Mountain House Books, 1991), 5; Robert Phelps, "All Hands Have Gone Downtown: Urban Places in Gold Rush California," *California History* 79, no. 2 (Summer 2000): 115; J. D. Borthwick, *The Gold Hunters: A First-Hand Picture of Life in California Mining Camps in the Early Fifties*, ed. Horace Kephart (New York: Outing Publishing, 1917), 210–211; Theodore Hittell, *History of California*, vol. 3 (San Francisco, 1897), 95. Parts of this chapter are drawn from Michael Luo, "The Dark Purpose Behind a Town Constable's Journal," *New Yorker*, January 28, 2022, https://www.newyorker.com/culture/photo-booth/the-dark-purpose-behind-a-town-constables-journal.

355 Downieville became notorious: William Downie, *Hunting for Gold: Reminiscences of Personal Experience and Research in the Early Days of the Pacific Coast from Alaska to Panama* (San Francisco, 1893), 152–153.

355 By 1852, Downieville's population: Bourdon Wilson, *Sierra County California* (San Francisco: Sunset Magazine Homeseekers' Bureau, n.d.), 25.

355 Chinese miners flocked to the region: Sinnott, *Downieville, Gold Town on the Yuba*, 9; *Sierra County Tribune*, May 24, 1883.

355 As the mining boom faded: "Population of California by Minor Civil Divisions," Census Bulletin, No. 10, October 24, 1900, Twelfth Census of the United States.

355 Yet the Chinese remained a sizable presence: Albert Dressler, *California's Pioneer Mountaineer of Rabbit Creek* (Campbell, CA: The Westerner Publisher, 1930), 67–68; James Galloway testimony, Committee of the Senate of the State of California, *Chinese Immigration: The Social, Moral, and Political Effect of Chinese Immigration* (Sacramento, CA: State Printing Office, 1876), 155; Sinnott, *Downieville, Gold Town on*

the Yuba, 106–109. See also occupations listed in John T. Mason, Photograph album of Chinese men and women in Sierra County, Vault-184, California Historical Society.

356 During the turbulence: *Sierra County Tribune*, March 19, 1886; Sinnott, *Downieville, Gold Town on the Yuba*, 106.

356 "The Chinese should be given to understand": *Mountain Messenger*, May 20, June 24, July 8, September 16, and December 16, 1893.

356 The constable in Downieville: John Thomas Mason, California, U.S., Pioneer and Immigrant Files, 1790–1950, California State Library, California History Section, via Ancestry.com; Dressler, *California's Pioneer Mountaineer of Rabbit Creek*, 67–68.

356 In the spring of 1889: Mason Ledger, 1–3.

356 On February 17, 1894: *Mountain Messenger*, February 24, 1894.

357 Over the course of the next week and a half: *Mountain Messenger*, March 3, 1894.

357 At the end of March: *Mountain Messenger*, March 31, 1894.

357 "Chinese Photographed by DD Beaty": Mason Journal, 4.

357 there is an entry for Quok Moon: Mason Journal, 56.

357 Census records point: Forest Township, Sierra County, California, Schedule No. 1—Population, Twelfth Census of the United States, June 6, 1900.

357 The youngest subject: Mason Journal, 104.

357 The last few photographs: Mason Journal, 106–109.

358 Nung Owen: Mason Journal, 25.

358 The photographer caught Jung Chung: Mason Journal, 60.

358 "froze to death": Mason Journal, 51.

358 The entry for Wong Fun: Mason Journal, 56.

358 In New York City: *The Evening World*, April 3, 1894.

358 In San Francisco: *SFCa*, April 21, 1894.

358 By the end of the day on May 3: U.S. Congress, House, *Report of the Commissioner of Internal Revenue for the Fiscal Year Ended June 30, 1895,* 54th Cong., 1st Sess., 1893, Doc. No. 11, serial 3395, 23–24.

359 In 1870: U.S. Census Bureau, 1870 Census, vol. 1, "The Statistics of the Population of the United States," Table 6, "Population of the United States (By States and Territories), Classified by Race and Place of Birth, Showing the Number of Persons Born in Each State and Territory and Specified Foreign Country," 328.

359 Three decades later: U.S. Census Bureau, 1900 Census, vol. 2, "Statistics of Population: Elements of the Population," xviii.

359 By 1920, native-born: Yumei Sun, "From Isolation to Participation: *Chung Sai Yat Po* [China West Daily] and San Francisco's Chinatown, 1900–1920" (PhD diss., University of Maryland, College Park, 1999), 74.

359 In May 1895: *SFCa,* May 11, 1895.

359 Within two months: *SFCa,* July 4 and 5, 1895, September 17, 1899.

359 Among the members: Robert Leon Park interview, January 31, 1921, File 12016/1908, CEACF, National Archives, San Bruno, CA; *SFCa,* September 17, 1899; Victor Low, *The Unimpressible Race: A Century of Educational Struggle by the Chinese in San Francisco* (San Francisco: East/West Publishing, 1982), 110; *SFE,* September 20, 1896; *SFCh,* November 29, December 5, 1951; *SFE,* September 20, 1896, November 29, 1951.

360 "We are Americans": *SFCa,* September 17, 1899.

360 "organize the better class": *The Inter Ocean* (Chicago), January 1, 1897.

360 two hundred "American-Chinamen": *Boston Evening Transcript,* January 27, 1897.

360 In May, Wong issued: *Evening Sentinel* (Santa Cruz, CA), May 28, 1897.

360 On November 27: *Chicago Chronicle,* November 28, 1897; *CT,* November 28, 1897. In 1898, Wong died in Hong Kong, at the age of fifty-one. Just before his death, he had been planning to return to the United States and had secured a passport as a naturalized citizen, only to have it revoked by an American consular official. See Scott D. Seligman, *The First Chinese American: The Remarkable Life of Wong Chin Foo* (Hong Kong: Hong Kong University Press, 2013), 284–285.

361 "permit the naturalization of Americanized Chinese": 31 Cong. Rec. 235, 237 (1897); *Evening Express* (Los Angeles), January 6, 1898; *CT,* February 14, 1898.

361 Habeas corpus petitions filed: Lucy E. Salyer, *Laws as Harsh as Tigers: Chinese Immigrants and the Shaping of Modern Immigration Law* (Chapel Hill: University of North Carolina Press, 1995), 98.

361 In November 1894, William Morrow: *Lem Moon Sing v. United States,* 158 U.S. 538, 541; *In re* Tom Yum (D.C.N.D. Cal. 1894), 490.

362 Wise warned his superiors: John Wise to Secretary of the Treasury, November 17, 1894, Letters sent to the Secretary of Treasury, 1869–1912, Records of the United States Customs Service, RG 36, National Archives, San Bruno, CA.

362 In the fall of 1870: Details of Wong Kim Ark's early life drawn from Form 2505, July 21, 1931, Wong Kim Ark interview, July 16, 1890, F. Bema statement, July 16, 1890, in Wong Kim Ark file 12017/42223 (hereafter cited as Wong Kim Ark file), Immigration and Naturalization Service, RG 85, National Archives, San Bruno, CA.

362 the couple decided to take their son: Application for preinvestigation of his status as a native, October 13, 1913, Wong Kim Ark file; Wong Yook Jim interview, July 23, 1926, Wong Yook Jim File 30980/7–5, and Wong Kim Ark interview, December 6, 1910, in Wong

Yook Fun file 10434/137 (hereafter cited as Wong Yook Fun file), Immigration and Naturalization Service, RG 85, National Archives, San Bruno, CA.

362 He "went to the country": Wong Kim Ark interview, August 31, 1895, Wong Kim Ark file.

363 he married a seventeen-year-old girl: See Form 2505, July 21, 1931, Wong Kim Ark file, in which Wong said Yee Shee was fifty-nine years old.

363 On July 8, 1890: Wong Kim Ark statement, November 5, 1894, Wong Kim Ark file.

363 Before his departure: Wong Kim Ark departure statement, November 5, 1894, Wong Kim Ark file.

363 Nevertheless, Wong made: Details of Wong's trip back to the United States drawn from Wong Kim Ark interview, August 31, 1895, Wong Kim Ark file; Amanda Frost, "By Accident of Birth: The Battle Over Birthright Citizenship After *United States v. Wong Kim Ark*," *Yale Journal of Law & the Humanities* 32, no. 1 (2021): 66; *SFCh*, September 1, 1895; *SFCa*, August 20, 25, September 1, 1895; *SFE*, September 1, 1895.

364 During Wong's interrogation: Wong Kim Ark interview, August 31, 1895, Wong Kim Ark file.

364 Notes added to Wong's arrival case file: Handwritten notes, n.d., Wong Kim Ark file.

364 On September 7: *SFCh*, September 8, 1895; *SFCa*, August 31, 1895.

364 Wise had continued: John Wise to Secretary of the Treasury, July 10, 1895, Letters sent to the Secretary of Treasury, 1869–1912, Records of the United States Customs Service, RG 36, National Archives, San Bruno, CA. Much thanks to Hardeep Dhillon, assistant professor of history at the University of Pennsylvania, whose correspondence with me about the Wong Kim Ark case helped lead me to this letter.

364 Over the next few weeks: Transcript of Record, Appeal from the District Court of the United States for the Northern District of California, United States v. Wong Kim Ark, Supreme Court of the United States, October 1897 Term, No. 132 (hereafter cited as Transcript), 2.

364 eager to bring a test case: *LAT*, October 1, 1895; *SFCa*, November 12, 1895, January 4, 1896; *Stockton Evening Mail*, October 1, 1895.

364 For years, however, George D. Collins: Lucy Salyer, "Wong Kim Ark: The Contest over Birthright Citizenship," in *Immigration Stories*, ed. David A. Martin and Peter H. Schuck (New York: Foundation Press, 2005), 58, 65–66; George Collins, "Citizenship by Birth," *American Law Review*, vol. 29 (St. Louis, 1895): 391 *SFCa*, November 14, 1895; Wise to Secretary of the Treasury, July 10, 1895.

365 On October 2: Transcript, 1; *SFCa*, October 27, 1894.

365 A little over a month later: H. S. Foote, Intervention, November 11, 1895, Wong Kim Ark file; *SFCa*, November 12, 1895.

365 the authorities released him: *SFE*, January 4, 1896.

365 "To hold that the Fourteenth Amendment": *United States v. Wong Kim Ark*, 169 U.S. 649 (1898), 169.

366 Charles Mehan, the Chinese immigration: *Albuquerque Citizen*, June 23, 1899; *SFE*, February 17, 1903; *Arizona Daily Star*, August 1, 1902.

366 At the turn of the century: Bureau of the Census, 1920 Census, Bulletin 127, *Chinese and Japanese in the United States 1910* (Washington, DC: Government Printing Office, 1914), 32; Erika Lee, "Enforcing the Borders: Chinese Exclusion Along the U.S. Borders with Canada and Mexico, 1882–1924," *Journal of American History* 89, no. 1 (June 2002): 60.

366 Immigration officials later reported: U.S. Congress, House, *Compilation from the Records of the U.S. Bureau of Immigration of Facts Concerning the Enforce-*

ment of the Chinese-Exclusion Laws, 59th Cong., 1st Sess., 1906, Doc. No. 847, 14.

366 it did not end his troubles: On the federal immigration bureaucracy's treatment of Wong Kim Ark and his family after *United States v. Wong Kim Ark,* see also Frost, "By Accident of Birth," 38–76.

366 On October 29: Arrest warrant, October 29, 1901, *United States v. Wong Kim Ark,* El Paso case 802(7), WTX097A1, Record of Proceedings Relating to Chinese Laborers Being Deported, National Archives, Fort Worth, TX.

366 On the day of Wong's arrest: *El Paso Times,* October 29, 1901.

366 Nearly a decade later: Wong Kim Ark affidavit, January 31, 1910, and Lee G. Dean to Inspector in Charge, Chinese Division, November 10, 1910, Wong Yook Fun file; *International Chinese Business Directory of the World for the Year 1913* (San Francisco: International Chinese Business Directory Co., 1913), 1542.

367 He wrote to his father: Yook Fun to Wong Kim Ock, December 4, 1910, Wong Yook Fun file.

367 didn't have the money: Immigration Inspector, Acting in Charge, to Commissioner of Immigration, San Francisco, November 17, 1910, Wong Yook Fun file.

367 The responses of father and son: Findings and Decree, December 27, 1910.

367 On January 9, 1911: Luther C. Steward to Supervising Inspector, Immigration Service, El Paso, January 10, 1910, Wong Yook Fun file.

367 Yook Jim, who crossed the Pacific: Form 2505, December 7, 1926, Wong Yook Jim file 30980/7-5.

367 His hair had grown wispy: Form 430, July 14, 1931, Wong Kim Ark file.

367 On August 26, 1936: Immigration officer's report, May 6, 1953, Wong Hang Juen (Wong Yook Sue), A12267981 File, RG 566 Records of U.S. Citizenship and Immigration Services, National Archives, San Bruno, CA.

Chapter 22: Ruin and Rebirth

368 his hair a shock of white: *Boston Evening Transcript,* September 30, 1904.

368 By the end of the nineteenth century: Heather Cox Richardson, *To Make Men Free: A History of the Republican Party* (New York: Basic Books, 2014), 115–152.

368 Mitchell was seeking: 35 Cong. Rec. 3656 (1902).

369 Senator Orville Platt: 35 Cong. Rec. 3945 (1902).

369 protesting "the unwarranted and unjust": Wu Ting-Fang to John Hay, March 22, 1902, Document 173, No. 240, PRFRUS, 1902.

369 In Hoar's old age: *Boston Evening Transcript,* September 30, 1904.

369 "I believe that everything": 35 Cong. Rec. 4208 (1902).

370 "every man's conscience": George Frisbie Hoar, *Autobiography of Seventy Years,* vol. 2 (New York: Charles Scribner's Sons, 1903), 125.

370 The congressional debate: George E. Paulsen, "The Abrogation of the Gresham-Yang Treaty," *Pacific Historical Review* 40, no. 4 (November 1971): 469–471.

370 The debate was "strenuous": 35 Cong. Rec. 4762 (1902).

370 "until otherwise provided by law": 35 Cong. Rec. 4761 (1902).

370 The following day: *SFCa,* April 30, 1902.

370 The cabinet of President Theodore Roosevelt: *NYT,* April 9, 1904.

370 Congress scrambled: 38 Cong. Rec. 5309 (1904); *SFCh,* April 28, 1904.

370 The total Chinese population: U.S. Census Bureau, 1920 Census, vol. 3, *Composition and Characteristics of the Population by States,* Table 7, 19; Census Office, 1890 Census, Part 1, *Sex, General Nativity, and Color,* Table 10, 397.

371 "Chinese population of the United States": W. S. Harwood, "The Passing of the Chinese," *The World's Work* 9 (December 1904): 5631.

371 The shrinking population: Chap. 551, "An act in amendment to the various

acts relative to immigration and the importation of aliens under contract or agreement to perform labor," *The Statutes at Large of the United States of America, from December, 1889, to March, 1891,* vol. 26 (Washington, DC, 1891), 1085; Mary Roberts Coolidge, *Chinese Immigration* (New York: Henry Holt and Company, 1909), 240; U.S. Congress, Senate, *A Compilation of the Laws, Treaty, and Regulations and Rulings of the Treasury Department Relating to the Exclusion of Chinese,* 57th Cong., 1st Sess., 1902, Doc. No. 291, serial 4239, 31; Nicholas A. Somma, "The Knights of Labor and Chinese Immigration" (PhD diss., June 1952, Catholic University of America), 58–59; Erika Lee, *At America's Gates: Chinese Immigration During the Exclusion Era, 1882–1943* (Chapel Hill: University of North Carolina Press, 2003), 65.

371 "It is my wish": *Washington Times,* January 1, 1902.

371 "a threat to our very civilization": F. P. Sargent, memorandum, c. 1905, File 52704/12, Subject Correspondence, 1906–32, Records of the U.S. Immigration and Naturalization Service, RG 85, National Archives, Washington, DC.

371 Chinese arrivals were required: Kitty Calavita, "The Paradoxes of Race, Class, Identity, and 'Passing': Enforcing the Chinese Exclusion Acts, 1882–1910," *Law & Social Inquiry* 25, no. 1 (Winter 2000): 22, 25–26, https://www.jstor.org/stable/829016.

372 "The Chinese immigrants coming to America": Liang Qichao, *Ji Huagong jinyue* in *Yinbingshi heji* (Collecting Writings from an Ice-drinker's Studio), zhuanji 22 (Shanghai: Zhonghua shuju, 1936), 162, as quoted in K. Scott Wong, "Liang Qichao and the Chinese of America: A Re-Evaluation of His *Selected Memoir of Travels in the New World,*" *Journal of American Ethnic History* 11, no. 4 (Summer 1992): 15–16, https://www.jstor.org/stable/27500979.

372 a detention shed to house them: *SFCa,* November 6, 1898.

372 "penned up": Ira M. Condit, *The Chinaman as We See Him* (Chicago, 1900), 87.

372 On September 17, 1899: Wu Ting-Fang to John Hay, December 9, 1901, Document 83, No. 218, PRFRUS, 1901; Dunn to Powderly, July 31, 1901, File 3576, Chinese General Correspondence, 1898–1908, Records of the U.S. Immigration and Naturalization Service, RG 85, National Archives, Washington, DC. (This archive will hereafter be cited as Chinese Correspondence.)

373 There were other outrages: Oliver P. Stidger affidavit, September 18, 1901, File 3758, Chinese Correspondence; Coolidge, *Chinese Immigration,* 321–322; *SFCa,* January 27, 1900; *SFB,* November 30, 1909.

373 The most notorious operation: *Boston Evening Transcript,* October 12, 13, and 15, 1903; *Boston Globe,* October 20, 1903.

374 mass meeting at Faneuil Hall: *Boston Evening Transcript,* October 16, 1903; *Boston Globe,* December 16, 1903.

374 Over the course of months: *Boston Globe,* October 29, 31, November 4, December 16, 1903, May 18, 1904; *Boston Post,* February 21, March 17, March 22, 1904.

374 A new voice emerged: *LAT,* July 23, 1899; *Oakland Tribune,* March 14, 1931; Alex Kerr to Rev. F. F. Ellinwood, November 15, 1884, BOFMS; J. H. Laughlin, "What America Has Meant to One Immigrant," *The Continent,* January 28, 1915, 108.

375 "The paper gave me a lever": M. B. Levick, "A Maker of New China," *Sunset, the Pacific Monthly* 28, no. 5 (May 1912).

375 In 1900, Ng returned: Yumei Sun, "From Isolation to Participation: *Chung Sai Yat Po* [China West Daily] and San Francisco's Chinatown, 1900–1920" (PhD diss., University of Maryland, College Park, 1999), 115; Charles F. Holder, "The Chinese Press in America," *Scientific American* 87, no. 15 (October 11, 1902): 241; *SFE,* August 3, 1901; *The Californian,* vol. 54, April 4, 1902.

375 "an influential organ": Holder, "The Chinese Press in America."

375 "debunk the myth": Corinne K. Hoexter, *From Canton to California: The Epic of Chinese Immigration* (New York: Four Winds Press, 1976), 181.

375 In the fall of 1901: *SFE*, December 5, 1901; L. Eve Armentrout, "Conflict and Contact Between the Chinese and Indigenous Communities in San Francisco, 1900–1911," in *The Life, Influence and the Role of the Chinese in the United States, 1776–1960* (San Francisco: Chinese Historical Society of America, 1976), 64.

376 The following year, Ng argued: Ng Poon Chew, "The Chinaman in America," *The Independent* 54 (April 1902): 801–802.

376 In the United States, *Chung Sai Yat Po:* Delber L. McKee, "The Chinese Boycott of 1905–1906 Reconsidered: The Role of Chinese Americans," *Pacific Historical Review* 55, no. 2 (May 1986): 177.

376 Ng became one of the boycott: McKee, "The Chinese Boycott of 1905–1906 Reconsidered," 178; Hoextra, *From Canton to California*, 192; Armentrout, "Conflict and Contact," 64; Summary of interview of Mansie Chew, daughter of Ng Poon Chew, July 27, 1973, carton 90:41, HMLRFA; L. Eve Armentrout Ma, *Revolutionaries, Monarchists, and Chinatowns: Chinese Politics in the Americas and the 1911 Revolution* (Honolulu: University of Hawaii Press, 1990), 173–174, footnote 100.

376 president issued instructions: Roosevelt to Francis B. Loomis, June 24, 1905, Series 2, Letterpress copybooks, vol. 56, Theodore Roosevelt Papers, Library of Congress.

376 On the afternoon of July 16, 1905: James L. Rodgers to Loomis, November 15, 1905, Despatches from U.S. Consuls in Shanghai, China, 1847–1906, vol. 52, General Records of the Department of State, RG 59, National Archives, College Park, MD. (This archive will hereafter be cited as Gen-

eral Records.) *Ta kung pao* (Tianjin edition), August 28, 1905; Keren He, "Dying Against Democracy: Suicide Protest and the 1905 Anti-American Boycott," *The Journal of Asian Studies* 80, no. 4 (November 2021): 869–870.

377 Two notes left: *Lat Pao*, September 20, 1905, as quoted in Wong Sin Kiong (Huang Xianqiang), *Hai wai hua ren de ang zheng: dui mei di zhi yun dong shi shi yu shi liao* (Singapore: Xinjiaopo ya zhou yan jiu xue hui, 2001), 221–222.

377 On October 15, 1905: Julius G. Lay to His Excellency Tsen, October 27, 1905, Despatches from U.S. Consuls in Canton, China, 1790–1906, vol. 19, General Records.

377 In November 1905: Patrick J. Healy and Ng Poon Chew, *A Statement for Non-Exclusion* (San Francisco: n.p., 1905); *SFE*, November 29, 1905.

377 Ng was the morning's first speaker: *NYT*, December 9, 1905.

378 In the end, the boycott: McKee, *Chinese Exclusion Versus the Open Door Policy*, 146–149; Tsai, *China and the Overseas Chinese*, 121–122; McKee, "The Chinese Boycott of 1905–1906 Reconsidered," 188–189; Yong Chen, *Chinese San Francisco, 1850–1943: A Transpacific Community* (Stanford, CA: Stanford University Press, 2000), 149.

378 Just past five o'clock in the morning: Joseph H. Harper, "Observations of the San Francisco Earthquake," January 11, 1908, delivered before the Montana Society of Engineers, Musuem of the City of San Francisco, https://sfmuseum.org/1906/harper.html; Harry Fielding Reid, *The California Earthquake of April 18, 1906, Report of the State Earthquake Investigation Commission in Two Volumes and Atlas*, vol. 2 (Washington, DC: Carnegie Institution of Washington, 1910), 3–4.

378 ribbon of land along the coast: Charles Derleth Jr., *The Destructive Extent of the California Earthquake* (San Francisco: A. M. Robertson, 1907), 1; Mary Lou Zoback, "The 1906 Earthquake and a

Century of Progress in Understanding Earthquakes and Their Hazards," *GSA Today* 16, no. 4/5 (April & May 2006): 4, https://doi.org/10.1130/GSAT01604.1.

378 The bell of St. Mary's: Ying Zi Pan, "The Impact of the 1906 Earthquake on San Francisco's Chinatown" (PhD diss., Brigham Young University, 1991), 49.

379 "Suddenly, I was rocking": Hugh Liang, "The Sign of the Times," unpublished manuscript, Chinese Historical Society of America, San Francisco, CA (hereafter cited as Liang MSS), 16.

379 "the American people did not want": Liang MSS, 10.

379 "It seemed that the whole": Liang MSS, 17.

379 A fire alarm operator: James C. Kelly to W. R. Hewitt, chief, Dept. of Electricity, May 14, 1906, Museum of the City of San Francisco, https://sfmuseum.org/conflag/falarm.html.

379 Liang dragged his father's trunk: Liang MSS, 18.

380 "whirlpool of fire": James C. Stetson, *Personal Recollections During the Eventful Days of April, 1906* (San Francisco: Murdock Press, 1906), 12.

380 The fire destroyed: *Chung Sai Yat Po*, May 11, 1906; Ying Zi Pan, "The Impact of the 1906 Earthquake on San Francisco's Chinatown," 52.

380 The newspaper's first article: *Chung Sai Yat Po*, April 26, 1906, as quoted in Sun, "From Isolation to Participation," 150.

380 The refugees who stayed behind: *SFCh*, April 22 and 23, 1906; Pan, "The Impact of the 1906 Earthquake," 65; *SFE*, April 23, 1906.

380 Alarmed by what he was hearing: *SFB*, April 23, 1906.

381 The military authorities prepared: *SFCh*, April 28, 1906.

381 Officials designated a new location: *SFCh*, April 29, 1906.

381 The *Oakland Enquirer* suggested: *Oakland Enquirer*, April 26, 1906.

381 continued to publish from Oakland: Sun, "From Isolation to Participation," 155.

381 "famous attorneys": *Chung Sai Yat Po*, April 29, 1906.

381 "Americans and foreigners": *Chung Sai Yat Po*, May 1, 1906, as quoted in Sun, "From Isolation to Participation," 170.

381 By early June: Pan, "The Impact of the 1906 Earthquake," 125–126.

Chapter 23: The Station

382 The first Chinese prisoner: *SFCa*, January 23, 1910; *SFE*, January 23, 1910; *SFCh*, January 23, 1910.

382 By the end of the day: There are conflicting accounts of the number of people transferred from the detention shed to Angel Island. The *San Francisco Call* and *Chinese World* reported a hundred and one; the *Examiner* said two hundred; and the *Chronicle* said four hundred.

382 a "serious evil": *SFCh*, November 18, 1902.

382 For immigration officials: *SFCh*, January 23, 1910; *Annual Report of the Commissioner-General of Immigration for the Fiscal Year Ended June 30, 1903* (Washington, DC: Government Printing Office, 1903), 63.

383 In March 1905: U.S. Congress, House, *Immigrant Station on Angel Island, California*, 59th Cong., 1st Sess., 1906, Doc. No. 786, serial 4990, 2.

383 Several months later, Sargent approved: Luther C. Steward to Commissioner-General of Immigration, December 19, 1910, File 59561/26-F, SPFINS.

383 Mathews's designs included: *Oakland Enquirer*, July 6, 1906; *SFCh*, August 18, 1907; Robert Eric Barde, *Immigration at the Golden Gate: Passenger Ships, Exclusion, and Angel Island* (Westport, CT: Praeger, 2008), 14–16.

383 "cheapest material obtainable": Richard Taylor to Commissioner-General of Immigration, July 1, 1909, File 52961/26-B, SPFINS.

383 Three years later: *The Daily Review* (Pacific Grove, CA), October 21, 1908.

383 "delightfully located": *Annual Report of the Commissioner-General of Immigration for the Fiscal Year Ended June 30,*

1909 (Washington, DC, Government Printing Office, 1909), 144.

383 Immigration officials decided: *SFCh*, October 8, 1909.

383 During a visit to San Francisco: *SFCa*, October 7, 1909; Taft to Charles Nagel, October 4, 1909, File 52961/26-B, SPFINS.

383 Immigration officials scrambled: *SFE*, October 10, 1909; Nagel to Taft, October 9, 1909, File 52961/26-B, SPFINS; *SFB*, January 28, 1910.

384 On the day of the station's opening: Hart Hyatt North to Commissioner-General of Immigration, January 27, 1910, and North to Immigration Bureau, Washington, telegram, January 24, 1910, File 52961/26-C, SPFINS; *SFE*, January 15, 1910; *Chinese World*, January 22, 1910; *SFE*, January 22, 1910; *SFCa*, January 22, 1910; North to Commissioner-General of Immigration, February 3, 1910, File 52961/26-D, SPFINS.

384 Upon arrival: *SFCa*, January 19, 1908. See Erika Lee and Judy Yung, *Angel Island: Immigrant Gateway to America* (New York: Oxford University Press, 2010), for a comprehensive examination of life on the immigration station.

384 On January 24: *Oakland Tribune*, February 16, 1916; Wong Chung Hong, File 10382/000–54, IACF.

385 Wong became the first: Lee and Yung, *Angel Island*, 3.

385 In more than half the cases: Author's analysis of *China* arrival case files, January 1910, IACF, boxes 394 and 395.

385 One passenger, a man named Liu Poy: File 10382/000-31, IACF.

385 Lau Tsan Tung: Lau Tsan Tung interview, January 24, 1910, File 10383/05756, IACF.

385 "On most carefully reviewing": Daniel J. Keefe, memorandum, March 31, 1910, File 10383/05756, IACF.

385 Chinese leaders in San Francisco: *SFE*, December 12, 1909.

385 Within days of the station's opening: *SFCh*, January 29, 1910; *The Recorder*

(San Francisco), January 29, 1910; *Los Angeles Record*, February 4, 1910; "Announcement of the Six Companies," February 4, 1910, File 52961/24, SPFINS.

386 In early February: *Los Angeles Record*, February 4, 1910; "Announcement of the Six Companies," February 4, 1910, File 52961/24, SPFINS.

386 "difficult situation for Chinese people": *Chinese World*, April 5, 1910; *Annual Report of the Commissioner-General of Immigration to the Secretary of Commerce and Labor for the Fiscal Year Ended June 30*, 1910 (Washington, DC: Government Printing Office, 1910), 132–133.

386 The station was at capacity: Commissioner of Immigration at San Francisco to Secretary of Commerce and Labor, February 16, 1910, and Commissioner-General of Immigration to Commissioner of Immigration at San Francisco, April 27, 1910, File 52961/26-D, SPFINS.

386 It did not take long: Glover to Acting Commissioner of Immigration at San Francisco, November 21 and December 17, 1910, File 52961/26-D, SPFINS; Acting Commissioner of Immigration at San Francisco to Commissioner-General of Immigration, December 9, 1910, 52961/26-F, SPFINS.

387 The slurry on the floor: "Transcript of Stenographic Notes Made Incident to the Visit to Angel Island Immigration Station June 6, 1911 of Committee Representing the Down Town Association," File 52961/24-D, SPFINS.

387 "fire traps": *SFB*, November 1, 1922. On the station's early history, see also Him Mark Lai, "Island of Immortals: Chinese Immigrants and the Angel Island Immigration Station," *California History* 57, no. 1 (Spring 1978): 89–93.

387 Chinese passengers accounted for: Robert Barde and Gustavo J. Bobonis, "Detention at Angel Island: First Empirical Evidence," *Social Science History* 30, no. 1 (Spring 2006): 113.

387 less than a quarter: Barde, *Immigration at the Golden Gate,* 22.

387 Among those who wound up: Barde and Bobonis, "Detention at Angel Island," 113, 116, 118.

387 In later years: Him Mark Lai, Genny Lim, and Judy Yung, eds., *Island: Poetry and History of Chinese Immigrants on Angel Island 1910–1940,* 2nd ed. (Seattle: University of Washington Press, 2014), 341.

387 "The inspector, to whom": Emery Sims, interview, June 29, 1977, Interview #47, AIOHP, in Judy Yung, *The Chinese Exclusion Act and Angel Island* (Boston: Bedford/St. Martin's, 2019), 111.

388 "wastefulness of the methods": John Birge Sawyer, February 13, 1917, diary, John Birge Sawyer diaries: holograph and typescript, 1910–1962, vol. 2, BANC FILM 2334, Bancroft Library, UC Berkeley.

388 "almost an impossibility": *The Chinese Defender* 1, no. 2 (October 1910).

388 "They ask so much": Mrs. Chin, December 18, 1975, interview, box 1, folder 2, AIOHP.

388 "With all due respect": The *Chinese Defender* 1, no. 10 (June 1911); Bulletin No. 1, Chinese League of Justice of America, CIC, Ethnic Studies Library, UC Berkeley.

388 On September 1, 1916: Chew Hoy Quong affidavit, September 22, 1916, case file, In the Matter of Quok Shee, no. 16290 (hereafter cited as Quok Shee court file), Admiralty Case Files, Records of District Courts of the United States, RG 21, National Archives, San Bruno, CA; Chew Hoy Quong interview, September 5, 1916, Quok Shee interview, September 5, 1916, Case 15330/6-29 (hereafter cited as Quok Shee case file), IACF. See also Robert Barde, "An Alleged Wife: One Immigrant in the Chinese Exclusion Era," *Prologue* 36, no. 1 (Spring 2004), and Barde, *Immigration at the Golden Gate,* 26–75.

389 W. H. Wilkinson, the chief inspector: W. H. Wilkinson, Memorandum for the Commissioner, September 15, 1916, Quok Shee case file.

389 On September 15: W. H. Wilkinson, confidential memorandum, September 15, 1916, Quok Shee case file.

389 The following day: Notice to Rejected Chinese Applicant, Under Rule 5, September 16, 1916, Quok Shee case file.

389 refused to let them: Acting Commissioner to McGowan and Worley, September 26, 1916, Quok Shee court file.

389 In December, a district court: Commissioner to Inspector in Charge, Deportation and Detention Division, Angel Island Station, December 19, 1916, Quok Shee case file.

389 Seven months into her detention: Handwritten note, n.d., Quok Shee case file, 147.

390 Two months later: Quok Shee interview, November 20, 1917, Quok Shee case file.

390 "Quok Shee is in a highly": Holm to Edward White, December 13, 1917, Quok Shee case file.

390 gave Quok Shee a legal opening: 240 F. 869 (9th Cir. 1918); Writ of Habeas Corpus, the President of the United States of America, to the Commissioner of Immigration, Port of San Francisco, Calif, Quok Shee court file.

390 On board was Wong Shee: Wong Shee interview, January 19, 1924, and Geo. A. McGowan to Commissioner of Immigration, January 17, 1924, and Form 2602, January 15, 1924, File 22969/9–17 (hereafter cited as Wong Shee case file), IACF; Connie Young Yu, "Lee Wong Sang, Laying Tracks to Follow," in Sue Lee and Connie Young Yu, eds., *Voices from the Railroad: Stories by Descendants of Chinese Railroad Workers* (San Francisco: Chinese Historical Society of America, 2019), 77–82.

391 In 1912, Lee Yoke Suey returned: Lee Yoke Suey interview, April 3, 1912, Wong Shee case file.

391 Wong Shee received a telegram: Wong Shee interview, February 20, 1925, Wong Shee case file.

391 The island's surgeon: Medical Certificate, January 17, 1924, Wong Shee case file.

391 The Chinese Chamber of Commerce: Tong Young Kew and B. S. Fong to John Nagle, January 19, 1924, Wong Shee case file.

391 Immigration officials ruled: W. W. Libray, Assistant Commissioner-General, February 8, 1924, and W. U. Smelser, February 7, 1924, Wong Shee case file.

391 A pair of lawyers: Petition for Writ, February 15, 1924, and Order to Show Cause, February 18, 1924, Wong Shee case file.

391 "Each month felt like": Connie Young Yu, "Rediscovered Voices: Chinese Immigrants and Angel Island," *Amerasia Journal* 4, no. 2 (1977): 129, https://doi.org/10.17953/amer.4.2.085p252p10l42316.

392 Wong Shee struggled: Meeting of a board of special inquiry, February 20, 1925, Wong Shee case file.

392 Wong Shee's lawyers: Charles Fickert and Geo. W. Gowan to John Nagle, March 3, 1925, Wong Shee case file.

392 emotional toll inflicted upon: Yu, "Rediscovered Voices," 129.

392 Sometimes despair: *SFCh,* October 7, 1919.

392 "She couldn't face": Edwar Lee interview, April 9, 1984, Felicia Lowe collection, box 1, folder 51, AIOHP.

392 On the island: Mr. Wong interview, July 16, 1977, box 1, folder 16, and Messrs. Dea, Chew, Jow, and Lee, 1976, box 1, folder 3, AIOHP.

393 "Besides listening to the birds": Mr. Lowe, 1977, typescript, box 1, folder 44, AIOHP.

393 In 1916, an official: Frank Hays to Commissioner of Immigration, March 4, 1916, carton 2, folder 1, Him Mark Lai Papers, 1778— (bulk 1970–1995), AAS ARC 2000/80, Ethnic Studies Library, UC Berkeley.

393 On August 11, 1931: Jann Mon Fang, record of sworn statement, June 2, 1959, Alien case file for Mon Fong Jann, File A11814436/566-2020-0074(13-0491) (hereafter cited as Jann case file), Alien Case Files, Records of U.S. Citizenship and Immigration Services, RG 566, National Archives, San Bruno, CA; Jann Mon Fong, "A Gold Mountain Man's Monologue," *Renjian Shi,* March 5, 1935, Marlon K. Hom, trans., in Yung, *The Chinese Exclusion Act and Angel Island,* 121.

393 He began to record: Poems are drawn from Yung, *The Chinese Exclusion Act and Angel Island,* 122–123; Him Mark Lai, Genny Lim, and Judy Yung, eds., *Island: Poetry and History of Chinese Immigrants on Angel Island, 1910–1940* (Seattle: University of Washington Press), 1980, 56.

394 His interrogation: Sue Sow Fong, interviews, August 28, 29, and 31, 1931, Jann case file; Yung, *The Chinese Exclusion Act and Angel Island,* 124.

394 Jann was a "paper son": Jann Mon Fang, record of sworn statement, June 2, 1959, Jann case file.

394 "The Chinaman, having been declared": U.S. Congress, House, *Compilation from the Records of the U.S. Bureau of Immigration of Facts Concerning the Enforcement of the Chinese-Exclusion Laws,* 59th Cong., 1st Sess., 1906, Doc. No. 847, 122.

395 After decades of decline: Barde, *Immigration at the Golden Gate,* 11; U.S. Census Bureau, 1930 Census, vol. 3, Population, Reports by States, 7.

Chapter 24: Becoming Chinese American

396 It was a plaintive plea: *LAT Magazine,* November 4, 1934.

396 In 1899, Leung's father: Louise Leung Larson, *Sweet Bamboo: A Memoir of a Chinese American Family* (Berkeley: University of California Press, 1989), 21–33; Jane Leung Larson email to author, January 24, 2024.

396 Tom Leung went on to become: Leung Larson, *Sweet Bamboo,* 44–45; Arnold B.

Larson, "Newspaper Reporting in the Twenties: Reflections," January 19, 1966, Oral History Program of the University of California Los Angeles, 180; Louise Larson, interview, August 28, 1979, box 3, folder 3, Chinese Historical Society of Southern California Southern California Chinese American Oral History Project, UCLA Library Special Collections (hereafter cited as Larson, 1979).

397 The state medical board: Leung Larson, *Sweet Bamboo,* 77; Louise Leung, "She Lost Her Papa at the Juncture of East and West," *LAT,* June 15, 1980.

397 Leung had a knack: Leung Larson, *Sweet Bamboo,* 19; Leung, *LAT,* June 15, 1980.

397 He later opened branch offices: Larson, 1979.

397 It was in elementary school: Leung Larson, *Sweet Bamboo,* 71.

397 "She didn't say why": Leung Larson, *Sweet Bamboo,* 133.

397 She rebelled against: Leung Larson, *Sweet Bamboo,* 71.

397 During her junior year: Louise Leung Larson interview, November 29, 1983, box 2, folder 10, Southern California Journalism Oral History Project, California State University, Northridge, Special Collections and Archives (hereafter cited as Larson, 1983); Louise Leung, "Capitalizing Liabilities," unpublished manuscript written for *Writer's Digest,* 1929, 2–3.

398 After college: Louise Leung interview, August 13, 1923, box 34, folder 63, SRR; Leung, "Capitalizing Liabilities," 3–7; *Los Angeles Record,* July 15, 1926; Unknown author, letter to "Boss" at *Honolulu Advertiser,* January 20, 1929, courtesy of Jane Larson; LL, 1983. On Leung's journalism career, see Yu-Li Chang Zacher, "First Chinese American Newspaperwoman: Mamie Louise Leung at the *Los Angeles Record,* 1926–1929," *Journalism History* 49, no. 4 (2023): 280–299, https://doi.org/10.1080/00947679.2023.2263729.

398 "I kept thinking": Larson, 1983.

398 She went on to work: Larson, 1983; *LAT,* Mamie Louise Leung, "A Brain Truster from China," September 2, 1934.

398 Over time, she came to embrace: *Editor & Publisher,* September 6, 1930, 57; Leung, "Capitalizing Liabilities," 4.

398 In 1930, she married: Leung Larson, *Sweet Bamboo,* 193; Larson, 1979.

399 "Papa succeeded": Leung, *LAT,* June 15, 1980.

399 "he looks like a Leung": Author interview with Jane Leung Larson, January 5, 2023.

399 In her *Los Angeles Times Sunday Magazine* article: *LAT Sunday Magazine,* November 4, 1934.

399 Even with years of tutoring: Leung Larson, *Sweet Bamboo,* 70, 123; Larson, 1979.

399 became close with: The pinyin romanization of Kit King Louis's name is Lei Jieqiong.

399 Louis's family had roots: Lily Xiao Hong Lee, ed., *Biographical Dictionary of Chinese Women: The Twentieth Century, 1912–2000* (New York: Routledge, 2015), 293; Leung Larson, *Sweet Bamboo,* 150; Haiming Liu, *The Transnational History of a Chinese Family: Immigrant Letters, Family Business, and Reverse Migration* (New Brunswick, NJ: Rutgers University Press, 2005), 179–180; Haiming Liu, "The Identity Formation of American-Born Chinese in the 1930s: A Review of Lei Jieqiong's (Kit King Louis) Master's Thesis," *Journal of Chinese Overseas* 3, no. 1 (May 2007): 119, footnote 1; "In Memoriam: Lei Jieqiong," *USC Trojan Family Magazine,* Spring 2011, 55.

400 "The American-born Chinese": Kit King Louis, "A Study of American-born and American-reared Chinese in Los Angeles" (master's thesis, University of Southern California, 1931), 5.

400 "Although American education": Louis, "A Study of American-born and American-reared Chinese in Los Angeles," 145.

400 "Legally we are American": Ibid., 85.

400 One college student: Ibid., 103.

401 "When I looked for a house": Ibid., 114.

401 "If I were a member": Ibid., 79.

401 Louis concluded: Ibid., 84.

401 "I feel that I am neither": Ibid., 134.

401 Four of the five sons: Leung Larson, *Sweet Bamboo*, 97–202.

401 Mamie went on to raise: Jane Leung Larson email to author, January 5, 2024.

401 In 1976, she visited: Louise Leung Larson, "My Ancestral Homeland," 1976, unpublished manuscript, courtesy of Jane Leung Larson.

401 The following year, she returned: *LAT*, March 13, 1978.

402 Chinese exclusion offered them: Erika Lee, "The Chinese Exclusion Example: Race, Immigration, and American Gatekeeping, 1882–1924," *Journal of American Ethnic History* 21, no. 3 (Spring 2002): 37; Erika Lee, *At America's Gates: Chinese Immigration During the Exclusion Era, 1882–1943*, 32–40.

402 "the Japanese is no more": *San Francisco Chronicle*, February 23, 1905.

402 A photograph taken: Chinese American Citizens Alliance delegation to hearings before the Committee on Immigration and Naturalization, House of Representatives, 1928, box 15, folder 2, HFP.

403 The group had begun: Outline of C.A.C.A. History, box Y19, folder 2, HFP; Sue Fawn Chung, "Fighting for Their American Rights: A History of the Chinese American Citizens Alliance," in *Claiming America: Constructing Chinese American Identities During the Exclusion Era*, ed. K. Scott Wong and Sucheng Chan (Philadelphia: Temple University Press, 1998), 102–103.

403 Hong's life embodied: David Pierson, "Chinatown Time Capsule," *LAT*, May 18, 2005; "Biography of Y. C. Hong," *The Chinese American*, Summer 1971, 13; John G. Tomlinson, "Four Lives in Legal Education, Community Lawyering, and Philanthropy," *USC Law*, Fall 1997, 13; *LAT*, March 15, 1923.

403 The citizens' alliance had appointed:

Xiaojian Zhao, *Remaking Chinese America: Immigration, Family, and Community, 1940–1965* (New Brunswick, NJ: Rutgers University Press, 2002), 17; "A Plea for Relief Together with a Supplement Containing Some Arguments in Support Thereof," in U.S. House of Representatives, *Wives of American Citizens of Oriental Race, Hearings Before the Committee on Immigration and Naturalization on H.R. 2404, H.R. 5654, H.R. 10524*, 71st Cong., 2nd sess., 563.

404 He characterized the first two: U.S. House of Representatives, *Wives of American Citizens of Oriental Race, Hearings Before the Commission on Immigration and Naturalization, on H.R. 6974*, 70th Cong., 1st sess., 10.

404 Two years passed: Act of June 14, 1930, ch. 476, 46 Stat. 581.

404 In a letter written: Y. C. Hong to Mabel Chin, April 25, 1929, box Y37, folder 15, HFP.

405 Over the next eight years: Rana Mitter, *China's War with Japan, 1937–1945: The Struggle for Survival* (London: Penguin Books, 2014), 5.

405 "from Anglo-Saxon imperialists": Xiaohua Ma, "The Sino-American Alliance During World War II and the Lifting of the Chinese Exclusion Acts," *American Studies International* 38, no. 2 (June 2000): 42.

406 Leaders in the Chinese community: Yong Chen, "China in America: A Cultural Study of Chinese San Francisco, 1850–1943" (PhD diss., Cornell University, August 1993), 315; K. Scott Wong, *Americans First: Chinese Americans and the Second World War* (Cambridge, MA: Harvard University Press, 2005), 80; Rose Hum Lee, "Chinese in the United States Today," *Survey Graphic* 31, no. 10 (October 1942): 419.

406 *Time* magazine published: *Time*, December 22, 1941, 34.

406 In February 1942: Charles Nelson Spinks, "Repeal Chinese Exclusion!" *Asia* 42, no. 2 (February 1942): 92, 94; *Harrisburg Telegraph*, August 18, 1939;

Fred Warren Riggs, *Pressures on Congress: A Study of the Repeal of Chinese Exclusion* (New York: King's Crown Press, 1950), 48.

406 That same month, Buck delivered: *New York Herald Tribune*, February 16, 1942; Peter Conn, *Pearl S. Buck: A Cultural Biography* (Cambridge: Cambridge University Press, 1996), 259–260.

406 "I myself do not know": Walsh to Julean Arnold, March 15, 1943, box 21, folder 3, Papers of Richard J. Walsh, RG 2, RJWP.

407 Walsh and H. J. Timperley: H. J. Timperley to W. B. Pettus, April 23, 1942, box 23, folder 24, RJWP.

407 In May, Walsh and Buck: Riggs, *Pressures on Congress*, 51; H. J. Timperley to Jean Lyon, May 20, 1942, box 23, folder 24, RJWP; Floyd Russel Goodno, "Walter H. Judd: Spokesman for China in the United States House of Representatives" (PhD diss., Oklahoma State University, 1970), 82; R. J. Walsh, "Our Great Wall Against the Chinese," *The New Republic*, November 23, 1942.

407 A widely distributed leaflet: 89 Cong. Rec. A3127 (1943).

407 By the late summer: Ling Yang, "Soong Mayling's 1943 American Speech Tour: A Study in the Rhetoric of Public Diplomacy" (PhD diss., University of Wisconsin-Madison, 2016), 77–85.

407 Madame Chiang, as she was known: *NYT*, April 21, 1940; *Evening Star* (Washington, DC), July 26, 1942.

407 Her father, Charlie: Yang, "Soong Mayling's 1943 American Speech Tour," 25; Laura Tyson Li, *Madam Chiang Kai-Shek: China's Eternal First Lady* (New York: Grove Press, 2006), 11–18.

408 Soong was suddenly: Tyson Li, *Madame Chiang Kai-shek*, 21–23; Jung Chang, *Big Sister, Little Sister, Red Sister: Three Women at the Heart of Twentieth-Century China* (New York: Anchor Books, 2019), 35–38.

408 All three daughters: Barbara Brannon, "China's Soong Sisters at Wesleyan," *Wesleyan Magazine*, Fall 1997; Juanjuan Peng, "Searching the Early Lives of the Soong Sisters in Macon, Georgia: Three Chinese Overseas Students in the American South," *International Journal of Asian Studies* 20 (2023): 779–783. The Soong sisters' names in Chinese have been romanized in a variety of ways. I have chosen to adopt here the versions they most commonly went by in the United States.

408 In 1917, she returned: Tyson Li, *Madame Chiang Kai-shek*, 43–44; Chang, *Big Sister, Little Sister, Red Sister*, 132–234; *NYT*, October 24, 2003.

408 In late November 1942, Madame Chiang: Tyson Li, *Madame Chiang Kai-shek*, 194; *NYT*, February 18, 1943.

409 On February 18, 1943: 89 Cong. Rec. 1081 (1943); *NYT*, February 19, 1943.

409 After her stint in Washington: *NYT*, March 3, 1943.

409 On April 4: *LADN*, April 5, 1943.

409 Shortly after her speech: Ling Yang, "Soong Mayling's 1943 American Speech Tour," 222–223; Riggs, *Pressures on Congress*, 116.

409 By the spring of 1943: Riggs, *Pressures on Congress*, 39; Goodno, "Walter H. Judd," 84.

410 Walsh, Buck, and their: Report to Members, August 15, 1943, in Citizens Committee to Repeal Chinese Exclusion and Place Immigration on a Quota Basis, *Miscellaneous Publications* (New York, 1943), New York Public Library; Riggs, *Pressures on Congress*, 56.

410 When Buck testified: U.S. House of Representatives, *Repeal of the Chinese Exclusion Acts, Hearings Before the Committee on Immigration and Naturalization on H.R. 1882 and H.R. 2309*, 78th Cong., 1st sess., 68–70.

410 Rep. A. Leonard Allen: *Repeal of the Chinese Exclusion Act Hearings*, 72.

410 James L. Wilmeth: *Repeal of the Chinese Exclusion Act Hearings*, 101.

411 "Probably not all Americans": *Repeal of the Chinese Exclusion Act Hearings*, 204.

411 "based on the fundamentals": *Repeal

of the Chinese Exclusion Act Hearings,
207.

411 Both Li and Yee: L. Ling-chi Wang,
"Politics of the Repeal of the Chinese
Exclusion Laws," *The Repeal and Its
Legacy: Proceedings of the Conference on
the 50th Anniversary of the Repeal of the
Exclusion Acts* (San Francisco: Chinese
Historical Society of America, 1994),
66–69.

411 During the Second World War: U.S.
Census Bureau, 1940 Census, vol. 2,
Characteristics of the Population, Table
4, 19.

411 On the evening of March 17, 1942:
NYT, March 18, 1942; *New York Journal-
American,* March 18, 1942; *New York
Daily News,* March 18 and 19, 1942.

412 As many as fifteen thousand: Wong,
Americans First, 58.

412 In an article for the magazine: Lee,
"Chinese in the United States Today,"
419, 444.

412 At the end of the House hearings:
Riggs, *Pressures on Congress,* 178–179.

413 "By the middle of August": Citizens
Committee, Report to Members,
August 15, 1943.

413 The committee produced: Citizens
Committee, Report to Members, September 20, 1943.

413 The committee decided: Riggs, *Pressures
on Congress,* 113; Jane H. Hong, *Opening
the Gates to Asia: A Transpacific History
of How America Repealed Asian Exclusion* (Chapel Hill: University of North
Carolina Press, 2019), 39–44.

413 The committee's files contain: Herbert
Chu to Citizens Committee, September 22, 1943, box 23, folder 9, RJWP;
Pearl S. Buck to Ko Lum See, December 13, 1943, box 23, folder 10, RJWP;
Dai Ming Lee to Pearl Buck, June 10,
1943, telegram, box 23, folder 11, RJWP;
Citizens Committee, Report to Members, August 15, 1943.

413 A report to members: Citizens Committee, Report to Members, September 20, 1943; Riggs, *Pressures on
Congress,* 113.

413 The committee's report: U.S. House of
Representatives, Committee on Immigration and Naturalization, *Repealing
the Chinese Exclusion Laws,* 78th Cong.,
1st Sess., H. Rep. 732, serial 10763, 2–3.

414 The *Chinese Press,* a weekly: *Chinese
Press,* June 11, August 20, September 10,
1943.

414 "In number there are not enough": Gilbert Woo, "One Hundred and Seven
Chinese," *Chinese Times,* September 7,
1943, in Judy Yung, Gordon H. Chang,
and Him Mark Lai, eds., *Chinese American Voices: From the Gold Rush to the
Present* (Berkeley: University of California Press, 2006), 222.

414 He framed the measure: Franklin D.
Roosevelt, Message to Congress
on Repeal of the Chinese Exclusion Laws, October 11, 1943, https://
www.presidency.ucsb.edu/documents
/message-congress-repeal-the-chinese
-exclusion-laws.

414 On December 3, a cablegram: 89 Cong.
Rec. 10292 (1943).

414 in Hawaii, Chinese Americans: *The
Nation,* March 11, 1944.

414 Fifty years later: Him Mark Lai,
"Unfinished Business: The Confes-
sion Program," in *The Repeal and Its
Legacy,* 47.

Chapter 25: Confession

415 After the war: K. Scott Wong, *Ameri-
cans First: Chinese Americans and the
Second World War* (Cambridge, MA:
Harvard University Press, 2005), 197;
Benson Tong, *The Chinese Americans,*
2nd ed. (Boulder: University Press of
Colorado, 2003), 106; Xiaojian Zhao,
*Remaking Chinese America: Immigra-
tion, Family, and Community, 1940–1965*
(New Brunswick, NJ: Rutgers Univer-
sity Press, 2002), 2.

415 During the hearings: John H. Ting,
"Intersectionality of Race and Gender:
A Story of Transnational Marriage and
Chinese 'War Brides' in Post WWII
America" (honors thesis, Rutgers Uni-
versity, 2010), 29–30; U.S. Congress,

Senate, *Placing Chinese Wives of American Citizens on a Nonquota Basis,* 79th Cong., 2nd sess., 1946, Report No. 1927, 1.

416 Over the next few years: Philip E. Wolgin and Irene Bloemraad, "'Our Gratitude to Our Soldiers': Military Spouses, Family Reunification, and Postwar Immigration Reform," *The Journal of Interdisciplinary History* 41, no. 1 (Summer 2010): 32; Zhao, *Remaking Chinese America,* 80–83.

416 A fire in 1940: *Palo Alto Times,* August 12, 1940.

416 Immigration officials in San Francisco: *SFCh,* July 30, 1940, September 24, 1948; *SFE,* June 19, 1940.

416 With the backlog of wives' cases: *SFCh,* January 28, 29, August 22, 1947, September 17, 1948; I. F. Wixon memorandum, September 21, 1943, in Leong Bick Ha, File 1566751–1300–78976 (hereafter cited as Leong file), CEACF, National Archives, San Bruno, CA.

416 Around three o'clock: *Oakland Tribune,* June 2, 1948; *Sacramento Union,* June 2, 1948; *SFCh,* June 2 and 9, 1948.

417 At the end of June: Record of Hearing, September 17 and 20, 1948, Leong File; Eng Lung Tuck, Statement of Applicant and Relative of Applicant for Entry, File 156675101300–78977 (hereafter cited as Eng Lung Tuck file), CEACF, San Bruno, CA.

417 Leong was hoping: Examination of Eng Bak Teung, August 4, 1948, in Leong file; U.S. Army, Certificate of Honorable Discharge, October 29, 1945, Eng Lung Tuck file.

417 After interviewing Leong: I. F. Wixon memorandum, September 21, 1948, Leong file.

417 On Friday, September 17: Record of Hearing, September 20, 1948, Leong file.

417 A doctor prescribed sedatives: I. F. Wixon memorandum, September 21, 1948, Leong file; *Stockton Daily Evening Record,* September 22, 1948.

417 A security officer checked: Celia Temple, statement, September 21, 1948, Leong file; *Oakland Tribune,* September 21, 1948.

417 More than a hundred: *New York Herald Tribune,* September 23, 1948.

417 Immigration officials promptly: Parole authorization, September 21, 1948, Eng Lung Tuck file.

417 In 1951, a district court: Law offices of Chow and Sing to District Director, Immigration Service, July 7, 1951, Eng Lung Tuck file.

418 The outcry: Tong, *The Chinese Americans,* 110; Zhao, *Remaking of Chinese America,* 92.

418 A new era of apprehension: On the Cold War's impact on Chinese immigration, see also Mae Ngai, *Impossible Subjects: Illegal Aliens and the Making of Modern America* (Princeton, NJ: Princeton University Press, 2004), 202–224; Zhao, *Remaking Chinese America,* 152–184.

418 Its primary mission: Jerome K. Holloway oral history, June 16, 1989, and John H. Holdridge oral history, 1989 and 1995, Foreign Affairs Oral History Collection, Association for Diplomatic Studies and Training, Arlington, VA, adst.org. (This archive will hereafter be cited as Foreign Affairs Collection.)

418 A backlog of several thousand: John Edward Torok, "'Chinese Investigations': Immigration Policy Enforcement in Cold War New York Chinatown, 1946–1965" (PhD diss., University of California, Berkeley, 2008), 155; James E. Fitzgerald statement, *Hearings Before the President's Commission on Immigration and Naturalization* (hereafter cited as Commission Hearings) (Washington, DC: Government Printing Office, 1952), 419; Lemont Eaton, "Inspections and Examinations Work of the Service," *Immigration and Naturalization Service Monthly Review* 3, no. 1 (July 1950): 31.

418 On February 9, 1950: "'Communists in Government Service,' McCarthy Says," on United States Senate website, https://www.senate.gov/about/powers

-procedures/investigations/mccarthy
-hearings/communists-in-government
-service.htm.

419 In August 1950: "Procedure for Documentation of Persons of Chinese Origin
Who Claim American Citizenship for
the First Time," Commission Hearings,
422–23; Everett Drumright, "Report on
the Problem of Fraud at Hong Kong,"
Department of State, photocopy, carton 34, folder 2, HMLRFA (hereafter
cited as Drumright Report), 43–45;
Boyd Reynolds statement, Commission
Hearings, 1242.

419 Unless they possessed: Fitzgerald statement, Commission Hearings, 420.

419 The number of consular officers:
Edward C. Ingraham oral history,
April 8, 1991, Foreign Affairs Collection.

419 "full field" investigations: Drumright
Report, 46.

419 Edward Ingraham, a young: Ingraham
oral history, Foreign Affairs Collection.

420 "You had twenty-five thousand": Holloway oral history, Foreign Affairs
Collection.

420 Drumright, an imposing: William
Andreas Brown, November 1998, For-
eign Affairs Collection; E. J. Kahn Jr.,
*The China Hands: America's Foreign Ser-
vice Officers and What Befell Them* (New
York: Viking Press, 1975), 38.

420 On December 9, 1955: Drumright
Report, 3, 14, 43, 52; *New York Daily
News*, March 4, 1956.

420 In a series of columns: *Chinese World*,
April 21 and June 21, 1956.

421 Congress earmarked: Torok, "Chinese
investigations," 164; Brown oral history,
Foreign Affairs Collection.

421 The fraud unit assembled: Donald M.
Anderson oral history, July 8 and Sep-
tember 2, 1992, and Brown oral history,
Foreign Affairs Collection.

421 On February 14, 1956: *New York Herald
Tribune*, February 15, 1956.

421 Their probe began: *SFE*, March 2, 1956;
SFCh, March 1, 1956.

422 Several days later: *SFCh*, March 7,
1956.

422 Fear settled over Chinatowns: *NYT*,
March 17, 1956; *Chinese World*,
March 13, 1956.

422 In late March: *SFCh*, March 21, 1956.

422 Yet prosecutors continued: U.S. Department of Justice, *Annual Report of the
Immigration and Naturalization Service for the Fiscal Year Ended June 30,
1955*, 12.

422 Over the coming months: U.S. Department of Justice, *Annual Report of the
Attorney General of the United States for
the Fiscal Year Ended June 30, 1957*, 122;
NYT, March 14, 1956; *SFCh*, July 6, 1956;
South China Morning Post, November 2,
1956.

423 Sing Kee was born: *San Jose Mercury
Herald*, October 3, 1918; Chellis V.
Smith, *Americans All: Nine Heroes Who
in the World War Showed That Ameri-
canism Is Above Race, Creed, or Condition* (Boston: Lothrop, Lee & Shepard,
1925), 119–120.

423 In the middle of August 1918: *SFE*,
June 14, 1919; *Honolulu Star Bulle-
tin*, October 5, 1918; *Los Angeles Her-
ald*, November 21, 1918; *Buffalo Evening
News*, April 28, 1919; *New York Herald*,
April 26, 1919; Ashlyn Weber, "Color
Sergeant Sing Lau Kee," *Valor Magazine*
2, no. 1 (June 23, 2021): 17–23.

423 He came home: *SFCh*, June 14, 1919.

423 After the war: Smith, *Americans All*, 123;
Charlotte Brooks, *Between Mao and
McCarthy: Chinese American Politics in
the Cold War Years* (Chicago: University
of Chicago Press, 2015), 39.

423 Prosecutors accused him: *NYT*, February 20, 1957; *Annual Report of the
Attorney General of the United States
for the Fiscal Year Ended June 30, 1957*,
122–123.

423 He appealed his case: *United States v.
Sing Kee*, 250 F.2d 236 (2d Cir. 1957).

423 He served his time: Andrew R. Chow,
"Overlooked No More: Lau Sing Kee,
War Hero Jailed for Helping Immi-
grants," *NYT*, August 21, 2019.

423 a longtime Chinese journalist: Y. K.
Chu, *Meiguo Huaqiao Kaishi* (New

York: China Times, 1975), 150–151; Brooks, *Between Mao and McCarthy*, 170–171. For more on Chu, see Ibid., 40–43.

424 In 1956, immigration officials: Department of Justice, *Annual Report of the Immigration and Naturalization Service*, 1957, 13; Fae Myenne Ng, *Orphan Bachelors: A Memoir* (New York: Grove Press, 2023), 66; Chu, *Meiguo Huaqiao Kaishi*, 151–152.

424 He'd arrived in the United States: Mr. Mock, interview, April 8, 1984, box 1, folder 42, AIOHP.

425 The confession of a single: *Time*, January 20, 1858, 17.

425 Then there were stories: Him Mark Lai, "The History of the Family of Tong Jung," August 17, 2008, carton 69, folder 13, HMLRFA, 1–6; Jean Dere, "Born Lucky: The Story of Laura Lai," *Chinese America: History & Perspectives—The Journal of the Chinese Historical Society of America* (San Francisco: Chinese Historical Society of America with UCLA Asian American Studies Center, 2011), 34–35.

425 Immigration officials reported: Zhao, *Remaking Chinese America*, 183.

Epilogue

427 "slur on the patriotism": *NYT*, June 26, 1952.

427 "generous," "fair," and: John F. Kennedy, *A Nation of Immigrants*, updated ed. (Harper Perennial Modern Classics, 2018), 65.

427 On July 23, 1963: *NYT*, July 24, 1963.

427 He had never demonstrated: William S. Stern, "H.R. 2580, the Immigration and Nationality Amendments of 1965— a Case Study" (PhD diss., New York University, 1975), 36–37.

428 Nevertheless, he saw himself: Jia Lynn Yang, *One Mighty and Irresistible Tide: The Epic Struggle over American Immigration, 1924–1965* (New York: W. W. Norton, 2020), 231; Tom Gjelten, *A Nation of Nations: A Great American Immigration Story* (New York:

Simon and Schuster, 2015), 108; Lyndon Johnson, "Annual Message to the Congress on the State of the Union," January 8, 1964, American Presidency Project, UC Santa Barbara, https://www.presidency.ucsb.edu/documents/annual-message-the-congress-the-state-the-union-25.

428 "The bill will not flood": U.S. Congress, Senate, Committee on the Judiciary, Subcommittee on Immigration and Naturalization, "Opening Statement of the Honorable Edward M. Kennedy to Hearings on S. 500," February 10, 1965, box 9, "S. 500 folder 1 of 11," Legislative Files, Committee on Judiciary, 89th Congress, Records of the U.S. Senate, RG 46, National Archives, Washington, DC.

428 "There will not be": 111 Cong. Rec. 21758 (1965).

429 Representative Michael Feighan: Stern, "H.R. 2580," 42–43, 48.

429 Under heavy pressure: David M. Reimers, *Still the Golden Door: The Third World Comes to America*, 2nd ed. (New York: Columbia University Press, 1992), 69–72; Stern, "H.R. 2580," 128–129; Yang, *One Might and Irresistible Tide*, 250; Gjelten, *A Nation of Nations*, 125; Michael G. Davis, "Impetus for Immigration Reform: Asian Refugees and the Cold War," *Journal of American-East Asian Relations* 7, no. 3/4 (Fall-Winter 1998): 149–150, https://www.jstor.org/stable/23612917.

429 On October 3, 1965: *NYT*, October 4, 1965.

429 By 1970: U.S. Census Bureau, *1970 Census—Subject Reports: Japanese, Chinese, and Filipinos in the United States*, July 1973, Table 16; U.S. Census Bureau, U.S. Census Bureau, *Supplementary Reports: Race of the Population of the United States, by States: .0. 1960*, September 7, 1961, Table 56.

429 The number would continue: Jane H. Hong, *Opening the Gates to Asia: A Transpacific History of How America Repealed Asian Exclusion* (Chapel Hill:

University of North Carolina Press, 2019), 187; "Modern Immigration Wave Brings 59 Million to U.S., Driving Population Growth and Change Through 2065," Pew Research Center, September 28, 2015, https://www.pewresearch.org/race-and-ethnicity/2015/09/28/modern-immigration-wave-brings-59-million-to-u-s-driving-population-growth-and-change-through-2065/; Abby Budiman and Neil G. Ruiz, "Asian Americans Are the Fastest-Growing Racial or Ethnic Group in the U.S.," Pew Research Center, April 9, 2021, https://www.pewresearch.org/short-reads/2021/04/09/asian-americans-are-the-fastest-growing-racial-or-ethnic-group-in-the-u-s/.

430 "Orientals Find Bias Is Down": *NYT,* December 13, 1970.

431 The historian Ellen D. Wu: Ellen D. Wu, *The Color of Success: Asian Americans and the Origins of the Model Minority Myth* (Princeton, NJ: Princeton University Press, 2014), 5. Parts of this epilogue are drawn from Michael Luo, "America Was Eager for Chinese Immigrants. What Happened?"

New Yorker, August 23, 2021, https://www.newyorker.com/magazine/2021/08/30/america-was-eager-for-chinese-immigrants-what-happened.

431 In 1974: Stanford Lyman, *Chinese Americans* (New York: Random House, 1974), 119, 137–138.

432 The surge in harassment, violence: Hyeyoung Lim, Claire Seungeun Lee, and Chunrye Kim, "Covid-19 Pandemic and Anti-Asian Racism & Violence in the 21st Century," *Race and Justice* 13, no. 1 (2023): 3–8.

432 The complicated racial dynamics: Mae Ngai, *The Chinese Question: The Gold Rushes and Global Politics* (New York: W. W. Norton, 2021), 306–313.

432 In 2023, Florida: Amy Quin and Patricia Mazzei, "When Buying a Home Is Treated as a National Security Threat," *NYT,* May 6, 2024, https://www.nytimes.com/2024/05/06/us/florida-land-law-chinese-homes.html; Alan Rappeport, "Spreading State Restrictions on China Show Depths of Distrust in the U.S.," *NYT,* August 21, 2023, https://www.nytimes.com/2023/08/21/us/politics/china-restrictions-distrust.html.

Index

Illustration Credits

Page 1: Courtesy of California Historical Society (top); Courtesy, California Historical Society, FN-00421 (middle); Library of Congress Prints and Photographs Division, Washington, D.C. (bottom)

Page 2: Courtesy of the Presbyterian Historical Society (top); Library of Congress Prints and Photographs Division, Washington, D.C. (middle and bottom)

Page 3: UC Berkeley, Bancroft Library (top); Library of Congress Prints and Photographs Division, Washington, D.C. (bottom)

Page 4: USC Digital Library, California Historical Society Collection (top); Security Pacific National Bank Collection/Los Angeles Public Library (middle); Connecticut Museum of Culture and History (bottom)

Page 5: Connecticut Museum of Culture and History (top); Ivy Close Images / Alamy Stock Photo (middle); American portraiture / Alamy Stock Photo (bottom)

Page 6: Courtesy of the San Diego History Center (top and middle); Gado Images / Alamy Stock Photo (bottom)

Page 7: Courtesy of the Clarke Historical Museum (top); Library of Congress Prints and Photographs Division, Washington, D.C. (middle); Courtesy of Sweetwater County Historical Museum (bottom)

Page 8: University of Washington Libraries, Special Collections, SOC0886 (top); University of Washington Libraries, Special Collections, CUR1691 (bottom)

Page 9: Courtesy of Janice Tong (J Tong Collection) (top); Courtesy, California Historical Society, Vault-184 (bottom)

Page 10: Heritage Image Partnership Ltd / Alamy Stock Photo (top); Genthe photograph collection, Library of Congress, Prints and Photographs Division (middle); Universal History Archive / UIG / Bridgeman Images (bottom)

Page 11: Genthe photograph collection, Library of Congress, Prints and Photographs Division (top and bottom)

Page 12: Courtesy of California State Library via California Digital Library (top); UC Berkeley, Ethnic Studies Library, photograph courtesy of Michael Luo (bottom)

Page 13: Records of the Public Health Service, National Archive (top and middle); The Jon B. Lovelace Collection of California Photographs in Carol M. Highsmith's America Project, Library of Congress, Prints and Photographs Division (bottom)

Page 14: Union Pacific Coal Company Collection, Western Wyoming Community College (top); Courtesy of the Larson family (bottom)

Page 15: Hong family papers, the Huntington Library, San Marino, CA. Gift of Roger S. Hong, June 2006 (top); AP Photo / George R. Skadding (bottom)

Page 16: LBJ Library, photograph by Yoichi Okamoto (top); Courtesy of Michael Luo (bottom)

About the Author

MICHAEL LUO is an executive editor at *The New Yorker* and writes regularly for the magazine on politics, religion, and Asian American issues. He joined *The New Yorker* in 2016. Before that, he spent thirteen years at *The New York Times*, as a metro reporter, national correspondent, and investigative reporter and editor. He is a recipient of a George Polk Award and a Livingston Award for Young Journalists.